Morality and the Good Life

AN INTRODUCTION TO ETHICS THROUGH CLASSICAL SOURCES

FOURTH EDITION

Robert C. Solomon
University of Texas at Austin

Clancy W. Martin
University of Missouri, Kansas City

Boston   Burr Ridge, IL   Dubuque, IA   Madison, WI   New York   San Francisco   St. Louis
Bangkok   Bogotá   Caracas   Kuala Lumpur   Lisbon   London   Madrid   Mexico City
Milan   Montreal   New Delhi   Santiago   Seoul   Singapore   Sydney   Taipei   Toronto

The McGraw-Hill Companies

Higher Education

MORALITY AND THE GOOD LIFE:
AN INTRODUCTION TO ETHICS THROUGH CLASSICAL SOURCES

Published by McGraw-Hill, a business unit of The McGraw-Hill Companies, Inc., 1221 Avenue of the Americas, New York, NY, 10020 Copyright © 2004, 1999, 1992, 1984, by The McGraw-Hill Companies, Inc. All rights reserved. No part of this publication may be reproduced or distributed in any form or by any means, or stored in a database or retrieval system, without the prior written consent of The McGraw-Hill Companies, Inc., including, but not limited to, in any network or other electronic storage or transmission, or broadcast for distance learning.

Some ancillaries, including electronic and print components, may not be available to customers outside the United States.

This book is printed on acid-free paper.

1 2 3 4 5 6 7 8 9 0 DOC/DOC 0 9 8 7 6 5 4 3

ISBN 0-07-283192-8

Publisher: *Christopher Freitag*
Sponsoring editor: *Jon-David Hague*
Marketing manager: *Lisa Berry*
Senior project manager: *Rebecca Nordbrock*
Production supervisor: *Janean A. Utley*
Coordinator of freelance design: *Mary E. Kazak*
Cover design: *Sarah Studnicki*
Cover image: © 2003 *Artists Rights Society (ARS), New York/ADAGP, Paris*
                    © *Smithsonian American Art Museum, Washington, DC/Art Resource, NY*
Typeface: *10/12 Times Roman*
Compositor: *GAC Indianapolis*
Printer: *R. R. Donnelley and Sons, Inc.*

Library of Congress Cataloging-in-Publication Data

Solomon, Robert C.
    Morality and the good life : an introduction to ethics through classical sources / Robert C. Solomon, Clancy W. Martin — 4th ed.
        p.   cm.
    Includes biographical references and index.
        ISBN 0-07-283192-8 (alk. paper)
        1. Ethics.   I. Martin, Clancy W.   II. Title.
    BJ1012.S57   2004
    170—dc21

                                                                                    2003045931

www.mhhe.com

About the Authors

ROBERT C. SOLOMON is Quincy Lee Centennial Professor at the University of Texas at Austin. He received his Ph.D. from the University of Michigan and has taught at Princeton University, the University of Pittsburgh, and the University of California. He is the author of *From Rationalism to Existentialism* (Harper & Row, 1972), *The Passions* (Doubleday, 1976), *In the Spirit of Hegel* (Oxford, 1983), and *About Love* (Simon and Schuster, 1988) as well as a number of textbooks in general philosophy.

CLANCY W. MARTIN is Assistant Professor of Philosophy at the University of Missouri, Kansas City. He received his Ph.D. from the University of Texas at Austin and has taught at the University of Texas at Austin and Southwestern University. He is the author of several articles on applied and general ethics.

For Kathleen
For Rebecca and Zelly

Preface

This is a textbook in ethics. It is intended as an introduction for students who have had no philosophical background but are capable of studying somewhat difficult yet indisputably important sources. The premise of this book is that the study of ethics is first of all participation in a long tradition that is based upon a (more or less) agreed-upon sequence of "great" philosophers. Of course, ethics is also an attempt to come to grips with certain perennial moral problems, but these too must be understood as part of a tradition of questions and answers as well as problems intrinsic to the human condition.

Ethics has never been a more urgent undertaking. We live at a time in which the very existence of morals—or at least any "correct" morals—has been thrown into question. But in the pedagogical attempts to capture this urgency with reference to current moral crises (the morality of abortion and euthanasia, the threat of nuclear war), too many introductory ethics courses have been made "relevant" only at the cost of ignoring the tradition that gives them significance. There is no disputing that questions such as "What is right and what should I do?" are utterly necessary and ought to be asked more often and with greater insight than they are in our "bottom-line"–minded society. But, on the one hand, it is not at all clear that the heavy intellectual artillery of philosophy is usually required or even suitable to answer the more usual variety of ethical queries (for example, "Why shouldn't I cheat on my test? Everyone else does"). On the other hand, it is not clear that a serious answer to such questions can be provided except *within* that long tradition that stretches from Plato and the Bible to the present.

The study of ethics is this synthesis of current problems and a long tradition of answers. It is a common error to think that ethical issues can be settled in a moral vacuum, without already shared values and a broad, if vague, general understanding of the nature of morality and the importance of being moral. But it is also an error to expect that the broad understanding of ethics—even when sharpened by the study of ethics—will provide concrete answers to pressing moral problems. (One leading American ethicist tells of the time when a student walked into his office and with obvious urgency asked, "Do you believe that suicide is ever justified?" As a matter of fact, the ethicist did believe that suicide was justifiable in certain cases, but it was equally clear to him that this was not the time to display philosophical subtleties.)

This is not to say that ethics is irrelevant to practical problems; indeed, it would be absurd if that were so. But solving problems is not the only concern of ethics or philosophy, and there are virtues of general understanding that need not be convertible into concrete solutions. It may be that no ethical theory or viewpoint is of any interest if it does not come to grips with our everyday moral concerns, but we should not thereby expect ready-made solutions to every personal problem. Indeed, one of the lessons of the history of ethics is that difficulties enter into solving even the simplest moral dilemma. The point of learning about various ethical theories or viewpoints is not to make solving problems easier for us. In fact, it may well make problem solving harder, as we come to appreciate more and more of the implications and considerations that enter into even the simplest ethical decision.

To study ethics, with the approach assumed in this text, is to participate in that long tradition (or, rather, traditions) that reach back over 3,000 years, to ancient religions and early philosophers. In those traditions we find early on the central questions of ethics, "What is the good?" "What is justice?" "What is happiness?" and "Why should one not simply follow one's own desires and interests, without regard for others?" Studying ethics is reading and thinking through such questions and the answers provided to them by the ancient scriptures, by Socrates and Plato, and by Plato's student Aristotle, by the Medieval philosophers, and by such modern philosophers as David Hume, Immanuel Kant, John Stuart Mill, Jean-Paul Sartre, Bertrand Russell, and John Rawls.

It is too often said today that students are no longer interested or willing (or sometimes able) to read original texts. But these are not so difficult as supposed, and if they seem to be, it is in part because students today are confronted less and less with original philosophy texts, which means that they have a harder time reading them, which means that they avoid them more, and so on *ad illiteratum.* At the same time, it is a pedagogical fact that students resist long tracts of original text and at least at first have considerable difficulty learning the kind of critical reading required in philosophy. Accordingly, we have tried to provide both substantial portions of original texts *and* a continuing sequence of comments and suggestions. This has the effect, however modest, of providing a tutor for each student as he or she reads through the material and encouraging him or her to participate in the process rather than just struggling with the text. We hope that the commentary will allow instructors not only more freedom in leading discussions but also more confidence that their students will have had at least some minimal exposure to a broad range of issues.

This book is composed of substantial texts coupled and broken up with background and commentary, suggestions, and study questions. The works are not complete but, given the context of an undergraduate course, more than sufficient to give the student substantial knowledge of the classical texts. This book is adequate for a full course in ethics, but it is concise enough to allow the instructor time to include other approaches—whether more contemporary authors and issues or particular moral dilemmas—in addition to the classic texts and materials presented here.

In this, the fourth edition, we have continued to improve the earlier reading and tried to add and vary the material. In the previous edition, we used improved translations and added more Plato and Saint Augustine as well as more Nietzsche. We also added material from John Rawls' classic *Theory of Justice* and improved the commentary. The most dramatic change in this edition is a new Prologue of ancient religious sources with commentary. We have tried to be very multicultural in doing this, using selections not only from the Hebrew Bible and New Testament but also from the Qur'an, from the Indian Vedas and Bhagavad Gita, from Confucius and Mencius and two Taoists, Lao-Tze and Chuang-Tze. Since we do not assume that most students are familiar with some of these texts, we have added considerable commentary as well. We have also added selections from Bertrand Russell, one of the great philosophers of the twentieth century, and we have added to the selections of both Hobbes and Hume. And we have, of course, tried to further improve the introduction and the commentary throughout the book.

It is appropriate to comment here on the typical use of the masculine noun "man" in many of the authors included here. Aristotle, for example, develops an ethics that is literally just for men. More modern authors—Hume, Kant, and Mill, for example—use "man" as a generic term for "humanity." This grates against our contemporary sensibilities, and we have accordingly used more neutral language in the commentaries. The original language has been left in the texts as a matter of accuracy, not as a matter of approval.

We would like to express our thanks for the many useful comments and suggestions provided by colleagues who reviewed this text during the course of its development, especially to Orville Clark, University of Wisconsin–Green Bay; James Fortuna, Forsyth Technical College; R. J. Hankinson, the University of Texas at Austin; Izchak Miller, University of Pennsylvania; Sharon Lee Staples, Utah Valley Community College; John J. Stuhr, Whitman College; James J. Valone, visiting associate professor, Loyola University of Chicago; and Stephen Voss, San José State University; and for this edition to John Teehan, Hofstra University; Michael Foley, Marywood University; Janice Capel Anderson, University of Idaho; and David Chadd, California State University, Long Beach.

We would especially like to thank Patricia Greenspan, Jennifer Greene, and Al Martinich, for their help with this and prior editions.

Robert C. Solomon
Clancy W. Martin

Contents

How to Use This Book

In the following pages, some of the classic texts in the history of ethics are presented with introductions and commentary to help the beginning student through the readings. It is not to be expected that most instructors will attempt to use all the readings; in fact, some may want to use only three or four of them. Several possible combinations are particularly recommended:

Basic Sequence

Prologue

Plato, *Crito*

Augustine, *City of God*

Kant, *Grounding*

Mill, *Utilitarianism*

Nietzsche, selections

Historical Survey

Prologue

Plato, *Crito, Republic*

Aristotle, *Ethics,* (Book I)

Augustine, *City of God*

Hobbes, *Leviathan* (first chapter)

Hume, *Treatise, Inquiry* (Book I)

Kant, *Grounding* (Sections 1 and 2)

Mill, *Utilitarianism* (Chapters 1 and 4)

Nietzsche, selections

Prologue: Ethics and Religion

Sartre, *Existentialism*

Rawls, *Theory of Justice*

Russell, selections

Emphasis on Justification

Aristotle, *Ethics* (Books I to III)

Augustine, *City of God*

Hobbes, *Leviathan* (first section)

Kant, *Grounding* (Sections 1 and 2)

Mill, *Utilitarianism* (Chapters 1 and 4)

Nietzsche, selections from *Beyond Good and Evil* and *Genealogy of Morals*

Individual and State

Plato, *Crito* and *Republic*

Aristotle, *Ethics* (Books I to III)

Hobbes, *Leviathan* (first section)

Hume, *Inquiry* (Chapters 2 and 3)

Kant, *Grounding* (Sections 1 and 2)

Mill, *Utilitarianism* (Chapters 1, 2, 5)

Sartre, *Existentialism* and *Bad Faith*

Rawls, *Theory of Justice*

The Virtues

Plato, *Crito*

Aristotle, *Ethics* (Books I to IV)

Augustine, *City of God*

Kant, *Grounding* (Chapters 1 and 2)

Mill, *Utilitarianism* (Chapters 1 to 3)

Nietzsche, selections

Sartre, *Existentialism*

Russell, selections

Ethos and Ethics

Plato, *Crito*

Aristotle, *Ethics* (Books I to IV)

Augustine, *City of God*

Kant, *Grounding* (Chapter 1)

Mill, *Utilitarianism* (Chapters 1 and 4)

Nietzsche, selections (esp. *Beyond Good and Evil*)

Sartre, *Existentialism*

Rawls, *Theory of Justice*

Happiness

Aristotle, *Ethics* (Books I to III)

Augustine, *City of God*

Hobbes, *Leviathan* (first section)

Kant, *Grounding* (Section 2)

Mill, *Utilitarianism* (Chapters 1, 2, 5)

Nietzsche, selections from *Beyond Good and Evil* and *Will to Power*

Russell, selections

Rawls, *Theory of Justice*

Freedom

Plato, *Crito*

Aristotle, *Ethics* (Books I to III)

Augustine, *City of God* (Problem of Evil)

Hobbes, *Leviathan*

Kant, *Grounding* (Sections 1 and 2)

Mill, *Utilitarianism* (Chapters 1 and 2)

Nietzsche, selections from *Beyond Good and Evil* and *Will to Power*

Sartre, *Existentialism*

Discussion and study questions are provided at the end of each chapter; thought questions appear in the discussions of the text as well. A glossary is provided at the end of the book, but new and technical terms are also explained when they are introduced in the text. The introduction is an attempt to provide a simple overview of ethics for the student who has no or little familiarity with the subject. Because of the complexity and difficulty of some of the material that follows, we will frequently interrupt the flow of text with notes and reference guides.

Introduction

*T*oday in a wood, we heard a Voice.

We hunted for it but could not find it. Adam said he had heard it before, but had never seen it. . . . It was Lord of the Garden, he said, . . . and it had said we must not eat of the fruit of a certain tree and that if we ate of it we would surely die. . . . Adam said it was the tree of good and evil.

"Good and evil?

"Yes."

"What is that?"

"What is what?"

"Why, those things. What is good?"

"I do not know. How should I know?"

"Well, then, what is evil?"

"I suppose it is the name of something, but I do not know what."

"But, Adam, you must have some idea of what it is."

"Why should I have some idea? I have never seen the thing, how am I to form any conception of it? What is your own notion of it?"

Of course I had none, and it was unreasonable of me to require him to have one. There was no way for either of us to guess what it might be. It was a new word, like the other; we had not heard them before, and they meant nothing to us.

—MARK TWAIN

Ethics, broadly speaking, is the study of values, rules, and justifications. It involves questions such as the ones Adam and Eve were just beginning to think about: What is good? What is evil? How do we know right from wrong? What is the good life? What makes a person good? As indicated by this broad range of questions, giving precise meaning to the study of ethics is a complicated business. We might begin to untangle some of its many aspects by looking at the distinction between "ethics" and "morality." Although the two terms are often used interchangeably, there is an important conceptual difference between them. *Morality* has to do specifically with rules of conduct. It is concerned, in other words, with the interpretation and implementation of our value system. Moral questions have to do with right and wrong, in contrast to larger questions about good and evil, ultimate sources of value, or means of justification. The study of *ethics* involves the question of *why* certain actions are deemed right whereas others are deemed wrong. And this is a call for justification. In philosophy, ethics refers to the theory behind our moral pronouncements.

That ethics and morality are often used interchangeably is not simply a matter of carelessness (although this is sometimes the case). Rather, the two disciplines are intimately related and, at least ideally, constantly influence one another. We cannot ask what "right" conduct is in a vacuum—to inquire about the right thing to do is to necessarily take into account the sort of agents involved in making the choice and the values to which they are attached. For example, to answer the question of whether physician-assisted suicide is morally permissible, we must go beyond the particular circumstances and delve deeper to ask about the value of life in general, whether that value is compromised by terminal illness, what rights the individual requesting assistance has, and what the duties are of those who attend that person. In other words, questions about "right" actions inevitably lead us to further questions about values and their place in human lives.

Conversely, many hold that the study of ethics is (or should be) influenced by existing morality and the problems that arise within morality. Taking the preceding example, assisted suicide and euthanasia in general have become a pressing problem (although such practices have existed for much longer) only with the advent of medical and technological advances that enable us to keep people alive far longer. Thus, our day-to-day lives and the rules we use to govern them are constantly presenting us with new questions for the theoretical discipline of ethics to investigate. Practice informs theory and vice versa.

The readings included in this volume are, for the most part, concerned with ethical, rather than strictly moral, questions. Although it is difficult to generalize across the 13 quite distinct approaches offered, the authors are (again for the most part) concerned with questions regarding the nature of the values we hold and their role in human lives. One way of putting this, which we shall see time and again, is to ask, What is the ultimate good—or *summum bonum* (literally, "greatest good")—for human beings? The answers to this question are enormously varied. St. Augustine holds it to be salvation in the next life, whereas John Stuart Mill claims it is happiness in this one. Immanuel Kant locates the ultimate good in reason alone, but David Hume states famously that "reason is, and ought to be, the slave of the passions." Aristotle and Plato both thought that we could determine the good for human beings "caught in the act." It is interesting to remember here that Jesus's father Joseph initially had believed his wife Mary to be an adulteress, but had "planned to dismiss her quietly" in order not "to expose her to public disgrace," when an angel of the Lord appeared to him in a dream and convinced him that her conception was not manmade, but divine.) The accused woman is brought before Jesus, and her captors tell him that according to the law, she must be stoned to death. As John relates, they tell this to Jesus not because they want his advice, but in the hope that he will disagree with what is commanded by the law, so that they may have legal grounds for bringing a charge of heresy against him. But Jesus neatly outwits them, and in so doing illustrates the Christian principle that, at least among the merely mortal (as opposed to the divine) forgiveness is more important than the law.

8 [53 Then each of them went home, 1 while Jesus went to the Mount of Olives. 2 Early in the morning he came again to the temple. All the people came to him and he sat down and began to teach them. 3 The scribes and the Pharisees brought a woman who had been caught in adultery; and making her stand before all of them, 4 they said to him, "Teacher, this woman was caught in the very act of committing adultery. 5 Now in the law Moses commanded us to stone such women. Now what do you say?" 6 They said this to test him, so that they might have some charge to bring against him. Jesus bent down and wrote with his finger on the ground. 7 When they kept on questioning him, he straightened up and said to them, "Let anyone among you who is without sin be the first to throw a stone at her." 8 And once again he bent down and wrote on the ground. 9 When they heard it, they went away, one by one, beginning with the elders; and Jesus was left alone with the woman standing before him. 10 Jesus straightened up and said to her, "Woman, where are they? Has no one condemned you?" 11 She said, "No one, sir." And Jesus said, "Neither do I condemn you. Go your way, and from now on do not sin again."]

[John 8:1–11]

Our next three selections are from two of Paul's most important letters: the letter to the Romans and the first letter to the Corinthians. In the first text, Paul explains the relationship between sin and the redemption from sin by Christ. In the second text, also from Romans, he argues that "one word" sums up all the other commandments (though it takes five words): "Love your neighbor as yourself." Love, Paul writes, is "the fulfilling of the law" given in the Hebrew tradition. The last passage gives Paul's justly famous description of love in his first letter to the Corinthians. The passage has been overquoted, no doubt, but we repeat it here because we believe that it remains one of the most important and powerful descriptions of love in the Western tradition. It culminates in Paul's summary of the Christian message: "And now faith, hope, and love abide, these three; and the greatest of these is love."

14 For we know that the law is spiritual; but I am of the flesh, sold into slavery under sin. [15] I do not understand my own actions. For I do not do what

[Romans 7:14 – 8:11]

I want, but I do the very thing I hate. [16] Now if I do what I do not want, I agree that the law is good. [17] But in fact it is no longer I that do it, but sin that dwells within me. [18] For I know that nothing good dwells within me, that is, in my flesh. I can will what is right, but I cannot do it. [19] For I do not do the good I want, but the evil I do not want is what I do. [20] Now if I do what I do not want, it is no longer I that do it, but sin that dwells within me.

21 So I find it to be a law that when I want to do what is good, evil lies close at hand. [22] For I delight in the law of God in my inmost self, [23] but I see in my members another law at war with the law of my mind, making me captive to the law of sin that dwells in my members. [24] Wretched man that I am! Who will rescue me from this body of death? [25] Thanks be to God through Jesus Christ our Lord! So then, with my mind I am a slave to the law of God, but with my flesh I am a slave to the law of sin.

8 There is therefore now no condemnation for those who are in Christ Jesus. [2] For the law of the Spirit of life in Christ Jesus has set you free from the law of sin and of death. [3] For God has done what the law, weakened by the flesh, could not do: by sending his own Son in the likeness of sinful flesh, and to deal with sin, he condemned sin in the flesh, [4] so that the just requirement of the law might be fulfilled in us, who walk not according to the flesh but according to the Spirit. [5] For those who live according to the flesh set their minds on the things of the flesh, but those who live according to the Spirit set their minds on the things of the Spirit. [6] To set the mind on the flesh is death, but to set the mind on the Spirit is life and peace. [7] For this reason the mind that is set on the flesh is hostile to God; it does not submit to God's law—indeed it cannot, [8] and those who are in the flesh cannot please God.

9 But you are not in the flesh; you are in the Spirit, since the Spirit of God dwells in you. Anyone who does not have the Spirit of Christ does not belong to him. [10] But if Christ is in you, though the body is dead because of sin, the Spirit is life because of righteousness. [11] If the Spirit of him who raised Jesus from the dead dwells in you, he who raised Christ from the dead will give life to your mortal bodies also through his Spirit that dwells in you.

[Romans 13:8–10]

8 Owe no one anything, except to love one another: for the one who loves another has fulfilled the law. [9] The commandments, 'You shall not commit adultery; You shall not murder; You shall not steal; You shall not covet"; and any other commandment, are summed up in this word, "Love your neighbor as yourself." [10] Love does no wrong to a neighbor; therefore, love is the fulfilling of the law.

[1 Corinthians 13:1–13]

13 If I speak in the tongues of mortals and of angels, but do not have love, I am a noisy gong or a clanging cymbal. [2] And if I have prophetic powers, and understand all mysteries and all knowledge, and if I have all faith, so as to remove mountains, but do not have love, I am nothing. [3] If I give away all my possessions, and if I hand over my body so that I may boast, but do not have love, I gain nothing.

4 Love is patient; love is kind; love is not envious or boastful or arrogant [5] or rude. It does not insist on its own way; it is not irritable or resentful; [6] it does not rejoice in wrongdoing, but rejoices in the truth. [7] It bears all things, believes all things, hopes all things, endures all things.

8 Love never ends. But as for prophecies, they will come to an end; as for tongues, they will cease; as for knowledge, it will come to an end. [9] For we know only in part, and we prophesy only in part; [10] but when the complete comes, the partial will come to an end. [11] When I was a child, I spoke like a child, I thought like a child, I reasoned like a child; when I became an adult, I put an end to childish ways. [12] For now we see in a mirror, dimly, but then we will see face to face. Now I know only in part; then I will know fully, even as I have been fully known. [13] And now faith, hope, and love abide, these three; and the greatest of these is love.

THE QUR'AN

Islam means "surrender" (it is etymologically related to *salam,* "peace") and it is this peaceful surrender to God's will that is the foundation of the Islamic religion and ethic. The founder of the religion of Islam is Muhammad, often called simply "The Prophet." Muhammad was born in approximately A.D. 570, in the city of *Makkah* (Mecca) in present day Saudi Arabia. His ministry began in 609 or 610 and continued until his death in 632. The *Qur'an* is the written record of his inspired utterances (made, according to tradition, when he was in a trancelike state), which are to be understood as the direct revelation of God to Muhammad. Thus the verses or *suras* of the *Qur'an* often begin with the command, "Say," indicating that it is not Muhammad who is the source of these words, but God himself who is instructing Muhammad to repeat what he is told. (Sometimes the book also speaks of God in the third person, which has led Muslim scholars to suggest that an angel or angels may at times speak through Muhammad.)

The central message of the *Qur'an* is familiar: that there is only one God (*Allah*), and that it is the duty of all humankind to worship and obey him. For a Muslim—one who practices the religion of Islam—the belief that there is one and only one God is revealed not only by the *Qur'an,* but also by the prior prophetic tradition of the Hebrew Bible and the New Testament. Of course, the *Qur'an* does not itself depend on those previous prophetic revelations (although it mentions many characters from the Hebrew Bible and the New Testament), but neither is it intended to refute them. Rather, the *Qur'an* is the culminating revelation of God and is intended to conclusively establish all that has been previously revealed.

Accordingly, the *Qur'an* does not propose to introduce a new ethic: like Christianity before it, it seeks not to repeal or revise, but rather to further illuminate the moral tradition that has long been established. True, there are many highly specific moral and even legal recommendations and proscriptions in the *Qur'an*. The books of *fiqh* (roughly, "law") separate human behavior into five categories, which address everything from murder to manners and from incest to the rules of pilgrimage and religious seclusion. Many—if not most—of the specific "dos and don'ts" of the *Qur'an* seem particularly relevant to the problems of Arabic society at the time. For example, there are repeated injunctions against infanticide, which had become a common practice, especially among the very poor. (The Hebrew Bible, we recall, has many similarly practical recommendations that seem to be grounded in their particular socio-historical situation, such as the various rules governing the purity of foods). But the ethical core of the *Qur'an* is very much of a kind with the Hebrew and Christian tradition that it affirms:

> We believe in God and what has been sent down to us, and what was sent down
> to Abraham, Ishmael, Isaac, and their descendants, and what was given Moses,
> Jesus, and the prophets by their Lord (*Qur'an* 3:84).

Islam does not affirm the divinity of any of these prophets—even Muhammad was just a man. Rather, it affirms that God has spoken through these men and revealed the truth (or a series of truths) to humankind. Those truths include monotheism, and the consequent moral authority of God (and God's revealed word); the divine creation of the universe; the belief in eternal life and in a day of judgement, which will result either in a heavenly salvation or a damnation to hell; the importance of helping others, and avoiding doing unjustified harm to others (the *Qur'an* permits doing harm to others in self-defense and recommends various corporal punishments for lawbreakers, including the death penalty for murderers); the need to act with justice or fairness, which is tempered by the moral virtue of forgiveness; and many similar beliefs that we have already seen in the Hebrew and Christian traditions. The point, again, is that the *Qur'an* and Islamic belief is intended to further a religious and moral tradition that the faithful Muslim understands as fundamentally continuous.

Crucial to the Muslim way of life are the famous "Five Pillars of Islam." These are Islamic duties prescribed by the Prophet and distilled by later commentators from a variety of different places in the *Qur'an.* They are:

1. *Shahada* or simply "faith," which is declared in the formula, "There is no god worthy of worship except God and Muhammad is his messenger."
2. *Salat,* "prayer" or "worship," which must be performed five times a day by every Muslim and which is considered to be the direct link between the worshipper and God.
3. *Zakat,* meaning both "purification" and "growth", is practiced by almsgiving or compulsory charity. This is a tax, paid once a year by all adult Muslims, assessed at 2.5 percent of one's wealth above a certain minimum (known as the *nisab*). In more recent Muslim tradition, the *zakat* is often assessed by each believer individually.
4. *Sawm,* or the fast during Ramadan. This takes place every year in the month of Ramadan (the ninth month of the lunar calendar) and requires all Muslims from puberty on to abstain from food, drink, and sexual relations during the daylight hours.
5. *Hajj,* or the pilgrimage to Makkah. All able adult Muslims are required to make the journey to Makkah at least once in their lifetime. This particularly

All translations are from Malauwi Sher Ali, *The Holy Qur'an.* (Islam International Publications Limited, UK, 1992).

demanding religious obligation has been relaxed over time in many Muslim sects, and it is now generally considered to be a duty only for those who are physically and financially capable of performing it. (That said, approximately two million people visit Makkah each year).

The *Qur'an* consists of a series of 114 *suras* (literally, "rows") or chapters, arranged roughly according to length, beginning with the longest chapters. An important exception to this rule, however, is the first *sura*, the *Fatiha* ("Opening"). The *Fatiha* is sometimes called the "Mother of Islam." It is repeated during each of the five daily prayers required of all Moslems, and is also frequently used as a meditative prayer between the formal prayers. For Muslims, the essence of Islam is captured by the *Fatiha*.

> 1. In the name of Allah. the Gracious, the Merciful.
> 2. All praise belongs to Allah, Lord of all the worlds,
> 3. The Gracious, the Merciful,
> 4. Master of the Day of Judgment.
> 5. Thee alone do we worship and Thee alone do we implore for help.
> 6. Guide us in the right path—
> 7. The path of those on whom Thou hast bestowed *Thy* blessings, those who have not incurred *Thy* displeasure, and those who have not gone astray.

[Qur'an 1:1–7]

Perhaps the most concise statement of an Islamic ethical code is found at *Qur'an* 6:151–153, in the *sura* known as "Livestock." In "Livestock" the *Qur'an* takes on a character reminiscent of the Hebrew Ten Commandments, offering specific moral injunctions such as showing kindness to parents and being just in speech (even to relatives!). Here, as in the Hebrew Bible (which it mentions a few lines later, saying "We gave Moses the Book") the ethical code is based on justice or fairness, rather than on the Christian ethic of forgiveness. However, included within the *Qur'an*'s "explanation of all necessary things" is both "a guidance and a mercy": God insists on moral principles, but he also forgives moral failures. Notice also the emphasis the *Qur'an* always places on its role in tradition, reminding the Moslem believers that "the Book" was sent down to "two peoples" (the Hebrews and the Christians) before them, and now is being sent to them.

> 152. Say, 'Come, I will rehearse to you what your Lord has forbidden: that you associate not anything as partner with Him and *that you do* good to parents, and that you kill not your children for *fear of* poverty—it is We Who provide for you and for them—and that you approach not foul deeds, whether open or secret: and that you kill not the life which Allah has made sacred, save by right. That is what He has enjoined upon you, that you may understand.

[Qur'an 6:152–164]

153. 'And approach not the property of the orphan, except in *a way* which is best, till he attains his maturity. And give full measure and weight with equity. We task not any soul except according to its capacity. And when you speak, observe justice, even if *the concerned person* be a relative, and fulfil the covenant of Allah. That is what He enjoins upon you, that you may remember.'

154. And *say,* 'This is My path *leading* straight. So follow it; and follow not *other* ways, lest they lead you away from His way. That is what He enjoins upon you, that you may *become able to* guard *against evils.*'

155. Again, We gave Moses the Book—completing the favour upon him who did good, and an explanation of all *necessary* things, and a guidance and a mercy—that they might believe in the meeting with their Lord.

156. And this is a Book which We have sent down; *it is* full of blessings. So follow it, and guard against *sin* that you may be shown mercy;

157. Lest you should say, 'The Book was sent down only to two peoples before us, and we were indeed unaware of their reading;'

158. Or lest you should say, 'Had the Book been sent down to us, we should surely have been better guided than they.' There has *now* come to you a clear evidence from your Lord, and a guidance and a mercy. Who, then, is more unjust than he who rejects the Signs of Allah and turns away from them? We will requite those who turn away from Our Signs with an evil punishment because of their turning away.

159. Do they expect aught but that angels should come to them or that thy Lord should come or that some of the Signs of thy Lord should come? The day when some of the Signs of thy Lord shall come, to believe in them shall not profit a soul which believed not before, nor earned any good by its faith. Say, 'Wait ye, we *too* are waiting.'

160. *As for* those who split up their religion and became *divided into* sects, thou hast no concern at all with them. Surely their case will come before Allah, then will He inform them of what they used to do.

161. Whoso does a good deed shall have ten times as much; but he who does an evil deed, shall have only a like reward; and they shall not be wronged.

162. Say, 'As for me, my Lord has guided me unto a straight path—a right religion, the religion of Abraham, the upright. And he was not of those who join gods *with God.*'

163. Say, 'My Prayer and my sacrifice and my life and my death are *all* for Allah, the Lord of the worlds.

164. 'He has no partner. And so am I commanded, and I am the first of those who submit.'

Although the "Five Pillars" are not located in any particular series of *suras* or verses of the *Qur'an*, we have included a sampling of representative verses drawn from several places in the book. (The exception to this is the first pillar, which is given according to the standard Islamic formula.)

> There is no god but God, and Muhammad is his prophet.

The Second Pillar, *Salat* or prayer:

> And when you have finished the Prayer, remember Allah while standing, and sitting, and lying on your sides. And when you are secure from danger, then observe prayer in the proscribed form; verily Prayer is enjoined on the believers to be performed at fixed hours. (4:104)
>
> And enjoin Prayer on thy people, and be constant therein. We ask thee not for provision; it is We that provide for thee. And the end is for righteousness. (20:133).

On prayer, recitation of the *Qur'an* and the *Zakat* (growth through charity):

> 21. Surely, thy Lord knows that thou standest up *praying* for nearly two-thirds of the night, and *sometimes* half or a third thereof, and also a party of those who are with thee. And Allah determines the measure of the night and the day. He knows that you cannot keep its *measure,* so He has turned to you in mercy. Recite, then, as much of the Qur'ān as is easy *for you.* He knows that there will be some among you who may be sick and others who may travel in the land seeking Allah's bounty, and others who may fight in the cause of Allah. So recite of it that which is easy *for you,* and observe Prayer, and pay the Zakāt, and lend to Allah a goodly loan. And whatever good you send on before you for your souls, you will find it with Allah. It *will be* better and greater in reward. And seek forgiveness of Allah. Surely, Allah is Most Forgiving, Merciful.

[Qur'an 73:21]

The Third Pillar, *Zakat:*

> The alms are only for the poor and the needy, and for those employed in connection therewith, and for those whose hearts are to be reconciled, and for the freeing of slaves, and for those in debt, and for the cause of Allah, and for the wayfarer—an ordinance from Allah. And Allah is All-Knowing, Wise. (9:60).

[Qur'an
23:1–12]

1. In the name of Allah, the Gracious, the Merciful.

2. Surely, success does come to the believers,

3. Who are humble in their Prayers,

4. And who shun all that which is vain,

5. And who are active in paying the Zakāt,

6. And who guard their chastity—

7. Except from their wives or what their right hands possess, for then they are not to be blamed;

8. But those who seek *anything* beyond that are the transgressors—

9. And who are watchful of their trusts and their covenants,

10. And who are strict in the observance of their Prayers.

11. These are the heirs,

12. Who will inherit Paradise. They will abide therein.

The Fourth Pillar, *Sawm,* the fast during Ramadan:

[Qur'an
2:184–186]

184. O ye who believe! fasting is prescribed for you, as it was prescribed for those before you, so that you may become righteous.

185. *The prescribed fasting* is for a fixed number of days, but whoso among you is sick or is on a journey *shall fast* the same number of other days; and for those who are able to fast *only* with great difficulty is an expiation—the feeding of a poor man. And whoso performs a good work with willing obedience, it is better for him. And fasting is good for you, if you only knew.

186. The month of Ramadān is that in which the Qur'ān was sent down as a guidance for mankind with clear proofs of guidance and discrimination. Therefore, whosoever of you is present *at home* in this month, let him fast therein. But whoso is sick or is on a journey, *shall fast* the same number of other days. Allah desires *to give* you facility and He desires not hardship for you, and that you may complete the number, and that you may exalt Allah for His having guided you and that you may be grateful.

The Fifth Pillar, *Hajj,* the pilgrimage to Makkah:

[Qur'an 3:98]

98. In it are manifest Signs; it is the place of Abraham; and whoso enters it, enters peace. And pilgrimage to the House is a duty which men—those who can find a way thither—owe to Allah. And whoever disbelieves, *let him remember* that Allah is surely independent of all creatures.

And the purpose of the pilgrimage:

28. 'And proclaim unto mankind the Pilgrimage. They will come to thee on foot, and on every lean camel, coming by every distant track,

29. 'That they may witness *its* benefits for them and may mention the name of Allah, during the appointed days, over the quadrupeds of *the class of* cattle that He has provided for them. Then eat ye thereof and feed the distressed, the needy.

30. 'Then let them accomplish their needful acts of cleansing, and fulfil their vows, and go around the Ancient House.'

31. That is *God's commandment.* And whoso honours the sacred things of Allah, it will be good for him with his Lord. And cattle are made lawful to you but not that which has been announced to you. Shun therefore the abomination of idols, and shun all words of untruth,

32. Remaining ever inclined to Allah, not associating anything with Him. And whoso associates anything with Allah, falls, as it were, from a height, and the birds snatch him up, or the wind blows him away to a distant place.

33. That *is so.* And whoso respects the sacred Signs of Allah—that indeed *proceeds* from the righteousness of hearts.

34. In them (offerings) are benefits for you for an appointed term, then their place of sacrifice is at the Ancient House.

[Qur'an 22:28–34]

ANCIENT ASIA

The religious philosophies of Asia were deeply concerned with ethics and daily life and in general tended to avoid abstract questions of theology. The philosophical worldviews of ancient China and India, although cited in every list of major world "religions," are not focused on humanity's relationship to God. Buddhism, in general, is a religion without God (although it is quite full of divinities, which should not be assumed to be comparable to the Western monotheistic conception of God.) Thus, the dominant Judeo-Christian-Islamic questions of revelation and salvation are all but irrelevant. The great Eastern traditions (especially Buddhism and Confucianism), like the western religions, are "religions of the book"; that is, they have essential texts or scriptures. One might be tempted to say that these Eastern traditions tend to focus instead, like the Greeks and the Romans, on the appropriate way to live in this world. But that already introduces a distinction between the secular and the sacred, which is a Western, not an Eastern, way of thinking. In Confucianism, for instance, the distinction between heaven and earth, although thematic, is not a dichotomy between radically different orders of being. So, too, the distinction between religion and daily ethics is not pronounced, insofar as it can be made out at all.

We have included below excerpts from the great texts of two major traditions in ancient Asia, from South Asia (Hinduism, Jainism, and Buddhism) and from East Asia (Confucianism, Taoism). Hinduism, Jainism, and Buddhism share a source in the ancient *Vedas,* excerpts of which we have included here. Buddhism has as its subsequent sources the teachings of the Buddha ("the Enlightened One"), and we have also included some of those. Starting in India (and subsequently in much of southeast and eastern Asia and then throughout the world), Buddhism became one of the most widespread religious philosophies and sources of ethics. From China, we have included four ancient sources: two from Confucius and his followers—one from Confucius and the other from his distant disciple Mencius—and two from the Taoists Lao-Tze and Chuang-Tze. The religious philosophies of China remained more contained (although China absorbed many influences from India and other parts of the world), but they remain the primary source of ethics for over nearly two billion people around the world.

INDIA: HINDUISM AND BUDDHISM

The three indigenous religious philosophies of India—Hinduism, Jainism, and Buddhism—share a great many evident similarities, including their notable differences from the monotheistic religions of the West. Hinduism is not as such a religion—that is, a distinctive set of beliefs, but rather a wide variety of philosophies, folk myths, practices, rituals and social structures based on the ancient *Vedas,* which we have excerpted here. Buddhism and Jainism begin from the same texts, and they are all, in this sense, religions of the *Vedas.* In *The Upanishads,* early interpretations of the *Vedas,* the central notion is Brahman, the Absolute, the One, and there has been a three-millennium debate about whether Brahman is God. But both Buddhism and Jainism ultimately reject Hindu interpretations of the *Vedas* and, in particular, the caste system which the *Vedas* have historically justified. So, too, Buddhists generally reject both the notion of God (or Brahman) and the notion of self (atman) that are so central to much of Hindu thought. Buddhism, by contrast, often defends a conception of anatman, or "no self." We have included some of the central Buddhist teachings on this topic as well.

All three religions are deeply concerned with the problem of suffering (duhkha). It was his perception of the suffering around him that set the young prince Gautama Siddhartha on his quest for enlightenment and understanding, and it is above all the principle of "do no harm" that defines Jainism. Hinduism often strikes Western observers as a religion that is indifferent to suffering and, with its harsh social hierarchy, even contributes to human suffering. Insofar as life is suffering, we can readily understand the desire to escape it. The belief that life happens not just once but over and over again only makes the need for liberation all the more imperative and difficult. Thus, all three religious philosophies have as a central theme the notion of "release" or "liberation" from the suffering of life (nirvana in Buddhism, moksha in Hinduism and Jainism) and discuss in great detail the experience of such liberation. The way to liberation is enormously varied. In some Buddhist sects or cults, years of intensive training and discipline are required for enlightenment. In some forms of Hinduism, by contrast, the advice is rather "whatever works for you." And all three religious philosophies are deeply concerned about the nature of the soul or self (or the absence of one), because it is having the correct notion of oneself that is the key to liberation, or what the Western religions would call salvation.

The following excerpts are from the oldest *Veda,* the *Rg Veda* (from roughly 1500 B.C.E.). One is a "Hymn of Creation," in which desire is cited as the "earliest seed of thought." The other is a cautionary moral tale about gambling, evidently a dangerous vice more than three millennia ago.

The Rg Veda*

Hymn of Creation

1. Non-being then existed not nor being:

    There was no air, nor sky that is beyond it.

    What was concealed? Wherein? In whose protection?

    And was there deep unfathomable water?

2. Death then existed not nor life immortal;

    Of neither night nor day was any token.

    By its inherent force the One breathed windless:

    No other thing than that beyond existed.

3. Darkness there was at first by darkness hidden;

    Without distinctive marks, this all was water.

    That which, becoming, by the void was covered,

    That One by force of heat came into being.

4. Desire entered the One in the beginning:

    It was the earliest seed, of thought the product.

    The sages searching in their hearts with wisdom,

    Found out the bond of being in non-being.

5. Their ray extended light across the darkness:

    But was the One above or was it under?

    Creative force was there, and fertile power:

    Below was energy, above was impulse.

6. Who knows for certain? Who shall here declare it?

    His praiser in prosperity has settled,

    As long as clays endure, as long as mornings.

    What has become of those our former friendships,

    When we two held erstwhile unbroken converse?

    O sovereign Varuna, thy lofty mansion,

    Thy home, I entered, with its thousand portals.

    Who is, O Varuna, thy constant kinsman,

---

*A. A. Macdonell, ed. and trans. *Hymns from the Rg Veda.* London: Oxford University Press, 1911.

Once dear, though sinful now, he claims thy friendships.

As guilty may we not, O wizard, suffer:

Do thou, O sage, grant shelter to thy praiser.

O may we, in these fixed abodes abiding,

Now from the lap of Aditi find favour.

May from his noose king Varuna release us.

Ye gods protect us evermore with blessings.

The Gambler

1. On high trees born and in a windy region

   The danglers, rolling on the diceboard, cheer me.

   Like Soma draught from Mūjavant's great mountain,

   The rousing nut Vibhīdaka has pleased me.

2. She wrangles not with me nor is she angry:

   To me and comrades she was ever kindly.

   For dice that only luckless throws effected

   I've driven away from home a wife devoted.

3. Her mother hates me, she herself rejects me:

   For one in such distress there is no pity.

   I find a gambling man is no more useful

   Than is an aged horse that's in the market.

4. Others embrace the wife of him whose chattels

   The eager dice have striven hard to capture;

   And father, mother, brothers say about him:

   "We know him not; lead him away a captive."

5. When to myself I think, "I'll not go with them,

   I'll stay behind my friends that go to gamble,"

   And those brown nuts, thrown down, have raised their voices,

   I go, like wench, straight to the place of meeting.

6. To the assembly hall the gambler sallies,

   And asking, "Shall I win?" he quakes and trembles.

And then the dice run counter to his wishes,

Giving the lucky throw to his opponent.

7. The dice attract the gambler, but deceive and wound,

Both paining men at play and causing them to pain.

Like boys they offer first and then take back their gifts:

With honey sweet to gamblers by their magic charm.

8. Their throng in triple fifties plays untrammelled,

Like Savitar the god whose laws are constant.

They yield not to the wrath of even the mighty:

A king himself on them bestows obeisance.

9. Downward they roll, then swiftly springing upward,

They overcome the man with hands, though handless.

Cast on the board like magic bits of charcoal,

Though cold themselves, they burn the heart to ashes.

10. Grieved is the gambler's wife by him abandoned,

Grieved, too, his mother as he aimless wanders.

Indebted, fearing, he desiring money

At night approaches other people's houses.

11. It pains the gambler when he sees a woman

Another's wife, and their well-ordered household.

He yokes those brown steeds early in the morning,

And when the fire is low sinks down a beggar.

12. To him who's general of your mighty forces,

As king becomes the chief of your battalions,

I hold my fingers ten extended forward:

"No money I withhold, this truth I tell thee."

13. Play not with dice, but cultivate thy tillage,

Enjoy thy riches, deeming them abundant.

There are thy cows; there is thy wife, O Gambler:

This counsel Savitar the noble gives me.

14. Make friends with us, we pray, to us be gracious;

Do not bewitch us forcibly with magic;

Let now your enmity, your anger slumber:

Let others be in brownies' toils entangled.

The great moral treatise of Hinduism is an epic poem called the *Bhagavad Gita,* "The Song of God" (200 B.C.E.) The "Gita" is an extended dialogue between Krishna, one of the *avatars,* or manifestations of God, and Arjuna, a great hero who is about to fight his greatest battle in defense of the rightful king. But the "enemy" is also his family and his friends, and Arjuna is thus in moral turmoil about what is the right thing to do. Krishna tells him to do the right thing, even if it means killing his own kin. His arguments suggest a lot about the Hindu view of the world and what should be important to us.

The Bhagavad Gitā*

Arjuna said:

3.1 Krishna, if you consider understanding superior to action, why then do you urge me on to an action so terrible?

3.2 It seems you would confuse my understanding with contradictory words. So tell me definitely that whereby I can attain the supreme good.

Krishna said:

3.3 There are in this world two fundamental stances declared by me of old, Arjuna: the yoga of knowledge for intellectuals, the yoga of action for yogins.

3.4 By abstaining from works, a person does not enjoy a mystical action-lessness; nor by renunciation alone is perfection attained.

3.5 For no one is able to remain even for a moment without acting; everyone willy-nilly is made to do work by the impulsions [*gunas,* "modes"] of nature.

3.6 Self-deluded is he who sits controlling the faculties of action while at the same time thinking about the objects of experience. He is a hypocrite.

3.7 But a person controlling his senses with the mind and commencing a disciplined work [*karma yoga*] with his faculties of action, unattached, that person excels, Arjuna.

3.8 Do controlled work, for action is better than inaction. The very maintenance of your body would not be accomplished without work.

3.9 Without personal attachment undertake action, Arjuna, for just one purpose, for the purpose of sacrifice. From work undertaken for purposes other than sacrifice, this world is bound to the law of *karma.*

3.15 Know works to have their origin in Brahman, and Brahman its foundation in the Immutable. Therefore is the omnipresent Brahman established through all time in sacrifice.

3.16 The wheel is thus set in motion. One who does not follow its rounds, evil in intentions, sensual in delights, he lives in vain, Arjuna.

3.17 But the person delighting only in his higher Self and satisfied living in it—for such a person, thoroughly contented in the Self alone, there is nothing that must be done.

3.18 Nor is there for him any gain in what he has done or not done. Nor do his interests depend in any way on anyone or anything else.

*Translated by Stephen H. Phillips.

3.19 Therefore, ever unattached do the work that has to be done. For the person who is unattached in performing action attains the supreme good.

3.21 Whatever the superior person does that indeed is what other folk try to do. The standard that he sets is what the world follows.

3.22 For me, there is nothing whatsoever that has to be done, Arjuna, in the three worlds; nor anything unattained that I need to attain. Still I continue in action.

3.23 For if I did not continue ever tirelessly in action, my example people would follow, Arjuna, as they always do.

3.24 Societies would come apart if I were not to do works, and I would be the author of chaos in the world. I would destroy these creatures.

3.25 The unenlightened, who are attached to their actions, proceed in works, Arjuna; so should the enlightened, unattached, to hold together society.

3.26 One should not engender a division in the understanding of ignorant folk who are attached to their works; rather, knowing one should inspire them, performing all actions, himself disciplined.

3.27 Works in every fashion are being done by the impulsions [*gunas*, "modes"] of nature. The person deluded by egotism thinks, "I am the doer of this work."

3.28 But the one who knows what is real, Arjuna, concerning those impulsions and the different types of action, realizing that the impulsions operate on themselves, he is not attached.

3.29 Deluded by the impulsions of nature, people are attached to its works. One whose knowledge is complete should not disturb the dull-witted whose knowledge is incomplete.

3.30 Concentrating on your higher Self, entrust all your actions to me. Be free of expectation and possessiveness. Fight, with your fever departed.

3.31 People who always follow this teaching of mine, with faith and without griping, they too are freed from [the karmic consequences of] their actions.

3.32 But those who finding fault with this teaching of mine do not follow it, know them as confused by every bit of knowledge, lost and unaware.

3.33 Even a person with knowledge acts in accord with his own nature. Beings follow nature; what would coercing it avail?

3.35 Better one's own right way [*dharma*] though flawed than the way of another perfectly followed; death following one's own way is better. The way of another is perilous.

BUDDHISM

Buddhism deserves special attention with regard to its elaborate speculations on the nature of suffering, the self, and liberation. Siddhartha Gautama, the Buddha, was deeply concerned about the horrible suffering he saw all around him, and he wanted social reform. He denounced the caste system and the excesses of the Hindu priesthood as inhuman and destructive institutions. The Buddha's basic philosophy, however, is concerned primarily with the individual's inner transformation, achieved by means of insight into the Four Noble Truths of Buddhism:

1. All of life is misery.
2. Misery arises from selfish craving.
3. Selfish craving can be eliminated.
4. The elimination of selfish craving results from following the right way.

This right way to liberation or enlightenment is called the **Eightfold Path** of Buddhism, which consists of the

right way of seeing,

right thinking,

right speech,

right action,

right effort,

right way of living,

right mindfulness, and

right meditation.

The aim of Buddhism is to free oneself from deluded belief in the ego and all that goes with it: desire and frustration, ambition and disappointment, pride and humiliation, and to gain enlightenment and the end of misery, a condition called Nirvana. Although Nirvana is typically described in terms of the negation of the egoistic perspective, as the cessation of suffering, it can be more positively understood as *bliss,* but would be misleading to characterize the aim of Buddhism in terms of the Western ideal of "happiness." The Buddhist conception of life is primarily concerned with suffering and its relief, and the ultimate ideal of the Buddhist, as it is for both Hindus and Jains, is escape from the toll of suffering.

Buddhists, more emphatically than most Hindus, believe that all of life is impermanent and the self and our individuality are unreal illusions. Reality amounts to a series of successive momentary existences; there are no enduring substances. This doctrine of impermanence helps to explain the pathos of our situation, as described in the Four Noble Truths. We desire objects that are themselves impermanent, with the result that we never get (or get to keep) what we want. But until we recognize that the things we want are only momentary existences, we will tend to take them seriously as goals, harming ourselves and others in our efforts.

The following selection is from *The Dhammapada,* "The Teacher."

The Teacher

XLVIII. The Dhammapada

This is the Dhammapada, the path of religion pursued by those who are followers of the Buddha:

Creatures from mind their character derive; mind-marshalled are they, mind-made. Mind is the source either of bliss or of corruption.

By oneself evil is done; by oneself one suffers; by oneself evil is left undone; by oneself one is purified. Purity and impurity belong to oneself, no one can purify another.

You yourself must make an effort. The Tathāgatas are only preachers. The thoughtful who enter the way are freed from the bondage of Māra.

He who does not rouse himself when it is time to rise; who, though young and strong, is full of sloth; whose will and thoughts are weak; that lazy and idle man will never find the way to enlightenment.

If a man hold himself dear, let him watch himself carefully; the truth guards him who guards himself.

If a man makes himself as he teaches others to be, then, being himself subdued, he may subdue others; one's own self is indeed difficult to subdue.

If some men conquer in battle a thousand times a thousand men, and if another conquer himself, he is the greatest of conquerors.

It is the habit of fools, be they laymen or members of the clergy, to think, "this is done by me. May others be subject to me. In this or that transaction a prominent part should be played by me." Fools do not care for the duty to be performed or the aim to be reached, but think of their self alone. Everything is but a pedestal of their vanity.

Bad deeds, and deeds hurtful to ourselves, are easy to do; what is beneficial and good, that is very difficult.

If anything is to be done, let a man do it, let him attack it vigorously!

Before long, alas! this body will lie on the earth, despised, without understanding, like a useless log; yet our thoughts will endure. They will be thought again, and will produce action. Good thoughts will produce good actions, and bad thoughts will produce bad actions.

Earnestness is the path of immortality, thoughtlessness the path of death. Those who are in earnest do not die; those who are thoughtless are as if dead already.

Those who imagine they find truth in untruth, and see untruth in truth, will never arrive at truth, but follow vain desires. They who know truth in truth, and untruth in untruth, arrive at truth, and follow true desires.

As rain breaks through an ill-thatched house, passion will break through an unreflecting mind. As rain does not break through a well-thatched house, passion will not break through a well-reflecting mind.

Well-makers lead the water wherever they like; fletchers bend the arrow; carpenters bend a log of wood; wise people fashion themselves; wise people falter not amidst blame and praise. Having listened to the law, they become serene, like a deep, smooth, and still lake.

If a man speaks or acts with an evil thought, pain follows him as the wheel follows the foot of the ox that draws the carriage.

An evil deed is better left undone, for a man will repent of it afterwards; a good deed is better done, for having done it one will not repent.

If a man commits a wrong let him not do it again; let him not delight in wrongdoing; pain is the outcome of evil. If a man does what is good, let him do it again; let him delight in it; happiness is the outcome of good.

Let no man think lightly of evil, saying in his heart, "It will not come nigh unto me." As by the falling of water-drops a water-pot is filled, so the fool becomes full of evil, though he gather it little by little.

Let no man think lightly of good, saying in his heart, "It will not come nigh unto me." As by the falling of water-drops a water-pot is filled, so the wise man becomes full of good, though he gather it little by little.

He who lives for pleasure only, his senses uncontrolled, immoderate in his food, idle, and weak, him Māra, the tempter, will certainly overthrow, as the wind throws down a weak tree. He who lives without looking for pleasures, his senses well-controlled, moderate in his food, faithful and strong, him Māra will certainly not overthrow, any more than the wind throws down a rocky mountain.

The fool who knows his foolishness, is wise at least so far. But a fool who thinks himself wise, he is a fool indeed.

To the evil-doer wrong appears sweet as honey; he looks upon it as pleasant so long as it bears no fruit; but when its fruit ripens, then he looks upon it as wrong. And so the good man looks upon the goodness of the Dharma as a burden and an evil so long as it bears no fruit; but when its fruit ripens, then he sees its goodness.

A hater may do great harm to a hater, or an enemy to an enemy; but a wrongly-directed mind will do greater mischief unto itself. A mother, a father, or any other relative will do much good; but a well-directed mind will do greater service unto itself.

He whose wickedness is very great brings himself down to that state where his enemy wishes him to be. He himself is his greatest enemy. Thus a creeper destroys the life of a tree on which it finds support.

Do not direct thy thought to what gives pleasure, that thou mayest not cry out when burning, "This is pain." The wicked man burns by his own deeds, as if burnt by fire.

Pleasures destroy the foolish; the foolish man by his thirst for pleasures destroys himself as if he were his own enemy. The fields are damaged by hurricanes and weeds; mankind is damaged by passion, by hatred, by vanity, and by lust.

Let no man ever take into consideration whether a thing is pleasant or unpleasant. The love of pleasure begets grief and the dread of pain causes fear; he who is free from the love of pleasure and the dread of pain knows neither grief nor fear.

He who gives himself to vanity, and does not give himself to meditation, forgetting the real aim of life and grasping at pleasure, will in time envy him who has exerted himself in meditation.

The fault of others is easily noticed, but that of oneself is difficult to perceive. A man winnows his neighbor's faults like chaff, but his own fault he hides, as a cheat hides the false die from the gambler.

If a man looks after the faults of others, and is always inclined to take offence, his own passions will grow, and he is far from the destruction of passions.

Not about the perversities of others, not about their sins of commission or omission, but about his own misdeeds and negligences alone should a sage be worried.

Good people shine from afar, like the snowy mountains; bad people are concealed, like arrows shot by night.

If a man by causing pain to others, wishes to obtain pleasure for himself, he, entangled in the bonds of selfishness, will never be free from hatred.

Let a man overcome anger by love, let him overcome evil by good; let him overcome the greedy by liberality, the liar by truth!

For hatred does not cease by hatred at any time; hatred ceases by not-hatred, this is an old rule.

Speak the truth, do not yield to anger; give, if thou art asked; by these three steps thou wilt become divine.

Let a wise man blow off the impurities of his self, as a smith blows off the impurities of silver, one by one, little by little, and from time to time.

Lead others, not by violence, but by righteousness and equity.

He who possesses virtue and intelligence, who is just, speaks the truth, and does what is his own business, him the world will hold dear.

As the bee collects nectar and departs without injuring the flower, or its color or scent, so let a sage dwell in the community.

If a traveller does not meet with one who is his better, or his equal, let him firmly keep to his solitary journey; there is no companionship with fools.

Long is the night to him who is awake; long is a mile to him who is tired; long is life to the foolish who do not know the true religion.

Better than living a hundred years, not seeing the highest truth, is one day in the life of a man who sees the highest truth.

Some form their Dharma arbitrarily and fabricate it artificially; they advance complex speculations and imagine that good results are attainable only by the acceptance of their theories; yet the truth is but one; there are not different truths in the world. Having reflected on the various theories, we have gone into the yoke with him who has shaken off all sin. But shall we be able to proceed together with him?

The best of ways is the eightfold path. This is the path. There is no other that leads to the purifying of intelligence. Go on this path! Everything else is the deceit of Māra, the tempter. If you go on this path, you will make an end of pain! Says the Tathāgata, The path was preached by me, when I had understood the removal of the thorn in the flesh.

Not only by discipline and vows, not only by much learning, do I earn the happiness of release which no worldling can know. Bhikkhu, be not confident as long as thou hast not attained the extinction of thirst. The extinction of evil desire is the highest religion.

The gift of religion exceeds all gifts; the sweetness of religion exceeds all sweetness; the delight in religion exceeds all delights; the extinction of thirst overcomes all pain.

Few are there among men who cross the river and reach the goal. The great multitudes are running up and down the shore; but there is no suffering for him who has finished his journey.

As the lily will grow full of sweet perfume and delight upon a heap of rubbish, thus the disciple of the truly enlightened Buddha shines forth by his wisdom among those who are like rubbish, among the people that walk in darkness.

Let us live happily then, not hating those who hate us! Among men who hate us let us dwell free from hatred!

Let us live happily then, free from all ailments among the ailing! Among men who are ailing let us dwell free from ailments!

Let us live happily, then, free from greed among the greedy! Among men who are greedy let us dwell free from greed!

The sun is bright by day, the moon shines by night, the warrior is bright in his armor, thinkers are bright in their meditation; but among all the brightest with splendor day and night is the Buddha, the Awakened, the Holy, Blessed.

CHINA: CONFUCIANISM AND TAOISM

The ideal of ethics in China might best be summarized in the word "harmony." Confucius focused on the ethical and social conduct that would be conducive to a harmonious community. The original Taoists, by contrast, were reclusive individuals who saw society as harmful and urged harmony in nature and within one's own nature. Lao-Tze acknowledged the desirability of social harmony, but he considered such harmony more likely to prevail if society were ruled by sages, wise men who had first found harmony within themselves. Indeed, according to the Taoists, such "rulers" need not rule, for the wise ruler is one who rules as little as possible. Confucius, on the other hand, saw his philosophy as first of all a philosophy for rulers. The main character in his many writings is the "authoritative" or "exemplary" person, one who has mastered the Tao. He often uses music and the harmony of voices as an analogy, and the wise ruler, he says, will orchestrate society. Nevertheless, the harmony of society depends on individual virtue, not only in the ruler but in every member of society. Confucius' philosophy, accordingly, is largely an exhortation to virtue. The emphasis on personal virtue within the context of a harmonious society is extremely important for understanding Chinese philosophy. It also provides an important link with the West. Two centuries later, in Greece, Aristotle would develop a similar conception of ethics, in which personal virtue was primary but was understood in the context of one's role in a harmoniously functioning community.

For Confucius, the single most important virtue in any society is good leadership. Good leadership requires the personal development of the ruler, who, in turn, inspires virtue in his subjects. The Confucian emphasis on self-realization should be understood in this social context. It is not individual enlightenment or personal perfection. It is through and through a *social* concern. By comparison, Judaism, Christianity, and Islam tend to be more individualistic and more concerned with the well-being of the individual soul (Christianity especially so). In Confucianism, there is no atomistic "soul" in the Western sense, for the individual cannot be distinguished from his or her social roles and relationships, especially relations within the *family.* Society as a whole, in Confucian thought, is like a gigantic extended family, even such an enormous society as China.

Because Chinese ethics is for the most part an ethics of virtue, a good way to get a handle on Chinese ethics is to consider the different virtues that Confucius and the Taoists defended, all of which are based on their shared central notion of the Tao. The Tao "the way," briefly, the right way to live. For the Confucians, it is living up to one's duties and obligations in society and, especially, in one's family. "Filial piety," respect and loyalty to one's parents, is one of the most important Confucian virtues. (Compare the sixth of the Ten Commandments, "Honor thy father and thy mother.") The Tao can be taught, if mainly by example. Many of Confucius' most famous sayings and parables have to do with exemplifying the social virtues, as he himself did famously. In Taoism, by contrast, the Tao is more of the way of nature and its goal, living "naturally."

Confucianism, like the Judeo-Christian-Islamic traditions, can be defined by a set of scriptures, namely, the classic texts that precede Confucius (the *Book of Changes,* the *Book of Odes,* the *Book of History, Rites, Music,* and the *Spring and Autumn Annals,* which provide an historical account of Confucius' home state, Lu), the four great books of Confucianism (the *Confucian Analects,* the *Book of Mencius,* the *Great Learning,* and the *Doctrine of the Mean*), and the many commentaries upon them. These books, however, are not considered to be divine revelations. Confucius is neither a prophet nor a god. Confucianism has virtually nothing to say about cosmology; and neither God nor Confucius sits or will sit in judgment over people. People rather do that themselves, every day, in the social context in which they display their *jen,* or fail to do so. Confucius himself, of course, is an example of an authoritative (or exemplary) human being.

The following selections are from *The Analects,* a compilation of Confucius' central teachings on ethics.

Confucius, from *The Analects*

Confucius said, "At 15 my heart-and-mind were set upon learning; at 30 I took my stance; at 40 I was no longer of two minds; at 50 I realized the order prevailing in the world; at 60 my ear was attuned; at 70 I could give my heart-and-mind free rein without overstepping the mark."

The exemplary person seeks harmony rather than agreement; the small person does the opposite.

Lead the people with administrative injunctions and organize them with penal law, and they will avoid punishments but will be without a sense of shame.

Lead them with excellence and organize them through roles and ritual practices, and they will develop a sense of shame, and moreover, will order themselves harmoniously.

Learn broadly yet be determined in your own dispositions; enquire with urgency yet reflect closely on the question at hand: becoming authoritative in your person lies in this.

If someone can recite the three hundred *Songs* but yet when you give him official responsibility, he fails you, or when you send him to distant quarters he is not able to act on his own initiative, then although he knows so much, what good is it to him?

To realize that you know something when you do, and to realize that you do not when you do not—this then is knowing.

Confucius presents his version of the "Golden Rule":

Tzu-kung asked, "Is there one expression that one can act on to the end of one's days?"

The Master replied, "There is deference: do not impose on other people what you yourself do not desire."

And, on friendship:

Confucius said, "Having three kinds of friends will bring personal improvement; three kinds will bring injury. To have friends who are straight, who are true to their word, and who are well-informed is to be improved; to have friends who are ingratiating, foppish, and superficial is to be injured."

The disciples of Tzu-hsia asked Tzu-chang about friendship. Tzu-chang queried, "What has Tzu-hsia told you?" They replied, "Join together with those from whom you can learn; spurn those from whom you can't." Tzu-chang says, "This is different from what I have heard. The exemplary person exalts the worthy and is tolerant of the common, praises those who are capable and is sympathetic to those who are not. If in comparison with others I am truly worthy, who am I unable to tolerate? If I am not worthy in the comparison, and people are going to spurn me, on what basis do I spurn them?"

It is the human being who broadens natural and moral order [*tao*], not natural and moral order that broadens the human being.

One of the central Confucian concepts is *li,* or ritual. *Li* involves more than the external observance of ceremonial forms; *li* requires an active sense of appropriateness to one's context, as well as grace in one's actions. Disciplined physical exercise is understood as a means of attaining spiritual mastery over oneself. Mind and body are complements, not opposites, in Confucian thought, both defined by *ch'i,* or "energy." Ceremony and music are considered particularly important by the Confucians, for not only do they bring society together; they also provide the rituals through which *jen* is learned, practiced, and cultivated.

> Having a sense of propriety as one's raw stuff, to practice it in ritual relations, to express it with humility, and to complete it in living up to one's word: this, then, is the exemplary person.
>
> Confucius said, "To discipline oneself through ritual practice is to become authoritatively human. If for the space of one day one were able to accomplish this, the world would turn to one as a model of humanity. However, becoming truly human emerges out of oneself; how could it emerge out of others?"
>
> What does one who is not authoritatively human have to do with ritual practice or with music?

Another central Confucian virtue is filial piety, respect for one's parents.

> Mêng Wu Po asked about the treatment of parents. The Master said, Behave in such a way that your father and mother have no anxiety about you, except concerning your health.
>
> Tzu-yu asked about the treatment of parents. The Master said, 'Filial sons' nowadays are people who see to it that their parents get enough to eat. But even dogs and horses are cared for to that extent. If there is no feeling of respect, wherein lies the difference?
>
> Someone asked Confucius, "Why are you not in government?" Confucius replied, "The *Book of Documents* says: 'Filiality! Simply extend filiality and fraternity into government.' This 'filiality' then, is also taking part in government. Why must one take part in formal government?"

Long before Western philosophy became fascinated with language, the Chinese philosophers recognized the central definitive role of language in the determination of our way(s) of seeing the world. It is through language that we define the world around us, especially the social world. According to Confucius, "the rectification of names" is essential for any society to be a good society.

> Since the exemplary person will be deemed wise or not because of one word, how could one be but careful about what one has to say?

He who does not understand the will of Heaven cannot be regarded as a gentleman. He who does not know the rites cannot take his stand. He who does not understand words, cannot understand people.

The exemplary person holds three things in awe: the natural order of things, the distinguished person, and the words of the sage.

And, finally, Confucius on worrying about death:

Chi-lu asked about serving the gods and the spirits of the dead, but the Master replied, "If you are not yet able to serve other people, how can you serve the spirits of the dead?" Chi-lu then asked about death, but the Master replied, "If you do not yet understand life, how can you understand death?"

Mencius (371–289 B.C.E.) was one of the great Confucian thinkers. He defended a particularly striking and optimistic portrait of human nature, not unlike that which we will see in some of the eighteenth century European philosophers, notably David Hume. Mencius argued that every human being, no matter how crude or even cruel, had within a natural sense of compassion or sympathy. We feel compassion not only for those close to us but even for complete strangers, and love for humanity is an extension of the more powerful love one feels for one's own family. Contending that human beings are essentially good, Mencius was optimistic about humanity's ability to be benevolent in all of their dealings with others. But it is not as if we can simply rely on our natural constitution to make us good. Being fully human is an achievement. But although he considered training and commitment to be essential if the innate goodness of human beings was to be realized in society, Mencius considered moral goodness and wisdom to be within the reach of everyone. What is necessary to become wise (a sage) is commitment. The following are some of the best known passages from his writings:

Mencius*

Mencius said, 'No man is devoid of a heart sensitive to the suffering of others. Such a sensitive heart was possessed by the Former Kings and this manifested itself in compassionate government. With such a sensitive heart behind compassionate government, it was as easy to rule the Empire as rolling it on your palm.

'My reason for saying that no man is devoid of a heart sensitive to the suffering of others is this. Suppose a man were, all of a sudden, to see a young child on the verge of falling into a well. He would certainly be moved to

*Translated by Roger T. Ames.

compassion, not because he wanted to get in the good graces of the parents, nor because he wished to win the praise of his fellow villagers or friends, nor yet because he disliked the cry of the child. From this it can be seen that whoever is devoid of the heart of compassion is not human, whoever is devoid of the heart of right and wrong is not human. The heart of compassion is the germ of benevolence; the heart of shame, of dutifulness; the heart of courtesy and modesty, of observance of the rites; the heart of right and wrong, of wisdom. Man has these four germs just as he has four limbs. For a man possessing these four germs to deny his own potentialities is for him to cripple himself; for him to deny the potentialities of his prince is for him to cripple his prince. If a man is able to develop all these four germs that he possesses, it will be like a fire starting up or a spring coming through. When these are fully developed, he can take under his protection the whole realm within the Four Seas, but if he fails to develop them, he will not be able even to serve his parents.'

Mencius said, 'Is the maker of arrows really more unfeeling than the maker of armour? He is afraid lest he should fail to harm people, whereas the maker of armour is afraid lest he should fail to protect them. The case is similar with the sorcerer-doctor and the coffin-maker. For this reason one cannot be too careful in the choice of one's calling.

'Confucius said, "The best neighbourhood is where benevolence is to be found. Not to live in such a neighbourhood when one has the choice cannot by any means be considered wise." Benevolence is the high honour bestowed by Heaven and the peaceful abode of man. Not to be benevolent when nothing stands in the way is to show a lack of wisdom. A man neither benevolent nor wise, devoid of courtesy and dutifulness, is a slave. A slave ashamed of serving is like a maker of bows ashamed of making bows, or a maker of arrows ashamed of making arrows. If one is ashamed, there is no better remedy than to practise benevolence. Benevolence is like archery: an archer makes sure his stance is correct before letting fly the arrow, and if he fails to hit the mark, he does not hold it against his victor. He simply seeks the cause within himself.'

For a person to realize fully one's heart-and-mind is to realize fully one's nature and character, and in so doing, one realizes Nature.

Nature's mandate is not immutable. (4A/7, citing the *Book of Songs*)

When enjoyment arises, it cannot be stopped. And when it cannot be stopped, one unconsciously taps it with his feet and dances it with his arms.

The mouth's propensity for tastes, the eye's for colors, the ear's for sounds, the nose's for smells, and the four limbs' for comfort—these are a matter of nature, yet basic conditions also have a part in it. That is why the exemplary person does not refer to these as one's nature. The relevance of authoritativeness to the father-son relationship, of appropriateness to the ruler-subject relationship, of ritual action to the guest-host relationship, of wisdom to the good and wise person, and of sages to the way of Nature, are basic conditions, yet one's nature also has a part in it. That is why the exemplary person does not refer to these as basic conditions.

What the exemplary person cultivates as nature and character is authoritative personhood, appropriateness, ritual propriety, and wisdom. These components are rooted in one's heart-and-mind, and the complexion that develops in the process is disclosed radiantly in one's face, manifested in one's posture, and extended throughout one's four limbs. One's four limbs thus communicate effectively without speaking.

The admirable person is called "good." The one who has integrity is called "true." To be totally genuine is called "beautiful," and to radiate this genuineness is called "greatness." Being great, to be transformed and transforming is called "sageliness." And being sagely, to be unfathomable is called "human spirituality and divinity."

Mencius said to Wan Chang, "The best people in one village will make friends with the best people in another village; the best people in one state will make friends with the best people in another state; the best people in the empire will make friends with other people in the empire like them. And not content with making friends with the best people in the empire, they go back in time and commune with the ancients. When one reads the poems and writings of the ancients, can it be right not to know something about them as persons? Hence one tries to understand the age in which they lived. This can be described as 'looking for friends in history.'"

Mencius said, "If you want to condemn the village worthy, you have nothing on him; if you want to criticize him, there is nothing to criticize. He chimes in with the practices of the day and blends in with the common world. Where he lives he seems to be conscientious and to live up to his word, and in what he does, he seems to have integrity. His community all like him, and he sees himself as being right. Yet one cannot pursue the way of Yao or Shun with such a person. Thus Confucius said he is 'the thief of virtue.' Confucius further said, 'As for my dislike and condemnation of what is specious, I dislike weeds lest they be confused with grain; I dislike flattery lest it be confused with what is proper for one to say; I dislike a glib tongue lest it be confused with integrity; I dislike the tunes of Cheng lest they be confused with music; I dislike purple lest it be confused with vermillion; I dislike the village worthy lest he be confused with the virtuous. The exemplary person simply reverts to the standard. Where the standard is upheld, the common people will flourish, and where they flourish, there will be no perversity or aberration.'"

CHINA: TAOISM

Although Confucianism, Taoism, and Buddhism represent the three major currents of Chinese thought and religion, we should not imagine that these traditions have spent two thousand years in competition for adherents. They are all central influences on Chinese ethics, and the Neo-Confucian thinkers of the Sung dynasty (960–1279 C.E.) sought to synthesize them. Consequently, Chinese thought has been characterized more by an amalgam of traditions than controversy among them. Nevertheless, we noted that Confucius and the Taoists had different conceptions of the proper relationship between the individual and society and different notions of the virtues that a person should pursue. Whereas Confucius emphasized the social, Lao-Tze emphasized nature and distinguished what was due to social cultivation from what was natural. Taoism teaches attuning the inner person to the rhythms of nature, the Tao, the Way of the universe. Simplicity, the avoidance of artificiality, was the way to wisdom. Even traditional moral concepts like "good" and "evil" can be obstacles to living in accordance with the Tao, as too often such concepts are understood so rigidly that they obscure more than they illuminate. In particular, they fail to reflect the subtle changes of the Tao.

The greatest virtue, according to Lao-Tze, is non-action (***wu-wei***). The ideal leader, paradoxically, does not lead. Lao-Tze was keenly aware of the foibles that can result from "overdoing it," especially where governmental policies and legal restrictions are concerned. Similarly, the ideal teacher does not teach. The virtuous individual does not act, in the sense of asserting him or herself. Avoiding all unnecessary effort, the wise individual "acts naturally," behaving spontaneously in accordance with nature as it exists within him or her. Such an individual adopts a stance of receptiveness, and this in turn allows the Way of the universe (the universal Tao) to act through him or her. In this way, the person achieves **te,** his or her own natural power.

Although the life span of Lao-Tze is disputed, the Taoist tradition most likely preceded him. The following is from Lao-Tze's *Tao Te Ching* (literally, *The Book of the Way and Power.*)

Lao-Tze: *Tao Te Ching**

> You carry the spiritual and sentient souls and unite them as one,
>
> But can you keep them together?
>
> You concentrate your vital forces and attain pliancy,
>
> But can you assume the bearing of a child?
>
> You cleanse the dark mirror of your mind,
>
> But can you be free of imperfection?
>
> You love the people and order the country properly,
>
> But can you be anarchic?
>
> Your senses are open to the world,
>
> But can you act the female?
>
> You are clear and penetrating in all things,
>
> But can you be ignorant? (10)
>
> The most excellent ruler—the people do not know he's around;
>
> The second most excellent—they love and praise him;
>
> The next—they fear him;
>
> And the worst—they look on him with contempt.
>
> When his integrity is inadequate,

*Translated by Roger T. Ames.

There will be those who do not trust him.

Relaxed, he is economical with his words.

When his accomplishments are full and the affairs of state are in proper order,

The common people all say, "We are naturally like this." (17)

You have to be bent to be made whole;

You have to be warped to be straightened;

You have to be hollow to be filled up;

You have to be broken to be renewed;

You have to have little to get a lot;

You have to have much to become confused;

Thus the Sage embraces One to be the model of the world.

It is because he does not show himself that he is brilliant;

It is because he does not assert himself that he is distinguished;

It is because he does not boast that he is accomplished;

It is because he is not conceited that he is enduring.

It is only because he does not compete that no one in the world is able to compete with him.

As the ancients said, "You have to be bent to be made whole."

How can this be empty talk?

This is really returning to it whole. (22)

One who understands masculinity and preserves femininity

Is the river gorge of the world.

As the river gorge of the world,

One's constant potency does not quit one,

And one returns to a state of infancy.

One who understands white and preserves black

Is the model of the world.

As the model of the world,

One's constant potency does not err,

And one returns to a state of boundlessness.

One who understands glory and preserves disgrace

Becomes the valley of the world.

As the valley of the world,

One's constant potency is thus sufficient,

And one returns to a state of unworked wood.

When unworked wood is splintered,

It becomes vessels.

The Sage uses it,

Only to become the chief of the officials.

Therefore, the best organization does not divide things up. (28)

Tao engenders one,

One engenders two,

Two engenders three,

And three engenders the myriad things.

The myriad things shoulder the *yin* and embrace the *yang*,

And in blending their psychophysical vapors, they achieve harmony. (42)

Another significant sage of early Taoism was Chuang-Tze (c. 369–286 B.C.E.), a contemporary of Mencius. Chuang-Tze was an anarchist, skeptical of all government that he considered obstacles to human happiness. Happiness depends on individual freedom to spontaneously express the nature within them. His writings often take the form of stories or fables, raising radical questions about ethical perspectives and defending a kind of intuitionism against the rationality of the Confucians and logicians of his day. Whereas Confucius taught that an essential part of wisdom was to be found in the clarification of language, Chuang-Tze argued that the highest happiness could be attained only by transcending language and the distinctions it makes. The initial step in overcoming distinctions is to recognize the partiality and relativity of all viewpoints. In some of Chuang-Tze's most celebrated stories, we are forced to consider a variety of very different perspectives. He also taught that death is part of the cyclical movement of *Tao,* so one should not be emotionally distressed at a loved one's death or in fear of one's own.

Chuang-Tze

Once Chuang-Tze dreamt he was a butterfly, a butterfly flitting and fluttering around, happy with himself and doing as he pleased. He didn't know he was Chuang-Tze. Suddenly he woke up and there he was, solid and unmistakable Chuang-Tze. But he didn't know if he was Chuang-Tze who had dreamt he was a butterfly, or a butterfly dreaming he was Chuang-Tze. Between Chuang-Tze and a butterfly there must be *some* distinction! This is called the Transformation of Things.

There is nothing which is not a "that" and nothing which is not a "this." Because we cannot see from a "that" perspective but can only know from our own perspective, it is said that "that" arises out of "this" and "this" further accommodates "that." This is the notion that "this" and "that" are born simultaneously. But being born entails dying, and vice versa; being acceptable entails being unacceptable, and vice versa; accommodating right is accommodating wrong, and vice versa. It is for this reason that the sage, illuminating this situation with the way things really are rather than going along with discriminations among them, is also a further case of accommodating what is right and what is "this." But "this" is also "that," and vice versa. And a "this's" "that" further has one set of right and wrong, while "this" has another. In truth, is there really such a thing as "this" and "that" or not?

Chuang-Tze and Hui Tze were strolling across the bridge over the Hao River. Chuang-Tze observed, "The minnows swim out and about as they please—this is the way they enjoy themselves."

Hui Tze replied, "You are not a fish—how do you know what they enjoy?"

Chuang-Tze returned, "You are not me—how do you know that I don't know what is enjoyable for the fish?"

Hui Tze said, "I am not you, so I certainly don't know what you know; but it follows that, since you are certainly not the fish, you don't know what is enjoyment for the fish either."

Chuang-Tze said "Let's get back to your basic question. When you asked '*From where* do you know what the fish enjoy?' you already knew that I know what the fish enjoy, or you wouldn't have asked me. I know it from here above the Hao River." (Chapter 17)

When Chuang-Tze's wife died, Hui Shih came to console him. As for Chuang-Tze, he was squatting with his knees out, drumming on a pot and singing.

"When you have lived with someone," said Hui Shih, "and brought up children, and grown old together, to refuse to bewail her death would be bad enough, but to drum on a pot and sing—could there be anything more shameful?"

Not so. When she first died, do you suppose that I was able not to feel the loss? I peered back into her beginnings; there was a time before there was a life. Not only was there no life, there was a time before there was a shape. Not only was there no shape, there was a time before there was energy. Mingled together in the amorphous, something altered, and there was the energy; by alteration in the energy, there was the shape; by alteration in the shape, there was the life. Now once more altered she has gone over to death. This is to be a companion with spring and autumn, summer and winter, in the procession of the four seasons. When someone was about to lie down and sleep in the greatest of mansions, I with my sobbing knew no better than to bewail her. The thought came to me that I was being uncomprehending towards destiny, so I stopped.

Discussion Questions

1. Why might the Hebrews have tended to blame themselves when disaster struck their people?
2. Suppose God had not stopped Abraham's hand, and Isaac had been sacrificed. How would the meaning of the parable change?
3. Compare the ethical code presented in the Qur'an's "Livestock" with that presented in the Hebrew Ten Commandments.
4. What does Arjuna's discussion with Krishna reveal about the Hindu understanding of the good life?
5. Why is that, as the Dhammapada asserts, "Bad deeds, and deeds hurtful to ourselves, are easy to do; what is beneficial and good, that is very difficult"?
6. Compare the Christian "Golden Rule" with the version offered by Confucius. Are the two rules different, or the same?
7. Why does Lao-Tze argue that the greatest virtue is nonaction? What does he mean? Should we simply be passive? What if terrible moral evils are taking place in the world (for example, the Holocaust)? Should we act then?

Study Questions

1. Name the five beliefs often taken to be central to Christian philosophy.
2. How does Christian moral philosophy revise Hebrew moral philosophy (if it does)? How does Islamic moral philosophy further revise the tradition (if it does)?
3. What is the problem of suffering? How do Hinduism and Buddhism respond to the problem?
4. Why does Confucius believe that the single most important virtue in any society is good leadership? How does he argue for the view?
5. Make a list of the virtues presented by Confucius and Mencius.
6. Why does Chuang-Tze drum on a pot and sing when his wife dies?
7. Does Lao-Tze have a moral philosophy? If not, why not? If so, try to explain it (using real-life examples).

1

Plato

Plato lived from 427 to 347 B.C. He was a student of Socrates during the tragic period of Socrates's trial and execution, and he used Socrates's teachings and dialogues for his own work. Plato founded the famous Academy in Athens for the purposes of presenting, preserving, and continuing Socrates's work, and he always used Socrates as the spokesman for his ideas. But the result of this practice was that Plato's thinking, which developed far beyond the relatively simple ideas of his teacher, was presented as Socrates's. The *Crito* is probably a relatively faithful transcription of the conversation that took place in Socrates's prison cell, but some of the other dialogues, for example, *The Republic,* are thought to be just as much Plato as Socrates, and it is not always possible to tell which ideas belong to which philosopher. Excerpts from both the *Crito* and *The Republic* are presented in this chapter.

Since Socrates himself did not write down his lectures and conversations, we know of his ethical views only through the writing of other philosophers who either knew him and heard him discuss these matters, or heard about him and his views from others. However, most of what we know of his work comes to us most directly in the form of "dialogues" written by Socrates's most illustrious student, Plato. In these dialogues, Socrates himself almost always plays the leading role. Socrates's general strategy—which has since come to be called "the Socratic method"—is for him to claim ignorance, urging his interlocutor (the person who is going to be utterly refuted in the course of the dialogue) to state his own opinion—for example, about what one ought to do in a certain situation or the meaning of a particular moral concept. Socrates then points out what is wrong with such an opinion, forcing the interlocutor to revise and restate his position in a better-thought-out form, which Socrates then attacks as well. Finally, by the end of each dialogue, the fallacies and inadequacies of various positions have been displayed, and Socrates suggests his own view, free from the errors that have been pointed out in the other's positions. In addition to this dialogal (or "dialectical") technique, Plato also uses a number of dramatic techniques—for instance, having Socrates take on the role of a muse or a goddess to make a point or, in the *Crito,* allowing him to be the spokesman for "the laws of Athens."

Socrates lived from 470 until 399 B.C. and spent virtually his entire life in Athens (except for various military campaigns, in which he took part). He lived most of his life in a modest way, living mainly on gifts from his students. He was known to be a brilliant debater and spent much of his life debating with the "Sophists" who wandered around Greece giving lessons in philosophy and argument. But where the Sophists were cynical and pessimistic about the possibility of finding the Good in ethics (often arguing such theses as "all men are selfish" or "there is no such thing as justice"), Socrates took a positive and optimistic view. He was always confident, despite his rhetorical strategy of feigning total ignorance— that the Good could be found and taught, and it was in the name of the Good, accordingly, that he died.

The ethical subject matter of many of Plato's Socratic dialogues is very abstract and metaethical, having to do with the meaning of such terms as "good" and "justice." We have included such discussions in the two selections from Plato's *The Republic,* which begins on page 81. In contrast, the subject of our first dialogue, *Crito,* could not be more down to earth and urgent in a life and death way.

CRITO*

The *Crito* depicts the fictionalized scene from Socrates's own life, after he has been tried by the court of Athens for "corrupting the youth" and sentenced to death. In the *Crito,* he is in prison, awaiting execution, when one of his good friends, Crito (the names of the Platonic dialogues are often based on the name of the interlocutor), informs Socrates that plans have been made for his escape. But Socrates, instead of being overjoyed or relieved at the news, is deeply troubled. On the one hand, he is still a healthy and vigorous man (his physical prowess and endurance were legendary). He had a family and many friends and lived what we would probably all agree was a very good life, filled with good dinners with his students, friends, excitement, conversation, and parties (one of which is recorded by Plato as *The Symposium,* in which the topic of the drunken evening is erotic love). Even as an old man of 70, Socrates still had much to live for. On the other hand, Socrates had made his career as a philosopher by arguing for the importance of such abstract ideals as honor and justice, and his idea of living well was not confined to the pleasures of life.

True happiness, in Socrates's view, has to do primarily with the soul rather than the body. Care for our soul includes being true to our principles, doing the right thing regardless of the effect it might have on our more ordinary concerns—in this case, the impending execution. Living well also included doing one's duty as a citizen, which obviously meant, among other things, obeying and respecting the law. But in his present situation, obeying and respecting the law included accepting the

---

*Plato, *Crito,* translated by Benjamin Jowett. Copyright 1892 by Oxford University Press.

(unjust) sentence of the Athenian court, which meant allowing himself to be killed when he ought not to have been. Socrates's dialogue with Crito (reported to Plato by Crito afterward) is essentially the all-important debate between the worth of life and its pleasures versus the value of duty and honor. It is important to note here that Socrates himself did not take this to be a difficult or painful decision to make. For duty and honor have to do with the health, or well-being, or our soul, which he believed to be immortal. The body, on the other hand, perishes at death. Its pleasures are not nearly as important as the care of the soul. As Socrates states in the *Phaedo*, the dialogue that describes his death as mandated by the Court, "The one aim of those who practice philosophy in the proper manner is to practice for dying and death." This points to a theme that recurs in many of the Platonic dialogues: namely, that acting ethically does not mean choosing the course of action that you least want to do. Rather, doing the right thing is in your own interest. It may not always appear to be so; in particular, it is often necessary to distinguish between short-term and long-term interests (the latter obviously being what Socrates has in mind when he worries about the condition of his immortal soul). Given the appropriate perspective, however, what is best for you and what is best in general come to the same thing in Socrates's mind.

Crito argues that Socrates should escape and go on living the good life (which includes both body and soul). Socrates argues that he has an obligation to respect the law, which overrides even the unjust nature of his sentence and his desire to continue to live and live well. How could he live well, he insists, if he has betrayed the principles that have made his life meaningful, if he has betrayed his own soul?

In the dialogue that follows, it is worth watching the various turns in Socrates's argument. Notice, for example, that Crito's emotional appeals to Socrates are inevitably ignored or rejected, as Socrates insists on pursuing a purely rational line of thought, free from his own feelings and as objective as possible. (This is the reason behind his dramatic device of speaking for the laws instead of just speaking for himself.) Notice, too, the different kinds of reasons Socrates and Crito give for their positions—arguments about duty, appeals to what the gods want, the nature of political obligation, entreaties to Socrates's and Crito's personal self-interests as well as to "what people will think," and entreaties on the basis of what would be good for everyone. Socrates may win the argument, but he is executed the next day, by means of a fast-acting poison derived from the hemlock plant. The execution itself is movingly described—also second-hand—by Plato in the *Phaedo.*

PERSONS OF THE DIALOGUE: *Socrates, Crito*
SCENE: The Prison of Socrates

SOCRATES: Why have you come at this hour Crito? It must be quite early?
CRITO: Yes, certainly.
SOC: What is the exact time?
CR: The dawn is breaking.
SOC: I wonder that the keeper of the prison would let you in.
CR: He knows me, because I often come, Socrates; moreover, I have done him a kindness.

Soc: And are you only just arrived?

Cr: No. I came some time ago.

Soc: Then why did you sit and say nothing, instead of at once awakening me?

Cr: I should not have liked myself. Socrates, to be in such great trouble and unrest as you are—indeed I should not: I have been watching with amazement your peaceful slumbers; and for that reason I did not awake you, because I wished to minimize the pain. I have always thought you to be of a happy disposition; but never did I see anything like the easy, tranquil manner in which you bear this calamity.

Soc: Why, Crito, when a man has reached my age he ought not be repining at the approach of death.

Cr: And yet other old men find themselves in similar misfortunes, and age does not prevent them from repining.

Soc: That is true. But you have not told me why you come at this early hour.

Cr: I come to bring you a message which is sad and painful; not, as I believe, to yourself, but to all of us who are your friends, and saddest of all to me.

Soc: What? Has the ship come from Delos, on the arrival of which I am to die?

Cr: No, the ship has not actually arrived, but she will probably be here to-day, as persons who have come from Sunium tell me that they left her there; and therefore tomorrow, Socrates, will be the last day of your life.

Soc: Very well, Crito if such is the will of God, I am willing; but my belief is that there will be a delay of a day.

Cr: Why do you think so?

Soc: I will tell you. I am to die on the day after the arrival of the ship.

Cr: Yes; that is what the authorities say.

Soc: But I do not think that the ship will be here until to-morrow; this I infer from a vision which I had last night, or rather only just now, when you fortunately allowed me to sleep.

Cr: And what was the nature of the vision?

Soc: There appeared to me the likeness of a woman, fair and comely, clothed in bright raiment, who called to me and said: O Socrates,

"The third day hence to fertile Phthia shalt thou go."

Cr: What a singular dream, Socrates!

Soc: There can be no doubt about the meaning, Crito, I think.

Cr: Yes; the meaning is only too clear. But, oh! my beloved Socrates, let me entreat you once more to take my advice and escape. For if you die I shall not only lose a friend who can never be replaced, but there is another evil: people who do not know you and me will believe that I might have saved you if I had been willing to give money, but that I did not care. Now, can there be a worse disgrace than this—that I should be thought to value money more than the life of a friend? For the many will not be persuaded that I wanted you to escape, and that you refused.

Soc: But why, my dear Crito, should we care about the opinion of the many? Good men, and they are the only persons who are worth considering, will think of these things truly as they occurred.

CR: But you see, Socrates, that the opinion of the many must be regarded, for what is now happening shows that they can do the greatest evil to any one who has lost their good opinion.

SOC: I only wish it were so, Crito; and that the many could do the greatest evil; for then they would also be able to do the greatest good—and what a fine thing this would be! But in reality they can do neither; for they cannot make a man either wise or foolish; and whatever they do is the result of chance.

CR: Well, I will not dispute with you; but please to tell me, Socrates, whether you are not acting out of regard to me and your other friends: are you not afraid that if you escape from prison we may get into trouble with the informers for having stolen you away, and lose either the whole or a great part of our property; or that even a worse evil may happen to us? Now, if you fear on our account, be at ease; for in order to save you, we ought surely to run this, or even a greater risk; be persuaded, then, and do as I say.

SOC: Yes, Crito, that is one fear which you mention, but by no means the only one.

CR: Fear not—there are persons who are willing to get you out of prison at no great cost; and as for the informers, they are far from being exorbitant in their demands—a little money will satisfy them. My means, which are certainly ample, are at your service, and if you have a scruple about spending all mine, here are strangers who will give you the use of theirs; and one of them, Simmias the Theban, has brought a large sum of money for this very purpose; and Cebes and many others are prepared to spend their money in helping you to escape. I say, therefore, do not hesitate on our account, and do not say, as you did in the court, that you will have a difficulty in knowing what to do with yourself anywhere else. For men will love you in other places to which you may go, and not in Athens only; there are friends of mine in Thessaly, if you like to go to them, who will value and protect you, and no Thessalian will give you any trouble. Nor can I think that you are at all justified, Socrates, in betraying your own life when you might be saved; in acting thus you are playing into the hands of your enemies, who are hurrying on your destruction. And further I should say that you are deserting your own children; for you might bring them up and educate them; instead of which you go away and leave them, and they will have to take their chance; and if they do not meet with the usual fate of orphans, there will be small thanks to you. No man should bring children into the world who is unwilling to persevere to the end in their nurture and education. But you appear to be choosing the easier part, not the better and manlier, which would have been more becoming in one who professes to care for virtue in all his actions, like yourself. And, indeed, I am ashamed not only of you, but of us who are your friends, when I reflect that the whole business will be attributed entirely to our want of courage. The trial need never have come on, or might have been managed differently; and this last act, of crowning folly, will seem to have occurred through our negligence and cowardice, who might have saved you, if we had been good for anything; and you might have saved yourself, for there was no difficulty at all. See now, Socrates, how sad and discreditable are the consequences, both to us and you. Make up your mind, then, or rather have your mind already made up, for the time of deliberation is over, and there is only one thing to be done, which must be done this very night, and if we delay at all will be no longer practicable or possible; I beseech you therefore, Socrates, be persuaded by me, and do as I say.

Soc: Dear Crito, your zeal is invaluable, if a right one; but if wrong, the greater the zeal the greater the danger; and therefore we ought to consider whether I shall or shall not do as you say. For I am and always have been one of those natures who must be guided by reason, whatever the reason may be which upon reflection appears to me to be the best; and now that this chance has befallen me, I cannot repudiate my own words: the principles which I have hitherto honoured and revered I still honour, and unless we can at once find other and better principles, I am certain not to agree with you; no, not even if the power of the multitude could inflict many more imprisonments, confiscations, deaths, frightening us like children with hobgoblin terrors. What will be the fairest way of considering the question? Shall I return to your old argument about the opinions of men?—we were saying that some of them are to be regarded, and others not. Now, were we right in maintaining this before I was condemned? And has the argument which was once good now proved to be talk for the sake of talking—mere childish nonsense? That is what I want to consider with your help. Crito:—whether, under my present circumstances, the argument appears to be in any way different or not; and is to be allowed by me or disallowed. That argument, which, as I believe, is maintained by many persons of authority, was to the effect, as I was saying, that the opinions of some men are to be regarded, and of other men not to be regarded. Now you, Crito, are not going to die tomorrow—at least, there is no human probability of this—and therefore you are disinterested and not liable to be deceived by the circumstances in which you are placed. Tell me, then, whether I am right in saying that some opinions, and the opinions of some men only, are to be valued, and that other opinions, and the opinions of other men, are not to be valued. I ask you whether I was right in maintaining this?

Cr: Certainly.

Soc: The good are to be regarded, and not the bad?

Cr: Yes.

Soc: And the opinions of the wise are good, and the opinions of the unwise are evil?

Cr: Certainly.

Soc: And what was said about another matter? Is the pupil who devotes himself to the practice of gymnastic supposed to attend to the praise and blame and opinion of every man, or of one man only—his physician or trainer, whoever he may be?

Cr: Of one man only.

Soc: And he ought to fear the censure and welcome the praise of that one only, and not of the many?

Cr: Clearly so.

Soc: And he ought to act and train, and eat and drink in the way which seems good to his single master who has understanding, rather than according to the opinion of all other men put together?

Cr: True.

SOC: And if he disobeys and disregards the opinion and approval of the one, and regards the opinion of the many who have no understanding, will he not suffer evil?

CR: Certainly he will.

SOC: And what will the evil be, whither tending and what affecting, in the disobedient person?

CR: Clearly, affecting the body; that is what is destroyed by the evil.

SOC: Very good; and is not this true, Crito, of other things which we need not separately enumerate? In questions of just and unjust, fair and foul, good and evil, which are the subjects of our present consultation, ought we to follow the opinion of the many and to fear them; or the opinion of the one man who has understanding? Ought we not to fear and reverence him more than all the rest of the world: and if we desert him shall we not destroy and injure that principle in us which may be assumed to be improved by justice and deteriorated by injustice;—there is such a principle?

CR: Certainly there is, Socrates.

SOC: Take a parallel instance:—if, acting under the advice of those who have no understanding, we destroy that which is improved by health and is deteriorated by disease, would life be worth having? And that which has been destroyed is—the body?

CR: Yes.

SOC: Could we live, having an evil and corrupted body?

CR: Certainly not.

SOC: And will life be worth having, if that higher part of man be destroyed, which is improved by justice and depraved by injustice? Do we suppose that principle, whatever it may be in man, which has to do with justice and injustice, to be inferior to the body?

CR: Certainly not.

SOC: More honourable than the body?

CR: Far more.

SOC: Then, my friend, we must not regard what the many say of us: but what he, the one man who has understanding of just and unjust, will say, and what the truth will say. And therefore you begin in error when you advise that we should regard the opinion of the man about just and unjust, good and evil, honourable and dishonourable.—"Well," some one will say, "but the many can kill us."

CR: Yes, Socrates; that will clearly be the answer.

SOC: And it is true: but still I find with surprise that the old argument is unshaken as ever. And I should like to know whether I may say the same of another proposition—that not life, but a good life, is to be chiefly valued?

CR: Yes, that also remains unshaken.

SOC: And a good life is equivalent to a just and honourable one—that holds also?

CR: Yes, it does.

SOC: From these premises I proceed to argue the question whether I ought or ought not to try to escape without the consent of the Athenians: and if I am clearly right in escaping, then I will make the attempt; but if not, I will abstain. The other considerations which you mention, of money and loss of character and the duty of educating one's children, are, I fear, only the doctrines of the multitude, who would be as ready to restore people to life, if they were able, as they are to put them to death—and with as little reason. But now, since the argument has thus far prevailed, the only question which remains to be considered is whether we shall do rightly either in escaping or in suffering others to aid in our escape and paying them in money and thanks, or whether in reality we shall not do rightly; and if the latter, then death or any other calamity which may ensue on my remaining here must not be allowed to enter into the calculation.

CR: I think that you are right, Socrates; how then shall we proceed?

SOC: Let us consider the matter together, and do you either refute me if you can, and I will be convinced; or else cease, my dear friend, from repeating to me that I ought to escape against the wishes of the Athenians: for I highly value your attempts to persuade me to do so, but I may not be persuaded against my own better judgment. And now please to consider my first position, and try how you can best answer me.

CR: I will.

SOC: Are we to say that we are never intentionally to do wrong, or that in one way we ought and in another way we ought not to do wrong, or is doing wrong always evil and dishonourable, as I was just now saying, and as has been already acknowledged by us? Are all our former admissions which were made within a few days to be thrown away? And have we, at our age, been earnestly discoursing with one another all our life long only to discover that we are no better than children? Or, in spite of the opinion of the many, and in spite of consequences whether better or worse, shall we insist on the truth of what was then said, that injustice is always an evil and dishonour to him who acts unjustly? Shall we say so or not?

CR: Yes.

SOC: Then we must do no wrong?

CR: Certainly not.

SOC: Nor when injured injure in return, as the many imagine; for we must injure no one at all?

CR: Clearly not.

SOC: Again, Crito, may we do evil?

CR: Surely not, Socrates.

SOC: And what of doing evil in return for evil, which is the morality of the many—is that just or not?

CR: Not just.

SOC: For doing evil to another is the same as injuring him?

CR: Very true.

SOC: Then we ought not to retaliate or render evil for evil to anyone, whatever evil we may have suffered from him. But I would have you consider, Crito, whether you really mean what you are saying. For this opinion has never been held, and never will be held, by any considerable number of persons; and those who are agreed and those who are not agreed upon this point have no common ground, and can only despise one another when they see how widely they differ. Tell me, then, whether you agree with and assent to my first principle, that neither injury nor retaliation nor warding off evil by evil is ever right. And shall that be the premise of our argument? Or do you decline and dissent from this? For so I have ever thought, and continue to think: but, if you are of another opinion, let me hear what you have to say. If, however, you remain of the same mind as formerly, I will proceed to the next step.

CR: You may proceed, for I have not changed my mind.

SOC: Then I will go on to the next point, which may be put in the form of a question:—Ought a man to do what he admits to be right, or ought he to betray the right?

CR: He ought to do what he thinks right.

SOC: But if this is true, what is the application? In leaving the prison against the will of the Athenians, do I wrong any? Or rather do I not wrong those whom I ought least to wrong? Do I not desert the principles which were acknowledged by us to be just—what do you say?

CR: I cannot tell, Socrates; for I do not know.

SOC: Then consider the matter in this way:—Imagine that I am about to play truant (you may call the proceeding by any name which you like), and the laws and the government come and interrogate me: "Tell us, Socrates," they say; "what are you about? are you not going by an act of yours to overturn us—the laws, and the whole state, as far as in you lies? Do you imagine that a state can subsist and not be overthrown, in which the decisions of law have no power, but are set aside and trampled upon by individuals?" What will be our answer, Crito, to these and the like words? Anyone, and especially a rhetorician, will have a good deal to say on behalf of the law which requires a sentence to be carried out. He will argue that this law should not be set aside; and shall we reply, "Yes; but the state has injured us and given an unjust sentence." Suppose I say that?

CR: Very good, Socrates.

SOC: "And was that our agreement with you?" the law would answer; "or were you to abide by the sentence of the state?" And if I were to express my astonishment at their words, the law would probably add: "Answer, Socrates, instead of opening your eyes—you are in the habit of asking and answering questions. Tell us,—What complaint have you to make against us which justifies you in attempting to destroy us and the state? In the first place did we not bring you into existence? Your father married your mother by our aid and begat you. Say whether you have any objection to urge against those of us who regulate marriage?" None, I should reply. "Or against those of us who after birth regulate the nurture and education of children, in which you also were trained? Were not the laws, which have the charge of education, right in commanding your father to train you in music and gymnastic?" Right, I should reply. "Well, then since you were brought into the world and nurtured and educated by us, can you deny in the first place that you are our child and slave, as your fathers were before you? And if this is true, you are not on equal terms with us; nor can you think that you have a right to do to us what we are doing to you. Would you have any right to strike or revile or do any other evil to your father or your master, if you had one, because you have been struck or reviled by him, or received some other evil at his hands?—you would not say this? And because we think right to destroy you, do you think that you have any right to destroy us in return, and your country as far as in you lies? Will you, O professor of true virtue, pretend that you are justified in this? Has a philosopher like you failed to discover that our country is more to be valued and higher and holier far than mother or father or any ancestor, and more to be regarded in the eyes of the gods and of men of understanding? Also to be soothed, and gently and reverently entreated when angry, even more than a father, and either to be persuaded, or if not persuaded, to be obeyed? And when we are punished by her, whether with imprisonment or stripes, the punishment is to be endured in silence; and if she lead us to wounds or death in battle, thither we follow as is right; neither may any one yield or retreat or leave his rank, but whether in battle or in a court of law, or in any other place, he must do what his city and his country order him; or he must change their view of what is just: and if he may do no violence to his father or mother, much less may he do violence to his country." What answer shall we make to this, Crito? Do the laws speak truly, or do they not?

CR: I think that they do.

SOC: Then the laws will say: "Consider, Socrates, if we are speaking truly that in your present attempt you are going to do us an injury. For, having brought you into the world, and nurtured and educated you, and given you and every other citizen a share in every good which we had to give, we further proclaim to any Athenian by the liberty which we allow him, that if he does not like us when he has become of age and has seen the ways of the city, and made our acquaintance, he may go where he pleases and take his goods with him. None of us laws will forbid him or interfere with him. Any of you who does not like us and the city, and who wants to emigrate to a colony or to any other city, may go where he likes, retaining his property. But he who has experience of the manner in which we order justice and administer the State, and still remains, has entered into an implied contract that he will do as we command him. And he who disobeys us is, as we maintain, thrice wrong; first, because in disobeying us he is disobeying his parents; secondly, because we are the authors of his education; thirdly, because he has made an agreement with us that he will duly obey our commands; and he neither obeys them nor convinces us that our commands are unjust; and we do not rudely impose them, but give him the alternative of obeying or convincing us;—that is what we offer, and he does neither.

"These are the sort of accusations to which, as we were saying, you, Socrates, will be exposed if you accomplish your intentions; you, above all other Athenians." Suppose now I ask, why I rather than anybody else? They will justly retort upon me that I above all other men have acknowledged the agreement. "There is clear proof," they will say, "Socrates, that we and the city were not displeasing to you. Of all Athenians you have been the most constant resident in the city, which, as you never leave, you may be supposed to love. For you never went out of the city either to see the games, except once when you went to the Isthmus, or to any other place unless when you were on military service; nor did you travel as other men do. Nor had you any curiosity to know other States or their laws: your affections did not go beyond us and our State; we were your special favourites, and you acquiesced in our government of you; and here in this city you begat your children, which is a proof of your satisfaction. Moreover, you might in the course of the trial, if you had liked, have fixed the penalty at banishment; the State which refuses to let you go now would have let you go then. But you pretended that you preferred death to exile and that you were not unwilling to die. And now you have forgotten these fine sentiments, and pay no respect to us, the laws, of whom you are the destroyer; and are doing what only a miserable slave would do, running away and turning your back upon the compacts and agreements which you made as a citizen. And, first of all, answer this very question: Are we right in saying that you agreed to be governed according to us in deed, and not in word only? Is that true or not?" How shall we answer, Crito? Must we not assent?

CR: We cannot help it, Socrates.

SOC: Then will they not say: "You, Socrates, are breaking the covenants and agreements which you made with us at your leisure, not in any haste or under any compulsion or deception, but after you have had seventy years to think of them, during which time you were at liberty to leave the city, if we were not to your mind, or if our covenants appeared to you to be unfair. You had your choice, and might have gone either to Lacedaemon or Crete, both which States are often praised by you for their good government, or to some other Hellenic or foreign State. Whereas you, above all other Athenians, seemed to be so fond of the State, or, in other words, of us, her laws (and who would care about a State which has no laws?), that you never stirred out of her; the halt, the blind, the maimed were not more stationary in her than you were. And now you run away and forsake your agreements. Not so, Socrates, if you will take our advice; do not make yourself ridiculous by escaping out of the city.

"For just consider, if you transgress and err in this sort of way, what good will you do either to yourself or to your friends? That your friends will be driven into exile and deprived of citizenship, or will lose their property, is tolerably certain; and you yourself, if you fly to one of the neighbouring cities, as, for example, Thebes or Megara, both of which are well governed, will come to them as an enemy, Socrates, and their government will be against you, and all patriotic citizens will cast an evil eye upon you as a subverter of the laws, and you will confirm in the minds of the judges the justice of their own condemnation of you. For he who is a corrupter of the laws is more than likely to be a corrupter of the young and foolish portion of mankind. Will you then flee from well-ordered cities and virtuous men? And is existence worth having on these terms? Or will you go to them without shame, and talk to them, Socrates? And what will you say to them? What you say here about virtue and justice and institutions and laws being the best things among men? Would that be decent of you? Surely not. But if you go away from well-governed States to Crito's friends in Thessaly, where there is great disorder and licence, they will be charmed to hear the tale of your escape from prison, set off with ludicrous particulars of the manner in which you were wrapped in a goatskin or some other disguise, and metamorphosed as the manner is of runaways; but will there be no one to remind you that in your old age you were not ashamed to violate the most sacred laws from a miserable desire of a little more life? Perhaps not, if you keep them in a good temper; but if they are out of temper you will hear many degrading things; you will live, but how?—as the flatterer of all men, and the servant of all men; and doing what?—eating and drinking in Thessaly, having gone abroad in order that you may get a dinner. And where will be your fine sentiments about justice and virtue? Say that you wish to live for the sake of your children—you want to bring them up and educate them—will you take them into Thessaly and deprive them of Athenian citizenship? Is this the benefit which you will confer upon them? Or are you under the impression that they will be better cared for and educated here if you are still alive, although absent from them; for your friends will take care of them? Do you fancy that if you are an inhabitant of Thessaly they will take care of them, and if you are an inhabitant of the other world that they will not take care of them? Nay; but if they who call themselves friends are good for anything, they will—to be sure they will.

"Listen, then, Socrates, to us who have brought you up. Think not of life and children first, and of justice afterwards, but of justice first, that you may be justified before the princes of the world below. For neither will you nor any that belong to you be happier or holier or juster in this life, or happier in another, if you do as Crito bids. Now you depart in innocence, a sufferer and not a doer of evil; a victim, not of the laws but of men. But if you go forth, returning evil for evil; and injury for injury, breaking the covenants and agreements which you have made with us, and wronging those whom you ought least of all to wrong, that is to say, yourself, your friends, your country, and us, we shall be angry with you while you live, and our brethren, the laws in the world below, will receive you as an enemy; for they will know that you have done your best to destroy us. Listen, then, to us and not to Crito."

This, dear Crito, is the voice which I seem to hear murmuring in my ears, like the sound of the flute in the ears of the mystic; that voice, I say, is humming in my ears, and prevents me from hearing any other. And I know that anything more which you may say will be vain. Yet speak, if you have anything to say.

CR: I have nothing to say, Socrates.

SOC: Leave me then, Crito, to fulfill the will of God, and to follow whither he leads.

DISCUSSION

The conflict presented in the *Crito* is the life-and-death struggle between self-preservation and honor. The fact that Socrates's punishment is so unjust colors the argument even more, for one would probably feel much more righteous running away from an unjust death sentence than from a sentence that one knew one deserved. If escaping when one has been *unjustly* convicted is justifiable, then Socrates would not be faced with the choice between acting rightly and saving his life; the two would be one and the same. This is precisely the conclusion that Crito attempts to impress upon his friend. If Crito's argument were right, it would seem that Socrates could both take good care of his soul and continue living in this world. This attempt to do away with the conflict at issue, however, ultimately fails. Socrates here introduces, for the first time that we know of, what was to become one of the most famous arguments for political obligation, that of tacit consent. When he assumes the persona of the laws of Athens, Socrates asks himself whether he has benefited from the existence of such laws and the institutions they make possible. The "laws" then press him on whether he was free to leave at any time if he did not approve of the laws. The fact that he did not leave (and enjoyed the benefits of the state) forms the basis for the claim that "he has made an agreement with us that he will duly obey our commands." In other words, not leaving the city is the equivalent to consenting, albeit tacitly. And consenting to obey the law includes accepting the judgments made possible by that law. No matter how unjust the sentence, then, Socrates is not entitled to escape; doing so would be acting dishonorably.

There is, however, another question at stake here, one which can be asked even in those cases in which a person rightly faces dishonor and punishment: Is life itself worth more than anything? Death rather than dishonor has been a central ethical code of a great many societies. The naval captain has always been expected to "go down with his ship," no matter how easily he could save himself. Some of the male passengers on the ill-fated *Titanic,* which sank in 1912, felt that dying with honor was preferable to taking a seat from a woman or child (there were not nearly enough lifeboats to accommodate everyone). The multimillionaire John Jacob Astor, for example, went down with the ship in the name of his honor, leaving behind an enviable life of wealth and power.

One of the essential ethical questions of all times has been, What is worth dying for? Ask yourself this question: Under what circumstances would you be willing to give up your life? If your parents were kidnapped and your life was the ransom, would you willingly give yourself up? If your country were attacked and you were assigned a certainly fatal mission, would you willingly go? If you were caught cheating on an exam, would you—like some of the Roman heroes—kill yourself to show your remorse? Under what kinds of circumstances would you consider risking or giving up your life? Under what circumstances would you consider such action foolish or "a waste"? What is worth dying for? (This is an indirect way of asking, What is ultimately worth living for?)

Finally, a less life-and-death question raised by the *Crito* is the moral status of law. In most societies, many of the laws will be in accordance with (if not derived directly from) morality, and most judicial decisions will agree with most people's moral opinions. But law and morality are not the same and are not always in agreement. There are immoral acts that are not usually illegal (for example, lying to your friends), and there are many laws whose concern is not primarily (or even secondarily) moral (most traffic laws, for example). There are some bad laws and bad judicial decisions, and the decision against Socrates was one of the most notorious of them. Should he therefore have refused to accept the decision and escaped? Does the argument from tacit consent already discussed really commit citizens to obeying *every* law, decree, or judgment regardless of its fairness? The notorious counterexample to absolute obligation of this sort is the legal system in Nazi Germany. Advocating obedience no matter what, so long as you have (tacitly) consented by not leaving or protesting, runs the risk of going too far in separating the questions of What is right? and What is law? On the other hand, if we are to maintain a legal system (and few of us would tolerate a system in which every law is open to debate), it must be enforceable to a large degree regardless of the reactions and opinions of those who are penalized by it. Can you think of a case in which you would feel obliged to break the law, in the name of morality or some higher ideal?

THE REPUBLIC*

The idea that pervades and defines all of Plato's work—and, we may surmise, Socrates's teachings—is that of the Good. In *The Republic,* Plato's most comprehensive Socratic dialogue, the ideas of the two men are difficult to distinguish. Plato probably wrote *The Republic* around 380 B.C. It is his best-known and most-debated work, not only because of his dramatic conception of the Good, but also because of his controversial vision of the Good society. It shocked many of the Athenians when he wrote it, and (for different reasons) it still shocks readers today. The book centers around the question, What is justice?—which has become one of the leading questions of ethics and social philosophy. But the word that Plato uses for justice, *dikaiosyne*—might just as well be translated as "righteousness." Thus, most, if not all, of Plato's (Socrates's) argument about the nature of justice might just as well be taken as an argument about the Good and the right way to live. Thus, Plato argues that justice is not just one virtue among many, but the most complete virtue, which ultimately consists in "performing the function(s) for which one's nature is best fitted."

WHAT IS JUSTICE?: BOOKS I, II, AND IV

In the opening books of *The Republic,* Socrates engages in casual conversation with some of his colleagues in the Athenian marketplace. His strategy, called "dialectic," involves provoking his companion (or "interlocutor") to define "justice." Then Socrates shows what is wrong or lacking in the definition and suggests another in its place. In the first conversation with Cephalus, an old man, Cephalus suggests that justice is paying your debts and giving each his due. Socrates quickly shows him that in some circumstances, it would not be just to pay a debt. Cephalus makes it clear that he is not quite up to the rigors of a philosophical argument and politely excuses himself from the discussion. The conversation continues between Socrates and Cephalus's son, Polemachus, who tries to salvage his father's meek attempt at a definition by arguing the more basic thesis that "it is just to give to each what is owed to him," adding that this means doing good to one's friends and doing harm to one's enemies. Socrates replies that it is wrong to harm anyone, so that this would mean that being just requires being unjust, an obvious contradiction. Then follows a famous exchange with Thrasymachus, a belligerent young man, who argues that justice is nothing but the interests of the strong. Socrates catches him in a contradiction, and Thrasymachus, his conversation punctuated by insults already, leaves with a final rebuff.

The subsequent dialogue with Glaucon, which in fact continues for the remainder of the book, focuses the discussion on the question, Why should one be just? Glaucon suggests, using the fabled "Ring of Gyges" as his example, that people would not be just if they could in fact get away with being unjust. Socrates is determined to argue, against Glaucon's sincere skepticism, that it is good to be just for its own sake and not for any further reason, and good for the person who is just as well.

This recurring Platonic theme—that it is in our own interest to do the right thing rather than that which is easy or pleasurable—goes for the other virtues as well. To support this claim, however, we must show that even if there are no *apparent* benefits to being just (or honorable or pious), indeed even if there are obvious costs attached to doing the right thing, it nevertheless benefits the actor to do so, at least in the long run. If a case can be made for this view (and Socrates spares no effort to do so), many recalcitrant moral problems turn out to be less difficult than first appeared. For instance, the question of whether moral duty should override self-interest (for example, whether you should give to charity or spend the money on luxuries for yourself) is neatly solved if the two come to the same thing. Likewise, the problem often discussed in political and legal philosophy of motivating large numbers of people to act rightly, whether it involves obeying the law or treating each other with minimal respect (for example, being committed to following social or legal rules even absent penalties), no longer seems intractable.

However, this view requires, among other things, that we be able to discern what the right thing to do actually is, and this determination should be fairly steady across time, circumstances, and players. It must be possible, in other words, to definitively answer the question, What should I do?

Against the skeptics (doubters) of the day, Socrates and Plato continued to believe in an absolute ideal that does not depend on the whims and feelings of individuals or on the conventions and customs of particular cities or societies. The project that Plato takes on in *The Republic* is to give this sort of objective account of the ideal of justice—one which is true no matter what, who, or where. The ideal defines whole societies as well as individuals, and the vision of *The Republic* is that of an ideal society composed of individuals, each of whom knows his proper place. In a short excerpt from Book IV, Plato (Socrates) provides his own theory of justice, a twin ideal in which the various parts of the republic and the various parts of the individual soul each does its own assigned task and works together in harmony for the good of the whole.

The dialogue begins as Socrates is discussing the virtues and disadvantages of old age with Cephalus, who is already a very old man. (Socrates is depicted as considerably younger.) Baited into a conversation about justice by Socrates, Cephalus casually suggests that justice is paying your debts. Socrates quickly shows him that it would not be just to give arms to a wicked or a crazed man, even if he were so owed. Cephalus, who is not equal to an intense argument with Socrates, departs politely and leaves the field to younger dialecticians.

Book I

> If it is moderate and contented, old age too is but moderately burdensome; if it is not, then both old age and youth are hard to bear.
>
> [Socrates] I wondered at his saying this and I wanted him to say more, so I urged him on by saying: Cephalus, when you say this, I don't think most people would agree with you; they think you endure old age easily not because of your manner of life but because you are wealthy, for the wealthy, they say, have many things to encourage them.

What you say is true, he said. They would not agree. And there is something in what they say, but not as much as they think. What Themistocles said is quite right: when a man from Seriphus was insulting him by saying that his high reputation was due to his city and not to himself, he replied that, had he been a Seriphian, he would not be famous, but neither would the other had he been an Athenian. The same can be applied to those who are not rich and find old age hard to bear—namely that a good man would not very easily bear old age in poverty, nor would a bad man, even if wealthy, be at peace with himself.

Did you inherit most of your wealth, Cephalus, I asked, or did you acquire it?

How much did I acquire, Socrates? As a moneymaker I stand between my grandfather and my father. My grandfather and namesake inherited about the same amount of wealth which I possess but multiplied it many times. My father, Lysanias, however, diminished that amount to even less than I have now. As for me, I am satisfied to leave to my sons here no less but a little more than I inherited.

The reason I asked, said I, is that you did not seem to me to be overfond of money, and this is generally the case with those who have not made it themselves. Those who have acquired it by their own efforts are twice as fond of it as other men. Just as poets love their own poems and fathers love their children, so those who have made their money are attached to it as something they have made themselves, besides using it as other men do. This makes them poor company, for they are unwilling to give their approval to anything but money.

What you say is true, he said.

It surely is, said I. Now tell me this much more: What is the greatest benefit you have received from the enjoyment of wealth?

I would probably not convince many people in saying this, Socrates, he said, but you must realize that when a man approaches the time when he thinks he will die, he becomes fearful and concerned about things which he did not fear before. It is then that the stories we are told about the underworld, which he ridiculed before—that the man who has sinned here will pay the penalty there—torture his mind lest they be true. Whether because of the weakness of old age, or because he is now closer to what happens there and has a clearer view, the man himself is filled with suspicion and fear, and he now takes account and examines whether he has wronged anyone. If he finds many sins in his own life, he awakes from sleep in terror, as children do, and he lives with the expectation of evil. However, the man who knows he has not sinned has a sweet and good hope as his constant companion, a nurse to his old age, as Pindar too puts it. The poet has expressed this charmingly, Socrates, that whoever lives a just and pious life

Sweet is the hope that nurtures his heart,

companion and nurse to his old age,

a hope which governs the rapidly changing thoughts of mortals.

This is wonderfully well said. It is in this connection that I would say that wealth has its greatest value, not for everyone but for a good and well-balanced man. Not to have lied to or deceived anyone even unwillingly, not to depart yonder in fear, owing either sacrifices to a god or money to a man: to this wealth makes a great contribution. It has many other uses, but benefit for benefit I would say that its greatest usefulness lies in this for an intelligent man, Socrates.

Beautifully spoken, Cephalus, said I, but are we to say that justice or right is simply to speak the truth and to pay back any debt one may have contracted? Or are these same actions sometimes right and sometimes wrong? I mean this sort of thing, for example: everyone would surely agree that if a friend has deposited weapons with you when he was sane, and he asks for them when he is out of his mind, you should not return them. The man who returns them is not doing right, nor is one who is willing to tell the whole truth to a man in such a state.

What you say is correct, he answered.

This then is not a definition of right or justice, namely to tell the truth and pay one's debts.

It certainly is, said Polemarchus interrupting, if we are to put any trust in Simonides.

And now, said Cephalus, I leave the argument to you, for I must go back and look after the sacrifice.

Do I then inherit your role? asked Polemarchus.

You certainly do, said Cephalus laughing, and as he said it he went off to sacrifice.

Then do tell us, Polemarchus, said I, as the heir to the argument, what it is that Simonides stated about justice which you consider to be correct.

He stated, said he, that it is just to give to each what is owed to him, and I think he was right to say so.

Well now, I said, it is hard not to believe Simonides, for he is a wise and inspired man, but what does he mean? Perhaps you understand him, but I do not. Clearly he does not mean what we were saying just now, that anything he has deposited must be returned to a man who is not in his right mind; yet anything he has deposited is owing to him. Is that not so?—Yes.

But it is not to be returned to him at all if he is out of his mind when he asks for it?—That's true.

Certainly Simonides meant something different from this when he says that to return what is owed is just.

He did indeed mean something different by Zeus, said he. He believes that one owes it to one's friends to do good to them, and not harm.

I understand, said I, that one does not give what is owed or due if one gives back gold to a depositor, when giving back and receiving are harmful, and the two are friends. Is that not what you say Simonides meant?—Quite.

Well then, should one give what is due to one's enemies?

By all means, said he, what is in fact due to them, and I believe that is what is properly due from an enemy to an enemy, namely something harmful.

It seems, I said, that Simonides was suggesting the nature of the just poetically and in riddles. For he thought this to be just, to give to each man what is proper to him, and he called this what is due.—Surely. . . . When you say friends, do you mean those whom a man believes to be helpful to him, or those who are helpful even if they do not appear to be so, and so with enemies?

Probably, he said, one is fond of those whom one thinks to be good and helpful to one, and one hates those whom one considers bad and harmful.

Surely people make mistakes about this, and consider many to be helpful when they are not, and often make the opposite mistake about enemies?—They do.

Then good men are their enemies, and bad people their friends?—Quite so.

And so it is just and right for these mistaken people to benefit the bad and harm the good?—It seems so.

But the good are just and able to do no wrong?—True.

But according to your argument it is just to harm those who do no wrong.

Never, Socrates, he said. It is the argument that is wrong.

It is just to harm the wrongdoers and to benefit the just?

That statement, Socrates, seems much more attractive than the other.

Then, Polemarchus, for many who are mistaken in their judgment it follows that it is just to harm their friends, for these are bad, and to benefit their enemies, who are good, and so we come to a conclusion which is the opposite of what we said was the meaning of Simonides.

That certainly follows, he said, but let us change our assumption; we have probably not defined the friend and the enemy correctly.

Where were we mistaken, Polemarchus?

When we said that a friend was one who was thought to be helpful.

How shall we change this now? I asked.

Let us state, he said, that a friend is one who is both thought to be helpful and also is; one who is thought to be, but is not, helpful is thought to be a friend but is not. And so also with the enemy.

According to this argument then, the good man will be a friend, and the bad man an enemy.—Yes.

You want us to add to what we said before about the just, namely that it is just to benefit one's friend and harm one's enemy; to this you want us to make an addition and say that it is just to benefit the friend who is good and to harm the enemy who is bad?

Quite so, he said. This seems to me to be well said.

But, I said, is it the part of the just man to harm anyone at all?

Why certainly, he said, those who are bad and one's enemies.

Do horses become better or worse when they are harmed?—Worse. . . .

Shall we not say so about men too, that when they are harmed they deteriorate in their human excellence?—Quite so.

And is not justice a human excellence?—Of course.

Then men who are harmed, my friend, necessarily become more unjust.—So it appears. . . .

Well then, can the just, by the practice of justice, make men unjust? Or, in a word, can good men, by the practice of their virtue, make men bad?—They cannot. . . .

It is not then the function of the just man, Polemarchus, to do harm to a friend or anyone else, but it is that of his opposite, the unjust man?—I think that you are entirely right, Socrates.

If, then, anyone tells us that it is just to give everyone his due, and he means by this that from the just man harm is due to his enemies and benefit due to his friends—the man who says that is not wise, for it is not true. We have shown that it is never just to harm anyone.—I agree. . . .

Thrasymachus, a belligerent young man, interrupts the conversation and immediately begins attacking Socrates. He attacks Socrates's method (of always "asking questions") and his vague answers (justice as "the needful, the advantageous, the beneficial"). He provides his own analysis of justice, which is in direct opposition to Socrates's claim that it can never be just to harm another, and that "the just is nothing else but the advantage of the stronger." Socrates asks him what he means by this, and again we see the master dialectician at work. Thrasymachus continues to insult Socrates, but Socrates pushes his notion that justice is a virtue and not merely self-interest (to which Thrasymachus blushingly agrees) and, by the end of the conversation, Socrates catches him in a flat-out contradiction. Injustice, he concludes, is never more advantageous than justice.

While we were speaking Thrasymachus often started to interrupt, but he was restrained by those who were sitting by him, for they wanted to hear the argument to the end. But when we paused after these last words of mine he could no longer keep quiet. He gathered himself together like a wild beast about to spring, and he came at us as if to tear us to pieces.

Polemarchus and I were afraid and flustered as he roared into the middle of our company: What nonsense have you two been talking, Socrates? Why do you play the fool in thus giving way to each other? If you really want to know what justice is, don't only ask questions and then score off anyone who answers, and refute him. You know very well that it is much easier to ask questions than to answer them. Give an answer yourself and tell us what you say justice is. And don't tell me that it is the needful, or the advantageous, or the beneficial, or the gainful, or the useful, but tell me clearly and precisely what you mean, for I will not accept it if you utter such rubbish.

His words startled me, and glancing at him I was afraid. I think if I had not looked at him before he looked at me, I should have been speechless. As it was I had glanced at him first when our discussion began to exasperate him, so I was able to answer him and I said, trembling: do not be hard on us, Thrasymachus, if we have erred in our investigation, he and I; be sure that we err unwillingly. You surely do not believe that if we were searching for gold we would be unwilling to give way to each other and thus destroy our chance of finding it, but that when searching for justice, a thing more precious than much gold, we mindlessly give way to one another, and that we are not thoroughly in earnest about finding it. You must believe that, my friend, for I think we could not do it. So it is much more seemly that you clever people should pity us than that you should be angry with us.

When he heard that he gave a loud and bitter laugh and said: By Heracles, that is just Socrates' usual irony. I knew this, and I warned these men here before that you would not be willing to answer any questions but would pretend ignorance, and that you would do anything rather than give an answer, if anyone questioned you. . . . Listen then, said he. I say that the just is nothing else than the advantage of the stronger. Well, why don't you praise me? But you will not want to.

I must first understand your meaning, said I, for I do not know it yet. You say that the advantage of the stronger is just. What do you mean, Thrasymachus? Surely you do not mean such a thing as this: Poulydamas, the pancratist athlete, is stronger than we are; it is to his advantage to eat beef to build up his physical strength. Do you mean that this food is also advantageous and just for us who are weaker than he is?

You disgust me, Socrates, he said. Your trick is always to take up the argument at the point where you can damage it most.

Not at all, my dear sir, I said, but tell us more clearly what you mean.

Do you not know, he said, that some cities are ruled by a despot, others by the people, and others again by the aristocracy?—Of course.

And this element has the power and rules in every city?—Certainly.

Yes, and each government makes laws to its own advantage: democracy makes democratic laws, a despotism makes despotic laws, and so with the others, and when they have made these laws they declare this to be just for their subjects, that is, their own advantage, and they punish him who transgresses the laws as lawless and unjust. This then, my good man, is what I say justice is, the same in all cities, the advantage of the established government, and correct reasoning will conclude that the just is the same everywhere, the advantage of the stronger.

Now I see what you mean, I said. Whether it is true or not I will try to find out. But you too, Thrasymachus, have given as an answer that the just is the advantageous whereas you forbade that answer to me. True, you have added the words "of the stronger."

Perhaps, he said, you consider that an insignificant addition!

It is not clear yet whether or not it is significant. Obviously, we must investigate whether what you say is true. I agree that the just is some kind of advantage, but you add that it is the advantage of the stronger. I do not know. We must look into this.—Go on looking, he said.

We will do so, said I. Tell me, do you also say that obedience to the rulers is just?—I do.

And are the rulers in all cities infallible, or are they liable to error?—No doubt they are liable to error.

When they undertake to make laws, therefore, they make some correctly and make others incorrectly?—I think so.

"Correctly" means that they make laws to their own advantage, and "incorrectly" not to their own advantage. Or how would you put it?—As you do.

And whatever laws they make must be obeyed by their subjects, and this is just?—Of course.

Then, according to your argument, it is just to do not only what is to the advantage of the stronger, but also the opposite, what is not to their advantage.

What is that you are saying? he asked.

The same as you, I think, but let us examine it more fully. Have we not agreed that, in giving orders to their subjects, the rulers are sometimes in error as to what is best for themselves, yet it is just for their subjects to do whatever their rulers order. Is that much agreed?—I think so.

Think then also, said I, that you have agreed that it is just to do what is to the disadvantage of the rulers and the stronger whenever they unintentionally give orders which are bad for themselves, and you say it is just for the others to obey their given orders. Does it not of necessity follow, my wise Thrasymachus, that it is just to do the opposite of what you said? The weaker are then ordered to do what is to the disadvantage of the stronger.

Yes by Zeus, Socrates, said Polemarchus, that is quite clear.

Yes, if you bear witness for him, interrupted Cleitophon.

What need of a witness? said Polemarchus. Thrasymachus himself agrees that the rulers sometimes give orders that are bad for themselves, and that it is just to obey them.

Thrasymachus maintained that it is just to obey the orders of the rulers, Polemarchus.

He also said that the just was the advantage of the stronger, Cleitophon. Having established those two points he went on to agree that the stronger sometimes ordered the weaker, their subjects, to do what was disadvantageous to themselves. From these agreed premises it follows that what is of advantage to the stronger is no more just than what is not.

But, Cleitophon replied, he said that the advantage of the stronger is what the stronger believes to be of advantage to him. This the weaker must do, and that is what he defined the just to be.

When we reached this point in our argument and it was clear to all that the definition of justice had turned into its opposite, Thrasymachus, instead of answering, said: Tell me, Socrates, do you have a nanny?

What's this? said I. Had you not better answer than ask such questions?

Because, he said, she is letting you go around with a snotty nose and does not wipe it when she needs to, if she leaves you without any knowledge of sheep or shepherds.

What is the particular point of that remark? I asked.

You think, he said, that shepherds and cowherds seek the good of their sheep or cattle, whereas their sole purpose in fattening them and looking after them is their own good and that of their master. Moreover, you believe that rulers in the cities, true rulers that is, have a different attitude towards their subjects than one has towards sheep, and that they think of anything else, night and day, than their own advantage. You are so far from understanding the nature of justice and the just, of injustice and the unjust, that you do not realize that the just is really another's good, the advantage of the stronger and the ruler, but for the inferior who obeys it is a personal injury. Injustice on the other hand exercises its power over those who are truly naive and just, and those over whom it rules do what is of advantage to the other, the stronger, and, by obeying him, they make him happy, but themselves not in the least.

You must look at it in this way, my naive Socrates: the just is everywhere at a disadvantage compared with the unjust. First, in their contracts with one another; wherever two such men are associated you will never find, when the partnership ends, the just man to have more than the unjust, but less. Then, in their relation to the city: when taxes are to be paid, from the same income the just man pays more, the other less; but, when benefits are to be received, the one gets nothing while the other profits much; whenever each of them holds a public office, the just man, even if he is not penalized in other ways, finds that his private affairs deteriorate through neglect while he gets nothing from the public purse because he is just; moreover, he is disliked by his household and his acquaintances whenever he refuses them an unjust favour. The opposite is true of the unjust man in every respect. I repeat what I said before: the man of great power gets the better deal. Consider him if you want to decide how much more it benefits him privately to be unjust rather than just. You will see this most easily if you turn your thoughts to the most complete form of injustice which brings the greatest happiness to the wrongdoer, while it makes those whom he wronged, and who are not willing to do wrong, most wretched. This most complete form is despotism; it does not appropriate other people's property little by little, whether secretly or by force, whether public or private, whether sacred objects or temple property, but appropriates it all at once.

When a wrongdoer is discovered in petty cases, he is punished and faces great opprobrium, for the perpetrators of these petty crimes are called temple robbers, kidnappers, housebreakers, robbers, and thieves, but when a man, besides appropriating the possessions of the citizens, manages to enslave the owners as well, then, instead of those ugly names he is called happy and blessed, not only by his fellow citizens but by all others who learn that he has run through the whole gamut of injustice. Those who give injustice a bad name do so because they are afraid, not of practising but of suffering injustice.

And so, Socrates, injustice, if it is on a large enough scale, is a stronger, freer, and more powerful thing than justice and, as I said from the first, the just is what is advantageous to the stronger, while the unjust is to one's own advantage and benefit.

Having said this and poured this mass of close-packed words into our ears as a bathman might a flood of water, Thrasymachus intended to leave, but those present did not let him, and made him stay for a discussion of his views. I too begged him to stay and I said: My dear Thrasymachus, after throwing such a speech at us, you want to leave before adequately instructing us or finding out whether you are right or not? Or do you think it a small thing to decide on a whole way of living, which, if each of us adopted it, would make him live the most profitable life?

Come then, Thrasymachus, I said, answer us from the beginning. You say that complete injustice is more profitable than complete justice?

I certainly do say that, he said, and I have told you why.

Well then, what about this: you call one of the two a virtue and the other a vice?—Of course.

That is, you call justice a virtue, and injustice a vice?

Is that likely, my good man, said he, since I say that injustice is profitable, and justice is not?

What then?—The opposite.

Do you call being just a vice?—No, but certainly high-minded foolishness.

And you call being unjust low-minded?—No, I call it good judgment.

You consider the unjust then, Thrasymachus, to be good and knowledgeable?

Yes, he said, those who are able to carry injustice through to the end, who can bring cities and communities of men under their power. Perhaps you think I mean purse-snatchers? Not that those actions too are not profitable, if they are not found out, but they are not worth mentioning in comparison with what I am talking about.

I am not unaware of what you mean, I said, but this point astonishes me: do you include injustice under virtue and wisdom, and justice among their opposites?—I certainly do.

That makes it harder, my friend, and it is not easy now to know what to say. If you had declared that injustice was more profitable, but agreed that it was a vice or shameful as some others do, we could have discussed it along the lines of general opinion. Now, obviously, you will say that it is fine and strong, and apply to it all the attributes which we used to apply to justice, since you have been so bold as to include it under virtue and wisdom.—Your guess, he said, is quite right.

We must not, however, shrink from pursuing our argument and looking into this, so long as I am sure that you mean what you say. For I do not think you are joking now, Thrasymachus, but are saying what you believe to be true.

What difference, said he, does it make to you whether I believe it or not? Is it not my argument you are refuting?

No difference, said I, but try to answer this further question: do you think that the just man wants to get the better of the just?

Never, said he, for he would not then be well mannered and simple, as he is now.

Does he want to overreach a just action?

Not a just action either, he said.

Would he want to get the better of an unjust man, and would he deem that just or not?

He would want to, he said, and he would deem it right, but he would not be able to.

That was not my question, said I, but whether the just man wants and deems it right to outdo not a just man, but an unjust one?—That is so.

What about the unjust man? Would he deem it right to outdo the just man and the just action?

Of course he does, he said, since he deems it right to get the better of everybody.

So the unjust man will get the better of another unjust man or an unjust action and he will strive to get all he can from everyone?—That is so.

Let us put it this way, I said. The just man does not try to get the better of one like him but of one unlike him, whereas the unjust man overreaches the like and the unlike?—Very well put.

The unjust man, I said, is knowledgeable and good, and the just man is neither?—That is well said too.

It follows, I said, that the unjust man is like the knowledgeable and the good, while the just man is unlike them?

Of course that will be so, he said, being such a man he will be like such men, while the other is not like them.

Good. Each of them has the qualities of those he is like?—Why not?

Very well, Thrasymachus. Now you speak of one man as musical, of another as unmusical?—I do indeed.

Which is knowledgeable and which is not?

Of course the musical man is knowledgeable, the unmusical is not. . . .

Do you think, my dear sir, that any musician when tuning his lyre, desires, in the tightening and relaxing of the strings, to do better than another musician or deems it right to get the better of him?—I don't think so.

But he wants to do better than the non-musician?—Necessarily. . . .

In matters involving any kind of knowledge, or ignorance, do you think that any expert would wish to achieve more than any other expert would do or say, rather than, in respect to the same action, achieve the same as anyone like himself?—Well perhaps, it must be as you say.

What about the non-expert? Does he not want to outdo the expert and the non-expert equally?—Perhaps.

The man with knowledge is wise?—I agree.

And the wise is good?—I agree.

Now Thrasymachus, I said, we found that the unjust man tries to get the better of both those like and those unlike him. Did you not say so?—I did.

Yes, and the just man will not get the better of his like, but of one unlike him?—Yes.

The just man then, I said, resembles the wise and good, while the unjust resembles the bad and ignorant?—It may be so.

Further, we agreed that each will be such as the man he resembles?—We did so agree.

So we find that the just man has turned out to be good and wise, and the unjust man ignorant and bad.

Thrasymachus agreed to all this, not easily as I am telling it, but reluctantly and after being pushed. It was summer and he was perspiring profusely. And then I saw something I had never seen before: Thrasymachus blushing. After we had agreed that justice was virtue and wisdom, and injustice vice and ignorance, I said: Very well, let us consider this as established, . . . Come now, consider this point next: There is a function of the soul which you could not fulfill by means of any other thing, as for example: to take care of things, to rule, to deliberate, and other things of the kind; could we entrust these things to any other agent than the soul and say that they belong to it?—To no other.

What of living? Is that not a function of the soul?—It most certainly is.

So there is also an excellence of the soul?—We say so.

And, Thrasymachus, will the soul ever fulfill its function well if it is deprived of its own particular excellence, or is this impossible?—Impossible.

It is therefore inevitable that the bad soul rules and looks after things badly and that the good soul does all these things well.—Inevitable.

Now we have agreed that justice is excellence of the soul, and that injustice is vice of the soul?—We have so agreed.

The just soul and the just man, then, will live well, and the unjust man will live badly.—So it seems, according to your argument.

Surely the one who lives well is blessed and happy, and the one who does not is the opposite.—Of course.

So the just man is happy, and the unjust one is wretched.—So be it.

It profits no one to be wretched, but to be happy.—Of course.

And so, my good Thrasymachus, injustice is never more profitable than justice.

Book II

Plato's brother, Glaucon, picks up the argument where Thrasymachus abandoned it, and the conversation begins to take a truly reflective, philosophical turn. Glaucon plays devil's advocate and argues, against Socrates, that it is not necessarily in one's own best interests to be just. If people could be unjust and get away with it, he suggests, then injustice would indeed be to their advantage. As a protracted illustration of this thesis, he introduces the myth of the "Ring of Gyges," which makes the wearer invisible and thus would allow a person to commit all sorts of crimes without getting caught.

I, before finding the answer to our first enquiry into the nature of justice, let that go and turned to investigate whether it was vice and ignorance or wisdom and virtue. Another argument came up after, that injustice was more profitable than justice, and I could not refrain from following this up and abandoning the previous one so that the result of our discussion for me is that I know nothing; for, when I do not know what justice is, I shall hardly know whether it is a kind of virtue or not, or whether the just man is unhappy or happy.

When I had said this I thought I had done with the discussion, but evidently this was only a prelude. Glaucon on this occasion too showed that boldness which is characteristic of him, and refused to accept Thrasymachus' abandoning the argument. He said: Do you, Socrates, want to appear to have persuaded us, or do you want truly to convince us that it is better in every way to be just than unjust?

I would certainly wish to convince you truly, I said, if I could.

They say that to do wrong is naturally good, to be wronged is bad, but the suffering of injury so far exceeds in badness the good of inflicting it that when men have done wrong to each other and suffered it, and have had a taste of both, those who are unable to avoid the latter and practice the former decide that it is profitable to come to an agreement with each other neither to inflict injury nor to suffer it. As a result they begin to make laws and covenants, and the law's command they call lawful and just. This, they say, is the origin and essence of justice; it stands between the best and the worst, the best being to do wrong without paying the penalty and the worst to be wronged without the power of revenge. The just then is a mean between two extremes; it is welcomed and honoured because of men's lack of the power to do wrong. The man who has that power, the real man, would not make a compact with anyone not to inflict injury or suffer it. For him that would be madness. This then, Socrates, is, according to their argument, the nature and origin of justice.

Even those who practise justice do so against their will because they lack the power to do wrong. This we could realize very clearly if we imagined ourselves granting to both the just and the unjust the freedom to do whatever they liked. We could then follow both of them and observe where their desires led them, and we would catch the just man redhanded travelling the same road as the unjust. The reason is the desire for undue gain which every organism by nature pursues as a good, but the law forcibly sidetracks him to honour equality. The freedom I just mentioned would most easily occur if these men had the power which they say the ancestor of the Lydian Gyges possessed. The story is that he was a shepherd in the service of the ruler of Lydia. There was a violent rainstorm and an earthquake which broke open the ground and created a chasm at the place where he was tending sheep. Seeing this and marvelling, he went down into it. He saw, besides many other wonders of which we are told, a hollow bronze horse. There were window-like openings in it; he climbed through them and caught sight of a corpse which seemed of more than human stature, wearing nothing but a ring of gold on its finger. This ring the shepherd put on and came out. He arrived at the usual monthly meeting which reported to the king on the state of the flocks, wearing the ring. As he was sitting among the others he happened to twist the hoop of the ring towards himself, to the inside of his hand, and as he did this he became invisible to those sitting near him and they went on talking as if he had gone. He marvelled at this and, fingering the ring, he turned the hoop outward again and became visible. Perceiving this he tested whether the ring had this power and so it happened: if he turned the hoop inwards he became invisible, but was visible when he turned it outwards. When he realized this, he at once arranged to become one of the messengers to the king. He went, committed adultery with the king's wife, attacked the king with her help, killed him, and took over the kingdom.

Now if there were two such rings, one worn by the just man, the other by the unjust, no one, as these people think, would be so incorruptible that he would stay on the path of justice or bring himself to keep away from other people's property and not touch it, when he could with impunity take whatever he wanted from the market, go into houses and have sexual relations with anyone he wanted, kill anyone, free all those he wished from prison, and do the other things which would make him like a god among men. His actions would be in no way different from those of the other and they would both follow the same path. This, some would say, is a great proof that no one is just willingly but under compulsion, so that justice is not one's private good, since wherever either thought he could do wrong with impunity he would do so. Every man believes that injustice is much more profitable to himself than justice, and any exponent of this argument will say that he is right. The man who did not wish to do wrong with that opportunity, and did not touch other people's property, would be thought by those who knew it to be very foolish and miserable. They would praise him in public, thus deceiving one another, for fear of being wronged. So much for my second topic.

As for the choice between the lives we are discussing, we shall be able to make a correct judgment about it only if we put the most just man and the most unjust man face to face; otherwise we cannot do so. By face to face I mean this: let us grant to the unjust the fullest degree of injustice and to the just the fullest justice, each being perfect in his own pursuit. First, the unjust man will act as clever craftsmen do—a top navigator, for example, or physician distinguishes what his craft can do and what it cannot; the former he will undertake, the latter he will pass by, and when he slips he can put things right. So the unjust man's correct attempts at wrongdoing must remain secret; the one who is caught must be considered a poor performer, for the extreme of injustice is to have a reputation for justice, and our perfectly unjust man must be granted perfection in injustice. We must not take this from him, but we must allow that, while committing the greatest crimes, he has provided himself with the greatest reputation for justice; if he makes a slip he must be able to put it right; he must be a sufficiently persuasive speaker if some wrongdoing of his is made public; he must be able to use force, where force is needed, with the help of his courage, his strength, and the friends and wealth with which he has provided himself.

Having described such a man, let us now in our argument put beside him the just man, simple as he is and noble, who, as Aeschylus put it, does not wish to appear just but to be so. We must take away his reputation, for a reputation for justice would bring him honour and rewards, and it would then not be clear whether he is what he is for justice's sake or for the sake of rewards and honour. We must strip him of everything except justice and make him the complete opposite of the other. Though he does no wrong, he must have the greatest reputation for wrongdoing so that he may be tested for justice by not weakening under ill repute and its consequences. Let him go his incorruptible way until death with a reputation for injustice throughout his life, just though he is, so that our two men may reach the extremes, one of justice, the other of injustice, and let them be judged as to which of the two is the happier.

Whew! My dear Glaucon, I said, what a mighty scouring you have given those two characters, as if they were statues in a competition.

Besides this, Socrates, look at another kind of argument which is spoken in private, and also by the poets, concerning justice and injustice. All go on repeating with one voice that justice and moderation are beautiful, but certainly difficult and burdensome, while incontinence and injustice are sweet and easy, and shameful only by repute and by law. They add that unjust deeds are for the most part more profitable than just ones. They freely declare, both in private and in public, that the wicked who have wealth and other forms of power are happy. They honour them but pay neither honour nor attention to the weak and the poor, though they agree that these are better men than the others. What men say about the gods and virtue is the most amazing of all, namely that the gods too inflict misfortunes and a miserable life upon many good men, and the opposite fate upon their opposites.

Book IV

Thus far, the conversation has presented us only with problems—what it means to be good or just and whether it is or is not in one's interest to be good or just. Socrates has insisted that justice (goodness) is desirable for its own sake but he has not yet either defined "justice" nor shown how it would not be against one's own interests (at least sometimes) to be good or just. In Book IV of *The Republic* Socrates begins to unfold his own vision and definition of justice. He does so by proposing that those in search of the essence of justice or goodness in the individual might profit by looking at a larger model first, that of the just society. After a long discussion of the ideal city and its parts, Socrates defines *justice* in terms of a persuasive metaphor, that of "harmony." The just city, then, is one in which each person performs that function for which he or she is best suited, creating a harmonious whole. Injustice is, in turn, defined as "meddling and exchange between the . . . established orders." The soul is likewise composed of parts that, in the good and happy person, are all in harmony, which means that reason dominates (but does not suppress) the appetites and the emotions (what Socrates calls the "spirited part"). Thus, the good and happy society or city is one whose parts are in harmony, and the good and happy person is one who fulfills his role in the good and happy society. Such is the idealism of *The Republic,* which has alternatively inspired and horrified readers for almost 2,500 years.

. . . everyone must pursue one occupation of those in the city, that for which his nature best fitted him.—Yes, we kept saying that.

Further, we have heard many people say, and have often said ourselves, that justice is to perform one's own task and not to meddle with that of others.—We have said that.

This then, my friend, I said, when it happens, is in some way justice, to do one's own job. And do you know what I take to be a proof of this?—No, tell me.

Look at it this way and see whether you agree: you will order your rulers to act as judges in the courts of the city?—Surely.

And will their exclusive aim in delivering judgment not be that no citizen should have what belongs to another or be deprived of what is his own?—That would be their aim.

That being just?—Yes.

In some way then possession of one's own and the performance of one's own task could be agreed to be justice.—That is so.

Consider then whether you agree with me in this: if a carpenter attempts to do the work of a cobbler, or a cobbler that of a carpenter, and they exchange their tools and the esteem that goes with the job, or the same man tries to do both, and all the other exchanges are made, do you think that this does any great harm to the city?—No.

But I think that when one who is by nature a worker or some other kind of moneymaker is puffed up by wealth, or by the mob, or by his own strength, or some other such thing, and attempts to enter the warrior class, or one of the soldiers tries to enter the group of counsellors and guardians, though he is unworthy of it, and these exchange their tools and the public esteem, or when the same man tries to perform all these jobs together, then I think you will agree that these exchanges and this meddling bring the city to ruin.—They certainly do.

The meddling and exchange between the three established orders does very great harm to the city and would most correctly be called wickedness.—Very definitely.

And you would call the greatest wickedness worked against one's own city injustice?—Of course.

That then is injustice. And let us repeat that the doing of one's own job by the moneymaking, auxiliary, and guardian groups, when each group is performing its own task in the city, is the opposite, it is justice and makes the city just.—I agree with you that this is so.

Do not let us, I said, take this as quite final yet. If we find that this quality, when existing in each individual man, is agreed there too to be justice, then we can assent to this—for what can we say?—but if not, we must look for something else. For the present, let us complete that examination which we thought we should make, that if we tried to observe justice in something larger which contains it, this would make it easier to observe it in the individual. We thought that this larger thing was a city, and so we established the best city we could, knowing well that justice would be present in the good city. It has now appeared to us there, so let us now transfer it to the individual and, if it corresponds, all will be well. But if it is seen to be something different in the individual, then we must go back to the city and examine this new notion of justice. By thus comparing and testing the two, we might make justice light up like fire from the rubbing of firesticks, and when it has become clear, we shall fix it firmly in our own minds.—You are following the path we set, and we must do so.

Well now, when you apply the same name to a thing whether it is big or small, are these two instances of it like or unlike with regard to that to which the same name applies?—They are alike in that, he said.

So the just man and the just city will be no different but alike as regards the very form of justice.—Yes, they will be.

Now the city was thought to be just when the three kinds of men within it each performed their own task, and it was moderate and brave and wise because of some other qualities and attitudes of the same groups.—True.

And we shall therefore deem it right, my friend, that the individual have the same parts in his own soul, and through the same qualities in those parts will correctly be given the same names.—That must be so.

Well, then, I said, we are surely compelled to agree that each of us has within himself the same parts and characteristics as the city? Where else would they come from? It would be ridiculous for anyone to think that spiritedness has not come to be in the city from individuals who are held to possess it, like the inhabitants of Thrace and Scythia and others who live to the north of us, or that the same is not true of the love of learning which one would attribute most to our part of the world, or the love of money which one might say is conspicuously displayed by the Phoenicians and the Egyptians.—Certainly, he said.

This then, is the case, I said, and it is not hard to understand.—No indeed.

But this is: whether we do everything with the same part of our soul, or one thing with one of the three parts, and another with another. Do we learn with one part of ourselves, get angry with another, and with some third part desire the pleasures of food and procreation and other things closely akin to them, or, when we set out after something, do we act with the whole of our soul in each case? This will be hard to determine satisfactorily.—I think so too.

Socrates proceeds to give a detailed argument for the conclusion that our soul has different "parts" or functions by showing that we sometimes find ourselves in the equivalent of an internal civil war. For instance, we often find ourselves tempted by desires we know we ought not to act upon. One part of us (our appetites) says "go," while the other (our reason) says "stop." But, Socrates asserts, one and the same thing cannot move in two directions at once; therefore, there must be at least two distinct parts or voices within us. There is also a third voice, neither appetitive nor reasonable, our "spirited part." This is the part of our soul with which we feel anger, courage, disgust, and other similar states, which, while emotions, are not the same as our basic appetites. Our spirited part lies somewhere between the appetites and reason, and in the just person comes to the aid of reason in ruling the appetites.

The position of the spirited part seems the opposite of what we thought a short time ago. Then we thought of it as something appetitive, but now we say it is far from being that; in the civil war of the soul it aligns itself far more with the reasonable part.—Very much so.

Is it different from that also, or is it some part of reason, so that there are two parts of the soul instead of three, the reasonable and the appetitive? Or, as we had three separate parts holding our city together, the money-making, the auxiliary and the deliberative, so in the soul the spirited is a third part, by nature the helper of reason, if it has not been corrupted by a bad upbringing?—It must be a third part.

Yes, I said, if it now appears to be different from the reasonable part, as earlier from the appetitive part.

It is not difficult, he said, to show that it is different. One can see this in children; they are full of spirit from birth, whereas a few of them seem to me never to acquire a share of reason, while the majority do not do so until late.

By Zeus, I said, that is very well put. One can see this also in animals. Besides, our earlier quotation from Homer bears witness to it, where he says:

Striking his chest, he addressed his heart,

for clearly Homer represents the part which reasons about the better and the worse course, and which strikes his chest, as different from that which is angry without reasoning.—You are definitely right.

We have now made our difficult way through a sea of argument to reach this point, and we have fairly agreed that the same kinds of parts, and the same number of parts, exist in the soul of each individual as in our city.—That is so.

It necessarily follows that the individual is wise in the same way, and in the same part of himself, as the city.—Quite so.

And the part which makes the individual brave is the same as that which makes the city brave, and in the same manner, and everything which makes for virtue is the same in both?—That necessarily follows.

Moreover, Glaucon, I think we shall say that a man is just in the same way as the city is just.—That too is inevitable.

We have surely not forgotten that the city was just because each of the three classes in it was fulfilling its own task.—I do not think, he said, that we have forgotten that.

We must remember then that each one of us within whom each part is fulfilling its own task will himself be just and do his own work.—We must certainly remember this.

Therefore it is fitting that the reasonable part should rule, it being wise and exercising foresight on behalf of the whole soul, and for the spirited part to obey it and be its ally.—Quite so.

Plato's analogy between the soul and the state is probably the most controversial aspect of *The Republic,* not so much because it has been disputed whether the soul can in fact be said to have three parts but rather because the "one man, one task" definition of justice flies in the face of everything we have come to believe about the success both of individuals and of their states. It is not at all clear (and there is much evidence the other way) that people are more productive and happy when their jobs and their roles in society are defined as so limited (even if the tasks Plato enumerates—for example, craftsman, farmer, soldier—are much broader and more varied than the specialized industrial jobs today). As a political entity, a state that is so fixed and "closed" is the very anathema of our ideal of a democracy where people are free to speak out and even to leave. (Plato, of course, thought very little of democracy, and listed it as one of the worst forms of government, second only to tyranny.) Thus, Sir Karl Popper bitterly complained about Plato's political theory—in his aptly titled book, *The Open Society and Its Enemies*—as being a recipe for totalitarianism. But although we may well reject the hierarchical ordering of Plato's closed society, most of us will probably find something very attractive in the metaphor of "harmony" that links the two parts of the analogy. Harmony of the soul—or "wisdom"—is a healthy ideal that we understand quite well, and it does not seem to be limited to any particular political or social system. The idea that the good person is the healthy person is an idea that we find very appealing, and it has much to do with the contemporary quest for "integrity" or (in more colloquial terms) "getting it all together." So, too, notice that Plato (Socrates) has finally given us a definition of justice (goodness) that does succeed in integrating what was right about the earlier, rejected definitions of Cephalus and his son: the idea that justice (goodness) is "giving what is due." But whereas Cephalus intended by this only the payment of debts and Polemarchus restricted it to personal relations, Plato has in mind the proper "due" of the soul itself, which is to be an active participant and contributor to the community by developing itself and its talents. Goodness is good for the soul.

THE MYTH OF THE CAVE: FROM BOOK VII

Our selections from *The Republic* conclude with the famous allegory in Book VII, the "Myth of the Cave," which dramatically introduces the theory of the Forms. Plato (Socrates) has already introduced the grand conception of the pure Idea or Form of the Good. An idea, for Plato, was not an idea in our minds but rather an independent existence in its own real world ("the world of being"), a world even more real than our own. Our everyday world ("the world of becoming") is unstable and always changing. People grow old and die. Great cities become corrupted and are destroyed. People's opinions seem to change with the times and with age. But the pure Ideas or Forms remain eternally the same: for being perfect, they are neither corruptible nor in need of any change for the better. The theory of the Forms supplies Socrates with what he has been searching for: an objective, unchanging account of justice and the other virtues that is true under all circumstances. The good man, accordingly, would seek out the Form of the Good (by way of finding its correct definition) whatever the state of society around him. (Socrates and Plato both had reason to be pessimistic about finding or establishing this idea in actual society, although both of them tried to do so: Socrates in Athens, Plato in Syracuse.) The Myth of the Cave is a dramatic image of the existence of the Form of the Good in the "intelligible world," standing apart from the mere shadows of our everyday life, and it is an ominous warning for the philosopher who would seek to define this good and make it clear to an unenlightened society.

> Next, I said, compare the effect of education and the lack of it upon our human nature to a situation like this: imagine men to be living in an underground cave-like dwelling place, which has a way up to the light along its whole width, but

the entrance is a long way up. The men have been there from childhood, with their neck and legs in fetters, so that they remain in the same place and can only see ahead of them, as their bonds prevent them turning their heads. Light is provided by a fire burning some way behind and above them. Between the fire and the prisoners, some way behind them and on a higher ground, there is a path across the cave and along this a low wall has been built, like the screen at a puppet show in front of the performers who show their puppets above it.—I see it.

See then also men carrying along that wall, so that they overtop it, all kinds of artifacts, statues of men, reproductions of other animals in stone or wood fashioned in all sorts of ways, and, as is likely, some of the carriers are talking while others are silent.—This is a strange picture, and strange prisoners.

They are like us, I said. Do you think, in the first place, that such men could see anything of themselves and each other except the shadows which the fire casts upon the wall of the cave in front of them?—How could they, if they have to keep their heads still throughout life?

And is not the same true of the objects carried along the wall?—Quite.

If they could converse with one another, do you not think that they would consider these shadows to be the real things?—Necessarily.

What if their prison had an echo which reached them from in front of them? Whenever one of the carriers passing behind the wall spoke, would they not think that it was the shadow passing in front of them which was talking? Do you agree?—By Zeus I do.

Altogether then, I said, such men would believe the truth to be nothing else than the shadows of the artifacts?—They must believe that.

Consider then what deliverance from their bonds and the curing of their ignorance would be if something like this naturally happened to them. Whenever one of them was freed, had to stand up suddenly, turn his head, walk, and look up toward the light, doing all that would give him pain; the flash of the fire would make it impossible for him to see the objects of which he had earlier seen the shadows. What do you think he would say if he was told that what he saw then was foolishness, that he was now somewhat closer to reality and turned to things that existed more fully, that he saw more correctly? If one then pointed to each of the objects passing by, asked him what each was, and forced him to answer, do you not think he would be at a loss and believe that the things which he saw earlier were truer than the things now pointed out to him?—Much truer.

If one then compelled him to look at the fire itself, his eyes would hurt, he would turn round and flee toward those things which he could see, and think that they were in fact clearer than those now shown to him.—Quite so.

And if one were to drag him thence by force up the rough and steep path, and did not let him go before he was dragged into the sunlight, would he not be in physical pain and angry as he was dragged along? When he came into the light, with the sunlight filling his eyes, he would not be able to see a single one of the things which are now said to be true.—Not at once, certainly.

I think he would need time to get adjusted before he could see things in the world above; at first he would see shadows most easily, then reflections of men and other things in water, then the things themselves. After this he would see objects in the sky and the sky itself more easily at night, the light of the stars and the moon more easily than the sun and the light of the sun during the day.—Of course.

Then, at last, he would be able to see the sun, not images of it in water or in some alien place, but the sun itself in its own place, and be able to contemplate it.—That must be so.

After this he would reflect that it is the sun which provides the seasons and the years, which governs everything in the visible world, and is also in some way the cause of those other things which he used to see.—Clearly that would be the next stage.

What then? As he reminds himself of his first dwelling place, of the wisdom there and of his fellow prisoners, would he not reckon himself happy for the change, and pity them?—Surely.

And if the men below had praise and honours from each other, and prizes for the man who saw most clearly the shadows that passed before them, and who could best remember which usually came earlier and which later, and which came together and thus could most ably prophesy the future, do you think our man would desire those rewards and envy those who were honoured and held power among the prisoners, or would he feel, as Homer put it, that he certainly wished to be "serf to another man without possessions upon the earth" and go through any suffering, rather than share their opinions and live as they do?—Quite so, he said, I think he would rather suffer anything.

Reflect on this too, I said. If this man went down into the cave again and sat down in the same seat, would his eyes not be filled with darkness, coming suddenly out of the sunlight?—They certainly would.

And if he had to contend again with those who had remained prisoners in recognizing those shadows while his sight was affected and his eyes had not settled down—and the time for this adjustment would not be short—would he not be ridiculed? Would it not be said that he had returned from his upward journey with his eyesight spoiled, and that it was not worthwhile even to attempt to travel upward? As for the man who tried to free them and lead them upward, if they could somehow lay their hands on him and kill him, they would do so.—They certainly would.

This whole image, my dear Glaucon, I said, must be related to what we said before. The realm of the visible should be compared to the prison dwelling, and the fire inside it to the power of the sun. If you interpret the upward journey and the contemplation of things above as the upward journey of the soul to the intelligible realm, you will grasp what I surmise since you were keen to hear it. Whether it is true or not only the god knows, but this is how I see it, namely that in the intelligible world the Form of the Good is the last to be seen, and with difficulty; when seen it must be reckoned to be for all the cause of all that is right and beautiful, to have produced in the visible world both light and the fount of light, while in the intelligible world it is itself that which produces and controls truth and intelligence, and he who is to act intelligently in public or in private must see it.—I share your thought as far as I am able.

Come then, share with me this thought also: do not be surprised that those who have reached this point are unwilling to occupy themselves with human affairs, and that their souls are always pressing upward to spend their time there, for this is natural if things are as our parable indicates.—That is very likely.

Further, I said, do you think it at all surprising that anyone coming to the evils of human life from the contemplation of the divine behaves awkwardly and appears very ridiculous while his eyes are still dazzled and before he is sufficiently adjusted to the darkness around him, if he is compelled to contend in court or some other place about the shadows of justice or the objects of which they are shadows, and to carry through the contest about these in the way these things are understood by those who have never seen Justice itself?—That is not surprising at all.

Anyone with intelligence, I said, would remember that the eyes may be confused in two ways and from two causes, coming from light into darkness as well as from darkness into light. Realizing that the same applies to the soul, whenever he sees a soul disturbed and unable to see something, he will not laugh mindlessly but will consider whether it has come from a brighter life and is dimmed because unadjusted, or has come from greater ignorance into greater light and is filled with a brighter dazzlement. The former he would declare happy in its life and experience, the latter he would pity, and if he should wish to laugh at it, his laughter would be less ridiculous than if he laughed at a soul that has come from the light above.—What you say is very reasonable.

DISCUSSION

The opening arguments of *The Republic* are intended to prepare the way for Plato's (Socrates's) own definition and discussion of justice—"righteousness" or goodness—although their initial result is a series of devastating refutations. And yet, those early positions are not wholly done away with. They are rather transformed and made more philosophical, and so we should not be surprised that Cephalus's casual suggestion that justice is paying your debts eventually surfaces (transformed) at the heart of Plato's (Socrates's) theory of justice as playing one's proper part in the good society. So, too, Glaucon's seeming defense of selfishness is, he himself tells us, not a position that he himself believes. It is rather to improve the debate (after Thrasymachus's belligerent ad hominem arguments) and provide Socrates with the best possible foils for his own discussion. The progression of the argument underscores Socrates's effort to find an adequate *definition* of justice (goodness), but the theories of Cephalus and his son Polemarchus are subject to easy counterexamples that show the inadequacies of those definitions familiar to Athenians. The main problem with Cephalus's definition is that he tries to define justice through one of its many specific instances, namely, paying one's debts. A proper definition is not just a list of proper and improper actions or "dos and don'ts"; rather it is a description of the necessary ingredients of *any* instance of justice. Thus, Socrates pushes Polemarchus to go beyond the simple "give what is owed" definition to a more general characterization. It is Thrasymachus who steps forward with a thesis that looks like such a theory, but Plato makes it very clear that Thrasymachus is no philosopher and is far more concerned with getting his way and impressing his friends than reaching the truth. Thus, it is fairly easy for Socrates to show that there is a contradiction involved in equating justice or what is *right* with anyone's advantage. Thrasymachus, it soon becomes apparent, does not believe that this is a definition of justice at all; it is rather a way of saying that there is no justice or "goodness," that the word is just a cover for whatever benefits the rulers of the society. It is here that Socrates begins to insist that justice is both real (in fact, more so than anything in "this world") and to be practiced for its own sake.

The central distinction that then emerges is the distinction between virtue and prudence, acting justly and acting in our own interests, respectively. What virtue requires, however, is an impersonal ideal that is not of our own making, not a course of action tailor-made to our own needs and interests. The two are often in agreement, of course; indeed, it is part of Plato's (Socrates's) argument in *The Republic* that virtue and happiness are inextricably interwoven. The Ring of Gyges discussion is an extreme illustration of pure prudence—we would call it "selfishness"—devoid of any concern for justice or goodness whatever. Glaucon uses this story to make his point that justice and individual happiness are quite distinct, even incompatible, to which Socrates will eventually reply that this involves an essential misunderstanding of what happiness requires.

The argument here is that, although we can imagine an isolated case in which a perfectly wicked man might be quite happy and a perfectly good man utterly miserable, the case to be made for justice cannot be based upon two such unusual—if not implausible—examples. (It is very difficult to be perfectly wicked; indeed, it is as hard as it is to be perfectly good.) The argument for justice must be a *general* argument, and in the rest of Book II Socrates shifts the terms from the image of a single person who is just or unjust to the question of what it is for the whole society to be just. Again, this is a form of argument that we will see in different guises throughout the history of ethics: the move from individual, personal concerns to more general, impersonal considerations. Why should we be just? Not because, in each individual case, it will necessarily make us happier but rather because—thinking prudentially—if we want to live in a livable society in which we will all be happier in general, justice is better than injustice. Socrates will introduce another argument, though, that is not a prudential argument but is what we later call a "moral" consideration. (Plato does not use this concept.) This is the insistence that a "noble" person will be just for justice's sake and not because of the usual rewards of having a good reputation. But it is notable that Plato does not make much of this argument, except to acknowledge it as a possibility; for him, justice and well-being go hand in hand, and Socrates criticizes Glaucon precisely for artificially forcing them apart ("scouring them . . . as if they were statues in a competition").

In the "Myth of the Cave" and in his theory of "Ideas" or "the Forms," Plato provides us with a spectacular answer to some of the most troubling and perennial problems in philosophy. One of the central questions of metaethics might simply be stated, What does the word "good" mean? There are various answers, some of them more or less "objective" (that is, that goodness is a property of the "object" itself). Others are more "subjective" (that is, that it is the attitude of the person who calls something good that makes it good). Advocates of the latter, more subjective position often argue that the word "good" is a sign of approval or recommendation (for example, "I approve of this and you should too"). Advocates of the more objective position insist that goodness is a real property of the object (the person or action judged to be good, for example), whether or not it is recognized by any number of subjects. The disadvantage of the former position is that it leaves us with no way of finding out what is really good, except perhaps by way of consensus and what people agree is good. The difficulty of the latter theory is trying to describe this property of "goodness." It is here that Plato's theory enters the picture.

Plato's theory of Ideas or the Forms is even more than an objective theory. Not only is the property goodness a real property of the object, but goodness is an object itself, an ideal object that is even more real than the things that are good. Why does Plato believe this? First of all, he firmly believes that goodness is objective and not dependent on individuals or social consensus. He utterly rejects Protagoras, in other words, who insists that "man is the measure of all things." But not only this, Plato also realizes that, if goodness is to be a real property of things, then it must have a definable set of characteristics, like other real properties. An animal has the property of being a dog, for example, because it has certain characteristics—four legs, fur, teeth, it barks, and so on. So, too, all good things have something in common, but what would this be? Could it be a simple property, like redness? But what simple property would all good things have in common? A good paperweight is heavy; a good crepe is light. Don't we have to say that goodness is a different property in different good things, depending on the kind of things that they are? Plato doesn't think so. Indeed, his theory is that if all good things didn't share some property in common, then we would have no right calling them all "good."

This property is participation in the Good; it is not a property of things but an Idea or Form that good things "imitate." Plato's analogy with the Sun and the shadows it casts is well chosen. The sun gives plants and ultimately all living things the power to live and to grow. It provides them with the light with which things can be seen. To think of the World of Forms ("of Being") as our conceptual Sun is a powerful way of seeing our ordinary, everchanging world as but a reflection of a more basic, enduring, unchanging realm, and our daily conceptions of the good, so rife with complications and confusions, as reflections of an eternal Form of the Good, which is absolute and perfect. The reasons behind Plato's metaphysical speculations on the independent reality of such ideas or Forms are beyond the scope of ethics, but the basic principle is clear enough: If good things are really good, and if they all deserve to be called by the same name, then they must have something in common, namely, that they all resemble, or imitate, the Idea of the Good. The "Myth of the Cave" is Plato's extremely dramatic way of suggesting to us the existence of an ideal world other than our own imperfect world—a vision that would later influence the development of Christianity. But the theory behind the myth is based on a metaethical concern—to try to account for our use of the word "good" and to explain how it is that we can call so many things good, including, not least, the good man and the good life for man.

Discussion Questions

1. What are Socrates's arguments against running away and for staying to be executed? Are they convincing arguments? What kinds of reasons appear in these arguments?

2. Does being born and staying and living in a community give a person an absolute obligation to obey the laws of that community?

3. What is wrong with the concept of justice, which says, in effect, "might makes right"? Why is it not just that a person should get what he or she can, without further qualification or restrictions?

4. Is being good simply obeying the law? Which laws, if any, should we not obey? Why or why not?

5. Define the word "good." Now take the role of Socrates and criticize your own definition. In what ways is it too broad? In what ways too narrow? Try again. (Then try the same with "justice.")

Study Questions

1. What is the argument in "The Ring of Gyges"? How would you answer Glaucon?

2. Why does Socrates (Plato) introduce the idea of the Form of the Good (and Justice) in his argument? Why not restrict attention to actual good acts? What philosophical power does the introduction of the Forms give the Socratic argument? What alternative positions is Socrates (Plato) attempting to cut off?

3. What does Plato's "Myth of the Cave" represent? What is the cave? What are the Sun and the Shadows? What is it that will allow us to "see the light," in more literal terms?

4. How does Socrates define justice in the city? In the individual? Are cities and persons enough alike to allow for the analogy?

5. What conclusions does Socrates draw from his belief that our souls are immortal?

2

Aristotle

Aristotle was born in 384 B.C. in northern Greece (in Stagira). His father was the physician to the king (Philip of Macedonia), and Aristotle later became tutor to Philip's son Alexander (later to become Alexander the Great). Aristotle studied with Plato for 18 years, but when Plato died, Aristotle turned much more to the sciences—biology in particular—and his various theories ruled Western science for almost 2,000 years. He set up his own school in Athens but when Alexander died and his empire started to fall apart, anti-Macedonian feeling in Athens was such that Aristotle beat a hasty retreat, supposedly remarking that the Athenians would not have a second chance to sin against philosophy. Aristotle's influence, however, came to rule not only Athens but all of Europe and the Mediterranean. Many of his views on science, for example, were not seriously challenged for 1,500 years, and his views on ethics still provide the touchstone to which moral philosophers return again and again.

Aristotle was a student in Plato's academy, but he ultimately grew to disagree with Plato almost entirely. The difference between them is enormous, in style as well as in substance. Plato's Socratic dialogues are literary as well as philosophical masterpieces, dramatic plays that could be performed as well as studied. Aristotle, on the other hand, wrote ponderous and technical philosophical treatises, brilliant but more difficult to read. (Actually, this is misleading; Aristotle wrote dialogues, too, but none of them have survived.) Many of Plato's ethical investigations, furthermore, were mainly concerned with the most metaethical questions—the definition of the Good and Justice. Aristotle, on the other hand, was more interested in the details of everyday life—how a good person should behave and what goes wrong when someone knows what should be done but doesn't do it (or knows what should not be done and does it anyway). The *Nicomachean Ethics* covers the entire spectrum of ethical issues, from the most general metaethical concerns about the nature of the Good to the most specific questions about the value of certain emotions (pride, for example) and the way one ought to act toward friends. Indeed, there has probably never been a book more complete on the subject of ethics than Aristotle's *Ethics*. (In fact, Aristotle wrote at least two treatises in ethics. The "Nicomachean" treatise—generally thought to have been edited by Aristotle's son Nicomachus and later named for him—is by far the better known. The other treatise, the "Eudemian Ethics" differs in some significant ways from The *Nicomachean Ethics,* but these differences will not concern us here, and we will simply refer to the better-known treatise as the *Ethics.*)

The stated purpose of the *Ethics* is to describe "the good for man." The emphasis on description here is extremely important, for Aristotle often begins an investigation by pointing to or describing "what most men think." However, this appeal to received opinion is only the starting point. Aristotle then analyzes the accepted views, checking their consistency with one another as well as with other securely held beliefs on related subjects, ultimately coming up with a conclusion or a definition that usually differs in important ways from any of the opinions with which he began. For instance, in determining the true nature of happiness, a state about which most people have an opinion, Aristotle begins by surveying the various candidates for the happy life. Some say it is a life built on wealth, others on honor, still others on pleasure. After showing the defects of each of these conceptions, Aristotle gives his own account of happiness, one that is grounded in large part on commonsensical observations but that is, at the same time, startlingly new. Although his ultimate definition of happiness is by no means "what most men think," his account of happiness is achieved in part by pointing to commonly observable characteristics of humans and the sorts of lives they tend to lead or are capable of leading.

One of the most important concepts in Aristotle's theory, that of a thing's *telos,* or end, is developed in a similar way. From his many studies of the natural world, Aristotle concluded that nature is purposive, that "she does nothing in vain." That is, everything (almost) has a particular purpose for which it is best suited, and that purpose or goal is what Aristotle calls its *telos.* Included in this account are not only natural objects such as plants and animals, but man-made artifacts as well. Moreover, we can inquire about the *telos* of particular parts of animals or objects as well. For instance, the purpose, or function, of the eye is to enable us to see; the ear, to provide hearing.

The way in which we ascertain the *telos* of something is again, empirically based. We look at the entity in question and ask, What is it for? or more precisely, What can it do either uniquely or best? In other words, we look for what it has that other things lack and that makes it better suited for a particular function. For example, there are a number of tools we might use in sharpening a pencil: a knife, our teeth, a nail file, a saw, scissors, or a pencil sharpener. Although we can get the job done by other means, it is clear that it is *best* done by the pencil sharpener. That is, of all the tools available, if the task at hand is pencil sharpening, we can do no better than to seek out a pencil sharpener. (Conversely, although we might accomplish other tasks with a pencil sharpener—trimming hair, for instance—it will not be the best tool for the job, for its function is reserved for pencil sharpening.) After we have determined what the function of a particular object or being is, we can see why it is built the way it is. The pencil sharpener, once again, has a sharp edge on the inside of a small hole *because* that is the arrangement of parts that is best for sharpening pencils. This provides us, then, with what is known as a *teleological explanation,* one that is given in terms of the thing's function or end.

But it also provides us (or Aristotle) with the starting point for developing a theory of the good. After we have identified the specific function of an artifact or natural object, we can talk about its effectiveness in achieving that function. That is, we can judge a thing's value by how well it fulfills its role or function. A good knife is not one that is decorative or fun for kids to play with, but rather one that cuts well. Consequently, a sharp knife is *better* than a dull one. For Aristotle, value is assessed in terms of function. To say something is a good *x* is to say that it accomplishes the task well for which *x*'s are intended. Although he does not always put it this way, Aristotle's use of the term "good" always presupposes knowledge of the thing's function. Again, Aristotle included not only objects, but species, including human beings, in his teleological account. The question with which we begin the *Ethics* then is, What is the good for man? To answer this we must first determine the *telos* of man, that is, that which human beings can do either uniquely or better than anything else. Only then can we make judgments about how well particular men fulfill that *telos.* And it will turn out on Aristotle's account that our unique quality is the ability to deploy reason, with regard to both practical and intellectual matters.

In subsequent books of the *Ethics,* Aristotle goes on to describe the central concepts of happiness *(eudaimonia)* and virtue or excellence *(arete)* and to list and describe the various virtues. He also spends considerable effort attacking the hedonist, who argues that the good for man is pleasure, and analyzing various pitfalls that plague our attempts to be good. Two full books are devoted to describing the virtues of friendship—an emphasis lacking in many ethical treatises that should make us stop and think about the usual neglect of this very important part of life. ("No one would choose to live without friends," he says.)

THE NICOMACHEAN ETHICS*

THE GOAL OF HUMAN ACTIVITY: FROM BOOK I

Aristotle begins his *Ethics* by clearly stating his teleological premise: Everything seems to aim at some good. This "teleology" provides the framework for his entire argument, and the main question is, Exactly what is this ultimate good? Notice that, for Aristotle, ethics and politics are part of the same discipline, and the good of the individual and the good of the society (the state) go hand in hand. More specifically, Aristotle tells us that Politics is the "master-art or master-science" because it determines what men will do in society. Although he does not discuss it explicitly in the *Ethics,* an important component of Aristotle's views on human nature is the claim that we are essentially social, or political, animals. As a result, anything that can be said to be a part of human happiness or flourishing will necessarily take place within a society. Because it is politics that determines what people will do in society, an inquiry into the good man, says Aristotle, is a "sort of political inquiry."

---

*Aristotle, *The Nicomachean Ethics of Aristotle,* translated by F. H. Peters with some revisions and changes in the paragraphing. Copyright 1901 by K. Paul, Trench, Trubner & Co.

1. Every art and every kind of inquiry, and likewise every act and purpose, seems to aim at some good; and so it has been well said that the good is that at which everything aims. But a difference is observable among these aims or ends. What is aimed at is sometimes the exercise of a faculty, sometimes a certain result beyond that exercise. And where there is an end beyond that act, there the result is better than the exercise of the faculty. Now since there are many kinds of actions and many arts and sciences, it follows that there are many ends also; *e.g.* health is the end of medicine, ships of shipbuilding, victory of the art of war, and wealth of economy. But when several of these are subordinated to some one art or science,—as the making of bridles and other trappings to the art of horsemanship, and this in turn, along with all else that the soldier does, to the art of war, and so on,—then the end of the master art is always more desired than the end of the subordinate arts, since these are pursued for its sake. And this is equally true whether the end in view be the mere exercise of a faculty or something beyond that, as in the above instances.

2. If then in what we do there be some end which we wish for on its own account, choosing all the others as means to this, but not every end without exception as a means to something else (for so we should go on *ad infinitum,* and desire would be left void and objectless),—this evidently will be the good or the best of all things. And surely from a practical point of view it much concerns us to know this good; for then, like archers shooting at a definite mark, we shall be more likely to attain what we want. If this be so, we must try to indicate roughly what it is, and first of all to which of the arts or sciences it belongs. It would seem to belong to the supreme art or science, that one which most of all deserves the name of master-art or master-science. Now Politics seems to this description. For it prescribes which of the sciences a state needs, and which each man shall study, and up to what point; and to it we see subordinated even the highest arts, such as economy, rhetoric, and the art of war. Since then it makes use of the other practical sciences, and since it further ordains what men are to do and from what to refrain, its end must include the ends of the others, and must be the proper good of man. For though this good is the same for the individual and the state, yet the good of the state seems a grander and more perfect thing both to attain and to secure; and glad as one would be to do this service for a single individual, to do it for a people and for a number of states is nobler and more divine.

This then is the aim of the present inquiry, which is a sort of political inquiry.

3. We must be content if we can attain to so much precision in our statement as the subject before us admits of; for the same degree of accuracy is no more to be expected in all kinds of reasoning than in all kinds of handicraft. Now the things that are noble and just (with which Politics deals) are so various and so uncertain, that some think these are merely conventional and not natural distinctions. There is a similar uncertainty also about what is good, because good things often do people harm: men have before now been ruined by wealth, and have lost their lives through courage. Our subject, then, and our data being of this nature, we must be content if we can indicate the truth roughly and in

outline, and if, in dealing with matters that are not amenable to immutable laws, and reasoning from premises that are but probable, we can arrive at probable conclusions. The reader, on his part, should take each of my statements in the same spirit; for it is the mark of an educated man to require, in each kind of inquiry, just so much exactness as the subject admits of: it is equally absurd to accept probable reasoning from a mathematician, and to demand scientific proof from an orator.

But each man can form a judgment about what he knows, and is called "a good judge" of that—of any special matter when he has received a special education therein, "a good judge" (without any qualifying epithet) when he has received a universal education. And hence a young man is not qualified to be a student of Politics; for he lacks experience of the affairs of life, which form the data and the subject-matter of Politics. Further, since he is apt to be swayed by his feelings, he will derive no benefit from a study whose aim is not speculative but practical. But in this respect young in character counts the same as young in years; for the young man's disqualification is not a matter of time, but is due to the fact that feeling rules his life and directs all his desires. Men of this character turn the knowledge they get to no account in practice, as we see with those we call incontinent; but those who direct their desires and actions by reason will gain much profit from the knowledge of these matters.

So much then by way of preface as to the student and the spirit in which he must accept what we say, and the object which we propose to ourselves.

Aristotle now returns to his main theme, the ultimate good. Everyone (the "masses" as well as "men of culture") agrees that it is happiness or *eudaimonia* (more accurately "doing or living well"). But most people ("the masses") take this happiness to be something very specific, such as pleasure, wealth, health, or fame, whereas the philosophers ("men of culture," mainly Plato) take the ultimate good to be something outside of human life (Plato's Form of the Good). Aristotle then looks at three examples of the good life, two of which he rejects (pleasure and honor); the third, the life of contemplation (living as a philosopher)—which he accepts—he postpones for future discussion. After reviewing and rejecting a number of candidates for the account of the good which he seeks, Aristotle again returns to his main point. (Remember that these were originally lectures, not written down as a book.) What is happiness? Recall that the state that we are trying to define is not a momentary burst of pleasure or a giddy feeling that, just now, our lives are as we'd like them to be. Rather the concept of *eudaimonia* (Aristotle's term for happiness) refers to a complete life well lived. While Aristotle does not deny the pleasures of the flesh, or the advantages of wealth and honors, the fleeting (not to mention corruptible) nature of such goods disqualifies them from constituting the sort of long-term well-being, or flourishing, which he believes is the ultimate goal of human beings.

Again, to ask about the final goal, or end, is to ask about a thing's function. Thus, happiness is to be found in terms of the function of man—that is, the ultimate end that is not just one good thing among others, but the goal of all good things in life. Here Aristotle's biological teleology is fully evident: Our function cannot be simply "to live," for this we share even with plants. It cannot be just to move around and experience the world, for even cows can do this. The one thing that is uniquely human (and note that our function must be unique in this sense) is our reason. Our function, then, is to be rational. This does not exclude other human activities, such as physical prowess, nor does it exclude pleasure (more on this later); indeed, Aristotle holds that if one is totally lacking in some important external good, such as wealth or honors, happiness will be impossible. Although many have criticized Aristotle for his elitism, his point is, in fact, a realistic one. It will be impossible to flourish if we are hungry all the time, living without friends, or without any meaningful activities. But all of this is not yet happiness, although these are the preconditions of happiness.

To be clear on Aristotle's sketch of happiness and its role in ethics and politics, we must finally make the connections between his most important concepts so far: the good, happiness *(eudaimonia),* the final goal *(telos),* and excellence *(arete).* The question with which ethics begins according to Aristotle is, What is the good for man? In other words, what goals should human beings strive for? What sort of life should they attempt to lead? (It is these sorts of formulations of the question that led Aristotle to claim that ethics and politics are intimately connected.) The answer to these first questions is one that is both obvious and widely agreed upon: happiness.

However, what exactly happiness amounts to is not so uncontroversial. It is at this point that Aristotle's teleology (and the assumptions it entails) comes into play. In particular, he assumes that you will achieve long-term well-being, *eudaimonia,* only if you are, as the U.S. Army put it, being "all that you can be." Although certain external goods such as wealth, honor, or fame might offer momentary satisfaction, true happiness, for Aristotle, can never be made up of such fleeting, often accidental, pleasures. Instead, it has to do with taking on and meeting certain challenges, of honing your skills, of developing your capacities, and most of all, of making use of your uniquely human attribute—reason. And all of this is based on the fact that we *have* such capacities. Thus, from the empirical observation that we have certain powers that other species lack, Aristotle concludes that our best and most noble activities are those that make use of our unique capacities (Why else would we have them?). It is for this reason that Aristotle inquires into our *telos,* asking what makes us unique, or uniquely capable of leading (and excelling at) a particular sort of life.

The final step to this account—which will occupy Aristotle for the remainder of the *Ethics*—is the determination of the sort of excellence of which rational animals are capable. Recall that for Aristotle "good" is not a concept that is meaningful independently of the objects to which it is attributed; rather it always presupposes the function of whatever it is applied to: a good knife has a very different sort of virtue (and thus, a very different meaning of the word "good") than a good person. Excellence is always tied to function. After Aristotle has determined the function of man to be rational activity, what needs to be filled in is what the excellence—or the virtue—of the rational soul consists of.

---

4. Since—to resume—all knowledge and all purpose aims at some good, what is this which we say is the aim of Politics; or, in other words, what is the

highest of all realizable goods? As to its name, I suppose nearly all men are agreed; for the masses and the men of culture alike declare that it is happiness, and hold that to "live well" or to "do well" is the same as to be "happy." But they differ as to what this happiness is, and the masses do not give the same account of it as the philosophers. The former take it to be something palpable and plain, as pleasure or wealth or fame: one man holds it to be this, and another that, and often the same man is of different minds at different times,—after sickness it is health, and in poverty it is wealth; while when they are impressed with the consciousness of their ignorance, they admire most those who say grand things that are above their comprehension. Some philosophers, on the other hand, have thought that, beside these several good things, there is an "absolute" good which is the cause of their goodness. As it would hardly be worthwhile to review all the opinions that have been held, we will confine ourselves to those which are most popular, or which seem to have some foundation in reason.

But we must not omit to notice the distinction that is drawn between the method of proceeding from your starting-points or principles, and the method of working up to them. Plato used with fitness to raise this question, and to ask whether the right way is from or to your starting-points, as in the race-course you may run from the judges to the boundary, or *vice versa*. Well, we must start from what is known. But "what is known" may mean two things: "what is known to us," which is one thing, or "what is known" simply, which is another. I think it is safe to say that *we* must start from what is known to *us*. And on this account nothing but a good moral training can qualify a man to study what is noble and just—in a word, to study questions of Politics. For the undemonstrated fact is here the starting-point, and if this undemonstrated fact be sufficiently evident to a man, he will not require a "reason why." Now the man who has had a good moral training either has already arrived at starting-points or principles of action, or will easily accept them when pointed out. But he who neither has them nor will accept them may hear what Hesiod says—

The best is he who of himself doth know;

Good too is he who listens to the wise;

But he who neither knows himself nor heeds

The words of others, is a useless man.

5. It seems that men not unreasonably take their notions of the good or happiness from the lives actually led, and that the masses who are the least refined suppose it to be pleasure, which is the reason why they aim at nothing higher than the life of enjoyment. For the most conspicuous kinds of life are three: this life of enjoyment, the life of the statesman, and, thirdly, the contemplative life. The mass of men show themselves utterly slavish in their preference for the life of brute beasts, but their views receive consideration because many of those in high places have the tastes of Sardanapalus. Men of refinement with a practical turn prefer honour; for I suppose we may say that honour is the aim of the statesman's life. But this seems too superficial to be the good we are seeking; for it appears to depend upon those who give rather than upon those who receive it;

while we have a presentiment that the good is something that is peculiarly a man's own and can scarce be taken away from him. Moreover, these men seem to pursue honour in order that they may be assured of their own excellence,—at least, they wish to be honoured by men of sense, and by those who know them, and on the ground of their virtue or excellence. It is plain, then, that in their view, at any rate, virtue or excellence is better than honour; and perhaps we should take this to be the end of the statesman's life, rather than honour. But virtue or excellence also appears too incomplete to be what we want; for it seems that a man might have virtue and yet be asleep or be inactive all his life, and, moreover, might meet with the greatest disasters and misfortunes; and no one would maintain that such a man is happy, except for argument's sake. But we will not dwell on these matters now, for they are sufficiently discussed in the popular treatises. The third kind of life is the life of contemplation: we will treat of it further on. As for the money-making life, it is something quite contrary to nature; and wealth evidently is not the good of which we are in search, for it is merely useful as a means to something else. So we might rather take pleasure and virtue or excellence to be ends than wealth; for they are chosen on their own account. But it seems that not even they are the end, though much breath has been wasted in attempts to show that they are. . . .

7. Leaving these matters, then, let us return once more to the question, what this good can be of which we are in search. It seems to be different in different kinds of action and in different arts,—one thing in medicine and another in war, and so on. What then is the good in each of these cases? Surely that for the sake of which all else is done. And that in medicine is health, in war is victory, in building is a house,—a different thing in each different case, but always, in whatever we do and in whatever we choose, the end. For it is always for the sake of the end that all else is done. If then there be one end of all that man does, this end will be the realizable good,—or these ends, if there be more than one.

By this generalization our argument is brought to the same point as before. This point we must try to explain more clearly. We see that there are many ends. But some of these are chosen only as means, as wealth, flutes, and the whole class of instruments. And so it is plain that not all ends are final. But the best of all things must, we conceive, be something final. If then there be only one final end, this will be what we are seeking,—or if there be more than one, then the most final of them. Now that which is pursued as an end in itself is more final than that which is pursued as means to something else, and that which is never chosen as means than that which is chosen both as an end in it-self and as means, and that is strictly final which is always chosen as an end in itself and never as means.

Happiness seems more than anything else to answer to this description: for we always choose it for itself, and never for the sake of something else; while honour and pleasure and reason, and all virtue or excellence, we choose partly indeed for themselves (for, apart from any result, we should choose each of them), but partly also for the sake of happiness, supposing that they will help to make us happy. But no one chooses happiness for the sake of these things, or as a means to anything else at all. We seem to be led to the same conclusion when we start from the notion of self-sufficiency. The final good is thought to be self-sufficing [or all-sufficing]. In applying this term we do not regard a man as an individual leading a solitary life, but we also take account of parents, children, wife, and, in short, friends and fellow-citizens generally, since man is naturally a social being. Some limit must indeed be set to this; for if you go on to parents and descendants and friends of friends, you will never come to a stop. But this we will consider further on: for the present we will take self-sufficing to mean what by itself makes life desirable and in want of nothing. And happiness is believed to answer to this description. And further, happiness is believed to be the most desirable thing in the world, and that not merely as one among other good things: if it were merely one among other good things [so that other things could be added to it], it is plain that the addition of the least of other goods must make it more desirable; for the addition becomes a surplus of good, and of two goods the greater is always more desirable. Thus it seems that happiness is something final and self-sufficing, and is the end of all that man does.

But perhaps the reader thinks that though no one will dispute the statement that happiness is the best thing in the world, yet a still more precise definition of it is needed. This will best be gained, I think, by asking, What is the function of man? For as the goodness and the excellence of a piper or a sculptor, or the practiser of any art, and generally of those who have any function or business to do, lies in that function, so man's good would seem to lie in his function, if he has one. But can we suppose that, while a carpenter and a cobbler has a function and a business of his own, man has no business and no function assigned him by nature? Nay, surely as his several members, eye and hand and foot, plainly have each his own function, so we must suppose that man also has some function over and above all these.

What then is it? Life evidently he has in common even with the plants, but we want that which is peculiar to him. We must exclude, therefore, the life of mere nutrition and growth. Next to this comes the life of sense; but this too he plainly shares with horses and cattle and all kinds of animals. There remains then the life whereby he acts—the life of his rational nature, with its two sides or divisions, one rational as obeying reason, the other rational as having and exercising reason. But as this expression is ambiguous, we must be understood to mean thereby the life that consists in the exercise [not the mere possession] of the faculties; for this seems to be more properly entitled to the name.

The function of man, then, is exercise of his vital faculties [or soul] on one side in obedience to reason, and on the other side with reason. But what is called the function of a man of any profession and the function of a man who is good in that profession are generically the same, *e.g.* of a harper and of a good harper; and this holds in all cases without exception, only that in the case of the latter his superior excellence at his work is added; for we say a harper's function is to harp, and a good harper's to harp well. Man's function then being, as we say, a kind of life—that is to say, exercise of his faculties and action of various kinds with reason—the good man's function is to do this well and beautifully [or nobly]. But the function of anything is done well when it is done in accordance with the proper excellence of that thing. If this be so the result is that the good of man is exercise of his faculties in accordance with excellence or virtue, or, if there be more than one, in accordance with the best and most complete virtue. But there must also be a full term of years for this exercise; for one swallow or one fine day does not make a spring, nor does one day or any small space of time make a blessed or happy man.

This, then, may be taken as a rough outline of the good; for this, I think, is the proper method,—first to sketch the outline, and then to fill in the details. But it would seem that, the outline once fairly drawn, any one can carry on the work and fit in the several items which time reveals to us or helps us to find. And this indeed is the way in which the arts and sciences have grown; for it requires no extraordinary genius to fill up the gaps. We must bear in mind, however, what was said above, and not demand the same degree of accuracy in all branches of study, but in each case so much as the subject-matter admits of and as is proper to that kind of inquiry. The carpenter and the geometer both look for the right angle, but in different ways: the former only wants such an approximation to it as his work requires, but the latter wants to know what constitutes a right angle, or what is its special quality; his aim is to find out the truth. And so in other cases we must follow the same course, lest we spend more time on what is immaterial than on the real business in hand. Nor must we in all cases alike demand the reason why; sometimes it is enough if the undemonstrated fact be fairly pointed out, as in the case of the starting-points or principles of a science. Undemonstrated facts always form the first step or starting-point of a science; and these starting-points or principles are arrived at some in one way, some in another—some by induction, others by perception, others again by some kind of training. But in each case we must try to apprehend them in the proper way, and do our best to define them clearly; for they have great influence upon the subsequent course of an inquiry. A good start is more than half the race, I think, and our starting-point of principle, once found, clears up a number of our difficulties.

8. We must not be satisfied, then, with examining this starting-point or principle of ours as a conclusion from our data, but must also view it in its relation to current opinions on the subject; for all experience harmonizes with a true principle, but a false one is soon found to be incompatible with the facts. Now, good things have been divided into three classes, external goods on the one hand, and on the other goods of the soul and goods of the body; and the goods of the soul are commonly said to be goods in the fullest sense, and more good than any other. But "actions and exercises of the vital faculties may be said to be of the soul." So our account is confirmed by this opinion, which is both of long standing and approved by all who busy themselves with philosophy. But, indeed, we secure the support of this opinion by the mere statement that certain actions and exercises are the end; for this implies that it is to be ranked among the goods of the soul, and not among external goods. Our account, again, is in harmony with the common saying that the happy man lives well and does well; for we may say that happiness, according to us, is living well and doing well. And, indeed, all the characteristics that men expect to find in happiness seem to belong to happiness as we define it. Some hold it to be virtue or excellence, some prudence, others a kind of wisdom; others, again, held it to be all or some of these, with the addition of pleasure, either as an ingredient or as a necessary

accompaniment; and some even include external prosperity in their account of it. Now, some of these views have the support of many voices and of old authority; others have few voices, but those of weight; but it is probable that neither the one side nor the other is entirely wrong, but that in some one point at least, if not in most, they are both right.

First, then, the view that happiness is excellence or a kind of excellence harmonizes with our account; for "exercise of faculties in accordance with excellence" belongs to excellence. But I think we may say that it makes no small difference whether the good be conceived as the mere possession of something, or as its use—as a mere habit or trained faculty, or as the exercise of that faculty. For the habit or faculty may be present, and yet issue in no good result, as when a man is asleep, or in any other way hindered from his function; but with its exercise this is not possible, for it must show itself in acts and in good acts. And as at the Olympic games it is not the fairest and strongest who receive the crown, but those who contend (for among these are the victors), so in life, too, the winners are those who not only have all the excellences, but manifest these in deed.

And, further, the life of these men is in itself pleasant. For pleasure is an affection of the soul, and each man takes pleasure in that which he is said to love,—he who loves horses in horses, he who loves sight-seeing in sight-seeing, and in the same way he who loves justice in acts of justice, and generally the lover of excellence or virtue in virtuous acts or the manifestation of excellence. And while with most men there is a perpetual conflict between the several things in which they find pleasure, since these are not naturally pleasant, those who love what is noble take pleasure in that which is naturally pleasant. For the manifestations of excellence are naturally pleasant, so that they are both pleasant to them and pleasant in themselves. Their life, then, does not need pleasure to be added to it as an appendage, but contains pleasure in itself.

Indeed, in addition to what we have said, a man is not good at all unless he takes pleasure in noble deeds. No one would call a man just who did not take pleasure in doing justice, nor generous who took no pleasure in acts of generosity, and so on. If this be so, the manifestations of excellence will be pleasant in themselves. But they are also both good and noble, and that in the highest degree—at least, if the good man's judgment about them is right, for this is his judgment. Happiness, then, is at once the best and noblest and pleasantest thing in the world, and these are not separated, as the Delian inscription would have them to be:

> What is most just is noblest, health is best,
>
> Pleasantest is to get your heart's desire.

For all these characteristics are united in the best exercises of our faculties; and these, or some one of them that is better than all the others, we identify with happiness.

But nevertheless happiness plainly requires external goods too, as we said; for it is impossible, or at least not easy, to act nobly without some furniture of fortune. There are many things that can only be done through instruments, so to speak, such as friends and wealth and political influence: and there are some things whose absence takes the bloom off our happiness, as good birth, the blessing of children, personal beauty; for a man is not very likely to be happy if he is very ugly in person, or of low birth, or alone in the world, or childless, and perhaps still less if he has worthless children or friends, or has lost good ones that he had. As we said, then, happiness seems to stand in need of this kind of prosperity; and so some identify it with good fortune, just as others identify it with excellence.

9. This has led people to ask whether happiness is attained by learning, or the formation of habits, or any other kind of training, or comes by some divine dispensation or even by chance. Well, if the Gods do give gifts to men, happiness is likely to be among the number, more likely, indeed, than anything else, in proportion as it is better than all other human things. This belongs more properly to another branch of inquiry; but we may say that even if it is not heaven-sent, but comes as a consequence of virtue or some kind of learning or training, still it seems to be one of the most divine things in the world; for the prize and aim of virtue would appear to be better than anything else and something divine and blessed. Again, if it is thus acquired it will be widely accessible; for it will then be in the power of all except those who have lost the capacity for excellence to acquire it by study and diligence. And if it be better that men should attain happiness in this way rather than by chance, it is reasonable to suppose that it is so, since in the sphere of nature all things are arranged in the best possible way, and likewise in the sphere of art, and of each mode of causation, and most of all in the sphere of the noblest mode of causation. And indeed it would be too absurd to leave what is noblest and fairest to the dispensation of chance.

But our definition itself clears up the difficulty; for happiness was defined as a certain kind of exercise of the vital faculties in accordance with excellence or virtue. And of the remaining goods [other than happiness itself], some must be present as necessary conditions, while others are aids and useful instruments to happiness. And this agrees with what we said at starting. We then laid down that the end of the art political is the best of all ends; but the chief business of that art is to make the citizens of a certain character—that is, good and apt to do what is noble. It is not without reason, then, that we do not call an ox, or a horse, or any brute happy; for none of them is able to share in this kind of activity. For the same reason also a child is not happy; he is as yet, because of his age, unable to do such things. If we ever call a child happy, it is because we hope he will do them. For, as we said, happiness requires not only perfect excellence or virtue, but also a full term of years for its exercise. For our circumstances are liable to many changes and to all sorts of chances, and it is possible that he who is now most prosperous will in his old age meet with great disasters, as is told of Priam in the tales of Troy; and a man who is thus used by fortune and comes to a miserable end cannot be called happy.

We tend to think of happiness as a feeling or sense of contentment. For Aristotle, it is "doing well," and not just for a while (your freshman year of college) but for a whole lifetime. Indeed, the insistence that we can be happy only after having lived a full life leads Aristotle to a curious question that would not even make sense to our more fleeting sense of happiness:

10. Are we, then, to call no man happy as long as he lives, but to wait for the end, as Solon said? And, supposing we have to allow this, do we mean that he actually is happy after he is dead? Surely that is absurd, especially for us who say that happiness is a kind of activity or life. But if we do not call the dead man happy, and if Solon meant not this, but that only then could we safely apply the term to a man, as being now beyond the reach of evil and calamity, then here too we find some ground for objection. For it is thought that both good and evil may in some sort befall a dead man (just as they may befall a living man, although he is unconscious of them), *e.g.* honours rendered to him, or the reverse of these, and again the prosperity or the misfortune of his children and all his descendants. But this, too, has its difficulties; for after a man has lived happily to a good old age, and ended as he lived, it is possible that many changes may befall him in the persons of his descendants, and that some of them may turn out good and meet with the good fortune they deserve, and others the reverse. It is evident too that the degree in which the descendants are related to their ancestors may vary to any extent. And it would be a strange thing if the dead man were to change with these changes and become happy and miserable by turns. But it would also be strange to suppose that the dead are not affected at all, even for a limited time, by the fortunes of their posterity.

But let us return to our former question; for its solution will, perhaps, clear up this other difficulty. The saying of Solon may mean that we ought to look for the end and then call a man happy, not because he now is, but because he once was happy. But surely it is strange that when he is happy we should refuse to say what is true of him, because we do not like to apply the term to living men in view of the changes to which they are liable, and because we hold happiness to be something that endures and is little liable to change, while the fortunes of one and the same man often undergo many revolutions: for, it is argued, it is plain that, if we follow the changes of fortune, we shall call the same man happy and miserable many times over, making the happy man "a sort of chameleon and one who rests on no sound foundation." We reply that it cannot be right thus to follow fortune. For it is not in this that our weal or woe lies; but, as we said, though good fortune is needed to complete man's life, yet it is the excellent employment of his powers that constitutes his happiness, as the reverse of this constitutes his misery.

But the discussion of this difficulty leads to a further confirmation of our account. For nothing human is so constant as the excellent exercise of our faculties. The sciences themselves seem to be less abiding. And the highest of these exercises are the most abiding, because the happy are occupied with them most of all and most continuously (for this seems to be the reason why we do not forget how to do them). The happy man, then, as we define him, will have this required property of permanence, and all through life will preserve his character; for he will be occupied continually, or with the least possible interruption, in excellent deeds and excellent speculations; and, whatever his fortune be, he will take it in the noblest fashion, and bear himself always and in all things suitably, since he is truly good and "foursquare without a flaw."

But the dispensations of fortune are many, some great, some small. The small ones, whether good or evil, plainly are of no weight in the scale; but the great ones, when numerous, will make life happier if they be good; for they help to give a grace to life themselves, and their use is noble and good; but, if they be evil, will enfeeble and spoil happiness; for they bring pain, and often impede the exercise of our faculties. But nevertheless true worth shines out even here, in the calm endurance of many great misfortunes, not through insensibility, but through nobility and greatness of soul. And if it is what a man does that determines the character of his life, as we said, then no happy man will become miserable; for he will never do what is hateful and base. For we hold that the man who is truly good and wise will bear with dignity whatever fortune sends, and will always make the best of his circumstances, as a good general will turn the forces at his command to the best account, and a good shoemaker will make the best shoe that can be made out of a given piece of leather, and so on with all other crafts. If this be so, the happy man will never become miserable, though he will not be truly happy if he meets with the fate of Priam.

But yet he is not unstable and lightly changed: he will not be moved from his happiness easily, nor by any ordinary misfortunes, but only by many heavy ones; and after such, he will not recover his happiness again in a short time, but if at all, only in a considerable period, which has a certain completeness, and in which he attains to great and noble things.

We shall meet all objections, then, if we say that a happy man is "one who exercises his faculties in accordance with perfect excellence, being duly furnished with external goods, not for any chance time, but for a full term of years": to which perhaps we should add, "and who shall continue to live so, and shall die as he lived," since the future is veiled to us, but happiness we take to be the end and in all ways perfectly final or complete. If this be so, we may say that those living men are blessed or perfectly happy who both have and shall continue to have these characteristics, but happy as men only.

11. Passing now from this question to that of the fortunes of descendants and of friends generally, the doctrine that they do not affect the departed at all seems too cold and too much opposed to popular opinion. But as the things that happen to them are many and differ in all sorts of ways, and some come home to them more and some less, so that to discuss them all separately would be a long, indeed an endless task, it will perhaps be enough to speak of them in general terms and in outline merely. Now, as of the misfortunes that happen to a man's self, some have a certain weight and influence on his life, while others are of less moment, so is it also with what happens to any of his friends. And, again, it always makes much more difference whether those who are affected by an occurrence are alive or dead than it does whether a terrible crime in a tragedy be enacted on the stage or merely supposed to have already taken place. We must therefore take these differences into account, and still more, perhaps, the fact that it is a doubtful question whether the dead are at all accessible to good and ill. For it appears that even if anything that happens, whether good or evil, does come home to them, yet it is something unsubstantial and slight to them if not in itself; or if not that, yet at any rate its influence is not of that magnitude or nature that it can make happy those who are not, or take away their happiness from those that are. It seems then—to conclude—that the prosperity, and likewise the adversity, of friends does affect the dead, but not in such a way or to such an extent as to make the happy unhappy, or to do anything of the kind. . . .

What is happiness? Happiness is an activity of the soul, in accordance with virtue or excellence. We now have to see what virtue is (the main topic of the next several books), with the preliminary understanding that virtue is primarily of the soul. (Aristotle's notion of the soul is appropriate to a biologist and is not that of a theologian, nor even of Plato.) Furthermore, there are two kinds of virtues, *intellectual* virtues (which have to do with rational principles and the ability to think) and *moral* virtues, which have to do with character and a person's ability to act correctly in accordance with reason (for example, being courageous). Note that "moral" here has nothing particularly to do with what we call "morality"—an impersonal set of principles that we are all bound to obey.

Like Plato, Aristotle proceeds to divide the soul according to function. The first main division is between the irrational and the rational parts of the soul, each of which are then further divided into two parts. The irrational "half" of the soul is made up of our vegetative faculty, which we share with plants and other animals and, as such, is of no interest to the ethicist. The other part of our irrational part is a bit more complicated: It "is irrational, and yet in some way partakes of reason." What Aristotle has in mind here is that part of us that produces desires independently of thought. He speaks of it as "the faculty of appetite or of desire in general." It is irrational insofar as we do not control the desires and appetites we come to have—they just seem to come upon us. However, this part of us is somewhat rational (it partakes in, or listens to reason) insofar as we then deliberate on and decide what to do about such desires. Finally, the rational "half" of our soul is divided into two faculties as well: those that are responsible for the intellectual and the moral excellences.

13. Since happiness is an exercise of the vital faculties in accordance with perfect virtue or excellence, we will now inquire about virtue or excellence; for this will probably help us in our inquiry about happiness. And indeed the true statesman seems to be especially concerned with virtue, for he wishes to make the citizens good and obedient to the laws. Of this we have an example in the Cretan and the Lacedaemonian lawgivers, and any others who have resembled them. But if the inquiry belongs to Politics or the science of the state, it is plain that it will be in accordance with our original purpose to pursue it.

The virtue or excellence that we are to consider is, of course, the excellence of man; for it is the good of man and the happiness of man that we started to seek. And by the excellence of man I mean excellence not of body, but of soul; for happiness we take to be an activity of the soul. If this be so, then it is evident that the statesman must have some knowledge of the soul, just as the man who is to heal the eye or the whole body must have some knowledge of them, and that the more in proportion as the science of the state is higher and better than medicine. But all educated physicians take much pains to know about the body. As statesmen and students of Politics, then, we must inquire into the nature of the soul, but in so doing we must keep our special purpose in view and go only so far as that requires; for to go into minuter detail would be too laborious for the present undertaking.

Now, there are certain doctrines about the soul which are stated elsewhere with sufficient precision, and these we will adopt. Two parts of the soul are distinguished, an irrational and a rational part. Whether these are separated as are the parts of the body or any divisible thing, or whether they are only distinguishable in thought but in fact inseparable, like concave and convex in the circumference of a circle, makes no difference for our present purpose.

Of the irrational part, again, one division seems to be common to all things that live, and to be possessed by plants—I mean that which causes nutrition and growth; for we must assume that all things that take nourishment have a faculty of this kind, even when they are embryos, and have the same faculty when they are full grown; at least, this is more reasonable than to suppose that they then have a different one. The excellence of this faculty, then, is plainly one that man shares with other beings, and not specifically human. And this is confirmed by the fact that in sleep this part of the soul, or this faculty, is thought to be most active, while the good and the bad man are undistinguishable when they are asleep (whence the saying that for half their lives there is no difference between the happy and the miserable; which indeed is what we should expect; for sleep is the cessation of the soul from those functions in respect of which it is called good or bad), except that they are to some slight extent roused by what goes on in their bodies, with the result that the dreams of the good man are better than those of ordinary people. However, we need not pursue this further, and may dismiss the nutritive principle, since it has no place in the excellence of man.

But there seems to be another vital principle that is irrational, and yet in some way partakes of reason. In the case of the continent and of the incontinent man alike we praise the reason or the rational part, for it exhorts them rightly and urges them to do what is best; but there is plainly present in them another principle besides the rational one, which fights and struggles against the reason. For just as a paralyzed limb, when you will to move it to the right, moves on the contrary to the left, so is it with the soul; the incontinent man's impulses run counter to his reason. Only whereas we see the refractory member in the case of the body, we do not see it in the case of the soul. But we must nevertheless, I think, hold that in the soul too there is something beside the reason, which opposes and runs counter to it (though in what sense it is distinct from the reason does not matter here). It seems, however, to partake of reason also, as we said: at least, in the continent man it submits to the reason; while in the temperate and courageous man we may say it is still more obedient; for in him it is altogether in harmony with the reason.

The irrational part, then, it appears, is twofold. There is the vegetative faculty, which has no share of reason; and the faculty of appetite or of desire in general, which in a manner partakes of reason or is rational as listening to reason and submitting to its sway,—rational in the sense in which we speak of rational obedience to father or friends, not in the sense in which we speak of rational apprehension of mathematical truths. But all advice and all rebuke and exhortation testify that the irrational part is in some way amenable to reason. If then we like to say that this part, too, has a share of reason, the rational part also will have two divisions: one rational in the strict sense as possessing reason in itself, the other rational as listening to reason as a man listens to his father. Now, on this division of the faculties is based the division of excellence; for we speak of intellectual excellences and of moral excellences; wisdom and understanding and prudence we call intellectual, liberality and temperance we call moral virtues or excellences. When we are speaking of a man's moral character we do not say that he is wise or intelligent, but that he is gentle or temperate. But we praise the wise man, too, for his habit of mind or trained faculty; and a habit or trained faculty that is praiseworthy is what we call an excellence or virtue.

DISCUSSION

In Book I, Aristotle has set out his central question and his general strategy for answering it. The question is, What is the good life for man?—by which he means, What is our ultimate goal in life? What do we really want? What will really make us happy? The strategy, already partially determined by the teleological form of this main question, is to examine various aspects of human life and put them in a kind of (teleo-) logical order. Thus, such different sides of our personalities as emotions, habits, intelligence, and skills are considered, and in each case their place in the overall scheme of the good life is determined.

The logical framework Aristotle has set up, then, is an overall teleological scheme. Everything we do has a goal, and all of the things that we do have an ultimate goal. This is called "happiness." The question then becomes, What is Happiness? Aristotle's answer is in terms of human "function," our unique characteristic, which is reason. Happiness is therefore living according to reason. But what does this mean? It does not mean just thinking (although, in the contemplative life, Aristotle gives great importance to thinking): Happiness is a life of *activity* in accordance with reason. But activity in accordance with reason is called *virtue* or *excellence,* which is a matter of cultivated habit as well as understandable in terms of rational principles. Thus, we have our middle term between abstract happiness and particular activities; happiness is the virtuous life, and with this general outline, Aristotle turns to the concept of virtue and the particular kinds of virtue.

As matter-of-fact as Aristotle makes all of this seem, his framework can be questioned in a number of ways. First, one can ask why we should accept the teleological scheme that he gives us. A person who believes that the purpose of life is to serve God and do His bidding, for example, will not accept Aristotle's strictly humanistic framework in which all human activity is aimed at satisfying *our* goals and functions. (It is worth noting, however, that St. Thomas Aquinas later turned Aristotle's arguments into a very Christian conception of morality.) Second, even if we do accept the teleological humanistic framework, does it follow that there is a single goal ("happiness") that is the "end" of all of our activities? Can you think of other goals? Third, must we accept the argument that happiness is necessarily tied to reason (again, even if we accept the teleological scheme)? What problems are there with Aristotle's conception of "reason" so far? Finally, why consider virtue so important? Important for whom? If a person can enjoy a life of slovenly but harmless vice, or can be content with a life of mediocrity and comfort, devoid of "excellence," why should we deny that person his or her conception of the good life? What kinds of arguments can you raise at this point for and against Aristotle's framework for "the good for man"?

The second book of the *Ethics*—and several chapters to follow—is concerned with "the moral virtues," those "excellences" that have to do with correct behavior. (The word "virtue" and the word "excellence" are used interchangeably as translations of *arete*.) It is in the list of moral virtues, perhaps more than anywhere else, that the vast differences between Aristotle's Athens and our modern society are most evident. Aristotle's society was only a few generations removed from comparatively primitive tribal times, and during his lifetime Greece was constantly involved in wars (both among the city-states and with other nations). Thus, military virtues such as courage are of primary importance. Moreover, many Christian virtues are absent from the list: Faith is not to be found, nor hope, humility, or charity. Indeed, some of these would be *vices* for an Aristotelian Greek. Athens was an elitist society with a privileged class of male citizens, and it was for them alone that Aristotle was writing. The moral virtues, therefore, are specific to an aristocratic, wealthy, and politically powerful brotherhood. It is worth pointing out, however, that the formal structure of virtues that he advocates (the doctrine of the mean) is independent of any particular society. In studying Aristotle's account of the virtues, it would be a good idea to write up your own list of virtues, marking the similarities and differences.

Aristotle begins the second book by repeating his distinction between the moral and intellectual virtues and characterizing the former by reference to "habit or custom." Indeed, this is a most important concept for Aristotle, which we will find to be quite absent from some later ethicists (Kant, for example). Being a good person is first of all doing the right things without even thinking about it. Aristotle would consider the plight of a person who has to "wrestle with his conscience" all the time to be absurd and not at all good (much less happy), even if, in the end, he did the right thing. Being virtuous is, first of all, having good habits, which means having had the luck to be brought up in the right way.

1. Excellence, then, being of these two kinds, intellectual and moral, intellectual excellence owes its birth and growth mainly to instruction, and so requires time and experience, while moral excellence is the result of habit or custom and has accordingly in our language received a name formed by a slight change from the word for custom. From this it is plain that none of the moral excellences or virtues is implanted in us by nature; for that which is by nature cannot be altered by training. For instance, a stone naturally tends to fall downwards, and you could not train it to rise upwards, though you tried to do so by throwing it up ten thousand times, nor could you train fire to move downwards, nor accustom anything which naturally behaves in one way to behave in any other way. The virtues, then, come neither by nature nor against nature, but nature gives the capacity for acquiring them, and this is developed by training.

Again, where we do things by nature we get the power first, and put this power forth in act afterwards: as we plainly see in the case of the senses; for it is not by constantly seeing and hearing that we acquire those faculties, but, on the contrary, we had the power first and then used it, instead of acquiring the power by the use. But the virtues we acquire by doing the acts, as is the case with the arts too. We learn an art by doing that which we wish to do when we have learned it; we become builders by building, and harpers by harping. And so by doing just acts we become just, and by doing acts of temperance and courage we become temperate and courageous. This is attested, too, by what occurs in states; for the legislators make their citizens good by training; *e.g.* this is the wish of all legislators, and those who do not succeed in this miss their aim, and it is this that distinguishes a good from a bad constitution.

Again, both the moral virtues and the corresponding vices result from and are formed by the same acts; and this is the case with the arts also. It is by harping that good harpers and bad harpers alike are produced: and so with builders and the rest; by building well they will become good builders, and bad builders by building badly. Indeed, if it were not so, they would not want anybody to teach them, but would all be born either good or bad at their trades. And it is just the same with the virtues also. It is by our conduct in our intercourse with other men that we become just or unjust, and by acting in circumstances of danger, and training ourselves to feel fear or confidence, that we become courageous or cowardly. So, too, with our animal appetites and the passion of anger; for by behaving in this way or in that on the occasions with which these passions are concerned, some become temperate and gentle, and others profligate and ill-tempered. In a word, acts of any kind produce habits or characters of the same kind. Hence we ought to make sure that our acts be of a certain kind; for the resulting character varies as they vary. It makes no small difference, therefore, whether a man be trained from his youth up in this way or in that, but a great difference, or rather all the difference.

Aristotle now seeks a general test for virtue. He has already characterized a virtue as involving activity in accordance with reason and said that virtue must be manifested in us as habit, as part of our character. But now, he asks, how can we tell what activities and habits are the rational ones? And how can we test to see whether someone has a virtue or not? The fact that a person does a virtuous act does not necessarily mean that he or she is virtuous. A soldier might not run in battle because he is more afraid of his commanding officer than he is of the enemy. This is not courage, even though he does what the courageous man does—stays in battle. A student who does not cheat on an exam because he or she is afraid of getting caught is not virtuous, even though he or she has done what virtuous students do, namely, not cheated on an exam.

Aristotle's theory of virtue is this: A virtue is neither too much nor too little; it is a "mean between the extremes." Too much perseverance in the face of an enemy isn't courage, but foolhardiness. Too little perseverence is cowardice. Having too much to drink is vulgar and ruinous but, Aristotle insists, refusing to drink altogether is not virtuous either. Virtue is having the right amount (of perseverence, of drink, of money, of humor, of strength, of pleasure). It is worth noting how Aristotle does not consider abstention itself to be a virtue; a man who does not enjoy himself he calls a "boor." Virtue is a kind of moderation, and this is cultivated, as we have seen, by habitually practicing moderation.

2. But our present inquiry has not, like the rest, a merely speculative aim; we are not inquiring merely in order to know what excellence or virtue is, but in order to become good; for otherwise it would profit us nothing. We must ask therefore about these acts, and see of what kind they are to be; for, as we said, it is they that determine our habits or character. First of all, then, that they must be in accordance with right reason is a common characteristic of them, which we shall here take for granted, reserving for future discussion the question what this right reason is, and how it is related to the other excellences.

But let it be understood, before we go on, that all reasoning on matters of practice must be in outline merely, and not scientifically exact: for, as we said at starting, the kind of reasoning to be demanded varies with the subject in hand; and in practical matters and questions of expediency there are no invariable laws, any more than in questions of health. And if our general conclusions are thus inexact, still more inexact is all reasoning about particular cases; for these fall under no system of scientifically established rules or traditional maxims, but the agent must always consider for himself what the special occasion requires, just as in medicine or navigation. But though this is the case we must try to render what help we can.

First of all, then, we must observe that, in matters of this sort, to fall short and to exceed are alike fatal. This is plain (to illustrate what we cannot see by what we can see) in the case of strength and health. Too much and too little exercise alike destroy strength; and to take too much meat and drink, or to take too little, is equally ruinous to health, but the fitting amount produces and increases and preserves them. Just so, then, is it with temperance also, and courage, and the other virtues. The man who shuns and fears everything and never makes a stand, becomes a coward; while the man who fears nothing at all, but will face anything, becomes foolhardy. So, too, the man who takes his fill of any kind of pleasure, and abstains from none, is a profligate, but the man who shuns all (like him whom we call a "boor") is devoid of sensibility. Thus temperance and courage are destroyed both by excess and defect, but preserved by moderation. But habits or types of character are not only produced and preserved and destroyed by the same occasions and the same means, but they will also manifest themselves in the same circumstances. This is the case with palpable things like strength. Strength is produced by taking plenty of nourishment and doing plenty of hard work, and the strong man, in turn, has the greatest capacity for these. And the case is the same with the virtues: by abstaining from pleasure we become temperate, and when we have become temperate we are best able to abstain. And so with courage: by habituating ourselves to despise danger, and to face it, we become courageous; and when we have become courageous, we are best able to face danger.

The test of virtue is this: A man who is virtuous *enjoys* being virtuous. A person is not more virtuous because he or she is in great pain, having been deprived of some desired goal (the regret of having said "no" or desperately wanting one [too many] more martini). The virtuous person prefers being virtuous and does not regret it. The courageous man enjoys being courageous (which is not to say, of course, that he has to enjoy the danger of battle). And again, this is a matter of upbringing; a person must be educated to enjoy virtue and not enjoy vice. (What would Aristotle say about a society such as ours, where entertainment for youths consists in the glorification of gratuitous violence?)

---

3. The pleasure or pain that accompanies the acts must be taken as a test of the formed habit or character. He who abstains from the pleasures of the body and rejoices in the abstinence is temperate, while he who is vexed at having to abstain is profligate; and again, he who faces danger with pleasure, or, at any rate, without pain, is courageous, but he to whom this is painful is a coward. For moral virtue or excellence is closely concerned with pleasure and pain. It is pleasure that moves us to do what is base, and pain that moves us to refrain from what is noble. And therefore, as Plato says, man needs to be so trained from his youth up as to find pleasure and pain in the right objects. This is what sound education means.

Another reason why virtue has to do with pleasure and pain is that it has to do with actions and passions or affections; but every affection and every act is accompanied by pleasure or pain. The fact is further attested by the employment of pleasure and pain in correction; they have a kind of curative property, and a cure is effected by administering the opposite of the disease.

Again, as we said before, every type of character [or habit or formed faculty] is essentially relative to, and concerned with, those things that form it for good or for ill; but it is through pleasure and pain that bad characters are formed—that is to say, through pursuing and avoiding the wrong pleasures and pains, or pursuing and avoiding them at the wrong time, or in the wrong manner, or in any other of the various ways of going wrong that may be distinguished. And hence some people go so far as to define the virtues as a kind of impassive or neutral state of mind. But they err in stating this absolutely, instead of qualifying it by the addition of the right and wrong manner, time, etc. We may lay down, herefore, that this kind of excellence [*i.e.* moral excellence] makes us to do what is best in matters of pleasure and pain, while vice or badness has the contrary effect. But the following considerations will throw additional light on the point.

There are three kinds of things that move us to choose, and three that move us to avoid them: on the one hand, the beautiful or noble, the advantageous, the pleasant; on the other hand, the ugly or base, the hurtful, the painful. Now, the good man is apt to go right, and the bad man to go wrong, about them all, but especially about pleasure: for pleasure is not only common to man with animals, but also accompanies all pursuit or choice; since the noble, and the advantageous also, are pleasant in idea. Again, the feeling of pleasure has been fostered in us all from our infancy by our training, and has thus become so engrained in our life that it can scarce be washed out. And, indeed, we all more or less make pleasure our test in judging of actions. For this reason too, then, our whole inquiry must be concerned with these matters; since to be pleased and pained in the right or the wrong way has great influence on our actions. Again, to fight with pleasure is harder than to fight with wrath (which Heraclitus says is hard), and virtue, like art, is always more concerned with what is harder; for the harder the task the better is success. For this reason also, then, both [moral] virtue or excellence and the science of the state must always be concerned with pleasures and pains; for he that behaves rightly with regard to them will be good, and he that behaves badly will be bad. We will take it as established, then, that [moral] excellence or virtue has to do with pleasures and pains; and that the acts which produce it develop it, and also, when differently done, destroy it; and that it manifests itself in the same acts which produced it.

Aristotle now pursues this idea, that virtue requires habituation of right activity. For an act to be virtuous,

- You must know what you are doing.
- You must deliberately choose to do it.
- You must do it for its own sake.
- It must be a manifestation of a state of character and not just an isolated incident.

4. But here we may be asked what we mean by saying that men can become just and temperate only by doing what is just and temperate: surely, it may be said, if their acts are just and temperate, they themselves are already just and temperate, as they are grammarians and musicians if they do what is grammatical and musical. We may answer, I think, firstly, that this is not quite the case even with the arts. A man may do something grammatical [or write something correctly] by chance, or at the prompting of another person: he will not be grammatical till he not only does something grammatical, but also does it grammatically [or like a grammatical person], *i.e.* in virtue of his own knowledge of grammar. But, secondly, the virtues are not in this point analogous to the arts. The products of art have their excellence in themselves, and so it is enough if when produced they are of a certain quality; but in the case of the virtues, a man is not said to act justly or temperately [or like a just or temperate man] if what he does merely be of a certain sort—he must be in a certain state of mind when he does it; *i.e.* first of all, he must know what he is doing; secondly, he must choose it, and choose it for itself; and, thirdly, his act must be the expression of a formed and stable character. Now, of these conditions, only one, the knowledge, is necessary for the possession of any art; but for the possession of the virtues knowledge is of little or no avail, while the other conditions that result from repeatedly doing what is just and temperate are not a little important, but all-important.

The thing that is done, therefore, is called just or temperate when it is such as the just or temperate man would do; but the man who does it is not just or temperate, unless he also does it in the spirit of the just or the temperate man. It is right, then, to say that by doing what is just a man becomes just, and temperate by doing what is temperate, while without doing thus he has no chance of ever becoming good. But most men, instead of doing thus, fly to theories, and fancy that they are philosophizing and that this will make them good, like a sick man who listens attentively to what the doctor says and then disobeys all his orders. This sort of philosophizing will no more produce a healthy habit of mind than this sort of treatment will produce a healthy habit of body.

What is a virtue? So far we have seen that it is (*a*) activity, (*b*) in accordance with reason, (*c*) the mean between the extremes, (*d*) a matter of habit, (*e*) and gives pleasure to the virtuous person. Aristotle now approaches this question again, asking whether a virtue is

1. A passion or an emotion.
2. A power or natural faculty.
3. A habit or trained faculty.

We already know the answer (number 3), but Aristotle gives us his reasons for rejecting the first two possibilities. (Why is it important to him that a virtue is not simply an emotion? What would follow if virtues were emotions?)

5. We have next to inquire what excellence or virtue is. A quality of the soul is either (1) a passion or emotion, or (2) a power or faculty, or (3) a habit or trained faculty; and so virtue must be one of these three. By (1) a passion or emotion we mean appetite, anger, fear, confidence, envy, joy, love, hate, longing, emulation, pity, or generally that which is accompanied by pleasure or pain; (2) a power of faculty is that in respect of which we are said to be capable of being affected in any of these ways, as, for instance, that in respect of which we are able to be angered or pained or to pity; and (3) a habit or trained faculty is that in respect of which we are well or ill regulated or disposed in the matter of our affections; as, for instance, in the matter of being angered, we are ill regulated if we are too violent or too slack, but if we are moderate in our anger we are well regulated. And so with the rest.

Now, the virtues are not emotions, nor are the vices—(1) because we are not called good or bad in respect of our emotions, but are called so in respect of our virtues or vices; (2) because we are neither praised nor blamed in respect of our emotions (a man is not praised for being afraid or angry, nor blamed for being angry simply, but for being angry in a particular way), but we are praised or blamed in respect of our virtues or vices; (3) because we may be angered or frightened without deliberate choice, but the virtues are a kind of deliberate choice, or at least are impossible without it; and (4) because in respect of our emotions we are said to be moved, but in respect of our virtues and vices we are not said to be moved, but to be regulated or disposed in this way or in that.

For these same reasons also they are not powers or faculties; for we are not called either good or bad for being merely capable of emotion, nor are we either praised or blamed for this. And further, while nature gives us our powers or faculties, she does not make us either good or bad. (This point, however, we have already treated.) If, then, the virtues be neither emotions nor faculties, it only remains for them to be habits or trained faculties.

Harking back to Book I, Aristotle defines excellence or virtue in general as that which makes a thing both good in itself and able to perform its proper function. Thus, the sort of moral virtue we seek is described by Aristotle as "the habit or trained faculty that makes a man good and makes him perform his function well." He now pursues his analysis of moral virtue as habitual rational activity and the choice of a mean between extremes. Although most moral systems stigmatize acting excessively (being too loud, too drunk, and so on), few have made the corollary claim that Aristotle points to, namely, that a deficiency can be just as bad. The person who is constantly belittling him- or herself is as just as bad, or imbalanced, as the one who is puffed up with unwarranted pride. Likewise, both a deficiency and an excess of self-esteem (to use a contemporary "virtue") can be problematic. The point is that there is a right combination of the extremes, so to speak, just as in a fine painting there is just the right amount of color, line, and so on—to *either* add to or subtract from it would be to make it worse. However, we must always take into account our own natures when looking for the proper mean.

But not all activities or motives can be moderated. You can drink just so much, not more or less, and you can stay in battle just so long. But you cannot commit just the right amount of adultery or theft, for any amount of such activities is wrong. Similarly, although a person can have a right amount of anger and be angry at the right things (which is a virtue), he or she cannot have a virtuous amount of envy, for envy is one of those emotions that is degrading in any amount.

6. We have thus found the genus to which virtue belongs; but we want to know, not only that it is a trained faculty, but also what species of trained faculty it is. We may safely assert that the virtue or excellence of a thing causes that thing both to be itself in good condition and to perform its function well. The excellence of the eye, for instance, makes both the eye and its work good; for it is by the excellence of the eye that we see well. So the proper excellence of the horse makes a horse what he should be, and makes him good at running, and carrying his rider, and standing a charge. If, then, this holds good in all cases, the proper excellence or virtue of man will be the habit or trained faculty that makes a man good and makes him perform his function well.

How this is to be done we have already said, but we may exhibit the same conclusion in another way, by inquiring what the nature of this virtue is. Now, if we have any quantity, whether continuous or discrete, it is possible to take either a larger [or too large], or a smaller [or too small], or an equal [or fair] amount, and that either absolutely or relatively to our own needs. By an equal or fair amount I understand a mean amount, or one that lies between excess and deficiency. By the absolute mean, or mean relatively to the thing itself, I understand that which is equidistant from both extremes, and this is one and the same for all. By the mean relatively to us I understand that which is neither too much nor too little for us; and this is not one and the same for all. For instance, if ten be too large and two too small, six is the mean relatively to the thing itself; for it exceeds one extreme by the same amount by which it is exceeded by the other extreme: and this is the mean in arithmetical proportion. But the mean relatively to us cannot be found in this way. If ten pounds of food is too much for a given man to eat, and two pounds too little, it does not follow that the trainer will order him six pounds: for that also may perhaps be too much for the man in question, or too little; too little for Milo, too much for the beginner. The same holds true in running and wrestling. And so we may say generally that a master in any art avoids what is too much and what is too little, and seeks for the mean and chooses it—not the absolute but the relative mean.

If, then, every art or science perfects its work in this way, looking to the mean and bringing its work up to this standard (so that people are wont to say of a good work that nothing could be taken from it or added to it, implying that excellence is destroyed by excess or deficiency, but secured by observing the mean; and good artists, as we say, do in fact keep their eyes fixed on this in all that they do), and if virtue, like nature, is more exact and better than any art, it follows that virtue also must aim at the mean—virtue of course meaning moral virtue or excellence; for it has to do with passions and actions, and it is these that admit of excess and deficiency and the mean. For instance, it is possible to feel fear, confidence, desire, anger, pity, and generally to be affected pleasantly and painfully, either too much or too little, in either case wrongly; but to be thus affected at the right times, and on the right occasions, and towards the right persons, and with the right object, and in the right fashion, is the mean course and the best course, and these are characteristics of virtue. And in the same way our outward acts also admit of excess and deficiency, and the mean or due amount. Virtue, then, has to deal with feelings or passions and with outward acts, in which excess is wrong and deficiency also is blamed, but the mean amount is praised and is right—both of which are characteristics of virtue. Virtue, then, is a kind of moderation inasmuch as it aims at the mean.

Again, there are many ways of going wrong (for evil is infinite in nature, to use a Pythagorean figure, while good is finite), but only one way of going right; so that the one is easy and the other hard—easy to miss the mark and hard to hit. On this account also, then, excess and deficiency are characteristic of vice, hitting the mean is characteristic of virtue.

Virtue, then, is a habit or trained faculty of choice, the characteristic of which lies in moderation or observance of the mean relatively to the persons concerned, as determined by reason, *i.e.* by the reason by which the prudent man would determine it. And it is a moderation, firstly, inasmuch as it comes in the middle or mean between two vices, one on the side of excess, the other on the side of defect; and, secondly, inasmuch as, while these vices fall short of or exceed the due measure in feeling and in action, it finds and chooses the mean, middling, or moderate amount. Regarded in its essence, therefore, or according to the definition of its nature, virtue is a moderation or middle state, but viewed in its relation to what is best and right it is the extreme of perfection.

But it is not all actions nor all passions that admit of moderation; there are some whose very names imply badness, as malevolence, shamelessness, envy, and, among acts, adultery, theft, murder. These and all other like things are blamed as being bad in themselves, and not merely in their excess or deficiency. It is impossible therefore to go right in them; they are always wrong: rightness and wrongness in such things (*e.g.* in adultery) does not depend upon whether it is the right person and occasion and manner, but the mere doing of any one of them is wrong. It would be equally absurd to look for moderation or excess or deficiency in unjust cowardly or profligate conduct; for then there would be moderation in excess or deficiency, and excess in excess, and deficiency in deficiency. The fact is that just as there can be no excess or deficiency in temperance or courage because the mean or moderate amount is, in a sense, an extreme, so in these kinds of conduct also there can be no moderation or excess or deficiency, but the acts are wrong however they be done. For, to put it generally, there cannot be moderation in excess or deficiency, nor excess or deficiency in moderation.

Aristotle now gives us his list of the virtues, and it is here that the reader would be well advised—if he or she has not done so already—to make out a comparable list of his or her own virtues, to see how it compares. Here is Aristotle's list:

- Courage (particularly, but not only, in battle).
- Temperance (self-control in such pleasant activities as eating, drinking, sex).
- Justice (being fair with others, and keeping one's promises and contracts).
- Liberality (spending money; notice that charity itself is not a virtue, and giving away all of one's money [like some of the saints did] would be considered not only excessive but insane).
- Magnificence (living well materially, driving a substantial but not too flashy chariot, living in a big [but not too big] house, giving good [but not too ridiculously lavish] parties).
- Pride (taking public pleasure in one's accomplishments and status. Notice that, for Aristotle, not doing so, being humble, is a vice).
- High-mindedness (not being petty).
- Aspiration (being ambitious but not too ambitious. Notice that Aristotle says that this virtue has no name in Greek and that what we call "ambition" is taken by him to be a vice. Why?).
- Gentleness (not wimpiness—Athens was a very "macho" society—but charm and concern for others, sensitivity).
- Truthfulness (not being a liar, particularly with regard to one's own accomplishments).
- Wittiness (having a sense of humor).

- Friendliness (properly pleasant and outgoing; this is different from having friends, which is much more than a moral virtue; it is one of the absolute necessities of the good life, whatever one's virtues).
- Modesty (not the same as humility, just not thinking too much of oneself).
- Righteous indignation (getting angry about the right things, and in proportion to the offense in question. Not getting angry at all [a Christian virtue] is considered a vice, if something is worth being angry about).

7. But it is not enough to make these general statements [about virtue and vice]: we must go on and apply them to particulars [*i.e.* to the several virtues and vices]. For in reasoning about matters of conduct general statements are too vague, and do not convey so much truth as particular propositions. It is with particulars that conduct is concerned: our statements, therefore, when applied to these particulars, should be found to hold good. These particulars then [*i.e.* the several virtues and vices and the several acts and affections with which they deal], we will take from the following list.

Moderation in the feelings of fear and confidence is courage: of those that exceed, he that exceeds in fearlessness has no name (as often happens), but he that exceeds in confidence is foolhardy, while he that exceeds in fear, but is deficient in confidence, is cowardly. Moderation in respect of certain pleasures and also (though to a less extent) certain pains is temperance, while excess is profligacy. But defectiveness in the matter of these pleasures is hardly ever found, and so this sort of people also have as yet received no name: let us put them down as "void of sensibility." In the matter of giving and taking money, moderation is liberality; excess and deficiency are prodigality and illiberality. But both vices exceed and fall short in giving and taking; while the illiberal man exceeds in taking, but falls short in spending. (For the present we are but giving an outline or summary, and aim at nothing more; we shall afterwards treat these points in greater detail.) But, besides these, there are other dispositions in the matter of money: there is a moderation which is called magnificence (for the magnificent is not the same as the liberal man: the former deals with large sums, the latter with small), and an excess which is called bad taste or vulgarity, and a deficiency which is called meanness; and these vices differ from those which are opposed to liberality: how they differ will be explained later. With respect to honour and disgrace, there is a moderation which is pride, an excess which may be called vanity, and a deficiency which is humility.

But just as we said that liberality is related to magnificence, differing only in that it deals with small sums, so here there is a virtue related to highmindedness, and differing only in that it is concerned with small instead of great honours. A man may have a due desire for honour, and also more or less than a due desire: he that carries this desire to excess is called ambitious, he that has not enough of it is called unambitious, but he that has the due amount has no name. There are also no abstract names for the characters, except "ambition," corresponding to ambitious. And on this account those who occupy the extremes lay claim to the middle place. And in common parlance, too, the moderate man is sometimes called ambitious and sometimes unambitious, and sometimes the ambitious man is praised and sometimes the unambitious. Why this is we will explain afterwards; for the present we will follow out our plan and enumerate the other types of character. In the matter of anger also we find excess and deficiency and moderation. The characters themselves hardly have recognized names, but as the moderate man is here called gentle, we will call his character gentleness; of those who go into extremes, we may take the term wrathful for him who exceeds, with wrathfulness for the vice, and wrathless for him who is deficient, with wrathlessness for his character.

Besides these, there are three kinds of moderation, bearing some resemblance to one another, and yet different. They all have to do with intercourse in speech and action, but they differ in that one has to do with the truthfulness of this intercourse, while the other two have to do with its pleasantness—one of the two with pleasantness in matters of amusement, the other with pleasantness in all the relations of life. We must therefore speak of these qualities also in order that we may the more plainly see how, in all cases, moderation is praiseworthy, while the extreme courses are neither right nor praiseworthy, but blamable. In these cases also names are for the most part wanting, but we must try, here as elsewhere, to coin names ourselves, in order to make our argument clear and easy to follow.

In the matter of truth, then, let us call him who observes the mean a true [or truthful] person, and observance of the mean truth [or truthfulness]: pretence, when it exaggerates, may be called boasting, and the person a boaster; when it understates, let the names be irony and ironical. With regard to pleasantness in amusement, he who observes the mean may be called witty, and his character wittiness; excess may be called buffoonery, and the man a buffoon; while boorish may stand for the person who is deficient, and boorishness for his character. With regard to pleasantness in the other affairs of life, he who makes himself properly pleasant may be called friendly, and his moderation friendliness; he that exceeds may be called obsequious if he have no ulterior motive, but a flatterer if he has an eye to his own advantage; he that is deficient in this respect, and always makes himself disagreeable, may be called a quarrelsome or peevish fellow.

Moreover, in mere emotions and in our conduct with regard to them, there are ways of observing the mean; for instance, shame is not a virtue, but yet the modest man is praised. For in these matters also we speak of this man as observing the mean, of that man as going beyond it (as the shame-faced man whom the least thing makes shy), while he who is deficient in the feeling, or lacks it altogether, is called shameless; but the term modest is applied to him who observes the mean. Righteous indignation, again, hits the mean between envy and malevolence. These have to do with feelings of pleasure and pain at what happens to our neighbours. A man is called righteously indignant when he feels pain at the sight of undeserved prosperity, but your envious man goes beyond him and is pained by the sight of any one in prosperity, while the malevolent man is so far from being pained that he actually exults in the misfortunes of his neighbours. But we shall have another opportunity of discussing these matters. As for justice, the term is used in more senses than one; we will, therefore, after disposing of the above questions, distinguish these various senses, and show how each of these kinds of justice is a kind of moderation. And then we will treat of the intellectual virtues in the same way.

8. There are, as we said, three classes of disposition, viz. two kinds of vice, one marked by excess, the other by deficiency, and one kind of virtue, the observance of the mean. Now, each is in a way opposed to each, for the extreme dispositions are opposed both to the mean or moderate disposition and to one another, while the moderate disposition is opposed to both the extremes. Just as a quantity which is equal to a given quantity is also greater when compared with a less, and less when compared with a greater quantity, so the mean or moderate dispositions exceed as compared with the defective dispositions, and fall short as compared with the excessive dispositions, both in feeling and in action; *e.g.* the courageous man seems foolhardy as compared with the coward, and cowardly as compared with the foolhardy; and similarly the temperate man appears profligate in comparison with the insensible, and insensible in comparison with the profligate man; and the liberal man appears prodigal by the side of the illiberal man, and illiberal by the side of the prodigal man. And so the extreme characters try to displace the mean or moderate character, and each represents him as falling into the opposite extreme, the coward calling the courageous man foolhardy, the foolhardy calling him coward, and so on in other cases. But while the mean and the extremes are thus opposed to one another, the extremes are strictly contrary to each other rather than to the mean; for they are further removed from one another than from the mean, as that which is greater than a given magnitude is further from that which is less, and that which is less is further from that which is greater, than either the greater or the less is from that which is equal to the given magnitude.

Sometimes, again, an extreme, when compared with the mean, has a sort of resemblance to it, as foolhardiness to courage, or prodigality to liberality; but there is the greatest possible dissimilarity between the extremes. Again, "things that are as far as possible removed from each other" is the accepted definition of contraries, so that the further things are removed from each other the more contrary they are.

In comparison with the mean, however, it is sometimes the deficiency that is the more opposed, and sometimes the excess; *e.g.* foolhardiness, which is excess, is not so much opposed to courage as cowardice, which is deficiency; but insensibility, which is lack of feeling, is not so much opposed to temperance as profligacy, which is excess.

The reasons for this are two. One is the reason derived from the nature of the matter itself: since one extreme is, in fact, nearer and more similar to the mean, we naturally do not oppose it to the mean so strongly as the other; *e.g.* as foolhardiness seems more similar to courage and nearer to it, and cowardice more dissimilar, we speak of cowardice as the opposite rather than the other: for that which is further removed from the mean seems to be more opposed to it. This, then, is one reason, derived from the nature of the thing itself. Another reason lies in ourselves: and it is this—those things to which we happen to be more prone by nature appear to be more opposed to the mean: *e.g.* our natural inclination is rather towards indulgence in pleasure, and so we more easily fall into profligate than into regular habits: those courses, then, in which we are more apt to run to great lengths are spoken of as more opposed to the mean; and thus profligacy, which is an excess, is more opposed to temperance than the deficiency is.

9. We have sufficiently explained, then, that moral virtue is moderation or observance of the mean, and in what sense, viz. (1) as holding a middle position between two vices, one on the side of excess, and the other on the side of deficiency, and (2) as aiming at the mean or moderate amount both in feeling and in action. And on this account it is a hard thing to be good; for finding the middle or the mean in each case is a hard thing, just as finding the middle or centre of a circle is a thing that is not within the power of everybody, but only of him who has the requisite knowledge. Thus any one can be angry—that is quite easy; any one can give money away or spend it: but to do these things to the right person, to the right extent, at the right time, with the right object, and in the right manner, is not what everybody can do, and is by no means easy; and that is the reason why right doing is rare and praiseworthy and noble. He that aims at the mean, then, should first of all strive to avoid that extreme which is more opposed to it, as Calypso bids Ulysses—

Clear of these smoking breakers keep thy ship.

For of the extremes one is more dangerous, the other less. Since then it is hard to hit the mean precisely, we must "row when we cannot sail," as the proverb has it, and choose the least of two evils; and that will be best effected in the way we have described. And secondly we must consider, each for himself, what we are most prone to—for different natures are inclined to different things—which we may learn by the pleasure or pain we feel. And then we must bend ourselves in the opposite direction; for by keeping well away from error we shall fall into the middle course, as we straighten a bent stick by bending it the other way.

But in all cases we must be especially on our guard against pleasant things, and against pleasure; for we can scarce judge her impartially. And so, in our behaviour towards her, we should imitate the behaviour of the old counsellors towards Helen, and in all cases repeat their saying: if we dismiss her we shall be less likely to go wrong.

This then, in outline, is the course by which we shall best be able to hit the mean. But it is a hard task, we must admit, especially in a particular case. It is not easy to determine, for instance, how and with whom one ought to be angry, and upon what grounds, and for how long; for public opinion sometimes praises those who fall short, and calls them gentle, and sometimes applies the term mainly to those who show a harsh temper. In fact, a slight error, whether on the side of excess or deficiency, is not blamed, but only a considerable error; for then there can be no mistake. But it is hardly possible to determine by reasoning how far or to what extent a man must err in order to incur blame; and indeed matters that fall within the scope of perception never can be so determined. Such matters lie within the region of particulars, and can only be determined by perception. So much then is plain, that the middle character is in all cases to be praised, but that we ought to incline sometimes towards excess, sometimes towards deficiency; for in this way we shall most easily hit the mean and attain to right doing.

DISCUSSION

The alternative translation for the word for "virtue" *(arete)* as "excellence" points to an extremely important feature of Aristotle's ethics. The good for Aristotle is defined not so much in terms of obeying certain laws or "being moral" as in terms of excelling as human beings. We have several times emphasized Aristotle's elitism—the fact that his ethics is aimed at an aristocratic, mainly male, Athenian class. But because of this, Aristotle's conception of virtue is not at all concerned with the good life or the virtues of people who are not in this privileged class. Unlike Christian ethics, for example, Aristotle's ethics is not concerned with that form of goodwill that is possible for everyone. The ordinary citizen and his or her virtues do not enter into his considerations. It is assumed that a shoemaker should be a good shoemaker and a baker should be a good baker, and, of course, husbands, wives, and children should be good husbands, wives, and children. But there is nothing in Aristotle that would generally count as "being a good person," without reference to role or rank, and Aristotle would have found such an idea (despite his own phrase, "the good for man") to be unintelligible. The virtues, accordingly, are tailored for men of leisure and considerable status and responsibility in the community. They are excellences in the sense that they measure a particular kind of social achievement and recognition ("honor"), and they demand of these privileged, accomplished, and already "noble" men that they not only exercise the virtues peculiar to their rank (social magnificence, for example) but also excel in those special skills (such as statesmanship and justice) appropriate for the leadership of society. Many of Aristotle's virtues would hardly apply to poor people (liberality—as well as stinginess and waste—refer to quite different traits and concerns in the poor). Let us note again that a number of Aristotle's virtues would not count as virtues for us at all, but, furthermore, let us note that Aristotle calls these excellences of character. How many of them would count as "moral" in our terms (in contrast to merely pleasant or charming traits, such as wittiness and friendliness)? What important moral virtues—in our sense of that term—have been left off of Aristotle's list?

FRIENDSHIP: FROM BOOKS VIII AND IX

Aristotle's discussion of friendship occupies the single greatest portion of the *Ethics*—two full chapters, or almost a quarter of the book. The extensiveness of the discussion attests to the importance of this most necessary component of the good life, "for no one would want to live without friends." Aristotle's ethics is first of all a *social* ethics in which it is all-important for people to get along with one another, help one another, and inspire one another to be even more virtuous. (Aristotle defends many of the virtues by commenting that our friends will approve of and appreciate virtuous action but will disdain vice.) Friendship, as something more than a single virtue, is the best manifestation of all of these concerns. Friends not only get along, they *like* (even *love*) each other. They help each other, and they also—ideally—inspire one another to ever-new heights of virtue. You will notice that Aristotle considers friendship much more than mere companionship and mutual help; it is a kind of love *(philia)* and is one of the most important determinants of character.

In Chapters 1 to 6 of Book VIII, Aristotle discusses the necessity of friendship for the good life and delineates three distinct kinds of friendship, from the merely useful to the ideal.

1. After what we have said, a discussion of friendship would naturally follow, since it is a virtue or implies virtue, and is besides most necessary with a view to living. For without friends no one would choose to live, though he had all other goods; even rich men and those in possession of office and of dominating power are thought to need friends most of all; for what is the use of such prosperity without the opportunity of beneficence, which is exercised chiefly and in its most laudable form towards friends? Or how can prosperity be guarded and preserved without friends? The greater it is, the more exposed is it to risk. And in poverty and in other misfortunes men think friends are the only refuge. It helps the young, too, to keep from error; it aids older people by ministering to their needs and supplementing the activities that are failing from weakness; those in the prime of life it stimulates to noble actions—'two going together'—for with friends men are more able both to think and to act. Again, parent seems by nature to feel it for offspring and offspring for parent, not only among men but among birds and among most animals; it is felt mutually by members of the same race, and especially by men, whence we praise lovers of their fellowmen. We may see even in our travels how near and dear every man is to every other. Friendship seems too to hold states together, and lawgivers to care more for it than for justice; for unanimity seems to be something like friendship, and this they aim at most of all, and expel faction as their worst enemy; and when men are friends they have no need of justice, while when they are just they need friendship as well, and the truest form of justice is thought to be a friendly quality.

But it is not only necessary but also noble; for we praise those who love their friends, and it is thought to be a fine thing to have many friends; and again we think it is the same people that are good men and are friends.

Not a few things about friendship are matters of debate. Some define it as a kind of likeness and say like people are friends, whence come the sayings 'like to like', 'birds of a feather flock together', and so on; others on the contrary say 'two of a trade never agree'. On this very question they inquire for deeper and more physical causes, Euripides saying that 'parched earth loves the rain, and stately heaven when filled with rain loves to fall to earth', and Heraclitus that 'it is what opposes that helps' and 'from different tones comes the fairest tune' and 'all things are produced through strife'; while Empedocles, as well as others, expresses the opposite view that like aims at like. The physical problems we may leave alone (for they do not belong to the present inquiry); let us examine those which are human and involve character and feeling, *e.g.* whether friendship can arise between any two people or people cannot be friends if they are wicked, and whether there is one species of friendship or more than one. Those who think there is only one because it admits of degrees have relied on an inadequate indication; for even things different in species admit of degree. We have discussed this matter previously.

2. The kinds of friendship may perhaps be cleared up if we first come to know the object of love. For not everything seems to be loved but only the lovable, and this is good, pleasant, or useful; but it would seem to be that by which some good or pleasure is produced that is useful, so that it is the good and the useful that are lovable as ends. Do men love, then, *the* good, or what is good for *them?* These sometimes clash. So too with regard to the pleasant. Now it is thought that each loves what is good for himself, and that the good is without qualification lovable, and what is good for each man is lovable for him; but each man loves not what is good for him but what seems good. This however will make no difference; we shall just have to say that this is 'that which seems lovable'. Now there are three grounds on which people love; of the love of lifeless objects we do not use the word 'friendship'; for it is not mutual love, nor is there a wishing of good to the other (for it would surely be ridiculous to wish wine well; if one wishes anything for it, it is that it may keep, so that one may have it oneself); but to a friend we say we ought to wish what is good for his sake. But to those who thus wish good we ascribe only goodwill, if the wish is not reciprocated; goodwill when it *is* reciprocal being friendship. Or must we add 'when it is recognized'? For many people have goodwill to those whom they have not seen but judge to be good or useful; and one of these might return this feeling. These people seem to bear goodwill to each other; but how could one call them friends when they do not know their mutual feelings? To be friends, then, they must be mutually recognized as bearing goodwill and wishing well to each other for one of the aforesaid reasons.

3. Now these reasons differ from each other in kind; so, therefore, do the corresponding forms of love and friendship. There are therefore three kinds of friendship equal in number to the things that are lovable; for with respect to each there is a mutual and recognized love, and those who love each other wish well to each other in that respect in which they love one another. Now those who love each other for their utility do not love each other for themselves but in virtue of some good which they get from each other. So too with those who love for the sake of pleasure; it is not for their character that men love ready-witted people, but because they find them pleasant. Therefore those who love for the sake of utility love for the sake of what is good for *themselves* and those who love for the sake of pleasure do so for the sake of what is pleasant to *themselves,* and not in so far as the other is the person loved but in so far as he is useful or pleasant. And thus these friendships are only incidental; for it is not as being the man he is that the loved person is loved, but as providing some good or pleasure. Such friendships, then, are easily dissolved, if the parties do not remain like themselves; for if the one party is no longer pleasant or useful the other ceases to love him.

Now the useful is not permanent but is always changing. Thus when the motive of the friendship is done away, the friendship is dissolved, inasmuch as it existed only for the ends in question. This kind of friendship seems to exist chiefly between old people (for at that age people pursue not the pleasant but the useful) and, of those who are in their prime or young, between those who pursue utility. And such people do not live much with each other either; for sometimes they do not even find each other pleasant; therefore they do not need such companionship unless they are useful to each other; for they are pleasant to each other only in so far as they rouse in each other hopes of something good to come. Among such friendships people also class the friendship of host and guest. On the other hand the friendship of young people seems to aim at pleasure; for they live under the guidance of emotion, and pursue above all what is pleasant to themselves and what is immediately before them; but with increasing age their pleasures become different. This is why they quickly become friends and quickly cease to be so; their friendship changes with the object that is found pleasant, and such pleasure alters quickly. Young people are amorous too; for the greater part of the friendship of love depends on emotion and aims at pleasure; this is why they fall in love and quickly fall out of love, changing often within a single day. But these people do wish to spend their days and lives together; for it is thus that they attain the purpose of their friendship.

Perfect friendship is the friendship of men who are good, and alike in virtue; for these wish well alike to each other *qua* good, and they are good in themselves. Now those who wish well to their friends for their sake are most truly friends; for they do this by reason of their own nature and not incidentally; therefore their friendship lasts as long as they are good—and goodness is an enduring thing. And each is good without qualification and to his friend, for the good are both good without qualification and useful to each other. So too they are pleasant; for the good are pleasant both without qualification and to each other, since to each his own activities and others like them are pleasurable, and the actions of the good *are* the same or like. And such a friendship is as might be expected permanent, since there meet in it all the qualities that friends should have. For all friendship is for the sake of good or of pleasure—good or pleasure either in the abstract or such as will be enjoyed by him who has the friendly feeling—and is based on a certain resemblance; and to a friendship of good men all the qualities we have named belong in virtue of the nature of the friends themselves; for in the case of this kind of friendship the other qualities also are alike in both friends, and that which is good without qualification is also without qualification pleasant, and these are the most lovable qualities. Love and friendship therefore are found most and in their best form between such men.

But it is natural that such friendships should be infrequent; for such men are rare. Further, such friendship requires time and familiarity; as the proverb says, men cannot know each other till they have 'eaten salt together'; nor can they admit each other to friendship or be friends till each has been found lovable and been trusted by each. Those who quickly show the marks of friendship to each other wish to be friends, but are not friends unless they both are lovable and know the fact; for a wish for friendship may arise quickly, but friendship does not.

4. This kind of friendship, then, is perfect both in respect of duration and in all other respects, and in it each gets from each in all respects the same as, or something like what, he gives; which is what ought to happen between friends. Friendship for the sake of pleasure bears a resemblance to this kind; for good

people too *are* pleasant to each other. So too does friendship for the sake of utility; for the good are also useful to each other. Among men of these inferior sorts too, friendships are most permanent when the friends get the same thing from each other (*e.g.* pleasure), and not only that but also from the same source, as happens between ready-witted people, not as happens between lover and beloved. For these do not take pleasure in the same things, but the one in seeing the beloved and the other in receiving attentions from his lover; and when the bloom of youth is passing the friendship sometimes passes too (for the one finds no pleasure in the sight of the other, and the other gets no attentions from the first); but many lovers on the other hand are constant, if familiarity has led them to love each other's characters, these being alike. But those who exchange not pleasure but utility in their amour are both less truly friends and less constant. Those who are friends for the sake of utility part when the advantage is at an end; for they were lovers not of each other but of profit.

For the sake of pleasure or utility, then, even bad men may be friends of each other, or good men of bad, or one who is neither good nor bad may be a friend to any sort of person, but for their own sake clearly only good men can be friends; for bad men do not delight in each other unless some advantage come of the relation.

The friendship of the good too and this alone is proof against slander; for it is not easy to trust any one's talk about a man who has long been tested by oneself; and it is among good men that trust and the feeling that 'he would never wrong me' and all the other things that are demanded in true friendship are found. In the other kinds of friendship, however, there is nothing to prevent evils arising.

For men apply the name of friends even to those whose motive is utility, in which sense states are said to be friendly (for the alliances of states seem to aim at advantage), and to those who love each other for the sake of pleasure, in which sense children are called friends. Therefore we too ought perhaps to call such people friends, and say that there are several kinds of friendship—firstly and in the proper sense that of good men *qua* good, and by analogy the other kinds; for it is in virtue of something good and something akin to what is found in true friendship that they are friends, since even the pleasant is good for the lovers of pleasure. But these two kinds of friendship are not often united, nor do the same people become friends for the sake of utility and of pleasure; for things that are only incidentally connected are not often coupled together.

Friendship being divided into these kinds, bad men will be friends for the sake of pleasure or of utility, being in this respect like each other, but good men will be friends for their own sake, *i.e.* in virtue of their goodness. These, then, are friends without qualification; the others are friends incidentally and through a resemblance to these.

5. As in regard to the virtues some men are called good in respect of a state of character, others in respect of an activity, so too in the case of friendship; for those who live together delight in each other and confer benefits on each other, but those who are asleep or locally separated are not performing, but are disposed to perform, the activities of friendship; distance does not break off the friendship absolutely, but only the activity of it. But if the absence is lasting, it

seems actually to make men forget their friendship; hence the saying 'out of sight, out of mind.' Neither old people nor sour people seem to make friends easily; for there is little that is pleasant in them, and no one can spend his days with one whose company is painful, or not pleasant, since nature seems above all to avoid the painful and to aim at the pleasant. Those, however, who approve of each other but do not live together seem to be well-disposed rather than actual friends. For there is nothing so characteristic of friends as living together (since while it is people who are in need that desire benefits, even those who are supremely happy desire to spend their days together; for solitude suits such people least of all); but people cannot live together if they are not pleasant and do not enjoy the same things, as friends who are companions seem to do.

The truest friendship, then, is that of the good, as we have frequently said; for that which is without qualification good or pleasant seems to be lovable and desirable, and for each person that which is good or pleasant to him; and the good man is lovable and desirable to the good man for both these reasons. Now it looks as if love were a feeling, friendship a state of character; for love may be felt just as much towards lifeless things, but mutual love involves choice and choice springs from a state of character; and men wish well to those whom they love, for their sake, not as a result of feeling but as a result of a state of character. And in loving a friend men love what is good for themselves; for the good man in becoming a friend becomes a good to his friend. Each, then, both loves what is good for himself, and makes an equal return in goodwill and in pleasantness; for friendship is said to be equality, and both of these are found most in the friendship of the good.

6. Between sour and elderly people friendship arises less readily, inasmuch as they are less good-tempered and enjoy companionship less; for these are thought to be the greatest marks of friendship and most productive of it. This is why, while young men become friends quickly, old men do not; it is because men do not become friends with those in whom they do not delight; and similarly sour people do not quickly make friends either. But such men may bear goodwill to each other; for they wish one another well and aid one another in need; but they are hardly *friends* because they do not spend their days together nor delight in each other, and these are thought the greatest marks of friendship.

One cannot be a friend to many people in the sense of having friendship of the perfect type with them, just as one cannot be in love with many people at once (for love is a sort of excess of feeling, and it is the nature of such only to be felt towards one person); and it is not easy for many people at the same time to please the same person very greatly, or perhaps even to be good in his eyes. One must, too, acquire some experience of the other person and become familiar with him, and that is very hard. But with a view to utility or pleasure it is possible that many people should please one; for many people are useful or pleasant, and these services take little time.

Of these two kinds that which is for the sake of pleasure is the more like friendship, when both parties get the same things from each other and delight in each other or in the same things, as in the friendships of the young; for generosity is more found in such friendships. Friendship based on utility is for the commercially minded. People who are supremely happy, too, have no need of useful friends, but do need pleasant friends: for they wish to live with *some one* and, though they can endure for a short time what is painful, no one could put up with it continuously, nor even with the Good itself if it were painful to him; this is why they look out for friends who are pleasant. Perhaps they should look out for friends who, being pleasant, are also good, and good for them, too; for so they will have all the characteristics that friends should have.

People in positions of authority seem to have friends who fall into distinct classes; some people are useful to them and others are pleasant, but the same people are rarely both; for they seek neither those whose pleasantness is accompanied by virtue nor those whose utility is with a view to noble objects, but in their desire for pleasure they seek for ready-witted people, and their other friends they choose as being clever at doing what they are told, and these characteristics are rarely combined. Now we have said that the good man is at the same time pleasant and useful; but such a man does not become the friend of one who surpasses him in station, unless he is surpassed also in virtue; if this is not so, he does not establish equality by being proportionally exceeded in both respects. But people who surpass him in both respects are not so easy to find.

However that may be, the aforesaid friendships involve equality; for the friends get the same things from one another and wish the same things for one another, or exchange one thing for another, *e.g.* pleasure for utility; we have said, however, that they are both less truly friendships and less permanent. But it is from their likeness and their unlikeness to the same thing that they are thought both to be and not to be friendships. It is by their likeness to the friendship of virtue that they seem to be friendships (for one of them involves pleasure and the other utility, and these characteristics belong to the friendship of virtue as well); while it is because the friendship of virtue is proof against slander and permanent, while these quickly change (besides differing from the former in many other respects), that they appear *not* to be friendships; *i.e.* it is because of their unlikeness to the friendship of virtue. . . .

Book IX

In Book IX, Aristotle continues his discussion of the dynamics of friendship, including questions of motivation and obligation. Crucial to this discussion is that perennial ethical debate between those who insist that all our actions—including acts of friendship—are ultimately motivated by self-interest and those who insist that there are genuine acts of altruism and friendship in which self-interest is not a motive. In Chapter 4 of the *Ethics,* Book IX, Aristotle finds a position between these two extremes and insists that friendship is based on "self-love." In Chapter 8, he then goes on to discuss the nature of true self-love.

4. Friendly relations to others, and all the characteristics by which friendship is defined, seem to be derived from our relations towards ourselves. A friend is sometimes described as one who wishes and does to another what is

good or seems good for that other's sake, or as one who wishes his friend to exist and to live for his (the friend's) sake. (This is what mothers feel towards their children, and what friends who have had a difference feel for one another.) Others describe a friend as one who lives with another and chooses what he chooses, or as one who sympathizes with the griefs and joys of his friend. (This, also, is especially the case with mothers.) And, similarly, friendship is usually defined by some one or other of these characteristics.

Now, every one of these characteristics we find in the good man's relations to himself (and in other men just so far as they suppose themselves to be good; but it seems, as we have said, that virtue and the good man are in everything the standard): for the good man is of one mind with himself, and desires the same things with all his soul, and wishes for himself what both is and seems good, and does that (for it is characteristic of him to work out that which is good) for his own sake—for the sake, that is to say, of the rational part of him, which seems to be a man's self. And he wishes his self to live and be preserved, and especially that part of his self by which he thinks: for existence is good to the good man. But it is for himself that each wishes the good; no one would choose to have all that is good (as *e.g.* God is in complete possession of the good) on condition of becoming someone else, but only on condition of still being just himself. But his reason would seem to be a man's self, or, at least, to be so in a truer sense than any other of his faculties.

Such a man also wishes to live with himself; for his own company is pleasant to him. The memory of his past life is sweet, and for the future he has good hopes; and such hopes are pleasant. His mind, moreover, is well stored with matter for contemplation: and he sympathizes with himself in sorrow and in joy; for at all seasons the same things give him pain and pleasure, not this thing now, and then another thing,—for he is, so to speak, not apt to change his mind.

Since, then, all these characteristics are found in the good man's relations to himself, and since his relations to his friend are the same as his relations to himself (for his friend is his second self), friendship is described by one or other of these characteristics, and those are called friends in whom these characteristics are found. The question whether friendship towards one's self is or is not possible may be dismissed at present; but that it is possible so far as one has two or more selves would seem to follow from what has been already said, and also from the fact that the extreme of friendship for another is likened to friendship for one's self.

But the characteristics we have mentioned appear to be found in the generality of men, though they are not good. Perhaps we may say that so far as they are agreeable to themselves, and believe they are good, so far do they share these characteristics. People who are utterly worthless and impious never have them, nor do they even seem to have them. But we might almost say roundly that they are wanting in all who are not good; for such men are not at one with themselves: they desire one thing while they wish another, as the incontinent do, for instance (for, instead of what they hold to be good, they choose what is pleasant though injurious). Others, again, through cowardice or laziness, shrink from doing that which they believe is the best for them; while those who have done many terrible things out of wickedness, hate life, and wish to get rid of it, and sometimes actually destroy themselves. Bad men try to find people with whom to spend their time, and eschew their own company; for there is much that is painful in the past on which they look back and in the future to which they look forward when they are by themselves, but the company of others diverts them from these thoughts. As there is nothing lovable in them, they have no friendly feelings towards themselves.

He who is not good, then, cannot sympathize with himself in joy or sorrow; for his soul is divided against itself: one part of him, by reason of its viciousness, is pained at being deprived of something, while another part of him is pleased; one part pulls this way, another that, tearing him to pieces, as it were, between them. Or if it be impossible to be pained and pleased at the same time, yet, at any rate, after a short interval he is pained that he was pleased, and wishes that he had never partaken of this pleasure; for those who are not good are full of remorse. Thus we may say roundly that he who is not good has no friendly feelings even for himself, as there is nothing lovable in him. If, then, to be in this state is utterly miserable, we ought to strain every nerve to avoid vice, and try to be good; for thus we may be friendly disposed towards ourselves, and make friends with others. . . .

8. Another question which is raised is, whether we ought most to love ourselves or others. We blame, it is said, those who love themselves most, and apply the term self-loving to them as a term of reproach: and, again, he who is not good is thought to have regard to himself in everything that he does, and the more so the worse he is; and so we accuse him of doing nothing disinterestedly. The good man on the other hand, it is thought, takes what is noble as his motive, and the better he is the more is he guided by this motive, and by regard for his friend, neglecting his own interest.

But this theory disagrees with facts, nor is it surprising that it should. For it is allowed that we ought to love him most who is most truly a friend, and that he is most truly a friend who, in wishing well to another, wishes well to him for his (the other's) sake, and even though no one should ever know. But all these characteristics, and all the others which go to make up the definition of a friend, are found in the highest degree in a man's relations to himself; for we have already seen how it is from our relations to ourselves that all our friendly relations to others are derived. Moreover, all the proverbs point to the same conclusion—such as "Friends have one soul," "Friends have all things in common," "Equality makes friendship," "The knee is nearer than the shin." All these characteristics are found in the highest degree in a man's relations to himself; for he is his own best friend: and so he must love himself better than any one else.

People not unnaturally are puzzled to know which of these two statements to adopt, since both appeal to them. Perhaps the best method of dealing with conflicting statements of this kind is first to make out the difference between them, and then to determine how far and in what sense each is right. So here, if we first ascertain what self-loving means in each statement, the difficulty will perhaps be cleared up. Those who use self-loving as a term of reproach apply the name to those who take more than their due of money, and honour, and bodily pleasures; for the generality of men desire these things, and set their hearts upon them as the best things in the world, so that they are keenly competed for. Those, then, who grasp at more than their share of these things indulge their animal appetites and their passions generally—in a word, the irrational part of their nature. But this is the character of the generality of men; and hence the term self-loving has come to be used in this bad sense from the fact that the greater part of mankind are not good. It is with justice, then, that we reproach those who are self-loving in this sense. That it really is to those who take more than their due of these things that the term is usually applied by the generality of men, may easily be shown; for if what a man always set his heart upon were that he, rather than another, should do what is just or temperate, or in any other way virtuous—if, in a word, he were always claiming the noble course of conduct, no one would call him self-loving and no one would reproach him.

And yet such a man would seem to be more truly self-loving. At least, he takes for himself that which is noblest and most truly good, and gratifies the ruling power in himself, and in all things obeys it. But just as the ruling part in a state or in any other system seems, more than any other part, to be the state or the system, so also the ruling part of a man seems to be most truly the man's self. He therefore who loves and gratifies this part of himself is most truly self-loving. Again, we call a man continent or incontinent, according as his reason has or has not the mastery, implying that his reason is his self; and when a man has acted under the guidance of his reason he is thought, in the fullest sense, to have done the deed himself, and of his own will. It is plain, then, that this part of us is our self, or is most truly our self, and that the good man more than any other loves this part of himself. He, then, more than any other, will be self-loving, in another sense than the man whom we reproach as self-loving, differing from him by all the difference that exists between living according to reason and living according to passion, between desiring what is noble and desiring what appears to be profitable.

Those who beyond other men set their hearts on noble deeds are welcomed and praised by all; but if all men were vieing with each other in the pursuit of what is noble, and were straining every nerve to act in the noblest possible manner, the result would be that both the wants of the community would be perfectly satisfied, and at the same time each individually would win the greatest of all good things—for virtue is that.

The good man, therefore, ought to be self-loving; for by doing what is noble he will at once benefit himself and assist others: but the bad man ought not; for he will injure both himself and his neighbours by following passions that are not good. Thus, with the bad man there is a discrepancy between what he ought to do and what he does: but with the good man what he ought to do is what he does; for reason always chooses that which is best for itself; and the good man obeys the voice of reason. Again, it is quite true to say of the good man that he does many things for the sake of his friends and of his country, and will, if need be, even die for them. He will throw away money and honour, and, in a word, all the good things for which men compete, claiming for himself that which is noble; for he will prefer a brief period of intense pleasure to a long period of mild pleasure, one year of noble life to many years of ordinary life, one great and noble action to many little ones. This, we may perhaps say, is what he gets who gives his life for others: and so he chooses for himself something that is noble on a grand scale.

Such a man will surrender wealth to enrich his friend: for while his friend gets the money, he gets what is noble; so he takes the greater good for himself. His conduct will be the same with regard to honours and offices: he will give up all to his friend; for this he deems noble and praiseworthy. Such a man, then, is not unreasonably considered good, as he chooses what is noble in preference to everything else. But, again, it is possible to give up to your friend an opportunity for action, and it may be nobler to cause your friend to do a deed than to do it yourself.

It is plain, then, that in all cases in which he is praised the good man takes for himself a larger share of what is noble. And in this sense, as we have said, a man ought to be self-loving, but not in the sense in which the generality of men are self-loving.

Discussion Questions

1. What is "teleology," and what is a teleological approach to ethics? How is Aristotle a teleologist, in this sense?
2. What does Aristotle mean by "happiness" *(eudaimonia)?* In what significant ways does his term radically differ from our own notion of happiness?
3. Why should we not look for "too much precision" in ethics? Is it because every rule has its exceptions? Or because of the complicated variety of human behavior? Why can ethics not be an exact science—like mathematics or geometry (Aristotle's models)?
4. Why is ethics wasted on the young? Isn't that where moral exhortation is most important, as a way of building character and conscience?
5. Why is *eudaimonia* not for everybody? What is wrong with being "happy as a clam"? (Could clams be *eudaimon?*) What are the necessary material and social conditions for happiness?
6. Why is making a lot of money not in itself the good life?
7. Aristotle keeps appealing to the fact that "everyone agrees" or "all men call this . . . ." Is this a valid form of ethical argument? What does it presuppose? What are its limitations?
8. Why does Aristotle insist (following Solon) that "no man can be called happy while he is still alive." What does this show about Aristotle's notion of happiness? Does it make any sense to call a man happy *after* he is dead? Why or why not?
9. Why should our goal in life not be simply to stay healthy and grow? How does Aristotle's teleology help him make this point? What contemporary examples of these same arguments can you find?
10. What is a "virtue"? Do we still have the concept of virtue—or has our notion of virtue changed drastically since Aristotle's time? What is a virtuous person—for us? What is a virtuous person—for Aristotle?
11. Why is the good life not the life of pleasure? Why is the good life inconceivable without pleasure? How do these two theses fit together in Aristotle's ethics? (In other words, what is the proper place of pleasure in the good life?)

12. If you have had the misfortune to be brought up vulgar and inconsiderate, is there any hope for you? What sort of people would you describe as "vulgar" and to what do you attribute their vulgarity?

13. Why is *pride* a virtue? Why is it not a vice?—or at least an emotion to be ignored in ethics? What is the difference between pride and *vanity?*

14. Do friends inevitably "use" one another? If you want very much to play a game of tennis and join up with an acquaintance to be able to do so, are you using him or her? Why or why not?

15. Could a person be happy without any friends at all?

Study Questions

1. Is it valid to infer from the statement that "every act and inquiry aims at some good (some goal)" that there is a single Good (or Goal) at which everything aims? Why or why not? What is the ethical advantage of accepting this idea of a single goal for all human behavior?

2. Why is the good life necessarily a *rational* life? What does Aristotle mean by "reason" here? In what sense is an activity rational? Why are the virtues rational?

3. What does it mean to say that something is "good in itself" (or intrinsically good)? What sorts of things might be good in themselves?

4. In what sense is virtue the "mean between the extremes"? Is this the same as saying "everything in moderation"? Give an example of a contemporary virtue, and explain how it is a mean between extremes. What are the extremes? What is the motive or activity of which these are extremes?

5. Why is a person painfully following his or her conscience not thereby virtuous, according to Aristotle?

6. What is courage?

7. What are Aristotle's two conditions for *voluntary* action? Can you think of others? Could an act fulfill both of Aristotle's conditions and still not be voluntary? Give examples.

8. What is deliberation? Can one deliberate over an action and not do it? What is the difference between deliberation and simply "mulling over various possibilities"?

9. What is so good about the life of contemplation? What *is* the life of contemplation?

3

Saint Augustine

Augustine was born in 354, in Africa. He was raised in Carthage and learned Christianity as a child, but he was also steeped in paganism and spent an admittedly wild youth in "the pleasures of the flesh." Eventually, he earned his living in Rome by teaching rhetoric. At the age of 30, however, he was deeply troubled and unhappy both with his life and with the pagan view of life. After two years of study and contemplation, he rather suddenly decided to embrace Christianity and was baptized on Easter, 387. He returned to Carthage and spent the rest of his life in Hippo, where he died during a siege in 430. He is generally recognized as the founder of Christian theology and, after only Saint Paul, the most powerful influence on the development of Christianity. His discussion of Christian ethics, while extreme, is the classic statement of the separation of the secular and the divine (in contrast to the more Aristotelian and synthetic teachings of Saint Thomas Aquinas, nearly 900 years later).

Questions of ethics are, among other things, concerned with ideals, the ideal of the Good, the ideal of Justice. But ideals are, by their very nature, not readily attainable in the complexities, confusions, and unexpected tragedies of everyday life. Many philosophers would say that these ideals are, in fact, unattainable, that they are to be striven for, but, in this life, it is not possible to achieve them (except, perhaps, in a tiny number of extremely exceptional cases). Accordingly, we can take the ultimate question of the Good in ethics—the *summum bonum*—in either of two directions: we can remain within the sphere of the secular and refocus the quest as the search for "the good for man," as Aristotle did; or we can continue to defend the pure ideals themselves, which our worldly performances, at best, approximate, as Plato did. Of course, Aristotle still believed in ideals, and Plato staunchly defended the importance of the secular manifestations of virtue. Nevertheless, the difference between them, albeit one of ethical emphasis, set the stage for the most dramatic single development in the whole history of ethics, the complete separation of secular assessments of good and evil and the "transcendent" values, best known to us through Christianity.

Although Christian ethics clearly places its emphasis upon the transcendent and the divine, this is not to the neglect of the secular. Few Christian spokesmen, for example, have ever suggested that worldly virtue is unimportant, because it is only through the practice of such virtue that we may hope to achieve true virtue in the next world. Nevertheless, the core of Christian ethics is the existence of a sphere of pure ideals that transcends the secular worldly stage of human action, ideals that our worldly performances at best approximate. This neo-Platonic vision is nowhere more powerfully developed than in the writings of the Christian Saint Augustine. In the midst of the fall of the mighty Roman Empire, he distinguished two "cities"— the city of man and the city of God. The first was worldly social and political life, the search for a purely secular happiness celebrated and given ethical articulation by Aristotle. The second, reminiscent of Plato's world of ideal forms ("World of Being"), was the Christian heaven, the domain of the Almighty, the realm of the Spirit and of true happiness and true virtue, the *summum bonum.*

Saint Augustine's two cities did not exist in harmony, except insofar as both sought peace in civic life. Each city's reasons for valuing peace, however, were very different. Those who lived in the city of man sought a well-ordered society so that they might be better able to pursue earthly pleasures, whereas the citizens of the heavenly city valued civic peace only because it made possible "the things necessary for the maintenance of this mortal life." Nor was human life simply the quest for individual virtue, even for those who "lived" in the city of God. For such a quest was always undermined by original sin, which could not be undone by any human effort but only by the grace of God. Indeed, one of the major battles of Augustine's career was a dispute with the British monk Pelagius and his followers (Pelagians), who denied original sin and emphasized good works (worldly virtues) as well as the grace of God. In Augustine's harsh ethics, we are essentially corrupt and helpless, and faith is our only salvation. Aristotle's quest for happiness in this life through virtuous activity is, therefore, only a delusion.

THE CITY OF GOD*

In "The City of God," Augustine distinguishes between two "cities"—secular and divine—and attacks the pagan philosophers, Aristotle and his followers ("peripatetics") in particular, for their belief that the highest good (the *summum bonum*) is to be found in this life rather than in the city of God. Augustine did not mean that these were actual cities in the sense of being identifiable by location and population. Rather, the secular city and the heavenly city are intended to describe two radically different ways of life, or what he calls "two kinds of human society." These two societies are created and distinguished by the beliefs, values, and goals of their members. Thus,

*Saint Augustine, *The City of God,* translated and edited by Marcus Dods. Copyright 1950 by Random House, Inc.

rather than there being the external connections of common laws, interests, and economies, Augustine's cities are united by the bond of shared beliefs. In particular, he distinguishes the two cities by the things that are loved in them: In the city of man, it is love of pleasure and the desire for earthly goods that unites the people, whereas in the heavenly city, the bond is formed from the love of God and the hope for a better life in the next world.

This division according to what people value is ultimately the basis for Augustine's judgment of human goodness. Those who love the right things, or whose love is "well-directed," are good, whereas those whose love is misdirected (to matters of the flesh) are bad. This view of the good person is radically different from traditional accounts, which tend to focus either on the traits of character (virtues) that constitute human goodness or on the sorts of actions taken by the good person. Although Augustine is deeply concerned with both actions and virtues (as his discussion of sin makes amply clear), they are not all that matter. More specifically, right actions and a virtuous character will neither buy you present happiness nor ensure that you are on the right path to future contentment. True happiness in this world is impossible, as we shall see, and blessedness in the future depends not only on how you comport yourself on earth, but on what you believe, or love. This has the interesting result that the life of hedonistic pleasure and the life of virtue are on a par, at least with regard to their ability to bring happiness: They both fall miserably short. Thus, Aristotle got it just as wrong as the hedonist.

THE CITY OF GOD: FROM BOOKS XIV, XIX, AND XXII

The Two Cities: From Book XIV

God, desiring not only that the human race might be able by their similarity of nature to associate with one another, but also that they might be bound together in harmony and peace by the ties of relationship, was pleased to derive all men from one individual, and created man with such a nature that the members of the race should not have died, had not the two first (of whom the one was created out of nothing, and the other out of him) merited this by their disobedience; for by them so great a sin was committed, that by it the human nature was altered for the worse, and was transmitted also to their posterity, liable to sin and subject to death. And the kingdom of death so reigned over men that the deserved penalty of sin would have hurled all headlong even into the second death, of which there is no end, had not the undeserved grace of God saved some therefrom. And thus it has come to pass, that though there are very many and great nations all over the earth, whose rites and customs, speech, arms, and dress, are distinguished by marked differences, yet there are no more than two kinds of human society, which we may justly call two cities, according to the language of our Scriptures. The one consists of those who wish to live after the flesh, the other of those who wish to live after the spirit; and when they severally achieve what they wish, they live in peace, each after their kind. . . .

He who resolves to love God, and to love his neighbor as himself, not according to man but according to God, is on account of this love said to be of a good will. . . .

The right will is, therefore, well-directed love, and the wrong will is ill-directed love. Love, then, yearning to have what is loved, is desire; and having and enjoying it, is joy; fleeing what is opposed to it, is fear; and feeling what is opposed to it, when it has befallen it, it is sadness. Now these motions are evil if the love is evil; good if the love is good. . . .

So that good and bad men alike will, are cautious, and contented; or, to say the same thing in other words, good and bad men alike desire, fear, rejoice, but the former in a good, the latter in a bad fashion, according as the will is right or wrong. Sorrow itself, too, which the Stoics would not allow to be represented in the mind of the wise man, is used in a good sense, and especially in our writings.

What the Christians Believe Regarding the Supreme Good and Evil, in Opposition to the Philosophers, Who Have Maintained That the Supreme Good Is in Themselves: From Book XIX

If, then, we be asked what . . . the supreme good and evil is, [we] will reply that life eternal is the supreme good, death eternal the supreme evil, and that to obtain the one and escape the other we must live rightly. And thus it is written, "The just lives by faith," for we do not as yet see our good, and must therefore live by faith; neither have we in ourselves power to live rightly, but can do so only if He who has given us faith to believe in His help do help us when we believe and pray (Hab. 2:4). As for those who have supposed that the sovereign good and evil are to be found in this life, and have placed it either in pleasure or in virtue, or in both; in repose or in virtue, or in both; in pleasure and repose, or in virtue, or in all combined; in the primary objects of nature, or in virtue, or in both,—all these have, with a marvellous shallowness, sought to find their blessedness in this life and in themselves. Contempt has been poured upon such ideas by the Truth, saying by the prophet, "The Lord knoweth the thoughts of men" (or, as the Apostle Paul cites the passage, "The Lord knoweth the thoughts of the *wise*") "that they are vain" (Ps. 94: 11; 1 Cor. 3:20).

For what flood of eloquence can suffice to detail the miseries of this life? Cicero, in the *Consolation* on the death of his daughter, has spent all his ability in lamentation; but how inadequate was even his ability here? For when, where, how, in this life can these primary objects of nature be possessed so that they may not be assailed by unforeseen accidents? Is the body of the wise man exempt from any pain which may dispel pleasure, from any disquietude which may banish repose? The amputation or decay of the members of the body puts an end to its integrity, deformity blights its beauty, weakness its health, lassitude its vigour, sleepiness or sluggishness its activity,—and which of these is it that may not assail the flesh of the wise man? Comely and fitting attitudes and movements of the body are numbered among the prime natural blessings; but what if some sickness makes the members tremble? What if a man suffers from curvature of the spine to such an extent that his hands reach the ground, and he goes upon all-fours like a quadruped? Does not this destroy all beauty and grace in the body, whether at rest or in motion? What shall I say of the fundamental blessings of the soul, sense and intellect, of which the one is given for the perception, and the other for the comprehension of truth? But what kind of sense is it that remains when a man becomes deaf and blind? Where are reason and intellect when disease makes a man delirious? We can scarcely, or not at all, refrain from tears, when we think of or see the actions and words of such frantic persons, and consider how different from and even opposed to their own sober judgment and ordinary conduct their present demeanour is. And what shall I say of those who suffer from demoniacal possession? Where is their own intelligence hidden and buried while the malignant spirit is using their body and soul according to his own will? And who is quite sure that no such thing can happen to the wise man in this life? Then, as to the perception of truth, what can we hope for even in this way while in the body, as we read in the true book of Wisdom, "The corruptible body weigheth down the soul, and the earthly tabernacle presseth down the mind that museth upon many things?" (Wisdom, 4:15). And eagerness, or desire of action, if this is the right meaning to put upon the Greek λ λρμ is also reckoned among the primary advantages of nature; and yet is it not this which produces those pitiable movements of the insane, and those actions which we shudder to see, when sense is deceived and reason deranged?

Having rendered such a harsh picture of human misery and the natural frailty of even the wisest people, Augustine goes on to present the now classical Christian portrait of sin, the locus of which is the body (flesh) as such. It is the body that makes us suffer, and the body that prevents us from attaining true spirituality, which is the aim of virtue. Thus, we are rent by an unending internal conflict, between spirit and the flesh, between virtue and vice. Vice is not just an external temptation but built right into us, and it is our mistake (and that of the great pagan philosophers) to think that happiness is possible in this life by prudent avoidance of temptation. Life is not happiness, but misery, and the true virtues are not prudence and temperance but the single-minded hope for salvation, which alone can be our "final happiness."

In what follows, Augustine continues to widen the dichotomy between the heavenly and the earthly cities, between spirit and the flesh. Prudence is that virtue that enables us to avoid the evil that surrounds us and, more ominously, is in us. But even if we avoid and abstain from evil, our lives are not happy and it is no wisdom (as many of the ancients argued) to see past the evils and misfortunes of life or to escape them even at one's own hand. Rather than pointing to the possibility of attaining happiness in this life, the advice of the ancients leads Augustine to draw the reverse conclusion—that earthly happiness is impossible. For virtue "holds the highest place among human good things," yet its goodness consists in its ability to fight off the vices. In other words, the very best life has to offer exists only to battle that which makes life miserable. Thus, if the highest possible human attainment necessarily involves misery, misery in this life is inevitable.

Finally, virtue itself, which is not among the primary objects of nature, but succeeds to them as the result of learning, though it holds the highest place among human good things, what is its occupation save to wage perpetual war with vices,—not those that are outside of us, but within; not other men's, but our own,—a war which is waged especially by that virtue which the Greeks call σωφροσύνη and we temperance, and which bridles carnal lusts, and prevents them from winning the consent of the spirit to wicked deeds? For we must not fancy that there is no vice in us, when, as the apostle says, "The flesh lusteth against the spirit" (Gal. 5:17); for to this vice there is a contrary virtue, when, as the same writer says, "The spirit lusteth against the flesh." "For these two," he says, "are contrary one to the other, so that you cannot do the things which you would." But what is it we wish to do when we seek to attain the supreme good, unless that the flesh should cease to lust against the spirit, and that there be no vice in us against which the spirit may lust? And as we cannot attain to this in the present life, however ardently we desire it, let us by God's help accomplish at least this, to preserve the soul from succumbing and yielding to the flesh that lusts against it, and to refuse our consent to the perpetration of sin. Far be it from us, then, to fancy that while we are still engaged in this intestine war, we have already found the happiness which we seek to reach by victory. And who is there so wise that he has no conflict at all to maintain against his vices?

What shall I say of that virtue which is called prudence? Is not all its vigilance spent in the discernment of good from evil things, so that no mistake may be admitted about what we should desire and what avoid? And thus it is itself a proof that we are in the midst of evils, or that evils are in us; for it teaches us that it is an evil to consent to sin, and a good to refuse this consent. And yet this evil, to which prudence teaches and temperance enables us not to consent, is removed from this life neither by prudence nor by temperance. And justice, whose office it is to render to every man his due, whereby there is in man himself a certain just order of nature, so that the soul is subjected to God, and the flesh to the soul, and consequently both soul and flesh to God,—does not this virtue demonstrate that it is as yet rather labouring towards its end than resting in its finished work? For the soul is so much the less subjected to God as it is less occupied with the thought of God; and the flesh is so much the less subjected to the spirit as it lusts more vehemently against the spirit. So long, therefore, as we are beset by this weakness, this plague, this disease, how shall we dare to say that we are safe? And if not safe, then how can we be already enjoying our final beatitude? Then that virtue which goes by the name of fortitude is the plainest proof of the ills of life, for it is these ills which it is compelled to bear patiently. And this holds good, no matter though the ripest wisdom co-exists with it. And I am at a loss to understand how the Stoic philosophers can presume to say that these are no ills, though at the same time they allow the wise man to commit suicide and pass out of this life if they become so grievous that he cannot or ought not to endure them. But such is the stupid pride of these men who fancy that the supreme good can be found in this life, and that they can become happy by their own resources, that their wise man, or at least the man whom they fancifully depict as such, is always happy, even though he become blind, deaf, dumb, mutilated, racked with pains, or suffer any conceivable calamity such as may compel him to make away with himself; and they are not ashamed to call the life that is beset with these evils happy. O happy life, which seeks the aid of death to end it! If it is happy, let the wise man remain in it; but if these ills drive him out of it, in what sense is it happy? Or how can they say that these are not evils which conquer the virtue of fortitude, and force it not only to yield, but so to rave that it in one breath calls life happy and recommends it to be given up? For who is so blind as not to see that if it were happy it would not be fled from? And if they say we should flee from it on account of the infirmities that beset it, why then do they not lower their pride and acknowledge that it is miserable? Was it, I would ask, fortitude or weakness which prompted Cato to kill himself? For he would not have done so had he not been too weak to endure Caesar's victory. Where, then, is his fortitude? It has yielded, it has succumbed, it has been so thoroughly overcome as to abandon, forsake, flee this happy life. Or was it no longer happy? Then it was miserable. How, then, were these not evils which made life miserable, and a thing to be escaped from?

And therefore those who admit that these are evils, as the Peripatetics do, and the Old Academy, the sect which Varro advocates, express a more intelligible doctrine; but theirs also is a surprising mistake, for they contend that this is a happy life which is beset by these evils, even though they be so great that he who endures them should commit suicide to escape them. "Pains and anguish of body," says Varro, "are evils, and so much the worse in proportion to their severity; and to escape them you must quit this life." What life, I pray? This life, he says, which is oppressed by such evils. Then it is happy in the midst of these very evils on account of which you say we must quit it? Or do you call it happy because you are at liberty to escape these evils by death? What, then, if by some secret judgment of God you were held fast and not permitted to die, nor suffered to live without these evils? In that case, at least, you would say that such a life was miserable. It is soon relinquished, no doubt, but this does not make it not miserable; for were it eternal, you yourself would pronounce it miserable. Its brevity, therefore, does not clear it of misery; neither ought it to be called happiness because it is a brief misery. Certainly there is a mighty force in these evils which compel a man—according to them, even a wise man—to cease to be a man that he may escape them, though they say, and say truly, that it is as it were the first and strongest demand of nature that a man cherish himself, and naturally therefore avoid death, and should so stand his own friend as to wish and vehemently aim at continuing to exist as a living creature, and subsisting in this union of soul and body. There is a mighty force in these evils to overcome this natural instinct by which death is by every means and with all a man's efforts avoided, and to overcome it so completely that what was avoided is desired, sought after, and if it cannot in any other way be obtained, is inflicted by the man on himself. There is a mighty force in these evils which make fortitude a homicide,—if indeed, that is to be called fortitude which is so thoroughly overcome by these evils, that it not only cannot preserve by patience the man whom it undertook to govern and defend, but is itself obliged to kill him. The wise man, I admit, ought to bear death with patience, but when it is inflicted by another. If, then, as those men maintain, he is obliged to inflict it on himself, certainly it must be owned that the ills which compel him to this are not only evils, but intolerable evils. The life, then, which is either subject to accidents, or environed with evils so considerable and grievous, could never have been called happy, if the men who give it this name had condescended to yield to the truth, and to be conquered by valid arguments, when they inquired after the happy life, as they yield to unhappiness, and are overcome by overwhelming evils, when they put themselves to death, and if they had not fancied that the supreme good was to be found in this mortal life; for the very virtues of this life, which are certainly its best and most useful possessions, are all the more telling proofs of its miseries in proportion as they are helpful against the violence of its dangers, toils, and woes. For if these are true virtues,—and such cannot exist save in those who have true piety,—they do not profess to be able to deliver the men who possess them from all miseries; for true virtues tell no such lies, but they profess that by the hope of the future world this life, which is miserably involved in the many and great evils of this world, is happy as it is also safe. For if not yet safe, how could it be happy? And therefore the Apostle Paul, speaking not of men without prudence, temperance, fortitude, and justice, but of those whose lives were regulated by true piety, and whose virtues were therefore true, says, "For we are saved by hope: now hope which is seen is not hope; for what a man seeth, why doth he yet hope for? But if we hope for that we see not, then do we with patience wait for it" (Rom. 8:24). As, therefore, we are saved, so we are made happy by hope. And as we do not as yet possess a present, but look for a future salvation, so is it with our happiness, and this "with patience"; for we are encompassed with evils, which we ought patiently to endure, until we come to the ineffable enjoyment of unmixed good; for there shall be no longer anything to endure. Salvation, such as it shall be in the world to come, shall itself be our final happiness. And this happiness these philosophers refuse to believe in, because they do not see it, and attempt to fabricate for themselves a happiness in this life, based upon a virtue which is as deceitful as it is proud.

Augustine continues to remind us of the inevitable unhappiness of (this) life. And the inevitability of human misery has, for Augustine, great normative value. It points us in the right direction ethically speaking: the next world. The impossibility of earthly happiness shows us not only why it is pointless to seek fulfillment on earth, but why it is important to act in such a way in this life that we can find fulfillment in the next. Thus, earthly misery shows us both the limits and the possibilities of human action.

Hell upon Earth: From Book XXII

That the whole human race has been condemned in its first origin, this life itself, if life it is to be called, bears witness by the host of cruel ills with which it is filled. Is not this proved by the profound and dreadful ignorance which produces all the errors that enfold the children of Adam, and from which no man can be delivered without toil, pain, and fear? Is it not proved by his love of so many vain and hurtful things, which produces gnawing cares, disquiet, griefs, fears, wild joys, quarrels, law-suits, wars, treasons, angers, hatreds, deceit, flattery, fraud, theft, robbery, perfidy, pride, ambition, envy, murders, parricides, cruelty, ferocity, wickedness, luxury, insolence, impudence, shamelessness, fornications, adulteries, incests, and the numberless uncleannesses and unnatural acts of both sexes, which it is shameful so much as to mention; sacrileges, heresies, blasphemies, perjuries, oppression of the innocent, calumnies, plots, falsehoods, false witnessings, unrighteous judgments, violent deeds, plunderings, and whatever similar wickedness has found its way into the lives of men, though it cannot find its way into the conception of pure minds? These are indeed the crimes of wicked men, yet they spring from that root of error and misplaced love which is born with every son of Adam. . . .

Who can conceive the number and severity of the punishments which afflict the human race,—pains which are not only the accompaniment of the wickedness of godless men, but are a part of the human condition and the common misery,—what fear and what grief are caused by bereavement and mourning, by losses and condemnations, by fraud and falsehood, by false suspicions, and all the crimes and wicked deeds of other men? For at their hands we suffer robbery, captivity, chains, imprisonment, exile, torture, mutilation, loss of sight, the violation of chastity to satisfy the lust of the oppressor, and many other dreadful evils. What numberless casualties threaten our bodies from without,—extremes of heat and cold, storms, floods, inundations, lightning, thunder, hail, earthquakes, houses falling; or from the stumbling, or shying, or vices of horses; from countless poisons in fruit, water, air, animals; from the painful or even deadly bites of wild animals; from the madness which a mad dog communicates, so that even the animal which of all others is most gentle and friendly to its own master, becomes an object of intenser fear than a lion or dragon, and the man whom it has by chance infected with this pestilential contagion becomes so rabid, that his parents, wife, children, dread him more than any wild beast! What disasters are suffered by those who travel by land or sea! What man can go out of his own house without being exposed on all hands to unforeseen accidents? Returning home sound in limb, he slips on his own door-step, breaks his leg, and never recovers. What can seem safer than a man sitting in his chair? Eli the priest fell from his, and broke his neck. How many accidents do farmers, or rather all men, fear that the crops may suffer from the weather, or the soil, or the ravages of destructive animals? Commonly they feel safe when the crops are gathered and housed. Yet, to my certain knowledge, sudden floods have driven the labourers away, and swept the barns clean of the finest harvest. Is innocence a sufficient protection against the various assaults of demons? That no man might think so, even baptized infants, who are certainly unsurpassed in innocence, are sometimes so tormented, that God, who permits it, teaches us hereby to bewail the calamities of this life, and to desire the felicity of the life to come. As to bodily diseases, they are so numerous that they cannot all be contained even in medical books. And in very many, or almost all of them, the cures and remedies are themselves tortures, so that men are delivered from a pain that destroys by a cure that pains. Has not the madness of thirst driven men to drink human urine, and even their own? Has not hunger driven men to eat human flesh, and that the flesh not of bodies found dead, but of bodies slain for the purpose? Have not the fierce pangs of famine driven mothers to eat their own children, incredibly savage as it seems? In fine, sleep itself, which is justly called repose, how little of repose there sometimes is in it when disturbed with dreams and visions; and with what terror is the wretched mind overwhelmed by the appearances of things which are so presented, and which, as it were, so stand out before the senses, that we cannot distinguish them from realities! How wretchedly do false appearances distract men in certain diseases! With what astonishing variety of appearances are even healthy men sometimes deceived by evil spirits, who produce these delusions for the sake of perplexing the senses of their victims, if they cannot succeed in seducing them to their side!

From this hell upon earth there is no escape, save through the grace of the Saviour Christ, our God and Lord. The very name Jesus shows this, for it means Saviour; and He saves us especially from passing out of this life into a more wretched and eternal state, which is rather a death than a life. For in this life, though holy men and holy pursuits afford us great consolations, yet the blessings which men crave are not invariably bestowed upon them, lest religion should be cultivated for the sake of these temporal advantages, while it ought rather to be cultivated for the sake of that other life from which all evil is excluded. . . .

Finally, Augustine contrasts this life of misery to the eternal happiness of Heaven (the city of God), which he compares to an endless "Sabbath"—the day of rest, free from toil and the hardships of life. In the actual city of God (Heaven), there will be no grief, no fear, no pain, but only love and joy. However, for those who live in the city of God in this life (that part of the heavenly city "which sojourns on earth and lives by faith"), such emotions are entirely appropriate, for how else should one respond to the misery one finds in this life?

No Peace of Mind in This Life: From Book XIV

According to the sacred Scriptures and sound doctrine, the citizens of the holy city of God, who live according to God in the pilgrimage of this life, both fear and desire, and grieve and rejoice. And because their love is rightly placed, all these affections of theirs are right. They fear eternal punishment, they desire eternal life; they grieve because they themselves groan within themselves, waiting for the adoption, the redemption of their body (Rom. 8:23); they rejoice in hope, because there "shall be brought to pass the saying that is written, Death is swallowed up in victory" (1 Cor. 15:54). In like manner they fear to sin, they desire to persevere; they grieve in sin, they rejoice in good works. . . .

But since these affections, when they are exercised in a becoming way, follow the guidance of right reason, who will dare to say that they are diseases or vicious passions. . . . So long as we wear the infirmity of this life, we are rather worse men than better if we have none of these emotions at all. For the apostle vituperated and abominated some who, as he said, were "without natural affection" (Rom. 1:31). The sacred Psalmist also found fault with those of whom he said, "I looked for some to lament with me, and there was none" (Ps. 69:30). For to be quite free from pain while we are in this place of misery is only purchased, as one of this world's literati perceived and remarked, at the price of blunted sensibilities both of mind and body. And therefore that which the Greeks call *apatheia,* and what the Latins call, if their language would allow them, *impassibilitas,* if it be taken to mean an impassibility of spirit and not of body, or, in other words, a freedom from those emotions which are contrary to reason and disturb the mind, then it is obviously a good and most desirable quality, but it is not one which is attainable in this life. For the words of the apostle are the confession, not of the common herd, but of the eminently pious, just, and holy men: "If we say we have no sin, we deceive ourselves, and the truth is not in us" (1 John 1:8). When there shall be no sin in a man, then there shall be this *apatheia.* At present it is enough if we live without crime; and he who thinks he lives without sin puts aside not sin, but pardon. And if that is to be called apathy, where the mind is the subject of no emotion, then who would not consider this insensibility to be worse than all vices? It may, indeed, reasonably be maintained that the perfect blessedness we hope for shall be free from all sting of fear or sadness; but who that is not quite lost to truth would say that neither love nor joy shall be experienced there? But if by apathy a condition be meant in which no fear terrifies nor any pain annoys, we must in this life renounce such a state if we would live according to God's will, but may hope to enjoy it in that blessedness which is promised as our eternal condition.

And since this is so,—since we must live a good life in order to attain to a blessed life,—a good life has all these affections right, a bad life has them wrong. But in the blessed life eternal there will be love and joy, not only right, but also assured; but fear and grief there will be none. Whence it already appears in some sort what manner of persons the citizens of the city of God must be in this their pilgrimage, who live after the spirit, not after the flesh,—that is to say, according to God, not according to man,—and what manner of persons they shall be also in that immortality whither they are journeying. And the city or society of the wicked, who live not according to God, but according to man, and who accept the doctrines of men or devils in the worship of a false and contempt of the true divinity, is shaken with those wicked emotions as by diseases and disturbances. And if there be some of its citizens who seem to restrain and, as it were, temper those passions, they are so elated with ungodly pride, that their disease is as much greater as their pain is less. And if some, with a vanity monstrous in proportion to its rarity, have become enamoured of themselves because they can be stimulated and excited by no emotion, moved or bent by no affection, such persons rather lose all humanity than obtain true tranquillity. For a thing is not necessarily right because it is inflexible, nor healthy because it is insensible.

What the Righteous Wish For: From Book XIV

We see that no one lives as he wishes but the blessed, and that no one is blessed but the righteous. But even the righteous himself does not live as he wishes, until he has arrived where he cannot die, be deceived, or injured, and until he is assured that this shall be his eternal condition. For this nature demands; and nature is not fully and perfectly blessed till it attains what it seeks. But what man is at present able to live as he wishes, when it is not in his power so much as to live? He wishes to live, he is compelled to die. How, then, does he live as he wishes who does not live as long as he wishes? Or if he wishes to die, how can he live as he wishes, since he does not wish even to live? Or if he wishes to die, not because he dislikes life, but that after death he may live better, still he is not yet living as he wishes, but only has the prospect of so living when, through death, he reaches that which he wishes. But admit that he lives as he wishes, because he has done violence to himself, and forced himself not to wish what he cannot obtain, and to wish only what he can (as Terence has it, "Since you cannot do what you will, will what you can"), is he therefore blessed because he is patiently wretched? For a blessed life is possessed only by the man who loves it. If it is loved and possessed, it must necessarily be more ardently loved than all besides; for whatever else is loved for the sake of the blessed life. And if it is loved as it deserves to be,—and the man is not blessed who does not love the blessed life as it deserves,—then he who so loves it but wish it to be eternal. Therefore it shall then only be blessed when it is eternal.

Of the Eternal Felicity of the City of God, and of the Perpetual Sabbath: From Book XXII

How great shall be that felicity, which shall be tainted with no evil, which shall lack no good, and which shall afford leisure for the praises of God, who shall be all in all! For I know not what other employment there can be where no lassitude shall slacken activity, nor any want stimulate to labour. I am admonished also by the sacred song, in which I read or hear the words, "Blessed are they that dwell in Thy house, O Lord; they will be still praising Thee." All the members and organs of the incorruptible body, which now we see to be suited to various necessary uses, shall contribute to the praises of God; for in that life necessity shall have no place, but full, certain, secure, everlasting felicity. For all those parts of the bodily harmony, which are distributed through the whole body, within and without, and of which I have just been saying that they at present elude our observation, shall then be discerned; and, along with the other great and marvellous discoveries which shall then kindle rational minds in praise of the great Artificer, there shall be the enjoyment of a beauty which appeals to the reason. What power of movement such bodies shall possess, I have not the audacity rashly to define, as I have not the ability to conceive. Nevertheless I will say that in any case, both in motion and at rest, they shall be, as in their appearance, seemly; for into that state nothing which is unseemly shall be admitted. One thing is certain, the body shall forthwith be wherever the spirit wills, and the spirit shall will nothing which is unbecoming either to the spirit or to the body. True honour shall be there, for it shall be denied to none who is worthy, nor yielded to any unworthy; neither shall any unworthy person so much as sue for it, for none but the worthy shall be there. True peace shall be there, where no one shall suffer opposition either from himself or any other. God Himself, who is the Author of virtue, shall there be its reward; for, as there is nothing greater or better, He has promised Himself. What else was meant by His word through the prophet, "I will be your God, and ye shall be my people" (Lev. 26:12), than, I shall be their satisfaction, I shall be all that men honourably desire,—life, and health, and nourishment, and plenty, and glory, and honour, and peace, and all good things? This, too, is the right interpretation of the saying of the apostle, "That God may be all in all" (1 Cor. 15:28). He shall be the end of our desires who shall be seen without end, loved without cloy, praised without weariness. This outgoing of affection, this employment, shall certainly be, like eternal life itself, common to all.

But who can conceive, not to say describe, what degrees of honour and glory shall be awarded to the various degrees of merit? Yet it cannot be doubted that there shall be degrees. And in that blessed city there shall be this great blessing, that no inferior shall envy any superior, as now the archangels are not envied by the angels, because no one will wish to be what he has not received, though bound in strictest concord with him who has received; as in the body the finger does not seek to be the eye, though both members are harmoniously included in the complete structure of the body. And thus, along with his gift, greater or less, each shall receive this further gift of contentment to desire no more than he has.

Neither are we to suppose that because sin shall have no power to delight them, free will must be withdrawn. It will, on the contrary, be all the more truly free, because set free from delight in sinning to take unfailing delight in not sinning. For the first freedom of will which man received when he was created upright consisted in an ability not to sin, but also in an ability to sin; whereas this last freedom of will shall be superior, inasmuch as it shall not be able to sin.

This, indeed, shall not be a natural ability, but the gift of God. For it is one thing to be God, another thing to be a partaker of God. God by nature cannot sin, but the partaker of God receives this inability from God. And in this divine gift there was to be observed this gradation, that man should first receive a free will by which he was able not to sin, and at last a free will by which he was not able to sin,—the former being adapted to the acquiring of merit, the latter to the enjoying of the reward. But the nature thus constituted, having sinned when it had the ability to do so, it is by a more abundant grace that is delivered so as to reach that freedom in which it cannot sin. For as the first immortality which Adam lost by sinning consisted in his being able not to die, while the last shall consist in his not being able to die, so the first free will consisted in his being able not to sin, the last in his not being able to sin. And thus piety and justice shall be as indefeasible as happiness. For certainly by sinning we lost both piety and happiness; but when we lost happiness, we did not lose the love of it. Are we to say that God Himself is not free because He cannot sin? In that city, then, there shall be free will, one in all the citizens, and indivisible in each, delivered from all ill, filled with all good, enjoying indefeasibly the delights of eternal joys, oblivious of sins, oblivious of sufferings, and yet not so oblivious of its deliverance as to be ungrateful to its Deliverer.

The soul, then, shall have an intellectual remembrance of its past ills; but, so far as regards sensible experience, they shall be quite forgotten. For a skillful physician knows, indeed, professionally almost all diseases; but experimentally he is ignorant of a great number which he himself has never suffered from. As, therefore, there are two ways of knowing evil things,—one by mental insight, the other by sensible experience, for it is one thing to understand all vices by the wisdom of a cultivated mind, another to understand them by the foolishness of an abandoned life,—so also there are two ways of forgetting evils. For a well-instructed and learned man forgets them one way, and he who has experimentally suffered from them forgets them another,—the former by neglecting what he has learned, the latter by escaping what he has suffered. And in this latter way the saints shall forget their past ills, for they shall have so thoroughly escaped them all, that they shall be quite blotted out of their experience. But their intellectual knowledge, which shall be great, shall keep them acquainted not only with their own past woes, but with the eternal sufferings of the lost. For if they were not to know that they had been miserable, how could they, as the Psalmist says, for ever sing the mercies of God? Certainly that city shall have no greater joy than the celebration of the grace of Christ, who redeemed us by His blood. There shall be accomplished the words of the psalm, "Be still, and know that I am God" (Ps. 66:10). There shall be the great Sabbath which has no evening, which God celebrated among His first works, as it is written, "And God rested on the seventh day from all His works which He had made. And God blessed the seventh day, and sanctified it; because that in it He had rested from all His work which God began to make" (Gen. 2:2,3). For we shall ourselves be the seventh day, when we shall be filled and replenished with God's blessing and sanctification. There shall we be still, and know that He is God; that He is that which we ourselves aspired to be when we fell away from Him, and listened to the voice of the seducer, "Ye shall be as Gods" (Gen. 3:5), and so abandoned God, who would have made us as gods, not by deserting Him, but by participating in Him. For without Him what have we accomplished, save to perish in His anger? But when we are restored by Him, and perfected with greater grace, we shall have eternal leisure to see that He is God, for we shall be full of Him when He shall be all in all. For even our good works, when they are understood to be rather His than ours, are imputed to us that we may enjoy this Sabbath rest. For if we attribute them to ourselves, they shall be servile; for it is said of the Sabbath, "Ye shall do no servile work in it." Wherefore also it is said by Ezekiel the prophet, "And I gave them my Sabbaths to be a sign between me and them, that they might know that I am the Lord who sanctify them." This knowledge shall be perfected when we shall be perfectly at rest, and shall perfectly know that He is God.

This Sabbath shall appear still more clearly if we count the ages as days, in accordance with the periods of time defined in Scripture, for that period will be found to be the seventh. The first age, as the first day, extends from Adam to the deluge; the second from the deluge to Abraham, equalling the first, not in length of time, but in the number of generations, there being ten in each. From Abraham to the advent of Christ there are, as the evangelist Matthew calculates, three periods, in each of which are fourteen generations—one period from Abraham to David, a second from David to the captivity, a third from the captivity to the birth of Christ in the flesh. There are thus five ages in all. The sixth is now passing, and cannot be measured by any number of generations, as it has been said, "It is not for you to know the times, which the Father hath put in His own power." After this period God shall rest as on the seventh day, when He shall give us (who shall be the seventh day) rest in Himself. But there is not now space to treat of these ages; suffice it to say that the seventh shall be our Sabbath, which shall be brought to a close, not by evening, but by the Lord's day, as an eighth and eternal day, consecrated by the resurrection of Christ, and prefiguring the eternal repose not only of the spirit, but also of the body. There we shall rest and see, see and love, love and praise. This is what shall be in the end without end. For what other end do we propose to ourselves than to attain to the kingdom of which there is no end?

DISCUSSION

For Augustine, faith is the most important element in a good life. Given the impossibility of achieving happiness on earth, the best we can do is hope for joy in the next life. But the only way of attaining such joy is to live the life of the faithful. Augustine's ethical system, then, is governed almost entirely by hope for the future in conjunction with rules—issued primarily by the Church—on how to get there. The person with faith is consequently well on the road to salvation and the eternal happiness that accompanies it. But faith alone is not sufficient to account for the details of ethical life. We know that God wants us to promote good and avoid what is evil, but what is good, and what is evil? In other words, knowing all values lie with God and holding God Himself as the highest Good *(summum bonum)* still leaves open the questions, What should one do in this life? How should one live? How does one do God's will, in addition to having faith in him? Augustine may have disagreed with Pelagius about the importance of good works, but nevertheless the way we behave in the details of life is as important to Augustine as to Aristotle. Where does our knowledge of these details—our knowledge of the Christian virtues—come from? How does faith in God entail an ethics that we mortals can know and thus act upon?

In one of his early dialogues—*Euthyphro*—Plato has Socrates debating the suggestion that "the Good is what the gods find pious." In Augustine's neo-Platonic Christian ethics, we might simply translate this as "the Good is what God wills." But this suggestion contains an essential ambiguity; it might mean: Whatever God wills (whatever the gods find pious) is good. Or it might mean: God always wills the Good (the gods always find the Good to be pious). In the first case, it is the fact that God wills something (for example, chastity or charity) that makes it good. In the second case, something is already good, and God wills it because it is good and, just as important, because He is (infinitely) good.

This distinction makes an enormous practical difference to us. Our answer to the question posed in the *Euthyphro* will determine how we go about assessing what is required of the faithful, or the good, in this life. If the Good is prior to God's will—if God wills something *because* it is already good—then although knowing what He wills will give us important hints regarding the nature of the Good, such knowledge will not necessarily give us the whole story. Rather we will have to look beyond God's will. But this simply brings back to the original question: What is good, and how do we know it? Although God's will may provide guidance, it does not on this view offer answers.

If, on the other hand, the Good is simply what God wills, gaining knowledge of good and evil is an entirely different matter. Our ethical categories are determined by what God wills, and that is the end of the matter. (As we shall see, this approach is plagued by the problem of understanding *why* God would will certain things, but that is another issue.) However, it then becomes of the utmost importance that we can know God's will. Where God gives us explicit commands (for example, in the scriptures, or through Moses, or, occasionally, through direct communication to some saintly figure), God's will is presumably straightforward (although serious problems of interpretation remain—as the whole history of Christianity has demonstrated in an often violent way). But even where God's will is seemingly explicit and straightforward—for example, in the Ten Commandments—the problem remains that we must interpret those commandments and understand their qualifications (for example, understand in what circumstances one can kill, despite the clarity of the commandment, "Thou shalt not kill").

We are therefore left with a deficit of knowledge under either interpretation of the connection between God's will and the Good. If the Good is independent of God's will, it remains for us to discover it, with or without the help of God. Alternatively, if God's will is prior to the Good (if His willing something makes it good), we would have to have clear guidelines for the interpretation of that will, something that has been notoriously lacking in all ages. The essential concerns of ethics are not resolved by religion; they are only given an infinitely larger stage on which to play their crucial roles in our lives and a divine realm of judgment, rewards, and punishments to give them even more weight and significance.

Having sharply distinguished the "city" of the secular and the "city" of God and so emphasized the misery found in the former, Augustine finds himself confronting what is probably the most difficult single problem for any believer in God's goodness: the source and origin of the misery in the world. This "Problem of Evil" is fundamental to Christian ethics and to any ethical system that believes in a powerful God who watches over the world. What cannot be denied—and Augustine certainly never questions it—is that there is evil in the world. There is suffering, there is misfortune, there is tragedy. But is God, the creator of the world, therefore responsible for the existence of evil? How could a caring, compassionate God allow this to be? One might think of the problem as a kind of paradox: Assuming that God is benevolent, all-knowing, and all-powerful, He would and could certainly prevent the evil in the world. It would seem that either He doesn't really care about human suffering, or He doesn't know about it (He lacks "prescience" or "foreknowledge" as Augustine puts it), or He is unable to do anything about it. It is a problem that has vexed and troubled believers for many centuries, and attempted solutions have varied from the argument that, appearances aside, this is in fact "the best of all possible worlds" (Leibniz, in the seventeenth century) to the more American idea that "he's too busy" (Rabbi Kushner in the twentieth century, in *Why Bad Things Happen to Good People*). But the most profound and provocative answer to the problem of evil was offered by Augustine, who formulated the problem itself in its classical version. Augustine argued that our own freedom, given to us as a gift by God, makes us responsible for the evil in the world. To be sure, we must distinguish between those "natural" evils ("acts of God") that befall us and those that we clearly bring upon ourselves. But it is human nature, not God, that must be confronted in our effort to understand the unhappiness of human life.

Book V

> But, let these perplexing debatings and disputations of the philosophers go on as they may, we, in order that we may confess the most high and true God Himself, do confess His will, supreme power, and prescience. Neither let us be afraid lest, after all, we do not do by will that which we do by will, because He, whose foreknowledge is infallible, foreknew that we would do it. It was this which Cicero was afraid of, and therefore opposed foreknowledge. The Stoics also maintained that all things do not come to pass by necessity, although they contended that all things happen according to destiny. What is it, then, that Cicero feared in the prescience of future things? Doubtless it was this—that if all future things have been foreknown, they will happen in the order in which they have been foreknown; and if they come to pass in this order, there is a certain order of things foreknown by God; and if a certain order of things, then a certain order of causes, for nothing can happen which is not preceded by some efficient cause. But if there is a certain order of causes according to which

everything happens which does happen, then by fate, says he, all things happen which do happen. But if this be so, then is there nothing in our own power, and there is no such thing as freedom of will; and if we grant that, says he, the whole economy of human life is subverted. In vain are laws enacted. In vain are reproaches, praises, chidings, exhortations had recourse to; and there is no justice whatever in the appointment of rewards for the good, and punishments for the wicked. And that consequences so disgraceful, and absurd, and pernicious to humanity may not follow, Cicero chooses to reject the foreknowledge of future things, and shuts up the religious mind to this alternative, to make choice between two things, either that something is in our own power, or that there is foreknowledge—both of which cannot be true; but if the one is affirmed, the other is thereby denied. He therefore, like a truly great and wise man, and one who consulted very much and very skilfully for the good of humanity, of those two chose the freedom of the will, to confirm which he denied the foreknowledge of future things; and thus, wishing to make men free, he makes them sacrilegious. But the religious mind chooses both, confesses both, and maintains both by the faith of piety. But how so? says Cicero; for the knowledge of future things being granted, there follows a chain of consequences which ends in this, that there can be nothing depending on our own free wills. And further, if there is anything depending on our wills, we must go backwards by the same steps of reasoning till we arrive at the conclusion that there is no foreknowledge of future things. For we go backwards through all the steps in the following order:— If there is free will, all things do not happen according to fate; if all things do not happen according to fate, there is not a certain order of causes; and if there is not a certain order of causes, neither is there a certain order of things foreknown by God—for things cannot come to pass except they are preceded by efficient causes—but, if there is no fixed and certain order of causes foreknown by God, all things cannot be said to happen according as He foreknew that they would happen. And further, if it is not true that all things happen just as they have been foreknown by Him, there is not, says he, in God any foreknowledge of future events.

Now, against the sacrilegious and impious darings of reason, we assert both that God knows all things before they come to pass, and that we do by our free will whatsoever we know and feel to be done by us only because we will it. But that all things come to pass by fate, we do not say; nay we affirm that nothing comes to pass by fate; for we demonstrate that the name of fate, as it is wont to be used by those who speak of fate, meaning thereby the position of the stars at the time of each one's conception or birth, is an unmeaning word, for astrology itself is a delusion. But an order of causes in which the highest efficiency is attributed to the will of God, we neither deny nor do we designate it by the name of fate, unless, perhaps, we may understand fate to mean that which is spoken, deriving it from *fari*, to speak; for we cannot deny that it is written in the sacred Scriptures, "God hath spoken once; these two things have I heard, that power belongeth unto God. Also unto Thee, O God, belongeth mercy: for Thou wilt render unto every man according to his works" [Ps. 62:11,12]. Now the expression, "Once hath He spoken," is to be understood as meaning *"immovably,"* that is, unchangeably hath He spoken, inasmuch as He knows unchangeably all things which shall be, and all things which He will do. We might, then, use the word fate in the sense it bears when derived from *fari,* to speak, had it not already come to be understood in another sense, into which I am unwilling that the hearts of men should unconsciously slide. But it does not follow that, though there is for God a certain order of all causes, there must therefore be nothing depending on the free exercise of our own wills, for our wills themselves are included in that order of causes which is certain to God, and is embraced by His foreknowledge, for human wills are also causes of human actions; and He who foreknew all the causes of things would certainly among those causes not have been ignorant of our wills. For even that very concession which Cicero himself makes is enough to refute him in this argument. For what does it help him to say that nothing takes place without a cause, but that every cause is not fatal, there being a fortuitous cause, a natural cause, and a voluntary cause? It is sufficient that he confesses that whatever happens must be preceded by a cause. For we say that those causes which are called fortuitous are not a mere name for the absence of causes, but are only latent, and we attribute them either to the will of the true God, or to that of spirits of some kind or other. And as to natural causes, we by no means separate them from the will of Him who is the author and framer of all nature. But now as to voluntary causes. They are referable either to God, or to angels, or to men, or to animals of whatever description, if indeed those instinctive movements of animals devoid of reason, by which, in accordance with their own nature, they seek or shun various things, are to be called wills. And when I speak of the wills of angels, I mean either the wills of good angels, whom we call the angels of God, or of the wicked angels, whom we call the angels of the devil, or demons. Also by the wills of men I mean the wills either of the good or of the wicked. And from this we conclude that there are no efficient causes of all things which come to pass unless voluntary causes, that is, such as belong to that nature, which is the spirit of life. For the air or wind is called spirit, but, inasmuch as it is a body, it is not the spirit of life. The spirit of life, therefore, which quickens all things, and is the creator of every body, and of every created spirit, is God Himself, the uncreated spirit. In His supreme will resides the power which acts on the wills of all created spirits, helping the good, judging the evil, controlling all, granting power to some, not granting it to others. For, as He is the creator of all natures, so also is He the bestower of all powers, not of all wills; for wicked wills are not from Him, being contrary to nature, which is from Him. As to bodies, they are more subject to wills; some to our wills, by which I mean the wills of all living mortal creatures, but more to the wills of men than of beasts. But all of them are most of all subject to the will of God, to whom all wills also are subject, since they have no power except what He has bestowed upon them. The cause of things, therefore, which makes but is not made, is God; but all other causes both make and are made. Such are all created spirits, and especially the rational. Material causes, therefore, which may rather be said to be made than to make, are not to be reckoned among efficient causes, because they can only do what the wills of spirits do by them. How, then, does an order of causes which is certain to the foreknowledge of God necessitate that there should be nothing which is dependent on our wills, when our wills themselves have a very important place in the order of causes? Cicero, then, contends with those who call this order of causes fatal, or rather designate this order itself by the name of fate; to which we have an abhorrence, especially on account of the word, which men have become accustomed to understand as meaning what is not true. But, whereas he denies that the order of all causes is most certain, and perfectly clear to the prescience of God, we detest his opinion more than the Stoics do. For he either denies that God exists—which, indeed, in an assumed personage, he has laboured to do, in his book *De Natura Deorum*—or if he confesses that He exists, but denies that He is prescient of future things, what is that but just "the fool saying in his heart there is no God?" For one who is not prescient of all future things is not God. Wherefore our wills also have just so much power as God willed and foreknew that they should have; and therefore whatever power they have, they have it within most certain limits; and whatever they are to do, they are most assuredly to do, for He whose fore-knowledge is infallible foreknew that they would have the power to do it, and would do it. Wherefore, if I should choose to apply the name of fate to anything at all, I should rather say that fate belongs to the weaker of two parties, will to the stronger, who has the other in his power, than that the freedom of our will is excluded by that order of causes, which, by an unusual application of the word peculiar to themselves, the Stoics call *Fate*.

Whether Our Wills Are Ruled by Necessity Wherefore, neither is that necessity to be feared, for dread of which the Stoics laboured to make such distinctions among the causes of things as should enable them to rescue certain things from the dominion of necessity, and to subject others to it. Among those things which they wished not to be subject to necessity they placed our wills, knowing that they would not be free if subjected to necessity. For if that is to be called our necessity which is not in our power, but even though we be unwilling effects what it can effect—as, for instance, the necessity of death—it is manifest that our wills by which we live uprightly or wickedly are not under such a necessity; for we do many things which, if we were not willing, we should certainly not do. This is primarily true of the act of willing itself—for if we will, it is; if we will not, it is not—for we should not will if we were unwilling. But if we define necessity to be that according to which we say that it is necessary that anything be of such or such a nature, or be done in such and such a manner, I know not why we should have any dread of that necessity taking away the freedom of our will. For we do not put the life of God or the foreknowledge of God under necessity if we should say that it is necessary that God should live for ever, and foreknow all things; as neither is His power diminished when we say that He cannot die or fall into error—for this is in such a way impossible to Him, that if it were possible for Him, He would be of less power. But assuredly He is rightly called omnipotent, though He can neither die nor fall into error. For He is called omnipotent on account of His doing what He wills, not on account of His suffering what He wills not; for if that should befall Him, He would by no means be omnipotent. Wherefore, He cannot do some things for the very reason that He is omnipotent. So also, when we say that it is necessary that, when we will, we will by free choice, in so saying we both affirm what is true beyond doubt, and do not still subject our wills thereby to a necessity which destroys liberty. Our wills, therefore, exist as wills, and do themselves whatever we do by willing, and which would not be done if we were unwilling. But when any one suffers anything, being unwilling, by the will of another, even in that case will retains its essential validity—we do not mean the will of the party who inflicts the suffering, for we resolve it into the power of God. For if a will should simply exist, but not be able to do what it wills, it would be overborne by a more powerful will. Nor would this be the case unless there had existed will, and that not the will of the other party, but the will of him who willed, but was not able to accomplish what he willed. Therefore, whatsoever a man suffers contrary to his own will, he ought not to attribute to the will of men, or of angels, or of any created spirit, but rather to His will who gives power to wills. It is not the case, therefore, that because God foreknew what would be in the power of our wills, there is for that reason nothing in the power of our wills. For he who foreknew this did not foreknow nothing. Moreover, if He who foreknew what would be in the power of our wills did not foreknow nothing, but something, assuredly, even though He did foreknow, there is something in the power of our wills. Therefore we are by no means compelled, either, retaining the prescience of God, to take away the freedom of the will, or, retaining the freedom of the will, to deny that He is prescient of future things, which is impious. But we embrace both. We faithfully and sincerely confess both. The former, that we may believe well; the latter, that we may live well. For he lives ill who does not believe well concerning God. Wherefore, be it far from us, in order to maintain our freedom, to deny the prescience of Him by whose help we are or shall be free. Consequently, it is not in vain that laws are enacted, and that reproaches, exhortations, praises, and vituperations are had recourse to; for these also He foreknew, and they are of great avail, even as great as He foreknew that they would be of. Prayers, also, are of avail to procure those things which He foreknew that He would grant to those who offered them; and with justice have rewards been appointed for good deeds, and punishments for sins. For a man does not therefore sin because God foreknew that he would sin. Nay, it cannot be doubted but that it is the man himself who sins when he does sin, because He, whose foreknowledge is infallible, foreknew not that fate, or fortune, or something else would sin, but that the man himself would sin, who, if he wills not, sins not. But if he shall not will to sin, even this did God foreknow.

Concerning the Universal Providence of God in the Laws of Which All Things Are Comprehended   Therefore God supreme and true, with His Word and Holy Spirit (which three are one), one God omnipotent, creator and maker of every soul and of every body; by whose gift all are happy who are happy through verity and not through vanity; who made man a rational animal consisting of soul and body, who, when he sinned, neither permitted him to go unpunished, nor left him without mercy; who has given to the good and to the evil, being in common with stones, vegetable life in common with trees, sensuous life in common with brutes, intellectual life in common with angels alone; from whom is every mode, every species, every order; from whom are measure, number, weight; from whom is everything which has an existence in nature, of whatever kind it be, and of whatever value; from whom are the seeds of forms and the forms of seeds, and the motion of seeds and of forms; who gave also to flesh its origin, beauty, health, reproductive fecundity, disposition of members, and the salutary concord of its parts; who also to the irrational soul has given memory, sense, appetite, but to the rational soul, in addition to these, has given intelligence and will; who has not left, not to speak of heaven and earth, angels and men, but not even the entrails of the smallest and most contemptible animal, or the feather of a bird, or the little flower of a plant, or the leaf of a tree, without an harmony, and, as it were, a mutual peace among all its parts;—that God can never be believed to have left the kingdoms of men, their dominations and servitudes, outside of the laws of His providence.

Augustine has been concerned with the question of who is ultimately responsible for the evil that we undoubtedly find in this world. More specifically, he wants to deny the argument made by Cicero that we have to choose between asserting God's foreknowledge on the one hand and human responsibility on the other. Cicero argued that if a supreme being really has foreknowledge of all that will take place, the good as well as the bad, such knowledge implies a causal sequence that is entirely independent of human action. Imagine that you are considering committing a crime. If it is the case that God knows all, He knows (even before you are born) whether you will in fact commit the crime. But if that is true, then (according to Cicero) your deliberations have no real effect. The course of events—including the commission of the crime or failure thereof—is already, as it were, written in stone in the form of God's foreknowledge. In this view, God's foreknowledge necessarily leads to the denial of human control, and hence, human responsibility. And a further consequence of this account is that God, not human beings, is the originator of evil. Not willing to allow that humans have no real control over their actions, Cicero concluded that any sort of prescience, whether of man or a higher being, was unintelligible. Thus, for Cicero foreknowledge precludes moral responsibility and moral responsibility makes foreknowledge impossible.

Clearly, this is not a view that Augustine can accept. If God has no foreknowledge, He lacks perfection. And if He lacks perfection, He is not God. However, neither does Augustine want to give up the notion of human responsibility. Like Cicero, he finds a world without the possibility of praise and blame impossible to accept. Augustine, therefore, needs to reconcile the two, and he does so through the notion of free will. God does in fact know all that will happen, but this need not preclude freedom of action on our part. Our wills can be both free and a part of the sequence of causes that God knows.

Augustine traces the existence of evil back to Adam and Eve, whose willfulness brought about the world of calamity and misery in which we now live. The key to the argument is that human suffering is the result of human choice, not the doing of God as such. And those human choices that lead to evil are not attributable to God because they are a "falling away from Him," rather than an "image of Him." Sin and evil are thus an *absence* of goodness rather than something existing in its own right.

Of the Fall of the First Man, in Whom Nature Was Created Good, and Can Be Restored Only by its Author But because God foresaw all things, and was therefore not ignorant that man also would fall, we ought to consider this holy city in connection with what God foresaw and ordained, and not according to our own ideas, which do not embrace God's ordination. For man, by his sin, could not disturb the divine counsel, nor compel God to change what He had decreed; for God's foreknowledge had anticipated both—that is to say, both how evil the man whom He had created good should become, and what good He Himself should even thus derive from him. For though God is said to change His determinations (so that in a topical sense the Holy Scripture says even that God repented), this is said with reference to man's expectation, or the order of natural causes, and not with reference to that which the Almighty had foreknown that He would do. Accordingly God, as it is written, made man upright, and consequently with a good will. For if he had not had a good will, he could not have been upright. The good will, then, is the work of God; for God created him with it. But the first evil will, which preceded all man's evil acts, was rather a kind of falling away from the work of God to its own works than any positive work. And therefore the acts resulting were evil, not having God, but the will itself for their end; so that the will or the man himself, so far as his will is bad, was as it were the evil tree bringing forth evil fruit. Moreover, the bad will, though it be not in harmony with, but opposed to nature, inasmuch as it is a vice or blemish, yet it is true of it as of all vice, that it cannot exist except in a nature, and only in a nature created out of nothing, and not in that which the Creator has begotten of Himself, as He begot the Word, by whom all things were made. For though God formed man of the dust of the earth, yet the earth itself, and every earthly material, is absolutely created out of nothing; and man's soul, too, God created out of nothing, and joined to the body, when He made a man. But evils are so thoroughly overcome by good, that though they are permitted to exist, for the sake of demonstrating how the most righteous foresight of God can make a good use even of them, yet good can exist without evil, as in the true and supreme God Himself, and as in every invisible and visible celestial creature that exists above this murky atmosphere; but evil cannot exist without good, because the natures in which evil exists, in so far as they are natures, are good. And evil is removed, not by removing any nature, or part of a nature, which had been introduced by the evil, but by healing and correcting that which had been vitiated and depraved. The will, therefore, is then truly free, when it is not the slave of vices and sins. Such was it given us by God; and this being lost by its own fault, can only be restored by Him who was able at first to give it. And therefore the truth says, "If the Son shall make you free, ye shall be free indeed" [John 8:36]; which is equivalent to saying, If the Son shall save you, ye shall be saved indeed. For He is our Liberator, inasmuch as He is our Saviour.

Man then lived with God for his rule in a paradise at once physical and spiritual. For neither was it a paradise only physical for the advantage of the body, and not also spiritual for the advantage of the mind; nor was it only spiritual to afford enjoyment to man by his internal sensations, and not also physical to afford him enjoyment through his external senses. But obviously it was both for both ends. But after that proud and therefore envious angel (of whose fall I have said as much as I was able in the eleventh and twelfth books of this work, as well as that of his fellows, who, from being God's angels, became his angels), preferring to rule with a kind of pomp of empire rather than to be another's subject, fell from the spiritual Paradise, and essaying to insinuate his persuasive guile into the mind of man, whose unfallen condition provoked him to envy now that himself was fallen, he chose the serpent as his mouthpiece in that bodily Paradise in which it and all the other earthly animals were living with those two human beings, the man and his wife, subject to them, and harmless; and he chose the serpent because, being slippery, and moving in tortuous windings, it was suitable for his purpose. And this animal being subdued to his wicked ends by the presence and superior force of his angelic nature, he abused as his instrument, and first tried his deceit upon the woman, making his assault upon the weaker part of that human alliance, that he might gradually gain the whole, and not supposing that the man would readily give ear to him, or be deceived, but that he might yield to the error of the woman. For as Aaron was not induced to agree with the people when they blindly wished him to make an idol, and yet yielded to constraint; and as it is not credible that Solomon was so blind as to suppose that idols should be worshipped, but was drawn over to such sacrilege by the blandishments of women; so we cannot believe that Adam was deceived, and supposed the devil's word to be truth, and therefore transgressed God's law, but that he by the drawings of kindred yielded to the woman, the husband to the wife, the one human being to the only other human being. For not without significance did the apostle say, "And Adam was not deceived, but the woman being deceived was in the transgression" [1 Tim. 2:14]; but he speaks thus, because the woman accepted as true what the serpent told her, but the man could not bear to be severed from his only companion, even though this involved a partnership in sin. He was not on this account less culpable, but sinned with his eyes open. And so the apostle does not say, "He did not sin," but "He was not deceived." For he shows that he sinned when he says, "By one man sin entered into the world" [Rom. 5:12], and immediately after more distinctly, "In the likeness of Adam's transgression." But he meant that those are deceived who do not judge that which they do to be sin; but he knew. Otherwise how were it true "Adam was not deceived"? But having as yet no experience of the divine severity, he was possibly deceived in so far as he thought his sin venial. And consequently he was not deceived as the woman was deceived, but he was deceived as to the judgment which would be passed on his apology: "The woman whom thou gavest to be with me, she gave me, and I did eat" [Gen. 3:12]. What need of saying more? Although they were not both deceived by credulity, yet both were entangled in the snares of the devil, and taken by sin.

Of the Nature of Man's First Sin   If any one finds a difficulty in understanding why other sins do not alter human nature as it was altered by the transgression of those first human beings, so that on account of it this nature is subject to the great corruption we feel and see, and to death, and is distracted and tossed with so many furious and contending emotions, and is certainly far different from what it was before sin, even though it were then lodged in an animal body—if, I say, any one is moved by this, he ought not to think that that sin was a small and light one because it was committed about food, and that not bad nor noxious, except because it was forbidden; for in that spot of singular felicity God could not have created and planted any evil thing. But by the precept He gave, God commended obedience, which is, in a sort, the mother and guardian of all the virtues in the reasonable creature, which was so created that sub-mission is advantageous to it, while the fulfillment of its own will in preference to the Creator's is destruction. And as this commandment enjoining abstinence from one kind of food in the midst of great abundance of other kinds was so easy to keep—so light a burden to the memory—and, above all, found no resistance to its observance in lust, which only afterwards sprung up as the penal consequence of sin, the iniquity of violating it was all the greater in proportion to the ease with which it might have been kept.

That in Adam's Sin an Evil Will Preceded the Evil Act   Our first parents fell into open disobedience because already they were secretly corrupted; for the evil act had never been done had not an evil will preceded it. And what is the origin of our evil will but pride? For "pride is the beginning of sin" [Eccles. 10:13]. And what is pride but the craving for undue exaltation? And this is undue exaltation, when the soul abandons Him to whom it ought to cleave as its end, and becomes a kind of end to itself. This happens when it becomes its own satisfaction. And it does so when it falls away from that unchangeable good which ought to satisfy it more than itself. This falling away is spontaneous; for if the will had remained stedfast in the love of that higher and changeless good by which it was illumined to intelligence and kindled into love, it would not have turned away to find satisfaction in itself, and so become frigid and benighted; the woman would not have believed the serpent spoke the truth, nor would the man have preferred the request of his wife to the command of God, nor have supposed that it was a venial transgression to cleave to the partner of his life even in a partnership of sin. The wicked deed, then—that is to say, the transgression of eating the forbidden fruit—was committed by persons who were already wicked. That "evil fruit" [Matt. 7:18] could be brought forth only by "a corrupt tree." But that the tree was evil was not the result of nature; for certainly it could become so only by the vice of the will, and vice is contrary to nature. Now, nature could not have been depraved by vice had it not been made out of nothing. Consequently, that it is a nature, this is because it is made by God; but that it falls away from Him, this is because it is made out of nothing. But man did not so fall away[1] as to become absolutely nothing; but being turned towards himself, his being became more contracted than it was when he clave to him who supremely is. Accordingly, to exist in himself, that is, to be his own satisfaction after abandoning God, is not quite to become a nonentity, but to ap-

[1]*Deficit.*

proximate to that. And therefore the holy Scriptures designate the proud by another name, "self-pleasers." For it is good to have the heart lifted up, yet not to one's self, for this is proud, but to the Lord, for this is obedient, and can be the act only of the humble. There is, therefore, something in humility which, strangely enough, exalts the heart, and something in pride which debases it. This seems, indeed, to be contradictory, that loftiness should debase and lowliness exalt. But pious humility enables us to submit to what is above us; and nothing is more exalted above us than God; and therefore humility, by making us subject to God, exalts us. But pride, being a defect of nature, by the very act of refusing subjection and revolting from Him who is supreme, falls to a low condition; and then comes to pass what is written: "Thou castedst them down when they lifted up themselves" [Ps. 73:18]. For he does not say, "when they had been lifted up," as if first they were exalted, and then afterwards cast down; but "when they lifted up themselves" even then they were cast down—that is to say, the very lifting up was already a fall. And therefore it is that humility is specially recommended to the city of God as it sojourns in this world, and is specially exhibited in the city of God, and in the person of Christ its King; while the contrary vice of pride, according to the testimony of the sacred writings, specially rules his adversary the devil. And certainly this is the great difference which distinguishes the two cities of which we speak, the one being the society of the godly men, the other of the ungodly, each associated with the angels that adhere to their party, and the one guided and fashioned by love of self, the other by love of God.

The devil, then, would not have ensnared man in the open and manifest sin of doing what God had forbidden, had man not already begun to live for himself. It was this that made him listen with pleasure to the words, "Ye shall be as gods" [Gen. 3:5], which they would much more readily have accomplished by obediently adhering to their supreme and true end than by proudly living to themselves. For created gods are gods not by virtue of what is in themselves, but by a participation of the true God. By craving to be more, man becomes less; and by aspiring to be self-sufficing, he fell away from Him who truly suffices him. Accordingly, this wicked desire which prompts man to please himself as if he were himself light, and which thus turns him away from that light by which, had he followed it, he would himself have become light—this wicked desire, I say, already secretly existed in him, and the open sin was but its consequence. For that is true which is written, "Pride goeth before destruction, and before honour is humility" [Prov. 18:12]; that is to say, secret ruin precedes open ruin, while the former is not counted ruin. For who counts exaltation ruin, though no sooner is the Highest forsaken than a fall is begun? But who does not recognise it as ruin, when there occurs an evident and indubitable transgression of the commandment? And consequently, God's prohibition had reference to such an act as, when committed, could not be defended on any pretence of doing what was righteous. And I make bold to say that it is useful for the proud to fall into an open and indisputable transgression, and so displease themselves, as already, by pleasing themselves, they had fallen. For Peter was in a healthier condition when he wept and was dissatisfied with himself, than when he boldly presumed and satisfied himself. And this is averred by the sacred Psalmist when he says, "Fill their faces with shame, that they may seek Thy name, O Lord;" that is, that they who have pleased themselves in seeking their own glory may be pleased and satisfied with Thee in seeking Thy glory.

And again, Augustine argues that it is our existence as "flesh" that causes our misery, but this should not be taken to mean that the cause of evil is the flesh. We are "corrupted" by the flesh but it is our choices—emanating from the soul—that make us responsible for the evil in the world. The flesh is ultimately the punishment, not the cause, of evil.

That Sin Is Caused Not by the Flesh, but by the Soul, and That the Corruption Contracted from Sin Is Not Sin, but Sin's Punishment But if any one says that the flesh is the cause of all vices and ill conduct, inasmuch as the soul lives wickedly only because it is moved by the flesh, it is certain he has not carefully considered the whole nature of man. For "the corruptible body, indeed, weigheth down the soul" [Wisd. 9:15]. Whence, too, the apostle, speaking of this corruptible body, of which he had shortly before said, "though our outward man perish" [2 Cor. 4:16], says, "We know that if our earthly house of this tabernacle were dissolved, we have a building of God, an house not made with hands, eternal in the heavens. For in this we groan, earnestly desiring to be clothed upon with our house which is from heaven: if so be that being clothed we shall not be found naked. For we that are in this tabernacle do groan, being burdened: not for that we would be unclothed, but clothed upon, that mortality might be swallowed up in life" [2 Cor. 5:1–4]. We are then burdened with this corruptible body; but knowing that the cause of this burdensomeness is not the nature and substance of the body, but its corruption, we do not desire to be deprived of the body, but to be clothed with its immortality. For then, also, there will be a body, but it shall no longer be a burden, being no longer corruptible. At present, then, "the corruptible body presseth down the soul, and the earthly tabernacle weigheth down the mind that museth upon many things," nevertheless they are in error who suppose that all the evils of the soul proceed from the body.

Virgil, indeed, seems to express the sentiments of Plato in the beautiful lines, where he says—

"A fiery strength inspires their lives,

An essence that from heaven derives,

Though clogged in part by limbs of clay,

An the dull 'vesture of decay;'"

but though he goes on to mention the four most common mental emotions—desire, fear, joy, sorrow—with the intention of showing that the body is the origin of all sins and vices, saying—

"Hence wild desires and groveling fears,

And human laughter, human tears,

Immured in dungeon-seeming night,

They look abroad, yet see no light,"

yet we believe quite otherwise. For the corruption of the body, which weighs down the soul, is not the cause but the punishment of the first sin; and it was not the corruptible flesh that made the soul sinful, but the sinful soul that made the flesh corruptible. And though from this corruption of the flesh there arise certain incitements to vice, and indeed vicious desires, yet we must not attribute to the flesh all the vices of a wicked life, in case we thereby clear the devil of all these, for he has no flesh. For though we cannot call the devil a fornicator or drunkard, or ascribe to him any sensual indulgence (though he is the secret instigator and prompter of those who sin in these ways), yet he is exceedingly proud and envious. And this viciousness has so possessed him, that on account of it he is reserved in chains of darkness to everlasting punishment. Now these vices, which have dominion over the devil, the apostle attributes to the flesh, which certainly the devil has not. For he says "hatred, variance, emulations, strife, envying" are the works of the flesh; and of all these evils pride is the origin and head, and it rules in the devil though he has no flesh. For who shows more hatred to the saints? who is more at variance with them? who more envious, bitter, and jealous? And since he exhibits all these works, though he has no flesh, how are they works of the flesh, unless because they are the works of man, who is, as I said, spoken of under the name of flesh? For it is not by having flesh, which the devil has not, but by living according to himself—that is, according to man—that man became like the devil. For the devil too, wished to live according to himself when he did not abide in the truth; so that when he lied, this was not of God, but of himself, who is not only a liar, but the father of lies, he being the first who lied, and the originator of lying as of sin.

Finally, Augustine argues that God cannot be blamed for creating us with wills that make the wrong choices. To create a will is to create it such that it can make independent choices, or in the technical language inherited from Aristotle, it can have no "efficient cause." Again, Augustine's intention is to separate completely the existence of evil from God's creation and rest the responsibility with us.

That We Ought Not to Expect to Find Any Efficient Cause of the Evil Will
Let no one, therefore, look for an efficient cause of the evil will; for it is not efficient, but deficient, as the will itself is not an effecting of something, but a defect. For defection from that which supremely is, to that which has less of being—this is to begin to have an evil will. Now, to seek to discover the causes of these defections—causes, as I have said, not efficient, but deficient—is as if

some one sought to see darkness, or hear silence. Yet both of these are known by us, and the former by means only of the eye, the latter only by the ear; but not by their positive actuality, but by their want of it. Let no one, then, seek to know from me what I know that I do not know; unless he perhaps wishes to learn to be ignorant of that of which all we know is, that it cannot be known. For those things which are known not by their actuality, but by their want of it, are known, if our expression may be allowed and understood, by not knowing them, that by knowing them they may be not known. For when the eyesight surveys objects that strike the sense, it nowhere sees darkness but where it begins not to see. And so no other sense but the ear can perceive silence, and yet it is only perceived by not hearing. Thus, too, our mind perceives intelligible forms by understanding them; but when they are deficient, it knows them by not knowing them; for "who can understand defects?"

DISCUSSION

The problem of evil begins with an apparent paradox: If God is omnipotent, omniscient, and just, then He would prevent undeserved suffering in the world, either by direct intervention (stopping an earthquake before it starts) or by originally creating a world in which the undeserved suffering of its creatures would not be possible. But there is such undeserved suffering in the world—how then can one believe in God? One answer, and an essential part of Augustine's response, is that much of the suffering in the world—including suffering imposed upon otherwise innocent people—is due to our own free will, our own decisions, many of which are motivated by greed and impiety, or "ill-directed love." God might be just, but we are not, and the world is unjust for that reason. But this raises a further question: Even if we are indeed free to choose what we will do—including unjust and even cruel courses of action, God (as omniscient) would certainly know in advance that we would so choose. Thus, either God is not omniscient (he did not know) or he is in an important sense complicitous in our evil, just as someone who knows that an acquaintance is about to commit a crime becomes an accomplice if he or she makes no effort to stop such behavior. One alternative, which Augustine rejects, is the possibility that our evil action may be unpredictable—even to God, for the very nature of causality requires that there be a series of "efficient causes" that can be, and are, known by God. Augustine maintains both that God knows our every action in advance and that we are nevertheless free to choose. He justifies this potentially contradictory view by claiming that evil is "nothing but the want of good," rather than something with positive existence that requires a creator.

These questions remain with us today, and they have force beyond a religious framework. For any action or event, we can look for its cause, and then for the cause of that cause and so on. But if there is such a series of causes that bring about our actions (and can be known by God), then does it make sense to say that we actually "choose" anything at all? We may have an experience of choosing. (Such an experience may be a link in the causal chain or, perhaps, a curious side effect—an "epiphenomenon," the American philosopher William James would later call it—which has nothing to do with the actual necessity of the action itself.) But if our action is necessitated by some sequence of antecedent conditions and events, what sense does it make to say that we could have chosen to do anything other than what we actually did? There have been a number of sophisticated attempts to respond to this question, now entitled "the free will problem," especially in its connection with moral responsibility. Many have disagreed with Augustine's solution, but one part of his answer is uncompromising: even if our actions were necessitated and even if God knows all about them in advance, we cannot and should not blame our sins on fate or fortune but only on ourselves.

Discussion Questions

1. Does the evil and injustice in the world contradict our faith in God? Should it do so? How is it possible to believe in a God who is all-powerful, all-knowing, and good in the face of all the needless suffering in the world?

2. What is "original sin"? What importance does it have for ethics? Why would the theology of good works (advanced by the monk Pelagius, for example) contradict the concept of original sin?

3. What would Augustine have to say about those theologians who claim that God will show his grace to those who believe by making them rich? What changes in Christianity are necessary to even condone—much less encourage—business activity (making a profit, selling one's skills or inventions to the highest bidder, lending money at the highest allowable interest rate)?

4. What is salvation? What are we saved *from?* Why believe in it? What is desirable about it?

5. How do we know what God wills? Do we have to know that God willed it to know that it is good?

6. How convincing do you find Augustine's claim that life on earth is inevitably miserable? Does it really follow from the fact that some misfortune will befall us, that all of earthly life will be unhappy? How is Augustine's ethical theory affected if it turns out that this claim is false?

7. Is Augustine's solution to the problem of evil persuasive? Can you think of an example of a wrong action that is better described as the absence of good rather than the presence of evil?

Study Questions

1. Does good mean "what God wills"? Is this what Augustine is arguing? What problems are there with such a definition? What would happen if God willed evil (for example, commanding Abraham to kill his son)?

2. Why can "happiness" *not* be the "good for man," according to Augustine?

3. What are the "two cities"? In what way are these parallel to Plato's "two worlds" (of everyday life and the Forms, respectively)?

4. The French philosopher Pascal advanced a "wager" that he thought demonstrated the rationality of believing in God. He argued, briefly, that one could choose to believe or not believe; not believing, he acknowledged, had certain secular advantages. Believing "paid off" spectacularly if God actually did exist. In graphic form, here is the bet—with odds—that Pascal is setting out for us:

	God Exists	God Does Not Exist
Believe	Infinite reward	Wasted piety
Not Believe	Infinite punishment	No wasted piety

What would Augustine say about this line of reasoning?

5. What is Augustine's view of virtue, and how does it differ from the one offered by Aristotle?

6. What sort of ethical conclusions does Augustine's view of the impossibility of earthly happiness lead him to draw?

4

Thomas Hobbes

Hobbes was born in 1588, graduated from Oxford University, and entered into a lifetime of study in the sciences and mathematics. He earned his living as a tutor (for a while, he was tutor to Prince Charles, the future Charles II of England). He often traveled to Europe and was a friend of Galileo and Gassendi, the leading scientists of the time. His early political writings had already gotten him into trouble, and so he prudently left England in the 1640s for France. But his politics also endangered him in France, and his irreligious materialism caused him to be condemned by the French church as well. Accordingly, he went back to England in 1651, when he published *Leviathan,* and lived relatively peacefully until his death in 1679.

For Plato and for Augustine, the Good in ethics had to be defined through metaphysics—by reference to a transcendent Idea or Form of "the Good" or by appeal to a transcendent almighty God. For Aristotle, the Good was identified as "the good for man," by appeal to human happiness. However, happiness was in turn defined by the *telos* of man, that activity of which humans are uniquely or best capable. Thus, not even Aristotle wholly made the move that has become the basis of much of modern ethics and moral philosophy—the appeal to human *psychological* nature, the actual springs and impulses that drive us and determine our goals and desires. Both Plato and Augustine were psychologically insightful, even brilliantly so. Aristotle certainly delved into the logic of deliberation and action as deeply as any philosopher before or since. But the idea of basing ethics wholly on psychology is a distinctively modern idea, and one of its first and foremost proponents was the English philosopher Thomas Hobbes. Hobbes was not an optimist on questions of human nature. He believed that our primary passion is *fear* and our natural tendencies are for self-interest and violence. He famously suggested that without the controlling force of government and society, our lives would be "nasty, brutish, and short" and there would be a "war of everyone against everyone." Although he was a proponent of strong government as an antidote to our less than benevolent natures, Hobbes was also a progressive thinker who rejected the conception of government as based on divine right of kings still popular in his time and advocated the radical new theory that the power of the sovereign is derived from the people. (This theory got him into considerable trouble.)

Hobbes's main work is a monumental treatise appropriately entitled *Leviathan* (1651). (A leviathan is a medieval sea monster, often conceived of as a snake or a whale. Hobbes uses the term to refer to the whole of society.) It begins as a treatise on psychology—the nature of the mind and of human nature; it then turns to ethics and, ultimately, to politics. Hobbes's psychology developed as part of a larger view of the universe as essentially mechanical in its workings, as "matter in motion." (Isaac Newton developed his own mechanical theory of the universe only a few years later.)

Hobbes's view of people as primarily egocentric and, more than anything else, afraid for their lives, dictated the ultimate principle of his ethics, which is that people must get together and form a society with a strong government in order to protect themselves from enemies and each other. Consequently, the basis for any sort of communal living (and this will come to include ethics as well as politics) is self-interest. This in turn sets up the basis of his political theory, that society is based on a *social contract* in which everyone gives up certain rights and privileges in return for the protection and advantages of society. (Other social-contract theories were developed in the following century by John Locke and Jean-Jacques Rousseau, from which evolved our own notion of the social contract—so evident in our Declaration of Independence, for example—"to secure these rights, Governments are instituted among Men, deriving their Just powers from the consent of the governed. . . .") Hobbes's ethics is one of the great examples of *psychological egoism,* the theory that all of our actions—good or bad, noble or vicious—are motivated by our own self-interest, especially, in Hobbes's view, the fear of violent death. His politics provided the justification of a strong central government that was becoming influential at the time. (But the Glorious Revolution in England was only 37 years later.)

LEVIATHAN*

In the following excerpts from *Leviathan,* Hobbes first outlines for us the mechanical basis of his psychology in terms of "motions," in particular, actions (or "endeavors") moved by "appetite or desire." He then provides us with a brief catalog of the reigning human passions and gives us his definition of that all-important ethical word, "good." According to Hobbes, "good" means "the object of any man's appetite or desire," and it is clearly a "subjective" matter whether something is good or not ("there being nothing simply and absolutely so"). By offering this sort of descriptive account of the concepts of good and evil, Hobbes manages to avoid many

*Thomas Hobbes, *Leviathan,* edited by Herbert W. Schneider. Copyright 1985 by Macmillan Publishing Company.

of the problems that plague those who subscribe to more metaphysically based accounts, including how we know what is really good, especially in the face of radical disagreement.

OF THE INTERIOR BEGINNINGS OF VOLUNTARY MOTIONS COMMONLY CALLED THE PASSIONS AND THE SPEECHES BY WHICH THEY ARE EXPRESSED

There be in animals, two sorts of *motions* peculiar to them: one called *vital;* begun in generation, and continued without interruption through their whole life; such as are the *course* of the *blood,* the *pulse,* the *breathing,* the *concoction, nutrition, excretion,* etc. to which motions there needs no help of imagination: the other is *animal motion,* otherwise called *voluntary motion;* as to *go,* to *speak,* to *move* any of our limbs, in such manner as is first fancied in our minds. That sense is motion in the organs and interior parts of man's body, caused by the action of the things we see, hear, etc.; and that fancy is but the relics of the same motion, remaining after sense, has been already said in the first and second chapters. And because *going, speaking,* and the like voluntary motions, depend always upon a precedent thought of *whither, which way,* and *what;* it is evident, that the imagination is the first internal beginning of all voluntary motion. And although unstudied men do not conceive any motion at all to be there, where the thing moved is invisible; or the space it is moved in is, for the shortness of it, insensible; yet that doth not hinder, but that such motions are. For let a space be never so little, that which is moved over a greater space, whereof that little one is part, must first be moved over that. These small beginnings of motion, within the body of man, before they appear in walking, speaking, striking, and other visible actions, are commonly called ENDEAVOUR.

This endeavour, when it is toward something which causes it, is called APPETITE, OR DESIRE; the latter, being the general name; and the other oftentimes restrained to signify the desire of food, namely *hunger* and *thirst.* And when the endeavour is fromward something, it is generally called AVERSION. These words, *appetite* and *aversion,* we have from the Latins; and they both of them signify the motions, one of approaching, the other of retiring. So also do the Greek words for the same, which are ὁρμή and ἀφορμή. For nature itself does often press upon men those truths, which afterwards, when they look for somewhat beyond nature, they stumble at. For the Schools find in mere appetite to go, or move, no actual motion at all: but because some motion they must acknowledge, they call it metaphorical motion; which is but an absurd speech: for though words may be called metaphorical; bodies and motions can not.

That which men desire, they are also said to LOVE: and to HATE those things for which they have aversion. So that desire and love are the same thing; save that by desire, we always signify the absence of the object; by love, most commonly the presence of the same. So also by aversion, we signify the absence; and by hate, the presence of the object.

Of appetites and aversions, some are born with men; as appetite of food, appetite of excretion, and exoneration, which may also and more properly be called aversions, from somewhat they feel in their bodies; and some other appetites, not many. The rest, which are appetites of particular things, proceed from experience, and trial of their effects upon themselves or other men. For of things we know not at all, or believe not to be, we can have no further desire, than to taste and try. But aversion we have for things, not only which we know have hurt us, but also that we do not know whether they will hurt us, or not.

Those things which we neither desire, nor hate, we are said to contemn; CONTEMPT being nothing else but an immobility, or contumacy of the heart, in resisting the action of certain things; and proceeding from that the heart is already moved otherwise, by other more potent objects; or from want of experience of them.

And because the constitution of a man's body is in continual mutation, it is impossible that all the same things should always cause in him the same appetites, and aversions: much less can all men consent, in the desire of almost any one and the same object.

But whatsoever is the object of any man's appetite or desire, that is it which he for his part calleth good: and the object of his hate and aversion, evil; and of his contempt, vile and inconsiderable. For these words of good, evil, and contemptible, are ever used with relation to the person that useth them: there being nothing simply and absolutely so; nor any common rule of good and evil, to be taken from the nature of the objects themselves; but from the person of the man, where there is no commonwealth; or, in a commonwealth, from the person that representeth it; or from an arbitrator or judge, whom men disagreeing shall by consent set up, and make his sentence the rule thereof. . . .

As, in sense, that which is really within us, is, as I have said before, only motion, caused by the action of external objects, but in apparence; to the sight light and colour; to the ear, sound; to the nostril, odour, &c.: so, when the action of the same object is continued from the eyes, ears, and other organs to the heart, the real effect there is nothing but motion, or endeavour; which consisteth in appetite, or aversion, to or from the object moving. But the apparence, or sense of that motion, is that we either call delight, or trouble of mind. . . .

Pleasure therefore, or delight, is the apparence, or sense of good; and molestation, or displeasure, the apparence, or sense of evil. And consequently all appetite, desire, and love, is accompanied with some delight more or less; and all hatred and aversion, with more or less displeasure and offence.

Of pleasures or delights, some arise from the sense of an object present; and those may be called pleasure of sense; the word sensual as it is used by those only that condemn them, having no place till there be laws. Of this kind are all onerations and exonerations of the body; as also all that is pleasant, in the sight, hearing, smell, taste, or touch. Others arise from the expectation, that proceeds from foresight of the end, or consequence of things; whether those things in the sense please or displease. And these are pleasures of the mind of him that draweth those consequences, and are generally called joy. In the like manner, displeasures are some in the sense, and called PAIN; others in the expectation of consequences, and are called GRIEF.

These simple passions called appetite, desire, love, aversion, hate, joy, and grief, have their names for divers considerations diversified. As first, when they one succeed another, they are diversely called from the opinion men have of the likelihood of attaining what they desire. Secondly, from the object loved or hated. Thirdly, from the consideration of many of them together. Fourthly, from the alteration or succession itself.

For appetite, with an opinion of attaining, is called HOPE.

The same, without such opinion, DESPAIR.

Aversion, with opinion of HURT from the object, FEAR. . . .

The "natural condition" of man, we have anticipated, is one of misery. Not only are we essentially self-centered, but we are all more or less equal—whatever the obvious differences between us—at least in the sense that almost everyone has the power to make life miserable—and dangerous—for everyone else. We do not enjoy each other so much as we interfere with one another in the pursuit of our own interests; we quarrel constantly, because we are competitive, because we are insecure, because we are vain. All in all, it is not a pretty portrait of the human race. It is, however, a realistic one, at least in Hobbes's mind. What impressed Hobbes most in his survey of political and ethical thought was not the force or clarity of any particular doctrine, but rather the absence of any one theory that commanded anything close to universal assent. Even in the sciences, human knowledge appeared to be very far from secure, thanks to the work of Galileo and his fellow scientists. If even the natural sciences lacked concrete, universally accepted truths, the prospects of finding such principles in the far less absolute "sciences" of human interaction seemed dim indeed. There was, however, one fact about human beings that Hobbes found to be universally true: Every human being feared for his or her life and would do almost anything to protect it. Prior to entering civil society, that protection would be based on force and cunning alone; it would be judged entirely on the basis of success, by whatever means necessary. That is why Hobbes claims that there is no right or wrong in the state of nature, only the more or less successful fight for survival. In other words, there is no such thing as natural justice, independent of social arrangements. Rather, as Hobbes states, "Where there is no common power, there is no law; where no law, no injustice."

OF THE NATURAL CONDITION OF MANKIND AS CONCERNING THEIR FELICITY AND MISERY

Nature hath made men so equal, in the faculties of the body, and mind; as that though there be found one man sometimes manifestly stronger in body, or of quicker mind than another; yet when all is reckoned together, the difference between man, and man, is not so considerable, as that one man can thereupon claim to himself any benefit, to which another may not pretend, as well as he. For as to the strength of body, the weakest has strength enough to kill the strongest, either by secret machination, or by confederacy with others, that are in the same danger with himself.

And as to the faculties of the mind, setting aside the arts grounded upon words, and especially that skill of proceeding upon general, and infallible rules, called science; which very few have, and but in few things; as being not a native faculty, born with us; nor attained, as prudence, while we look after somewhat else, I find yet a greater equality amongst men, than that of strength. For prudence, is but experience; which equal time, equally bestows on all men, in those things they equally apply themselves unto. That which may perhaps make such equality incredible, is but a vain conceit of one's own wisdom, which almost all men think they have in a greater degree, than the vulgar; that is, than all men but themselves, and a few others, whom by fame, or for concurring with themselves, they approve. For such is the nature of men, that howsoever they may acknowledge many others to be more witty, or more eloquent, or more learned; yet they will hardly believe there be many so wise as themselves; for they see their own wit at hand, and other men's at a distance. But this proveth rather that men are in that point equal, than unequal. For there is not ordinarily a greater sign of the equal distribution of any thing, than that every man is contented with his share.

From this equality of ability, ariseth equality of hope in the attaining of our ends. And therefore if any two men desire the same thing, which nevertheless they cannot both enjoy, they become enemies; and in the way to their end, which is principally their own conservation, and sometimes their delectation only, endeavour to destroy, or subdue one another. And from hence it comes to pass, that where an invader hath no more to fear, than another man's single power; if one plant, sow, build, or possess a convenient seat, others may probably be expected to come prepared with forces united, to dispossess, and deprive him, not only of the fruit of his labour, but also of his life, or liberty. And the invader again is in the like danger of another.

And from this difference of one another, there is no way for any man to secure himself, so reasonable, as anticipation; that is, by force, or wiles, to master the persons of all men he can, so long, till he see no other power great enough to endanger him: and this is no more than his own conservation requireth, and is generally allowed. Also because there be some, that taking pleasure in contemplating their own power in the acts of conquest, which they pursue farther than their security requires; if others, that otherwise would be glad to be at ease within modest bounds, should not by invasion increase their power, they would not be able, long time, by standing only on their defence, to subsist. And by consequence, such augmentation of dominion over men being necessary to a man's conservation, it ought to be allowed him.

Again, men have no pleasure, but on the contrary a great deal of grief, in keeping company, where there is no power able to over-awe them all. For every man looketh that his companion should value him, at the same rate he sets upon himself: and upon all signs of contempt, or undervaluing, naturally endeavours, as far as he dares (which amongst them that have no common power to keep them in quiet, is far enough to make them destroy each other), to extort a greater value from his contemners, by damage; and from others, by the example.

So that in the nature of man, we find three principal causes of quarrel. First, competition; secondly, diffidence; thirdly, glory.

The first, maketh men invade for gain; the second, for safety; and the third, for reputation. The first use violence, to make themselves masters of other men's persons, wives, children, and cattle; the second, to defend them; the third, for trifles, as a word, a smile, a different opinion, and any other sign of under-value, either direct in their persons, or by reflection in their kindred, their friends, their nation, their profession, or their name.

Hereby it is manifest, that during the time men live without a common power to keep them all in awe, they are in that condition which is called war; and such a war, as is of every man, against every man. For WAR, consisteth not in battle only, or the act of fighting; but in a tract of time, wherein the will to contend by the battle is sufficiently known; and therefore the notion of *time,* is to be considered in the nature of war, as it is in the nature of weather. For as the nature of foul weather, lieth not in a shower or two of rain; but in an inclination thereto of many days together: so the nature of war, consisteth not in actual fighting; but in the known disposition thereto, during all the time there is no as-surance to the contrary. All other time is PEACE.

Whatsoever therefore is consequent to a time of war, where every man is enemy to every man; the same is consequent to the time, wherein men live with-out other security, than what their own strength, and their own invention shall furnish them withal. In such condition, there is no place for industry; because the fruit thereof is uncertain: and consequently no culture of the earth; no navi-gation, nor use of the commodities that may be imported by sea; no commodi-ous building; no instruments of moving, and removing, such things as require much force; no knowledge of the face of the earth; no account of time; no arts; no letters; no society; and which is worst of all, continual fear, and danger of vi-olent death; and the life of man, solitary, poor, nasty, brutish, and short.

It may seem strange to some man, that has not well weighed these things; that nature should thus dissociate, and render men apt to invade, and destroy one another: and he may therefore, not trusting to this inference, made from the pas-sions, desire perhaps to have the same confirmed by experience. Let him there-fore consider with himself, when taking a journey, he arms himself, and seeks to go well accompanied; when going to sleep, he locks his doors; when even in his house he locks his chests; and this when he knows there be laws, and public offi-cers, armed, to revenge all injuries shall be done him; what opinion he has of his fellow-subjects, when he rides armed; of his fellow citizens, when he locks his doors; and of his children, and servants, when he locks his chests. Does he not there as much accuse mankind by his actions, as I do by my words? But neither of us accuse man's nature in it. The desires, and other passions of man, are in themselves no sin. No more are the actions, that proceed from those passions, till they know a law that forbids them: which till laws be made they cannot know: nor can any law be made, till they have agreed upon the person that shall make it.

It may peradventure be thought, there was never such a time, nor condition of war as this; and I believe it was never generally so, over all the world: but there are many places, where they live so now. For the savage people in many places of America, except the government of small families, the concord whereof dependeth on natural lust, have no government at all; and live at this day in that brutish manner, as I said before. Howsoever, it may be perceived what manner of life there would be, where there were no common power to fear, by the manner of life, which men that have formerly lived under a peaceful government, use to degenerate into, in a civil war.

But though there had never been any time, wherein particular men were in a condition of war one against another; yet in all times, kings, and persons of sovereign authority, because of their independency, are in continual jealousies, and in the state and posture of gladiators; having their weapons pointing, and their eyes fixed on one another; that is, their forts, garrisons, and guns upon the frontiers of their kingdoms; and continual spies upon their neighbours; which is a posture of war. But because they uphold thereby, the industry of their subjects; there does not follow from it, that misery, which accompanies the liberty of particular men.

To this war of every man, against every man, this also is consequent; that nothing can be unjust. The notions of right and wrong, justice and injustice have there no place. Where there is no common power, there is no law: where no law, no injustice. Force, and fraud, are in war the two cardinal virtues. Justice, and injustice are none of the faculties neither of the body, nor mind. If they were, they might be in a man that were alone in the world, as well as his senses, and passions. They are qualities, that relate to men in society, not in solitude. It is consequent also to the same condition, that there be no propriety, no dominion, no *mine* and *thine* distinct; but only that to be every man's that he can get; and for so long, as he can keep it. And thus much for the ill condition, which man by mere nature is actually placed in; though with a possibility to come out of it, consisting partly in the passions, partly in his reason.

The passions that incline men to peace, are fear of death; desire of such things as are necessary to commodious living; and a hope by their industry to obtain them. And reason suggesteth convenient articles of peace, upon which men may be drawn to agreement. These articles, are they, which otherwise are called the Laws of Nature: whereof I shall speak more particularly, in the following chapters.

Hobbes next spells out for us the notion of "natural law" and examines the origins of the "social contract." A law of nature, as Hobbes uses the term, describes a duty that is obligatory not because of any coercive power of a created state but rather by force of reason alone. (He describes it as "a precept or general rule, found out by reason.") Recall, however, what Hobbes thought one could say about concepts such as "good" and "evil," which form a part of the idea of a duty. In the state of nature, they are entirely relative—prior to entering society, "good" simply means that which a person desires and "bad" that to which he or she is averse. There does not seem to be, then, much for reason to find out here about what the law of nature obliges us to do. But there is Hobbes's one absolute truth regarding human beings: They all desire to preserve their lives; therefore, they all call continued existence "good." This self-interested desire will form the basis for Hobbes's entire ethical and political theory.

The law of nature thus dictates self-preservation, and in a "war of every one against every one," a person has a *right* to use any means whatever to protect and defend him or herself. But such insecurity is clearly to virtually everyone's disadvantage, and so the reasonable thing for everyone to want is peace, if possible, or, if not, the means to defend ourselves. Given our first preference for peace, we are willing to lay down our rights to self-defense, just so long as everyone else sets aside their combative means as well. This reciprocity is the key to the formation of the social contract, which Hobbes calls "the first and fundamental law of nature."

From this first law of nature, "to seek peace and follow it," Hobbes derives not only those constraints necessary to form a political community but all of the traditional moral virtues as well. If we accept the first fundamental law of nature, we must also accept that which is necessary to achieve its goal, self-preservation through peace. Thus, the second law of nature requires that we lay down our natural right to defend ourselves, and the third that we keep our word in the covenant required to ensure that peace (the social contract). In all, Hobbes offers 19 laws of nature, all of which are characterized as simply the logical means to realizing one's own security. What is so interesting about Hobbes's account is that the acceptance of these laws is based entirely on self-interest, yet the result is the restoration of traditional Christian virtues, which seem very far from egocentric, including mercy, modesty, equity, and justice.

OF THE FIRST AND SECOND NATURAL LAWS AND OF CONTRACTS

The right of nature, which writers commonly call *jus naturale,* is the liberty each man hath, to use his own power, as he will himself, for the preservation of his own nature; that is to say, of his own life; and consequently, of doing any thing, which in his own judgment, and reason, he shall conceive to be the aptest means thereunto.

By liberty, is understood, according to the proper signification of the word, the absence of external impediments: which impediments, may oft take away part of a man's power to do what he would; but cannot hinder him from using the power left him, according as his judgment, and reason shall dictate to him.

A law of nature, *lex naturalis,* is a precept or general rule, found out by reason, by which a man is forbidden to do that, which is destructive of his life, or taketh away the means of preserving the same; and to omit that, by which he thinketh it may be best preserved. For though they that speak of this subject, use to confound *jus,* and *lex, right* and *law:* yet they ought to be distinguished; because RIGHT, consisteth in liberty to do, or to forbear; whereas LAW, determineth, and bindeth to one of them: so that law, and right, differ as much, as obligation, and liberty, which in one and the same matter are inconsistent.

And because the condition of man, as hath been declared in the precedent chapter, is a condition of war of every one against every one: in which case every one is governed by his own reason; and there is nothing he can make use of, that may not be a help unto him, in preserving his life against his enemies; it followeth, that in such a condition, every man has a right to every thing; even to one another's body. And therefore, as long as this natural right of every man to every thing endureth, there can be no security to any man, how strong or wise soever he be, of living out the time, which nature ordinarily alloweth men to live. And consequently it is a precept, or general rule of reason, *that every man, ought to endeavour peace, as far as he has hope of obtaining it; and when he cannot obtain it, that he may seek, and use, all helps, and advantages of war.* The first branch of which rule, containeth the first, and fundamental law of nature; which is, to *seek peace, and follow it.* The second, the sum of the right of nature; which is, *by all means we can, to defend ourselves.*

From this fundamental law of nature, by which men are commanded to endeavour peace, is derived this second law; *that a man be willing, when others are so too, as far-forth, as for peace, and defence of himself he shall think it necessary, to lay down this right to all things; and be contented with so much liberty against other men, as he would allow other men against himself.* For as long as every man holdeth this right, of doing any thing he liketh; so long are all men in the condition of war. But if other men will not lay down their right, as well as he; then there is no reason for any one, to divest himself of his: for that were to expose himself to prey, which no man is bound to, rather than to dispose himself to peace. This is that law of the Gospel; *whatsoever you require that others should do to you, that do ye to them.* And that law of all men, *quod tibi fieri non vis, alteri ne feceris.*

To *lay down* a man's *right* to any thing, is to *divest* himself of the *liberty,* of hindering another of the benefit of his own right to the same. For he that renounceth, or passeth away his right, giveth not to any other man a right which he had not before; because there is nothing to which every man had not right by nature: but only standeth out of his way, that he may enjoy his own original right, without hindrance from him; not without hindrance from another. So that the effect which redoundeth to one man, by another man's defect of right, is but so much diminution of impediments to the use of his own right original.

Right is laid aside, either by simply remouncing it; or by transferring it to another. By *simply* RENOUNCING; when he cares not to whom the benefit thereof redoundeth. By TRANSFERRING; when he intendeth the benefit thereof to some certain person, or persons. And when a man hath in either manner abandoned, or granted away his right; then is he said to be OBLIGED, or BOUND, not to hinder those, to whom such right is granted, or abandoned, from the benefit of it: and that he *ought,* and it is his DUTY, not to make void that voluntary act of his own: and that such hindrance is INJUSTICE, and INJURY, as being *sine jure;* the right being before renounced, or transferred. So that *injury,* or *injustice,* in the controversies of the world, is somewhat like to that, which in the disputations of scholars is called *absurdity.* For as it is there called an absurdity, to contradict what one maintained in the beginning: so in the world, it is called injustice, and injury, voluntarily to undo that, which from the beginning he had voluntarily done. The way by which a man either simply renounceth, or transferreth his right, is a declaration, or signification, by some voluntary and sufficient sign, or signs, that he doth so renounce, or transfer; or hath so renounced, or transferred the same, to him that accepted it. And these signs are either words only, or actions only; or, as it happenneth most often, both words, and actions. And the same are the BONDS, by which men are bound, and obliged: bonds, that have their strength, not from their own nature, for nothing is more easily broken than a man's word, but from fear of some evil consequence upon the rupture.

Whensoever a man transferreth his right, or renounceth it; it is either in consideration of some right reciprocally transferred to himself; or for some other good he hopeth for thereby. For it is a voluntary act: and of the voluntary acts of every man, the object is some *good to himself.* And therefore there be some rights, which no man can be understood by any words, or other signs, to have abandoned, or transferred. As first a man cannot lay down the right of resisting them, that assault him by force, to take away his life; because he cannot be understood to aim thereby, at any good to himself. The same may be said of wounds, and chains, and imprisonment; both because there is no benefit consequent to such patience; as there is to the patience of suffering another to be wounded, or imprisoned: as also because a man cannot tell, when he seeth men proceed against him by violence, whether they intend his death or not. And lastly the motive, and end for which this renouncing, and transferring of right is introduced, is nothing else but the security of a man's person, in his life, and in the means of so preserving life, as not to be weary of it. And therefore if a man by words, or other signs, seem to despoil himself of the end, for which those signs were intended; he is not to be understood as if he meant it, or that it was his will; but that he was ignorant of how such words and actions were to be interpreted.

The mutual transferring of right, is that which men call CONTRACT.

There is difference between transferring of right to the thing: and transferring, or tradition, that is delivery of the thing itself. For the thing may be delivered together with the translation of the right; as in buying and selling with ready-money; or exchange of goods, or lands: and it may be delivered some time after.

Again, one of the contractors, deliver the thing contracted for on his part, and leave the other to perform his part at some determinate time after, and in the mean time be trusted; and then the contract on his part, is called PACT, or COVENANT: or both parts may contract now, to perform hereafter: in which cases, he that is to perform in time to come, being trusted, his performance is called *keeping of promise,* or faith: and the failing of performance, if it be voluntary, *violation of faith.* . . .

These are the laws of nature dictating peace for a means of the conservation of men in multitudes, and which only concern the doctrine of civil society. There be other things tending to the destruction of particular men—as drunkenness and all other parts of intemperance—which may therefore also be reckoned among those things which the law of nature has forbidden, but are not necessary to be mentioned nor are pertinent enough to this place.

And though this may seem too subtle a deduction of the laws of nature to be taken notice of by all men—whereof the most part are too busy in getting food and the rest too negligent to understand—yet to leave all men inexcusable they have been contracted into one easy sum, intelligible even to the meanest capacity, and that is *Do not that to another which you would not have done to yourself;* which shows him that he has no more to do in learning the laws of nature but, when weighing the actions of other men with his own they seem too heavy, to put them into the other part of the balance and his own into their place, that his own passions and self-love may add nothing to the weight, and then there is none of these laws of nature that will not appear unto him very reasonable. . . .

The laws of nature are immutable and eternal, for injustice, ingratitude, arrogance, pride, iniquity, acception of persons, and the rest can never be made lawful. For it can never be that war shall preserve life and peace destroy it.

The same laws, because they oblige only to a desire and endeavor—I mean an unfeigned and constant endeavor—are easy to be observed. For in that they require nothing but endeavor, he that endeavors their performance fulfills them; and he that fulfills the law is just.

And the science of them is the true and only moral philosophy. For moral philosophy is nothing else but the science of what is *good* and *evil* in the conversation and society of mankind. *Good* and *evil* are names that signify our appetites and aversions, which in different tempers, customs, and doctrines of men are different; and divers men differ not only in their judgment on the senses of what is pleasant and unpleasant to the taste, smell, hearing, touch, and sight but also of what is conformable or disagreeable to reason in the actions of common life. Nay, the same man in divers times differs from himself, and one time praises—that is, calls good—what another time he dispraises and calls evil; from whence arise disputes, controversies, and at last war. And therefore so long as a man is in the condition of mere nature, which is a condition of war, private appetite is the measure of good and evil; and consequently all men agree on this: that peace is good, and therefore also the way or means of peace, which, as I have showed before, are *justice, gratitude, modesty, equity, mercy,* and the rest of the laws of nature, are good—that is to say, *moral virtues*—and their contrary *vices* evil. Now the science of virtue and vice is moral philosophy; and therefore the true doctrine of the laws of nature is the true moral philosophy. But the writers of moral philosophy, though they acknowledge the same virtues and vices, yet, not seeing wherein consisted their goodness nor that they come to be praised as the means of peaceable, sociable, and comfortable living, place them in a mediocrity of passions; as if not the cause but the degree of daring made fortitude, or not the cause but the quantity of a gift made liberality.

These dictates of reason men used to call by the name of laws, but improperly, for they are but conclusions or theorems concerning what conduces to the conservation and defense of themselves, whereas law, properly, is the word of him that by right has command over others. But yet if we consider the same theorems as delivered in the word of God, that by right commands all things, then are they properly called laws. . . .

As a result of the social contract, we bond together to form a society for the security of all, a "commonwealth," in which the rights and powers that we once had alone (and ineffectively) are now concentrated in the hands of "the sovereign," who can use that power very effectively to ensure everyone's (physical) security. It is only when such a sovereign exists—when there is, in Hobbes's terms, a common power to compel obedience—that any sort of ethical relations are possible.

OF THE CAUSES, GENERATION, AND DEFINITION OF A COMMONWEALTH

The final cause, end, or design of men, who naturally love liberty, and dominion over others, in the introduction of that restraint upon themselves, in which we see them live in commonwealths, is the foresight of their own preservation, and of a more contented life thereby; that is to say, of getting themselves out from that miserable condition of war, which is necessarily consequent, as hath been shown in chapter XIII, to the natural passions of men, when there is no visible power to keep them in awe, and tie them by fear of punishment to the performance of their covenants, and observation of those laws of nature set down in the fourteenth and fifteenth chapters.

For the laws of nature, as *justice, equity, modesty, mercy,* and, in sum, *doing to others, as we would be done to,* of themselves, without the terror of some power, to cause them to be observed, are contrary to our natural passions, that carry us to partiality, pride, revenge, and the like. And covenants, without the sword, are but words, and of no strength to secure a man at all. Therefore notwithstanding the laws of nature, which every one hath then kept, when he has the will to keep them, when he can do it safely, if there be no power erected, or not great enough for our security; every man will, and may lawfully rely on his own strength and art, for caution against all other men. And in all places, where men have lived by small families, to rob and spoil one another, has been a trade, and so far from being reputed against the law of nature, that the greater spoils they gained, the greater was their honour; and men observed no other laws therein, but the laws of honour; that is, to abstain from cruelty, leaving to men their lives, and instruments of husbandry. And as small families did then; so now do cities and kingdoms which are but greater families, for their own security, enlarge their dominions, upon all pretences of danger, and fear of invasion, or assistance that may be given to invaders, and endeavour as much as they can, to subdue, or weaken their neighbours, by open force, and secret arts, for want of other caution, justly; and are remembered for it in after ages with honour. . . .

The only way to erect such a common power, as may be able to defend them from the invasion of foreigners, and the injuries of one another, and thereby to secure them in such sort, as that by their own industry, and by the fruits of the earth, they may nourish themselves and live contentedly; is, to confer all their power and strength upon one man, or upon one assembly of men, that may reduce all their wills, by plurality of voices, unto one will: which is as much as to say, to appoint one man, or assembly of men, to bear their person; and every one to own, and acknowledge himself to be author of whatsoever he that so beareth their person, shall act, or cause to be acted, in those things which concern the common peace and safety; and therein to submit their wills, every one to his will, and their judgments, to his judgment. This is more than consent, or concord; it is a real unity of them all, in one and the same person, made by covenant of every man with every man, in such manner, as if every man should say to every man, *I authorize and give up my right of governing myself, to this man, or to this assembly of men, on this condition, that thou give up thy right to him, and authorize all his actions in like manner.* This done, the multitude so united in one person, is called a COMMONWEALTH, in Latin CIVITAS. This is the generation of that great LEVIATHAN, or rather, to speak more reverently, of that *mortal god,* to which we owe under the *immortal God,* our peace and defence. For by this authority, given him by every particular men in the commonwealth, he hath the use of so much power and strength conferred on him, that by terror thereof, he is enabled to perform the wills of them all, to peace at home, and mutual aid against their enemies abroad. And in him consisteth the essence of the commonwealth; which, to define it, is *one person, of whose acts a great multitude, by mutual covenants one with another, have made themselves every one the author, to the end he may use the strength and means of them all, as he shall think expedient, for their peace and common defence.*

And he that carrieth this person, is called SOVEREIGN, and said to have *sovereign power;* and every one besides, his SUBJECT.

The attaining to this sovereign power, is by two ways. One, by natural force; as when a man maketh his children, to submit themselves, and their children to his government, as being able to destroy them if they refuse; or by war subdueth his enemies to his will, giving them their lives on that condition. The other, is when men agree amongst themselves, to submit to some man, or assembly of men, voluntarily, on confidence to be protected by him against all others. This latter, may be called a political commonwealth, or commonwealth by *institution;* and the former, a commonwealth by *acquisition.* . . .

The problem with any theory in which fear and force are primary motives is the question of what happens to individual *freedom* (or liberty). In a commonwealth (a society), what is a person free to do, or not to do? Does a person give up a substantial amount of freedom when he or she agrees to obey the laws, or could it be argued that we are much freer within the restrictions of society than outside of it in our "natural condition"?

Much of the answer to these sorts of questions depends on what one takes liberty to mean. Consistent with his refusal to posit any transcendent ethical truths, Hobbes denies that there is anything more to the loss of liberty than obvious physical impediments such as imprisonment, chains, or (physical) force. If you are free from these sorts of hindrances—if there is an "absence of opposition"—you are free. To talk about the freedom of your soul, mind, conscience, or any other non-physical aspect is to talk nonsense.

For Hobbes, then, freedom is both clearly identifiable and relatively easy to attain, because it consists in no more than corporal liberty. It leaves out entirely those intangible forms of freedom that are often discussed today such as the freedom to realize one's potential or to make truly autonomous choices. This minimalist conception of liberty leads Hobbes to defend a heavily authoritarian power vested in the sovereign (or at least potentially so). As long as the sovereign does not threaten your life or physical well-being, he or she does you no wrong (in particular, does not limit your freedom) and is within the proper boundaries of sovereign power. However, the initial motivation for entering civil society—the desire to save yourself—remains as the basis of, and justification for, any political power. "The obligation of subjects to the sovereign, is understood to last as long, and no longer, than the power lasteth, by which he is able to protect them."

OF THE LIBERTY OF SUBJECTS

LIBERTY, or FREEDOM, signifieth, properly, the absence of opposition; by opposition, I mean external impediments of motion; and may be applied no less to irrational, and inanimate creatures, than to rational. For whatsoever is so tied, or environed, as it cannot move but within a certain space, which space is determined by the opposition of some external body, we say it hath not liberty to go further. And so of all living creatures, whilst they are imprisoned, or restrained, with walls, or chains; and of the water whilst it is kept in by banks, or vessels, that otherwise would spread itself into a larger space, we use to say, they are not at liberty, to move in such manner, as without those external impediments they would. But when the impediment of motion, is in the constitution of the thing itself, we use not to say; it wants the liberty; but the power to move; as when a stone lieth still, or a man is fastened to his bed by sickness.

And according to this proper, and generally received meaning of the word, a FREE-MAN, is *he, that in those things, which by his strength and wit he is able to do, is not hindered to do what he has a will to.* But when the words *free,* and *liberty,* are applied to any thing but *bodies,* they are abused; for that which is not subject to motion, is not subject to impediment: and therefore, when it is said, for example, the way is free, no liberty of the way is signified, but of those that walk in it without stop. And when we say a gift is free, there is not meant any liberty of the gift, but of the giver, that was not bound by any law or covenant

to give it. So when we *speak freely,* it is not the liberty of voice, or pronunciation, but of the man, whom no law hath obliged to speak otherwise than he did.
Lastly, from the use of the word *free-will,* no liberty can be inferred of the will,
desire, or inclination, but the liberty of the man; which consisteth in this, that he
finds no stop, in doing what he has the will, desire, or inclination to do.

Fear and liberty are consistent; as when a man throweth his goods into the
sea for *fear* the ship should sink, he doth it nevertheless very willingly, and may
refuse to do it if he will: it is therefore the action of one that was *free:* so a man
sometimes pays his debt, only for *fear* of imprisonment, which because nobody
hindered him from detaining, was the action of a man at *liberty.* And generally
all actions which men do in commonwealths, for *fear* of the law, are actions,
which the doers had *liberty* to omit.

Liberty, and *necessity* are consistent: as in the water, that hath not only *liberty,* but a *necessity* of descending by the channel; so likewise in the actions
which men voluntarily do: which, because they proceed from their will, proceed
from *liberty;* and yet, because every act of man's will, and every desire, and inclination proceedeth from some cause, and that from another cause, in a continual chain, whose first link is in the hand of God the first of all causes, proceed
from *necessity.* So that to him that could see the connexion of those causes, the
necessity of all men's voluntary actions, would appear manifest. And therefore
God, that seeth, and disposeth all things, seeth also that the *liberty* of man in doing what he will, is accompanied with the *necessity* of doing that which God
will, and no more, nor less. For though men may do many things, which God
does not command, nor is therefore author of them; yet they can have no passion, nor appetite to anything, of which appetite God's *liberty,* which only is
properly called *liberty.*

But as men, for the attaining of peace, and conservation of themselves
thereby, have made an artificial man, which we call a commonwealth; so also
have they made artificial chains, called *civil laws,* which they themselves, by
mutual conventants, have fastened at one end, to the lips of that man, or assembly, to whom they have given the sovereign power; and at the other end to their
own ears. These bonds, in their own nature but weak, may nevertheless be made
to hold, by the danger, though not by the difficulty of breaking them.

In relation to these bonds only it is, that I am to speak now, of the *liberty* of
subjects. For seeing there is no commonwealth in the world, wherein there be
rules enough set down, for the regulating of all the actions, and words of men;
as being a thing impossible: to followeth necessarily, that in all kinds of actions
by the laws praetermitted, men have the liberty, of doing what their own reasons
shall suggest, for the most profitable to themselves. For if we take liberty in the
proper sense, for corporal liberty; that is to say, freedom from chains and prison;
it were very absurd for men to clamour as they do, for the liberty they so manifestly enjoy. Again, if we take liberty, for an exemption from laws, it is no less
absurd, for men to demand as they do, that liberty, by which all other men may
be masters of their lives. And yet, as absurd as it is, this is it they demand; not
knowing that the laws are of no power to protect them, without a sword in the
hands of a man, or men, to cause those laws to be put in execution. The liberty

of a subject, lieth therefore only in those things, which in regulating their actions, the sovereign hath praetermitted: such as is the liberty to buy, and sell, and otherwise contract with one another; to choose their own abode, their own diet, their own trade of life, and institute their children as they themselves think fit; and the like. . . .

To come now to the particulars of the true liberty of a subject; that is to say, what are the things, which though commanded by the sovereign, he may nevertheless, without injustice, refuse to do; we are to consider, what rights we pass away, when we make a commonwealth; or, which is all one, what liberty we deny ourselves, by owning all the actions, without exception, of the man, or assembly we make our sovereign. For in the act of our *submission,* consisteth both our *obligation,* and our *liberty;* which must therefore be inferred by arguments taken from thence; there being no obligation on any man, which ariseth not from some act of his own; for all men equally, are by nature free. And because such arguments, must either be drawn from the express words, *I authorize all his actions,* or from the intention of him that submitteth himself to his power, which intention is to be understood by the end for which he so submitteth; the obligation, and liberty of the subject, is to be derived, either from those words, or others equivalent; or else from the end of the institution of sovereignty, namely, the peace of the subjects within themselves, and their defence against a common enemy.

First therefore, seeing sovereignty by institution, is by covenant of every one to everyone; and sovereignty by acquisition, by covenants of the vanquished to the victor, or child to the parent; it is manifest, that every subject has liberty in all those things, the right whereof cannot by covenant be transferred. I have shown before in the 14th chapter, that covenants, not to defend a man's own body, are void. Therefore,

If the sovereign command a man, though justly condemned, to kill, wound, or maim himself; or not to resist those that assault him; or to abstain from the use of food, air, medicine, or any other thing, without which he cannot live; yet hath that man the liberty to disobey.

If a man be interrogated by the sovereign, or his authority, concerning a crime done by himself, he is not bound, without assurance of pardon, to confess it; because no man, as I have shown in the same chapter, can be obliged by covenant to accuse himself.

Again, the consent of a subject to sovereign power, is contained in these words, *I authorize, or take upon me, all his actions;* in which there is no restriction at all, of his own former natural liberty: for by allowing him to *kill me,* I am not bound to kill myself when he commands me. It is one thing to say, *kill me,* or *my fellow, if you please;* another thing to say, *I will kill myself, or my fellow.* It followeth therefore, that

No man is bound by the words themselves, either to kill himself, or any other man; and consequently, that the obligation a man may sometimes have, upon the command of the sovereign to execute any dangerous, or dishonourable office, dependeth not on the words of our submission; but on the intention, which is to be understood by the end thereof. When therefore our refusal to obey, frustrates the end for which the sovereignty was ordained; then there is no liberty to refuse: otherwise there is.

Upon this ground, a man that is commanded as a soldier to fight against the enemy, though his sovereign have right enough to punish his refusal with death, may nevertheless in many cases refuse, without injustice; as when he substituteth a sufficient soldier in his place: for in this case he deserteth not the service of the commonwealth. And there is allowance to be made for natural timorousness; not only to women, of whom no such dangerous duty is expected, but also to men of feminine courage. When armies fight, there is on one side, or both, a running away; yet when they do it not out of treachery, but fear, they are not esteemed to do it unjustly, but dishonourably. For the same reason, to avoid battle, is not injustice, but cowardice. But he that inrolleth himself a soldier, or taketh imprest money, taketh away the excuse of a timorous nature; and is obliged, not only to go to the battle, but also not to run from it, without his captain's leave. And when the defence of the commonwealth, requireth at once the help of all that are able to bear arms, every one is obliged; because otherwise the institution of the commonwealth, which they have not the purpose, or courage to preserve, was in vain.

To resist the sword of the commonwealth, in defence of another man, guilty, or innocent, no man hath liberty; because such liberty, takes away from the sovereign, the means of protecting us; and is therefore destructive of the very essence of government. But in case a great many men together, have already resisted the sovereign power unjustly, or committed some capital crime, for which every one of them expecteth death, whether have they not the liberty then to join together, and assist, and defend one another? Certainly they have: for they but defend their lives, which the guilty man may as well do, as the innocent. There was indeed injustice in the first breach of their duty; their bearing of arms subsequent to it, though it be to maintain what they have done, is no new unjust act. And if it be only to defend their persons, it is not unjust at all. But the offer of pardon taketh from them, to whom it is offered, the plea of self-defence, and maketh their perseverance in assisting, or defending the rest, unlawful.

As for other liberties, they depend on the silence of the law. In cases where the sovereign has prescribed no rule, there the subject hath the liberty to do, or forbear, according to his own discretion. And therefore such liberty is in some places more, and in some less; and in some times more, in other times less, according as they that have the sovereignty shall think most convenient. As for example, there was a time, when in England a man might enter into his own land, and dispossess such as wrongfully possessed it, by force. But in aftertimes, that liberty of forcible entry, was taken away by a statute made, by the king, in parliament. And in some places of the world, men have the liberty of many wives: in other places, such liberty is not allowed.

If a subject have a controversy with his sovereign, of debt, or of right of possession of lands or goods, or concerning any service required at his hands, or concerning any penalty, corporal, or pecuniary, grounded on a precedent law; he hath the same liberty to sue for his right, as if it were against a subject; and before such judges, as are appointed by the sovereign. For seeing the sovereign demandeth by force of a former law, and not by virtue of his power; he declareth thereby, that he requireth no more, than shall appear to be due by that law. The suit therefore is not contrary to the will of the sovereign: and consequently the subject hath the liberty to demand the hearing of his cause; and sentence, according to that law. But if he demand, or take anything by pretence of his power; there lieth, in that case, no action of law; for all that is done by him in virtue of his power, is done by the authority of every subject, and consequently he that brings an action against the sovereign, brings it against himself.

If a monarch, or sovereign assembly, grant a liberty to all, or any of his subjects, which grant standing, he is disabled to provide for their safety, the grant is void; unless he directly renounce, or transfer the sovereignty to another. For in that he might openly, if it had been his will, and in plain terms, have renounced, or transferred it, and did not: it is to be understood it was not his will, but that the grant proceeded from ignorance of the repugnancy between such a liberty and the sovereign power; and therefore the sovereignty is still retained; and consequently all those powers, which are necessary to the exercising thereof; such as are the power of war, and peace, of judicature, of appointing officers, and councillors, of levying money, and the rest named in the 18th chapter.

The obligation of subjects to the sovereign, is understood to last as long, and no longer, than the power lasteth, by which he is able to protect them. For the right men have by nature to protect themselves, when none else can protect them, can by no covenant be relinquished. The sovereignty is the soul of the commonwealth; which once departed from the body, the members do no more receive their motion from it. The end of obedience is protection; which, wheresoever a man seeth it, either in his own, or in another's sword, nature applieth his obedience to it, and his endeavour to maintain it. And though sovereignty, in the intention of them that make it, be immortal; yet is it in its own nature not only subject to violent death, by foreign war; but also through the ignorance and passions of men, it hath in it, from the very institution, many seeds of a natural mortality, by intestine discord.

In the passage below, Hobbes presents an objection to his social contract theory in the mouth of "the fool." The fool poses a question: Suppose it is the case that telling lies and breaking promises always works to my benefit? The fool believes that, in fact, experience teaches us that liars, promise breakers, and other violators of contracts often find that such behavior works to their advantage. And so, the fool thinks, it is not in one's interest to follow the rules of the contract.

Although Hobbes's reply to this objection is not as clear as we might like, he seems to argue that, although it is true that experience might confirm the fool's proposal, reason will contradict him. Because Hobbes is searching for the rational principles that underlie and justify a society—like the rational principles that underlie natural laws—experience alone will not reveal the truth about how one ought to behave within the social contract. The fool's unjust behavior may (or indeed, may not) work to his advantage in experience, but the rational principles of a just society contradict him.

The fool hath said in his heart, there is no such thing as justice; and sometimes also with his tongue; seriously alleging, that every man's conservation, and contentment, being committed to his own care, there could be no reason, why every man might not do what he thought conduced thereunto: and therefore also to make, or not make; keep, or not keep covenants, was not against reason, when it conduced to one's benefit. He does not therein deny, that there be covenants; and that they are sometimes broken, sometimes kept; and that such breach of them may be called injustice, and the observance of them justice: but he questioneth, whether injustice, taking away the fear of God, for the same fool hath said in his heart there is no God, may not sometimes stand with that reason, which dictateth to every man his own good; and particularly then, when it conduceth to such a benefit, as shall put a man in a condition, to neglect not only the dispraise, and revilings, but also the power of other men. The kingdom of God is gotten by violence: but what if it could be gotten by unjust violence? were it against reason so to get it, when it is impossible to receive hurt by it? and if it be not against reason, it is not against justice; or else justice is not to be approved for good. From such reasoning as this, successful wickedness hath obtained the name of virtue: and some that in all other things have disallowed the violation of faith; yet have allowed it, when it is for the getting of a kingdom. And the heathen that believed, that Saturn was deposed by his son Jupiter, believed nevertheless the same Jupiter to be the avenger of injustice: somewhat like to a piece of law in Coke's *Commentaries on Littleton;* where he says, if the right heir of the crown be attainted of treason; yet the crown shall descend to him, and *eo instante* the attainder be void: from which instances a man will be very prone to infer; that when the heir apparent of a kingdom, shall kill him that is in possession, though his father; you may call it injustice, or by what other name you will; yet it can never be against reason, seeing all the voluntary actions of men tend to the benefit of themselves; and those actions are most reasonable, that conduce most to their ends. This specious reasoning is nevertheless false.

For the question is not of promises mutual, where there is no security of performance on either side; as when there is no civil power erected over the parties promising; for such promises are no covenants: but either where one of the parties has performed already; or where there is a power to make him perform; there is the question whether it be against reason, that is, against the benefit of the other to perform, or not. And I say it is not against reason. For the mnanifestation whereof, we are to consider; first, that when a man doth a thing, which notwithstanding any thing can be foreseen, and reckoned on, tendeth to his own destruction, howsoever some accident which he could not expect, arriving may turn it to his benefit; yet such events do not make it reasonably or wisely done. Secondly, that in a condition of war, wherein every man to every man, for want of a common power to keep them all in awe, is an enemy, there is no man who can hope by his own strength, or wit, to defend himself from destruction, without the help of confederates; where every one expects the same defence by the confederation, that any one else does: and therefore he which declares he thinks it reason to deceive those that help him, can in reason expect no other means of safety, than what can be had from his own single power. He therefore that breaketh his covenant, and consequently declareth that he thinks he may with reason do so, cannot be received into any society, that unite themselves for peace and defence, but by the error of them that receive him; nor when he is received, be retained in it, without seeing the danger of their error; which errors a man cannot reasonably reckon upon as the means of his security: and therefore if he be left, or cast out of society, he perisheth; and if he live in society, it is by the errors of other men, which he could not foresee, nor reckon upon; and consequently against the reason of his preservation; and so, as all men that contribute not to his destruction, forbear him only out of ignorance of what is good for themselves.

As for the instance of gaining the secure and perpetual felicity of heaven, by any way; it is frivolous: there being but one way imaginable; and that is not breaking, but keeping of covenant.

And for the other instance of attaining sovereignty by rebellion; it is manifest, that though the event follow, yet because it cannot reasonably be expected, but rather the contrary; and because by gaining it so, others are taught to gain the same in like manner, the attempt thereof is against reason. Justice therefore, that is to say, keeping of covenant, is a rule of reason, by which we are forbidden to do any thing destructive to our life; and consequently a law of nature.

There be some that proceed further; and will not have the law of nature, to be those rules which conduce to the preservation of man's life on earth; but to the attaining of an eternal felicity after death; to which they think the breach of covenant may conduce; and consequently be just and reasonable; such are they that think it a work of merit to kill, or depose, or rebel against, the sovereign power constituted over them by their own consent. But because there is no natural knowledge of man's estate after death; much less of the reward that is then to be given to breach of faith; but only a belief grounded upon other men's saying, that they know it supernaturally, or that they know those, that knew them, that knew others, that knew it supernaturally; breach of faith cannot be called a precept of reason, or nature.

DISCUSSION

In these excerpts from *Leviathan,* Hobbes presents us with (at least) two theses that are radically at odds with the accounts of virtue we found in Plato and Aristotle (and, of course, in Augustine). First, Hobbes gives us a psychological account of human nature in which self-interest—even selfishness—is the sole motive for every action. In Plato and Aristotle's account of virtuous action, on the other hand, it is quite clear that—whether virtuous action is also in one's self-interest or not—it is action that is motivated just by the fact that it is virtuous and certainly not—as in Hobbes—out of fear or defensiveness. (The Greek virtue of courage, for instance, becomes unintelligible on Hobbes's account.) Second, Hobbes gives us an account of the formation of society and social bonds out of a "state of nature" in which each of us is a miserable, independent, but defensive animal, coming together for mutual protection and peace. In Plato and Aristotle, it is assumed from the outset that our natural condition *is* to be social and in society. (Aristotle famously defines man as "the social animal.") Societies are not created by individuals; individuals are born into and, in an important sense, created by, society.

These two differences mark a series of debates that have characterized ethics since ancient times. We can find a straightforward version of Hobbes's egoism, for example, in Plato's *Republic,* in his telling of "the ring of Gyges"—about a ring that allows a person to be invisible and thus immune from capture and punishment for whatever crimes and selfish actions. Glaucon's argument, when he presents this story, is that people are just only because they are afraid of being caught and punished. They are wary of the sanctions of society, but they do not act justly for the sake of being virtuous. Plato rejects this account, though not on psychological grounds, because it fails to account for the importance of justice in society in general. The more psychological answer would be that we do not, in fact, act out of selfish motives alone and that we do sometimes act out of consideration for other people's welfare, for the good of society, and for the sake of impersonal principles. Plato and Aristotle took social action as natural human behavior, but in modern ethics, beginning with Hobbes, the very possibility of altruism has become a major issue. Do we ever act unselfishly, however seemingly noble our motives?

This issue is called psychological egoism. (It has sometimes been suggested that Hobbes is also an *ethical egoist*—arguing that we ought to act in our own selfish interests. He says, for example, "It is natural, *and so reasonable,* for each individual to aim solely at his own preservation or pleasure" [emphasis added].) It is true, of course, that people in society often act for the benefit of others; indeed, Hobbes even allows that they ought to do so because of the rules to which they have (tacitly) agreed because of the social contract. But such behavior is nevertheless motivated by selfish motives, by the desire to protect oneself and maximize security and power in society. Thus the egoist need not argue that every act in itself must be carried out for purely selfish motives; it is enough that one's overall behavior in society is motivated by the desire for personal peace and well-being.

This view has the further consequence that the description of the way people actually do act provides the foundation for Hobbes's account of the way they *should* act, of the virtues. Rather than beginning with an ideal of human behavior, as Plato and Aristotle do, Hobbes takes the psychological character of human beings as the starting point and shows how acting ethically is nevertheless in the individual's own interests. Not only does this approach avoid the problem of basing ethical action on unprovable metaphysical assumptions (such as the existence of Plato's Forms, Aristotle's *telos,* or Augustine's God), but it leads to a theory in which ethics is a matter of human convention rather than some ideal to which people are naturally motivated. Whatever the advantage of theories based on natural altruism, there is clearly something philosophically attractive about a theory that relies only on undisputed, empirically supported premises (if Hobbes's theory in fact does).

However, egoism has been attacked vigorously ever since it became popular. One of the classic attacks on the egoist position was launched soon after Hobbes's death by Bishop Joseph Butler in England. In *Fifteen Sermons* (1726), he rejected

psychological egoism on several grounds; he began by accepting the distinction between (1) "private good and a person's own preservation and happiness" and
(2) "respect to society and the promotion of public good and happiness of society."
But these are not always in conflict, as the egoist too easily presumes; harking back
to Plato and Aristotle, Butler argues that, to the contrary, they are almost always
in harmony.

Butler's arguments might be condensed to three main points, all of which are
still being debated today (for example, in Thomas Nagel's recent book, *The Possibility of Altruism*). First, he says, the disposition to compassion and benevolence is
just as natural in us as our motives of self-interest. Moreover, so much of our self-
interest depends on the good will and approval (if not also affection) of other people that the two motives—egoism and altruism—are almost always in agreement.
Second, most of our interests in personal gain also (whether we intend them to or
not) benefit the rest of society. (This is a position that economist Adam Smith would
also argue, 50 years later, in his suggestion that capitalism works because, even
though every person pursues only his or her financial interest, there is nonetheless
"an invisible hand" that coordinates these interests for the good of all and "the
wealth of the nation.") Third, Butler argues, the egoist neglects the important influence of what he calls "conscience" (many psychologists today would call it "the
superego") in correcting our behavior and leading us to do the right thing. Butler
agrees that there are occasional villains in the world who do in fact seem to be actual egoists, but they should not be taken as examples, rather as exceptions. Most of
us are not egoists, although we are not perfect altruists either. Acting on our desires
does not make us selfish, because, as Plato and Aristotle simply assumed, most of
those desires are cultivated by and for the good of society as a whole. Virtue is as
natural to us as prudence, and the desire to be good as important (if not as traumatic)
as the fear of death.

Hobbes's theory of the formation of society (the "Leviathan") goes far beyond
the scope of ethics, but the basic concern is clearly central to every ethical theory.
Whether or not one agrees with Hobbes's egoism (and by no means are all social
contract theorists egoists), the idea that society is formed by already preexisting individuals (whether this is taken as literal history or only as a theoretical fiction) is
one of those fundamental frameworks within which all the rest of ethics gets
formed. If one accepts any such theory, it becomes inevitable that the individual and
his or her desires and needs will be the primary consideration in ethics. (Our Declaration of Independence is again an example: "We hold these truths to be self-
evident, that all men are created equal and endowed by their creator with certain
inalienable rights. . . . ") On the other hand, if one conceives of society itself as
primary—as Plato and Aristotle do—then the significance of the individual is
determined by society, and the good of society—not the desires and needs of the
individual—becomes primary. This is emphatically not to say that, on the latter
view, the desires and needs of the individual do not count; indeed, proponents of the
socially oriented theory would answer that this conception of ethics provides a
much better way of fulfilling people's real desires and needs. Nor is it the case that
the individualist conception necessarily cares more for the individual; Hobbes, because of his deeply pessimistic view of human nature, gives much less credit to
sympathy and compassion than does Aristotle, who sees virtue and nobility as natural human traits.

Discussion Questions

1. What is "the state of nature"? Is it important for Hobbes's argument that there ever actually existed such a presocietal state? What theory of human nature underlies Hobbes's view that the state of nature is a "war of all against all"? Do you accept this? Why or why not?
2. What is the basis of the state, according to Hobbes? What alternative conceptions of the foundation of society can you think of? Does society need a "foundation," in this sense?
3. What is the "leviathan"? Why does Hobbes use this image?
4. What is the "social contract"? Who signed it? Give examples of real, historical social contracts, and explain what they do.
5. Why is there no justice in the state of nature? What does this say about the nature of justice? Would it make a difference if God looked over (and created) the state of nature?

Study Questions

1. Why does Hobbes begin a treatise on ethics and politics with a discussion of the passions? Why not just start out discussing what is good and what is bad?
2. What is pleasure, according to Hobbes? Is pleasure necessarily good?
3. In what sense are we all equal, according to Hobbes? Why is this essential to his theory of society, human nature, and the social contract?
4. Are we all basically selfish? Are our actions basically founded on fear and insecurity? Does Hobbes mean that literally *every* act is selfish?
5. What is a "right"? How does one have a right? Under what circumstances can a right be taken away? Can a person *give* a right away? When and how?
6. What is a "commonwealth"? How is it formed? Is every state a commonwealth?
7. What does Hobbes mean by "liberty" ("freedom")? Would a person be freer if there were no laws and no state restricting his or her actions?

5

David Hume

Hume was born in 1711, in Scotland, where he spent most of his life. But he also traveled extensively as a popular spokesman for the Enlightenment, and he was as well known in Paris and London as he was in his home city of Edinburgh. He confessed that the ruling passion of his life was the desire for "literary fame," but his first book, the *Treatise,* "fell stillborn from the press," as he put it, and his later philosophical works did not fare much better. Because of his atheism, Hume was never able to secure a university position, and his published works earned him the title of "the great infidel." His literary fame in his lifetime was based on his ambitious *History of England* rather than on his philosophical writings, and it was only later that he received his recognition as one of the greatest minds in the history of philosophy. Hume died in 1776, the year of a colonial revolution of which, as a conservative, he could not wholly approve.

David Hume commands an impressive but curious position in the world of philosophy. On the one hand, he has often been admired—for example, by the great twentieth-century philosopher Bertrand Russell—as the outstanding genius of British philosophy; on the other hand, he has just as often been denounced as the ultimate skeptic who reduced all philosophical inquiry to nonsense and thus confirmed the tragic divorce between philosophy and our practical, everyday beliefs and affairs. Historically, Hume was a prominent spokesman for the Enlightenment, that largely eighteenth-century intellectual movement that celebrated reason and critical thinking. But in his conclusions, Hume seriously challenged the abilities of reason and critical thinking to provide us with justifications of even the most basic beliefs and so undermined precisely that movement in which he was widely known as the ultimate spokesman and befriended as "le bon David." But by rejecting reason, Hume proposed a shift in ethics (and philosophy in general) from abstract thinking to concrete experience. Ethics, in other words, was to become something of a *science* (which was very much in accord with Enlightenment thinking).

The key to Hume's philosophical method is *empiricism*—the appeal to the facts of experience to justify all knowledge; his primary conclusion, however, is *skepticism*—the denial that ultimate justification is possible. We cannot *prove* that we know anything about the world; we cannot even prove that there is in fact an external world beyond our senses. But whatever the limitations of philosophical reason, "nature," Hume assures us, gives us the good sense to live in the world and believe what we must believe—whether or not the philosophers can prove it true. He finishes his great book—his *Treatise of Human Nature*—exclaiming,

> Most fortunately it happens, that since reason is incapable of dispelling these clouds, nature herself suffices to that purpose, and cures me of this philosophical melancholy and delirium, either by relaxing this bent of mind, or by some avocation, and lively impression of my senses, which obliterate all these chimeras. I dine, I play a game of backgammon, I converse, and am merry with my friends; and when after three or four hours' amusement, I would return to these speculations they appear so cold, and strained, and ridiculous, that I cannot find in my heart to enter into them any farther.

Nevertheless, Hume's arguments for skepticism were so powerful that Bertrand Russell wrote of him, in 1945, that

> Hume's skeptical conclusions . . . are equally difficult to refute and to accept. The result was a challenge to philosophers, which, in my opinion, has still not been adequately met.

In the realm of morality, Hume's skepticism takes a similar form; we cannot *know* by reason alone that the moral principles that govern our actions are right. The ends of human action

> can never, in any case, be accounted for by *reason,* but recommend themselves entirely to the sentiments and affections of mankind, without any dependence on the intellectual faculties.

Accordingly, Hume even goes so far as to argue that, "Tis, not contrary to reason to prefer the destruction of the whole world to the scratching of my finger."

Moral skepticism is the view that there is no rational justification of our ethical opinions. But, as in his skeptical views about knowledge, Hume offers us an escape from this troubling conclusion; "nature," once again, provides us with the good sense to live well and act rightly, even if the Good and the Right are beyond the reach of reason. Our "sentiments and affections," not the deliberations of reason, guide our actions. But for Hume, in contrast to Hobbes, our natural sentiments are not all selfish but also sympathetic and compassionate. Indeed, in his most famous phrase, Hume tells us that "reason is, and ought to be, the slave of the passions." He may be a moral skeptic, but morals still have a basis, not in reason, perhaps, but in our emotions and our desires.

It would not be either wrong or insulting to call Hume a pagan in his moral philosophy. He was a vehement atheist and wrote polemical treatises against Christianity (especially his *Dialogues on Natural Religion,* which were published only after his death). He was a great admirer of the ancient Greeks and was steeped in the study of classical literature. Most importantly, his ethics was far more concerned with the nature of a person's character than with the abstract rules that make up morality. Hume far more resembles Aristotle in his moral philosophy than he does many modern-day moralists. Indeed, he sometimes referred to himself as a "pagan." It is good character and the virtues that provide us with the elements of ethics, not abstract and absolute principles. It is not morality but morals that are crucial to Hume, the concern for "personal merit" and agreeable "qualities"—such as a good sense of humor and trustworthiness. Hume, like Aristotle, begins with a view of people as social and sociable beings. Unlike Hobbes, he does not see human nature in terms of selfishness and the need for laws to keep us from murdering one another. Our basic instincts are rather those of sympathy and fellow-feeling, and morals are essentially those useful and agreeable characteristics that make it not only possible but necessary and even delightful for us to live together.

How does Hume's moral skepticism tie into his pagan ethics? First, it must be pointed out that skepticism for Hume is a limited doctrine; it denies the possibility of an exclusively rational justification of morals, but it does not reject their importance or necessity. Indeed, Hume was very much a conservative in both his politics and ethics, emphasizing the importance of tradition and continuity. Furthermore, it should be emphasized that Hume is much more skeptical in his early *Treatise of Human Nature* (1739) than he is in his later work, *An Inquiry Concerning the Principles of Morals* (both presented here). The emphasis in the *Treatise* is on the distinctions between reason and sentiment and between judgments of value and judgments of fact, with the conclusion that morals are matters of sentiment and value and cannot be justified through reason alone. The emphasis in the *Inquiry,* however, is on the positive substance of ethics, an investigation into those sentiments and qualities that make up morals, including especially our sense of benevolence and justice and those qualities of character that are most agreeable to ourselves and others. The early skepticism purges moral philosophy of what Hume considered an excessive emphasis on rationality; the later ethical inquiry replaces the proper emphasis on moral character and our more sociable feelings about one another. The two works are not opposed but complement one another; Hume's skepticism and his paganism are of a single piece—however unthinkable the former might have been to Aristotle.

We began by saying that Hume was, in his method, an *empiricist,* appealing all knowledge to experience. His empiricism helps give substance to his skepticism, because experience deals in facts, whereas ethics is concerned with values, which Hume sharply distinguishes from facts. Nevertheless, Hume's empiricism also provides him with the "experimental" method that is evident throughout the *Inquiry*— as it was so evident in Aristotle's *Ethics*—a descriptive method that relies heavily on what ordinary people in fact do feel rather than a rational discourse on what they ought to feel. It is the fact that we are benevolent creatures, concerned for others as well as for ourselves, that provides the starting point of Hume's ethics. Nevertheless, this undeniable fact does not constitute a justification of morals. It means only that this is the way we do act and do think, not that we ought to do so. In another of Hume's famous phrases, there is no deriving an "ought" from an "is."

The body of Hume's *Inquiry* is a detailed exploration of the variety and complexity of human behavior, with the intent to "deduce general maxims from a comparison of particular instances." These general maxims (which are not the same as moral principles) essentially include the concept of a virtue, which is "a quality of the mind agreeable to or approved of by everyone who considers or contemplates it." This emphasis on what is "agreeable" and "approved of" in turn forms the basic quest of Hume's ethics, which is to discover "those universal principles from which all censure and approbation is ultimately derived." These principles can be summarized in two words, "happiness" and "utility." Like Aristotle, Hume insists that happiness is the end of all human activity. And like John Stuart Mill and the utilitarians who succeed Hume in English philosophy, he takes the usefulness of certain qualities to be their sole basis in ethics. Justice, for instance, is often defended in part by appeal to public utility, but Hume goes much further and insists that utility is "the sole foundation of its [justice's] merit."

Hume's "experimental" method was derived most immediately from his empiricist predecessor John Locke, but his real intellectual hero was the great British scientist, Sir Isaac Newton. In the *Treatise,* Hume tried self-consciously to derive a theory of human nature on a par with Newton's grand mechanistic theory of nature. The aim of the *Inquiry* is more modest, but it is still directed at the reduction of the variety of human behavior to a single principle. Agreeableness and approval are the basis of ethical judgments, but they are not yet its ultimate principle. Happiness and utility are primary considerations, but they too are not yet ultimate. What is the ultimate principle for Hume? It is the simple fact of "social sympathy in human nature" (Section V, Part ii). There is no need and no point to "push our researches" beyond this, for there is no rational justification or divine design behind this simple fact. As he points out in the conclusion of the *Inquiry,* the truths of the account of ethics he advocates "represent virtue in all her genuine and most engaging charms and make us approach her with ease, familiarity, and affection." We are social and sociable creatures "by nature," and that is the end (and the beginning) of our ethical inquiries.

TREATISE OF HUMAN NATURE*

This selection on morals from Hume's *Treatise* of 1739 follows a lengthy analysis of the nature and limits of human knowledge in which Hume presents and defends his empiricist views. The empiricist holds that all knowledge is ultimately reducible to experience; reason does not and cannot operate without input from the senses. For Hume, all mental activity can be divided into two categories: impressions and ideas, a distinction he characterizes in the beginning of the *Treatise* as one with which we are all familiar, that between feeling and thinking, or in his terms, between sentiment and reason. Impressions are those experiences or sensations that simply come upon us and include emotions as well as simple awareness of sense data, such as seeing the page of this book. Ideas, on the other hand, have a more reflective quality. They are in the end copies of impressions (and this is why Hume is at bottom an empiricist—with very few exceptions, all knowledge can be traced back to experience) but are subject to manipulation insofar as they can be joined or separated, added to or subtracted from. The possibility of this sort of manipulation provides Hume with the distinction between simple and complex ideas, the former being more or less exact copies of impressions, whereas the latter are copies that have been transformed by reason.

*David Hume, *A Treatise of Human Nature.* Printed for John Noon, London, 1739.

The problem with which he begins in our selection is what he calls the "general foundation of morals," that is, the question of where our moral principles come from and how we come to know them. The view that is adamantly argued against in this selection holds that moral rules are known through reason alone, that they prescribe "eternal fitnesses," and most importantly, that they do not essentially involve the emotions. Hume first shows why this cannot be the correct account of morality, then offers his own view in which the passions, not reason, rule.

Active reason is the manipulation and comparison of our ideas (in Hume's sense of the word), whether with each other or with matters of fact. Because this is essentially a matter of examination and comparison, Hume claims that reason alone is impotent—it has no power to make us *want* to act in one way rather than another. But moral rules do impose duties and prohibitions; that is, they encourage certain sorts of actions and discourage others. Thus, Hume claims that it cannot be the case that such rules are based on such an impotent faculty as reason alone.

OF VIRTUE AND VICE IN GENERAL

Moral Distinctions Not Derived from Reason: From Section I

It has been observed that nothing is ever present to the mind but its perceptions; and that all the actions of seeing, hearing, judging, loving, hating, and thinking, fall under this denomination. The mind can never exert itself in any action which we may not comprehend under the term of *perception;* and consequently that term is no less applicable to those judgments by which we distinguish moral good and evil, than to every other operation of the mind. To approve of one character, to condemn another, are only so many different perceptions.

Now, as perceptions resolve themselves into two kinds, viz., *impressions* and *ideas,* this distinction gives rise to a question, with which we shall open up our present inquiry concerning morals, whether it is by means of our *ideas* or *impressions* we distinguish betwixt vice and virtue, and pronounce an action blamable or praiseworthy? This will immediately cut off all loose discourses and declamations, and reduce us to something precise and exact on the present subject.

Those who affirm that virtue is nothing but a conformity to reason; that there are eternal fitnesses and unfitnesses of things which are the same to every rational being that considers them; that the immutable measure of right and wrong imposes an obligation, not only on human creatures, but also on the Deity himself: all these systems concur in the opinion that morality, like truth, is discerned merely by ideas, and by their juxtaposition and comparison. In order, therefore, to judge of these systems, we need only consider whether it be possible from reason alone to distinguish betwixt moral good and evil, or whether there must concur some other principles to enable us to make that distinction.

If morality had naturally no influence on human passions and actions, it were in vain to take such pains to inculcate it; and nothing would be more fruitless than that multitude of rules and precepts with which all moralists abound. Philosophy is commonly divided into *speculative* and *practical;* and as morality is always comprehended under the latter division, it is supposed to influence our passions and actions, and to go beyond the calm and indolent judgments of the understanding. And this is confirmed by common experience, which informs us that men are often governed by their duties, and are deterred from some actions by the opinion of injustice, and impelled to others by that of obligation.

Since morals, therefore, have an influence on the actions and affections, it follows that they cannot be derived from reason. . . . Morals excite passions, and produce or prevent actions. Reason of itself is utterly impotent in this particular. The rules of morality, therefore, are not conclusions of our reason.

No one, I believe, will deny the justness of this inference; nor is there any other means of evading it than by denying that principle on which it is founded. As long as it is allowed that reason has no influence on our passions and actions, it is in vain to pretend that morality is discovered only by a deduction of reason. An active principle can never be founded on an inactive; and if reason be inactive in itself, it must remain so in all its shapes and appearances, whether it exerts itself in natural or moral subjects, whether it considers the powers of external bodies or the actions of rational beings. . . .

Reason is the discovery of truth or falsehood. Truth or falsehood consists in an agreement or disagreement either to the *real* relations of ideas, or to *real* existence and matter of fact. Whatever, therefore, is not susceptible of this agreement or disagreement is incapable of being true or false, and can never be an object of our reason. Now, it is evident our passions, volitions, and actions, are not susceptible of any such agreement or disagreement; being original facts and realities, complete in themselves, and implying no reference to other passions, volitions, and actions. It is impossible, therefore, they can be pronounced either true or false, and be either contrary or conformable to reason.

This argument is of double advantage to our present purpose. For it proves *directly* that actions do not derive their merit from a conformity to reason, nor their blame from a contrariety to it; and it proves the same truth more *indirectly,* by showing us that as reason can never immediately prevent or produce any action by contradicting or approving of it, it cannot be the source of moral good and evil, which are found to have that influence. Actions may be laudable or blamable, but they cannot be reasonable or unreasonable: laudable or blamable, therefore, are not the same with reasonable or unreasonable. The merit and demerit of actions frequently contradict, and sometimes control our natural propensities. But reason has no such influence. Moral distinctions, therefore, are not the offspring of reason. Reason is wholly inactive, and can never be the source of so active a principle as conscience, or a sense of morals. . . .

Before offering his own theory of the foundation of morals, Hume gives us two more arguments against the view that moral principles are discoverable by reason alone. Both arguments are based on the limited powers of reason and its consequent inability to generate any of the ingredients necessary for moral action.

The first of these arguments begins by showing that reason's influence over actions is very limited indeed. Reason can be what Hume calls the "mediate cause" of an action in one of two ways: It can direct the passions (which in turn will result in action) toward an object, or it can tell us how to get the coveted object, a sort of means/end reasoning. These are the only ways in which reason can cause action. Now consider when it is appropriate to assign moral blame to a person. Surely, Hume says, it is not when that person makes a factual error with regard to either those things that ought to be pursued or the best means of attaining them. These are mistakes of fact, not instances of moral culpability. But these are just the ways—and the only ways—in which reason can cause action. Thus, if failures (and successes) in this regard are not the source of moral assessments, morality cannot be derived from reason alone.

The second argument has a similar form and the same conclusion. This time Hume begins with the powers of reason in itself rather than its effect on passions and actions. Again, there are two possibilities that must be investigated, neither of which turn out to be a good candidate for accounting for our moral lives. This leads Hume to conclude that morality is not based on reason. There are two "operations of human understanding": the ability to compare ideas, in particular with regard to relations between things, and the ability to draw conclusions regarding matters of fact. Neither of these powers can do more than *describe* a situation; they cannot recommend or discourage action. That is, they have no normative force and therefore cannot be the source of morality. This is what Hume means when he claims that one cannot derive "an 'ought' from an 'is.'"

It has been observed that reason, in a strict and philosophical sense, can have an influence on our conduct only after two ways: either when it excites a passion by informing us of the existence of something which is a proper object of it; or when it discovers the connection of causes and effects so as to afford us means of exerting any passion. These are the only kinds of judgment which can accompany our actions, or can be said to produce them in any manner; and it must be allowed that these judgments may often be false and erroneous. A person may be affected with passion, by supposing a pain or pleasure to lie in an object which has no tendency to produce either of these sensations, or which produces the contrary to what is imagined. A person may also take false measures for the attaining of his end, and may retard by his foolish conduct instead of forwarding the execution of any object. These false judgments may be thought to affect the passions and actions, which are connected with them, and may be said to render them unreasonable, in a figurative and improper way of speaking. But though this be acknowledged, it is easy to observe that these errors are so far from being the source of all immorality that they are commonly very innocent, and draw no manner of guilt upon the person who is so unfortunate as to fall into them. They extend not beyond a mistake of *fact,* which moralists have not generally supposed criminal, as being perfectly involuntary. I am more to be lamented than blamed if I am mistaken with regard to the influence of objects in producing pain or pleasure, or if I know not the proper means of satisfying my desires. No one can ever regard such errors as a defect in my moral character. A fruit, for instance, that is really disagreeable appears to me at a distance, and, through mistake, I fancy it to be pleasant and delicious. Here is one error. I choose certain means of reaching this fruit which are not proper for my end. Here is a second error; nor is there any third one which can ever possibly enter into our reasonings concerning actions. I ask, therefore, if a man in this situation, and guilty of these two errors, is to be regarded as vicious and criminal, however unavoidable they might have been? Or if it be possible to imagine that such errors are the sources of all immorality? . . .

Thus, upon the whole, it is impossible that the distinction betwixt moral good and evil can be made by reason; since that distinction has an influence upon our actions, of which reason alone is incapable. Reason and judgment may, indeed, be the mediate cause of an action, by prompting or by directing a passion; but it is not pretended that a judgment of this kind, either in its truth or falsehood, is attended with virtue or vice. And as to the judgments which are caused by our judgments, they can still less bestow those moral qualities on the actions which are their causes. . . .

Of all crimes that human creatures are capable of committing, the most horrid and unnatural is ingratitude, especially when it is committed against parents, and appears in the more flagrant instances of wounds and death. This is acknowledged by all mankind, philosophers as well as the people. The question only arises among philosophers, whether the guilt or moral deformity of this action be discovered by demonstrative reasoning, or be felt by an internal sense and by means of some sentiment which the reflecting on such an action naturally occasions. This question will soon be decided against the former opinion, if we can show the same relations in other objects without the notion of any guilt or iniquity attending them. Reason or science is nothing but the comparing of ideas, and the discovery of their relations; and if the same relations have different characters it must evidently follow that those characters are not discovered merely by reason. To put the affair, therefore, to this trial, let us choose any inanimate object, such as an oak or elm, and let us suppose that by the dropping of its seed it produces a sapling below it which, springing up by degrees, at last overtops and destroys the parent tree: I ask if in this instance there be wanting any relation which is discoverable in parricide or ingratitude? Is not the one tree the cause of the other's existence; and the latter the cause of the destruction of the former in the same manner as when a child murders his parent? It is not sufficient to reply that a choice or will is wanting. For in the case of parricide, a will does not give rise to any *different* relations, but is only the cause from which the action is derived; and consequently produces the *same* relations that in the oak or elm arise from some other principles. It is a will or choice that determines a man to kill his parent; and they are the laws of matter and motion that determine a sapling to destroy the oak from which it sprung. Here then the same relations have different causes; but still the relations are the same; and as their discovery is not in both cases attended with a notion of immorality, it follows that that notion does not arise from such a discovery.

But to choose an instance still more resembling; I would fain ask anyone why incest in the human species is criminal, and why the very same action and the same relations in animals have not the smallest moral turpitude and deformity? If it be answered that this action is innocent in animals, because they have not reason sufficient to discover its turpitude, but that man being endowed with that faculty which *ought* to restrain him to his duty, the same action instantly becomes criminal to him. Should this be said, I would reply that this is evidently arguing in a circle. For before reason can perceive this turpitude, the turpitude must exist, and consequently is independent of the decisions of our reason, and is their object more properly than their effect. According to this system, then, every animal that has sense, and appetite, and will, that is, every animal must be susceptible of all the same virtues and vices for which we ascribe praise and blame to human creatures. All the difference is that our superior reason may serve to discover the vice or virtue, and by that means may augment the blame or praise; but still this discovery supposes a separate being in these moral distinctions, and a being which depends only on the will and appetite, and which, both in thought and reality, may be distinguished from reason. Animals are susceptible of the same relations with respect to each other as the human species, and therefore would also be susceptible of the same morality if the essence of morality consisted in these relations. Their want of a sufficient degree of reason may hinder them from perceiving the duties and obligations of morality; but can never hinder these duties from existing; since they must antecedently exist in order to their being perceived. Reason must find them, and can never produce them. This argument deserves to be weighed as being, in my opinion, entirely decisive.

Nor does this reasoning only prove that morality consists not in any relations that are the objects of science; but, if examined, will prove with equal certainty that it consists not in any *matter of fact* which can be discovered by the understanding. This is the *second* part of our argument; and if it can be made evident, we may conclude that morality is not an object of reason. But can there be any difficulty in proving that vice and virtue are not matters of fact whose existence we can infer by reason? Take any action allowed to be vicious—willful murder, for instance. Examine it in all lights, and see if you can find that matter of fact or real existence which you call *vice*. In whichever way you take it, you find only certain passions, motives, volitions, and thoughts. There is no other matter of fact in the case. The vice entirely escapes you, as long as you consider the object. You never can find it till you turn your reflection into your own breast and find a sentiment of disapprobation which arises in you towards this action. Here is a matter of fact; but it is the object of feeling, not of reason. It lies in yourself, not in the object. So that when you pronounce any action or character to be vicious, you mean nothing, but that from the constitution of your nature you have a feeling or sentiment of blame from the contemplation of it. Vice and virtue, therefore, may be compared to sounds, colours, heat, and cold, which, according to modern philosophy, are not qualities in objects but perceptions in the mind: and this discovery in morals, like that other in physics, is to be regarded as a considerable advancement of the speculative sciences; though, like that too, it has little or no influence on practice. Nothing can be more real, or concern us more, than our own sentiments of pleasure and uneasiness; and if these be favourable to virtue, and unfavourable to vice, no more can be requisite to the regulation of our conduct and behaviour.

I cannot forbear adding to these reasonings an observation which may, perhaps, be found of some importance. In every system of morality which I have hitherto met with, I have always remarked that the author proceeds for some time in the ordinary way of reasoning, and establishes the being of a god, or makes observations concerning human affairs; when of a sudden I am surprised to find that instead of the usual copulations of propositions *is* and *is not,* I meet with no proposition that is not connected with an *ought* or an *ought not.* This change is imperceptible, but is, however, of the last consequence. For as this *ought* or *ought not* expresses some new relation or affirmation, it is necessary that it should be observed and explained; and at the same time that a reason should be given for what seems altogether inconceivable, how this new relation can be a deduction from others which are entirely different from it. But as authors do not commonly use this precaution, I shall presume to recommend it to the readers; and am persuaded that this small attention would subvert all the vulgar systems of morality and let us see that the distinction of vice and virtue is not founded merely on the relations of objects, nor is perceived by reason.

Hume now proceeds to give us his own theory—that morality is first of all a matter of emotion. The difference between virtuous and vicious actions, in the end, lies simply in the way they make us feel: Good actions cause us pleasure, bad ones pain. Of course, as Hume rightly points out, to get a full account of the nature of moral principles, we still need to discover *why* we have such reactions; that such reactions are the essence of moral distinctions Hume takes to be obvious.

Moral Distinctions Derived from a Moral Sense: From Section II

Thus the course of the argument leads us to conclude that since vice and virtue are not discoverable merely by reason, or the comparison of ideas, it must be by means of some impression or sentiment they occasion, that we are able to mark the difference betwixt them. Our decisions concerning moral rectitude and depravity are evidently perceptions; and as all perceptions are either impressions or ideas, the exclusion of the one is a convincing argument for the other. Morality, therefore, is more properly felt than judged of; though this feeling or sentiment is commonly so soft and gentle that we are apt to confound it with an idea, according to our common custom of taking all things for the same which have any near resemblance to each other.

The next question is of what nature are these impressions, and after what manner do they operate upon us? Here we cannot remain long in suspense, but must pronounce the impression arising from virtue to be agreeable, and that proceeding from vice to be uneasy. Every moment's experience must convince us of this. There is no spectacle so fair and beautiful as a noble and generous action; nor any which gives us more abhorrence than one that is cruel and treacherous. No enjoyment equals the satisfaction we receive from the company of those we love and esteem; as the greatest of all punishments is to be obliged to pass our lives with those we hate or contemn. A very play or romance may afford us instances of this pleasure which virtue conveys to us; and pain which arises from vice.

Now, since the distinguishing impressions by which moral good or evil is known are nothing but *particular* pains or pleasures, it follows that in all inquiries concerning these moral distinctions it will be sufficient to show the principles which make us feel a satisfaction or uneasiness from the survey of any character, in order to satisfy us why the character is laudable or blamable. An action, or sentiment, or character, is virtuous or vicious; why? Because its view causes a pleasure or uneasiness of a particular kind. In giving a reason, therefore, for the pleasure or uneasiness, we sufficiently explain the vice or virtue. To have the sense of virtue is nothing but to *feel* a satisfaction of a particular kind from the contemplation of a character. The very *feeling* constitutes our praise or admiration. We go no further; nor do we inquire into the cause of the satisfaction. We do not infer a character to be virtuous because it pleases; but in feeling that it pleases after such a particular manner we in effect feel that it is virtuous. The case is the same as in our judgments concerning all kinds of beauty, and tastes, and sensations. Our approbation is implied in the immediate pleasure they convey to us.

I have objected to the system, which establishes eternal rational measures of right and wrong, that 'tis impossible to shew, in the actions of reasonable creatures, any relations, which are not found in external objects; and therefore, if morality always attended these relations, 'twere possible for inanimate matter to become virtuous or vicious. Now it may, in like manner, be objected to the present system, that if virtue and vice be determin'd by pleasure and pain, these qualities must, in every case, arise from the sensations; and consequently any object, whether animate or inanimate, rational or irrational, might become morally good or evil, provided it can excite a satisfaction or uneasiness. But tho' this objection seems to be the very same, it has by no means the same force, in the one case as in the other. For, *first,* 'tis evident, that under the term *pleasure* we comprehend sensations, which are very different from each other, and which have only such a distant resemblance, as is requisite to make them be express'd by the same abstract term. A good composition of music and a bottle of good wine equally produce pleasure; and what is more, their goodness is determin'd merely by the pleasure. But shall we say upon that account, that the wine is harmonious, or the music of a good flavour? In like manner an inanimate object, and the character or sentiments of any person may, both of them, give satisfaction; but as the satisfaction is different, this keeps our sentiments concerning them from being confounded, and makes us ascribe virtue to the one, and not to the other. Nor is every sentiment of pleasure or pain, which arises from characters and actions, of that *peculiar* kind, which makes us praise or condemn. The good qualities of an enemy are hurtful to us; but may still command our esteem and respect. 'Tis only when a character is considered in general, without reference to our particular interest, that it causes such a feeling or sentiment, as denominates it morally good or evil. 'Tis true, those sentiments, from interest and morals, are apt to be confounded, and naturally run into one another. It seldom happens, that we do not think an enemy vicious, and can distinguish betwixt his opposition to our interest and real villainy or baseness. But this hinders not, but that the sentiments are, in themselves, distinct; and a man of temper and judgment may preserve himself from these illusions. In like manner, tho' 'tis certain a musical voice is nothing but one that naturally gives a *particular* kind of pleasure; yet 'tis difficult for a man to be sensible, that the voice of an enemy is agreeable, or to allow it to be musical. But a person of a fine ear, who has the command of himself, can separate these feelings, and give praise to what deserves it. . . .

Thus we are still brought back to our first position that virtue is distinguished by the pleasure, and vice by the pain, that any action, sentiment, or character, gives us by the mere view and contemplation. This decision is very commodious; because it reduces us to this simple question, *why any action or sentiment, upon the general view or survey, gives a certain satisfaction or uneasiness,* in order to show the origin of its moral recitude or depravity, without looking for any incomprehensible relations and qualities which never did exist in nature, nor even in our imagination, by any clear and distinct conception? I flatter myself I have executed a great part of my present design by a statement of the question which appears to me so free from ambiguity and obscurity.

We may begin with considering anew the nature and force of *sympathy.* The minds of all men are similar in their feelings and operations, nor can any one be actuated by any affection, of which all others are not, in some degree susceptible. As in strings equally wound up, the motion of one communicates itself to the rest; so all the affections readily pass from one person to another, and beget correspondent movements in every human creature. When I see the *effects* of passion in the voice and gesture of any person, my mind immediately passes from these effects to their causes, and forms such a lively idea of the passion, as is presently converted into the passion itself. In like manner, when I perceive the *causes* of any emotion, my mind is convey'd to the effects, and is actuated with a like emotion. Were I present at any of the more terrible operations of surgery, 'tis certain, that even before it begun, the preparation of the instruments, the laying of the bandages in order, the heating of the irons, with all the signs of anxiety and concern in the patients and assistants, would have a great effect upon my mind, and excite the strongest sentiments of pity and terror. No passion of another discovers itself immediately to the mind. We are only sensible of its causes or effects. From *these* we infer the passion: And consequently *these* give rise to our sympathy. . . .

Thus it appears, *that* sympathy is a very powerful principle in human nature, . . . and *that* it produces our sentiment of morals in all the artificial virtues. From thence we may presume, that it also gives rise to many of the other virtues; and that qualities acquire our approbation, because of their tendency to the good of mankind. This presumption must become a certainty, when we find that most of those qualities, which we *naturally* approve of, have actually that tendency, and render a man a proper member of society: While the qualities, which we *naturally* disapprove of, have a contrary tendency, and render any intercourse with the person dangerous or disagreeable. For having found, that such tendencies have force enough to produce the strongest sentiment of morals, we can never reasonably, in these cases, look for any other cause of approbation or blame; it being an inviolable maxim in philosophy, that where any particular cause is sufficient for an effect, we ought to rest satisfied with it, and ought not to multiply causes without necessity. . . .

There have been many systems of morality advanc'd by philosophers in all ages; but if they are strictly examin'd, they may be reduc'd to two, which alone merit our attention. Moral good and evil are certainly distinguish'd by our *sentiments,* not by *reason:* But these sentiments may arise either from the mere species or appearance of characters and passions, or from reflexions on their tendency to the happiness of mankind, and of particular persons. My opinion is, that both these causes are intermix'd in our judgments of morals; after the same manner as they are in our decisions concerning most kinds of external beauty: Tho' I am also of opinion, that reflexions on the tendencies of actions have by far the greatest influence, and determine all the great lines of our duty. There are, however, instances, in cases of less moment, wherein this immediate taste or sentiment produces our approbation. Wit, and a certain easy and disengag'd behaviour, are qualities *immediately agreeable* to others, and command their love and esteem. Some of these qualities produce satisfaction in others by particular *original* principles of human nature, which cannot be accounted for: Others may be resolv'd into principles, which are more general. This will best appear upon a particular enquiry.

In Book II of the *Treatise,* "Of The Passions," Hume proceeds to elaborate his theory of the sentiments. In the next two readings, from Part II of the work, Hume brilliantly analyzes two of the most important moral sentiments, love and hatred. (Between these two sections he conducts a number of fascinating "experiments" concerning what we today would call the psychology of love and hatred. Although space prevents us from including them here, we recommend them highly to readers interested in this subject).

OF LOVE AND HATRED

Of the Objects and Causes of Love and Hatred

'Tis altogether impossible to give any definition of the passions of *love* and *hatred;* and that because they produce merely a simple impression, without any mixture or composition. 'Twou'd be as unnecessary to attempt any description of them, drawn from their nature, origin, causes and objects; and that both because these are the subjects of our present enquiry, and because these passions of themselves are sufficiently known from our common feeling and experience. This we have already observ'd concerning pride and humility, and here repeat it concerning love and hatred; and indeed there is so great a resemblance betwixt these two sets of passions, that we shall be oblig'd to begin with a kind of abridgment of our reasonings concerning the former, in order to explain the latter.

As the immediate *object* of pride and humility is self or that identical person, of whose thoughts, actions, and sensations we are intimately conscious; so the *object* of love and hatred is some other person, of whose thoughts, actions, and sensations we are not conscious. This is sufficiently evident from experience. Our love and hatred are always directed to some sensible being external to us; and when we talk of *self-love,* 'tis not in a proper sense, nor has the sensation it produces any thing in common with that tender emotion, which is excited by a friend or mistress. 'Tis the same case with hatred. We may be mortified by our own faults and follies; but never feel any anger or hatred, except from the injuries of others.

But tho' the object of love and hatred be always some other person, 'tis plain that the object is not, properly speaking, the *cause* of these passions, or alone sufficient to excite them. For since love and hatred are directly contrary in their sensation, and have the same object in common, if that object were also their cause, it wou'd produce these opposite passions in an equal degree; and as they must, from the very first moment, destroy each other, none of them wou'd ever be able to make its appearance. There must, therefore, be some cause different from the object.

If we consider the causes of love and hatred, we shall find they are very much diversify'd, and have not many things in common. The virtue, knowledge, wit, good sense, good humour of any person, produce love and esteem; as the opposite qualities, hatred and contempt. The same passions arise from bodily accomplishments, such as beauty, force, swiftness, dexterity; and from their contraries; as likewise from the external advantages and disadvantages of family, possessions, cloaths, nation and climate. There is not one of these objects, but what by its different qualities may produce love and esteem, or hatred and contempt.

From the view of these causes we may derive a new distinction betwixt the *quality* that operates, and the *subject* on which it is plac'd. A prince, that is possess'd of a stately palace, commands the esteem of the people upon that account; and that *first,* by the beauty of the palace, and *secondly,* by the relation of property, which connects it with him. The removal of either of these destroys the passion; which evidently proves that the cause is a compounded one.

'Twou'd be tedious to trace the passions of love and hatred, thro' all the observations which we have form'd concerning pride and humility, and which are equally applicable to both sets of passions. 'Twill be sufficient to *remark* in general, that the object of love and hatred is evidently some thinking person; and that the sensation of the former passion is always agreeable, and of the latter uneasy. We may also *suppose* with some shew of probability, *that the cause of both these passions is always related to a thinking being,* and that the cause of the former produce a separate pleasure, and of the latter a separate uneasiness.

One of these suppositions, *viz.* that the cause of love and hatred must be related to a person or thinking being, in order to produce these passions, is not only probable, but too evident to be contested. Virtue and vice, when consider'd in the abstract; beauty and deformity, when plac'd on inanimate objects; poverty and riches, when belonging to a third person, excite no degree of love or hatred, esteem or contempt towards those, who have no relation to them. A person looking out at a window, sees me in the street, and beyond me a beautiful palace, with which I have no concern: I believe none will pretend, that this person will pay me the same respect, as if I were owner of the palace.

'Tis not so evident at first sight, that a relation of impressions is requisite to these passions, and that because in the transition the one impression is so much confounded with the other, that they become in a manner undistinguishable. But as in pride and humility, we have easily been able to make the separation, and to prove, that every cause of these passions produces a separate pain or pleasure, I might here observe the same method with the same success, in examining particularly the several causes of love and hatred. But as I hasten to a full and decisive proof of these systems, I delay this examination for a moment: And in the mean time shall endeavour to convert to my present purpose all my reasonings concerning pride and humility, by an argument that is founded on unquestionable experience.

There are few persons, that are satisfy'd with their own character, or genius, or fortune, who are not desirous of shewing themselves to the world, and of acquiring the love and approbation of mankind. Now 'tis evident, that the very same qualities and circumstances, which are the causes of pride or self-esteem, are also the causes of vanity or the desire of reputation; and that we always put to view those particulars with which in ourselves we are best satisfy'd. But if love and esteem were not produc'd by the same qualities as pride, according as these qualities are related to ourselves or others, this method of proceeding wou'd be very absurd, nor cou'd men expect a correspondence in the sentiments of every other person, with those themselves have entertain'd. 'Tis true, few can form exact systems of the passions, or make reflexions on their general nature and resemblances. But without such a progress in philosophy, we are not subject to many mistakes in this particular, but are sufficiently guided by common experience, as well as by a kind of *presensation;* which tells us what will operate on others, by what we feel immediately in ourselves. Since then the same qualities that produce pride or humility, cause love or hatred; all the arguments that have been employ'd to prove, that the causes of the former passions excite a pain or pleasure independent of the passion, will be applicable with equal evidence to the causes of the latter.

Difficulties Solv'd

After so many and such undeniable proofs drawn from daily experience and observation, it may seem superfluous to enter into a particular examination of all the causes of love and hatred. I shall, therefore, employ the sequel of this part, *First,* In removing some difficulties, concerning particular causes of these passions. *Secondly,* In examining the compound affections, which arise from the mixture of love and hatred with other emotions.

Nothing is more evident, than that any person acquires our kindness, or is expos'd to our ill-will, in proportion to the pleasure or uneasiness we receive from him, and that the passions keep pace exactly with the sensations in all their changes and variations. Whoever can find the means either by his services, his beauty, or his flattery, to render himself useful or agreeable to us, is sure of our affections: As on the other hand, whoever harms or displeases us never fails to excite our anger or hatred. When our own nation is at war with any other, we detest them under the character of cruel, perfidious, unjust and violent: But always esteem ourselves and allies equitable, moderate, and merciful. If the general of our enemies be successful, 'tis with difficulty we allow him the figure and character of a man. He is a sorcerer: He has a communication with daemons; as is reported of *Oliver Cromwell* and the *Duke of Luxembourg:* He is bloody-minded, and takes a pleasure in death and destruction. But if the success be on our side, our commander has all the opposite good qualities, and is a pattern of virtue, as well as of courage and conduct. His treachery we call policy: His cruelty is an evil insepararable from war. In short, every one of his faults we either endeavour to extenuate, or dignify it with the name of that virtue, which approaches it. 'Tis evident the same method of thinking runs thro' common life.

There are some, who add another condition, and require not only that the pain and pleasure arise from the person, but likewise that it arise knowingly, and with a particular design and intention. A man, who wounds and harms us by accident, becomes not our enemy upon that account, nor do we think ourselves bound by any ties of gratitude to one, who does us any service after the same manner. By the intention we judge of the actions, and according as that is good or bad, they become causes of love and hatred.

But here we must make a distinction. If that quality in another, which pleases or displeases, be constant and inherent in his person and character, it will cause love or hatred independent of the intention: But otherwise a knowledge and design is requisite, in order to give rise to these passions. One that is disagreeable by his deformity or folly is the object of our aversion, tho' nothing be more certain, than that he has not the least intention of displeasing us by these qualities. But if the uneasiness proceed not from a quality, but an action, which is produc'd and annihilated in a moment, 'tis necessary, in order to produce some relation, and connect this action sufficiently with the person, that it be deriv'd from a particular fore-thought and design. 'Tis not enough, that the action arise from the person, and have his for its immediate cause and author. This relation alone is too feeble and inconstant to be a foundation for these passions. It reaches not the sensible and thinking part, and neither proceeds from any thing *durable* in him, nor leaves any thing behind it; but passes in a moment, and is as if it had never been. On the other hand, an intention shews certain qualities, which remaining after the action is perform'd, connect it with the person, and facilitate the transition of ideas from one to the other. We can never think of him without reflecting on these qualities; unless repentance and a change of life have produc'd an alteration in that respect: In which case the passion is likewise alter'd. This therefore is one reason, why an intention is requisite to excite either love or hatred.

But we must farther consider, that an intention, besides its strengthening the relation of ideas, is often necessary to produce a relation of impressions, and give rise to pleasure and uneasiness. For 'tis observable, that the principal part of an injury is the contempt and hatred, which it shews in the person, that injures us; and without that, the mere harm gives us a less sensible uneasiness. In like manner, a good office is agreeable, chiefly because it flatters our vanity, and is a proof of the kindness and esteem of the person, who performs it. The removal of the intention, removes the mortification in the one case, and vanity in the other; and must of course cause a remarkable diminution in the passions of love and hatred.

I grant, that these effects of the removal of design, in diminishing the relations of impressions and ideas, are not entire, nor able to remove every degree of these relations. But then I ask, if the removal of design be able entirely to remove the passion of love and hatred? Experience, I am sure, informs us of the contrary, nor is there any thing more certain, than that men often fall into a violent anger for injuries, which they themselves must own to be entirely involuntary and accidental. This emotion, indeed, cannot be of long continuance; but still is sufficient to shew, that there is a natural connexion betwixt uneasiness and anger, and that the relation of impressions will operate upon a very small relation of ideas. But when the violence of the impression is once a little abated, the defect of the relation begins to be better felt; and as the character of a person is no wise interested in such injuries as are casual and involuntary, it seldom happens that on their account, we entertain a lasting enmity.

To illustrate this doctrine by a parallel instance, we may observe, that not only the uneasiness, which proceeds from another by accident, has but little force to excite our passion, but also that which arises from an acknowledg'd necessity and duty. One that has a real design of harming us, proceeding not from hatred and ill-will, but from justice and equity, draws not upon him our anger, if we be in any degree reasonable; notwithstanding he is both the cause, and the knowing cause of our sufferings. Let us examine a little this phenomenon.

'Tis evident in the first place, that this circumstance is not decisive; and tho' it may be able to diminish the passions, 'tis seldom it can entirely remove them. How few criminals are there, who have no ill-will to the person, that accuses them, or to the judge, that condemns them, even tho' they be conscious of their own deserts? In like manner our antagonist in a law-suit, and our competitor for any office, are commonly regarded as our enemies, tho' we must acknowledge, if we wou'd but reflect a moment, that their motive is entirely as justifiable as our own.

Besides we may consider, that when we receive harm from any person, we are apt to imagine him criminal, and 'tis with extreme difficulty we allow of his justice and innocence. This is a clear proof, that, independent of the opinion of iniquity, any harm or uneasiness has a natural tendency to excite our hatred, and that afterwards we seek for reasons upon which we may justify and establish the passion. Here the idea of injury produces not the passion, but arises from it.

Nor is it any wonder that passion should produce the opinion of injury; since otherwise it must suffer a considerable diminution, which all the passions avoid as much as possible. The removal of injury may remove the anger, without proving that the anger arises from only the injury. The harm and the justice are two contrary objects, of which the one has a tendency to produce hatred, and the other love; and 'tis according to their different degrees, and our particular turn of thinking, that either of the objects prevails, and excites its proper passion.

DISCUSSION

At the end of another book (*An Inquiry Concerning Human Understanding,* 1748) Hume also announces, "Morals and criticism are not so properly objects of the understanding as of taste and sentiment. Beauty, whether moral or natural, is felt more properly than perceived." This sharp distinction between judgments of fact (by way of "understanding") and judgments of value (through taste and sentiment) is the key to Hume's moral philosophy. It is, first of all, a kind of psychological theory about the origins and motivation of value judgments, but it is, much more importantly, a logical thesis about their nature and justification. In the *Treatise,* "sentiment" is sharply distinguished from "reason," which Hume continuously dismisses as "impotent" and incapable of directly "producing any action or volition." "Reason is, and ought to be, the slave of the passions, and can never pretend to any other office than to serve and obey them," he insists. Morals and actions are motivated by our emotions, desires, and instincts; reason is mere calculation of connections between ideas. No fact or mere idea can motivate us to do or want to do anything, Hume claims. At most, reason may be called in to deliberate the *means* to get what we want; it cannot (as Aristotle, for example, believed) establish our *ends.*

Hume's central logical argument in the *Treatise* (and his opening argument in the *Inquiry*) turns on the essential and often neglected distinction between judgments of fact and judgments of value. It is one thing to know that a thing has a certain quality (for example, that the fish has rotted or that Mr. Scrooge never gives Christmas presents), something quite different to be repulsed or attracted to that thing because of that quality. Virtue and vice are not the same as—and cannot be deduced from—the qualities themselves. Rather it is our reactions to those qualities that constitute moral judgments. This difference between facts and values can be demonstrated too in a logical distinction which, according to Hume, has been ignored by even the greatest moral philosophers.

In every system of morality, which I have hitherto met with, . . . the author proceeds for some time in the ordinary way of reasoning . . . when all of a sudden I am surprised to find that, instead of the usual copulations of propositions *is* and *is not,* I meet with no proposition that is not connected with an *ought* or an *ought not.* This change is imperceptible; but it is, however, of the last consequence. For as this *ought* or *ought not* expresses some new relation or affirmation, it is necessary that it should be observed and explained; and that at the same time a reason should be given, for what seems altogether inconceivable, how this new relation can be a deduction from others which are entirely different from it.

The *Inquiry* does not reiterate this point, but nevertheless the distinction between fact and value continues to be central to Hume's position. The argument—recently dubbed "the naturalistic fallacy"—is that no statement that something is good or bad, right or wrong, follows logically from a purely descriptive statement about what something is. Even the most extreme case—a description of the massacre of a defenseless village by bandits—does not yet warrant the conclusion that this is bad or wrong. (Imagine the same basic description supplied by a household exterminator, reporting to a homeowner on the treatment of a termite colony.) Psychologically, what must be added to the factual description to move us to repulsion are our feelings of human sympathy; logically, what must be added to the description is at least one premise that connects the "is" of description to the "ought" of morals, such as:

> (Factual premise) Three thousand creatures were killed.
>
> (Value premise) Killing is wrong.
>
> (Conclusion) Something wrong has been done.

But many moral philosophers commit the *naturalistic fallacy* with arguments such as the following (which are usually sufficiently complex so that the fallacy isn't so obvious):

> (Factual premise) The Bible says "thou shalt not kill."
>
> (Value conclusion) Therefore, do not kill.

or,

> (Factual premise) People are basically selfish.
>
> (Value conclusion) Therefore, people ought to do what is in their own best interests.

There are premises missing here: "You should do whatever the Bible says." And, "If people are selfish, then they ought to do what is in their own best interests." But these premises can be disputed, and thus the arguments are, at best, debatable if not fallacious. Sometimes, this "fallacy" is the core of an entire ethics, for example, in Aristotle (and Kant). Aristotle begins with certain "facts" about human nature and deduces, in just the way forbidden by Hume, conclusions about what is good and right and what one ought to do. (Kant begins with a factual premise about our rational faculties and similarly deduces that what we ought to do is to act rationally.) But is this "fallacy" really a fallacy? Or is Hume too strictly enforcing a too-narrow distinction and ignoring the *context* in which "is" and "ought" claims are made? Could we save the traditional arguments with an added premise, for example, that says that we *ought* to do what is *natural,* thus undercutting the so-called naturalistic fallacy by introducing nature into the argument itself (the teleological position, in effect)? Or consider the following sequence of statements, formulated by the American philosopher John Searle as a counterexample to Hume's "is-ought" argument:

1. Jones uttered the words "I hereby promise to pay you, Smith, five dollars."
2. Jones promised to pay Smith five dollars.
3. Jones placed himself under an obligation to pay Smith five dollars.
4. Jones is under an obligation to pay Smith five dollars.
5. Jones ought to pay Smith five dollars.

Searle claims that this sequence moves from purely factual statements to a conclusion that is clearly an "ought" type judgment of value. How is this possible? Is there a concealed evaluative premise somewhere in the argument, for instance, the value judgment that one ought to keep one's promises? (Searle claims that this is merely a tautology—a purely trivial statement.) Are there implicit conditions (for example, our own cultural expectations and understanding of promises) that provide unspoken premises? Indeed, how many other such arguments can you formulate in which the facts about certain institutions or established behavior seem to yield clear "ought" type value judgments? How defensible is Hume's "is-ought" distinction? And what does this imply about the general distinction between facts and values?

AN INQUIRY CONCERNING THE PRINCIPLES OF MORALS*

OF THE GENERAL PRINCIPLES OF MORALS, BENEVOLENCE, AND JUSTICE: SECTIONS I, II, AND III

Hume begins his *Inquiry* of 1751, as he began his earlier *Treatise*, by marking the distinction between reason and sentiment, and he again insists that the basis of morals can be only our feelings, not reason. On this basis, he again insists that virtually the whole of moral philosophy has been mistaken; but here in the *Inquiry* his emphasis is primarily on the positive, on the "scientific" approach to ethics and a study of "the estimable [and] blamable qualities of men" (Section I). He begins with two of the most estimable qualities—benevolence and justice (Sections II and III). Justice, Hume claims, is founded solely on *utility,* a claim that is calculated to challenge the whole history of the subject, from Plato until the present. Finally, Hume corrects his British compatriot Hobbes, who argued that political society is based on the force of *law,* originating with "the social contract," but political society is rather based, like justice, on the foundation of utility. Utility, Hume argues, inspires our approval and not our obedience. Utility "pleases"; it does not command.

Of the General Principles of Morals: Section I

> Disputes with men pertinaciously obstinate in their principles are, of all others, the most irksome, except, perhaps, those with persons entirely disingenuous, who really do not believe the opinions they defend, but engage in the controversy from affectation, from a spirit of opposition, or from a desire of showing wit and ingenuity superior to the rest of mankind. The same blind adherence to their own arguments is to be expected in both: the same contempt of their

*David Hume, *An Inquiry Concerning the Principles of Morals,* edited by L.A. Selby-Bigge. Copyright 1951 by Clarendon Press.

antagonists, and the same passionate vehemence in enforcing sophistry and falsehood. And as reasoning is not the source whence either disputant derives his tenets, it is in vain to expect that any logic which speaks not to the affections will ever engage him to embrace sounder principles.

Those who have denied the reality of moral distinctions may be ranked among the disingenuous disputants; nor is it conceivable that any human creature could ever seriously believe that all characters and actions were alike entitled to the affection and regard of everyone. The difference which nature has placed between one man and another is so wide, and this difference is still so much further widened by education, example, and habit that, where the opposite extremes come at once under our apprehension, there is no skepticism so scrupulous, and scarce any assurance so determined, as absolutely to deny all distinction between them. Let a man's insensibility be ever so great, he must often be touched with the images of *right* and *wrong;* and let his prejudices be ever so obstinate, he must observe that others are susceptible of like impressions. The only way, therefore, of converting an antagonist of this kind is to leave him to himself. For, finding that nobody keeps up the controversy with him, it is probable he will at last of himself, from mere weariness come over to the side of common sense and reason.

There has been a controversy started of late, much better worth examination, concerning the general foundation of *morals;* whether they be derived from *reason* or from *sentiment;* whether we attain the knowledge of them by a chain of argument and induction or by an immediate feeling and finer internal sense; whether, like all sound judgment of truth and falsehood, they should be the same to every rational, intelligent being, or whether, like the perception of beauty and deformity, they be founded entirely on the particular fabric and constitution of the human species.

The ancient philosophers, though they often affirm that virtue is nothing but conformity to reason, yet, in general, seem to consider morals as deriving their existence from taste and sentiment. On the other hand, our modern inquirers, though they also talk much of the beauty of virtue and deformity of vice, yet have commonly endeavored to account for these distinctions by metaphysical reasonings and by deductions from the most abstract principles of the understanding. Such confusion reigned in these subjects that an opposition of the greatest consequence could prevail between one system and another, and even in the parts of almost each individual system, and yet nobody, till very lately, was ever sensible of it. The elegant Lord Shaftesbury, who first gave occasion to remark this distinction, and who, in general, adhered to the principles of the ancients, is not himself entirely free from the same confusion.

It must be acknowledged that both sides of the question are susceptible of specious arguments. Moral distinctions, it may be said, are discernible by pure *reason:* else, whence the many disputes that reign in common life, as well as in philosophy, with regard to this subject; the long chain of proofs often produced on both sides, the examples cited, the authorities appealed to, the analogies employed, the fallacies detected, the inferences drawn, and the several conclusions adjusted to their proper principles? Truth is disputable, not taste: what exists in the nature of things is the standard of sentiment. Propositions in geometry may be proved, systems in physics may be controverted, but the harmony of verse, the tenderness of passion, the brilliancy of wit must give immediate pleasure. No man reasons concerning another's beauty, but frequently concerning the justice or injustice of his actions. In every criminal trial, the first object of the prisoner is to disprove the facts alleged and deny the actions imputed to him; the second, to prove that, even if these actions were real, they might be justified as innocent and lawful. It is confessedly by deductions of the understanding that the first point is ascertained: how can we suppose that a different faculty of the mind is employed in fixing the other?

On the other hand, those who would resolve all moral determinations into *sentiments* may endeavor to show that it is impossible for reason ever to draw conclusions of this nature. To virtue, say they, it belongs to be *amiable,* and vice *odious.* This forms their very nature or essence. But can reason or argumentation distribute these different epithets to any subjects and pronounce beforehand that this must produce love, and that hatred? Or what other reason can we ever assign for these affections but the original fabric and formation of the human mind, which is naturally adapted to receive them?

The end of all moral speculations is to teach us our duty, and, by proper representations of the deformity of vice and beauty of virtue, beget correspondent habits, and engage us to avoid the one, and embrace the other. But is this ever to be expected from inferences and conclusions of the understanding, which of themselves have no hold of the affections or set in motion the active powers of men? They discover truths. But where the truths which they discover are indifferent and beget no desire or aversion, they can have no influence on conduct and behavior. What is honorable, what is fair, what is becoming, what is noble, what is generous takes possession of the heart and animates us to embrace and maintain it. What is intelligible, what is evident, what is probable, what is true procures only the cool assent of the understanding, and, gratifying a speculative curiosity, puts an end to our researches.

Extinguish all the warm feelings and prepossessions in favor of virtue, and all disgust or aversion to vice; render men totally indifferent toward these distinctions; and morality is no longer a practical study, nor has any tendency to regulate our lives and actions.

These arguments on each side (and many more might be produced) are so plausible that I am apt to suspect they may, the one as well as the other, be solid and satisfactory, and that *reason* and *sentiment* concur in almost all moral determinations and conclusions. The final sentence, it is probable, which pronounces characters and actions amiable or odious, praiseworthy or blamable; that which stamps on them the mark of honor or infamy, approbation or censure; that which renders morality an active principle and constitutes virtue our happiness, and vice our misery—it is probable, I say, that this final sentence depends on some internal sense or feeling which nature has made universal in the whole species. For what else can have an influence of this nature? But in order to pave the way for such a sentiment and give a proper discernment of its object, it is often necessary, we find, that much reasoning should precede, that nice distinctions be made, just conclusions drawn, distant comparisons formed, complicated relations examined, and general facts fixed and ascertained. Some species of beauty, especially the natural kinds, on their first appearance command our affection and approbation; and where they fail of this effect, it is impossible for any reasoning to redress their influence or adapt them better to our taste and sentiment. But in many orders of beauty, particularly those of the finer arts, it is requisite to employ much reasoning in order to feel the proper sentiment; and a false relish may frequently be corrected by argument and reflection. There are just grounds to conclude that moral beauty partakes much of this latter species and demands the assistance of our intellectual faculties in order to give it a suitable influence on the human mind.

But though this question concerning the general principles of morals be curious and important, it is needless for us at present to employ further care in our researches concerning it. For if we can be so happy, in the course of this inquiry, as to discover the true origin of morals, it will then easily appear how far either sentiment or reason enters into all determinations of this nature. In order to attain this purpose, we shall endeavor to follow a very simple method: we shall analyze that complication of mental qualities which form what, in common life, we call "personal merit"; we shall consider every attribute of the mind which renders a man an object either of esteem and affection or of hatred and contempt; every habit or sentiment or faculty which, if ascribed to any person, implies either praise or blame and may enter into any panegyric or satire of his character and manners. The quick sensibility, which, on this head, is so universal among mankind, gives a philosopher sufficient assurance that he can never be considerably mistaken in framing the catalogue or incur any danger of misplacing the objects of his contemplation: he needs only enter into his own breast for a moment and consider whether or not he should desire to have this or that quality ascribed to him, and whether such or such an imputation would proceed from a friend or an enemy. The very nature of language guides us almost infallibly in forming a judgment of this nature; and as every tongue possesses one set of words which are taken in a good sense, and another in the opposite, the least acquaintance with the idiom suffices, without any reasoning, to direct us in collecting and arranging the estimable or blamable qualities of men. The only object of reasoning is to discover the circumstances on both sides which are common to these qualities—to observe that particular in which the estimable qualities agree, on the one hand, and the blamable, on the other; and thence to reach the foundation of ethics and find those universal principles from which all censure or approbation is ultimately derived. As this is a question of fact, not of abstract science, we can only expect success by following the experimental method and deducing general maxims from a comparison of particular instances. The other scientifical method, where a general abstract principle is first established, and is afterwards branched out into a variety of inferences and conclusions, may be more perfect in itself, but suits less the imperfection of human nature and is a common source of illusion and mistake, in this as well as in other subjects. Men are now cured of their passion for hypotheses and systems in natural philosophy, and will hearken to no arguments but those which are derived from experience. It is full time they should attempt a like reformation in all moral disquisitions and reject every system of ethics, however subtle or ingenious, which is not founded on fact and observation.

We shall begin our inquiry on this head by the consideration of the social virtues; Benevolence and Justice. The explication of them will probably give us an opening by which the others may be accounted for.

Of Benevolence: Section II

Part I It may be esteemed, perhaps, a superfluous task to prove that the benevolent or softer affections are *estimable* and, wherever they appear, engage the approbation and good will of mankind. The epithets, *sociable, good-natured, humane, merciful, grateful, friendly, generous, beneficent,* or their equivalents, are known in all languages, and universally express the highest merit which human nature is capable of attaining. Where these amiable qualities are attended with birth and power and eminent abilities, and display themselves in the good government or useful instruction of mankind, they seem even to raise the possessors of them above the rank of *human nature* and make them approach, in some measure, to the divine. Exalted capacity, undaunted courage, prosperous success—these may only expose a hero or politician to the envy and ill will of the public. But as soon as the praises are added of humane and beneficent, when instances are displayed of lenity, tenderness, or friendship, envy itself is silent or joins the general voice of approbation and applause.

When Pericles, the great Athenian statesman and general, was on his deathbed, his surrounding friends, deeming him now insensible, began to indulge their sorrow for their expiring patron by enumerating his great qualities and successes, his conquests and victories, the unusual length of his administration, and his nine trophies erected over the enemies of the republic. *You forget,* cries the dying hero who had heard all, *you forget the most eminent of my praises, while you dwell so much on those vulgar advantages in which fortune had a principal share. You have not observed that no citizen has ever yet worn mourning on my account.*

In men of more ordinary talents and capacity, the social virtues become, if possible, still more essentially requisite, there being nothing eminent, in that case, to compensate for the want of them, or preserve the person from our severest hatred as well as contempt. A high ambition, an elevated courage is apt, says Cicero, in less perfect characters, to degenerate into a turbulent ferocity. The more social and softer virtues are there chiefly to be regarded. These are always good and amiable.

The principal advantage which Juvenal discovers in the extensive capacity of the human species is that it renders our benevolence also more extensive and gives us larger opportunities of spreading our kindly influence than what are indulged to the inferior creation. It must, indeed, be confessed that by doing good only can a man truly enjoy the advantages of being eminent. His exalted station, of itself, but the more exposes him to danger and tempest. His sole prerogative is to afford shelter to inferiors who repose themselves under his cover and protection.

But I forget that it is not my present business to recommend generosity and benevolence, or to paint in their true colors all the genuine charms of the social virtues. These, indeed, sufficiently engage every heart, on the first apprehension of them; and it is difficult to abstain from some sally or panegyric, as often as they occur in discourse or reasoning. But our object here being more the speculative than the practical part of morals, it will suffice to remark (what will readily, I believe, be allowed) that no qualities are more entitled to the general good will and approbation of mankind than beneficence and humanity, friendship and gratitude, natural affection and public spirit, or whatever proceeds from a tender sympathy with others and a generous concern for our kind and species. These, wherever they appear, seem to transfuse themselves, in a manner, into each beholder, and to call forth, in their own behalf, the same favorable and affectionate sentiments which they exert on all around.

Part II   We may observe that in displaying the praises of any humane, beneficent man there is one circumstance which never fails to be amply insisted on—namely, the happiness and satisfaction derived to society from his intercourse and good offices. To his parents, we are apt to say, he endears himself by his pious attachment and duteous care still more than by the connections of nature. His children never feel his authority but when employed for their advantage. With him, the ties of love are consolidated by beneficence and friendship. The ties of friendship approach, in a fond observance of each obliging office, to those of love and inclination. His domestics and dependents have in him a sure resource, and no longer dread the power of fortune but so far as she exercises it over him. From him the hungry receive food, the naked clothing, the ignorant and slothful skill and industry. Like the sun, an inferior minister of Providence, he cheers, invigorates, and sustains the surrounding world.

If confined to private life, the sphere of his activity is narrower, but his influence is all benign and gentle. If exalted into a higher station, mankind and posterity reap the fruit of his labors.

As these topics of praise never fail to be employed, and with success, where we would inspire esteem for anyone, may it not thence be concluded that the *utility* resulting from the social virtues forms, at least, a *part* of their merit, and is one source of that approbation and regard so universally paid to them?

When we recommend even an animal or a plant as *useful* and *beneficial,* we give it an applause and recommendation suited to its nature. As, on the other hand, reflection on the baneful influence of any of these inferior beings always inspires us with the sentiment of aversion. The eye is pleased with the prospect of cornfields and loaded vineyards, horses grazing, and flocks pasturing; but flies the view of briars and brambles affording shelter to wolves and serpents.

A machine, a piece of furniture, a vestment, a house well contrived for use and convenience is so far beautiful and is contemplated with pleasure and approbation. An experienced eye is here sensible to many excellences which escape persons ignorant and uninstructed.

Can anything stronger be said in praise of a profession, such as merchandise or manufacture, than to observe the advantages which it procures to society? And is not a monk and inquisitor enraged when we treat his order as useless or pernicious to mankind?

The historian exults in displaying the benefit arising from his labors. The writer of romance alleviates or denies the bad consequences ascribed to his manner of composition.

In general, what praise is implied in the simple epithet "useful"! What reproach in the contrary!

Your gods, says Cicero, in opposition to the Epicureans, cannot justly claim any worship or adoration with whatever imaginary perfections you may suppose them endowed. They are totally useless and inactive. Even the Egyptians, whom you so much ridicule, never consecrated any animal but on account of its utility.

The skeptics assert, though absurdly, that the origin of all religious worship was derived from the utility of inanimate objects, as the sun and moon to the support and well-being of mankind. This is also the common reason assigned by historians for the deification of eminent heroes and legislators.

To plant a tree, to cultivate a field, to beget children—meritorious acts, according to the religion of Zoroaster.

In all determinations of morality, this circumstance of public utility is ever principally in view; and wherever disputes arise, either in philosophy or common life, concerning the bounds of duty, the question cannot, by any means, be decided with greater certainty than by ascertaining, on any side, the true interests of mankind. If any false opinion, embraced from appearances, has been found to prevail, as soon as further experience and sounder reasoning have given us juster notions of human affairs, we retract our first sentiment and adjust anew the boundaries of moral good and evil.

Giving alms to common beggars is naturally praised, because it seems to carry relief to the distressed and indigent. But when we observe the encouragement thence arising to idleness and debauchery, we regard that species of charity rather as a weakness than a virtue.

Tyrannicide, or the assassination of usurpers and oppressive princes, was highly extolled in ancient times, because it both freed mankind from many of these monsters and seemed to keep the others in awe whom the sword or poniard could not reach. But history and experience having since convinced us that this practice increases the jealousy and cruelty of princes, a Timoleon and a Brutus, though treated with indulgence on account of the prejudices of their times, are now considered as very improper models for imitation.

Liberality in princes is regarded as a mark of beneficence. But when it occurs that the homely bread of the honest and industrious is often thereby converted into delicious cakes for the idle and the prodigal, we soon retract our heedless praises. The regrets of a prince for having lost a day were noble and generous; but had he intended to have spent it in acts of generosity to his greedy courtiers, it was better lost than misemployed after that manner.

Luxury, or a refinement on the pleasures and conveniences of life, had long been supposed the source of every corruption in government, and the immediate cause of faction, sedition, civil wars, and the total loss of liberty. It was therefore universally regarded as a vice, and was an object of declamation to all satirists and severe moralists. Those who prove, or attempt to prove, that such refinements rather tend to the increase of industry, civility, and arts regulate anew our *moral* as well as *political* sentiments and represent as laudable or innocent what had formerly been regarded as pernicious and blamable.

Upon the whole, then, it seems undeniable that nothing can bestow more merit on any human creature than the sentiment of benevolence in an eminent degree, and that a *part,* at least, of its merit arises from its tendency to promote the interests of our species and bestow happiness on human society. We carry our view into the salutary consequences of such a character and disposition; and whatever has so benign an influence and forwards so desirable an end is beheld with complacency and pleasure. The social virtues are never regarded without their beneficial tendencies, nor viewed as barren and unfruitful. The happiness of mankind, the order of society, the harmony of families, the mutual support of friends are always considered as the result of the gentle dominion over the breasts of men.

How considerable a *part* of their merit we ought to ascribe to their utility will better appear from future disquisitions as well as the reason why this circumstance has such a command over our esteem and approbation (Section V).

Benevolence is a personal sense toward others, but justice is something more abstract, concerning the structure of the entire society. Both, however, serve general *utility,* justice by human design, benevolence "by nature." In this section, Hume argues further that utility is the *only* basis for justice. That is, if justice did not produce concrete benefits for human beings, it would not exist. It is entirely founded on social utility.

Of Justice: Section III

Part I   That Justice is useful to society, and consequently that *part* of its merit, at least, must arise from that consideration, it would be a superfluous undertaking to prove. That public utility is the *sole* origin of Justice, and that reflections on the beneficial consequences of this virtue are the *sole* foundation of its merit, this proposition, being more curious and important, will better deserve our examination and inquiry.

Let us suppose that nature has bestowed on the human race such profuse *abundance* of all *external* conveniences that, without any uncertainty in the event, without any care or industry on our part, every individual finds himself fully provided with whatever his most voracious appetites can want or luxurious imagination wish or desire. His natural beauty, we shall suppose, surpasses all acquired ornaments: the perpetual clemency of the seasons renders useless all clothes or covering; the raw herbage affords him the most delicious fare; the clear fountain the richest beverage. No laborious occupation required: no tillage, no navigation. Music, poetry, and contemplation form his sole business; conversation, mirth, and friendship, his sole amusement.

It seems evident that in such a happy state every other social virtue would flourish and receive tenfold increase; but the cautious, jealous virtue of justice would never once have been dreamed of. For what purpose make a partition of goods where everyone has already more than enough? Why give rise to property where there cannot possibly be any injury? Why call this object *mine* when, upon the seizing of it by another, I need but stretch out my hand to possess myself of what is equally valuable? Justice, in that case, being totally *useless,* would be an idle ceremonial and could never possibly have place in the catalogue of virtues.

We see, even in the present necessitous condition of mankind, that, wherever any benefit is bestowed by nature in an unlimited abundance, we leave it always in common among the whole human race and make no subdivisions of right and property. Water and air, though the most necessary of all objects, are not challenged as the property of individuals; nor can any man commit injustice by the most lavish use and enjoyment of these blessings. In fertile, extensive countries, with few inhabitants, land is regarded on the same footing. And no topic is so much insisted on, by those who defend the liberty of the seas, as the unexhausted use of them in navigation. Were the advantages procured by navigation as inexhaustible, these reasoners had never had any adversaries to refute, nor had any claims ever been advanced of a separate, exclusive dominion over the ocean.

It may happen in some countries, at some periods, that there be established a property in water, none in land, if the latter be in greater abundance than can be used by the inhabitants, and the former be found with difficulty and in very small quantities.

Again: suppose that, though the necessities of the human race continue the same as at present, yet the mind is so enlarged and so replete with friendship and generosity that every man has the utmost tenderness for every man, and feels no more concern for his own interest than for that of his fellows: It seems evident that the *use* of Justice would, in this case, be suspended by such an extensive benevolence, nor would the divisions and barriers of property and obligation have ever been thought of. Why should I bind another, by a deed or promise, to do me any good office when I know that he is already prompted by the strongest inclination to seek my happiness and would of himself perform the desired service, except the hurt he thereby receives be greater than the benefit accruing to me; in which case he knows that, from my innate humanity and friendship, I should be the first to oppose myself to his imprudent generosity? Why raise landmarks between my neighbor's field and mine when my heart has made no division between our interests, but shares all his joys and sorrows with the same force and vivacity as if originally my own? Every man, upon this supposition, being a second self to another, would trust all his interests to the discretion of every man without jealousy, without partition, without distinction. And the whole human race would form only one family where all would lie in common and be used freely, without regard to property; but cautiously too, with an entire regard to the necessities of each individual, as if our own interests were most intimately concerned.

In the present disposition of the human heart, it would perhaps be difficult to find complete instances of such enlarged affections; but still we may observe that the case of families approaches toward it; and the stronger the mutual benevolence is among the individuals, the nearer it approaches, till all distinction of property be, in a great measure, lost and confounded among them. Between married persons, the cement of friendship is by the laws supposed so strong as to abolish all division of possessions, and has often, in reality, the force ascribed to it. And it is observable that, during the ardor of new enthusiasms, when every principle is inflamed into extravagance, the community of goods has frequently been attempted; and nothing but experience of its inconveniences, from the returning or disguised selfishness of men, could make the imprudent fanatics adopt anew the ideas of justice and of separate property. So true is it that this virtue derives its existence entirely from its necessary *use* to the intercourse and social state of mankind.

To make this truth more evident, let us reverse the foregoing suppositions and, carrying everything to the opposite extreme, consider what would be the effect of these new situations. Suppose a society to fall into such want of all common necessaries that the utmost frugality and industry cannot preserve the greater number from perishing and the whole from extreme misery: it will readily, I believe, be admitted that the strict laws of justice are suspended in such a pressing emergency and give place to the stronger motives of necessity and self-preservation. Is it any crime, after a shipwreck, to seize whatever means or instrument of safety one can lay hold of, without regard to former limitations of property? Or if a city besieged were perishing with hunger, can we imagine that men will see any means of preservation before them and lose their lives from a scrupulous regard to what, in other situations, would be the rules of equity and justice? The *use* and *tendency* of that virtue is to procure happiness and security, by preserving order in society. But where the society is ready to perish from extreme necessity, no greater evil can be dreaded from violence and injustice, and every man may now provide for himself by all the means which prudence can dictate or humanity permit. The public, even in less urgent necessities, opens granaries without the consent of proprietors, as justly supposing that the authority of magistracy may, consistent with equity, extend so far. But were any number of men to assemble without the tie of laws or civil jurisdiction, would an equal partition of bread in a famine, though effected by power and even violence, be regarded as criminal or injurious?

Suppose, likewise, that it should be a virtuous man's fate to fall into the society of ruffians, remote from the protection of laws and government, what conduct must he embrace in that melancholy situation? He sees such a desperate rapaciousness prevail, such a disregard to equity, such contempt of order, such stupid blindness to future consequences, as must immediately have the most tragical conclusion and must terminate in destruction to the greater number and in a total dissolution of society to the rest. He, meanwhile, can have no other expedient than to arm himself, to whomever the sword he seizes, or the buckler, may belong; to make provision of all means of defense and security. And his particular regard to justice being no longer of *use* to his own safety or that of others, he must consult the dictates of self-preservation alone, without concern for those who no longer merit his care and attention.

When any man, even in political society, renders himself by his crimes obnoxious to the public, he is punished by the laws in his goods and person; that is, the ordinary rules of justice are, with regard to him, suspended for a moment, and it becomes equitable to inflict on him for the *benefit* of society, what otherwise he could not suffer without wrong or injury.

The rage and violence of public war, what is it but a suspension of justice among the warring parties who perceive that this virtue is now no longer of any *use* or advantage to them? The laws of war, which then succeed to those of equity and justice, are rules calculated for the *advantage* and *utility* of that particular state in which men are now placed. And were a civilized nation engaged with barbarians who observed no rules even of war, the former must also suspend their observance of them where they no longer serve to any purpose, and must render every action or rencounter as bloody and pernicious as possible to the first aggressors.

Thus the rules of equity or justice depend entirely on the particular state and condition in which men are placed, and owe their origin and existence to that *utility* which results to the public from their strict and regular observance. Reverse, in any considerable circumstance, the condition of men: produce extreme abundance or extreme necessity, implant in the human breast perfect moderation and humanity or perfect rapaciousness and malice; by rendering justice totally *useless,* you thereby totally destroy its essence and suspend its obligation upon mankind.

The common situation of society is a medium amidst all these extremes. We are naturally partial to ourselves and to our friends, but are capable of learning the advantage resulting from a more equitable conduct. Few enjoyments are given us from the open and liberal hand of nature; but by art, labor, and industry we can extract them in great abundance. Hence the ideas of property become necessary in all civil society; hence justice derives its usefulness to the public; and hence alone arises its merit and moral obligation. . . . The more we vary our views of human life, and the newer and more unusual the lights are in which we survey it, the more shall we be convinced that the origin here assigned for the virtue of justice is real and satisfactory. . . .

The convenience, or rather necessity, which leads to justice is so universal and everywhere points so much to the same rules that the habit takes place in all societies; and it is not without some scrutiny that we are able to ascertain its true origin. The matter, however, is not so obscure but that, even in common life, we have every moment recourse to the principle of public utility and ask, *What must become of the world, if such practices prevail? How could society subsist under such disorders?* Were the distinction or separation of possessions entirely useless, can anyone conceive that it ever should have obtained in society?

Thus we seem, upon the whole, to have attained a knowledge of the force of that principle here insisted on, and can determine what degree of esteem or moral approbation may result from reflections on public interest and utility. The necessity of justice to the support of society is the *sole* foundation of that virtue; and since no moral excellence is more highly esteemed, we may conclude that this circumstance of usefulness has, in general, the strongest energy and most entire command over our sentiments. It must therefore be the source of a considerable part of the merit ascribed to humanity, benevolence, friendship, public spirit, and other social virtues of that stamp; as it is the *sole* source of the moral approbation paid to fidelity, justice, veracity, integrity, and those other estimable and useful qualities and principles. It is entirely agreeable to the rules of philosophy, and even of common reason, where any principle has been found to have a great force and energy in one instance, to ascribe to it a like energy in all similar instances. This indeed is Newton's chief rule of philosophizing.

DISCUSSION

Hume begins his *Inquiry* by distinguishing once again the roles of reason and sentiment in morals, but his treatment here is much less polemical than in the *Treatise* and reason is given a more generous role in the ascertaining of utility, at least. He maintains throughout, however, that moral judgments come from sentiment and not reason, and reminds us that "truth is disputable, not taste." The method of the *Inquiry,* however, is not to pursue this central distinction between reason and sentiment so much as to study in detail the particular sentiments that motivate our actions. Always the scientist, Hume conscientiously abstains from moralizing:

> But I forget that it is not my present business to recommend generosity and benevolence, or to paint in their true colors all the genuine charms of the social virtues. . . . Our object here being more speculative than the practical part of morals, it will suffice to remark (what will readily, I believe, be allowed) that no qualities are more entitled to the general good will and approbation of mankind than beneficence and humanity, friendship and gratitude, natural affection and public spirit, or whatever proceeds from a tender sympathy with others and a generous concern for our kind and our species.

The *Inquiry,* in other words, is a description of our moral feelings rather than an attempt to praise and evoke them. Like Aristotle, he bases his argument on what people generally agree to, rather than his own moral arguments or feelings. Nevertheless, the writing of the *Inquiry* makes it quite obvious that Hume is also doing the latter, encouraging these good feelings as well as describing them. Again, like Aristotle.

The analysis of the key sentiments of benevolence and justice involves a potentially troublesome circle; benevolence is explained in terms of its utility, but then later (in Section V) it is made quite clear to us that utility pleases us because it serves our general feeling of benevolence. (Hume might well be able to avoid this circularity by pointing to the difference between sympathy and benevolence and claiming that it is the former on which utility is ultimately based. In other words, it is our fellow-feeling [our sympathy with others], rather than the more specific desire to benefit others that forms the basis of our moral judgments, our assessments of the pleasing and the displeasing. Indeed, Hume does base his defense of utility on sympathy for the most part, but there is no denying that he also makes reference to our "natural sentiment of benevolence.") Regardless of possible problems with circularity, however, the thrust of Hume's analysis is clearly pointed: *morality is first of all a question of good character,* "personal merit," and most of the virtues Hume praises are not what we would usually call "moral" virtues but rather *social* virtues—those that allow us to get along and enjoy each other's company. In this, again, he most resembles Aristotle and least resembles the Christian moralists of his own day, against whom Hume was vigorously reacting. Benevolence, of course, is an essential ingredient in Christian ethics as well. But Hume makes it clear that it is not "loving thy neighbor" as a divine duty, but rather as a natural affection, that is the key to morals.

Hume's heavy emphasis on utility becomes much more problematic when he turns to the virtue of justice. "Justice," Hume begins, "is useful to society." But Hume then goes on to say that "utility is the *sole* origin (and foundation) of Justice," which he insists is a "more curious and important" claim, deserving of our attention. If the world were more generous and if we all had everything that we wanted, Hume says, there would be no need for justice. Furthermore—again harking back to Aristotle—Hume suggests that if there were universal benevolence, for instance, if all of us were friends, there would be no use for justice either. Justice and benevolence are thereby distinguished; justice comes in when benevolence runs out. But can justice be attributed solely to utility?

The utility of justice is directed in every instance (though not always successfully) to "the good of mankind." But the argument that justice is necessary to the support of society (which Hume demonstrates through a large variety of considerations) does not demonstrate his polemical claim that utility is the *sole* foundation of justice. What he shows persuasively is the importance of justice and the wide variety of arrangements that might be just—because they are practical or convenient—in different societies and different circumstances. But he makes no mention of the particular aspect of justice that dominates modern discussions of the concept—the question of *rights.* Hume rejects the ideal of universal equality as "impractical," and he points to the utility of considerations of *merit.* But he does not consider those cases in which justice demands a respect for rights that is clearly against the general utility, perhaps even destructive to the whole society. The death-row inmate's right to appeal, for instance, is one that is often taken to decrease rather than increase overall utility (if, for example, it is virtually certain that the inmate is guilty and that the appeal will be unsuccessful); yet many hold that our system of justice requires that such a right cannot be sacrificed simply to achieve other more popular, and perhaps productive, societal goals (such as saving taxpayers' money). Hume could argue that respect for such rights will, in the long run, prove to be useful, but this is an argument that he does not make for himself and that has often been disputed. In any case, it would seem that justice sometimes demands respect for such rights, *whatever the effects of general utility.* Justice consists of a number of competing claims, among them claims to rights, an insistence on some kind of equality (before the law, for example), demands of merit and desert, contractual obligations, and a number of other, related concerns. To suggest that justice is solely a matter of utility is either to ignore these complications or to so stretch the concept of "utility" that it no longer means that singular concern around which Hume builds his ethics.

Why is Hume so adamant about this? His last sentence (in Section III) gives it away: "This indeed is Newton's chief rule of philosophizing." It is the scientific elegance of a single explanatory principle that leads Hume to his single-mindedness, and one might well suggest that "mutual agreeableness" plays the same role in Hume's social philosophy that "gravity" plays in Newton's physics.

WHY UTILITY PLEASES: FROM SECTION V

Having reduced morality to "utility," Hume now faces the critical question of how to explain the desirability of utility itself. After remarking on the curiosity that this principle has so often been ignored in morals, he goes on to assert the importance of *self-love*. (See also Appendix II, pages 239 to 242 in the *Inquiry*.) But self-love does not mean selfishness, and Hume takes great care to emphasize that hand in hand with self-love go our natural sentiments of sympathy and benevolence. It is our approval and repulsion of other people's behavior (for example, in studying the heroic and evil figures in history) that determine much of our feelings about ourselves, and it is a concern for the public good that motivates many of our actions, as part of our own good, too:

> It appears that a tendency to public good and to the promoting of peace, harmony and order in society does always, by affecting the benevolent principles of our frame, engage us on the side of the social virtues. And it appears, as an additional confirmation, that these principles of humanity and sympathy enter so deeply into all our sentiments and have so powerful an influence as may enable them to excite the strongest censure and applause.

Part I It seems so natural a thought to ascribe to their utility the praise which we bestow on the social virtues that one would expect to meet with this principle everywhere in moral writers as the chief foundation of their reasoning and inquiry. In common life we may observe that the circumstance of utility is always appealed to, nor is it supposed that a greater eulogy can be given to any man than to display his usefulness to the public and enumerate the services which he has performed to mankind and society. What praise, even of an inanimate form, if the regularity and elegance of its parts destroy not its fitness for any useful purpose! And how satisfactory an apology for any disproportion or seeming deformity if we can show the necessity of that particular construction for the use intended! A ship appears more beautiful to an artist, or one moderately skilled in navigation, where its prow is wide and swelling beyond its poop, than if it were framed with a precise geometrical regularity, in contradiction to all the laws of mechanics. A building whose doors and windows were exact squares would hurt the eye by that very proportion as ill-adapted to the figure of a human creature, for whose service the fabric was intended. What wonder then that a man whose habits and conduct are hurtful to society and dangerous or pernicious to everyone who has an intercourse with him should, on that account, be an object of disapprobation and communicate to every spectator the strongest sentiment of disgust and hatred?

But perhaps the difficulty of accounting for these effects of usefulness, or its contrary, has kept philosophers from admitting them into their systems of ethics, and has induced them rather to employ any other principle in explaining the origin or moral good and evil. But it is no just reason for rejecting any principle confirmed by experience that we cannot give a satisfactory account of its origin, nor are able to resolve it into other, more general principles. And if we would employ a little thought on the present subject we need be at no loss to account for the influence of utility and to deduce it from principles the most known and avowed in human nature.

From the apparent usefulness of the social virtues it has readily been inferred by skeptics, both ancient and modern, that all moral distinctions arise from education, and were at first invented, and afterwards encouraged, by the art of politicians in order to render men tractable and subdue their natural ferocity and selfishness, which incapacitated them for society. This principle, indeed, of precept and education must so far be owned to have a powerful influence that it may frequently increase or diminish, beyond their natural standard, the sentiments of approbation or dislike; and may even, in particular instances, create, without any natural principle, a new sentiment of this kind, as is evident in all superstitious practices and observances. But that *all* moral affection or dislike arises from this origin will never surely be allowed by any judicious inquirer. Had nature made no such distinction, founded on the original constitution of the mind, the words *honorable* and *shameful, lovely* and *odious, noble* and *despicable* had never had place in any language, nor could politicians, had they invented these terms, ever have been able to render them intelligible or make them convey any idea to the audience. So that nothing can be more superficial than this paradox of the skeptics; and it were well if, in the abstruser studies of logic and metaphysics, we could as easily obviate the cavils of that sect as in the practical and more intelligible sciences of politics and morals.

The social virtues must, therefore, be allowed to have a natural beauty and amiableness, which at first, antecedent to all precept or education, recommends them to the esteem of uninstructed mankind and engages their affections. And as the public utility of these virtues is the chief circumstance whence they derive their merit, it follows that the end which they have a tendency to promote must be some way agreeable to us and take hold of some natural affection. It must please either from considerations of self-interest or from more generous motives and regards.

It has often been asserted that as every man has a strong connection with society and perceives the impossibility of his solitary subsistence, he becomes, on that account, favorable to all those habits or principles which promote order in society and ensure to him the quiet possession of so inestimable a blessing. As much as we value our own happiness and welfare, as much must we applaud the practice of justice and humanity by which alone the social confederacy can be maintained and every man reap the fruits of mutual protection and assistance.

This deduction of morals from self-love, or a regard to private interest, is an obvious thought and has not arisen wholly from the wanton sallies and sportive assaults of the skeptics. To mention no others, Polybius, one of the gravest and most judicious as well as most moral writers of antiquity, has assigned this selfish origin of all our sentiments of virtue. But though the solid, practical sense of that author and his aversion to all vain subtleties render his authority on the present subject very considerable, yet is not this an affair to be decided by authority; and the voice of nature and experience seems plainly to oppose the selfish theory.

We frequently bestow praise on virtuous actions performed in very distant ages and remote countries, where the utmost subtlety of imagination would not discover any appearance of self-interest or find any connection of our present happiness and security with events so widely separated from us.

A generous, a brave, a noble deed performed by an adversary commands our approbation, while, in its consequences, it may be acknowledged prejudicial to our particular interest.

When private advantage concurs with general affection for virtue, we readily perceive and avow the mixture of these distinct sentiments, which have a very different feeling and influence on the mind. We praise, perhaps, with more alacrity where the generous, humane action contributes to our particular interest; but the topics of praise, which we insist on, are very wide of this circumstance. And we may attempt to bring over others to our sentiments, without endeavoring to convince them that they reap any advantage from the actions which we recommend to their approbation and applause.

Frame the model of a praiseworthy character consisting of all the most amiable moral virtues; give instances in which these display themselves after an eminent and extraordinary manner; you readily engage the esteem and approbation of all your audience, who never so much as inquire in what age and country the person lived who possessed these noble qualities—a circumstance, however, of all others the most material to self-love, or a concern for our own individual happiness.

Once on a time a statesman, in the shock and contest of parties, prevailed so far as to procure by his eloquence the banishment of an able adversary; whom he secretly followed, offering him money for his support during his exile and soothing him with topics of consolation in his misfortunes. *Alas!* cries the banished statesman, *with what regret must I leave my friends in this city where even enemies are so generous!* Virtue, though in an enemy, here pleased him; and we also give it the just tribute of praise and approbation; nor do we retract these sentiments when we hear that the action passed at Athens about two thousand years ago, and that the persons' names were Aeschines and Demosthenes.

What is that to me? There are few occasions when this question is not pertinent; and had it that universal, infallible influence supposed, it would turn into ridicule every composition, and almost every conversation, which contained any praise or censure of men and manners.

It is but a weak subterfuge, when pressed by these facts and arguments, to say that we transport ourselves, by the force of imagination, into distant ages and countries and consider the advantage which we should have reaped from these characters had we been contemporaries and had any commerce with the persons. It is not conceivable how a *real* sentiment or passion can ever arise from a known *imaginary* interest, especially when our *real* interest is still kept in view and is often acknowledged to be entirely distinct from the imaginary, and even sometimes opposite to it.

A man brought to the brink of a precipice cannot look down without trembling; and the sentiment of *imaginary* danger actuates him, in opposition to the opinion and belief of *real* safety. But the imagination is here assisted by the presence of a striking object, and yet prevails not, except it be also aided by novelty and the unusual appearance of the object. Custom soon reconciles us to heights and precipices, and wears off these false and delusive terrors. The reverse is observable in the estimates which we form of characters and manners; and the more we habituate ourselves to an accurate scrutiny of morals, the more delicate feeling do we acquire of the most minute distinctions between vice and virtue. Such frequent occasion, indeed, have we in common life to pronounce all kinds of moral determinations that no object of this kind can be new or unusual to us, nor could any *false* views or prepossessions maintain their ground against an experience so common and familiar. Experience being chiefly what forms the associations of ideas, it is impossible that any association could establish and support itself in direct opposition to that principle.

Usefulness is agreeable and engages our approbation. This is a matter of fact confirmed by daily observation. But *useful?* For what? For somebody's interest surely. Whose interest then? Not our own only, for our approbation frequently extends further. It must therefore be the interest of those who are served by the character or action approved of; and these, we may conclude, however remote, are not totally indifferent to us. By opening up this principle we shall discover one great source of moral distinctions.

Part II Self-love is a principle in human nature of such extensive energy, and the interest of each individual is in general so closely connected with that of the community, that those philosophers were excusable who fancied that all our concern for the public might be resolved into a concern for our own happiness and preservation. They saw, every moment, instances of approbation or blame, satisfaction or displeasure toward characters and actions; they denominated the objects of these sentiments *virtues* or *vices;* they observed that the former had a tendency to increase the happiness, and the latter the misery of mankind; they asked whether it were possible that we could have any general concern for society or any disinterested resentment of the welfare or injury of others; they found it simpler to consider all these sentiments as modifications of self-love, and they discovered a pretense at least for this unity of principle in that close union of interest which is so observable between the public and each individual.

But notwithstanding this frequent confusion of interests, it is easy to attain what natural philosophers, after Lord Bacon, have affected to call the *experimentum crucis,* or that experiment which points out the right way in any doubt or ambiguity. We have found instances in which private interest was separate from public in which it was even contrary, and yet we observed the moral sentiment to continue, notwithstanding this disjunction of interests. And wherever these distinct interests sensibly concurred, we always found a sensible increase of the sentiment and a more warm affection to virtue and detestation of vice, or what we properly call "gratitude" and "revenge." Compelled by these instances we must renounce the theory which accounts for every moral sentiment by the principle of self-love. We must adopt a more public affection and allow that the interests of society are not, even on their own account, entirely indifferent to us. Usefulness is only a tendency to a certain end; and it is a contradiction in terms that anything pleases as means to end where the end itself nowise affects us. If usefulness, therefore, be a source of moral sentiment, and if this usefulness be not always considered with a reference to self, it follows that everything which contributes to the happiness of society recommends itself directly to our approbation and good will. Here is a principle which accounts, in great part, for the origin of morality: and what need we seek for abstruse and remote systems when there occurs one so obvious and natural?

Have we any difficulty to comprehend the force of humanity and benevolence? Or to conceive that the very aspect of happiness, joy, prosperity gives pleasure; that of pain, suffering, sorrow communicates uneasiness? The human countenance, says Horace, borrows smiles or tears from the human countenance. Reduce a person to solitude and he loses all enjoyment, except either of the sensual or speculative kind; and that because the movements of his heart are not forwarded by correspondent movements in his fellow creatures. The signs of sorrow and mourning, though arbitrary, affect us with melancholy, but the natural symptoms, tears and cries and groans, never fail to infuse compassion and uneasiness. And if the effects of misery touch us in so lively a manner, can we be supposed altogether insensible or indifferent toward its causes when a malicious or treacherous character and behavior are presented to us?

We enter, I shall suppose, into a convenient, warm, well-contrived apartment: we necessarily receive a pleasure from its very survey because it presents us with the pleasing ideas of ease, satisfaction, and enjoyment. The hospitable, good-humored, humane landlord appears. This circumstance surely must embellish the whole, nor can we easily forbear reflecting, with pleasure, on the satisfaction which results to everyone from his intercourse and good offices.

His whole family, by the freedom, ease, confidence, and calm enjoyment diffused over their countenances, sufficiently express their happiness. I have a pleasing sympathy in the prospect of so much joy, and can never consider the source of it without the most agreeable emotions.

He tells me that an oppressive and powerful neighbor had attempted to dispossess him of his inheritance and had long disturbed all his innocent and social pleasures. I feel an immediate indignation arise in me against such violence and injury.

But it is no wonder, he adds, that a private wrong should proceed from a man who had enslaved provinces, depopulated cities, and made the field and scaffold stream with human blood. I am struck with horror at the prospect of so much misery and am actuated by the strongest antipathy against its author.

In general, it is certain that wherever we go, whatever we reflect on or converse about, everything still presents us with the view of human happiness or misery and excites in our breast a sympathetic movement of pleasure or uneasiness. In our serious occupations, in our careless amusements, this principle still exerts its active energy.

A man who enters the theater is immediately struck with the view of so great a multitude participating of one common amusement, and experiences, from their very aspect, a superior sensibility or disposition of being affected with every sentiment which he shares with his fellow creatures.

He observes the actors to be animated by the appearance of a full audience and raised to a degree of enthusiasm which they cannot command in any solitary or calm moment.

Every movement of the theater, by a skillful poet, is communicated, as it were, by magic to the spectators, who weep, tremble, resent, rejoice, and are inflamed with all the variety of passions which actuate the several personages of the drama.

Where any event crosses our wishes and interrupts the happiness of the favorite characters, we fell a sensible anxiety and concern. But where their sufferings proceed from the treachery, cruelty, or tyranny of an enemy, our breasts are affected with the liveliest resentment against the author of these calamities.

It is here esteemed contrary to the rules of art to represent anything cool and indifferent. A distant friend, or a confidant, who has no immediate interest in the catastrophe ought, if possible, to be avoided by the poet, as communicating a like indifference to the audience and checking the progress of the passions.

Few species of poetry are more entertaining than *pastoral;* and everyone is sensible that the chief source of its pleasure arises from those images of a gentle and tender tranquillity which it represents in its personages, and of which it communicates a like sentiment to the reader. Sannazarius, who transferred the scene to the seashore, though he presented the most magnificent object in nature, is confessed to have erred in his choice. The idea of toil, labor, and danger suffered by the fisherman is painful, by an unavoidable sympathy which attends every conception of human happiness or misery.

When I was twenty, says a French poet, Ovid was my favorite. Now I am forty, I declare for Horace. We enter, to be sure, more readily into sentiments which resemble those we feel every day; but no passion, when well represented, can be entirely indifferent to us, because there is none of which every man has not within him at least the seeds and first principles. It is the business of poetry to bring every affection near to us by lively imagery and representation, and make it look like truth and reality; a certain proof that, wherever the reality is found, our minds are disposed to be strongly affected by it.

Any recent event or piece of news by which the fate of states, provinces, or many individuals is affected is extremely interesting even to those whose welfare is not immediately engaged. Such intelligence is propagated with celerity, heard with avidity, and inquired into with attention and concern. The interest of society appears, on this occasion, to be in some degree the interest of each individual. The imagination is sure to be affected, though the passions excited may not always be so strong and steady as to have great influence on the conduct and behavior.

The perusal of a history seems a calm entertainment, but would be no entertainment at all did not our hearts beat with correspondent movements to those which are described by the historian.

Thucydides and Guicciardin support with difficulty our attention while the former describes the trivial rencounters of the small cities of Greece and the latter the harmless wars of Pisa. The few persons interested, and the small interest, fill not the imagination and engage not the affections. The deep distress of the numerous Athenian army before Syracuse, the danger which so nearly threatens Venice—these excite compassion; these move terror and anxiety.

The indifferent, uninteresting style of Suetonius, equally with the masterly pencil of Tacitus, may convince us of the cruel depravity of Nero or Tiberius; but what a difference of sentiment! While the former coldly relates the facts, the latter sets before our eyes the venerable figures of a Soranus and a Thrasea, intrepid in their fate and only moved by the melting sorrows of their friends and kindred. What sympathy then touches every human heart! What indignation against the tyrant whose causeless fear or unprovoked malice gave rise to such detestable barbarity!

If we bring these subjects nearer, if we remove all suspicion of fiction and deceit, what powerful concern is excited, and how much superior, in many instances, to the narrow attachments of self-love and private interest! Popular sedition, party seal, a devoted obedience to factious leaders—these are some of the most visible, though less laudable, effects of this social sympathy in human nature.

The frivolousness of the subject, too, we may observe, is not able to detach us entirely from what carries an image of human sentiment and affection.

When a person stutters and pronounces with difficulty, we even sympathize with this trivial uneasiness and suffer for him. And it is a rule in criticism that every combination of syllables or letters which gives pain to the organs of speech in the recital appears also, from a species of sympathy, harsh and disagreeable to the ear. Nay, when we run over a book with our eye, we are sensible of such unharmonious composition, because we still imagine that a person recites it to us and suffers from the pronunciation of these jarring sounds. So delicate is our sympathy! . . .

If any man, from a cold insensibility or narrow selfishness of temper, is unaffected with the images of human happiness or misery, he must be equally indifferent to the images of vice and virtue; as, on the other hand, it is always found that a warm concern for the interests of our species is attended with a delicate feeling of all moral distinctions—a strong resentment of injury done to men, a lively approbation of their welfare. In this particular, though great superiority is observable of one man above another, yet none are so entirely indifferent to the interests of their fellow creatures as to perceive no distinctions of moral good and evil, in consequence of the different tendencies of actions and principles. How, indeed, can we suppose it possible in anyone who wears a human heart that, if there be subjected to his censure one character or system of conduct which is beneficial, and another which is pernicious to his species or community, he will not so much as give a cool preference to the former or ascribe to it the smallest merit or regard? Let us suppose a person ever so selfish, let private interest have engrossed ever so much his attention, yet in instances where that is not concerned he must unavoidably feel *some* propensity to the good of mankind and make it an object of choice, if everything else be equal. Would any man who is walking alone tread as willingly on another's gouty toes, whom he has no quarrel with, as on the hard flint and pavement? There is here surely a difference in the case. We surely take into consideration the happiness and misery of others in weighing the several motives of action, and incline to the former where no private regards draw us to seek our own promotion or advantage by the injury of our fellow creatures. And if the principles of humanity are capable, in many instances, of influencing our actions, they must, at all times, have *some* authority over our sentiments and give us a general approbation of what is useful to society, and blame of what is dangerous or pernicious. The degrees of these sentiments may be the subject of controversy, but the reality of their existence, one should think, must be admitted in every theory or system. . . .

The more we converse with mankind, and the greater social intercourse we maintain, the more shall we be familiarized to these general preferences and distinctions without which our conversation and discourse could scarcely be rendered intelligible to each other. Every man's interest is peculiar to himself, and the aversions and desires which result from it cannot be supposed to affect others in a like degree. General language, therefore, being formed for general use, must be molded on some more general views and must affix the epithets of praise or blame in conformity to sentiments which arise from the general interests of the community. And if these sentiments, in most men, be not so strong as those which have a reference to private good, yet still they must make some distinction, even in persons the most depraved and selfish, and must attach the notion of good to a beneficent conduct, and of evil to the contrary. Sympathy, we shall allow, is much fainter than our concern for ourselves, and sympathy with persons remote from us much fainter than that with persons near and contiguous; but for this very reason it is necessary for us, in our calm judgments and discourse concerning the characters of men, to neglect all these differences and render our sentiments more public and social. Besides that we ourselves often change our situation in this particular; we every day meet with persons who are in a situation different from us, and who could never converse with us were we to remain constantly in that position and point of view which is peculiar to ourselves. The intercourse of sentiments, therefore, in society and conversation makes us form some general unalterable standard by which we may approve or disapprove of characters and manners. And though the heart takes not part entirely with those general notions, nor regulates all its love and hatred by the universal, abstract differences of vice and virtue without regard to self or the persons with whom we are more intimately connected, yet have these moral differences a considerable influence; and being sufficient, at least, for discourse, serve all our purposes in company, in the pulpit, in the theater, and in the schools.

Thus, in whatever light we take this subject, the merit ascribed to the social virtues appears still uniform and arises chiefly from that regard which the natural sentiment of benevolence engages us to pay to the interests of mankind and society. If we consider the principles of the human make, such as they appear to daily experience and observation, we must, *a priori,* conclude it impossible for such a creature as man to be totally indifferent to the well or ill-being of his fellow creatures, and not readily, of himself, to pronounce, where nothing gives him any particular bias, that what promotes their happiness is good, what tends to their misery is evil, without any further regard or consideration. Here then are the faint rudiments at least, or outlines, of a *general* distinction between actions, and in proportion as the humanity of the person is supposed to increase, his connection with those who are injured or benefited, and his lively conception of their misery or happiness, his consequent censure or approbation acquires proportionable vigor. There is no necessity that a generous action, barely mentioned in an old history or remote gazette, should communicate any strong feelings of applause and admiration. Virtue, placed at such a distance, is like a fixed star which, though to the eye of reason it may appear as luminous as the sun in his meridian, is so infinitely removed as to affect the senses neither with light nor heat. Bring this virtue nearer, by our acquaintance or connection with the persons, or even by an eloquent recital of the case, our hearts are immediately caught, our sympathy enlivened, and our cool approbation converted into the warmest sentiments of friendship and regard. These seem necessary and infallible consequences of the general principles of human nature, as discovered in common life and practice. . . .

It appears also that in our general approbation of characters and manners the useful tendency of the social virtues moves us not by any regards to self-interest, but has an influence much more universal and extensive. It appears that a tendency to public good and to the promoting of peace, harmony, and order in society does always, by affecting the benevolent principles of our frame, engage us on the side of the social virtues. And it appears, as an additional confirmation, that these principles of humanity and sympathy enter so deeply into all our sentiments and have so powerful an influence as may enable them to excite the strongest censure and applause. The present theory is the simple result of all these inferences, each of which seems founded on uniform experience and observation.

Were it doubtful whether there were any such principle in our nature as humanity or a concern for others, yet when we see, in numberless instances, that whatever has a tendency to promote the interest of society is so highly approved of, we ought thence to learn the force of the benevolent principle, since it is impossible for anything to please as means to an end where the end is totally indifferent. On the other hand, were it doubtful whether there were implanted in our nature any general principle of moral blame and approbation, yet when we see, in numberless instances, the influence of humanity, we ought thence to conclude that it is impossible, but that everything which promotes the interests of society must communicate pleasure, and what is pernicious give uneasiness. But when these different reflections and observations concur in establishing the same conclusion, must they not bestow an undisputed evidence upon it?

It is, however, hoped that the progress of this argument will bring a further confirmation of the present theory, by showing the rise of other sentiments of esteem and regard from the same or like principles.

DISCUSSION

The concept of utility is clearly central to Hume's analysis, and he envisions it as a moral analog to the concept of force in Newton's physics—a singular explanatory concept that will explain a wide variety of diverse phenomena. But Newton's concept of force is precisely defined (in terms of mass and movement); Hume's concept of utility is not. Sometimes, he appeals to utility in the most obvious sense—as "usefulness." Education is useful, for example, in training people to do certain jobs. Sometimes he refers to a broad sense of social function, in which society is more efficient, or more harmonious, or better able to defend itself against enemies. He finally appeals the concept of utility to "self-love" and the satisfaction of individual desires, though the connection with the broader senses of utility is not obvious. (Does the general utility consist of the satisfaction of individual desires, as the later utilitarians argued? If everyone cannot be equally satisfied, what principle determines whose interests should be satisfied and whose should not?) But then Hume also refers to the less obvious utility of beautiful and noble things and the satisfaction of our "more generous motives and regards." The French novelist Stendhal later said that "beauty is the promise of happiness," but is this true, or even plausible in many cases? We cannot disagree with Hume that a person's sense of humor and sociability are extremely desirable characteristics, but in what sense do they serve utility? Is there a way to define utility as precisely as Newton defines force (Force = Mass × Acceleration)?

In what sense are such virtues as generosity and mercy useful? How would Hume show that mere utility is not best served by an extremely efficient and orderly totalitarian society (for example, as depicted in George Orwell's *1984* or Aldous Huxley's drug-numbed *Brave New World*)?

Why does utility please us? Because it serves our self-interests, Hume suggests, but also because it serves our general sense of benevolence or sympathy. But by Hume's own account so far, it would seem that these are quite different and sometimes opposed, and the appeal of utility would seem to depend quite heavily on what kind of utility is in question. The appeal of utility, in other words, would seem to be as varied and imprecise as the concept of utility itself. In the excerpt that follows, Hume attempts to make clear the particular sort of utility that is involved in morality.

VIRTUE, APPROVAL, AND SELF-LOVE: FROM SECTION IX AND APPENDIX II

The final chapters of the *Inquiry* are detailed discussions of the various virtues. Hume concludes the *Inquiry* by again emphasizing the importance of personal merit and its relation to utility. In the Appendixes, he further analyzes his critical notion of the "moral sentiments" (a view that he shared with many philosophers of his time, most notably Frances Hutcheson before him and later Adam Smith, who wrote his *Theory of the Moral Sentiments* before he began his great economic treatise, *Wealth of Nations*).

Part I   It may justly appear surprising that any man in so late an age should find it requisite to prove, by elaborate reasoning, that *personal merit* consists altogether in the possession of mental qualities, *useful* or *agreeable* to the *person himself* or to *others.* It might be expected that this principle would have occurred even to the first, rude, unpracticed inquirers concerning morals, and been received from its own evidence without any argument or disputation. Whatever is valuable in any kind, so naturally classes itself under the division of *useful* or *agreeable,* the *utile* or the *dulce,* that it is not easy to imagine why we should ever seek further, or consider the question as a matter of nice research or inquiry. And as everything useful or agreeable must possess these qualities with regard either to the *person himself* or to *others,* the complete delineation or description of merit seems to be performed as naturally as a shadow is cast by the sun, or an image is reflected upon water. If the ground on which the shadow is cast be not broken and uneven, nor the surface from which the image is reflected disturbed and confused, a just figure is immediately presented without any art or attention. And it seems a reasonable presumption that systems and hypotheses have perverted our natural understanding when a theory so simple and obvious could so long have escaped the most elaborate examination. . . .

And as every quality which is useful or agreeable to ourselves or others is, in common life, allowed to be a part of personal merit, so no other will ever be received where men judge of things by their natural, unprejudiced reason, without the delusive glosses of superstition and false religion. Celibacy, fasting, penance, mortification, self-denial, humility, silence, solitude, and the whole train of monkish virtues—for what reason are they everywhere rejected by men of sense but because they serve to no manner of purpose; neither advance a man's fortune in the world, nor render him a more valuable member of society; neither qualify him for the entertainment of company nor increase his power of self-enjoyment? We observe, on the contrary, that they cross all these desirable ends, stupefy the understanding and harden the heart, obscure the fancy and sour the temper. We justly, therefore, transfer them to the opposite column and place them in the catalogue of vices; nor has any superstition force sufficient among men of the world to pervert entirely these natural sentiments. A gloomy, harebrained enthusiast, after his death, may have a place in the calendar, but will scarcely ever be admitted when alive into intimacy and society, except by those who are as delirious and dismal as himself.

It seems a happiness in the present theory that it enters not into that vulgar dispute concerning the *degrees* of benevolence or self-love which prevail in human nature—a dispute which is never likely to have any issue, both because men who have taken part are not easily convinced, and because the phenomena which can be produced on either side are so dispersed, so uncertain, and subject to so many interpretations that it is scarcely possible accurately to compare them or draw from them any determinate inference or conclusion. It is sufficient for our present purpose, if it be allowed, what surely, without the greatest absurdity, cannot be disputed, that there is some benevolence, however small, infused into our bosom; some spark of friendship for humankind; some particle of the dove kneaded into our frame, along with the elements of the wolf and serpent. Let these generous sentiments be supposed ever so weak, let them be insufficient to move even a hand or finger of our body, they must still direct the determinations of our mind and, where everything else is equal, produce a cool preference of what is useful and serviceable to mankind above what is pernicious and dangerous. A *moral distinction,* therefore, immediately arises; a general sentiment of blame and approbation; a tendency, however faint, to the objects of the one, and a proportionable aversion to those of the other. Nor will those reasoners who so earnestly maintain the predominant selfishness of humankind be anywise scandalized at hearing of the weak sentiments of virtue implanted in our nature. On the contrary, they are found as ready to maintain the one tenet as the other; and their spirit of satire (for such it appears, rather than of corruption) naturally gives rise to both opinions, which have, indeed, a great and almost an indissoluble connection together.

Avarice, ambition, vanity, and all passions vulgarly, though improperly, comprised under the denomination of *self-love* are here excluded from our theory concerning the *origin* of morals, not because they are too weak, but because they have not a proper direction for that purpose. The notion of morals implies some sentiment common to all mankind, which recommends the same object to general approbation and makes every man, or most men, agree in the same opinion or decision concerning it. It also implies some sentiment so universal and comprehensive as to extend to all mankind, and render the actions and conduct, even of the persons the most remote, an object of applause or censure, according as they agree or disagree with that rule of right which is established. These two requisite circumstances belong alone to the sentiment of humanity here insisted on. The other passions produce, in every breast, many strong sentiments of desire and aversion, affection and hatred, but these neither are felt so much in common nor are so comprehensive as to be the foundation of any general system and established theory of blame or approbation.

When a man denominates another his *enemy,* his *rival,* his *antagonist,* his *adversary,* he is understood to speak the language of self-love and to express sentiments peculiar to himself and arising from his particular circumstances and situation. But when he bestows on any man the epithets of *vicious* or *odious* or *depraved,* he then speaks another language and expresses sentiments in which he expects all his audience are to concur with him. He must here, therefore, depart from his private and particular situation and must choose a point of view common to him with others: he must move some universal principle of the human frame and touch a string to which all mankind have an accord and symphony. If he mean, therefore, to express that this man possesses qualities whose tendency is pernicious to society, he has chosen this common point of view and has touched the principle of humanity in which every man, in some degree, concurs. While the human heart is compounded of the same elements as at present, it will never be wholly indifferent to public good, nor entirely unaffected with the tendency of characters and manners. And though this affection of humanity may not generally be esteemed so strong as vanity or ambition, yet being common to all men, it can alone be the foundation of morals or of any general system of blame or praise. One man's ambition is not another's ambition, nor will the same event or object satisfy both; but the humanity of one man is the humanity of everyone; and the same object touches this passion in all human creatures.

But the sentiments which arise from humanity are not only the same in all human creatures and produce the same approbation or censure, but they also comprehend all human creatures; nor is there anyone whose conduct or character is not, by their means, an object, to everyone, of censure or approbation. On the contrary, those other passions, commonly denominated selfish, both produce different sentiments in each individual, according to his particular situation, and also contemplate the greater part of mankind with the utmost indifference and unconcern. Whoever has a high regard and esteem for me flatters my vanity; whoever expresses contempt, mortifies and displeases me. But as my name is known but to a small part of mankind there are few who come within the sphere of this passion, or excite, on its account, either my affection or disgust. But if you represent a tyrannical, insolent, or barbarous behavior, in any country or in any age of the world, I soon carry my eye to the pernicious tendency of such a conduct and feel the sentiment of repugnance and displeasure toward it. No character can be so remote as to be, in this light, wholly indifferent to me. What is beneficial to society or to the person himself must still be preferred. And every quality or action of every human being must by this means be ranked under some class or denomination expressive of general censure or applause.

What more, therefore, can we ask to distinguish the sentiments dependent on humanity from those connected with any other passion, or to satisfy us why the former are the origin of morals, not the latter? Whatever conduct gains my approbation, by touching my humanity, procures also the applause of all mankind by affecting the same principle in them; but what serves my avarice or ambition pleases these passions in me alone and affects not the avarice and ambition of the rest of mankind. There is no circumstance of conduct in any man, provided it have a beneficial tendency, that is not agreeable to my humanity, however remote the person; but every man, so far removed as neither to cross nor serve my avarice and ambition, is regarded as wholly indifferent by those passions. The distinction, therefore, between these species of sentiment being so great and evident, language must soon be molded upon it and must invent a peculiar set of terms in order to express those universal sentiments of censure or approbation which arise from humanity, or from views of general usefulness and its contrary. *Virtue* and *vice* become then known: morals are recognized; certain general ideas are framed of human conduct and behavior; such measures are expected from men in such situations: this action is determined to be conformable to our abstract rule; that other, contrary. And by such universal principles are the particular sentiments of self-love frequently controlled and limited.

Another spring of our constitution that brings a great addition of force to moral sentiment is the love of fame, which rules with such uncontrolled authority in all generous minds, and is often the grand object of all their designs and undertakings. By our continual and earnest pursuit of a character, a name, a reputation in the world, we bring our own deportment and conduct frequently in review and consider how they appear in the eyes of those who approach and regard us. This constant habit of surveying ourselves, as it were in reflection, keeps alive all the sentiments of right and wrong, and begets in noble natures a certain reverence for themselves as well as others, which is the surest guardian of every virtue. The animal conveniences and pleasures sink gradually in their value, while every inward beauty and moral grace is studiously acquired and the mind is accomplished in every perfection which can adorn or embellish a rational creature.

Here is the most perfect morality with which we are acquainted; here is displayed the force of many sympathies. Our moral sentiment is itself a feeling chiefly of that nature and our regard to a character with others seems to arise only from a care of preserving a character with ourselves; and in order to attain this end, we find it necessary to prop our tottering judgment on the correspondent approbation of mankind.

But that we may accommodate matters and remove, if possible, every difficulty, let us allow all these reasonings to be false. Let us allow that, when we resolve the pleasure which arises from views of utility into the sentiments of humanity and sympathy, we have embraced a wrong hypothesis. Let us confess it necessary to find some other explication of that applause which is paid to objects, whether inanimate, animate, or rational, if they have a tendency to promote the welfare and advantage of mankind. However difficult it be to conceive that an object is approved of on account of its tendency to a certain end, while the end itself is totally indifferent, let us swallow this absurdity and consider what are the consequences. The preceding delineation or definition of *personal merit* must still retain its evidence and authority: It must still be allowed that every quality of the mind which is *useful* or *agreeable* to the *person himself* or to *others* communicates a pleasure to the spectator, engages his esteem, and is admitted under the honorable denomination of virtue or merit. Are not justice, fidelity, honor, veracity, allegiance, chastity esteemed solely on account of their tendency to promote the good of society? Is not that tendency inseparable from humanity, benevolence, lenity, generosity, gratitude, moderation, tenderness, friendship, and all the other social virtues? Can it possibly be doubted that industry, discretion, frugality, secrecy, order, perseverance, forethought, judgment, and this whole class of virtues and accomplishments of which many pages would not contain the catalogue—can it be doubted, I say, that the tendency of these qualities to promote the interest and happiness of their possessor is the sole foundation of their merit? Who can dispute that a mind which supports a perpetual serenity and cheerfulness, a noble dignity and undaunted spirit, a tender affection and good will to all around, as it has more enjoyment within itself, is also a more animating and rejoicing spectacle than if dejected with melancholy, tormented with anxiety, irritated with rage, or sunk into the most abject baseness and degeneracy? And as to the qualities immediately *agreeable to others,* they speak sufficiently for themselves; and he must be unhappy indeed, either in his own temper, or in his situation and company, who has never perceived the charms of a facetious wit or flowing affability, of a delicate modesty or decent genteelness of address and manner.

I am sensible that nothing can be more unphilosophical than to be positive or dogmatical on any subject, and that, even if *excessive* skepticism could be maintained, it would not be more destructive to all just reasoning and inquiry. I am convinced that where men are the most sure and arrogant, they are commonly the most mistaken, and have there given reins to passion without that proper deliberation and suspense which can alone secure them from the grossest absurdities. Yet I must confess that this enumeration puts the matter in so strong a light that I cannot, *at present,* be more assured of any truth which I learn from reasoning and argument, than that personal merit consists entirely in the usefulness or agreeableness of qualities to the person himself possessed of them, or to others who have any intercourse with him. But when I reflect that though the bulk and figure of the earth have been measured and delineated, though the motions of the tides have been accounted for, the order and economy of the heavenly bodies subjected to their proper laws, and *infinite* itself reduced to calculation yet men still dispute concerning the foundation of their moral duties—when I reflect on this, I say, I fall back into diffidence and skepticism, and suspect that an hypothesis so obvious, had it been a true one, would long ere now have been received by the unanimous suffrage and consent of mankind.

Having argued that the specific sentiments upon which moral judgments are based (and the utility that accrues to them) must not only be "common to all mankind" but also universal insofar as they apply to all persons at all times, Hume goes on to discuss the manner in which actions corresponding to such assessments of virtue are obligatory. In particular, what he needs to account for is why the pursuit of our own happiness (or interests) will necessarily lead to following rules that concern the happiness of others.

Part II Having explained the moral *approbation* attending merit or virtue, there remains nothing but briefly to consider our interested *obligation* to it, and to inquire whether every man who has any regard to his own happiness and welfare will not best find his account in the practice of every moral duty. If this can be clearly ascertained from the foregoing theory, we shall have the satisfaction to reflect that we have advanced principles which not only, it is hoped will stand the test of reasoning and inquiry, but may contribute to the amendment of men's lives and their improvement in morality and social virtue. And though the philosophical truth of any proposition by no means depends on its tendency to promote the interests of society, yet a man has but a bad grace who delivers a theory, however true, which he must confess leads to a practice dangerous and pernicious. Why rake into those corners of nature which spread a nuisance all around? Why dig up the pestilence from the pit in which it is buried? The ingenuity of your researches may be admired, but your systems will be detested, and mankind will agree, if they cannot refute them, to sink them at least in eternal silence and oblivion. Truths which are *pernicious* to society, if any such there be, will yield to errors which are salutary and *advantageous.*

But what philosophical truths can be more advantageous to society than those here delivered, which represent virtue in all her genuine and most engaging charms and make us approach her with ease, familiarity, and affection? The dismal dress falls off, with which many divines and some philosophers have covered her, and nothing appears but gentleness, humanity, beneficence, affability, nay, even at proper intervals, play, frolic, and gaiety. She talks not of useless austerities and rigors, suffering, and self-denial. She declares that her sole purpose is to make her votaries, and all mankind, during every instant of their existence, if possible, cheerful and happy; nor does she ever willingly part with any pleasure but in hopes of ample compensation in some other period of their lives. The sole trouble which she demands is that of just calculation and a steady preference of the greater happiness. And if any austere pretenders approach her, enemies to joy and pleasure, she either rejects them as hypocrites and deceivers, or, if she admit them in her train, they are ranked, however, among the least favored of her votaries.

And, indeed, to drop all figurative expression, what hopes can we ever have of engaging mankind to a practice which we confess full of austerity and rigor? Or what theory of morals can ever serve any useful purpose unless it can show, by a particular detail, that all the duties which it recommends are also the true interest of each individual? The peculiar advantage of the foregoing system seems to be that it furnishes proper mediums for that purpose.

That the virtues which are immediately *useful* or *agreeable* to the person possessed of them are desirable in a view to self-interest, it would surely be superfluous to prove. Moralists, indeed, may spare themselves all the pains which they often take in recommending these duties. To what purpose collect arguments, to evince that temperance is advantageous and the excesses of pleasure hurtful? When it appears that these excesses are only denominated such because they are hurtful, and that if the unlimited use of strong liquors, for instance, no more impaired health or the faculties of mind and body, than the use of air or water, it would not be a whit more vicious or blamable.

It seems equally superfluous to prove that the *companionable* virtues of good manners and wit, decency and genteelness are more desirable than the contrary qualities. Vanity alone, without any other consideration, is a sufficient motive to make us wish for the possession of these accomplishments. No man was ever willingly deficient in this particular. All our failures here proceed from bad education, want of capacity, or a perverse and unpliable disposition. Would you have your company coveted, admired, followed rather than hated, despised, avoided? Can anyone seriously deliberate in the case? As no enjoyment is sincere without some reference to company and society, so no society can be agreeable, or even tolerable, where a man feels his presence unwelcome and discovers all around him symptoms of disgust and aversion.

But why, in the greater society or confederacy of mankind, should not the case be the same as in particular clubs and companies? Why is it more doubtful that the enlarged virtues of humanity generosity, beneficence are desirable, with a view to happiness and self-interest than the limited endowments of ingenuity and politeness? Are we apprehensive lest those social affections interfere in a greater and more immediate degree than any other pursuits with private utility, and cannot be gratified without some important sacrifice of honor and advantage? If so, we are but ill instructed in the nature of the human passions, and are more influenced by verbal distinctions than by real differences.

Whatever contradiction may vulgarly be supposed between the *selfish* and *social* sentiments or dispositions, they are really no more opposite than selfish and ambitious, selfish and revengeful, selfish and vain. It is requisite that there be an original propensity of some kind, in order to be a basis to self-love, by giving a relish to the objects of its pursuit; and none more fit for this purpose than benevolence or humanity. The goods of fortune are spent in one gratification or another: the miser who accumulates his annual income and lends it out at interest has really spent it in the gratification of his avarice. And it would be difficult to show why a man is more a loser by a generous action than by any other method of expense, since the utmost which he can attain by the most elaborate selfishness is the indulgence of some affection.

Now if life without passion must be altogether insipid and tiresome, let a man suppose that he has full power of modeling his own disposition and let him deliberate what appetite or desire he would choose for the foundation of his happiness and enjoyment. Every affection, he would observe, when gratified by success, gives a satisfaction proportioned to its force and violence; but besides this advantage, common to all, the immediate feeling of benevolence and friendship, humanity and kindness is sweet, smooth, tender, and agreeable, independent of all fortune and accidents. These virtues are, besides, attended with a pleasing consciousness or remembrance and keep us in humor with ourselves as well as others, while we retain the agreeable reflection of having done our part toward mankind and society. And though all men show a jealousy of our success in the pursuits of avarice and ambition, yet are we almost sure of their good will and good wishes so long as we persevere in the paths of virtue and employ ourselves in the execution of generous plans and purposes. What other passion is there where we shall find so many advantages united: an agreeable sentiment, a pleasing consciousness, a good reputation? But of these truths, we may observe, men are of themselves pretty much convinced; nor are they deficient in their duty to society because they would not wish to be generous, friendly, and humane, but because they do not feel themselves such.

Treating vice with the greatest candor and making it all possible concessions, we must acknowledge that there is not, in any instance, the smallest pretext for giving it the preference above virtue with a view to self-interest, except, perhaps, in the case of justice where a man, taking things in a certain light, may often seem to be a loser by his integrity. And though it is allowed that, without a regard to property, no society could subsist, yet, according to the imperfect way in which human affairs are conducted, a sensible knave, in particular incidents, may think that an act of iniquity or infidelity will make a considerable addition to his fortune without causing any considerable breach in the social union and confederacy. That *honesty is the best policy* may be a good general rule, but is liable to many exceptions. And he, it may perhaps be thought, conducts himself with most wisdom who observes the general rule and takes advantage of all the exceptions.

I must confess that if a man think that this reasoning much requires an answer, it will be a little difficult to find any which will to him appear satisfactory and convincing. If his heart rebel not against such pernicious maxims, if he feel no reluctance to the thoughts of villany or baseness he has indeed lost a considerable motive to virtue; and we may expect that his practice will be answerable to his speculation. But in all ingenuous natures the antipathy to treachery and roguery is too strong to be counterbalanced by any views of profit or pecuniary advantage. Inward peace of mind, consciousness of integrity, a satisfactory review of our own conduct—these are circumstances very requisite to happiness and will be cherished and cultivated by every honest man who feels the importance of them.

Such a one has, besides, the frequent satisfaction of seeing knaves, with all their pretended cunning and abilities, betrayed by their own maxims; and while they purpose to cheat with moderation and secrecy, a tempting incident occurs—nature is frail—and they give in to the snare, whence they can never extricate themselves without a total loss of reputation and the forfeiture of all future trust and confidence with mankind.

But were they ever so secret and successful, the honest man, if he has any tincture of philosophy, or even common observation and reflection, will discover that they themselves are, in the end, the greatest dupes, and have sacrificed the invaluable enjoyment of a character with themselves at least, for the acquisition of worthless toys and gewgaws. How little is requisite to supply the *necessities* of nature? And in a view to *pleasure,* what comparison between the unbought satisfaction of conversation, society, study, even health and the common beauties of nature, but above all, the peaceful reflection on one's own conduct? What comparison, I say, between these and the feverish, empty amusements of luxury and expense? These natural pleasures, indeed, are really without price, both because they are below all price in their attainment and above it in their enjoyment.

Finally, Hume offers his own arguments against psychological egoism, the "selfish hypothesis."

Of Self-Love: Appendix II

There is a principle, supposed to prevail among many, which is utterly incompatible with all virtue or moral sentiment; and as it can proceed from nothing but the most depraved disposition, so in its turn it tends still further to encourage that depravity. This principle is that all *benevolence* is mere hypocrisy, friendship a cheat, public spirit a farce, fidelity a snare to procure trust and confidence; and that, while all of us, at bottom, pursue only our private interest, we wear these fair disguises in order to put others off their guard and expose them the more to our wiles and machinations. What heart one must be possessed of who professes such principles, and who feels no internal sentiment that belies so pernicious a theory, it is easy to imagine; and also, what degree of affection and benevolence he can bear to a species whom he represents under such odious colors and supposes so little susceptible of gratitude or any return of affection. Or, if we should not ascribe these principles wholly to a corrupted heart, we must at least account for them from the most careless and precipitate examination. Superficial reasoners, indeed, observing many false pretenses among mankind, and feeling, perhaps, no very strong restraint in their own disposition, might draw a general and a hasty conclusion that all is equally corrupted, and that men, different from all other animals, and indeed from all other species of existence, admit of no degrees of good or bad, but are, in every instance, the same creatures under different disguises and appearances.

There is another principle somewhat resembling the former, which has been much insisted on by philosophers, and has been the foundation of many a system—that, whatever affection one may feel, or imagine he feels for others, no passion is, or can be, disinterested; that the most generous friendship, however sincere, is a modification of self-love; and that, even unknown to ourselves, we seek only our own gratification while we appear the most deeply engaged in schemes for the liberty and happiness of mankind. By a turn of imagination, by a refinement of reflection, by an enthusiasm of passion, we seem to take part in the interests of others and imagine ourselves divested of all selfish considerations. But, at bottom, the most generous patriot, and most niggardly miser, the bravest hero, and most abject coward have, in every action, an equal regard to their own happiness and welfare.

Whoever concludes from the seeming tendency of this opinion that those who make profession of it cannot possibly feel the true sentiments of benevolence, or have any regard for genuine virtue, will often find himself, in practice, very much mistaken. Probity and honor were no strangers to Epicurus and his sect. Atticus and Horace seem to have enjoyed from nature, and cultivated by reflection, as generous and friendly dispositions as any disciple of the austerer schools; and among the modern, Hobbes and Locke, who maintained the selfish system of morals, lived irreproachable lives, though the former lay not under any restraint of religion which might supply the defects of his philosophy. An Epicurean or a Hobbist readily allows that there is such a thing as friendship in the world without hypocrisy or disguise, though he may attempt, by a philosophical chemistry, to resolve the elements of this passion, if I may so speak, into those of another and explain every affection to be self-love twisted and molded by a particular turn of imagination into a variety of appearances. But as the same turn of imagination prevails not in every man, nor gives the same direction to the original passion, this is sufficient, even according to the selfish system, to make the widest difference in human characters and denominate one man virtuous and humane, another vicious and meanly interested. I esteem the man whose self-love, by whatever means, is so directed as to give him a concern for others and render him serviceable to society, as I hate or despise him who has no regard to anything beyond his own gratifications and enjoyments. In vain would you suggest that these characters, though seemingly opposite, are at bottom the same, and that a very inconsiderable turn of thought forms the whole difference between them. Each character, notwithstanding these inconsiderable differences, appears to me, in practice, pretty durable and untransmutable; and I find not in this more than in other subjects that the natural sentiments, arising from the general appearances of things, are easily destroyed by subtle reflections concerning the minute origin of these appearances. Does not the lively, cheerful color of a countenance inspire me with complacency and pleasure, even though I learn from philosophy that all difference of complexion arises from the most minute differences of thickness in the most minute parts of the skin, by means of which a superficies is qualified to reflect one of the original colors of light, and absorb the others?

But though the question concerning the universal or partial selfishness of man be not so material, as is usually imagined, to morality and practice, it is certainly of consequence in the speculative science of human nature, and is a proper object of curiosity and inquiry. It may not, therefore, be unsuitable, in this place, to bestow a few reflections upon it.

The most obvious objection to the selfish hypothesis is that as it is contrary to common feeling and our most unprejudiced notions, there is required the highest stretch of philosophy to establish so extraordinary a paradox. To the most careless observer there appear to be such dispositions as benevolence and generosity, such affections as love, friendship, compassion, gratitude. These sentiments have their causes, effects, objects, and operations marked by common language and observation, and plainly distinguished from those of the selfish passions. And as this is the obvious appearance of things, it must be admitted till some hypothesis be discovered which, by penetrating deeper into human nature, may prove the former affections to be nothing but modifications of the latter. All attempts of this kind have hitherto proved fruitless, and seem to have proceeded entirely from that love of *simplicity* which has been the source of much false reasoning in philosophy. I shall not here enter into any detail on the present subject. Many able philosophers have shown the insufficiency of these systems; and I shall take for granted what, I believe, the smallest reflection will make evident to every impartial inquirer.

But the nature of the subject furnishes the strongest presumption that no better system will ever, for the future, be invented in order to account for the origin of the benevolent from the selfish affections, and reduce all the various emotions of the human mind to a perfect simplicity. The case is not the same in this species of philosophy as in physics. Many a hypothesis in nature, contrary to first appearances, has been found on more accurate scrutiny solid and satisfactory. Instances of this kind are so frequent that a judicious as well as witty philosopher has ventured to affirm, if there be more than one way in which any phenomenon may be produced, that there is a general presumption for its arising from the causes which are the least obvious and familiar. But the presumption always lies on the other side in all inquiries concerning the origin of our passions and of the internal operations of the human mind. The simplest and most obvious cause which can there be assigned for any phenomenon is probably the true one. When a philosopher, in the explication of his system, is obliged to have recourse to some very intricate and refined reflections, and to suppose them essential to the production of any passion or emotion, we have reason to be extremely on our guard against so fallacious a hypothesis. The affections are not susceptible of any impression from the refinements of reason or imagination; and it is always found that a vigorous exertion of the latter faculties, necessarily from the narrow capacity of the human mind, destroys all activity in the former. Our predominant motive or intention is, indeed, frequently concealed from ourselves when it is mingled and confounded with other motives which the mind, from vanity or self-conceit, is desirous of supposing more prevalent. But there is no instance that a concealment of this nature has ever arisen from the abstruseness and intricacy of the motive. A man that has lost a friend and patron may flatter himself that all his grief arises from generous sentiments, without any mixture of narrow or interested considerations; but a man that grieves for a valuable friend who needed his patronage and protection—how can we suppose that his passionate tenderness arises from some metaphysical regards to a self-interest which has no foundation or reality? We may as well imagine that minute wheels and springs, like those of a watch, give motion to a loaded wagon, as account for the origin of passion from such abstruse reflections.

Animals are found susceptible of kindness, both to their own species and to ours; nor is there, in this case, the least suspicion of disguise or artifice. Shall we account for all *their* sentiments, too, from refined deductions of self-interest? Or if we admit a disinterested benevolence in the inferior species, by what rule of analogy can we refuse it in the superior?

Love between the sexes begets a complacency and good will very distinct from the gratification of an appetite. Tenderness to their offspring in all sensible beings, is commonly able alone to counterbalance the strongest motives of self-love, and has no manner of dependence on that affection. What interest can a fond mother have in view who loses her health by assiduous attendance on her sick child, and afterwards languishes and dies of grief when freed, by its death, from the slavery of that attendance?

Is gratitude no affection of the human breast, or is that a word merely without any meaning or reality? Have we no satisfaction in one man's company above another's, and no desire of the welfare of our friend even though absence or death should prevent us from all participation in it? Or what is it commonly that gives us any participation in it, even while alive and present, but our affection and regard to him?

These and a thousand other instances are marks of a general benevolence in human nature, where no *real* interest binds us to the object. And how an *imaginary* interest, known and avowed for such, can be the origin of any passion or emotion seems difficult to explain. No satisfactory hypothesis of this kind has yet been discovered, nor is there the smallest probability that the future industry of men will ever be attended with more favorable success.

But further, if we consider rightly of the matter, we shall find that the hypothesis which allows of a disinterested benevolence, distinct from self-love, has really more *simplicity* in it and is more conformable to the analogy of nature than that which pretends to resolve all friendship and humanity into this latter principle. There are bodily wants or appetites acknowledged by everyone, which necessarily precede all sensual enjoyment and carry us directly to seek possession of the object. Thus hunger and thirst have eating and drinking for their end; and from the gratification of these primary appetites arises a pleasure which may become the object of another species of desire or inclination that is secondary and interested. In the same manner, there are mental passions by which we are impelled immediately to seek particular objects, such as fame, or power, or vengeance, without any regard to interest; and when these objects are attained, a pleasing enjoyment ensues as the consequence of our indulged affections. Nature must, by the internal frame and constitution of the mind, give an original propensity to fame ere we can reap any pleasure from that acquisition or pursue it from motives of self-love and a desire of happiness. If I have no vanity, I take no delight in praise; if I be void of ambition, power gives me no enjoyment; if I be not angry, the punishment of an adversary is totally indifferent to me. In all these cases there is a passion which points immediately to the object and constitutes it our good or happiness, as there are other secondary passions which afterwards arise and pursue it as a part of our happiness when once it is constituted such by our original affections. Were there no appetite of any kind antecedent to self-love, that propensity could scarcely ever exert itself, because we should, in that case, have felt few and slender pains or pleasures, and have little misery or happiness to avoid or to pursue.

Now, where is the difficulty in conceiving that this may likewise be the case with benevolence and friendship, and that, from the original frame of our temper, we may feel a desire of another's happiness or good, which, by means of that affection, becomes our own good and is afterwards pursued from the combined motives of benevolence and self-enjoyment? Who sees not that vengeance, from the force alone of passion, may be so eagerly pursued as to make us knowingly neglect every consideration of ease, interest, or safety, and, like some vindictive animals, infuse our very souls into the wounds we give an enemy? And what a malignant philosophy must it be that will not allow to humanity and friendship the same privileges which are indisputably granted to the darker passions of enmity and resentment? Such a philosophy is more like a satire than a true delineation or description of human nature, and may be a good foundation for paradoxical wit and raillery, but is a very bad one for any serious argument or reasoning.

DISCUSSION

Throughout the *Inquiry*, benevolence is juxtaposed with self-love, and, in the conclusion, Hume explicitly plays them against one another, concerned to show that there is at least "some benevolence, however small, infused into our bosom." But this contrast threatens the intended unity of Hume's moral philosophy, and he therefore takes considerable pains to minimize the conflict. He does this through a rather extensive discussion of self-love, which permeates the whole of the *Inquiry* but finally becomes the focus of attention only in the conclusion and a special appendix. At the same time, Hume is concerned to further explain his conception of the moral sentiments, such as benevolence, in order to show that these are not to be construed as *against* our self-interest but rather in agreement with it.

It is worth making one short comment on Hume's list of virtues (in the omitted Sections VI to VIII). Hume makes it quite clear that those qualities "useful and agreeable to ourselves" are virtually identical to those qualities "useful and agreeable to others"; thus, having a sense of humor, being honest and generous, being courteous and reasonable are all advantageous to the person who has such qualities and to those around him or her. But along with this list of virtues, Hume also gives us a list of *false* virtues—the cardinal virtues of Christianity. He lists, for instance, celibacy, penance, self-denial, and humility (which receives extended treatment in Book II of the *Treatise*). These "monkish virtues" are "everywhere rejected by men of sense" because "they serve no manner or purpose." Hume excludes from his account of the qualities of self-love the "vulgar" passions of avarice, ambition, and vanity, precisely because they are not "common to all mankind" and agreeable to everyone. In other words, the mutual agreeableness of the virtues to ourselves and others functions as something of a criterion for Hume. A virtue is not a virtue unless it is useful or agreeable both to the person who has that virtue and to others, unless it commands a certain sort of universal assent. Thus, self-love becomes more and more a sense of feeling good about oneself in society rather than the satisfaction of selfish interests, and the moral sentiments and social virtues become more and more the qualities that most satisfy our self-interest.

As self-love is made more sociable, the moral sentiments are defended, too. Hume rejects that "depraved" view that "all benevolence is mere hypocrisy, friendship a cheat, public spirit a farce, fidelity a snare to procure trust and confidence." If the distinction between our own interests and the interests of others becomes exaggerated, then there is always the danger that—because in fact our motives are typically an amalgam of both—a cynic can plausibly argue that even our most generous and altruistic actions are in fact motivated by self-interest, and thus (in terms of their altruistic facade) hypocritical and fraudulent. But benevolence is real, Hume argues, precisely because it is not so sharply opposed to our self-love. Indeed, it is our benevolence that provides us with one of the most important sources of our self-love. Self-love is not that greedy selfishness that has always been condemned by moralists; it is rather feeling good about oneself for the qualities one has and the sentiments one feels. And it is the limits of self-love, not in humility or self-denial but simply in indifference, that makes benevolence so readily understandable. Few people may be wholly satisfied with what they have, but few people are out for themselves in the unbridled way suggested by some cynical philosophers. The proponents of selfishness (egoism) are not only advancing a dubious theory of human motivation, but they are also seriously misperceiving the simple facts of human behavior.

How does reason fit into all of this? In the *Treatise,* Hume is largely concerned with emphasizing reason's impotence; here in the *Inquiry* he corrects that antagonism by pointing out how important reason is, for example, in fixing the laws of justice. Accurate reason and good judgment (Plato and Aristotle's *phronesis*) thus become virtues in their own right. He continues to reject the idea that reason is the "sole source of morals," but he no longer excludes it from the center of the moral stage.

Discussion Questions

1. What is "moral skepticism"? In what ways is Hume a moral skeptic? In what ways is he not?
2. Hume claims (in the *Treatise*) that reason is "impotent"? Does he really deny reason any place in ethics? What does he mean when he says (also in the *Treatise*) that "reason is, and ought to be, the slave of the passions"?
3. Does it matter that Hume is an atheist—as far as his moral philosophy is concerned? Does he believe, as Dostoevsky wrote in the following century, "If there is no God, then everything is permitted"?
4. Why does Hume insist that "sentiment" is the basis of morality? What problems can you see with basing morals on sentiment?
5. What does it mean to say that "you can't derive an 'ought' from an 'is'"? Can you? Why or why not?
6. The basis of Hume's ethics is the sense of "fellow-feeling" and our need to get along well with one another. How does this differ from and how is it similar to Aristotle's ethics? To Hobbes's?
7. What does Hume mean by "utility"? Why is utility desirable? ("Why utility pleases.")
8. What is the connection between utility and fellow-feeling, for Hume? Which concept is the more fundamental?
9. Is Hume a utilitarian? In what ways? In what ways not? (See chapter VII, John Stuart Mill, *Utilitarianism.*)
10. Hume often said that his intellectual model was Isaac Newton. In what ways is his moral philosophy similar to Newton's philosophy of physics?

Study Questions

1. What is Hume's vision of "human nature"? Do you agree with it?
2. How would Hume explain the existence of wickedness and evil? What would he urge us to do about it?
3. What is the link between utility and benevolence? Is benevolence based on utility, or is utility based on benevolence? What considerations does Hume offer for each?
4. Is justice based on utility? Why does Hume think that the sole foundation of justice is utility? What problems do you see in this?
5. Is society based on a "social contract" according to Hume? Was there such a thing as justice before the formation of a legal (law-governed) society?
6. Is it irrational for me to prefer the destruction of the whole world to the scratching of my little finger? Why or why not?
7. If people in another society feel differently about an activity that we find repulsive (for example, cannibalism or human sacrifice), is it *right for them?* What does this mean?
8. What are the "moral" sentiments? Are all emotions moral sentiments? What distinguishes those that are from those that are not?
9. What is "self-love"? Is it the same as selfishness? What is Hume saying when he insists that all actions—including what we would call "altruistic" actions—are based first of all on self-love?
10. What role does society play in Hume's moral theory? Would it be possible for the hermit to lead a virtuous life?
11. Utility is the cornerstone of Hume's ethics, but he appeals to at least two kinds of utility. What are they, and how does Hume reconcile them? Which one is the most important?
12. What are the "monkish virtues," and why does Hume claim they are not virtues at all? Where do qualities that lead to our own good at the expense of others (such as greed) stand in Hume's account of the virtues?

Immanuel Kant

Immanuel Kant was a Prussian and a Lutheran Pietist who lived through most of the eighteenth century (1724–1804). He was a lifelong bachelor who was reputedly so regular in his habits that his neighbors set their clocks by his daily three o'clock walks. He lived his entire life in the east Prussian port city of Königsberg, but the city was sufficiently cosmopolitan that Kant could claim, late in his life, that he had seen "every type of humanity" at one time or another. And yet, from his safe distance, he was enthusiastic about the French Revolution, and he was no less of a revolutionary himself in the realm of the intellect. (The German poet Heine compared him with Robespierre.) He published the first volume of his monumental philosophical system, *The Critique of Pure Reason,* in 1781, followed by *The Critique of Practical Reason* in 1788 and *The Critique of Judgment* in 1790. *The Grounding of the Metaphysics of Morals* was published in 1785. By the time he died, he had set the tone of German philosophy for a century or more to come.

The heart of Kant's ethics is his emphasis on the importance of *reason* and the unqualified *rational* nature of moral principles. Morality is not to be confused with self-interest—no matter how "enlightened"—and the dictates of reason are not to be conflated with the pangs of Humean "sentiment" or with mere utility. The meaning of morality is *duty,* and duty for the sake of duty. It is a strict, hard-headed, and uncompromising view of morality, but Kant's ambition was to set morality on a rational, objective basis and establish a single set of moral principles "for all rational beings," once and for all. ("Oh Duty,/why hast thou not the visage/of a sweetie or a cutie," wrote the popular American poet Ogden Nash.)

Kant's philosophical work and reputation are based upon three voluminous critiques (*The Critique of Pure Reason, The Critique of Practical Reason,* and *The*

6

Critique of Judgment), all written in the last two decades of the eighteenth century. It is the second critique, *The Critique of Practical Reason,* that contains his ethics (although this presumes the theory of knowledge in the first book and anticipates the teleological view of the third). But before he published the second critique itself, Kant wrote a brief, more clearly written pamphlet on ethics—which serves as an introduction to the *Critique*—titled *The Grounding of the Metaphysics of Morals.* It is this shorter work that we have included here; in its essential features it is the same as the much larger volume.

Kant once described the critical moment in his own philosophical education as a debt to Hume, "who awakened me from my philosophical slumbers." It was Hume's doubts about the justifiability of both knowledge and morality that prompted Kant onto the path that resulted in the three critiques, and the first two volumes are in part a refutation of Hume's doubts, first with regard to knowledge, then with regard to morality. Hume's doubts about knowledge (his *skepticism*) were drawn from the question of whether we could ever prove that our "ideas" corresponded to reality; Kant's elaborate response developed the "revolutionary" view that we could know that we know reality precisely because we "constitute" reality through the concepts of our understanding. In ethics, Hume had doubted that reason alone could ever justify morality, because morality was based on our passions and "reason is, and ought to be, the slave of the passions." Kant's reply, which we shall study here, is that Hume misunderstood the nature of morality, that morality is based on reason, not passion, and the correctness of our moral principles is indeed provable by reason.

What is wrong with a view of morality based on passion or sentiments? Hume himself pointed out that such a view precludes a rational justification of morality. But it also leaves open the possibility that people with very different sentiments might have very different morals, equally correct. It was this sort of relativist view that Kant found unthinkable. Killing is wrong, everywhere; it does not matter if some perverse people somewhere enjoy killing and mutually approve of it. Lying is wrong, not just as a matter of social consensus or feeling, but because the suggestion that lying is permissible is itself *incomprehensible.* Kant's ethical theory, therefore, is aimed first at providing a rational basis for morality that will be correct for all people at all times and in all circumstances.

Second, however, Kant wanted to provide a general criterion for moral principles, a test that could be used to determine which principles were indeed morally correct and, at the same time, prove rationally that they were correct. It is to this end that he develops his theory of *the categorical imperative,* not only to stress the unconditional nature of moral principles, but also to establish a way of proving them. Finally, Kant wants to establish the *presuppositions* of morality—those conditions without which there could be no morality and which themselves *must* be believed in the moral life.

In Kant's ethics, morality consists of the dictates of practical reason. This means that morality does not depend on particular circumstances or the facts of a situation, and it means that morality does not depend on the customs of a particular society or the feelings engendered in its members. Kant's theory is what we have called a *deontological* theory, and so its central concept is that of *duty.* And yet, it is crucial to Kant's ethics that morality is also *autonomous*—that is, presupposes the ability of every rational being to ascertain for him- or herself the rightness or wrongness of a principle or an action. Morality is made up of rational principles that are freely arrived at through practical reason.

Because morality is a matter of reason, the "moral worth" of a person's behavior cannot depend on the contingencies of fate that dictate the success or failure of an action or, for that matter, on the fortune or misfortune of birth, talent, social status, and abilities. Thus, Kant could not be more opposed to Plato and Aristotle in this, for they believed that "the good man" included a very definite set of conditions in terms of sex, birth, citizenship, health, and good fortune of all kinds. If I try to save a baby from drowning, according to Kant, but I am tripped on the wharf by a clumsy sailor and drown the baby by accident, the consequences of my act may have been disastrous but, nonetheless, I behaved in a moral way. Likewise, if I somehow accidentally save the baby without meaning to, the consequences are good, but the action is not moral. Contrary to the utilitarians, Kant argues that it is never the consequences of an action that determine its "moral worth" but always the intentions and principles ("the maxim") that lie behind it. Thus Kant begins,

> Nothing can be conceived in the world, or even out of it, which can be called good without qualification, except a *good will*.

He thus dismisses out of hand all those features that the Greeks called happiness and turns instead to the characterization of the rational will as the basis of ethical theory.

Kant's ethics is essentially a formalization of Christian ethics, but with a number of startling variations. First and foremost, notice in the preceding quotation that Kant includes the curious phrase, "or even out of it." Elsewhere he speaks of "any rational creature." What he has in mind is the *primacy* of morality, that is, the rational justifiability of morality independent of God or divine commandments. Traditional Judeo-Christian morality presented morality as the commandments of God and that was their justification (as well as their ultimate sanction). But Kant is arguing the other way around—that God is moral and gave us moral commandments *because he is rational.* Kant never hesitates in his piety, but this reversal of God and morality will have momentous consequences in the future of moral thinking.

Other aspects of Kant's ethics display dramatically the central features of the Judeo-Christian tradition, however. His rejection of all "external" factors in determining moral worth and—ultimately—happiness is essential to the biblical emphasis on the goodness of one's soul as opposed to the gifts and punishments of fortune. His insistence on the autonomy and equality of every individual, while not in accordance with some traditional church teachings, is certainly in line with the Lutheran Pietism Kant learned at his mother's knee. And yet, Kant also defends a conception of morality that is wholly self-contained and not dependent on God or gods or, in one sense, on anything outside of the human will. Indeed, that is the ultimate challenge for Kant's philosophy—whether a theory so restricted and pure can capture the rich complexity of our daily moral life.

GROUNDING FOR THE METAPHYSICS OF MORALS*

EMPIRICAL AND A PRIORI ETHICS: PREFACE

In the short preface to the *Grounding,* Kant distinguishes two parts to ethics, based on a central distinction from his work in the theory of knowledge. The distinction, which will also be important for his ethics, is between

1. Empirical—based on experience, and
2. a priori—literally "before" experience; a priori principles are those which provide the framework within which all experience is to be understood.

In ethics, the distinction between the two parts is thus:

1. The empirical has to do with the details of our practical life, the circumstances in which we find ourselves, and the skills we develop to cope with them. Kant suggests that the empirical part of ethics might be called "practical anthropology."
2. The a priori has to do with the strictly *rational* part of ethics, that is, the principles provided by practical reason that form the framework for all of our practical behavior. Kant calls this a priori part of ethics "morality."

Kant adds that the two parts of ethics are almost always mixed together; nevertheless, it is possible and important to construct a "pure moral philosophy, perfectly cleared of everything that is only empirical and that belongs to anthropology." This philosophy will be based on the everyday concept of duty and moral laws. Thus, the commandment, "Thou shalt not steal," like the rule, "Don't lie," is a priori insofar as it is the basis of obligations that we do not find in situations but rather bring to them (thus "before" experience or "a priori"). Only such principles can properly be called *moral laws.*

Morality, Kant then continues, is action in obedience to moral principles. But, because morality is a priori, it is not enough that an action should merely happen to conform to the law (for example, when a person doesn't cheat because he or she didn't know how or forgot to do it). The action must be done for the sake of the law; in other words, one must have the moral principle in some sense "in mind" as the basis for action. The other motives that go into every action (and Kant never denies their influence) are not part of morality or moral philosophy. Hume's sentiments, for example, would have no place in morality. ("I felt sorry for him" would not be a *reason* for being moral.) So far as the a priori part of ethics is concerned, Kant is analyzing a "pure rational will," though, of course, such a pure will is an idealization.

The *Grounding* is the "popular" introduction to this conception of moral philosophy; but it is also the search for a practical test, "the supreme principle of morality," which is the singular key to every moral decision.

Ancient Greek philosophy was divided into three sciences: physics, ethics, and logic. This division is perfectly suitable to the nature of the subject, and the only improvement that can be made in it is perhaps only to supply its principle so that there will be a possibility on the one hand of ensuring its completeness and on the other of correctly determining its necessary subdivisions.

All rational knowledge is either material and concerned with some object, or formal and concerned only with the form of understanding and of reason themselves and with the universal rules of thought in general without regard to differences of its objects. Formal philosophy is called logic. Material philosophy, however, has to do with determinate objects and with the laws to which these objects are subject; and such philosophy is divided into two parts, because these laws are either laws of nature or laws of freedom. The science of the former is called physics, while that of the latter is called ethics; they are also called doctrine of nature and doctrine of morals respectively.

Logic cannot have any empirical part, i.e., a part in which the universal and necessary laws of thought would be based on grounds taken from experience; for in that case it would not be logic, i.e., a canon for understanding and reason, which is valid for all thinking and which has to be demonstrated. Natural and moral philosophy, on the contrary, can each have an empirical part. The former has to because it must determine the laws of nature as an object of experience, and the latter because it must determine the will of man insofar as the will is affected by nature. The laws of the former are those according to which everything does happen, while the laws of the latter are those according to which everything ought to happen, although these moral laws also consider the conditions under which what ought to happen frequently does not.

All philosophy insofar as it is founded on experience may be called empirical, while that which sets forth its doctrines as founded entirely on a priori principles may be called pure. The latter, when merely formal, is called logic; but when limited to determinate objects of the understanding, it is called metaphysics.

In this way there arises the idea of a twofold metaphysics: a metaphysics of nature and a metaphysics of morals. Physics will thus have its empirical part, but also a rational one. Ethics will too, though here the empirical part might more specifically be called practical anthropology, while the rational part might properly be called morals.

All industries, crafts, and arts have gained by the division of labor, viz., one man does not do everything, but each confines himself to a certain kind of work that is distinguished from all other kinds by the treatment it requires, so that the work may be done with the highest perfection and with greater ease. Where work is not so distinguished and divided, where everyone is a jack of all trades, there industry remains sunk in the greatest barbarism. Whether or not pure philosophy in all its parts requires its own special man might well be in itself a subject worthy of consideration. Would not the whole of this learned industry be better off if those who are accustomed, as the public taste demands, to purvey a mixture of the empirical with the rational in all sorts of proportions unknown even to themselves and who style themselves independent thinkers, while giving the name of hair-splitters to those who apply themselves to the purely rational part, were to be given warning about pursuing simultaneously two jobs which are quite different in their technique, and each of which perhaps requires a special talent that when combined with the other talent produces nothing but bungling? But I only ask here whether the nature of science does not require that the empirical part always be carefully separated from the rational part. Should not physics proper (i.e., empirical physics) be preceded by a metaphysics of nature, and practical anthropology by a metaphysics of morals? Both of these metaphysics must be carefully purified of everything empirical in order to know how much pure reason can accomplish in each case and from what sources it draws its a priori teaching, whether such teaching be conducted by all moralists (whose name is legion) or only by some who feel a calling thereto.

Since I am here primarily concerned with moral philosophy, the foregoing question will be limited to a consideration of whether or not there is the utmost necessity for working out for once a pure moral philosophy that is wholly cleared of everything which can only be empirical and can only belong to anthropology. That there must be such a philosophy is evident from the common idea of duty and of moral laws. Everyone must admit that if a law is to be morally valid, i.e., is to be valid as a ground of obligation, then it must carry with it absolute necessity. He must admit that the command, "Thou shalt not lie," does not hold only for men, as if other rational beings had no need to abide by it, and so with all the other moral laws properly so called. And he must concede that the ground of obligation here must therefore be sought not in the nature of man nor in the circumstances of the world in which man is placed, but must be sought a priori solely in the concepts of pure reason; he must grant that every other precept which is founded on principles of mere experience—even a precept that may in certain respects be universal— insofar as it rests in the least on empirical grounds—perhaps only in its motive—can indeed be called a practical rule, but never a moral law.

Thus not only are moral laws together with their principles essentially different from every kind of practical cognition in which there is anything empirical, but all moral philosophy rests entirely on its pure part. When applied to man, it does not in the least borrow from acquaintance with him (anthropology) but gives a priori laws to him as a rational being. To be sure, these laws require, furthermore, a power of judgment sharpened by experience, partly in order to distinguish in what cases they are applicable, and partly to gain for them access to the human will as well as influence for putting them into practice. For man is affected by so many inclinations that, even though he is indeed capable of the idea of a pure practical reason, he is not so easily able to make that idea effective *in concreto* in the conduct of his life.

A metaphysics of morals is thus indispensably necessary, not merely because of motives of speculation regarding the source of practical principles which are present a priori in our reason, but because morals themselves are liable to all kinds of corruption as long as the guide and supreme norm for correctly estimating them are missing. For in the case of what is to be morally good, that it conforms to the moral law is not enough; it must also be done for the sake of the moral law. Otherwise that conformity is only very contingent and uncertain, since the non-moral ground may now and then produce actions that conform with the law but quite often produces actions that are contrary to the law. Now the moral law in its purity and genuineness (which is of the utmost concern in the practical realm) can be sought nowhere but in a pure philosophy. Therefore, pure philosophy (metaphysics) must precede; without it there can be no moral philosophy at all. That philosophy which mixes pure principles with empirical ones does not deserve the name of philosophy (for philosophy is distinguished from ordinary rational knowledge by its treatment in a separate science of what the latter comprehends only confusedly). Still less does it deserve the name of moral philosophy, since by this very confusion it spoils even the purity of morals and counteracts its own end. . . .

The present *Grounding [Grundlegung]* is, however, intended for nothing more than seeking out and establishing the supreme principle of morality. This constitutes by itself a task which is complete in its purpose and should be kept separate from every other moral inquiry. The application of this supreme principle to the whole ethical system would, to be sure, shed much light on my conclusions regarding this central question, which is important but has not heretofore been at all satisfactorily discussed; and the adequacy manifested by the principle throughout such application would provide strong confirmation for the principle. Nevertheless, I must forgo this advantage, which after all would be more gratifying for myself than helpful for others, since ease of use and apparent adequacy of a principle do not provide any certain proof of its soundness, but do awaken, rather, a certain bias which prevents any rigorous examination and estimation of it for itself without any regard to its consequences.

The method adopted in this work is, I believe, one that is most suitable if we proceed analytically from ordinary knowledge to a determination of the supreme principle and then back again synthetically from an examination of this principle and its sources to ordinary knowledge where its application is found. Therefore, the division turns out to be the following:

1. First Section.   Transition from the Ordinary Rational Knowledge of Morality to the Philosophical
2. Second Section.   Transition from Popular Moral Philosophy to a Metaphysics of Morals
3. Third Section.   Final Step from a Metaphysics of Morals to a Critique of Pure Practical Reason.

DISCUSSION

In his preface, Kant admits that while the distinction between a priori and empirical elements is essential to ethics, the distinction is virtually impossible to make out in practice. Furthermore, from a more personal viewpoint, we would consider overly harsh this separation of moral (a priori, principled) considerations from immediate questions of consequences and interpersonal relationships. The very idea of deciding what one ought to do in the absence of any particular circumstances, personal feelings, or local customs or rules seems to us impossible, or at least peculiar. Why, then, does Kant so insist on it?

The answer has two parts: one of them, appropriately, abstract and philosophical, though not a priori; the other, strictly historical and cultural. The philosophical answer is that our concept of morality—as Kant himself points out—is an idealistic and "pure" concept that, it may be admitted, few if any of us ever achieve, though most of us make some effort to do so, at least some of the time. The analysis of the ideal is therefore necessarily distinct from the empirical details of our actual behavior, for, as Kant also points out, one can never get a clear picture of an ideal by trying to abstract from the confusion of actual examples. One must have a clear picture of the concept itself, and, in this instance, the concept of morality is the subject for analysis. The question is not whether anyone has ever been perfectly moral, any more than, in physics, the question is not whether there actually is an "ideal gas" or whether a person could travel at the speed of light. Nevertheless, our abstract understanding of an ideal can make an enormous difference to our actual behavior because understanding the moral ideal *is* understanding the basis of our (less than ideal) intentions and behavior.

The historical-cultural explanation of Kant's hard-headed conception of morality takes us back to that period we keep referring to as the Enlightenment (or, in Germany, the *Aufklärung*). This powerful movement preoccupied European intellectual and cultural life during most of the seventeenth and eighteenth centuries. Its foremost concept—and weapon—was *criticism* (thus, Kant's three great books were all called "critiques"). The Enlightenment was to a large extent the expression of a newly prospering and increasingly powerful middle class (between the royalty and the aristocracy on top, and the peasants and workers on the bottom). The members of the middle class were for the most part professionals—lawyers, doctors, teachers, clerks, bankers, businesspeople—and they held jobs in which they generally served the public (which meant, vaguely, society in general). Thus, they came to think of themselves as "the universal class" (an expression later picked up by Hegel and then Marx, who called the working class "the universal class"). The speakers for the Enlightenment—in part because they were professionals and critical of the inefficiency and inequity of the older regimes—made every attempt to break down class and national barriers to better government and better business, attacking every belief that seemed to them to be an inefficient relic of the past as "superstition" and rejecting everything provincial in favor of what was universal or "cosmopolitan" (literally, "of the universal city"). With this in mind, we can easily understand that Kant—who was one of the foremost spokesmen of the Enlightenment in Germany—was trying to capture in his ethics just that universal sense that the Enlightenment was promoting. The ethical truths he sought, in other words, were those that applied to all persons at all times. He offers an account of moral rules that are valid in all cases; for Kant, empirical circumstances are utterly independent of questions about the right thing to do. His attempt to bypass everything circumstantial and get to the heart of morality for all of humanity was part and parcel of the Enlightenment program, and we might add, very much in tune with Kant's French Enlightenment predecessor and intellectual hero—Jean Jacques Rousseau. Several years before, Rousseau had stunned

Europe with his intriguing theory of an "inherent natural goodness" in everyone, which modern society had "corrupted." Kant, too, sought that "inner goodness" in all people, not in the realm of sentiment (which Rousseau, like Hume, defended) but in the more rigorous realm of reason and the will.

THE RATIONAL BASIS OF MORALITY: FROM SECTION 1

The first part of the *Grounding* begins with the sentence we have already quoted: "Nothing can possibly be conceived in the world, or out of it, which can be called good without qualification, except a *good will*." In this single sentence, Kant captures the heart of his a priori conception of morals, the fact that it is our intentions that are moral or immoral, not the empirical fortunes of our lives, our abilities, and our successes and failures. It is what we *try* to do that counts. Indeed, what Aristotle called the essence of moral virtue, namely *character,* is dismissed immediately by Kant as not being morally good at all. Character is desirable, of course, but character, like all other abilities and talents, involves too much luck—having been born into the right family and with a good disposition and so on, not a matter of will. A good will is thus contrasted with good fortune, which altogether we call "happiness." But here Kant makes an important qualification: that although good will (morality) is wholly distinct from good fortune (happiness), we naturally expect that the two will go together; indeed, we are repulsed by the very idea of a person who has no good intentions enjoying prosperity. "Thus," Kant concludes, "a good will appears to constitute the indispensable condition even of being *worthy* of happiness" (emphasis added).

Transition from the Ordinary Rational Knowledge of Morality to the Philosophical

There is no possibility of thinking of anything at all in the world, or even out of it, which can be regarded as good without qualification, except a *good will*. Intelligence, wit, judgment, and whatever talents of the mind one might want to name are doubtless in many respects good and desirable, as are such qualities of temperament as courage, resolution, perseverance. But they can also become extremely bad and harmful if the will, which is to make use of these gifts of nature and which in its special constitution is called character, is not good. The same holds with gifts of fortune; power, riches, honor, even health, and that complete well-being and contentment with one's condition which is called happiness make for pride and often hereby even arrogance, unless there is a good will to correct their influence on the mind and herewith also to rectify the whole principle of action and make it universally conformable to its end. The sight of a being who is not graced by any touch of a pure and good will but who yet enjoys an uninterrupted prosperity can never delight a rational and impartial spectator. Thus a good will seems to constitute the indispensable condition of being even worthy of happiness.

Some qualities are even conducive to this good will itself and can facilitate its work. Nevertheless, they have no intrinsic unconditional worth; but they always presuppose, rather, a good will, which restricts the high esteem in which they are otherwise rightly held, and does not permit them to be regarded as absolutely good. Moderation in emotions and passions, self-control, and calm deliberation are not only good in many respects but even seem to constitute part of the intrinsic worth of a person. But they are far from being rightly called good without qualification (however unconditionally they were commended by the ancients). For without the principles of a good will, they can become extremely bad; the coolness of a villain makes him not only much more dangerous but also immediately more abominable in our eyes than he would have been regarded by us without it.

A good will is good not because of what it effects or accomplishes, nor because of its fitness to attain some proposed end; it is good only through its willing, i.e., it is good in itself. When it is considered in itself, then it is to be esteemed very much higher than anything which it might ever bring about merely in order to favor some inclination, or even the sum total of all inclinations. Even if, by some especially unfortunate fate or by the niggardly provision of stepmotherly nature, this will should be wholly lacking in the power to accomplish its purpose; if with the greatest effort it should yet achieve nothing, and only the good will should remain (not, to be sure, as a mere wish but as the summoning of all the means in our power), yet would it, like a jewel, still shine by its own light as something which has its full value in itself. Its usefulness or fruitlessness can neither augment nor diminish this value. Its usefulness would be, as it were, only the setting to enable us to handle it in ordinary dealings or to attract to it the attention of those who are not yet experts, but not to recommend it to real experts or to determine its value.

But there is something so strange in this idea of the absolute value of a mere will, in which no account is taken of any useful results, that in spite of all the agreement received even from ordinary reason, yet there must arise the suspicion that such an idea may perhaps have as its hidden base merely some high-flown fancy, and that we may have misunderstood the purpose of nature in assigning to reason the governing of our will. Therefore, this idea will be examined from this point of view.

Although Kant is a deontologist in his ethical theory (that is, his ethics is based on duty and the rational authority of morality rather than the consequences of our actions), he is also a teleologist in his vision of the world, much like Aristotle. This is a view that he defends mainly in his third critique, *The Critique of Judgment,* but it is manifested here in his ethics, too. The teleological view of the world is simply, in Kant's words (from the third critique), that "nature does nothing in vain." Thus, when he refers to "the purpose of nature in assigning reason as governor of our will" in the preceding paragraph, he is not just waxing poetic. He does see in all of nature a purpose, and he assumes that whatever nature does is done for a reason. The argument that follows is almost identical to the one employed by Aristotle: If we are rational creatures, it must be for a reason. Nature must have intended us to use our reason for a purpose. What purpose? Reason cannot have the job of making us happy, since our ability to reason and calculate and plot and brood has obviously caused more of us to be unhappy than happy. Indeed, who could be happier than a "dumb" animal, a dog romping in the woods or a kitten playing with a ball of yarn. Therefore reason must have some more exalted purpose, over and above the pursuit of happiness. This is, of course, morality.

In the natural constitution of an organized being, i.e., one suitably adapted to the purpose of life, let there be taken as a principle that in such a being no organ is to be found for any end unless it be the most fit and the best adapted for that end. Now if that being's preservation, welfare, or, in a word, its happiness, were the real end of nature in the case of a being having reason and will, then nature would have hit upon a very poor arrangement in having the reason of the creature carry out this purpose. For all the actions which such a creature has to perform with this purpose in view, and the whole rule of his conduct would have been prescribed much more exactly by instinct; and the purpose in question could have been attained much more certainly by instinct than it ever can be by reason. And if in addition reason had been imparted to this favored creature, then it would have had to serve him only to contemplate the happy constitution of his nature, to admire that nature, to rejoice in it, and to feel grateful to the cause that bestowed it; but reason would not have served him to subject his faculty of desire to its weak and delusive guidance nor would it have served him to meddle incompetently with the purpose of nature. In a word, nature would have taken care that reason did not strike out into a practical use nor presume, with its weak insight, to think out for itself a plan for happiness and the means for attaining it. Nature would have taken upon herself not only the choice of ends but also that of the means, and would with wise foresight have entrusted both to instinct alone.

And, in fact, we find that the more a cultivated reason devotes itself to the aim of enjoying life and happiness, the further does man get away from true contentment. Because of this there arises in many persons, if only they are candid enough to admit it, a certain degree of misology, i.e., hatred of reason. This is especially so in the case of those who are the most experienced in the use of reason, because after calculating all the advantages they derive, I say not from the invention of all the arts of common luxury, but even from the sciences (which in the end seem to them to be also a luxury of the understanding), they yet find that they have in fact only brought more trouble on their heads than they have gained in happiness. Therefore, they come to envy, rather than despise, the more common run of men who are closer to the guidance of mere natural instinct and who do not allow their reason much influence on their conduct. And we must admit that the judgment of those who would temper, or even reduce below zero, the boastful eulogies on behalf of the advantages which reason is supposed to provide as regards the happiness and contentment of life is by no means morose or ungrateful to the goodness with which the world is governed: There lies at the root of such judgments, rather, the idea that existence has another and much more worthy purpose, for which, and not for happiness, reason is quite properly intended, and which must, therefore, be regarded as the supreme condition to which the private purpose of men must, for the most part, defer.

Reason, however, is not competent enough to guide the will safely as regards its objects and the satisfaction of all our needs (which it in part even multiplies); to this end would an implanted natural instinct have led much more certainly. But inasmuch as reason has been imparted to us as a practical faculty, i.e., as one which is to have influence on the will, its true function must be to produce a will which is not merely good as a means to some further end, but is good in itself. To produce a will good in itself reason was absolutely necessary, inasmuch as nature in distributing her capacities has everywhere gone to work in a purposive manner. While such a will may not indeed be the sole and complete good, it must, nevertheless, be the highest good and the condition of all the rest, even of the desire for happiness. In this case there is nothing inconsistent with the wisdom of nature that the cultivation of reason, which is requisite for the first and unconditioned purpose, may in many ways restrict, at least in this life, the attainment of the second purpose, viz., happiness, which is always conditioned. Indeed happiness can even be reduced to less than nothing, without nature's failing thereby in her purpose; for reason recognizes as its highest practical function the establishment of a good will, whereby in the attainment of this end reason is capable only of its own kind of satisfaction, viz., that of fulfilling a purpose which is in turn determined only by reason, even though such fulfillment were often to interfere with the purposes of inclination.

Kant now introduces his all-important distinction between acting in conformity with duty versus acting for the sake of duty. A grocer, for example, might abstain from cheating his customers, but only because he is afraid of getting caught and losing business. He acts in conformity with duty; his action "agrees" with the moral principle "don't steal," but his reason for obeying is not that stealing is wrong, which would be acting for the sake of duty. Morality consists of the latter, not the former.

Contrasted with reason are the *inclinations;* that is, all our desires, instincts, emotions, ambitions, compulsions—in short what we *want*. These are strictly empirical, and so of no moral worth. This phrase, "moral worth," is critical in Kant. When he says that an act "has no moral worth," he is not saying that it is a bad act but rather an amoral one. The grocer who does not cheat his customers because he is afraid of getting caught is not doing wrong; he is just not *morally* praiseworthy, which is Kant's concern.

A great many actions are motivated by both duty and inclination. For example, Kant suggests that self-preservation is both a duty and one of our most basic instincts. Usually, we stay alive because we want to (from "inclination"), but sometimes, if we are very depressed and considering suicide, we might stay alive out of duty alone. Then our refraining from committing suicide has "moral worth," but not otherwise. So too, being kind ("beneficent") is often a matter of sympathy (and thus an inclination), but it is when one does not feel kindly that kindness has moral worth. This is where Kant's notion of "moral worth" starts bothering many people's intuitions. Is a philanthropist who gives to charity out of duty morally superior to one who gives just because he wants to?

It is important, however, to remember exactly what Kant takes himself to be doing. His project is an attempt to give a clear account of the concept, or true essence, of morality prior to the empirical circumstances of everyday life. He is not in the business, then, of explaining or accounting for our usual reactions or characterizations. To say that an action has no moral worth, or is amoral, is simply to say that it is not a true instance of the concept of morality, although it may be worthwhile or pleasing in other ways. In fact, Kant states that those actions done in accordance with duty, rather than for the sake of it, ought to be praised and encouraged; but if done from inclination, they are nevertheless not deserving of moral esteem.

The concept of a will estimable in itself and good without regard to any further end must now be developed. This concept already dwells in the natural sound understanding and needs not so much to be taught as merely to be elucidated. It always holds first place in estimating the total worth of our actions and constitutes the condition of all the rest. Therefore, we shall take up the concept of *duty,* which includes that of a good will, though with certain subjective restrictions and hindrances, which far from hiding a good will or rendering it unrecognizable, rather bring it out by contrast and make it shine forth more brightly.

I here omit all actions already recognized as contrary to duty, even though they may be useful for this or that end; for in the case of these the question does not arise at all as to whether they might be done from duty, since they even conflict with duty. I also set aside those actions which are really in accordance with duty, yet to which men have no immediate inclination, but perform them because they are impelled thereto by some other inclination. For in this [second] case to decide whether the action which is in accord with duty has been done from duty or from some selfish purpose is easy. This difference is far more difficult to note in the [third] case where the action accords with duty and the subject has in addition an immediate inclination to do the action. For example, that a dealer should not overcharge an inexperienced purchaser certainly accords with duty; and where there is much commerce, the prudent merchant does not overcharge but keeps to a fixed price for everyone in general, so that a child may buy from him just as well as everyone else may. Thus customers are honestly served, but this is not nearly enough for making us believe that the merchant has acted this way from duty and from principles of honesty; his own advantage required him to do it. He cannot, however, be assumed to have in addition [as in the third case] an immediate inclination toward his buyers, causing him, as it were, out of love to give no one as far as price is concerned any advantage over another. Hence the action was done neither from duty nor from immediate inclination, but merely for a selfish purpose.

On the other hand, to preserve one's life is a duty; and, furthermore, everyone has also an immediate inclination to do so. But on this account the often anxious care taken by most men for it has no intrinsic worth, and the maxim of their action has no moral content. They preserve their lives, to be sure, in accordance with duty, but not from duty. On the other hand, if adversity and hopeless sorrow have completely taken away the taste for life, if an unfortunate man, strong in soul and more indignant at his fate than despondent or dejected, wishes for death and yet preserves his life without loving it—not from inclination or fear, but from duty—then his maxim indeed has a moral content.

Kant's translator here explains:

Four different cases have been distinguished in the two foregoing paragraphs. Case 1 involves those actions which are contrary to duty (lying, cheating, stealing, etc.). Case 2 involves those which accord with duty but for which a person perhaps has no immediate inclination, though he does have a mediate inclination thereto (one pays his taxes not because he likes to but in order to avoid the penalties set for delinquents; one treats his fellows well not because he really likes them but because he wants their votes when at some future time he runs for public office, etc.). A vast number of so-called "morally good" actions actually belong to this case 2—they accord with duty because of self-seeking inclinations. Case 3 involves those which accord with duty and for which a person does have an immediate inclination (one does not commit suicide because all is going well with him; one does not commit adultery because he considers his wife to be the most desirable creature in the whole world, etc.). Case 4 involves those actions which accord with duty but are contrary to some immediate inclination (one does not commit suicide even when he is in dire distress; one does not commit adultery even though his wife has turned out to be an impossible shrew, etc.). Now case 4 is the crucial test case of the will's possible goodness—but Kant does not claim that one should lead his life in such a way as to encounter as many such cases as possible in order constantly to test his virtue (deliberately marry a shrew [in order] to be able to resist the temptation to commit adultery). Life itself forces enough such cases upon a person without his seeking them out. But when there is a conflict between duty and inclination, duty should always be followed. Case 3 makes for the easiest living and the greatest contentment, and anyone would wish that life might present him with far more of these cases than with cases 2 or 4. But yet one should not arrange his life in such a way as to avoid case 4 at all costs and to seek out case 3 as much as possible (become a recluse [in order] to avoid the possible rough and tumble involved with frequent association with one's fellows, avoid places where one might encounter the sick and the poor [in order] to spare oneself the pangs of sympathy and the need to exercise the virtue of benefiting those in distress, etc.). For the purpose of philosophical analysis Kant emphasizes case 4 as being the test case of the will's possible goodness, but he is not thereby advocating puritanism.

Kant continues:

To be beneficent where one can is a duty; and besides this, there are many persons who are so sympathetically constituted that, without any further motive of vanity or self-interest, they find an inner pleasure in spreading joy around them and can rejoice in the satisfaction of others as their own work. But I maintain that in such a case an action of this kind, however dutiful and amiable it may be, has nevertheless no true moral worth. It is on a level with such actions as arise from other inclinations, e.g., the inclination for honor, which if fortunately directed to what is in fact beneficial and accords with duty and is thus honorable, deserves praise and encouragement, but not esteem; for its maxim lacks the moral content of an action done not from inclination but from duty. Suppose then the mind of this friend of mankind to be clouded over with his own sorrow so that all sympathy with the lot of others is extinguished, and suppose him still to have the power to benefit others in distress, even though he is not touched by their trouble because he is sufficiently absorbed with his own; and now suppose that, even though no inclination moves him any longer, he nevertheless tears himself from this deadly insensibility and performs the action without any inclination at all, but solely from duty—then for the first time his action has genuine moral worth. Further still, if nature has put little sympathy in this or that man's heart, if (while being an honest man in other respects) he is by temperament cold and indifferent to the sufferings of others, perhaps because as regards his own sufferings he is endowed with the special gift of patience and fortitude and expects or even requires that others should have the same; if such a man (who would truly not be nature's worst product) had not been exactly fashioned by her to be a philanthropist, would he not yet find in himself a source from which he might give himself a worth far higher than any that a good-natured temperament might have? By all means, because just here does the worth of the character come out; this worth is moral and incomparably the highest of all, viz., that he is beneficent, not from inclination, but from duty.

Duty can therefore either coincide with the inclinations or be opposed to them. In the case of coincidence, the act that follows is amoral, but when duty is chosen *over* the inclinations, the act is moral. In what follows, Kant gives us his curious argument that although duty and happiness are distinct, a person has a duty to be happy. The reason is that people who are miserable are less likely to do their duty. In most cases, this duty to pursue happiness coincides with a person's inclinations and hence has no moral worth. However, in the rare cases in which the relevant inclinations fail, the duty remains, and acting on that duty is morally worthy.

To secure one's own happiness is a duty (at least indirectly); for discontent with one's condition under many pressing cares and amid unsatisfied wants might easily become a great temptation to transgress one's duties. But here also do men of themselves already have, irrespective of duty, the strongest and deepest inclination toward happiness, because just in this idea are all inclinations combined into a sum total. But the precept of happiness is often so constituted as greatly to interfere with some inclinations, and yet men cannot form any definite and certain concept of the sum of satisfaction of all inclination that is called happiness. Hence there is no wonder that a single inclination which is determinate both as to what it promises and as to the time within which it can be satisfied may outweigh a fluctuating idea; and there is no wonder that a man, e.g., a gouty patient, can choose to enjoy what he likes and to suffer what he may, since by his calculation he has here at least not sacrificed the enjoyment of the present moment to some possibly groundless expectations of the good fortune that is supposed to be found in health. But even in this case, if the universal inclination to happiness did not determine his will and if health, at least for him, did not figure as so necessary an element in his calculations; there still remains here, as in all other cases, a law, viz., that he should promote his happiness not from inclination but from duty, and thereby for the first time does his conduct have real moral worth.

Now, in a passage famous because it is somewhat shocking, Kant turns to the biblical injunction that we should "love our neighbors." But love is an inclination and not rational, not a matter of will. Therefore, Kant suggests that we distinguish two kinds of love, "practical" and "pathological," and only the first has moral worth. (The phrase "pathological love" comes from the Greek word *pathos,* which means "feeling" in general as well as "suffering," from which we get our medical word "pathology.") Pathological love, which includes all of those romantic and family feelings of intimacy and tenderness, is (as inclination) irrelevant to morality. And the reason it is irrelevant is that it cannot be "commanded." That is, emotions, desires, longings, and so on simply come upon us. Although we can be judged on what we do as a result of those feelings, we cannot be held responsible simply for having them; they just happen to us. (Can one *make* oneself feel love or jealousy or anger?) Yet moral assessments are intimately connected with the notions of praise and blame, which are in turn connected with the concept of responsibility. If I say you were wrong to do something, I mean both that you ought not to have done it and that you could have avoided doing it. The latter judgment is precisely what is precluded in the emotional realm according to Kant. If inclinations are not something that we can command, they are not something that we can avoid having. They are, therefore, not the proper subject matter of morality. The dictates of reason, on the other hand, are very much in our control, and hence something for which we can be held responsible.

Undoubtedly in this way also are to be understood those passages of Scripture which command us to love our neighbor and even our enemy. For love as an inclination cannot be commanded; but beneficence from duty, when no inclination impels us and even when a natural and unconquerable aversion opposes such beneficence, is practical, and not pathological, love. Such love resides in the will and not in the propensities of feeling, in principles of action and not in tender sympathy; and only this practical love can be commanded.

Although Kant did not list it as such, the proposition that to have "moral worth" an action must be done for the sake of duty was the first in a series of propositions that structure this part of the *Grounding*. The second, which distinguishes between formal and material principles, follows.

The distinction here is between the purpose and the maxim of an action. What Kant means by "purpose" is what the various teleological theorists have in mind when they talk about the "aim" of an action, what it is trying to achieve. But neither the purpose (the aim) nor the actual consequences themselves are a part of moral consideration according to Kant. The aim, like the results of action, is empirical (Kant uses the phrase *a posteriori,* which means "empirical" but is a direct contrast to a priori and means literally "after"). The maxim, on the other hand, is not an aim but a principle, that is, the general grounds upon which one acts. Thus, the grocer might have as his aim satisfying his customer and making a profit on the sale, but the maxim on which he acts (if he is being moral) is that one should be honest. It is the intention (to act according to what duty demands), not any repercussions of the act, that is the essentially moral aspect of an action.

The second proposition is this: An action done from duty has its moral worth, not in the purpose that is to be attained by it, but in the maxim according to which the action is determined. The moral worth depends, therefore, not on the realization of the object of the action, but merely on the principle of volition according to which, without regard to any objects of the faculty of desire, the action has been done. From what has gone before it is clear that the purposes which we may have in our actions, as well as their effects regarded as ends and incentives of the will, cannot give to actions any unconditioned and moral worth. Where, then, can this worth lie if it is not to be found in the will's relation to the expected effect? Nowhere but in the principle of the will, with no regard to the ends that can be brought about through such action. For the will stands, as it were, at a crossroads between its a priori principle, which is formal, and its a posteriori incentive, which is material; and since it must be determined by something, it must be determined by the formal principle of volition, if the action is done from duty—and in that case every material principle is taken away from it.

The third proposition, which follows from the other two, can be expressed thus: Duty is the necessity of an action done out of respect for the law. I can indeed have an inclination for an object as the effect of my proposed action; but I can never have respect for such an object, just because it is merely an effect and is not an activity of the will. Similarly, I can have no respect for inclination as such, whether my own or that of another. I can at most, if my own inclination, approve it; and, if that of another, even love it, i.e., consider it to be favorable to my own advantage. An object of respect can only be what is connected with my will solely as ground and never as effect—something that does not serve my inclination but, rather, outweighs it, or at least excludes it from consideration when some choice is made—in other words, only the law itself can be an object of respect and hence can be a command. Now an action done from duty must altogether exclude the influence of inclination and therewith every object of the will. Hence there is nothing left which can determine the will except objectively the law and subjectively pure respect for this practical law, i.e., the will can be subjectively determined by the maxim that I should follow such a law even if all my inclinations are thereby thwarted.

Thus the moral worth of an action does not lie in the effect expected from it nor in any principle of action that needs to borrow its motive from this expected effect. For all these effects (agreeableness of one's condition and even the furtherance of other people's happiness) could have been brought about also through other causes and would not have required the will of a rational being, in which the highest and unconditioned good can alone be found. Therefore, the pre-eminent good which is called moral can consist in nothing but the representation of the law in itself, and such a representation can admittedly be found only in a rational being insofar as this representation, and not some expected effect, is the determining ground of the will. This good is already present in the person who acts according to this representation, and such good need not be awaited merely from the effect.

Kant here adds, as a footnote:

There might be brought against me here an objection that I take refuge behind the word "respect" in an obscure feeling, instead of giving a clear answer to the question by means of a concept of reason. But even though respect is a feeling, it is not one received through any outside influence but is, rather, one that is self-produced by means of a rational concept; hence it is specifically different from all feelings of the first kind, which can all be reduced to inclination or fear. What I recognize immediately as a law for me, I recognize with respect; this means merely the consciousness of the subordination of my will to a law without the mediation of other influences upon my sense. The immediate determination of the will by the law, and the consciousness thereof, is called respect, which is hence regarded as the effect of the law upon the subject and not as the cause of the law. Respect is properly the representation of a worth that thwarts my self-love. Hence respect is something that is regarded as an object of neither inclination nor fear, although it has at the same time something analogous to both. The object of respect is, therefore, nothing but the law—indeed that very law which we impose on ourselves and yet recognize as necessary in itself. As law, we are subject to it without consulting self-love; as imposed on us by ourselves, it is a consequence of our will. In the former aspect, it is analogous to fear; in the latter, to inclination. All respect for a person is properly only respect for the law (of honesty, etc.) of which the person provides an example. Since we regard the development of our talents as a duty, we think of a man of talent as being also a kind of example of the law (the law of becoming like him by practice), and that is what constitutes our respect for him. All so-called moral interest consists solely in respect for the law.

Then the text continues:

But what sort of law can that be the thought of which must determine the will without reference to any expected effect, so that the will can be called absolutely good without qualification? Since I have deprived the will of every impulse that might arise for it from obeying any particular law, there is nothing left to serve the will as principle except the universal conformity of its actions to law as such, i.e., *I should never act except in such a way that I can also will that my maxim should become a universal law* [italics added]. Here mere conformity to law as such (without having as its basis any law determining particular actions) serves the will as principle and must so serve it if duty is not to be a vain delusion and a chimerical concept. The ordinary reason of mankind in its practical judgments agrees completely with this, and always has in view the aforementioned principle.

For example, take this question. When I am in distress, may I make a promise with the intention of not keeping it? I readily distinguish here the two meanings which the question may have; whether making a false promise conforms with prudence or with duty. Doubtless the former can often be the case. Indeed I clearly see that escape from some present difficulty by means of such a promise is not enough. In addition I must carefully consider whether from this lie there may later arise far greater inconvenience for me than from what I now try to escape. Furthermore, the consequences of my false promise are not easy to forsee, even with all my supposed cunning; loss of confidence in me might prove to be far more disadvantageous than the misfortune which I now try to avoid. The more prudent way might be to act according to a universal maxim and to make it a habit not to promise anything without intending to keep it. But that such a maxim is, nevertheless, always based on nothing but a fear of consequences becomes clear to me at once. To be truthful from duty is, however, quite different from being truthful from fear of disadvantageous consequences; in the first case the concept of the action itself contains a law for me, while in the second I must first look around elsewhere to see what are the results for me that might be connected with the action. For to deviate from the principle of duty is quite certainly bad; but to abandon my maxim of prudence can often be very advantageous for me, though to abide by it is certainly safer. The most direct and infallible way, however, to answer the question as to whether a lying promise accords with duty is to ask myself whether I would really be content if my maxim (of extricating myself from difficulty by means of a false promise) were to hold as a universal law for myself as well as for others, and could I really say to myself that everyone may promise falsely when he finds himself in a difficulty from which he can find no other way to extricate himself. Then I immediately become aware that I can indeed will the lie but can not at all will a universal law to lie. For by such a law there would really be no promises at all, since in vain would my willing future actions be professed to other people who would not believe what I professed, or if they over-hastily did believe, then they would pay me back in like coin. Therefore, my maxim would necessarily destroy itself just as soon as it was made a universal law.

Therefore, I need no far-reaching acuteness to discern what I have to do in order that my will may be morally good. Inexperienced in the course of the world and incapable of being prepared for all its contingencies, I only ask myself whether I can also will that my maxim should become a universal law. If not, then the maxim must be rejected, not because of any disadvantage accruing to me or even to others but because it cannot be fitting as a principle in a possible legislation of universal law and reason exacts from me immediate respect for such legislation. Indeed I have as yet no insight into the grounds of such respect (which the philosopher may investigate). But I at least understand that respect is an estimation of a worth that far outweighs any worth of what is recommended by inclination, and that the necessity of acting from pure respect for the practical law is what constitutes duty, to which every other motive must give way because duty is the condition of a will good in itself, whose worth is above all else.

Finally, Kant summarizes the importance of such moral thinking, even though most people do not think of it in such "abstract and universal form." Yet most people implicitly employ such reasoning and philosophers do so as a matter of necessity. (That is what makes them philosophers.) But is all of this necessary? Couldn't people be morally good without this rational apparatus? "Innocence is a glorious thing," Kant responds, but it is lost eventually and "easily seduced." The assurance of morality is that it is based on will power and reason and does not depend on good feelings and inclinations, which are themselves undependable.

Thus within the moral cognition of ordinary human reason we have arrived at its principle. To be sure, such reason does not think of this principle abstractly in its universal form, but does always have it actually in view and does use it as the standard of judgment. It would here be easy to show how ordinary reason, with this compass in hand, is well able to distinguish, in every case that occurs, what is good or evil, in accord with duty or contrary to duty, if we do not in the least try to teach reason anything new but only make it attend, as Socrates did, to its own principle—and thereby do we show that neither science nor philosophy is needed in order to know what one must do to be honest and good, and even wise and virtuous. Indeed we might even have conjectured beforehand that cognizance of what every man is obligated to do, and hence also to know, would be available to every man, even the most ordinary. Yet we cannot but observe with admiration how great an advantage the power of practical judgment has over the theoretical in ordinary human understanding. In the theoretical, when ordinary reason ventures to depart from the laws of experience and the perceptions of sense, it falls into sheer inconceivabilities and self-contradictions, or at least into a chaos of uncertainty, obscurity, and instability. In the practical, however, the power of judgment first begins to show itself to advantage when ordinary understanding excludes all sensuous incentives from practical laws. Such understanding then becomes even subtle, whether in quibbling with its own con-science or with other claims regarding what is to be called right, or whether in wanting to determine correctly for its own instruction the worth of various ac-tions. And the most extraordinary thing is that ordinary understanding in this practical case may have just as good a hope of hitting the mark as that which any philosopher may promise himself. Indeed it is almost more certain in this than even a philosopher is, because he can have no principle other than what ordinary understanding has, but he may easily confuse his judgment by a multitude of foreign and irrelevant considerations and thereby cause it to swerve from the right way. Would it not, therefore, be wiser in moral matters to abide by the or-dinary rational judgment or at most to bring in philosophy merely for the pur-pose of rendering the system of morals more complete and intelligible and of presenting its rules in a way that is more convenient for use (especially in dis-putation), but not for the purpose of leading ordinary human understanding away from its happy simplicity in practical matters and of bringing it by means of philosophy into a new path of inquiry and instruction?

Innocence is indeed a glorious thing; but, unfortunately, it does not keep very well and is easily led astray. Consequently, even wisdom—which consists more in doing and not doing than in knowing—needs science, not in order to learn from it, but in order that wisdom's precepts may gain acceptance and per-manence. Man feels within himself a powerful counterweight to all the com-mands of duty, which are presented to him by reason as being so pre-eminently worthy of respect; this counterweight consists of his needs and inclinations, whose total satisfaction is summed up under the name of happiness. Now rea-son irremissibly commands its precepts, without thereby promising the inclina-tions anything; hence it disregards and neglects these impetuous and at the same time so seemingly plausible claims (which do not allow themselves to be sup-pressed by any command). Hereby arises a natural dialectic, i.e., a propensity to quibble with these strict laws of duty, to cast doubt upon their validity, or at least upon their purity and strictness, and to make them, where possible, more compatible with our wishes and inclinations. Thereby are such laws corrupted in their very foundations and their whole dignity is destroyed—something which even ordinary practical reason cannot in the end call good.

Thus is ordinary human reason forced to go outside its sphere and take a step into the field of practical philosophy, not by any need for speculation (which never befalls such reason so long as it is content to be mere sound rea-son) but on practical grounds themselves. There it tries to obtain information and clear instruction regarding the source of its own principle and the correct determination of this principle in its opposition to maxims based on need and inclination, so that reason may escape from the perplexity of opposite claims and may avoid the risk of losing all genuine moral principles through the am-biguity into which it easily falls. Thus when ordinary practical reason cultivates itself, there imperceptibly arises in it a dialectic which compels it to seek help in philosophy. The same thing happens in reason's theoretical use; in this case, just as in the other, peace will be found only in a thorough critical examination of our reason.

Aristotle presented us with an ethics that was extremely specific to a certain kind of society and a particularly privileged class within that society. The good life was for them, and there was no conception of "virtue" that was not tied to specific roles and responsibilities and that did not presuppose certain particular circumstances and skills within which those virtues made sense and served society. In Kant, we see exactly the opposite, a view of virtue in which *all* such particularities are eliminated from consideration and in which all questions of good fortune and fate are neutralized. A person might be miserable, but he or she has as good a chance as anyone else to be morally good. A person might be incapacitated from acting in all but the most nominal ways, but that doesn't stop him or her from having a good will. A person might have all sorts of terrible problems, but that need not and should not interfere with his or her efforts to be rational, to do the right thing even in the most adverse circumstances. Even in distress—perhaps especially in distress—people are judged to behave well or badly, morally or immorally.

The conditions of morality for Kant are nothing other than being a human being—or, more accurately—being a rational being (on the assumption that we are primarily talking about ourselves). Aristotle insisted that there are all sorts of preconditions for the good life and virtue—a good upbringing, a leisurely life, adequate wealth, health, and social status. For Kant, one only needs a working brain, and not much more. One knows what is right because one is rational, because one knows—presumably without having yet read Kant—that one's duty is what one ought to do, whatever one's personal inclinations. And one knows too that duty is impersonal, in that anyone, in similar circumstances, would have the same duty, whatever their inclinations. We can leave it an open question how much this is simply a matter of certain languages and the concept of "duty" (*pflicht* in German) and, more speculatively, how much reason itself is bound to language and culture and not universal at all. But Kant certainly thought that reason and duty were universal (as did most of the Enlightenment), and, within our society at any rate, duty does seem to have such a meaning, such that duties apply to anyone in certain circumstances, whatever they would rather do.

Furthermore, Kant is surely right in basing his theory on the idea that we value people, at least as moral agents, on the basis of their good intentions. No matter how consistently good he may act, we would certainly never praise a man who did the right thing only because he was always looking askance and worrying about being punished ("shifty-eyed," we would call him). Conversely, we would continue to praise a person who at least always tried to do the right thing (although we would surely lose patience—at least—after consistent failures). Perhaps Kant overplays the emphasis on good intentions ("a good will") and underplays the importance—even the moral importance—of good results. But, then, he is after the "pure" conception of morals, not a diagnosis of our own impatience with human frailty and failure.

What is crucial to morals, he insists, is the will; all else is irrelevant. We might object that this totally ignores the fact that what is most important, to most of us, is not so much people's moral status but the results of their actions. What good is a "good man" if his every action makes us worse off than before? But Kant is not supposing, of course, that a good will would usually have disastrous consequences; the assumption, if anything is being assumed here, is that good intentions do usually lead to beneficial actions, and he even says that concern for duty is, in part, concern for the promotion of happiness. (The obvious contrast here is the utilitarianism of John Stuart Mill, for whom happiness and good consequences *are* the criteria of right action.) What is crucial to a good will is acting on principle, not on the basis of "sympathy" or any other personal (or interpersonal) feeling. We might object strenuously to this in the context of close family ties or a romantic relationship, but, in a world where so many of our dealings are with strangers (in contrast to Aristotle's *polis*), such a demand at least seems reasonable. (In fact, if we think of an administrative position—giving grants to students, for example—acting on the basis of personal ties and feelings rather than impersonal principles is the height of immorality.)

The exclusive emphasis on rationality and a priori considerations nevertheless yields questionable results, even when we limit our concern to the clearly more impersonal cases, in which personal feelings and particular circumstances are excluded. Are there rules that can be applied to everyone, regardless of any attention to particular circumstances? Does this emphasis on rationality in fact only encourage that impersonal and uncaring bureaucratic attitude that so many people deeply resent at least as much as they resent emotional immorality and personal injustice? (In fact, bureaucracy was a relatively new phenomenon in Kant's day, and, unlike today, it was looked upon with great favor by most people as an impersonal antidote to the personal abuses of power and privilege by the aristocracy.) And for ourselves, are we to consider as most moral those acts that we have to think and deliberate about? Do we in fact have principles (even if implicit and merely subjective) in all our actions, or is it more as Aristotle suggested—that the habitual act comes first, the principles and ability to deliberate later on? What kind of a portrait is Kant giving us here of ourselves as moral beings? Is it a portrait we can recognize, and one that we are willing to accept?

One way to think about these questions is to notice that in Kant's theory there will be far fewer "moral" actions. Many of the acts we might usually characterize as morally good, such as giving to charity, for instance, may well turn out to be amoral rather than moral on his account. But is this a problem? It is not that actions that are characterized as morally good in other theories turn out to be morally bad in the Kantian view. Nor is it the case that there is no good in such actions, because not only does one gratify one's own desire (inclination), but Kant admits a role for social praise and encouragement. All that is lost, it would seem, is the designation of *morally* worthy. Given Kant's purpose of discovering the essence of truly moral action, it may not be surprising that some types of action drop out.

THE CATEGORICAL IMPERATIVE: FROM SECTION 2

Kant has argued that an act has moral worth insofar as it is done for the sake of duty alone. But do we ever act out of so pure a motive? Kant is perfectly willing to admit that we do not, that even our most dutiful and morally self-conscious actions may still have reference to "the dear self" of self-interest and prudence. Indeed, he is even willing to say that "it is absolutely impossible to make out by experience with complete certainty a single case in which the maxim of an action, however right in itself, rested simply on moral grounds and on the conception of duty." Kant anticipates his future colleague, Sigmund Freud, in speculating on the "secret springs of action," unconscious impulses of which we may not be aware even in the noblest action. But if none of our actions is purely moral, it does not follow (as "those who ridicule all morality" would argue) that all of our actions are selfish either. Acting from pure duty may be an ideal, but this need not mean that we never act dutifully. It may be, for example, that none of us has ever made a friend without some self-interested motive (if only that we have a good time together); but this is not to say that none of us has ever been a friend. It is only to say that morality is an ideal, which is never to be found in pure form in the mixed motives of actual human behavior.

Transition from Popular Moral Philosophy to a Metaphysics of Morals

If we have so far drawn our concept of duty from the ordinary use of our practical reason, one is by no means to infer that we have treated it as a concept of experience. On the contrary, when we pay attention to our experience of the way human beings act, we meet frequent and—as we ourselves admit—justified complaints that there cannot be cited a single certain example of the disposition to act from pure duty; and we meet complaints that although much may be done that is in accordance with what duty commands, yet there are always doubts as to whether what occurs has really been done from duty and so has moral worth. Hence there have always been philosophers who have absolutely denied the reality of this disposition in human actions and have ascribed everything to a more or less refined self-love. Yet in so doing they have not cast doubt upon the rightness of the concept of morality. Rather, they have spoken with sincere regret as to the frailty and impurity of human nature, which they think is noble enough to take as its precept an idea so worthy of respect but yet is too weak to follow this idea: reason, which should legislate for human nature, is used only to look after the interest of inclinations, whether singly or, at best, in their greatest possible harmony with one another.

In fact there is absolutely no possibility by means of experience to make out with complete certainty a single case in which the maxim of an action that may in other respects conform to duty has rested solely on moral grounds and on the representation of one's duty. It is indeed sometimes the case that after the keenest self-examination we can find nothing except the moral ground of duty that could have been strong enough to move us to this or that good action and to such great sacrifice. But there cannot with certainty be at all inferred from this that some secret impulse of self-love, merely appearing as the idea of duty, was not the actual determining cause of the will. We like to flatter ourselves with the false claim to a more noble motive; but in fact we can never, even by the strictest examination, completely plumb the depths of the secret incentives of our actions. For when moral value is being considered, the concern is not with the actions, which are seen, but rather with their inner principles, which are not seen.

Moreover, one cannot better serve the wishes of those who ridicule all morality as being a mere phantom of human imagination getting above itself because of self-conceit than by conceding to them that the concepts of duty must be drawn solely from experience (just as from indolence one willingly persuades himself that such is the case as regards all other concepts as well). For by so conceding, one prepares for them a sure triumph. I am willing to admit out of love for humanity that most of our actions are in accordance with duty; but if we look more closely at our planning and striving, we everywhere come upon the dear self, which is always turning up, and upon which the intent of our actions is based rather than upon the strict command of duty (which would often require self-denial). One need not be exactly an enemy of virtue, but only a cool observer who does not take the liveliest wish for the good to be straight off its realization, in order to become doubtful at times whether any true virtue is actually to be found in the world. Such is especially the case when years increase and one's power of judgment is made shrewder by experience and keener in observation. Because of these things nothing can protect us from a complete falling away from our ideas of duty and preserve in the soul a well-grounded respect for duty's law except the clear conviction that, even if there never have been actions springing from such pure sources, the question at issue here is not whether this or that has happened but that reason of itself and independently of all experience commands what ought to happen. Consequently, reason unrelentingly commands actions of which the world has perhaps hitherto never provided an example and whose feasibility might well be doubted by one who bases everything upon experience; for instance, even though there might never yet have been a sincere friend, still pure sincerity in friendship is nonetheless required of every man, because this duty, prior to all experience, is contained as duty in general in the idea of a reason that determines the will by means of a priori grounds.

If morality is an ideal of pure reason, it follows that it applies not just to human beings but to "all rational creatures." (This would include angels, talking animals, and, of course, God.) And as an ideal of pure reason, morality cannot be understood just on the basis of actual experience, first because we have probably never seen an example of pure dutiful action, but second—and more importantly—because we would need our a priori standard of moral perfection in order to recognize an ideal example if we found one—for example, in Christ as a moral ideal. Thus, once again, the basis of morality must be found a priori, as an "absolute necessity."

There may be noted further that unless we want to deny to the concept of morality all truth and all reference to a possible object, we cannot but admit that the moral law is of such widespread significance that it must hold not merely for men but for all rational beings generally, and that it must be valid not merely under contingent conditions and with exceptions but must be absolutely necessary. Clearly, therefore, no experience can give occasion for inferring even the possibility of such apodeictic laws. For with what right could we bring into unlimited respect as a universal precept for every rational nature what is perhaps valid only under the contingent conditions of humanity? And how could laws for the determination of our will be regarded as laws for the determination of a rational being in general and of ourselves only insofar as we are rational beings, if these laws were merely empirical and did not have their source completely a priori in pure, but practical, reason?

Moreover, worse service cannot be rendered morality than that an attempt be made to derive it from examples. For every example of morality presented to me must itself first be judged according to principles of morality in order to see whether it is fit to serve as an original example, i.e., as a model. But in no way can it authoritatively furnish the concept of morality. Even the Holy One of the gospel must first be compared with our ideal of moral perfection before he is recognized as such. Even he says of himself, "Why do you call me (whom you see) good? None is good (the archetype of the good) except God only (whom you do not see)." But whence have we the concept of God as the highest good? Solely from the idea of moral perfection, which reason frames a priori and connects inseparably with the concept of a free will. Imitation has no place at all in moral matters. And examples serve only for encouragement, i.e., they put beyond doubt the feasibility of what the law commands and they make visible what the practical rule expresses more generally. But examples can never justify us in setting aside their true original, which lies in reason, and letting ourselves be guided by them.

Thus, a pure moral philosophy is necessary, even if it may not be, in the usual sense, a "popular" philosophy.

If there is then no genuine supreme principle of morality that must rest merely on pure reason, independently of all experience, I think it is unnecessary even to ask whether it is a good thing to exhibit these concepts generally *(in abstracto),* which, along with the principles that belong to them, hold a priori, so far as the knowledge involved is to be distinguished from ordinary knowledge and is to be called philosophical. But in our times it may well be necessary to do so. For if one were to take a vote as to whether pure rational knowledge separated from everything empirical, i.e., metaphysics of morals, or whether popular practical philosophy is to be preferred, one can easily guess which side would be preponderant.

This descent to popular thought is certainly very commendable once the ascent to the principles of pure reason has occurred and has been satisfactorily accomplished. That would mean that the doctrine of morals has first been grounded on metaphysics and that subsequently acceptance for morals has been won by giving it a popular character after it has been firmly established. But it is quite absurd to try for popularity in the first inquiry, upon which depends the total correctness of the principles. Not only can such a procedure never lay claim to the very rare merit of a true philosophical popularity, inasmuch as there is really no art involved at all in being generally intelligible if one thereby renounces all basic insight, but such a procedure turns out a disgusting mishmash of patchwork observations and half-reasoned principles in which shallowpates revel because all this is something quite useful for the chitchat of everyday life. Persons of insight, on the other hand, feel confused by all this and turn their eyes away with a dissatisfaction which they nevertheless cannot cure. Yet philosophers, who quite see through the delusion, get little hearing when they summon people for a time from this pretended popularity in order that they may be rightfully popular only after they have attained definite insight.

One need only look at the attempts to deal with morality in the way favored by popular taste. What he will find in an amazing mixture is at one time the particular constitution of human nature (but along with this also the idea of a rational nature in general), at another time perfection, at another happiness; here moral feeling, and there the fear of God; something of this, and also something of that. But the thought never occurs to ask whether the principles of morality are to be sought at all in the knowledge of human nature (which can be had only from experience). Nor does the thought occur that if these principles are not to be sought here but to be found, rather, completely a priori and free from everything empirical in pure rational concepts only, and are to be found nowhere else even to the slightest extent—then there had better be adopted the plan of undertaking this investigation as a separate inquiry, i.e., as pure practical philosophy or (if one may use a name so much decried) as a metaphysics of morals. It is better to bring this investigation to full completeness entirely by itself and to bid the public, which demands popularity, to await the outcome of this undertaking.

But such a completely isolated metaphysics of morals, not mixed with any anthropology, theology, physics, or hyperphysics, and still less with occult qualities (which might be called hypophysical), is not only an indispensable substratum of all theoretical and precisely defined knowledge of duties, but is at the same time a desideratum of the highest importance for the actual fulfillment of their precepts. For the pure thought of duty and of the moral law generally, unmixed with any extraneous addition of empirical inducements, has by the way of reason alone (which first becomes aware hereby that it can of itself be practical) an influence on the human heart so much more powerful than all other incentives which may be derived from the empirical field that reason in the consciousness of its dignity despises such incentives and is able gradually to become their master. On the other hand, a mixed moral philosophy, compounded both of incentives drawn from feelings and inclinations and at the same time of rational concepts, must make the mind waver between motives that cannot be brought under any principle and that can only by accident lead to the good but often can also lead to the bad.

The analysis that follows, therefore, is of the pure conception of duty, based solely on reason. And yet, such a "speculative" endeavor is nevertheless of the greatest practical importance; by gaining such a pure understanding of duty and its principles, we can clarify the nature of morality for ourselves (and not only for ourselves but "for every rational creature"), and we can teach ourselves and our children the ideal, with an eye to producing "pure moral dispositions, and to engraft them on men's minds to the promotion of the greatest possible good in the world."

It is clear from the foregoing that all moral concepts have their seat and origin completely a priori in reason, and indeed in the most ordinary human reason just as much as in the most highly speculative. They cannot be abstracted from any empirical, and hence merely contingent, cognition. In this purity of their origin lies their very worthiness to serve us as supreme practical principles; and to the extent that something empirical is added to them, just so much is taken away from their genuine influence and from the absolute worth of the corresponding actions. Moreover, it is not only a requirement of the greatest necessity from a theoretical point of view, when it is a question of speculation, but also of the greatest practical importance, to draw these concepts and laws from pure reason, to present them pure and unmixed, and indeed to determine the extent of this entire practical and pure rational cognition, i.e., to determine the whole faculty of pure practical reason. The principles should not be made to depend on the particular nature of human reason, as speculative philosophy may permit and even sometimes finds necessary; but, rather, the principles should be derived from the universal concept of a rational being in general, since moral laws should hold for every rational being as such. In this way all morals, which require anthropology in order to be applied to humans, must be entirely expounded at first independently of anthropology as pure philosophy, i.e., as metaphysics (which can easily be done in such distinct kinds of knowledge). One knows quite well that unless one is in possession of such a metaphysics, then the attempt is futile, I shall not say to determine exactly for speculative judgment the moral element of duty in all that accords with duty, but that the attempt is impossible, even in ordinary and practical usage, especially in that of moral instruction, to ground morals on their genuine principles and thereby to produce pure moral dispositions and engraft them on men's minds for the promotion of the highest good in the world.

In this study we must advance by natural stages not merely from ordinary moral judgment (which is here ever so worthy of respect) to philosophical judgment, as has already been done, but also from popular philosophy, which goes no further than it can get by groping about with the help of examples, to metaphysics (which does not permit itself to be held back any longer by what is empirical, and which, inasmuch as it must survey the whole extent of rational knowledge of this kind, goes right up to ideas, where examples themselves fail us). In order to make such an advance, we must follow and clearly present the practical faculty of reason from its universal rules of determination to the point where the concept of duty springs from it.

The strategy for doing this is to describe the basic rules of practical reason, the laws according to which our duties are prescribed and known. All of nature operates according to laws, Kant tells us, but only rational beings also have a conception of laws and the will to act according to them. That is, like other natural objects, rational beings are subject to the laws of nature, but unlike nonrational things, they have the further capacity to understand and be reflective about those laws. Most importantly, rational beings can choose whether to be bound by laws, to act knowingly in accordance with them. For instance, using an example from Aristotle's *Nicomachean Ethics,* a stone is subject to the law of gravity just as we are subject to the laws of reason. But it would be pointless to even consider that the stone might do anything but fall downward, because "you could not train it to rise upwards, though you tried to do so by throwing it up ten thousand times." With rational beings, on the other hand, it is meaningful to ask whether a law will be understood and followed. This capacity to act according to principle is found in the will, and it is, for Kant, the seat of our moral faculty. The will is practical reason, Kant says, that is, the ability to choose what is right.

Kant distinguishes between two sorts of wills: those that are absolutely good (holy wills) and those that, while subject to the same objective laws, do not invariably follow them (human wills). Again, the crucial distinction is between reason and the inclinations. In holy wills, the two come to the same thing—the inclinations (the subjective principles) coincide with what reason dictates (the objective principles). Kant says of such wills that "the *ought* is here out of place, because the *would* is already of itself necessarily in agreement with the law." Humans, however, often find that inclination and reason lead in opposite directions. To do the right thing—to follow the objective laws—reason must win out over the inclinations; there must be a command to follow because we won't always be naturally inclined to do as the law requires. For this reason, Kant introduces his central notion of the categorical imperative.

Everything in nature works according to laws. Only a rational being has the power to act according to his conception of laws, i.e., according to principles, and thereby has he a will. Since the derivation of actions from laws requires reason, the will is nothing but practical reason. If reason infallibly determines the will, then in the case of such a being actions which are recognized to be objectively necessary are also subjectively necessary, i.e., the will is a faculty of choosing only that which reason, independently of inclination, recognizes as being practically necessary, i.e., as good. But if reason of itself does not sufficiently determine the will, and if the will submits also to subjective conditions (certain incentives) which do not always agree with objective conditions; in a word, if the will does not in itself completely accord with reason (as is actually the case with men), then actions which are recognized as objectively necessary are subjectively contingent, and the determination of such a will according to objective laws is necessitation. That is to say that the relation of objective laws to a will not thoroughly good is represented as the determination of the will of a rational being by principles of reason which the will does not necessarily follow because of its own nature.

The representation of an objective principle insofar as it necessitates the will is called a command (of reason), and the formula of the command is called an imperative.

All imperatives are expressed by an *ought* and thereby indicate the relation of an objective law of reason to a will that is not necessarily determined by this law because of its subjective constitution (the relation of necessitation). Imperatives say that something would be good to do or to refrain from doing, but they say it to a will that does not always therefore do something simply because it has been represented to the will as something good to do. That is practically good which determines the will by means of representations of reason and hence not by subjective causes, but objectively, i.e., on grounds valid for every rational being as such. It is distinguished from the pleasant as that which influences the will only by means of sensation from merely subjective causes, which hold only for this or that person's senses but do not hold as a principle of reason valid for everyone.

A perfectly good will would thus be quite as much subject to objective laws (of the good), but could not be conceived as thereby necessitated to act in conformity with law, inasmuch as it can of itself, according to its subjective constitution, be determined only by the representation of the good. Therefore no imperatives hold for the divine will, and in general for a holy will; the *ought* is here out of place, because the *would* is already of itself necessarily in agreement with the law. Consequently, imperatives are only formulas for expressing the relation of objective laws of willing in general to the subjective imperfection of the will of this or that rational being, e.g., the human will.

Now all imperatives command either hypothetically or categorically. The former represent the practical necessity of a possible action as a means for attaining something else that one wants (or may possibly want). The categorical imperative would be one which represented an action as objectively necessary in itself, without reference to another end.

Every practical law represents a possible action as good and hence as necessary for a subject who is practically determinable by reason; therefore all imperatives are formulas for determining an action which is necessary according to the principle of a will that is good in some way. Now if the action would be good merely as a means to something else, so is the imperative hypothetical. But if the action is represented as good in itself, and hence as necessary in a will which of itself conforms to reason as the principle of the will, then the imperative is categorical.

An imperative thus says what action possible by me would be good, and it presents the practical rule in relation to a will which does not forthwith perform an action simply because it is good, partly because the subject does not always know that the action is good and partly because (even if he does know it is good) his maxims might yet be opposed to the objective principles of practical reason.

A hypothetical imperative thus says only that an action is good for some purpose, either possible or actual. In the first case it is a problematic practical principle; in the second case an assertoric one. A categorical imperative, which declares an action to be of itself objectively necessary without reference to any purpose, i.e., without any other end, holds as an apodeictic practical principle.

In other words, a hypothetical imperative applies to a person only if he or she fulfills the "if . . ." clause, as in "if you want to stay slim, don't drink too much German beer." If you don't care about staying slim, the imperative ("don't drink too much German beer") does not apply to you. It is thus, in part, optional. On the other hand, a categorical imperative has no such "if . . ." clause and applies to everyone under whatever circumstances. A commandment such as "Honor thy father and thy mother" is a categorical imperative because it does not have any exclusions or conditions, such as "if they were generous with you . . ." or "if you want to get your inheritance. . . ." Everyone is bound by reason to obey, whatever one's parents have been like, whatever one might expect from them in the future.

Most of practical behavior consists of hypothetical imperatives, that is, acting toward an end. But the number of ends or goals of our activities are almost innumerable.

Whatever is possible only through the powers of some rational being can be thought of as a possible purpose of some will. Consequently, there are in fact infinitely many principles of action insofar as they are represented as necessary for attaining a possible purpose achievable by them. All sciences have a practical part consisting of problems saying that some end is possible for us and of imperatives telling us how it can be attained. These can, therefore, be called in general imperatives of skill. Here there is no question at all whether the end is reasonable and good, but there is only a question as to what must be done to attain it. The prescriptions needed by a doctor in order to make his patient thoroughly healthy and by a poisoner in order to make sure of killing his victim are of equal value so far as each serves to bring about its purpose perfectly. Since there cannot be known in early youth what ends may be presented to us in the course of life, parents especially seek to have their children learn many different kinds of things, and they provide for skill in the use of means to all sorts of arbitrary ends, among which they cannot determine whether any one of them could in the future become an actual purpose for their ward, though there is always the possibility that he might adopt it. Their concern is so great that they commonly neglect to form and correct their children's judgment regarding the worth of things which might be chosen as ends.

There is, however, one end that can be presupposed as actual for all rational beings (so far as they are dependent beings to whom imperatives apply); and thus there is one purpose which they not merely can have but which can certainly be assumed to be such that they all do have by a natural necessity, and this is happiness. A hypothetical imperative which represents the practical necessity of an action as means for the promotion of happiness is assertoric. It may be expounded not simply as necessary to an uncertain, merely possible purpose, but as necessary to a purpose which can be presupposed a priori and with certainty as being present in everyone because it belongs to his essence. Now skill in the choice of means to one's own greatest well-being can be called prudence in the narrowest sense. And thus the imperative that refers to the choice of means to one's own happiness, i.e., the precept of prudence, still remains hypothetical; the action is commanded not absolutely but only as a means to a further purpose.

Categorical imperatives command without conditions. Morality thus consists of categorical imperatives that must be obeyed for their own sake, whatever the consequences. Properly speaking, only morality commands. (Skills have rules; prudence has advice or "counsel.")

Finally, there is one imperative which immediately commands a certain conduct without having as its condition any other purpose to be attained by it. This imperative is categorical. It is not concerned with the matter of the action and its intended result, but rather with the form of the action and the principle from which it follows; what is essentially good in the action consists in the mental disposition, let the consequences be what they may. This imperative may be called that of morality. . . .

If I think of a hypothetical imperative in general, I do not know beforehand what it will contain until its condition is given. But if I think of a categorical imperative, I know immediately what it contains. For since, besides the law, the imperative contains only the necessity that the maxim should accord with this law, while the law contains no condition to restrict it, there remains nothing but the universality of a law as such with which the maxim of the action should conform. This conformity alone is properly what is represented as necessary by the imperative.

Hence, there is only one categorical imperative and it is this: *Act only according to that maxim whereby you can at the same time will that it should become a universal law* (italics added).

Now if all imperatives of duty can be deduced from this one imperative as their principle, then there can at least be shown what is understood by the concept of duty is not merely a vain notion, yet at least we shall be able to show what we understand by it and what this notion means.

The universality of the law according to which effects are produced constitutes what is properly called *nature* in the most general sense (as to form)—that is, the existence of things so far as it is determined by universal law. Accordingly, the universal imperative of duty may be expressed thus: *Act as if the maxim of your action were to become through your will a universal law of nature* (italics added).

Although Kant states that there is "only one categorical imperative," he offers in the end no fewer than five formulations of it (depending on how one interprets them—many commentators find only three versions, whereas others claim that there are in fact four), two of which are given here. They look quite similar at first glance, but the slight variation in wording makes an enormous difference. The first refers simply to "a universal law." In other words, what if everyone were to adopt this as his or her maxim? What Kant asks us to do here is to consider whether the maxim in question is one that privileges our own interests (in which case it would not pass the categorical imperative test), or one that *could* be fairly applied to any rational being. The second says, "a universal law of nature." In Kant's philosophy, the realm of morality (freedom and the will) is radically separated from the world of nature (the world of science and causality). The law of nature formulation is thus concerned not with the maxim of action but rather with the actual universal achievement of the maxim. It is one thing to ask, What if everyone tried to do that?—something quite different to ask, What if everyone actually *did* that?

Kant now gives us four illustrations, a mixed batch of examples whose point is not always clear (but then, we should be delighted to get a few examples; Kant does not give us many of them).

We shall now enumerate some duties, following the usual division of them into duties to ourselves and to others and into perfect and imperfect duties.

1. A man reduced to despair by a series of misfortunes feels sick of life but is still so far in possession of his reason that he can ask himself whether taking his own life would not be contrary to his duty to himself. Now he asks whether the maxim of his action could become a universal law of nature. But his maxim is this: from self-love I make as my principle to shorten my life when its continued duration threatens more evil than it promises satisfaction. There only remains the question as to whether this principle of self-love can become a universal law of nature. One sees at once a contradiction in a system of nature whose law would destroy life by means of the very same feeling that acts so as to stimulate the furtherance of life, and hence there could be no existence as a system of nature. Therefore, such a maxim cannot possibly hold as a universal law of nature and is, consequently, wholly opposed to the supreme principle of all duty.

2. Another man in need finds himself forced to borrow money. He knows well that he won't be able to repay it, but he sees also that he will not get any loan unless he firmly promises to repay it within a fixed time. He wants to make such a promise, but he still has conscience enough to ask himself whether it is not permissible and is contrary to duty to get out of difficulty in this way. Suppose, however, that he decides to do so. The maxim of his action would then be expressed as follows: when I believe myself to be in need of money, I will borrow money and promise to pay it back, although I know that I can never do so. Now this principle of self-love or personal advantage may perhaps be quite compatible with one's entire future welfare, but the question is now whether it is right. I then transform the requirement of self-love into a universal law and put the question thus: how would things stand if my maxim were to become a universal law? He then sees at once that such a maxim could never hold as a universal law of nature and be consistent with itself, but must necessarily be self-contradictory. For the universality of a law which says that anyone believing himself to be in difficulty could promise whatever he pleases with the intention of not keeping it would make promising itself and the end to be attained thereby quite impossible, inasmuch as no one would believe what was promised him but would merely laugh at all such utterances as being vain pretenses.

3. A third finds in himself a talent whose cultivation could make him a man useful in many respects. But he finds himself in comfortable circumstances and prefers to indulge in pleasure rather than to bother himself about broadening and improving his fortunate natural aptitudes. But he asks himself further whether his maxim of neglecting his natural gifts, besides agreeing of itself with his propensity to indulgence, might agree also with what is called duty. He then sees that a system of nature could indeed always subsist according to such a universal law, even though every man (like South Sea Islanders) should let his talents rust and resolve to devote his life entirely to idleness, indulgence, propagation, and, in a word, to enjoyment. But he cannot possibly will that this should become a universal law of nature or be implanted in us as such a law by a natural instinct. For as a rational being he necessarily wills that all his faculties should be developed, inasmuch as they are given him for all sorts of possible purposes.

4. A fourth man finds things going well for himself but sees others (whom he could help) struggling with great hardships; and he thinks; what does it matter to me? Let everybody be as happy as Heaven wills or as he can make himself; I shall take nothing from him nor even envy him; but I have no desire to contribute anything to his well-being or to his assistance when in need. If such a way of thinking were to become a universal law of nature, the human race admittedly could very well subsist and doubtless could subsist even better than when everyone prates about sympathy and benevolence and even on occasion exerts himself to practice them but, on the other hand, also cheats when he can, betrays the rights of man, or otherwise violates them. But even though it is possible that a universal law of nature could subsist in accordance with that maxim, still it is impossible to will that such a principle should hold everywhere as a law of nature. For a will which resolved in this way would contradict itself, inasmuch as cases might often arise in which one would have need of the love and sympathy of others and in which he would deprive himself, by such a law of nature springing from his own will, of all hope of the aid he wants for himself.

Let's look at these examples again.

1. Suppose a man is miserable and is contemplating suicide. The maxim of his intended action is "for my own sake, I will end my life if I am only going to be miserable." Could this be a universal law of nature? No, Kant argues, because nature could not maintain life if living things were unwilling to endure hardship to survive. Recall that Kant holds a teleological view of nature—"nature does nothing in vain." It is doubtless that at least part of the purpose of self-love is to ensure survival. In a purposive universe, then, it is not possible that the very instinct for survival should lead one to suicide. Therefore, the maxim could not become a universal law of nature. Notice that it is the "law of nature" formulation that Kant uses here; it is not clear how the "first formulation" (universal law) would work in the same case.

2. Here we see repeated in more detail the example already used in section 1. A person needs money and is forced to borrow, falsely promising to repay when he knows that he cannot. The maxim would be, "If I need money, I will make a false promise to repay it." Universalized, it becomes, "Anyone who needs money can make false promises to get it, even knowing that repayment is impossible." We have already noted the sense in which such a law contradicts itself. Kant puts it with unusual charm, "No one would consider that anything was promised to him, but would ridicule all such statements as vain pretenses." This is the key example. Note again that it is not the inconvenience of the projected universal results that makes the act immoral. It is the logical *inconsistency* of the universalized maxim. To believe both in the institution of promising and in the universal practice of false promising is simply illogical—the two are contradictory. Thus, the test of a maxim, as an attempted instance of the categorical imperative, is this:

1. State the maxim of your action.
2. Universalize it as a law for everyone.
3. Ask yourself whether the intended action would still be possible after such universalization. Could you continue to make such promises? Would *you* be able to think of them as "promises"?

The whole process is not much different in strategy than the grandmotherly admonition, "What if everyone did that?" The difference, of course, is that Kant has a theory about why it matters to ask such a question which does not so easily allow the usual reply, "But everyone *won't* do it!" Because it is a logical condition and not merely speculation on the results of mass conformity, Kant is not so easily answered as Grandmother (who is probably worried about actual consequences).

3. The third example again returns to the second formulation. Notice that Kant appeals to his overall teleological vision, the idea that our talents have been given to us for a purpose. In fact, the usual test of the categorical imperative seems *not* to work here, because Kant even admits that we could universalize our laziness as a law of nature and all be like (what Kant fantasizes as) the South Pacific natives who do little but lie in the sun and enjoy themselves. The argument, then, is not that the universalized maxim contradicts itself but rather that it contradicts nature's purposes—a very different matter.

4. The fourth example is, ironically, a conservative political philosophy that has become more (but has always been) popular in the United States, usually under the all-purpose banner of "liberty." It is the view that everyone should make his or her own way in the world and be as happy as he or she can be, but without expecting help from anyone else. It is a philosophy, not surprisingly, usually espoused by those who are already rich and well-off, or soon plan to be. Could such an attitude be universalized as law? (Kant remarks that the resulting world might not be as bad as a world in which everyone liberally espoused sympathetic platitudes about the poor but never did a damned thing themselves about it.) Notice that here again it is primarily the law of nature formulation (why?) and notice again that the contradiction involved is less than convincing. The argument (which has been made into the basis of an elaborate theory of justice by American Kantian philosopher John Rawls) is that none of us, no matter how rich or well-off, would be willing to universalize the attitude that "each person should get what he or she can, but without expecting any help from others" because one never knows when he or she might *need* the help of others. (Rawls sets up the conditions of the just society such that everyone could agree to its conditions without knowing his or her own role or place. It is an immensely expanded version of the childhood lesson in justice, in which the older child is asked to cut the cake, with the understanding that the other children will get the first choices.) As Kant presents the case, however, justice is not the issue. It is rather whether one might oneself claim just the help that this attitude now denies to others and thus contradict oneself. One might well argue, however, that one could consistently hold this position, even, when—unhappily—one finds oneself in precisely the downtrodden position that one never before considered (though not every conservative carries this through in practice).

Out of four examples, only one (keeping promises) fully employs the first and primary formulation of the categorical imperative, and, perhaps not coincidentally, it is the only one of the examples that seems to illustrate adequately the thesis that Kant has been arguing. It is in this one that we get the sharp, logical contradiction— that which will show us that it is not *rational* to will such a course of action, regardless of our present desires. Nevertheless, Kant seems contented with the argument, even commenting that "it has been completely shown by these examples how all duties depend . . . on the same principle."

> These are some of the many actual duties, or at least what are taken to be such, whose derivation from the single principle cited above is clear. We must be able to will that a maxim of our action become a universal law; this is the canon for morally estimating any of our actions. Some actions are so constituted that their maxims cannot without contradiction even be thought as a universal law of nature, much less be willed as what should become one. In the case of others this internal impossibility is indeed not found, but there is still no possibility of willing that their maxim should be raised to the universality of a law of nature, because such a will would contradict itself. There is no difficulty in seeing that the former kind of action conflicts with strict or narrow [perfect] (irremissible) duty, while the second kind conflicts only with broad [imperfect] (meritorious) duty. By means of these examples there has thus been fully set forth how all duties depend as regards the kind of obligation (not the object of their action) upon the one principle.

If what Kant says about the categorical imperative is true, then how is it possible that we ever do anything knowingly wrong? (This is very much the kind of question asked by Socrates, Plato, and Aristotle under the name "incontinence.") The problem is not that we do not know the moral principle in question or that we (conveniently) forget it. Nor is it the kind of incontinence focused on by Plato and Aristotle, when desire or passion blinds us to what we ought to do. It is rather that, as rationalizing as well as rational beings, we make *exceptions* of ourselves. This is, perhaps, the most familiar and widespread *abuse* of the categorical imperative.

> If we now attend to ourselves in any transgression of a duty, we find that we actually do not will that our maxim should become a universal law—because this is impossible for us—but rather that the opposite of this maxim should remain a law universally. We only take the liberty of making an exception to the law for ourselves (or just for this one time) to the advantage of our inclination.

Consequently, if we weighed up everything from one and the same standpoint, namely, that of reason, we would find a contradiction in our own will, viz., that a certain principle be objectively necessary as a universal law and yet subjectively not hold universally but should admit of exceptions. But since we at one moment regard our action from the standpoint of a will wholly in accord with reason and then at another moment regard the very same action from the standpoint of a will affected by inclination, there is really no contradiction here. Rather, there is an opposition *(antagonismus)* of inclination to the precept of reason, whereby the universality *(universalitas)* of the principle is changed into a mere generality *(generalitas)* so that the practical principle of reason may meet the maxim halfway. Although this procedure cannot be justified in our own impartial judgment, yet it does show that we actually acknowledge the validity of the categorical imperative and (with all respect for it) merely allow ourselves a few exceptions which, as they seem to us, are unimportant and forced upon us.

We have thus at least shown that if duty is a concept which is to have significance and real legislative authority for our actions, then such duty can be expressed only in categorical imperatives but not at all in hypothetical ones. We have also—and this is already a great deal—exhibited clearly and definitely for every application what is the content of the categorical imperative, which must contain the principle of all duty (if there is such a thing at all). But we have not yet advanced far enough to prove a priori that there actually is an imperative of this kind, that there is a practical law which of itself commands absolutely and without any incentives, and that following this law is duty.

In order to attain this proof there is the utmost importance in being warned that we must not take it into our mind to derive the reality of this principle from the special characteristics of human nature. For duty has to be a practical, unconditioned necessity of action; hence it must hold for all rational beings (to whom alone an imperative is at all applicable) and for this reason only can it also be a law for all human wills. On the other hand, whatever is derived from the special natural condition of humanity, from certain feelings and propensities, or even, if such were possible, from some special tendency peculiar to human reason and not holding necessarily for the will of every rational being—all of this can indeed yield a maxim valid for us, but not a law. This is to say that such can yield a subjective principle according to which we might act if we happen to have the propensity and inclination, but cannot yield an objective principle according to which we would be directed to act even though our every propensity, and inclination, and natural tendency were opposed to it. In fact, the sublimity and inner worth of the command are so much the more evident in a duty, the fewer subjective causes there are for it and the more they oppose it; such causes do not in the least weaken the necessitation exerted by the law or take away anything from its validity.

Here philosophy is seen in fact to be put in a precarious position, which should be firm even though there is neither in heaven nor on earth anything upon which it depends or is based. Here philosophy must show its purity as author of its laws, and not as the herald of such laws as are whispered to it by an implanted sense or by who knows what tutelary nature. Such laws may be better than nothing at all, but they can never give us principles dictated by reason. These principles must have an origin that is completely a priori and must at the same time derive from such origin their authority to command. They expect nothing from the inclination of men but, rather, expect everything from the supremacy of the law and from the respect owed to the law. Without the latter expectation, these principles condemn man to self-contempt and inward abhorrence.

Hence everything empirical is not only quite unsuitable as a contribution to the principle of morality, but is even highly detrimental to the purity of morals. For the proper and inestimable worth of an absolutely good will consists precisely in the fact that the principle of action is free of all influences from contingent grounds, which only experience can furnish. This lax or even mean way of thinking which seeks its principle among empirical motives and laws cannot too much or too often be warned against, for human reason in its weariness is glad to rest upon this pillow. In a dream of sweet illusions (in which not Juno but a cloud is embraced) there is substituted for morality some bastard patched up from limbs of quite varied ancestry and looking like anything one wants to see in it but not looking like virtue to him who has once beheld her in her true form.

Therefore, the question is this: is it a necessary law for all rational beings always to judge their actions according to such maxims as they can themselves will that such should serve as universal laws? If there is such a law, then it must already be connected (completely a priori) with the concept of a rational being in general. But in order to discover this connection we must, however reluctantly, take a step into metaphysics, although into a region of it different from speculative philosophy, i.e., we must enter the metaphysics of morals. In practical philosophy the concern is not with accepting grounds for what happens but with accepting laws of what ought to happen, even though it never does happen—that is, the concern is with objectively practical laws. Here there is no need to inquire into the grounds as to why something pleases or displeases, how the pleasure of mere sensation differs from taste, and whether taste differs from a general satisfaction of reason, upon what does the feeling of pleasure and displeasure rest, and how from this feeling desires and inclinations arise, and how, finally, from these there arise maxims through the cooperation of reason. All of this belongs to an empirical psychology, which would constitute the second part of the doctrine of nature, if this doctrine is regarded as the philosophy of nature insofar as this philosophy is grounded on empirical laws. But here the concern is with objectively practical laws, and hence with the relation of a will to itself insofar as it is determined solely by reason. In this case everything related to what is empirical falls away of itself, because if reason entirely by itself determines conduct (and the possibility of such determination we now wish to investigate), then reason must necessarily do so a priori.

Two terms often employed by Kant, and by many philosophers and philosophy students, are the words "subjective" and "objective." The maxim of an action, for example, is described as a "subjective" principle, as opposed to a law, which is "objective." Similarly, in his first critique, Kant is concerned to show that our subjective experiences and beliefs are in fact objective knowledge. "Subjective" means literally "pertaining to the subject," the individual person. Subjective experience therefore includes personal biases and misinformation, and the maxims (that is, subjective principles) of our actions inevitably contain selfish or at least self-centered concerns. Moral laws are free from any selfish or self-referential concerns, just as objective knowledge is free from such biases and misinformation. In the following passage, Kant also distinguishes between the subjective "springs" of action and the objective "motive." (We will see much more of these terms in the pages to follow.)

> The will is thought of as a faculty of determining itself to action in accordance with the representation of certain laws, and such a faculty can be found only in rational beings. Now what serves the will as the objective ground of its self-determination is an end; and if this end is given by reason alone, then it must be equally valid for all rational beings. On the other hand, what contains merely the ground of the possibility of the action, whose effect is an end, is called the means. The subjective ground of desire is the incentive; the objective ground of volition is the motive. Hence there arises the distinction between subjective ends, which rest on incentives, and objective ends, which depend on motives valid for every rational being. Practical principles are formal when they abstract from all subjective ends; they are material, however, when they are founded upon subjective ends, and hence upon certain incentives. The ends which a rational being arbitrarily proposes to himself as effects of this action (material ends) are all merely relative, for only their relation to a specially constituted faculty of desire in the subject gives them their worth. Consequently, such worth cannot provide any universal principles, which are valid and necessary for all rational beings and, furthermore, are valid for every volition, i.e., cannot provide any practical laws. Therefore, all such relative ends can be grounds only for hypothetical imperatives.

We are now ready to introduce a third formulation of the categorical imperative, one that is as important as the first. The principle is that we should always treat people as ends, never (merely) as means. In other words, don't "use" people. We have already seen that Kant considers the concern for (our own) happiness to be only a hypothetical imperative. But the concern for happiness in general is nevertheless the basis for this categorical imperative. (Notice that Kant uses the word "humanity" to refer to individual human beings as well as the human species in general.)

> But let us suppose that there were something whose existence has in itself an absolute worth, something which as an end in itself could be a ground of determinate laws. In it, and in it alone, would there be the ground of a possible categorical imperative, i.e., of a practical law.

Now I say that man, and in general every rational being, exists as an end in himself and not merely as a means to be arbitrarily used by this or that will. He must in all his actions, whether directed to himself or to other rational beings, always be regarded at the same time as an end. All the objects of inclinations have only a conditioned value; for if there were not these inclinations and the needs founded on them, then their object would be without value. But the inclinations themselves, being sources of needs, are so far from having an absolute value such as to render them desirable for their own sake that the universal wish of every rational being must be, rather, to be wholly free from them. Accordingly, the value of any object obtainable by our action is always conditioned. Beings whose existence depends not on our will but on nature have, nevertheless, if they are not rational beings, only a relative value as means and are therefore called things. On the other hand, rational beings are called persons inasmuch as their nature already marks them out as ends in themselves, i.e., as something which is not to be used merely as means and hence there is imposed thereby a limit on all arbitrary use of such beings, which are thus objects of respect. Persons are, therefore, not merely subjective ends, whose existence as an effect of our actions has a value for us; but such beings are objective ends, i.e., exist as ends in themselves. Such an end is one for which there can be substituted no other end to which such beings should serve merely as means, for otherwise nothing at all of absolute value would be found anywhere. But if all value were conditioned and hence contingent, then no supreme practical principle could be found for reason at all.

If then there is to be a supreme practical principle and, as far as the human will is concerned, a categorical imperative, then it must be such that from the conception of what is necessarily an end for everyone because this end is an end in itself it constitutes an objective principle of the will and can hence serve as a practical law. The ground of such a principle is this: rational nature exists as an end in itself. In this way man necessarily thinks of his own existence; thus far is it a subjective principle of human actions. But in this way also does every other rational being think of his existence on the same rational ground that holds also for me; hence it is at the same time an objective principle, from which, as a supreme practical ground, all laws of the will must be able to be derived. The practical imperative will therefore be the following: *Act in such a way that you treat humanity, whether in your own person or in the person of another, always at the same time as an end and never simply as a means* (italics added). We now want to see whether this can be carried out in practice.

Kant now returns to his previous examples and tests them according to this new formulation.

Let us keep to our previous examples.

First, as regards the concept of necessary duty to oneself, the man who contemplates suicide will ask himself whether his action can be consistent with the idea of humanity as an end in itself. If he destroys himself in order to escape from a difficult situation, then he is making use of his person merely as a means so as to maintain a tolerable condition till the end of his life. Man, however, is not a thing and hence is not something to be used merely as a means; he must in all his actions always be regarded as an end in himself. Therefore, I cannot dispose of man in my own person by mutilating, damaging, or killing him. (A more exact determination of this principle so as to avoid all misunderstanding, e.g., regarding the amputation of limbs in order to save oneself, or the exposure of one's life to danger in order to save it, and so on, must here be omitted; such questions belong to morals proper.)

Second, as concerns necessary or strict duty to others, the man who intends to make a false promise will immediately see that he intends to make use of another man merely as a means to an end which the latter does not likewise hold. For the man whom I want to use for my own purposes by such a promise cannot possibly concur with my way of acting toward him and hence cannot himself hold the end of this action. This conflict with the principle of duty to others becomes even clearer when instances of attacks on the freedom and property of others are considered. For then it becomes clear that a transgressor of the rights of men intends to make use of the persons of others merely as a means, without taking into consideration that, as rational beings, they should always be esteemed at the same time as ends, i.e., be esteemed only as beings who must themselves be able to hold the very same action as an end.

Third, with regard to contingent (meritorious) duty to oneself, it is not enough that the action does not conflict with humanity in our own person as an end in itself; the action must also harmonize with this end. Now there are in humanity capacities for greater perfection which belong to the end that nature has in view as regards humanity in our own person. To neglect these capacities might perhaps be consistent with the maintenance of humanity as an end in itself, but would not be consistent with the advancement of this end.

Fourth, concerning meritorious duty to others, the natural end that all men have is their own happiness. Now humanity might indeed subsist if nobody contributed anything to the happiness of others, provided he did not intentionally impair their happiness. But this, after all, would harmonize only negatively and not positively with humanity as an end in itself, if everyone does not also strive, as much as he can, to further the ends of others. For the ends of any subject who is an end in himself must as far as possible be my ends also, if that conception of an end in itself is to have its full effect in me.

The basis for this new formulation lies in the distinction between those things that are valuable in and of themselves regardless of their use and those things in which value arises solely from the use that can be made of them. Only rational beings belong to the former group and have value no matter what; all other objects are only contingently or circumstantially valuable. As a result, there are limits on the ways that one can treat rational beings (oneself or others) because they alone have intrinsic value. And those limitations are given in the form of a prohibition against treating persons as though they were mere objects or ignoring the fact that they are ends in themselves.

Returning to Kant's examples, again there are oddities. (1) A man who commits suicide is said to be "using himself," an odd argument at the least. (We might be using someone else as a mere means if we kill him in order to help our career or steal his valuables, but it is hard to argue that killing oneself is on a logical par.) What Kant has in mind, however, is the lack of respect for the intrinsic value of any rational being, even if it is one's miserable own self. Suicide is impermissible because it fails to recognize that the life of a rational being can never be treated as a mere stepping stone to a further goal. (2) As with the illustration of the previous formulations, the case is more convincing. It is using someone in a malicious and immoral way to make false promises. Cheating that person out of his money precludes him from deciding for himself what to do with it; that is, it precludes his acting as a rational being. (3) Again he invokes the teleological viewpoint (in this case, the "advancement" of humanity). Here the emphasis is not so much on the prohibition against using rational beings simply as a means but rather on the additional requirement that we (sometimes at least) further the ends of those rational beings (again including ourselves). Failing to develop our talents would not result in the obviously impermissible sort of maltreatment that making false promises does, but it nonetheless fails to respect the inherent value of rational beings. (4) This one is similar to part 3 insofar as it focuses on the furtherance of ends rather than on restrictions on how humanity can be treated. Like part 3, Kant is concerned about the level of respect accorded to rational beings. To refuse to help others when one can is to fail to see them as intrinsically valuable, which is in turn to miss the whole point regarding the special status of rational beings.

What happens now has been interpreted by some Kant scholars as a fourth formulation of the categorical imperative, although Kant calls it "the third practical principle of the will." (The numbering or counting of the various formulations of the categorical imperative has been the source of a good deal of scholarly dispute but need not concern us here.) It is not stated as such, but it clearly has some of the same features as the first three formulations. The actual formulation might read, "Act as a universal legislator." In this formulation, the focus is not so much on the duty to limit the ways in which we might act (for instance, to those actions that can be universalized or that show genuine respect for persons) but rather on where those limits come from. Kant argues that there is a difference in motivation between laws that are simply imposed upon us from without and those that we take on ourselves. In the former case, there must be some additional incentive, "some interest functioning as an attracting stimulus." For instance, many people obey the speed limit not out of respect for the limits it imposes (most people think that others might need such rules, but good drivers like themselves are perfectly safe at higher speeds) but because of their interest in avoiding traffic fines. In the case of laws that are arrived at and adopted voluntarily, however, such incentive is not needed. If one is the author or legislator, one already understands the reasonableness and necessity of the law. Moreover, having adopted it on the basis of reason alone, one eliminates the temptation to claim exceptions to the law.

This notion of formulating and accepting a universal law for oneself in contrast to externally imposed laws leads Kant to the central concept of *autonomy*. Autonomy literally means "self-rule" and is generally taken to indicate a certain degree of freedom from interference. Different conceptions of autonomy will point to different forms of interference: An autonomous nation is one that is not ruled by foreign powers, autonomy on the job means little interference from the boss and co-workers, an autonomous decision is one that is freely made without undue influence, and so on. For Kant, the interference that is relevant in the moral realm comes from our own emotions. An autonomous will is one that acts upon reason alone and that is entirely unaffected by the passions and inclinations. A will that is so affected Kant calls "heteronomous." Thus, again we see that morality is based solely upon reason.

This principle of humanity and of every rational nature generally as an end in itself is the supreme limiting condition of every man's freedom of action. This principle is not borrowed from experience, first, because of its universality, inasmuch as it applies to all rational beings generally, and no experience is capable of determining anything about them; and, secondly, because in experience (subjectively) humanity is not thought of as the end of men, i.e., as an object that we of ourselves actually make our end which as a law ought to constitute the supreme limiting condition of all subjective ends (whatever they may be); and hence this principle must arise from pure reason [and not from experience]. That is to say that the ground of all practical legislation lies objectively in the rule and in the form of universality, which (according to the first principle) makes the rule capable of being a law (say, for example, a law of nature). Subjectively, however, the ground of all practical legislation lies in the end; but . . . the subject of all ends is every rational being as an end in himself. From this there now follows the third practical principle of the will as the supreme condition of the will's conformity with universal practical reason, viz., *the idea of the will of every rational being as a will that legislates universal law* (italics added).

According to this principle all maxims are rejected which are not consistent with the will's own legislation of universal law. The will is thus not merely subject to the law but is subject to the law in such a way that it must be regarded also as legislating for itself and only on this account as being subject to the law (of which it can regard itself as the author).

In the previous formulations of imperatives, viz., that based on the conception of the conformity of actions to universal law in a way similar to a natural order and that based on the universal prerogative of rational beings as ends in themselves, these imperatives just because they were thought of as categorical excluded from their legislative authority all admixture of any interest as an incentive. They were, however, only assumed to be categorical because such an assumption had to be made if the concept of duty was to be explained. But that there were practical propositions which commanded categorically could not itself be proved, nor can it be proved anywhere in this section. But one thing could have been done, viz., to indicate that in willing from duty the renunciation of all interest is the specific mark distinguishing a categorical imperative from a hypothetical one and that such renunciation was expressed in the imperative itself by means of some determination contained in it. This is done in the present . . . formulation of the principle, namely, in the idea of the will of every rational being as a will that legislates universal law.

When such a will is thought of, then even though a will which is subject to law may be bound to this law by means of some interest, nevertheless a will that is itself a supreme lawgiver is not able as such to depend on any interest. For a will which is so dependent would itself require yet another law restricting the interest of its self-love to the condition that such interest should itself be valid as a universal law.

Thus the principle that every human will is a will that legislates universal law in all its maxims, provided it is otherwise correct, would be well suited to being a categorical imperative in the following respect: just because of the idea of legislating universal law such an imperative is not based on any interest, and therefore it alone of all possible imperatives can be unconditional. Or still better, the proposition being converted, if there is a categorical imperative (i.e., a law for the will of every rational being), then it can only command that everything be done from the maxim of such a will as could at the same time have as its object only itself regarded as legislating universal law. For only then are the practical principle and the imperative which the will obeys unconditional, inasmuch as the will can be based on no interest at all.

When we look back upon all previous attempts that have been made to discover the principle of morality, there is no reason now to wonder why they one and all had to fail. Man was viewed as bound to laws by his duty; but it was not seen that man is subject only to his own, yet universal, legislation and that he is bound only to act in accordance with his own will, which is, however, a will purposed by nature to legislate universal laws. For when man is thought as being merely subject to a law (whatever it might be), then the law had to carry with it some interest functioning as an attracting stimulus or as a constraining force for obedience, inasmuch as the law did not arise as a law from his own will. Rather, in order that his will conform with law, it had to be necessitated by something else to act in a certain way. By this absolutely necessary conclusion, however, all the labor spent in finding a supreme ground for duty was irretrievably lost; duty was never discovered, but only the necessity of acting from a certain interest. This might be either one's own interest or another's, but either way the imperative had to be always conditional and could never possibly serve as a moral command. I want, therefore, to call my principle the principle of the autonomy of the will, in contrast with every other principle, which I accordingly count under heteronomy.

And finally, a fifth formulation of the categorical imperative, a somewhat utopian vision that says, in effect, that we should act as if we were all members of the perfectly moral community.

The concept of every rational being as one who must regard himself as legislating universal law by all his will's maxims, so that he may judge himself and his actions from this point of view, leads to another very fruitful concept, which depends on the aforementioned one, viz., that of a kingdom of ends.

By "kingdom" I understand a systematic union of different rational beings through common laws. Now laws determine ends as regards their universal validity; therefore, if one abstracts from the personal differences of rational beings and also from all content of their private ends, then it will be possible to think of a whole of all ends in systematic connection (a whole both of rational being as ends in themselves and also of the particular ends which each may set for himself); that is, one can think of a kingdom of ends that is possible on the aforesaid principles.

For all rational beings stand under the law that each of them should treat himself and all others never merely as means but always at the same time as an end in himself. Hereby arises a systematic union of rational beings through common objective laws, i.e., a kingdom that may be called a kingdom of ends (certainly only an ideal), inasmuch as these laws have in view the very relation of such beings to one another as ends and means.

A rational being belongs to the kingdom of ends as a member when he legislates in it universal laws while also being himself subject to these laws. He belongs to it as sovereign, when as legislator he is himself subject to the will of no other.

A rational being must always regard himself as legislator in a kingdom of ends rendered possible by freedom of the will, whether as member or as sovereign. The position of the latter can be maintained not merely through the maxims of his will but only if he is a completely independent being without needs and with unlimited power adequate to his will.

Hence morality consists in the relation of all action to that legislation whereby alone a kingdom of ends is possible. This legislation must be found in every rational being and must be able to arise from his will, whose principle then is never to act on any maxim except such as can also be a universal law and hence such as the will can thereby regard itself as at the same time the legislator of universal law. If now the maxims do not by their very nature already necessarily conform with this objective principle of rational beings as legislating universal laws, then the necessity of acting on that principle is called practical necessitation, i.e., duty. Duty does not apply to the sovereign in the kingdom of ends, but it does apply to every member and to each in the same degree.

What is so "perfect" about the kingdom of ends (which is sometimes interpreted as Heaven) is not just that everyone wills and does what is right but that everyone *respects* everyone else. This is the point of the third formulation ("people as ends, not merely means") as well, but it can be summarized in a very different word—"dignity." Dignity, however, is not to be considered a mere "value," for it has no market price; it cannot be bought or sold. Kant is here reacting to early capitalism in Europe (the market society was just beginning to go strong at the end of the eighteenth century). He is saying, in modern terms, that "human life and dignity do not have a price. They are absolute and have intrinsic worth."

The practical necessity of acting according to this principle, i.e., duty, does not rest at all on feelings, impulses, and inclinations, but only on the relation of rational beings to one another, a relation in which the will of a rational being must always be regarded at the same time as legislative, because otherwise he could not be thought of as an end in himself. Reason, therefore, relates every maxim of the will as legislating universal laws to every other will and also to every action toward oneself; it does so not on account of any other practical motive or future advantage but rather from the idea of the dignity of a rational being who obeys no law except what he at the same time enacts himself.

In the kingdom of ends everything has either a price or a dignity. Whatever has a price can be replaced by something else as its equivalent; on the other hand, whatever is above all price, and therefore admits of no equivalent, has a dignity.

Whatever has reference to general human inclinations and needs has a market price; whatever, without presupposing any need, accords with a certain taste, i.e., a delight in the mere unpurposive play of our mental powers, has an affective price; but that which constitutes the condition under which alone something can be an end in itself has not merely a relative worth, i.e., a price, but has an intrinsic worth, i.e., dignity.

Now morality is the condition under which alone a rational being can be an end in himself, for only thereby can he be a legislating member in the kingdom of ends. Hence morality and humanity, insofar as it is capable of morality, alone have dignity. Skill and diligence in work have a market price; wit, lively imagination, and humor have an affective price; but fidelity to promises and benevolence based on principles (not on instinct) have intrinsic worth. Neither nature nor art contain anything which in default of these could be put in their place; for their worth consists, not in the effects which arise from them, nor in the advantage and profit which they provide, but in mental dispositions, i.e., in the maxims of the will which are ready in this way to manifest themselves in action, even if they are not favored with success. Such actions also need no recommendation from any subjective disposition or taste so as to meet with immediate favor and delight; there is no need of any immediate propensity or feeling toward them. They exhibit the will performing them as an object of immediate respect; and nothing but reason is required to impose them upon the will, which is not to be cajoled into them, since in the case of duties such cajoling would be a contradiction. This estimation, therefore, lets the worth of such a disposition be recognized as dignity and puts it infinitely beyond all price, with which it cannot in the least be brought into competition or comparison without, as it were, violating its sanctity.

What then is it that entitles the morally good disposition, or virtue, to make such lofty claims? It is nothing less than the share which such a disposition affords the rational being of legislating universal laws, so that he is fit to be a member in a possible kingdom of ends, for which his own nature has already determined him as an end in himself and therefore as a legislator in the kingdom of ends. Thereby is he free as regards all laws of nature, and he obeys only those laws which he gives to himself. Accordingly, his maxims can belong to a universal legislation to which he at the same time subjects himself. For nothing can have any worth other than what the law determines. But the legislation itself which determines all worth must for that very reason have dignity, i.e., unconditional and incomparable worth; and the word "respect" alone provides a suitable expression for the esteem which a rational being must have for it. Hence autonomy is the ground of the dignity of human nature and of every rational nature. . . .

Autonomy of the will is the property that the will has of being a law to itself (independently of any property of the objects of volition). The principle of autonomy is this: Always choose in such a way that in the same volition the maxims of the choice are at the same time present as universal law. That this practical rule is an imperative, i.e., that the will of every rational being is necessarily bound to the rule as a condition, cannot be proved by merely analyzing the concepts contained in it, since it is a synthetic proposition. For proof one would have to go beyond cognition of objects to a critical examination of the subject, i.e., go to a critique of pure practical reason, since this synthetic proposition which commands apodeictically must be capable of being cognized completely a priori. This task, however, does not belong to the present section. But that the above principle of autonomy is the sole principle of morals can quite well be shown by mere analysis of the concepts of morality; for thereby the principle of morals is found to be necessarily a categorical imperative, which commands nothing more nor less than this very autonomy.

DISCUSSION

The categorical imperative is the true key to Kant's moral philosophy. In two words, it summarizes the deontological orientation of his ethics: a moral principle is an "unconditional command." The categorical imperative is also the condensed statement of morality in general, particularly in its first formulation, which commands us to always act as we would will others to act too ("Act as if the maxim of your action were to be a universal law for everyone"). The resemblance to the biblical Golden Rule is more than superficial, and Kant himself comments on the kinship between the two.

The role of the categorical imperative in ethics, however, is something more specific as well. It is a test of moral principles, a kind of criterion. The conditions Kant imposes on the categorical imperative—not only its unconditional nature but its form as a universal principle—also mark the conditions that any moral principle—any particular maxim—must fulfill. A moral maxim must be universalizable as moral law. What determines a moral law, Kant argues, are purely formal conditions. That is, one need not (and should not) look at the particular circumstances or consequences or feelings of the agent, nor should one consult authorities or the customs of the locale. A maxim that has the wrong form cannot be universalized, and a maxim that is not moral cannot be universalized without inconsistency. Inconsistency or contradiction is a purely formal flaw in principles and thus appropriate, as Kant's analysis demands, for a purely rational test of a purely rational endeavor, morality.

There are, however, some problems. What Kant demands is clear enough; moral principles are a priori principles of reason and so must be established independently of empirical concerns (such as the feelings or fortunes of the participants). But what he means by "inconsistency" or "contradiction" is not at all clear, as evidenced by his often obscure applications to the four examples. And whether the categorical imperative test will work for even a small subsection of what we consider the moral realm, as one tries it out on more and more examples, is open to question.

Consider, for example, the moral question of adultery. Suppose one is considering having an illicit affair and, following Kant's test, universalizes his or her maxim. What is the result? One might argue that the institution of marriage as we know it would be changed considerably; sexual fidelity would no longer be a part of it (not even the pretense of fidelity). But would this count as an inconsistency? A contradiction? It does not seem so. (Kant does discuss sexual morality in his various lectures on ethics, but his view is harsh and conservative, and he would certainly object to this line of questioning.) Consider the troublesome example of a shoplifter about to steal a gadget from a department store. He or she being Kantian universalizes the maxim and asks, What if everyone would steal? A plausible answer would be that if everyone would take whatever he or she wanted, without considering who owned anything, then the very notion of ownership would seem to collapse, and ownership would be nothing but possession ("ten-tenths of the law," one might say). Stealing would therefore be impossible, because stealing is a violation of ownership, which would no longer exist.

This imagined consequence, however, is more problematic than it looks at first. It does seem as if we have a contradiction of just the sort Kant envisioned, but now suppose that we present our deliberations to a Marxist, who believes that private property is itself illegitimate and immoral. The Marxist will say, "Good, then everyone ought to steal." Kant would reply that this is an illicit appeal to consequences, namely, the Marxist's hoped-for improvement of the human lot with the abolition of private property. But suppose the Marxist, ready for this reply, responds as follows, "If that is a contradiction, it is only because you begin by *assuming* the legitimacy of the institution of private property. In other words, the categorical imperative has the result, no matter how 'formal' its appearance, of protecting already established institutions, whatever they may be." The real question, we can then imagine our Marxist insisting, is whether those institutions themselves are good. The categorical imperative simply begs the ethical question.

Perhaps the most troublesome objection to Kant's categorical imperative is aimed at the one part of the theory that we have so far taken at face value—the maxim itself. What is the maxim of a particular action? It is not, Kant insists, the end of the action, its purpose or desired result. It is not intention or motivation in the sense of desire or the "springs" of action. It is rather its implicit principle, its subjective characterization, or the rule one takes oneself to be acting upon. But how is this determined? Consider an example: A man cannot afford medicine for his sick wife. The pharmacy has refused him credit; the pharmacist has just left the prescription desk to answer the telephone. The man spies the medicine on the inside counter, within an easy stretch. A Kantian, he pauses a moment to deliberate, What if everyone were to . . .? To what? To steal? To steal medicine? To steal medicine that is desperately needed? To steal medicine desperately needed that one cannot afford? To steal this particular medicine that one's wife desperately needs and that one cannot afford? Which is the correct implicit principle of the intended action? Which is the maxim?

Part of the problem is that the maxim is implicit; it does not appear in consciousness fully articulated but is rather formulated afterward, as a description of one's intention. But even leaving aside the psychological nuances of unconscious and deceptive maxims (for example, "to steal medicine from this bastard who turned me down in my hour of need"), the variety of alternative maxims is bewildering. The maxim might include only the most general, value-neutral description of the action, "to take medicine from a pharmacy without paying for it," or it might be extremely detailed and specific, "to take this medicine from this pharmacy under the nose of this pharmacist who had just turned down a request for credit in the face of this desperate situation in which one's wife has this disease with these symptoms. . . ." In the process of universalization, of course, one would presumably take out all of the particular references (to "this" pharmacy and pharmacist, for instance), but one might retain their substance, nevertheless, with a detailed description ("a pharmacist about 40 years old, slightly balding at the top, wearing tortoise-shell glasses"). The first step of Kant's test of a moral principle, "take the maxim of your action," is extremely problematic. How specific—or how general—should a maxim be?

This objection, that the maxim does not appear fully articulated and can be characterized in any of a variety of ways, is not just a technical difficulty. It undermines the whole point of the categorical imperative. This becomes evident as soon as we take several of these competing maxims and universalize them. If the man in the pharmacy asks, "What if everyone were to take medicine without paying for it?" the economic consequences for the drug companies might be disturbing, but the consistency of the universal law does not seem to be called into question. Even with the more loaded description, "to steal medicine," one can presume that the free market system and the institution of private property do not depend upon the pharmaceutical industry, and no contradiction is even on the horizon. "To steal" implies unethical behavior in a way that "to take" does not. Generalized to the description, "to steal," of course, the contradiction does arise in Kant's sense, but why is "to steal" a more accurate description of the intended act than "to steal medicine that one desperately needs." If we universalize the latter, it is hard to imagine anything remotely resembling a contradiction in Kant's sense. But what this means is that the logical or formal consequences of universalizing the maxim of one's action depend on the detail and nature of the characterization of the maxim. This, however, requires just that attention to empirical elements that Kant tried to eliminate, an attention to circumstances and personal need, for example. The man might settle for the general description, "to steal," and then try to make an exception of himself, as Kant suggested. But he need not do this, and if he is a clever Kantian, he will rather alter his description of his intended action such that he is not an exception at all. Thus, it is possible, by way of a suitable framing of one's universal principles, to always find or create a principle that passes Kant's test and, nevertheless, is wholly designed to satisfy one's personal inclinations.

The purely formal test devised by Kant seems to collapse against the force of this objection. This is not, however, an argument against Kant's deontological ethics or against the categorical imperative (as Mill charges, for instance). It is only an argument against the adequacy of the first formulation of the categorical imperative alone as a standard for what—specifically—we ought to do. The general theory of morality as formal and a priori has not thus been refuted; what has been shown—barring a successful reply—is that the general theory by itself has no fixed rule of application to particular cases. (If there were such a rule, would we need a rule for the application of rules? This question worried Kant and has worried many of his critics since.) Even if we accept the moral principle that one should not steal, it still remains open for us to decide, in each particular case, what counts as stealing and whether all kinds of stealing are equally prohibited. Note, however, that the same problem does not occur with the third formulation, the prohibition against using persons. Regardless of the circumstances, to take the medicine after the pharmacist has refused to give it to you is to treat him as a means only.

A further problem arises as a result of Kant's absolutism. Because he does not allow circumstances, relationships, or emotions of any kind to play a role in our moral deliberations, there are no exceptions, even for extraordinary circumstances. This is usually considered a welcome result and was especially valued by Kant. However, consider the following situation.

Suppose you have to decide whether to lie about your friend's whereabouts to the Nazis, the alternative being to have a hand in your friend's death. As evidenced by the false-promising example, Kant believed that there is an absolute duty not to lie. However, most people would also assert a duty to protect innocent people from certain death. Even if we agree on the proper characterization of the alternative maxims and principles involved, how can we decide which takes (a priori) priority? The well-being of the friend is not a permissible consideration (nor is the question of how you will be able to live with yourself later). If the decision—as a moral decision—must rest on purely formal criteria, what could they be?

One suggestion that Kant makes is the distinction between "perfect" and "imperfect" duties. A perfect duty is one that cannot be violated universally. (Lying is the usual example because universal lying makes impossible the very act of lying.) An imperfect duty is one whose violation one cannot *will* universally; nevertheless, it might be possible for everyone to violate it. Complicity to murder (or even murder) would, on this account, not be a violation of a perfect duty (because everyone might try to murder each other in a way that everyone could not try to lie to one another). But this has an intolerable consequence for our preceding example; the perfect duty not to lie takes priority over the imperfect duty not to be an accomplice in your friend's death.

One Kantian reply that bears more consideration than is usually given is the insistence that the first formulation of the categorical imperative alone is not meant to provide the test of morality; only the various formulations together do this. Thus, the lying versus murder example may not be decided in a palatable way by the first formulation, but the second ("law of nature") formulation does give us our preferred answer. The "ends not merely means" formulation further provides an important set of considerations not included in the first two, most importantly some (formal) concern for the well-being of the people involved. (But aren't we "using" the Nazi by lying to him?) Together, the various formulations give us a much more complete moral picture and a more complete moral test. Nevertheless, duties obviously can conflict, and the hardest situations are those in which we find ourselves with not one but two conflicting obligations.

In the third and last section of the *Grounding,* Kant actually takes up the metaphysics of his moral philosophy, the basic principles that form the foundations of morality. In his earlier *Critique of Pure Reason,* Kant had summarized the basic concerns of metaphysics in a phrase, "God, Freedom, and Immortality." The first and last of these—God and immortality—are a brief summary of what in fact is the essence of Christianity: the belief in an all-powerful, all-knowing, and beneficent God, who is also our ultimate moral judge, and belief in the immortality of the human soul, which will survive the death of the body and be able to reap the rewards—or punishments—that we have earned here in life. The second metaphysical principle—freedom—is the condition without which the very concept of morality would make no sense at all. "Ought implies can," writes Kant, meaning that it makes no sense to say that a person ought to do something unless he or she is free to do it—or not to do it. It would make no sense to say that a person ought to break the law of gravity, for example, but neither would it make sense to tell a person that he or she ought to obey it. Where there is no freedom to choose, there are no moral considerations. Freedom, Kant tells us, is "the key to the explanation of the autonomy of the will."

In *The Critique of Pure Reason,* Kant had argued that every event in the universe must have its sufficient natural cause; in other words, it had to happen in a certain way because of all the other events and conditions preceding it. But this idea of universal causality—although undeniable in science—is intolerable in the realm of human action, where we would like to think (and must think, if we are to make sense of moral freedom) that we are the cause of our behavior, however influenced we may be by our circumstances, our upbringing, and any number of other causal factors. Thus, Kant makes a sharp distinction in his philosophy between the "sensible" world of nature, which is ruled by causality, and the "intelligible" world of freedom, which is the world of the will, our autonomous choices, which are not determined by anything foreign to the will itself.

But freedom from external determination of our choices and actions is only part of the meaning of this all-important condition of morality; Kant calls this a "negative" sense of freedom, freedom from external causes of our actions. But there is also a "positive" concept of freedom, which is the freedom to will in accordance with the moral law. Here Kant again distinguishes between the moral law—which is central to the world of freedom and morality—and the laws of nature—which are within the domain of causality. It is of the utmost importance for Kant to keep these always separate, because it is the separation of freedom from nature (and our inclinations) that forms the foundation of his entire moral philosophy.

Transition from a Metaphysics of Morals to a Critique of Pure Practical Reason

The Concept of Freedom Is the Key for an Explanation of the Autonomy of the Will   The will is a kind of causality belonging to living beings insofar as they are rational; freedom would be the property of this causality that makes it effective independent of any determination by alien causes. Similarly, natural necessity is the property of the causality of all non-rational beings by which they are determined to activity through the influence of alien causes.

The foregoing explanation of freedom is negative and is therefore unfruitful for attaining an insight regarding its essence; but there arises from it a positive concept, which as such is richer and more fruitful. The concept of causality involves that of laws according to which something that we call cause must entail something else—namely, the effect. Therefore freedom is certainly not lawless, even though it is not a property of will in accordance with laws of nature. It must, rather, be a causality in accordance with immutable laws, which, to be sure, is of a special kind; otherwise a free will would be something absurd. As we have already seen [in the preceding paragraph], natural necessity is a heteronomy of efficient causes, inasmuch as every effect is possible only in accordance with the law that something else determines the efficient cause to exercise its causality. What else, then, can freedom of the will be but autonomy, i.e., the property that the will has of being a law to itself? The proposition that the will is in every action a law to itself expresses, however, nothing but the principle of acting according to no other maxim than that which can at the same time have itself as a universal law for its object. Now this is precisely the formula of the categorical imperative and is the principle of morality. Thus a free will and a will subject to moral laws are one and the same. . . .

Freedom Must Be Presupposed as a Property of the Will of All Rational Beings   It is not enough to ascribe freedom to our will, on whatever ground, if we have not also sufficient reason for attributing it to all rational beings. For inasmuch as morality serves as a law for us only insofar as we are rational beings, it must also be valid for all rational beings. And since morality must be derived solely from the property of freedom, one must show that freedom is also the property of the will of all rational beings. It is not enough to prove freedom from certain alleged experiences of human nature (such a proof is indeed absolutely impossible, and so freedom can be proved only a priori). Rather, one must show that freedom belongs universally to the activity of rational beings endowed with a will. Now I say that every being which cannot act in any way other than under the idea of freedom is for this very reason free from a practical point of view. This is to say that for such a being all the laws that are inseparably bound up with freedom are valid just as much as if the will of such a being could be declared to be free in itself for reasons that are valid for theoretical philosophy. Now I claim that we must necessarily attribute to every rational being who has a will also the idea of freedom, under which only can such a being act. For in such a being we think of a reason that is practical, i.e., that has causality in reference to its objects. Now we cannot possibly think of a reason that consciously lets itself be directed from outside as regards its judgments; for in that case the subject would ascribe the determination of his faculty of judgment not to his reason, but to an impulse. Reason must regard itself as the author of its principles independent of foreign influences. Therefore as practical reason or as the will of a rational being must reason regard itself as free. This is to say that the will of a rational being can be a will of its own only under the idea of freedom, and that such a will must therefore, from a practical point of view, be attributed to all rational beings.

Concerning the Interest Attached to the Ideas of Morality   We have finally traced the determinate concept of morality back to the idea of freedom, but we could not prove freedom to be something actual in ourselves and in human nature. We saw merely that we must presuppose it if we want to think of a being as rational and as endowed with consciousness of its causality as regards actions, i.e., as endowed with a will. And so we find that on the very same ground we must attribute to every being endowed with reason and a will this property of determining itself to action under the idea of its own freedom.

Now there resulted from the presupposition of this idea of freedom also the consciousness of a law of action: that the subjective principles of actions, i.e., maxims, must always be so adopted that they can also be valid objectively, i.e., universally, as principles, and can therefore serve as universal laws of our own legislation. But why, then, should I subject myself to this principle simply as a rational being and by so doing also subject to this principle all other beings endowed with reason? I am willing to grant that no interest impels me to do so, because this would not give a categorical imperative. But nonetheless I must necessarily take an interest in it and discern how this comes about, for this *ought* is properly a *would* which is valid for every rational being, provided that reason is practical for such a being without hindrances. In the case of beings who, like ourselves, are also affected by sensibility, i.e., by incentives of a kind other than the purely rational, and who do not always act as reason by itself would act, this necessity of action is expressed only as an *ought,* and the subjective necessity is to be distinguished from the objective.

It therefore seems as if we have in the idea of freedom actually only presupposed the moral law, namely, the principle of the autonomy of the will, and as if we could not prove its reality and objective necessity independently. In that case we should indeed still have gained something quite considerable by at least determining the genuine principle more exactly than had previously been done. But as regards its validity and the practical necessity of subjecting oneself to it, we would have made no progress. We could give no satisfactory answer if asked the following questions: why must the universal validity of our maxim taken as a law be a condition restricting our actions; upon what do we base the worth that we assign to this way of acting—a worth that is supposed to be so great that there can be no higher interest; how does it happen that by this alone does man believe that he feels his own personal worth, in comparison with which that of an agreeable or disagreeable condition is to be regarded as nothing.

DISCUSSION

When Kant calls the realm of morality "the world of freedom," he is clearly stating, once again, the basic proposition of his entire conception of morality. Morality means acting *willfully* and not because one is in any way compelled to act, whether by external forces or by one's own inclinations. And morality means *autonomy,* that is, accepting the moral law for oneself and by oneself, on the basis of reason alone. The impetus behind this radical emphasis on freedom is the entire Enlightenment, as well as the independent spirit of Kant's Pietist Lutheranism. But the philosophical emphasis is clearly directed against that whole history of ethics, from Aristotle to Hume, that would reduce morals to a matter of inclination—to the search for happiness and the satisfaction of desires. For Aristotle and Hume, nothing is more essential to morality than participation in a community, which sets the customs and expectations, which cultivates in us the proper sentiments and gives moral behavior both its purpose and sanction. (A similar view is defended by Hegel—against Kant—only a few years later.) But for Kant, participation in a community has nothing to do with morality. Moral principles are a matter of the rational will, which means that we must be free to see beyond and even reject the customs and expectations we have learned. We must sometimes fight our sentiments and inclinations in general; indeed, our moral worth is tested in our ability to do so. The purpose of moral behavior, Kant insists, is not utility but rationality itself, in which freedom and autonomy are the key ingredients. As for sanctions, it is not a matter of morality if we behave correctly because of fear of censure or embarrassment. This, too, is a denial of freedom—that is, the freedom to do what we will independently of any causal influences, of which punishment is a primary example. (Kant and his German followers, including Hegel, were very concerned with the nature of punishment, which they felt turned a person into an "object" and denied his or her free will.)

It is important to ask, however, whether Kant goes too far in the direction of freedom and autonomy. Even if there are universal moral principles, for example, does it make sense to suppose that we can discover them through reason alone, without the context (as well as the education) of some particular community? And is freedom really the essence of morals? Why so dismiss the Aristotelian vision of a society of people who are "naturally" good just because they have been taught to be good, not because they "will" it, perhaps against all inclination? Is "moral worth" so important? Are consequences really so unimportant morally speaking? Is autonomy really the inescapable basis of ethics? Or is it possible that Kant's ideal ultimately leaves us in a moral vacuum, with a sense of ourselves devoid of any ethos, attachment, or belonging?

Discussion Questions

1. What is the "categorical imperative"? How is a categorical imperative distinguished from a "hypothetical" imperative? Why does Kant talk about *the* categorical imperative rather than simply talking about categorical imperatives ("Don't lie," "Don't cheat") in general?
2. What is "duty"? How do we distinguish duties from other acts that we think we should do? What does Kant mean by "acting for the sake of duty" (rather than "in accordance with duty")?
3. Why are *principles* so central to Kant's conception of morality? Why does he talk so little about "good character" and "personal merit," as Aristotle and Hume do? Why does he dismiss consequences as irrelevant to moral worth?
4. What is "moral worth"? Can an act be good in any sense but not show moral worth? Can a person be good in any sense if he or she does not have moral worth? A person

who wants to do what is right, but for reasons of inclination rather than a sense of duty, does not thereby have moral worth; why does Kant insist on this? Is he saying that we are not acting morally unless we do not want to do what we ought to do, but do it because we have to?

5. Why does Kant call his ethical treatise a work on "the metaphysics of morals"? Why does he call it a "metaphysics"?

6. Why does Kant reject Hume's moral skepticism? How does he reject it? What role do the sentiments play in Kant's ethics?

7. Why is freedom a presupposition of morality (a "postulate of practical reason")? Does the development of good habits and "character"—as in Aristotle—mean that we are not acting freely? Does "freedom" in Kant mean that we are free to choose anything? What restrictions does he place on this freedom?

8. What does it mean to say that morality is a function of "practical reason"? As opposed to what? What does this mean about the form of moral principles?

9. Why must there be a God and an immortal soul in order for there to be morality? In what sense are these presuppositions of duty? In what ways do these two "postulates of practical reason" threaten the central thesis of Kant's moral philosophy?

10. What is a "deontological" theory of morals? How is Kant's ethics an example of such a moral theory?

11. What is "autonomy"? What is necessary for a being to be autonomous? If a person accepts the idea that the Ten Commandments are the direct commandments of God, does that make him or her less autonomous? If a person resolves to obey the law and defend his or her country ("right or wrong"), does that mean less autonomy?

12. Is seeking the advice and opinions of other people acting in accordance with Kant's moral philosophy? Should we do this? Must we do this?

13. Why does Kant say that the only thing good "without qualification" is a good will? Why is being born rich not good "without qualification"? Why not being in good health or successful?

14. Do religious commandments tell us our duty because they are given by God? Or has God given them to us because they do in fact tell us what is good? What moral and religious questions depend on the answer to this question?

15. Is God rational? Why or why not?

16. Are we rational? In what senses? In what senses not? What does Kant mean by rationality?

Study Questions

1. Why not lie? Is it ever right to lie? How does Kant's categorical imperative act as a test in cases in which we are tempted to lie (even for good reasons)? In what sense is it inconsistent to will that everyone, in similar circumstances, ought to lie?

2. What is the connection—if any—between the various formulations of the categorical imperative? Which formulations are most important? Or are they all of equal importance? Why not just stick with the first (and best known) formulation and treat the others as corollaries or subsidiary principles?

3. Is Kant a teleologist? In what sense? What purpose does reason serve, and why does it not primarily serve to make us happy, according to Kant?

4. What are "inclinations," and why are they of no moral worth?

5. What does it mean to urge love as "practical" (as opposed to "pathological")? Why does Kant insist on this?

6. Why should one not commit suicide, according to Kant, even if life is very painful and unpromising and seems much more trouble than it's worth?

7. In what peculiar sense does Kant claim to have a "popular philosophy"? (Nietzsche wrote: "Kant's joke; he defended the common man in language which the common man could not possibly understand.")

8. Why should we help other people, according to Kant? What should motivate us, if our actions are morally worthy? What is the place of sympathy?

9. What is a "maxim"? Give some examples of maxims of actions. When does a maxim become a moral law?

10. What is the "kingdom of ends"? What ideal role does it play in Kant's ethics? In his religious vision of the *summum bonum?*

11. If I promised my friend that I would go to the movies with him, but my brother gets ill and asks me to stay with him, what should I do, according to Kant? How do I decide what to do?

7

John Stuart Mill

Mill was born in 1806 into a hard-driving, intellectual family. His accomplishments by the age of 10 would have been admirable in a 60-year-old scholar; he learned languages and higher mathematics; he studied the sciences and could discuss the latest theories and discoveries in science with the most brilliant academicians in London. But he pushed himself and was pushed so hard that he suffered a nervous breakdown at the age of 20 and turned his attention from the hard sciences to the more emotionally expressive study of poetry. He also became involved in political reform and the early feminist movement, with his wife Harriet Taylor. He is best known for his ethical and political writings, particularly *On Liberty* (1859) and *Utilitarianism* (1863), but his works on logic, mathematics, and the philosophy of science represent the best efforts of the British empiricist tradition in the nineteenth century. John Stuart Mill died in 1873.

Whereas the concept of "utility" has been employed by any number of modern authors in ethics (David Hume, for instance), the name "utilitarianism" is inevitably associated with one author more than any other, John Stuart Mill. (He also made up the word, although he admits adopting it "from a passing expression" in a popular book of the time.) The idea that happiness (or pleasure) and the general well-being should be the basis and the ultimate aim of ethics has been prominent since at least Aristotle; nevertheless, it was Mill who took this teleological (that is, goal-oriented) ethical standard and turned it into a precise contemporary theory. Indeed, many moral philosophers would insist that utilitarianism is one of the very few commonly agreed-upon candidates for a general ethical theory. Whether one believes that it can overcome certain now-standard objections, utilitarianism—in much the form that Mill defended it over a century ago—is one of the most plausible and prominent ethical viewpoints.

Utilitarianism was, in more primitive form, the ethical philosophy of the Enlightenment, particularly in England and France, during most of the seventeenth and eighteenth centuries. (It is worth noting that it had comparatively little influence in Germany, where Kant was the foremost defender of Enlightenment thinking.) Hume was only one of many secular, business-minded reformers who insisted that utility—what is useful—is the only reasonable general standard for social rules, laws, and moral principles, and by the time of Jeremy Bentham, at the end of the eighteenth century, this idea was generally accepted among the liberal-minded. It was Bentham who turned the idea into a rigorous decision procedure, however, and, with Mill's father—James Mill—initiated a kind of movement aimed primarily at legal reform in England. By the time John Stuart joined this movement (he always rejected the idea of utilitarianism as a single sectarian viewpoint), it was, on the one hand, already well established but, on the other hand, it was being profoundly challenged by an antithetical countermovement from Germany. That countermovement was Kant's deontological (that is, duty-based) ethics, which rejected the premise of the utilitarian philosophy, the so-called "principle of utility" (named by Bentham)—"the principle which approves or disapproves of every action whatsoever, according to the tendency which it appears to have to augment or diminish the happiness of the party whose interest is in question."

Not surprisingly, therefore, Mill begins his classic treatise (simply titled *Utilitarianism,* published in 1863) defining and defending utilitarianism with a few general remarks about the obviousness of the principle of utility and the fact that even Kant felt compelled to recognize it in his ethics. The argument between Kant and Mill is one of the most basic arguments in ethics—if not *the* basic argument in ethical theory—but it involves several dimensions, not just "duty versus utility," and so the confrontation between them is often based on misunderstandings and failure to address the same question. First, as the very names tell us, Mill's ethics of utility is a teleological ethics concerned with human happiness and desires, whereas Kant's deontological ethics explicitly rejects utility as a measure of moral worth and instead emphasizes duty *even to the exclusion of utility and happiness.* But this head-on collision is not as it seems. Notice that what Kant rejects is the idea that moral worth is measured by utility; that is, his position is that the moral goodness of an act is not a question of how useful it is but rather how good the intentions of the agent are and the morality of the principles (maxims) that define those intentions. Kant does not reject the idea that the natural goodness of the action (not the person) may be measured by utility; indeed, he would be willing to admit that, in such a context, the very meaning of a "good" act is its contribution to happiness, *so long as it is not also taken as a measure of moral worth.*

And Mill, on his side, does not reject the idea that we do evaluate persons according to their intentions as well as according to the utility of their actions. What he rejects is the Kantian emphasis on intentions instead of usefulness, as if a person could be perfectly good even if his or her good intentions consistently resulted in the most awful circumstances. (Dostoevsky wrote a novel, about the same time, about just such a fellow; the novel was appropriately called *The Idiot.*) The collision thus seems more of a sideswipe; there is certainly a deep disagreement in emphasis but not the wholesale contradiction suggested by many proponents of one view or the other.

The same might be said of the utilitarian emphasis on consequences, which Kant rejects as being irrelevant to morality. It is not that Mill is unconcerned with the intentions (or the good will) behind a person's actions, but he is concerned with such intentions only insofar as they have a bearing on utility. Would we be so concerned about a misanthrope's malicious intentions, for example, if every expression of his contempt was in fact a great boon to everyone? And it is not as if Kant is unconcerned with happiness in his emphasis on duty alone as the measure of moral worth. Indeed, some of his arguments even suggest that one justification of the emphasis on duty is the promotion of happiness (for example, with regard to the duty to help others, Kant specifically justifies it in terms of concern for the happiness of others). Moreover, Kant both begins and ends his *Grounding* with the observation that we find it intolerable that virtue should not be commensurate with happiness, and it is on this basis that Mill considers him, in effect, a closet utilitarian, for whom "utilitarian arguments are indispensable." (You will notice that Mill intentionally misunderstands Kant's insistence that it is the logical inconsistency of universalized maxims, not their consequences, that is the test of the categorical imperative.)

Jeremy Bentham's version of utilitarianism was a purely quantitative calculus ("the happiness calculus") in which the sheer amounts of pleasure and pain that result from an action *were the measure of its goodness or badness.* Mill rejects this purely quantitative calculus insisting that the *quality* of pleasure and pain is equally important. He recognized that, as a general ethical theory (in contrast to a theory of punishment, for example), there had to be some essential distinction made between the indulgent pleasures of gluttons and libertines and the more "refined" pleasures of artists, philosophers, and saints. (Note the agreement here with Kant's third example, concerned with developing one's talents rather than lying around naked and contented in the sun.) The revision tended to take some of the "vulgarity" out of utilitarianism, but at a considerable cost. The primary virtue of Bentham's theory was its simplicity, the fact that all ethical decisions could be appealed to a single standard—the *summum bonum* of pleasure and pain. But as Mill adds the dimension of quality to the utilitarian calculus, we find ourselves with two standards instead of just one: the *amount* of pleasure and pain and the *quality* of the pleasures and pains. But where there are two standards, one must have a way of weighing them against one another. How much artistic suffering—Rembrandt agonizing over an unfinished portrait—is balanced by how much pleasure? (A trip to southern France? Dinner at the luxurious Shwarte Shaep restaurant?) Or are we comparing apples and bananas? Can one compare the joys of reading Joyce with the pleasures of a good glass of wine? The problem with adding a conception of the quality of pleasure is that it destroys just that simple evaluation device that seemed to be the most obvious virtue of utilitarianism. And, in deciding the relative quality of pleasures, is there not also the tendency to slip into just that a priori mode of thinking that Mill was so concerned to reject? (For example: "It doesn't matter what the consequences are, art is good in itself." Or in the lingo of the late nineteenth century, "Art for art's sake.")

In *Utilitarianism,* Mill first defines what he means by the name of his theory, but then he also goes on to "prove" and defend it. The "proof" is qualified by the fact that—as Mill tells us—one cannot actually prove ultimate principles. Bentham had claimed this, too, that defending the principle of utility was "as impossible as it is needless." It was a simple fact of nature, Bentham had argued, that everything we do was governed by "the two sovereign masters, pleasure and pain." ("In words a man may pretend to abjure their empire; but in reality he will remain subject to it all the while.") Nevertheless, Mill does provide us with a proof, and it has become perhaps the single most controversial element of his ethics. We will encounter and discuss it in chapter 4, "Of What Sort of Proof the Principle of Utility Is Susceptible." Finally, Mill takes on one of the most damaging objections to utilitarianism— its apparent inability to adequately account for justice. After all, if the only measures of right and wrong are the amounts and qualities of pleasure and pain, what grounds are there for people's rights (for example, the right to a fair share or the right not to be tortured) when these do not promote "the greatest good for the greatest number"? (See Mill's chapter 5.)

UTILITARIANISM*

HAPPINESS AND THE *SUMMUM BONUM:* CHAPTER 1

In his General Remarks in chapter 1, Mill addresses the question of the *summum bonum,* the "foundation of morality." He points out that utilitarianism has been a viable candidate for that exalted conceptual position ever since Socrates and the Sophists, but it has often been confused. He asserts the resolutely teleological orientation of his ethics: "All action is for the sake of some end." "Rules of action," he adds, "take their whole character and color from the end to which they are subservient." Having thus attacked Kant's position (though not yet Kant by name), he then claims that "all those *a priori* moralists" ("who deem it necessary to argue at all") in fact find utilitarian arguments "indispensable" to them, whether or not they admit this. Finally referring to Kant with great respect, Mill points out that even he could not defend an ethic of pure duty that would allow him to deduce any substantial specific conclusion.

There are few circumstances among those which make up the present condition of human knowledge more unlike what might have been expected, or more significant of the backward state in which speculation on the most important subjects still lingers, than the little progress which has been made in the decision of the controversy respecting the criterion of right and wrong. From the dawn of philosophy, the question concerning the *summum bonum,* or, what is the same thing, concerning the foundation of morality, has been accounted the main problem in speculative thought, has occupied the most gifted intellects and divided them into sects and schools, carrying on a vigorous warfare against one another. And after more than two thousand years the same discussions continue, philosophers are still ranged under the same contending banners, and neither thinkers nor mankind at large seem nearer to being unanimous on the subject than when the youth Socrates listened to the old Protagoras, and asserted (if Plato's dialogue be grounded on a real conversation) the theory of utilitarianism against the popular morality of the so-called sophist.

*J. S. Mill, *Utilitarianism,* edited by George Sher. Copyright 1979 by Hacket Publishing Company, Inc.

It is true that similar confusion and uncertainty and, in some cases, similar discordance exist respecting the first principles of all the sciences, not excepting that which is deemed the most certain of them—mathematics, without much impairing, generally indeed without impairing at all, the trustworthiness of the conclusions of those sciences. An apparent anomaly, the explanation of which is that the detailed doctrines of a science are not usually deduced from, nor depend for their evidence upon, what are called its first principles. Were it not so, there would be no science more precarious, or whose conclusions were more insufficiently made out, than algebra, which derives none of its certainty from what are commonly taught to learners as its elements, since these, as laid down by some of its most eminent teachers, are as full of fictions as English law, and of mysteries as theology. The truths which are ultimately accepted as the first principles of a science are really the last results of metaphysical analysis, practised on the elementary notions with which the science is conversant; and their relation to the science is not that of foundations to an edifice, but of roots to a tree, which may perform their office equally well though they be never dug down to and exposed to light. But though in science the particular truth precede the general theory, the contrary might be expected to be the case with a practical art, such as morals or legislation. All action is for the sake of some end, and rules of action, it seems natural to suppose, must take their whole character and color from the end to which they are subservient. When we engage in a pursuit, a clear and precise conception of what we are pursuing would seem to be the first thing we need, instead of the last we are to look forward to. A test of right and wrong must be the means, one would think, of ascertaining what is right or wrong, and not a consequence of having already ascertained it.

The difficulty is not avoided by having recourse to the popular theory of a natural faculty, a sense or instinct, informing us of right and wrong. For—besides that the existence of such a moral instinct is itself one of the matters in dispute—those believers in it who have any pretensions to philosophy have been obliged to abandon the idea that it discerns what is right or wrong in the particular case in hand, as our other senses discern the sight or sound actually present. Our moral faculty, according to all those of its interpreters who are entitled to the name of thinkers, supplies us only with the general principles of moral judgments; it is a branch of our reason, not of our sensitive faculty; and must be looked to for the abstract doctrines of morality, not for perception of it in the concrete. The intuitive, no less than what may be termed the inductive, school of ethics insists on the necessity of general laws. They both agree that the morality of an individual action is not a question of direct perception, but of the application of a law to an individual case. They recognize also, to a great extent, the same moral laws, but differ as to their evidence and the source from which they derive their authority. According to the one opinion, the principles of morals are evident *a priori,* requiring nothing to command assent except that the meaning of the terms be understood. According to the other doctrine, right and wrong, as well as truth and falsehood, are questions of observation and experience. But both hold equally that morality must be deduced from principles; and the intuitive school affirm as strongly as the inductive that there is a science of morals.

Yet they seldom attempt to make out a list of the *a priori* principles which are to serve as the premises of the science; still more rarely do they make any effort to reduce those various principles to one first principle, or common ground of obligation. They either assume the ordinary precepts of morals as of *a priori* authority, or they lay down as the common groundwork of those maxims, some generality much less obviously authoritative than the maxims themselves, and which has never succeeded in gaining popular acceptance. Yet to support their pretensions there ought either to be some one fundamental principle or law at the root of all morality, or, if there be several, there should be a determinate order of precedence among them; and the one principle, or the rule for deciding between the various principles when they conflict, ought to be self-evident.

To inquire how far the bad effects of this deficiency have been mitigated in practice, or to what extent the moral beliefs of mankind have been vitiated or made uncertain by the absence of any distinct recognition of an ultimate standard, would imply a complete survey and criticism of past and present ethical doctrine. It would, however, be easy to show that whatever steadiness or consistency these moral beliefs have attained has been mainly due to the tacit influence of a standard not recognized. Although the non-existence of an acknowledged first principle has made ethics not so much a guide as a consecration of men's actual sentiments, still, as men's sentiments, both in favor and of aversion, are greatly influenced by what they suppose to be the effect of things upon their happiness, the principle of utility, or, as Bentham latterly called it, the greatest happiness principle, has had a large share in forming the moral doctrines even of those who most scornfully reject its authority. Nor is there any school of thought which refuses to admit that the influence of actions on happiness is a most material and even predominant consideration in many of the details, of morals, however unwilling to acknowledge it as the fundamental principle of morality and the source of moral obligation. I might go much further and say that to all those *a priori* moralists who deem it necessary to argue at all, utilitarian arguments are indispensable. It is not my present purpose to criticize these thinkers; but I cannot help referring, for illustration, to a systematic treatise by one of the most illustrious of them, the *Metaphysics of Ethics* by Kant. This remarkable man, whose system of thought will long remain one of the landmarks in the history of philosophical speculation, does, in the treatise in question, lay down a universal first principle as the origin and ground of moral obligation; it is this: "So act that the rule on which thou actest would admit of being adopted as a law by all rational beings." But when he begins to deduce from this precept any of the actual duties of morality, he fails, almost grotesquely, to show that there would be any contradiction, any logical (not to say physical) impossibility, in the adoption by all rational beings of the most outrageously immoral rules of conduct. All he knows is that the *consequences* of their universal adoption would be such as no one would choose to incur.

On the present occasion, I shall, without further discussion of the other theories, attempt to contribute something towards the understanding and appreciation of the "utilitarian" or "happiness" theory, and towards such proof as it is susceptible of. It is evident that this cannot be proof in the ordinary and popular meaning of the term. Questions of ultimate ends are not amenable to direct proof. Whatever can be proved to be good must be so by being shown to be a means to something admitted to be good without proof. The medical art is proved to be good by its conducing to health; but how is it possible to prove that health is good? The art of music is good, for the reason, among others, that it produces pleasure; but what proof is it possible to give that pleasure is good? If, then, it is asserted that there is a comprehensive formula, including all things which are in themselves good, and that whatever else is good is not so as an end but as a means, the formula may be accepted or rejected, but is not a subject of what is commonly understood by proof. We are not, however, to infer that its acceptance or rejection must depend on blind impulse, or arbitrary choice. There is a larger meaning of the word "proof," in which this question is as amenable to it as any other of the disputed questions of philosophy. The subject is within the cognizance of the rational faculty; and neither does that faculty deal with it solely in the way of intuition. Considerations may be presented capable of determining the intellect either to give or withhold its assent to the doctrine; and this is equivalent to proof.

We shall examine presently of what nature are these considerations; in what manner they apply to the case, and what rational grounds, therefore, can be given for accepting or rejecting the utilitarian formula. But it is a preliminary condition of rational acceptance or rejection, that the formula should be correctly understood. I believe that the very imperfect notion ordinarily formed of its meaning, is the chief obstacle which impedes its reception; and that could it be cleared, even from only the grosser misconceptions, the question would be greatly simplified, and a proportion of its difficulties removed. Before, therefore, I attempt to enter into the philosophical grounds which can be given for assenting to the utilitarian standard, I shall offer some illustrations of the doctrine itself; with the view of showing more clearly what it is, distinguishing it from what it is not, and disposing of such of the practical objections to it as either originate in, or are closely connected with, mistaken interpretations of its meaning. Having thus prepared the ground, I shall afterwards endeavour to throw such light as I can upon the question, considered as one of philosophical theory.

DISCUSSION

Mill, like Aristotle, begins his ethics with a clear statement of a teleological position. There is an ultimate good—a *summum bonum*—and all our actions are aimed (well or foolishly) toward that good. Like Aristotle, too, Mill insists that this good is happiness, but for Mill and most modern thinkers, happiness refers more to a state of mind than to achievements or circumstances as Aristotle might have thought. It is essential, Mill insists, that we look to the actual consequences of our actions, but the value of these consequences depends on their effect on us, whether we are satisfied or frustrated, pleased or displeased, caused pleasure or pain. Thus Mill, unlike Aristotle, allows for different interpretations of what it means to be happy; we all want happiness, but it is up to the individual to define what that happiness will look like.

How can Mill prove that the ultimate goal of all of our actions is happiness? He does appeal to the general agreement that this is so (as Aristotle does), but this does not constitute a proof. He considers the views of such moral philosophers as Kant, but these are acceptable only insofar as they too advance happiness. Finally, Mill acknowledges that there may be no proper "proof" of an ultimate principle, because if there were, those principles used to establish the purportedly "ultimate principle" would in turn require proof, and so on *ad infinitum.* Nevertheless Mill is confident that he can give us good reasons for accepting the principle that happiness is the sole value in life. In fact, he offers us a very famous "proof" (in chapter 4) that philosophers have been picking apart ever since. But whether or not it is provable, the happiness principle—that what we all want and what all ethics is aimed at is happiness—is well established as the starting point of Mill's utilitarianism.

WHAT UTILITARIANISM IS: CHAPTER 2

In chapter 2, Mill presents his doctrine concerning the *quality* of pleasures, attacking those who say that utilitarianism celebrates only the vulgar pleasures and ignores the "higher" values in life. Mill's model here is the ancient philosopher Epicurus (from whose name we get our word "epicurean" for someone fond of luxury and the good life). Epicurus (341–270 B.C.) also taught that the good life is the life of pleasure, but he too had to convince his critics that he did not mean only mindless bodily pleasures but intellectual and spiritual pleasures as well. Indeed, Epicurus spent considerable time lecturing his students on the abuses of hedonism (the life of pleasure) and the dangers of excess, and he spent equal time lauding the pleasures of philosophy and the arts. Mill makes the same point: that those who accuse utilitarianism of vulgarity are themselves degrading human life by supposing that only the "lower" pleasures are indeed pleasurable.

It is here too that Mill provides us with his actual criterion for deciding the quality of pleasures: "It is better to be a human being dissatisfied than a pig satisfied: better to be a Socrates dissatisfied than a fool satisfied." But how can we know this? Isn't this just a fraternal expression of support of one philosopher by another? But Mill gives us a test; Socrates knows *both* the life of bodily pleasure and the more difficult life of the mind and *chooses* the latter. The fool and the pig, however, "know only their own side of the question." The test, in other words, is which pleasure is to be chosen by those who know both of them.

The problem is *why* they choose. When Socrates chooses the pleasures of the mind—however dissatisfying—over the pleasures of the body, on what grounds does he do so? If the former are simply more pleasurable, then we are back to a purely quantitative measure, not a qualitative test. Does Socrates's choice reflect a difference in the quality of pleasures or only his (and Mill's) preference? And is it true that Socrates (or Mill, or we) have a choice, or are we abstract-minded creatures just as caught up in our life of reflection (however modest in its quality) as the fool and the pig are caught up in their life of vulgar hedonism?

Notice that Mill—in direct opposition to Kant—denies that there is any particular virtue to acting "for the sake of duty"; it is important only that our actions are *in accordance with* duty. It is results that count, and although the motive may be relevant to our opinion of the agent, it is irrelevant to the worth of the action.

Mill begins, briefly and sarcastically, by attacking those critics who, on the other side, object that utility is a concept opposed to pleasure (as in the emphasis on mere efficiency demanded by some people, to the exclusion of any enjoyment). Mill essentially calls them stupid and not worth attending to and then pronounces his quality of pleasure doctrine, finally turning once again to his critics (including Thomas Carlyle, one of the great writers and thinkers of the time).

A passing remark is all that needs be given to the ignorant blunder of supposing that those who stand up for utility as the test of right and wrong use the term in that restricted and merely colloquial sense in which utility is opposed to pleasure. An apology is due to the philosophical opponents of utilitarianism, for even the momentary appearance of confounding them with anyone capable of so absurd a misconception; which is the most extraordinary, inasmuch as the contrary accusation, of referring everything to pleasure, and that, too, in its grossest form, is another of the common charges against utilitarianism: and, as has been pointedly remarked by an able writer, the same sort of persons, and often the very same persons, denounce the theory "as impracticably dry when the word 'utility' precedes the word 'pleasure,' and as too practically voluptuous when the word 'pleasure' precedes the word 'utility'." Those who know anything about the matter are aware that every writer, from Epicurus to Bentham, who maintained the theory of utility, meant by it, not something to be contradistinguished from pleasure, but pleasure itself, together with exemption from pain; and instead of opposing the useful to the agreeable or the ornamental, have always declared that the useful means these, among other things. Yet the common herd, including the herd of writers, not only in newspapers and periodicals, but in books of weight and pretension, are perpetually falling into this shallow mistake. Having caught up the word "utilitarian" while knowing nothing whatever about it but its sound they habitually express by it the rejection or the neglect of pleasure in some of its forms: of beauty, or ornament or of amusement. Nor is the term thus ignorantly misapplied solely in disparagement, but occasionally in compliment, as though it implied superiority to frivolity and the mere pleasures of the moment. And this perverted use is the only one in which the word is popularly known, and the one from which the new generation are acquiring their sole notion of its meaning. Those who introduced the word, but who had for many years discontinued it as a distinctive appellation, may well feel themselves called upon to resume it if by doing so they can hope to contribute anything towards rescuing it from this utter degradation.

The creed which accepts as the foundation of morals "utility" or the "greatest happiness principle" holds that actions are right in proportion as they tend to promote happiness, wrong as they tend to produce the reverse of happiness. By happiness is intended pleasure, and the absence of pain; by unhappiness, pain, and the privation of pleasure. To give a clear view of the moral standard set up by the theory, much more requires to be said; in particular, what things it includes in the ideas of pain and pleasure; and to what extent this is left an open question. But these supplementary explanations do not affect the theory of life on which this theory of morality is grounded—namely, that pleasure and freedom from pain are the only things desirable as ends; and that all desirable things (which are as numerous in the utilitarian as in any other scheme) are desirable either for the pleasure inherent in themselves, or as means to the promotion of pleasure and the prevention of pain.

Now such a theory of life excites in many minds, and among them in some of the most estimable in feeling and purpose, inveterate dislike. To suppose that life has (as they express it) no higher end than pleasure—no better and nobler object of desire and pursuit—they designate as utterly mean and groveling; as a doctrine worthy only of swine, to whom the followers of Epicurus were, at a very early period, contemptuously likened; and modern holders of the doctrine are occasionally made the subject of equally polite comparisons by its German, French, and English assailants.

When thus attacked, the Epicureans have always answered that it is not they, but their accusers, who represent human nature in a degrading light, since the accusation supposes human beings to be capable of no pleasures except those of which swine are capable. If this supposition were true, the charge could not be gainsaid, but would then be no longer an imputation; for if the sources of pleasure were precisely the same to human beings and to swine, the rule of life which is good enough for the one would be good enough for the other. The comparison of the Epicurean life to that of beasts is felt as degrading, precisely because a beast's pleasures do not satisfy a human being's conceptions of happiness. Human beings have faculties more elevated than the animal appetites and, when once made conscious of them, do not regard anything as happiness which does not include their gratification. I do not, indeed, consider the Epicureans to have been by any means faultless in drawing out their scheme of consequences from the utilitarian principle. To do this in any sufficient manner, many Stoic, as well as Christian, elements require to be included. But there is no known Epicurean theory of life which does not assign to the pleasures of the intellect, of the feelings and imagination, and of the moral sentiments, a much higher value of pleasures than to those of mere sensation. It must be admitted, however, that utilitarian writers in general have placed the superiority of mental over bodily pleasures chiefly in the greater permanency, safety, uncostliness, etc., of the former—that is, in their circumstantial advantages rather than in their intrinsic nature. And on all these points utilitarians have fully proved their case; but they might have taken the other and, as it may be called, higher ground with entire consistency. It is quite compatible with the principle of utility to recognize the fact that some kinds of pleasure are more desirable and more valuable than others. It would be absurd that, while, in estimating all other things, quality is considered as well as quantity, the estimation of pleasures should be supposed to depend on quantity alone.

If I am asked what I mean by difference of quality in pleasures, or what makes one pleasure more valuable than another, merely as a pleasure, except its being greater in amount, there is but one possible answer. Of two pleasures, if there be one to which all or almost all who have experience of both give a decided preference, irrespective of a feeling of moral obligation to prefer it, that is the more desirable pleasure. If one of the two is, by those who are competently acquainted with both, placed so far above the other that they prefer it, even though knowing it to be attended with a greater amount of discontent, and would not resign it for any quantity of the other pleasure which their nature is capable of, we are justified in ascribing to the preferred enjoyment a superiority in quality so far outweighing quantity as to render it, in comparison, of small account.

Now it is an unquestionable fact that those who are equally acquainted with and equally capable of appreciating and enjoying both, do give a most marked preference to the manner of existence which employs their higher faculties. Few human creatures would consent to be changed into any of the lower animals for a promise of the fullest allowance of a beast's pleasures; no intelligent human being would consent to be a fool, no instructed person would be an ignoramus, no person of feeling and conscience would be selfish and base, even though they should be persuaded that the fool, the dunce, or the rascal is better satisfied with his lot than they are with theirs. They would not resign what they possess more than he for the most complete satisfaction of all the desires which they have in common with him. If they ever fancy they would, it is only in cases of unhappiness so extreme that to escape from it they would exchange their lot for almost any other, however undesirable in their own eyes. A being of higher faculties requires more to make him happy, is capable probably of more acute suffering, and certainly accessible to it at more points, than one of an inferior type; but in spite of these liabilities, he can never really wish to sink into what he feels to be a lower grade of existence. We may give what explanation we please of this unwillingness; we may attribute it to pride, a name which is given indiscriminately to some of the most and to some of the least estimable feelings of which mankind are capable: we may refer it to the love of liberty and personal independence, an appeal to which was with the Stoics one of the most effective means for the inculcation of it; to the love of power or to the love of excitement, both of which do really enter into and contribute to it; but its most appropriate appellation is a sense of dignity, which all human beings possess in one form or other, and in some, though by no means in exact, proportion to their higher faculties, and which is so essential a part of the happiness of those in whom it is strong that nothing which conflicts with it could be otherwise than momentarily an object of desire to them. Whoever supposes that this preference takes place at a sacrifice of happiness—that the superior being, in anything like equal circumstances, is not happier than the inferior—confounds the two very different ideas of happiness and content. It is indisputable that the being whose capacities of enjoyment are low has the greatest chance of having them fully satisfied; and a highly endowed being will always feel that any happiness which he can look for, as the world is constituted, is imperfect. But he can learn to bear its imperfections, if they are at all bearable; and they will not make him envy the being who is indeed unconscious of the imperfections, but only because he feels not at all the good which those imperfections qualify. It is better to be a human being dissatisfied than a pig satisfied: better to be Socrates dissatisfied than a fool satisfied. And if the fool, or the pig, are of a different opinion, it is because they only know their own side of the question. The other party to the comparison knows both sides.

It may be objected that many who are capable of the higher pleasures occasionally, under the influence of temptation, postpone them to the lower. But this is quite compatible with a full appreciation of the intrinsic superiority of the higher. Men often, from infirmity of character, make their election for the nearer good, though they know it to be the less valuable; and this no less when the choice is between two bodily pleasures than when it is between bodily and mental. They pursue sensual indulgences to the injury of health, though perfectly aware that health is the greater good. It may be further objected that many who begin with youthful enthusiasm for everything noble, as they advance in years, sink into indolence and selfishness. But I do not believe that those who undergo this very common change voluntarily choose the lower description of pleasures in preference to the higher. I believe that, before they devote themselves exclusively to the one, they have already become incapable of the other. Capacity for the nobler feelings is in most natures a very tender plant, easily killed, not only by hostile influences, but by mere want of sustenance; and in the majority of young persons it speedily dies away if the occupations to which their position in life has devoted them, and the society into which it has thrown them, are not favorable to keeping that higher capacity in exercise. Men lose their high aspirations as they lose their intellectual tastes, because they have not time or opportunity for indulging them; and they addict themselves to inferior pleasures, not because they deliberately prefer them, but because they are either the only ones to which they have access, or the only ones which they are any longer capable of enjoying. It may be questioned whether any one who has remained equally susceptible to both classes of pleasures, ever knowingly and calmly preferred the lower, though many, in all ages, have broken down in an ineffectual attempt to combine both.

From this verdict of the only competent judges, I apprehend there can be no appeal. On a question which is the best worth having of two pleasures, or which of two modes of existence is the most grateful to the feelings, apart from its moral attributes and from its consequences, the judgment of those who are qualified by knowledge of both, or, if they differ, that of the majority of them, must be admitted as final. And there needs be the less hesitation to accept this judgment respecting the quality of pleasures, since there is no other tribunal to be referred to even on the question of quantity. What means are there of determining which is the acutest of two pains, or the intensest of two pleasurable sensations, except the general suffrage of those who are familiar with both? Neither pains nor pleasures are homogeneous, and pain is always heterogeneous with pleasure. What is there to decide whether a particular pleasure is worth purchasing at the cost of a particular pain, except the feelings and judgment of the experienced? When, therefore, those feelings and judgment declare the pleasures derived from the higher faculties to be preferable *in kind,* apart from the question of intensity, to those of which the animal nature, disjoined from the higher faculties, is susceptible, they are entitled on this subject to the same regard.

Mill now introduces a crucial further component to utilitarian theory—the requirement that one consider everyone's happiness equally. The theory does not, in other words, prompt us to pursue our own happiness at the expense of the happiness of others, but rather requires us to be "a disinterested and benevolent spectator," viewing our own interests as on a par with those of others. Thus, Mill argues, even if it were not the case that the noble pleasures lead to greater happiness for the individual, it is obvious that the pursuit of such pleasures will bring greater happiness to society as a whole. For instance (returning again to Kant's example of developing one's talents), the person who develops her musical or artistic abilities clearly contributes more to society than the one who simply works on her beer-drinking skills.

After briefly making this point (he will develop it further later), Mill goes on to consider the objection that happiness cannot be the ultimate good because it is unattainable. His response to this is that it depends on what you mean by "happiness." In the utilitarian view, it is neither a life without any pain whatsoever nor one of constant rapture; both conceptions are highly unrealistic. Rather, the sort of life Mill has in mind as the goal to be aimed at is one in which there is a reasonable balance of tranquility (absence of pain) and genuine enjoyment of lasting pleasures. And this sort of happiness should be attainable by every member of society (here again, Mill's requirement that everyone's interests are to count equally is important). Many, if not all, the impediments to the attainment of this goal can be overcome by better education, better laws, and a more just distribution of wealth. It is, in other words, very much within our power to do away with most of the sources of pain. Mill was in fact very much involved in a social reform movement at the time, called "philosophic radicalism," that sought to do just this through political, legal, and social means.

Finally, Mill considers and answers various other objections that have been made against utilitarianism.

I have dwelt on this point, as being a necessary part of a perfectly just conception of utility or happiness considered as the directive rule of human conduct. But it is by no means an indispensable condition to the acceptance of the utilitarian standard; for that standard is not the agent's own greatest happiness, but the greatest amount of happiness altogether; and if it may possibly be doubted whether a noble character is always the happier for its nobleness, there can be no doubt that it makes other people happier, and that the world in general is immensely a gainer by it. Utilitarianism, therefore, could only attain its end by the general cultivation of nobleness of character, even if each individual were only benefited by the nobleness of others, and his own, so far as happiness is concerned, were a sheer deduction from the benefit. But the bare enunciation of such an absurdity as this last, renders refutation superfluous.

According to the Greatest Happiness Principle, as above explained, the ultimate end, with reference to and for the sake of which all other things are desirable (whether we are considering our own good or that of other people), is an existence exempt as far as possible from pain, and as rich as possible in enjoyments, both in point of quantity and quality; the test of quality, and the rule for measuring it against quantity, being the preference felt by those who, in their opportunities of experience, to which must be added their habits of self-consciousness and self-observation, are best furnished with the means of comparison. This, being, according to the utilitarian opinion, the end of human action, is necessarily also the standard of morality; which may accordingly be defined, the rules and precepts for human conduct, by the observance of which an existence such as has been described might be, to the greatest extent possible, secured to all mankind; and not to them only, but, so far as the nature of things admits, to the whole sentient creation.

Against this doctrine, however, rises another class of objectors, who say that happiness, in any form, cannot be the rational purpose of human life and action; because, in the first place, it is unattainable: and they contemptuously ask, What right hast thou to be happy? a question which Mr. Carlyle clenches by the addition, What right, a short time ago, hadst thou even *to be?* Next, they say, that men can do *without* happiness; that all noble human beings have felt this, and could not have become noble but by learning the lesson of *Entsagen,* or renunciation; which lesson, thoroughly learnt and submitted to, they affirm to be the beginning and necessary condition of all virtue.

The first of these objections would go to the root of the matter were it well founded; for if no happiness is to be had at all by human beings, the attainment of it cannot be the end of morality, or of any rational conduct. Though, even in that case, something might still be said for the utilitarian theory; since utility includes not solely the pursuit of happiness, but the prevention or mitigation of unhappiness; and if the former aim be chimerical, there will be all the greater scope and more imperative need for the latter, so long at least as mankind think fit to live, and do not take refuge in the simultaneous act of suicide recommended under certain conditions by Novalis. When, however, it is thus positively asserted to be impossible that human life should be happy, the assertion, if not something like a verbal quibble, is at least an exaggeration. If by happiness be meant a continuity of highly pleasurable excitement, it is evident enough that this is impossible. A state of exalted pleasure lasts only moments, or in some cases, and with some intermissions, hours or days, and is the occasional brilliant flash of enjoyment, not its permanent and steady flame. Of this the philosophers who have taught that happiness is the end of life were as fully aware as those who taunt them. The happiness which they meant was not a life of rapture; but moments of such, in an existence made up of few and transitory pains, many and various pleasures, with a decided predominance of the active over the passive, and having as the foundation of the whole, not to expect more from life than it is capable of bestowing. A life thus composed, to those who have been fortunate enough to obtain it, has always appeared worthy of the name of happiness. And such an existence is even now the lot of many, during some considerable portion of their lives. The present wretched education, and wretched social arrangements, are the only real hindrance to its being attainable by almost all.

The objectors perhaps may doubt whether human beings, if taught to consider happiness as the end of life, would be satisfied with such a moderate share of it. But great numbers of mankind have been satisfied with much less. The main constituents of a satisfied life appear to be two, either of which by itself is often found sufficient for the purpose: tranquillity, and excitement. With much tranquillity, many find that they can be content with very little pleasure: with much excitement, many can reconcile themselves to a considerable quantity of pain. There is assuredly no inherent impossibility in enabling even the mass of mankind to unite both; since the two are so far from being incompatible that they are in natural alliance, the prolongation of either being a preparation for, and exciting a wish for, the other. It is only those in whom indolence amounts to a vice, that do not desire excitement after an interval of repose; it is only those in whom the need of excitement is a disease, that feel the tranquillity which follows excitement dull and insipid, instead of pleasurable in direct proportion to the excitement which preceded it. When people who are tolerably fortunate in their outward lot do not find in life sufficient enjoyment to make it valuable to them, the cause generally is, caring for nobody but themselves. To those who have neither public nor private affections, the excitements of life are much curtailed, and in any case dwindle in value as the time approaches when all selfish interests must be terminated by death: while those who leave after them objects of personal affection, and especially those who have also cultivated a fellow-feeling with the collective interests of mankind, retain as lively an interest in life on the eve of death as in the vigour of youth and health. Next to selfishness, the principal cause which makes life unsatisfactory, is want of mental cultivation. A cultivated mind—I do not mean that of a philosopher, but any mind to which the fountains of knowledge have been opened, and which has been taught, in any tolerable degree, to exercise its faculties—finds sources of inexhaustible interest in all that surrounds it; in the objects of nature, the achievements of art, the imaginations of poetry, the incidents of history, the ways of mankind past and present, and their prospects in the future. It is possible, indeed, to become indifferent to all this, and that too without having exhausted a thousandth part of it; but only when one has had from the beginning no moral or human interest in these things and has sought in them only the gratification of curiosity.

Now there is absolutely no reason in the nature of things why an amount of mental culture sufficient to give an intelligent interest in these objects of contemplation, should not be the inheritance of every one born in a civilised country. As little is there an inherent necessity that any human being should be a selfish egotist, devoid of every feeling or care but those which centre in his own miserable individuality. Something far superior to this is sufficiently common even now, to give ample earnest of what the human species may be made. Genuine private affections, and a sincere interest in the public good, are possible, though in unequal degrees, to every rightly brought up human being. In a world in which there is so much to interest, so much to enjoy, and so much also to correct and improve, everyone who has this moderate amount of moral and intellectual requisites is capable of an existence which may be called enviable, and unless such a person, through bad laws, or subjection to the will of others, is denied the liberty to use the sources of happiness within his reach, he will not fail to find this enviable existence, if he escape the positive evils of life, the great sources of physical and mental suffering—such as indigence, disease, and the unkindness, worthlessness, or premature loss of objects of affection. The main stress of the problem lies, therefore, in the contest with these calamities, from which it is a rare good fortune entirely to escape; which, as things now are cannot be obviated, and often cannot be in any material degree mitigated. Yet no one whose opinion deserves a moment's consideration can doubt that most of the great positive evils of the world are in themselves removable, and will, if human affairs continue to improve, be in the end reduced within narrow limits. Poverty, in any sense implying suffering, may be completely extinguished by the wisdom of society, combined with the good sense and providence of individuals. Even that most intractable of enemies, disease, may be indefinitely reduced in dimensions by good physical and moral education, and proper control of noxious influences; while the progress of science holds out a promise for the future of still more direct conquests over this detestable foe. And every advance in that direction relieves us from some, not only of the chances which cut short our own lives, but, what concerns us still more, which deprive us of those in whom our happiness is wrapt up. As for vicissitudes of fortune, and other disappointments connected with worldly circumstances, these are principally the effect either of gross imprudence, of ill-regulated desires, or of bad or imperfect social institutions. All the grand sources, in short, of human suffering are in a great degree, many of them almost entirely, conquerable by human care and effort; and though their removal is grievously slow—though a long succession of generations will perish in the breach before the conquest is completed, and this world becomes all that, if will and knowledge were not wanting, it might easily be made—yet every mind sufficiently intelligent and generous to bear a part, however small and inconspicuous, in the endeavour, will draw a noble enjoyment from the contest itself, which he would not for any bribe in the form of selfish indulgence consent to be without.

And this leads to the true estimation of what is said by the objectors concerning the possibility and the obligation, of learning to do without happiness. Unquestionably it is possible to do without happiness; it is done involuntarily by nineteen-twentieths of mankind, even in those parts of our present world which are least deep in barbarism; and it often has to be done voluntarily by the hero or the martyr, for the sake of something which he prizes more than his individual happiness. But this something, what is it, unless the happiness of others, or some of the requisites of happiness? It is noble to be capable of resigning entirely one's own portion of happiness, or chances of it: but, after all, this self-sacrifice must be for some end; it is not its own end; and if we are told that its end is not happiness, but virtue, which is better than happiness, I ask, would the sacrifice be made if the hero or martyr did not believe that it would earn for others immunity from similar sacrifices? Would it be made, if he thought that his renunciation of happiness for himself would produce no fruit for any of his fellow creatures, but to make their lot like his, and place them also in the condition of persons who have renounced happiness? All honour to those who can abnegate for themselves the personal enjoyment of life, when by such renunciation they contribute worthily to increase the amount of happiness in the world; but he who does it, or professes to do it, for any other purpose, is no more deserving of admiration than the ascetic mounted on his pillar. He may be an inspiring proof of what men *can* do, but assuredly not an example of what they *should.*

Though it is only in a very imperfect state of the world's arrangements that any one can best serve the happiness of others by the absolute sacrifice of his own, yet so long as the world is in that imperfect state, I fully acknowledge that the readiness to make such a sacrifice is the highest virtue which can be found in man. I will add, that in this condition of the world, paradoxical as the assertion may be, the conscious ability to do without happiness gives the best prospect of realising such happiness as is attainable. For nothing except that consciousness can raise a person above the chances of life, by making him feel that, let fate and fortune do their worst, they have not power to subdue him: which, once felt, frees him from excess of anxiety concerning the evils of life, and enables him, like many a Stoic in the worst times of the Roman Empire, to cultivate in tranquillity the sources of satisfaction accessible to him, without concerning himself about the uncertainty of their duration, any more than about their inevitable end.

Meanwhile, let utilitarians never cease to claim the morality of self-devotion as a possession which belongs by as good a right to them, as either to the Stoic or to the Transcendentalist. The utilitarian morality does recognise in human beings the power of sacrificing their own greatest good for the good of others. It only refuses to admit that the sacrifice is itself a good. A sacrifice which does not increase, or tend to increase, the sum total of happiness, it considers as wasted. The only self-renunciation which it applauds is devotion to the happiness, or to some of the means of happiness, of others; either of mankind collectively, or of individuals within the limits imposed by the collective interests of mankind.

I must again repeat, what the assailants of utilitarianism seldom have the justice to acknowledge, that the happiness which forms the utilitarian standard of what is right in conduct, is not the agent's own happiness, but that of all concerned. As between his own happiness and that of others, utilitarianism requires him to be as strictly impartial as a disinterested and benevolent spectator. In the golden rule of Jesus of Nazareth, we read the complete spirit of the ethics of utility. To do as one would be done by, and to love one's neighbour as oneself constitute the ideal perfection of utilitarian morality. As the means of making the nearest approach to this ideal, utility would enjoin, first, that laws and social arrangements should place the happiness, or (as speaking practically it may be called) the interest, of every individual, as nearly as possible in harmony with the interest of the whole; and secondly, that education and opinion, which have so vast a power over human character, should so use that power as to establish in the mind of every individual an indissoluble association between his own happiness and the good of the whole; especially between his own happiness and the practice of such modes of conduct, negative and positive, as regard for the universal happiness prescribes: so that not only he may be unable to conceive the possibility of happiness to himself, consistently with conduct opposed to the general good, but also that a direct impulse to promote the general good may be in every individual one of the habitual motives of action, and the sentiments connected therewith may fill a large and prominent place in every human being's sentient existence. If the impugners of the utilitarian morality represented it to their own minds in this its true character, I know not what recommendation possessed by any other morality they could possibly affirm to be wanting to it: what more beautiful or more exalted developments of human nature any other ethical system can be supposed to foster, or what springs of action, not accessible to the utilitarian, such systems rely on for giving effect to their mandates.

The objectors to utilitarianism cannot always be charged with representing it in a discreditable light. On the contrary, those among them who entertain anything like a just idea of its disinterested character, sometimes find fault with its standard as being too high for humanity. They say it is exacting too much to require that people shall always act from the inducement of promoting the general interests of society. But this is to mistake the very meaning of a standard of morals, and to confound the rule of action with the motive of it. It is the business of ethics to tell us what are our duties, or by what test we may know them; but no system of ethics requires that the sole motive of all we do shall be a feeling of duty; on the contrary, ninety-nine hundredths of all our actions are done from other motives, and rightly so done, if the rule of duty does not condemn them. It is the more unjust to utilitarianism that this particular misapprehension should be made a ground of objection to it, inasmuch as utilitarian moralists have gone beyond almost all others in affirming that the motive has nothing to do with the morality of the action, though much with the worth of the agent. He who saves a fellow creature from drowning does what is morally right, whether his motive be duty, or the hope of being paid for his trouble: he who betrays the friend that trusts him, is guilty of a crime, even if his object be to serve another friend to whom he is under greater obligations. But to speak only of actions done from the motive of duty, and in direct obedience to principle: it is a misapprehension of the utilitarian mode of thought, to conceive it as implying that people should fix their minds upon so wide a generality as the world, or society at large. The great majority of good actions are intended, not for the benefit of the world, but for that of individuals, of which the good of the world is made up; and the thoughts of the most virtuous man need not on these occasions travel beyond the particular persons concerned, except so far as is necessary to assure himself that in benefiting them he is not violating the rights—that is, the legitimate and authorized expectations—of any one else. The multiplication of happiness is, according to the utilitarian ethics, the object of virtue: the occasions on which any person (except one in a thousand) has it in his power to do this on an extended scale, in other words, to be a public benefactor, are but exceptional; and on these occasions alone is he called on to consider public utility; in every other case, private utility, the interest or happiness of some few persons, is all he has to attend to. Those alone the influence of whose actions extends to society in general, need concern themselves habitually about so large an object. In the case of abstinences indeed—of things which people forbear to do, from moral considerations, though the consequences in the particular case might be beneficial—it would be unworthy of an intelligent agent not to be consciously aware that the action is of a class which, if practised generally, would be generally injurious, and that this is the ground of the obligation to abstain from it. The amount of regard for the public interest implied in this recognition is no greater than is demanded by every system of morals; for they all enjoin to abstain from whatever is manifestly pernicious to society.

The same considerations dispose of another reproach against the doctrine of utility, founded on a still grosser misconception of the purpose of a standard of morality, and of the very meaning of the words right and wrong. It is often affirmed that utilitarianism renders men cold and unsympathizing; that it chills their moral feelings towards individuals; that it makes them regard only the dry and hard consideration of the consequences of actions, not taking into their moral estimate the qualities from which those actions emanate. If the assertion means that they do not allow their judgment respecting the rightness or wrongness of an action to be influenced by their opinion of the qualities of the person who does it, this is a complaint not against utilitarianism, but against any standard of morality at all; for certainly no known ethical standard decides an action to be good or bad because it is done by a good or a bad man, still less because done by an amiable, a brave, or a benevolent man, or the contrary. These considerations are relevant, not to the estimation of actions, but of persons; and there is nothing in the utilitarian theory inconsistent with the fact that there are other things which interest us in persons besides the rightness and wrongness of their actions. The Stoics, indeed, with the paradoxical misuse of language which was part of their system, and by which they strove to raise themselves above all concern about anything but virtue, were fond of saying that he who has that has everything; that he, and only he, is rich, is beautiful, is a king. But no claim of this description is made for the virtuous man by the utilitarian doctrine. Utilitarians are quite aware that there are other desirable possessions and qualities besides virtue, and are perfectly willing to allow to all of them their full worth. They are also aware that a right action does not necessarily indicate a virtuous character, and that actions which are blameable often proceed from qualities entitled to praise. When this is apparent in any particular case, it modifies their estimation, not certainly of the act, but of the agent. I grant that they are, notwithstanding, of opinion, that in the long run the best proof of a good character is good actions; and resolutely refuse to consider any mental disposition as good, of which the predominant tendency is to produce bad conduct. This makes them unpopular with many people; but it is an unpopularity which they must share with every one who regards the distinction between right and wrong in a serious light; and the reproach is not one which a conscientious utilitarian need be anxious to repel.

If no more be meant by the objection than that many utilitarians look on the morality of actions, as measured by the utilitarian standard, with too exclusive a regard, and do not lay sufficient stress upon the other beauties of character which go towards making a human being loveable or admirable, this may be admitted. Utilitarians who have cultivated their moral feelings, but not their sympathies nor their artistic perceptions, do fall into this mistake; and so do all other moralists under the same conditions. What can be said in excuse for other moralists is equally available for them, namely, that if there is to be any error, it is better that it should be on that side. As a matter of fact, we may affirm that among utilitarians as among adherents of other systems, there is every imaginable degree of rigidity and of laxity in the application of their standard: some are even puritanically rigorous, while others are as indulgent as can possibly be desired by sinner or by sentimentalist. But on the whole, a doctrine which brings prominently forward the interest that mankind have in the repression and prevention of conduct which violates the moral law is likely to be inferior to no other in turning the sanctions of opinion against such violations. It is true, the question, What does violate the moral law? is one on which those who recognise different standards of morality are likely now and then to differ. But difference of opinion on moral questions was not first introduced into the world by utilitarianism, while that doctrine does supply, if not always an easy, at all events a tangible and intelligible mode of deciding such differences.

It may not be superfluous to notice a few more of the common misapprehensions of utilitarian ethics, even those which are so obvious and gross that it might appear impossible for any person of candour and intelligence to fall into them: since persons, even of considerable mental endowments, often give themselves so little trouble to understand the bearings of any opinion against which they entertain a prejudice, and men are in general so little conscious of this voluntary ignorance as a defect, that the vulgarest misunderstandings of ethical doctrines are continually met with in the deliberate writings of persons of the greatest pretensions both to high principle and to philosophy. We not uncommonly hear the doctrine of utility inveighed against as a *godless* doctrine. If it be necessary to say anything at all against so mere an assumption, we may say that the question depends upon what idea we have formed of the moral character of the Deity. If it be a true belief that God desires, above all things, the happiness of his creatures, and that this was his purpose in their creation, utility is not only not a godless doctrine, but more profoundly religious than any other. If it be meant that utilitarianism does not recognize the revealed will of God as the supreme law of morals, I answer, that a utilitarian who believes in the perfect goodness and wisdom of God necessarily believes that whatever God has thought fit to reveal on the subject of morals, must fulfill the requirements of utility in a supreme degree. But others besides utilitarians have been of opinion that the Christian revelation was intended, and is fitted, to inform the hearts and minds of mankind with a spirit which should enable them to find for themselves what is right, and incline them to do it when found, rather than to tell them, except in a very general way, what it is: and that we need a doctrine of ethics, carefully followed out, to *interpret* to us the will of God. Whether this opinion is correct or not, it is superfluous here to discuss; since whatever aid religion, either natural or revealed, can afford to ethical investigation, is as open to the utilitarian moralist as to any other. He can use it as the testimony of God to the usefulness or hurtfulness of any given course of action, by as good a right as others can use it for the indication of a transcendental law, having no connection with usefulness or with happiness.

Again, Utility is often summarily stigmatized as an immoral doctrine by giving it the name of Expediency, and taking advantage of the popular use of that term to contrast it with Principle. But the Expedient, in the sense in which it is opposed to the Right, generally means that which is expedient for the particular interest of the agent himself; as when a minister sacrifices the interests of his country to keep himself in place. When it means anything better than this, it means that which is expedient for some immediate object, some temporary purpose, but which violates a rule whose observance is expedient in a much higher degree. The Expedient, in this sense, instead of being the same thing with the useful, is a branch of the hurtful. Thus, it would often be expedient, for the purpose of getting over some momentary embarrassment, or attaining some object immediately useful to ourselves or others, to tell a lie. But inasmuch as the cultivation in ourselves of a sensitive feeling on the subject of veracity is one of the most useful, and the enfeeblement of that feeling one of the most hurtful, things to which our conduct can be instrumental; and inasmuch as any, even unintentional, deviation from truth, does that much towards weakening the trustworthiness of human assertion, which is not only the principal support of all present social well-being, but the insufficiency of which does more than any one thing that can be named to keep back civilisation, virtue, everything on which human happiness on the largest scale depends; we feel that the violation, for a present advantage, of a rule of such transcendent expediency, is not expedient, and that he who, for the sake of convenience to himself or to some other individual, does what depends on him to deprive mankind of the good, and inflict upon them the evil, involved in the greater or less reliance which they can place in each other's word, acts the part of one of their worst enemies. Yet that even this rule, sacred as it is, admits of possible exceptions is acknowledged by all moralists; the chief of which is when the withholding of some fact (as of information from a malefactor, or of bad news from a person dangerously ill) would preserve some one (especially a person other than oneself) from great and unmerited evil, and when the withholding can only be effected by denial. But in order that the exception may not extend itself beyond the need, and may have the least possible effect in weakening reliance on veracity, it ought to be recognised, and, if possible, its limits defined; and if the principle of utility is good for anything, it must be good for weighing these conflicting utilities against one another, and marking out the region within which one or the other preponderates.

Again, defenders of utility often find themselves called upon to reply to such objections as this—that there is not time, previous to action, for calculating and weighing the effects of any line of conduct on the general happiness. This is exactly as if any one were to say that it is impossible to guide our conduct by Christianity, because there is not time, on every occasion on which anything has to be done, to read through the Old and New Testaments. The answer to the objection is that there has been ample time, namely, the whole past duration of the human species. During all that time mankind have been learning by experience the tendencies of actions; on which experience all the prudence, as well as all the morality of life, is dependent. People talk as if the commencement of this course of experience had hitherto been put off, and as if, at the moment when some man feels tempted to meddle with the property or life of another, he had to begin considering for the first time whether murder and theft are injurious to human happiness. Even then I do not think that he would find the question very puzzling; but, at all events, the matter is now done to his hand. It is truly a whimsical supposition, that if mankind were agreed in considering utility to be the test of morality, they would remain without any agreement as to what *is* useful, and would take no measures for having their notions on the subject taught to the young, and enforced by law and opinion. There is no difficulty in proving any ethical standard whatever to work ill, if we suppose universal idiocy to be conjoined with it, but on any hypothesis short of that, mankind must by this time have acquired positive beliefs as to the effects of some actions on their happiness; and the beliefs which have thus come down are the rules of morality for the multitude, and for the philosopher until he has succeeded in finding better. That philosophers might easily do this, even now, on many subjects; that the received code of ethics is by no means of divine right; and that mankind have still much to learn as to the effects of actions on the general happiness, I admit, or rather, earnestly maintain. The corollaries from the principle of utility, like the precepts of every practical art, admit of indefinite improvement, and, in a progressive state of the human mind, their improvement is perpetually going on. But to consider the rules of morality as improvable is one thing; to pass over the intermediate generalisations entirely, and endeavour to test each individual action directly by the first principle, is another. It is a strange notion that the acknowledgment of a first principle is inconsistent with the admission of secondary ones. To inform a traveller respecting the place of his ultimate destination is not to forbid the use of landmarks and direction-posts on the way. The proposition that happiness is the end and aim of morality does not mean that no road ought to be laid down to that goal, or that persons going thither should not be advised to take one direction rather than another. Men really ought to leave off talking a kind of nonsense on this subject, which they would neither talk nor listen to on other matters of practical concernment. Nobody argues that the art of navigation is not founded on astronomy, because sailors cannot wait to calculate the Nautical Almanack. Being rational creatures, they go to sea with it ready calculated; and all rational creatures go out upon the sea of life with their minds made up on the common questions of right and wrong, as well as on many of the far more difficult questions of wise and foolish. And this, as long as foresight is a human quality, it is to be presumed they will continue to do. Whatever we adopt as the fundamental principle of morality, we require subordinate principles to apply it by: the impossibility of doing without them, being common to all systems, can afford no argument against any one in particular: but gravely to argue as if no such secondary principles could be had, and as if mankind had remained till now, and always must remain, without drawing any general conclusions from the experience of human life, is as high a pitch, I think, as absurdity has ever reached in philosophical controversy.

The remainder of the stock arguments against utilitarianism mostly consists in laying to its charge the common infirmities of human nature, and the general difficulties which embarrass conscientious persons in shaping their course through life. We are told that a utilitarian will be apt to make his own particular case an exception to moral rules, and, when under temptation, will see a utility in the breach of a rule greater than he will see in its observance. But is utility the only creed which is able to furnish us with excuses for evil doing, and means of cheating our own conscience? They are afforded in abundance by all doctrines which recognise as a fact in morals the existence of conflicting considerations; which all doctrines do, that have been believed by sane persons. It is not the fault of any creed, but of the complicated nature of human affairs, that rules of conduct cannot be so framed as to require no exceptions, and that hardly any kind of action can safely be laid down as either always obligatory or always condemnable. There is no ethical creed which does not temper the rigidity of its laws, by giving a certain latitude, under the moral responsibility of the agent, for accommodation to peculiarities of circumstances; and under every creed, at the opening thus made, self-deception and dishonest casuistry get in. There exists no moral system under which there do not arise unequivocal cases of conflicting obligation. These are the real difficulties, the knotty points both in the theory of ethics, and in the conscientious guidance of personal conduct. They are overcome practically with greater or with less success according to the intellect and virtue of the individual; but it can hardly be pretended that any one will be the less qualified for dealing with them, from possessing an ultimate standard to which conflicting rights and duties can be referred. If utility is the ultimate source of moral obligations, utility may be invoked to decide between them when their demands are incompatible. Though the application of the standard may be difficult, it is better than none at all: while in other systems, the moral laws all claiming independent authority, there is no common umpire entitled to interfere between them; their claims to precedence one over another rest on little better than sophistry, and unless determined, as they generally are, by the unacknowledged influence of considerations of utility, afford a free scope for the action of personal desires and partialities. We must remember that only in these cases of conflict between secondary principles is it requisite that first principles should be appealed to. There is no case of moral obligation in which some secondary principle is not involved; and if only one, there can seldom be any real doubt which one it is, in the mind of any person by whom the principle itself is recognised.

DISCUSSION

It was David Hume who argued that "utility" was the sole basis of ethics, the foundation of justice and benevolence as well as our more self-interested actions. Bentham turned the concept into the full-fledged philosophy of "utilitarianism." His colleague was James Mill, John Stuart Mill's father, and Mill literally grew up with the idea. But "utility" is not the central concept of utilitarianism, as it was in Hume's ethics; pleasure is the crucial concept (which Hume discusses only in a casual way). It is here that Mill differs most from Aristotle, who emphatically denied that what he called "happiness" *(eudaimonia)* was to be identified with pleasure. Mill's harsh rebuttal of those who try to make utilitarianism sound vulgar or voluptuous because of its emphasis on pleasure reflects the disapproval of hedonism throughout the history of ethics, and the heart of Mill's theory is his attempt to make the notion of "pleasure" (which he equates with happiness) more respectable.

It is with this in mind that he introduces his novel theory of the "quality" of pleasure to supplement Bentham's quantitative theory. It is worth noting how negligible a role "utility" plays in Mill's discussion. He does not suggest that some pleasures are more "useful" than others; in fact, the utility of pleasure seems not to be at all in question, particularly because the "higher" pleasures typically consist of such activities as reading and thinking and enjoying the arts, which may be laudable but hardly useful. By contrast, Mill hardly discusses at all the pleasures of physical work and economic production, although he was, we might add, one of the leading economists of the nineteenth century. He seems to have viewed physical labor as relentless drudgery (a view much more extreme than that of Karl Marx—who was in London about the same time).

There can be no mistaking what Mill means by "higher" pleasures; these are those enjoyments that are more intellectual, artistic, or spiritual (although Mill was basically an atheist) as opposed to those that are more physical and physiological. The pleasures of good food, sex, and other physical activities are not excluded, but they are given a distinctly lower value on Mill's "quality" scale of pleasures. He does not exclude or ignore noble actions as sources of pleasure, but he clearly suggests that nobility and intellect go hand in hand and that "men lose their high aspirations as they lose their intellectual tastes." Socrates supplies Mill with his most prominent example of the "higher" pleasures—however dissatisfied the great philosopher may have been with his own intellectual accomplishments—and a pig provides the paradigm of enjoyment of the "lower" pleasures, thus setting up the scale in the most biased possible way. But are all pleasures of the intellect so noble? And must we consider all physical pleasures as piglike? Is enjoying an excellent bottle of Bordeaux really on a par with wallowing in the mud? And are the joys of abstruse metaphysics necessarily "higher" (that is, better) than the simple physical pleasure of receiving—or giving—an effective back rub?

The real problem with Mill's conception of "quality" of pleasures is not the bias of his scale in favor of the intellectual and against the physical, however. We can still readily agree to some distinction between quality of pleasures—for example, we would agree that the pleasure one gets from having cooked and served a good dinner to one's friends is much better than the pleasures of a sadist, even if the sadist should get more enjoyment out of his or her perversions. And isn't there something debatably "better" about enjoying Mozart than "picking one's toes in Poughkeepsie"? But it is Mill's *criterion* for distinguishing the qualities of pleasures that is dubious; he says that the former is preferred to the latter by all or most competent judges who have experienced both kinds of pleasure. But is it all that clear that we would or do choose the higher pleasures? And what do we mean by "choose"? Public television often broadcasts Shakespearean plays opposite network series of undeniable worthlessness, and a vast audience of those who have experienced both choose to watch the worthlessness. What does this mean? If questioned, surely most people who have read, seen, and appreciated Shakespeare will say that they prefer the "higher" pleasure of Shakespeare. What they do however, is watch MTV or *The Simpsons*. Which counts as a choice? And how does either succeed as a plausible test of quality? Indeed, isn't the (indisputable) difference in quality assumed beforehand? And don't people choose in part because of that difference? The sad fact seems to be that most people choose on the basis of the quantity of simple pleasure (or the simplicity of quantity of pleasure), but the philosophic point is that the choice—on whatever grounds—is not the test of quality; if anything, quality survives despite the majority's choices.

What Mill has tried to do is to reduce the vulgarity and "voluptuousness" of Bentham's quantitative pleasure model of ethics and replace it with a two-dimensional model of both quantity and quality. But the beauty of Bentham's ethics was that it reduced all ethical calculations to a single dimension, and this is just what Mill has undone. How will we tell when one pleasure is of a greater quality than another? How can we tell when quality overrides quantity, or vice versa? When is extravagant physical pleasure more desirable than a modest intellectual or artistic pleasure? When is a good philosophy lecture worth more than a day at the beach? And since "utility" is not even mentioned as a criterion—and would be implausible as a defense of most of Mill's preferred "higher" pleasures anyway—have we not moved back to square one and opened up—rather than solved—the question of the *summum bonum* all over again?

THE ULTIMATE SANCTION OF THE PRINCIPLE OF UTILITY: CHAPTER 3

A *sanction* is a motive for action that we otherwise might not perform (although it often has a more negative meaning—as a threat of punishment for wrongdoing). Mill distinguishes two kinds of sanctions, *external* and *internal*. External sanctions are the law, social disapproval, and punishment (including divine punishment); the internal sanction is one's conscience—feeling good when you do right and feeling guilty when you do wrong. It is this internal sanction, Mill argues, that is the ultimate sanction, and Mill suggests that conscience be cultivated precisely in order to make wrongdoing painful for the agent. Again, we see Mill's great faith in the possible achievements of social reform, including educating people to have the right feelings.

The question is often asked, and properly so, in regard to any supposed moral standard—What is its sanction? what are the motives to obey? or, more specifically, what is the source of its obligation? whence does it derive its binding force? It is a necessary part of moral philosophy to provide the answer to this question, which, though frequently assuming the shape of an objection to the utilitarian morality, as if it had some special applicability to that above others, really arises in regard to all standards. It arises, in fact, whenever a person is called on to *adopt* a standard, or refer morality to any basis on which he has not been accustomed to rest it. For the customary morality, that which education and opinion have consecrated, is the only one which presents itself to the mind with the feeling of being in *itself* obligatory; and when a person is asked to believe that this morality *derives* its obligation from some general principle round which custom has not thrown the same halo, the assertion is to him a paradox; the supposed corollaries seem to have a more binding force than the original theorem; the superstructure seems to stand better without than with what is represented as its foundation. He says to himself, I feel that I am bound not to rob or murder, betray or deceive; but why am I bound to promote the general happiness? If my own happiness lies in something else, why may I not give that the preference?

If the view adopted by the utilitarian philosophy of the nature of the moral sense be correct, this difficulty will always present itself until the influences which form moral character have taken the same hold of the principle which they have taken of some of the consequences—until, by the improvement of education, the feeling of unity with our fellow creatures shall be (what it cannot be denied that Christ intended it to be) as deeply rooted in our character, and to our own consciousness as completely a part of our nature, as the horror of crime is in an ordinarily well-brought-up young person. In the meantime, however, the difficulty has no peculiar application to the doctrine of utility, but is inherent in every attempt to analyze morality and reduce it to principles; which, unless the principle is already in men's minds invested with as much sacredness as any of its applications, always seems to divest them of a part of their sanctity.

The principle of utility either has, or there is no reason why it might not have, all the sanctions which belong to any other system of morals. Those sanctions are either external or internal. Of the external sanctions it is not necessary to speak at any length. They are the hope of favor and the fear of displeasure from our fellow creatures or from the Ruler of the universe, along with whatever we may have of sympathy or affection for them, or of love and awe of Him, inclining us to do His will independently of selfish consequences. There is evidently no reason why all these motives for observance should not attach themselves to the utilitarian morality as completely and as powerfully as to any other. Indeed, those of them which refer to our fellow creatures are sure to do so, in proportion to the amount of general intelligence; for whether there be any other ground of moral obligation than the general happiness or not, men do desire happiness; and however imperfect may be their own practice, they desire and commend all conduct in others toward themselves by which they think their happiness is promoted. With regard to the religious motive, if men believe, as most profess to do, in the goodness of God, those who think that conduciveness to the general happiness is the essence or even only the criterion of good must necessarily believe that it is also that which God approves. The whole force therefore of external reward and punishment, whether physical or moral, and whether proceeding from God or from our fellow men, together with all that the capacities of human nature admit of disinterested devotion to either, become available to enforce the utilitarian morality, in proportion as that morality is recognized; and the more powerfully, the more the appliances of education and general cultivation are bent to the purpose.

So far as to external sanctions. The internal sanction of duty, whatever our standard of duty may be, is one and the same—a feeling in our own mind; a pain, more or less intense, attendant on violation of duty, which in properly cultivated moral natures rises, in the more serious cases, into shrinking from it as an impossibility. This feeling, when disinterested and connecting itself with the pure idea of duty, and not with some particular form of it, or with any of the merely accessory circumstances, is the essence of conscience; though in that complex phenomenon as it actually exists, the simple fact is in general all encrusted over with collateral associations derived from sympathy, from love, and still more from fear; from all the forms of religious feeling; from the recollections of child-hood and of all our past life; from self-esteem, desire of the esteem of others, and occasionally even self-abasement. This extreme complication is, I apprehend, the origin of the sort of mystical character which, by a tendency of the human mind of which there are many other examples, is apt to be attributed to the idea of moral obligation, and which leads people to believe that the idea cannot possibly attach itself to any other objects than those which, by a supposed mysterious law, are found in our present experience to excite it. Its binding force, however, con-sists in the existence of a mass of feeling which must be broken through in order to do what violates our standard of right, and which, if we do nevertheless vio-late that standard, will probably have to be encountered afterwards in the form of remorse. Whatever theory we have of the nature or origin of conscience, this is what essentially constitutes it.

The ultimate sanction, therefore, of all morality (external motives apart) be-ing a subjective feeling in our own minds, I see nothing embarrassing to those whose standard is utility in the question, What is the sanction of that particular standard? We may answer, the same as of all other moral standards—the con-scientious feelings of mankind. Undoubtedly this sanction has no binding effi-cacy on those who do not possess the feelings it appeals to; but neither will these persons be more obedient to any other moral principle than to the utilitar-ian one. On them morality of any kind has no hold but through the external sanctions. Meanwhile the feelings exist, a fact in human nature, the reality of which, and the great power with which they are capable of acting on those in whom they have been duly cultivated, are proved by experience. No reason has ever been shown why they may not be cultivated to as great intensity in con-nection with the utilitarian as with any other rule of morals.

There is, I am aware, a disposition to believe that a person who sees in moral obligation a transcendental fact, an objective reality belonging to the province of "things in themselves," is likely to be more obedient to it than one who believes it to be entirely subjective, having its seat in human conscious-ness only. But whatever a person's opinion may be on this point of ontology, the force he is really urged by is his own subjective feeling, and is exactly mea-sured by its strength. No one's belief that duty is an objective reality is stronger than the belief that God is so; yet the belief in God, apart from the expectation of actual reward and punishment, only operates on conduct through, and in pro-portion to, the subjective religious feeling. The sanction, so far as it is disinter-ested, is always in the mind itself; and the notion, therefore, of the transcendental moralists must be that this sanction will not exist *in* the mind un-less it is believed to have its root out of the mind; and that if a person is able to say to himself, "That which is restraining me and which is called my con-science is only a feeling in my own mind," he may possibly draw the conclu-sion that when the feeling ceases the obligation ceases, and that if he find the feeling inconvenient, he may disregard it and endeavor to get rid of it. But is this danger confined to the utilitarian morality? Does the belief that moral obligation has its seat outside the mind make the feeling of it too strong to be got rid of? The fact is so far otherwise that all moralists admit and lament the ease with which, in the generality of minds, conscience can be silenced or stifled. The question, "Need I obey my conscience?" is quite as often put to themselves by persons who never heard of the principle of utility as by its adherents. Those whose conscientious feelings are so weak as to allow of their asking this question, if they answer it affirmatively, will not do so because they believe in the transcendental theory, but because of the external sanctions.

It is not necessary, for the present purpose, to decide whether the feeling of duty is innate or implanted. Assuming it to be innate, it is an open question to what objects it naturally attaches itself; for the philosophic supporters of that theory are now agreed that the intuitive perception is of principles of morality and not of the details. If there be anything innate in the matter, I see no reason why the feeling which is innate should not be that of regard to the pleasures and pains of others. If there is any principle of morals which is intuitively obligatory, I should say it must be that. If so, the intuitive ethics would coincide with the utilitarian, and there would be no further quarrel between them. Even as it is, the intuitive moralists, though they believe that there are other intuitive moral obligations, do already believe this to be one; for they unanimously hold that a large *portion* of morality turns upon the consideration due to the interests of our fellow creatures. Therefore, if the belief in the transcendental origin of moral obligation gives any additional efficacy to the internal sanction, it appears to me that the utilitarian principle has already the benefit of it.

On the other hand, if, as is my own belief, the moral feelings are not innate but acquired, they are not for that reason the less natural. It is natural to man to speak, to reason, to build cities, to cultivate the ground, though these are acquired faculties. The moral feelings are not indeed a part of our nature in the sense of being in any perceptible degree present in all of us; but this, unhappily, is a fact admitted by those who believe the most strenuously in their transcendental origin. Like the other acquired capacities above referred to, the moral faculty, if not a part of our nature, is a natural outgrowth from it; capable, like them, in a certain small degree, of springing up spontaneously; and susceptible of being brought by cultivation to a high degree of development. Unhappily it is also susceptible, by a sufficient use of the external sanctions and of the force of early impressions, of being cultivated in almost any direction so that there is hardly anything so absurd or so mischievous that it may not, by means of these influences, be made to act on the human mind with all the authority of conscience. To doubt that the same potency might be given by the same means to the principle of utility, even if it had no foundation in human nature, would be flying in the face of all experience.

But moral associations which are wholly of artificial creation, when the intellectual culture goes on, yield by degrees to the dissolving force of analysis; and if the feeling of duty, when associated with utility, would appear equally arbitrary; if there were no leading department of our nature, no powerful class of sentiments, with which that association would harmonize, which would make us feel it congenial and incline us not only to foster it in others (for which we have abundant interested motives), but also to cherish it in ourselves—if there were not, in short, a natural basis of sentiment for utilitarian morality, it might well happen that this association also, even after it had been implanted by education, might be analyzed away.

But there *is* this basis of powerful natural sentiment; and this it is which, when once the general happiness is recognized as the ethical standard, will constitute the strength of the utilitarian morality. This firm foundation is that of the social feelings of mankind—the desire to be in unity with our fellow creatures, which is already a powerful principle in human nature, and happily one of those which tend to become stronger, even without express inculcation, from the influences of advancing civilization. The social state is at once so natural, so necessary, and so habitual to man, that, except in some unusual circumstances or by an effort of voluntary abstraction, he never conceives himself otherwise than as a member of a body; and this association is riveted more and more, as mankind are further removed from the state of savage independence. Any condition, therefore, which is essential to a state of society becomes more and more an inseparable part of every person's conception of the state of things which he is born into, and which is the destiny of a human being. Now society between human beings, except in the relation of master and slave, is manifestly impossible on any other footing than that the interests of all are to be consulted. Society between equals can only exist on the understanding that the interests of all are to be regarded equally. And since in all states of civilization, every person, except an absolute monarch, has equals, everyone is obliged to live on these terms with somebody; and in every age some advance is made toward a state in which it will be impossible to live permanently on other terms with anybody. In this way people grow up unable to conceive as possible to them a state of total disregard of other people's interests. They are under a necessity of conceiving themselves as at least abstaining from all the grosser injuries, and (if only for their own protection) living in a state of constant protest against them. They are also familiar with the fact of co-operating with others and proposing to themselves a collective, not an individual, interest as the aim (at least for the time being) of their actions. So long as they are co-operating, their ends are identified with those of others; there is at least a temporary feeling that the interests of others are their own interests. Not only does all strengthening of social ties, and all healthy growth of society, give to each individual a stronger personal interest in practically consulting the welfare of others, it also leads him to identify his *feelings* more and more with their good, or at least with an even greater degree of practical consideration for it. He comes, as though instinctively, to be conscious of himself as a being who *of course* pays regard to others. The good of others becomes to him a thing naturally and necessarily to be attended to, like any of the physical conditions of our existence. Now, whatever amount of this feeling a person has, he is urged by the strongest motives both of interest and of sympathy to demonstrate it, and to the utmost of his power encourage it in others; and even if he has none of it himself, he is as greatly interested as anyone else that others should have it. Consequently, the smallest germs of the feeling are laid hold of and nourished by the contagion of sympathy and the influences of education; and a complete web of corroborative association is woven round it by the powerful agency of the external sanctions. This mode of conceiving ourselves and human life, as civilization goes on, is felt to be more and more natural. Every step in political improvement renders it more so, by removing the sources of opposition of interest and leveling those inequalities of legal privilege between individuals or classes, owing to which there are large portions of mankind whose happiness it is still practicable to disregard. In an improving state of the human mind, the influences are constantly on the increase which tend to generate in each individual a feeling of unity with all the rest; which, if perfect, would make him never think of, or desire, any beneficial condition for himself in the benefits of which they are not included. If we now suppose this feeling of unity to be taught as a religion, and the whole force of education, of institutions, and of opinion directed, as it once was in the case of religion, to make every person grow up from infancy surrounded on all sides both by the profession and the practice of it, I think that no one who can realize this conception will feel any misgiving about the sufficiency of the ultimate sanction for the happiness morality. To any ethical student who finds the realization difficult, I recommend, as a means of facilitating it, the second of M. Comte's two principal works, the *Traité de politique positive.* I entertain the strongest objections to the system of politics and morals set forth in that treatise, but I think it has superabundantly shown the possibility of giving to the service of humanity, even without the aid of belief in a Providence, both the psychological power and the social efficacy of a religion, making it take hold of human life, and color all thought, feeling, and action in a manner of which the greatest ascendancy ever exercised by any religion may be but a type and foretaste; and of which the danger is, not that it should be insufficient, but that it should be so excessive as to interfere unduly with human freedom and individuality.

Neither is it necessary to the feeling which constitutes the binding force of the utilitarian morality on those who recognize it to wait for those social influences which would make its obligation felt by mankind at large. In the comparatively early state of human advancement in which we now live, a person cannot, indeed, feel that entireness of sympathy with all others which would make any real discordance in the general direction of their conduct in life impossible, but already a person in whom the social feeling is at all developed cannot bring himself to think of the rest of his fellow creatures as struggling rivals with him for the means of happiness, whom he must desire to see defeated in their object in order that he may succeed in his. The deeply rooted conception which every individual even now has of himself as a social being tends to make him feel it one of his natural wants that there should be harmony between his feelings and aims and those of his fellow creatures. If differences of opinion and of mental culture make it impossible for him to share many of their actual feelings—perhaps make him denounce and defy those feelings—he still needs to be conscious that his real aim and theirs do not conflict; that he is not opposing himself to what they really wish for, namely, their own good, but is, on the contrary, promoting it. This feeling in most individuals is much inferior in strength to their selfish feelings, and is often wanting altogether. But to those who have it, it possesses all the characters of a natural feeling. It does not present itself to their minds as a superstition of education or a law despotically imposed by the power of society, but as an attribute which it would not be well for them to be without. This conviction is the ultimate sanction of the greatest happiness morality. This it is which makes any mind of well-developed feelings work with, and not against, the outward motives to care for others, afforded by what I have called the external sanctions; and, when those sanctions are wanting or act in an opposite direction, constitutes in itself a powerful internal binding force, in proportion to the sensitiveness and thoughtfulness of the character, since few but those whose mind is a moral blank could bear to lay out their course of life on the plan of paying no regard to others except so far as their own private interest compels.

DISCUSSION

The problem that concerns Mill is that of obligation, in this case the obligation to promote the greatest happiness for the greatest number. The question is, Where does it come from? What is there in the theory that makes such disinterested promotion of the general good something each individual will feel he or she *must* do? As Mill rightly points out, this is not a problem unique to utilitarianism, although it may not seem quite so obvious in other theories. For instance, in those "transcendental theories," which posit some greater reality, such as God, it may first appear that there are stronger sanctions than in utilitarianism, which locates the primary obligation in the subjective feelings of the individual. But how does belief in God affect our actions? Through the "subjective religious feelings," Mill answers. The point is that regardless of the theory and its principles, to make sense of moral duty, we must always revert to the individual conscience. Thus, utilitarianism is no worse off on this count than any other theory.

For Mill, this internal sanction (conscience) is socially constructed rather than innate. It begins with the recognition of humans as necessarily social animals, which in turn leads to the "social feelings of mankind—the desire to be in unity with our fellow creatures." On the positive side, it encourages us to promote the good of others, to see their interests as valid as our own, and to realize the deep interconnectedness of everyone's happiness. And it seems plausible to claim, as Mill does, that these sorts of social feelings are self-perpetuating—the rewards of doing good for others lead us to continue to want to do so. There is a "contagion of sympathy."

However, the negative aspect of relying on such sanctions seems equally, if not more, important. What is required is a feeling, or set of feelings, that will prevent us from doing what is harmful to the general good (although beneficial to ourselves). Mill is surely right that, for most of us, "pangs of conscience" serve as an effective deterrent, causing a pain of sorts that offsets the pleasure gained from many a minor indiscretion. But there is a problem in treating the pain of a bad conscience as a pain in the sense that is important to utilitarianism. Pangs of conscience are not just pain and not just internal punishment. If we think about it, the pain of guilt is rather difficult to specify; it is unpleasant, to be sure, and one might note the discomfort of that choked-up, flushed feeling that often accompanies guilt. But this would hardly seem to be a deterrent to self-interested action, and, because it is internal, it would be easy enough to assuage the guilt by taking certain drugs or having a stiff martini. Why doesn't this work? It is not because the guilty feelings last so long (one can always take another drink). It is rather because guilt is not just a pain; it is a much more pervasive aspect of our lives. Guilt is painful because it reflects an intolerable view of ourselves, as a rotten person or, at least, as a person who has done something rotten. Eliminating the pain of guilt is not yet to eliminate the guilt, and the pain of a pang of conscience is not a sanction so much as it is part and parcel of our moral sense itself. Does this mean that guilt cannot play the role that Mill thinks it does—as an internal punishment? The suggestion that it is the ultimate sanction of our actions may be circular: Do we feel guilt the same way we feel pain? It seems more often as if we do not come to believe that what we did was wrong because we feel guilty, but that we feel guilty because we know that what we did was wrong.

THE "PROOF" OF UTILITARIANISM: CHAPTER 4

Although he began *Utilitarianism* with the reminder that there can be no "proof" of ultimate ends, Mill now proceeds to give us a proof of sorts. To establish the greatest happiness principle as *the* rule of morality, Mill needs to show that happiness is the ultimate end, the one and only value to which we should appeal in running our (moral) lives. And to say something is an ultimate end is, according to Mill, to say that it is desirable. Thus, Mill needs to show two things: (1) that happiness is desirable and (2) that it is the only thing that is desirable. The steps of the argument are not entirely clear, and generations of critics and defenders of Mill have struggled to recast the argument in its strongest form. Mill's own attention, however, is not focused on the formal validity of the argument so much as it is on the most common objections to number 2, in particular, the question whether such desirable goods as virtue, power, and fame must be considered as distinct from happiness or rather desirable components of it.

It has already been remarked that questions of ultimate ends do not admit of proof, in the ordinary acceptation of the term. To be incapable of proof by reasoning is common to all first principles, to the first premises of our knowledge, as well as to those of our conduct. But the former, being matters of fact, may be the subject of a direct appeal to the faculties which judge of fact—namely, our senses and our internal consciousness. Can an appeal be made to the same faculties on questions of practical ends? Or by what other faculty is cognizance taken of them?

Questions about ends are, in other words, questions about what things are desirable. The utilitarian doctrine is that happiness is desirable, and the only thing desirable, as an end; all other things being only desirable as means to that end. What ought to be required of this doctrine, what conditions is it requisite that the doctrine should fulfill—to make good its claim to be believed?

The only proof capable of being given that an object is visible is that people actually see it. The only proof that a sound is audible is that people hear it; and so of the other sources of our experience. In like manner, I apprehend, the sole evidence it is possible to produce that anything is desirable is that people do actually desire it. If the end which the utilitarian doctrine proposes to itself were not, in theory and in practice, acknowledged to be an end, nothing could ever convince any person that it was so. No reason can be given why the general happiness is desirable, except that each person, so far as he believes it to be attainable, desires his own happiness. This, however, being a fact, we have not only all the proof which the case admits of, but all which it is possible to require, that happiness is a good; that each person's happiness is a good to that person, and the general happiness, therefore, a good to the aggregate of all persons. Happiness had made out its title as *one* of the ends of conduct, and consequently one of the criteria of morality.

But it has not, by this alone, proved itself to be the sole criterion. To do that, it would seem, by the same rule, necessary to show, not only that people desire happiness, but that they never desire anything else. Now it is palpable that they do desire things which, in common language, are decidedly distinguished from happiness. They desire, for example, virtue and the absence of vice, no less really than pleasure and the absence of pain. The desire of virtue is not as universal, but it is as authentic a fact as the desire of happiness. And hence the opponents of the utilitarian standard deem that they have a right to infer that there are other ends of human action besides happiness, and that happiness is not the standard of approbation and disapprobation.

But does the utilitarian doctrine deny that people desire virtue, or maintain that virtue is not a thing to be desired? The very reverse. It maintains not only that virtue is to be desired, but that it is to be desired disinterestedly, for itself. Whatever may be the opinion of utilitarian moralists as to the original conditions by which virtue is made virtue, however they may believe (as they do) that actions and dispositions are only virtuous because they promote another end than virtue, yet this being granted, and it having been decided, from considerations of this description, what *is* virtuous, they not only place virtue at the very head of the things which are good as means to the ultimate end, but they also recognize as a psychological fact the possibility of its being, to the individual, a good in itself, without looking to any end beyond it; and hold that the mind is not in a right state, not in a state conformable to utility, not in the state most conducive to the general happiness, unless it does love virtue in this manner—as a thing desirable in itself, even although, in the individual instance, it should not produce those other desirable consequences which it tends to produce, and on account of which it is held to be virtue. This opinion is not, in the smallest degree, a departure from the happiness principle. The ingredients of happiness are very various, and each of them is desirable in itself, and not merely when considered as swelling an aggregate. The principle of utility does not mean that any given pleasure, as music, for instance, or any given exemption from pain, as for example health, is to be looked upon as means to a collective something termed happiness, and to be desired on that account. They are desired and desirable in and for themselves; besides being means, they are a part of the end. Virtue, according to the utilitarian doctrine, is not naturally and originally part of the end, but it is capable of becoming so; and in those who love it disinterestedly it has become so, and is desired and cherished, not as a means to happiness, but as a part of their happiness.

To illustrate this further, we may remember that virtue is not the only thing originally a means, and which if it were not a means to anything else would be and remain indifferent, but which by association with what it is a means to comes to be desired for itself, and that too with the utmost intensity. What, for example, shall we say of the love of money? There is nothing originally more desirable about money than about any heap of glittering pebbles. Its worth is solely that of the things which it will buy; the desires for other things than itself, which it is a means of gratifying. Yet the love of money is not only one of the strongest moving forces of human life, but money is, in many cases, desired in and for itself; the desire to possess it is often stronger than the desire to use it, and goes on increasing when all the desires which point to ends beyond it, to be compassed by it, are falling off. It may, then, be said truly that money is desired not for the sake of an end, but as part of the end. From being a means to happiness, it has come to be itself a principal ingredient of the individual's conception of happiness. The same may be said of the majority of the great objects of human life: power, for example, or fame, except that to each of these there is a certain amount of immediate pleasure annexed, which has at least the semblance of being naturally inherent in them—a thing which cannot be said of money. Still, however, the strongest natural attraction, both of power and of fame, is the immense aid they give to the attainment of our other wishes; and it is the strong association thus generated between them and all our objects of desire which gives to the direct desire of them the intensity it often assumes, so as in some characters to surpass in strength all other desires. In these cases the means have become a part of the end, and a more important part of it than any of the things which they are means to. What was once desired as an instrument for the attainment of happiness has come to be desired for its own sake. In being desired for its own sake it is, however, desired as *part* of happiness. The person is made, or thinks he would be made, happy by its mere possession; and is made unhappy by failure to obtain it. The desire of it is not a different thing from the desire of happiness any more than the love of music or the desire of health. They are included in happiness. They are some of the elements of which the desire of happiness is made up. Happiness is not an abstract idea but a concrete whole; and these are some of its parts. And the utilitarian standard sanctions and approves their being so. Life would be a poor thing, very ill provided with sources of happiness, if there were not this provision of nature by which things originally indifferent, but conducive to, or otherwise associated with, the satisfaction of our primitive desires, become in themselves sources of pleasure more valuable than the primitive pleasures, both in permanency, in the space of human existence that they are capable of covering, and even in intensity.

Virtue, according to the utilitarian conception, is a good of this description. There was no original desire of it, or motive to it, save its conduciveness to pleasure, and especially to protection from pain. But through the association thus formed it may be felt a good in itself, and desired as such with as great intensity as any other good; and with this difference between it and the love of money, of power, or of fame, that all of these may, and often do, render the individual noxious to the other members of the society to which he belongs, whereas there is nothing which makes him so much a blessing to them as the cultivation of the disinterested love of virtue. And consequently, the utilitarian standard, while it tolerates and approves those other acquired desires, up to the point beyond which they would be more injurious to the general happiness than promotive of it, enjoins and requires the cultivation of the love of virtue up to the greatest strength possible, as being above all things important to the general happiness.

It results from the preceding considerations that there is in reality nothing desired except happiness. Whatever is desired otherwise than as a means to some end beyond itself, and ultimately to happiness, is desired as itself a part of happiness, and is not desired for itself until it has become so. Those who desire virtue for its own sake desire it either because the consciousness of it is a pleasure, or because the consciousness of being without it is a pain, or for both reasons united; as in truth the pleasure and pain seldom exist separately, but almost always together—the same person feeling pleasure in the degree of virtue attained, and pain in not having attained more. If one of these gave him no pleasure, and the other no pain, he would not love or desire virtue, or would desire it only for the other benefits which it might produce to himself or to persons whom he cared for.

We have now, then, an answer to the question, of what sort of proof the principle of utility is susceptible. If the opinion which I have now stated is psychologically true—if human nature is so constituted as to desire nothing which is not either a part of happiness or a means of happiness, we can have no other proof, and we require no other, that these are the only things desirable. If so, happiness is the sole end of human action, and the promotion of it the test by which to judge of all human conduct; from whence it necessarily follows that it must be the criterion of morality, since a part is included in the whole.

And now to decide whether this is really so, whether mankind do desire nothing for itself but that which is a pleasure to them, or of which the absence is a pain, we have evidently arrived at a question of fact and experience, dependent, like all similar questions, upon evidence. It can only be determined by practised self-consciousness and self-observation, assisted by observation of others. I believe that these sources of evidence, impartially consulted, will declare that desiring a thing and finding it pleasant, aversion to it and thinking of it as painful, are phenomena entirely inseparable or rather two parts of the same phenomenon; in strictness of language, two different modes of naming the same psychological fact; that to think of an object as desirable (unless for the sake of its consequences) and to think of it as pleasant are one and the same thing; and that to desire anything except in proportion as the idea of it is pleasant, is a physical and metaphysical impossibility.

So obvious does this appear to me that I expect it will hardly be disputed; and the objection made will be, not that desire can possibly be directed to anything ultimately except pleasure and exemption from pain, but that the will is a different thing from desire; that a person of confirmed virtue or any other person whose purposes are fixed carries out his purposes without any thought of the pleasure he has in contemplating them or expects to derive from their fulfillment, and persists in acting on them, even though these pleasures are much diminished by changes in his character or decay of his passive sensibilities, or are outweighed by the pains which the pursuit of the purposes may bring upon him. All this I fully admit and have stated it elsewhere as positively and emphatically as anyone. Will, the active phenomenon, is a different thing from desire, the state of passive sensibility, and, though originally an offshoot from it, may in time take root and detach itself from the parent stock, so much so that in the case of a habitual purpose, instead of willing the thing because we desire it, we often desire it only because we will it. This, however, is but an instance of that familiar fact, the power of habit, and is nowise confined to the case of virtuous actions. Many indifferent things which men originally did from a motive of some sort they continue to do from habit. Sometimes this is done unconsciously, the consciousness coming only after the action; at other times with conscious volition, but volition which has become habitual and is put in operation by the force of habit, in opposition perhaps to the deliberate preference, as often happens with those who have contracted habits of vicious or hurtful indulgence. Third and last comes the case in which the habitual act of will in the individual instance is not in contradiction to the general intention prevailing at other times, but in fulfillment of it, as in the case of the person of confirmed virtue and of all who pursue deliberately and consistently any determinate end. The distinction between will and desire thus understood is an authentic and highly important psychological fact; but the fact consists solely in this—that will, like all other parts of our constitution, is amenable to habit, and that we may will from habit what we no longer desire for itself, or desire only because we will it. It is not the less true that will, in the beginning, is entirely produced by desire, including in that term the repelling influence of pain as well as the attractive one of pleasure. Let us take into consideration no longer the person who has a confirmed will to do right, but him in whom that virtuous will is still feeble, conquerable by temptation, and not to be fully relied on; by what means can it be strengthened? How can the will to be virtuous, where it does not exist in sufficient force, be implanted or awakened? Only by making the person *desire* virtue—by making him think of it in a pleasurable light, or of its absence in a painful one. It is by associating the doing right with pleasure, or the wrong with pain, or by eliciting and impressing and bringing home to the person's experience the pleasure naturally involved in the one or the pain in the other, that it is possible to call forth that will to be virtuous which, when confirmed, acts without any thought of either pleasure or pain. Will is the child of desire, and passes out of the dominion of its parents only to come under that of habit. That which is the result of habit affords no presumption of being intrinsically good; and there would be no reason for wishing that the purpose of virtue should become independent of pleasure and pain were it not that the influence of the pleasurable and painful associations which prompt to virtue is not sufficiently to be depended on for unerring constancy of action until it has acquired the support of habit. Both in feeling and in conduct, habit is the only thing which imparts certainty; and it is because of the importance to others of being able to rely absolutely on one's feelings and conduct, and to oneself of being able to rely on one's own, that the will to do right ought to be cultivated into this habitual independence. In other words, this state of the will is a means to good, not intrinsically a good; and does not contradict the doctrine that nothing is a good to human beings but in so far as it is either itself pleasurable or a means of attaining pleasure or averting pain.

But if this doctrine be true, the principle of utility is proved. Whether it is so or not must now be left to the consideration of the thoughtful reader.

DISCUSSION

Despite Mill's disclaimers, his "proof" certainly has the appearance of a standard deductive argument, and it has been interpreted as such by many moral philosophers. There are many reformulations of the argument, some of them more flattering and more generous than others. One of the most common reformulations, in more straightforward deductive form, is this:

1. The only test of something's being desirable is its being desired.
2. Everyone desires his or her own happiness.
3. (Therefore) the general happiness is desired by all.
4. For anything desired, it is either a means to happiness, or a part of it.
5. (Therefore) the only thing desired is (the general) happiness.
6. (Therefore) the only test of the rightness and wrongness of actions is their tendency to promote the general happiness ("the greatest good for the greatest number").

There are several serious problems with the proof. Statement 1 is the focus of the most frequent criticisms and discussions of Mill's proof because it contains a suspicious ambiguity. Statement 1 functions as a premise, but it is also an argument that

> The sole evidence it is possible to produce that anything is desirable is that people actually do desire it.

Mill argues by analogy that just as an object is visible only if people see it, a thing is desirable only if people desire it. But "visible" means *able to be seen;* "desirable" does not mean *able to be desired.* It means *should be desired.* One might alter the wording cautiously and suggest that "desirable" does mean *worthy* of being desired. We should also remember that Mill himself does not exactly say that "desirable" *means* "desired"; he just points out that the *test* of desirability must have something to do with being desired. But no matter how it is argued—the critics claim—this crucial premise involves the unwarranted leap from the simple fact that people desire something to the value judgment that it is worth desiring. (This is often taken as an illustration of the "naturalistic fallacy," the inference of a value judgment from a strictly factual statement, or in Hume's terms, the derivation of an "ought" from an "is.") On the other hand, could one possibly say that people's desires are *irrelevant* to what is good? Many people desire to drive at unsafe speeds, but it does not follow from that that reckless driving is desirable.

A second problem arises in the move from statement 2 to statement 3. Mill takes statement 2 to be a "metaphysical necessity," in fact, a simple statement of psychological egoism and hedonism—that each person desires his or her own happiness.

Statement 3 is presented as an inference from statement 2. But it too betrays a fallacy, which logicians call "the fallacy of composition." The confusion is in Mill's so easily slipping from a statement that

a. All individuals want their own happiness,

to

b. All individuals want everyone's happiness.

The phrase "the general happiness" is ambiguous between these two very different statements, and a sentence such as "everyone desires the happiness of all" only makes things more confusing. Notice that so far we have argued only a *fact* about people; no mention has been made of what they *should* desire. Mill might respond by reminding us of the role of education discussed in chapter 2. Properly implemented, social reform and education have the potential "to establish in the mind of every individual an indissoluble association between his own happiness and the good of the whole." However, more needs to be said in order to make the move from statement 2 to statement 3 as obvious and natural as Mill takes it to be.

What are we to make of this flawed attempt, about which Mill himself clearly had reservations? The logical inadequacy of the "proof" does not end its obvious appeal. There is something undeniable in the claim that any doctrine about what we ought to want has to be based on what we actually want. And there is something equally undeniable—perhaps even trivial—in the claim that each of us wants to be happy, that is, wants his or her own happiness. Mill is right, no doubt, that our individual happiness is not incompatible with the happiness of others, and it is equally clear that the happiness of others is often bound up with our own. (It is much easier to have fun at a party when everyone else is enjoying themselves, too.) But how can these plausible claims be put together in a valid argument? Or is "the principle of utility," for all of its initial appeal, an inadequate principle of ethics because it cannot be proved?

JUSTICE AND UTILITY: CHAPTER 5

Justice and utility are typically placed opposite one another, as in the following example: A wealthy neighborhood finds itself the occasional victim of a small crime wave, the perpetrators of which are found to live in a small pocket of poor minority families. To stop the crime and to prevent any likelihood of further criminal activity, the wealthy majority band together and quite easily—and by means of the law—force the minority families out of their homes. The action succeeds; the crime wave stops. And the suffering of the few evicted families is exceeded by the relief of the wealthy majority. In terms of utility ("the greatest happiness of the greatest number"), the right thing has been done; the amount of pleasure now exceeds the balance of suffering, and the balance of pleasure under the new arrangement now exceeds the balance of pleasure had things remained as they were. Nevertheless, we feel quite strongly that justice has been violated. Some innocent people—even if they were a poor minority—have been unfairly treated. They have *rights* that have been violated, and no argument for utility can compensate them for that. The "greatest good for the greatest number" is not the same thing as—and may even be incompatible with—*justice.*

John Stuart Mill was, as a matter of fact, one of the great defenders of individual rights; his essay *On Liberty* (published a few years before *Utilitarianism*) established the doctrine of individual liberty—including the rights of the minority in the face of an overwhelming majority—more persuasively than any other modern document. It is of the utmost importance to him, therefore, to show that justice and utility are not incompatible because his whole ethics is committed to the proposition that there is only one *summum bonum*—the happiness of all, and his whole life was dedicated to the importance of individual rights and justice.

In all ages of speculation one of the strongest obstacles to the reception of the doctrine that utility or happiness is the criterion of right and wrong has been drawn from the idea of justice. The powerful sentiment and apparently clear perception which that word recalls with a rapidity and certainty resembling an instinct have seemed to the majority of thinkers to point to an inherent quality in things; to show that the just must have an existence in nature as something absolute, generically distinct from every variety of the expedient and, in idea, opposed to it, though (as is commonly acknowledged) never, in the long run, disjoined from it in fact.

In the case of this, as of our other moral sentiments, there is no necessary connection between the question of its origin and that of its binding force. That a feeling is bestowed on us by nature does not necessarily legitimate all its promptings. The feeling of justice might be a peculiar instinct, and might yet require, like our other instincts, to be controlled and enlightened by a higher reason. If we have intellectual instincts leading us to judge in a particular way, as well as animal instincts that prompt us to act in a particular way, there is no necessity that the former should be more infallible in their sphere than the latter in theirs; it may as well happen that wrong judgments are occasionally suggested by those, as wrong actions by these. But though it is one thing to believe that we have natural feelings of justice, and another to acknowledge them as an ultimate criterion of conduct, these two opinions are very closely connected in point of fact. Mankind are always predisposed to believe that any subjective feeling, not otherwise accounted for, is a revelation of some objective reality. Our present object is to determine whether the reality to which the feeling of justice corresponds is one which needs any such special revelation, whether the justice or injustice of an action is a thing intrinsically peculiar and distinct from all its other qualities or only a combination of certain of those qualities presented under a peculiar aspect. For the purpose of this inquiry it is practically important to consider whether the feeling itself, of justice and injustice, is *sui generis* like our sensations of color and taste or a derivative feeling formed by a combination of others. And this it is the more essential to examine, as people are in general willing enough to allow that objectively the dictates of justice coincide with a part of the field of general expediency; but inasmuch as the subjective mental feeling of justice is different from that which commonly attaches to simple expediency, and, except in the extreme cases of the latter, is far more imperative in its demands, people find it difficult to see in justice only a particular kind or branch of general utility, and think that its superior binding force requires a totally different origin.

To throw light upon this question, it is necessary to attempt to ascertain what is the distinguishing character of justice, or of injustice; what is the quality, or whether there is any quality, attributed in common to all modes of conduct designated as unjust (for justice, like many other moral attributes, is best defined by its opposite), and distinguishing them from such modes of conduct as are disapproved, but without having that particular epithet of disapprobation applied to them. If in everything which men are accustomed to characterize as just or unjust some one common attribute or collection of attributes is always present, we may judge whether this particular attribute or combination of attributes would be capable of gathering round it a sentiment of that peculiar character and intensity by virtue of the general laws of our emotional constitution, or whether the sentiment is inexplicable and requires to be regarded as a special provision of nature. If we find the former to be the case, we shall, in resolving this question, have resolved also the main problem; if the latter, we shall have to seek for some other mode of investigating it:

To find the common attributes of a variety of objects, it is necessary to begin by surveying the objects themselves in the concrete. Let us therefore advert successively to the various modes of action and arrangements of human affairs which are classed, by universal or widely spread opinion, as just or as unjust. The things well known to excite the sentiments associated with those names are of a very multifarious character. I shall pass them rapidly in review, without studying any particular arrangement.

In the first place, it is mostly considered unjust to deprive anyone of his personal liberty, his property, or any other thing which belongs to him by law. Here, therefore, is one instance of the application of the terms "just" and "unjust" in a perfectly definite sense, namely, that it is just to respect, unjust to violate, the *legal rights* of anyone. But this judgment admits of several exceptions, arising from the other forms in which the notions of justice and injustice present themselves. For example, the person who suffers the deprivation may (as the phrase is) have *forfeited* the rights which he is so deprived of—a case to which we shall return presently. But also—

Secondly, the legal rights of which he is deprived may be rights which *ought* not to have belonged to him; in other words, the law which confers on him these rights may be a bad law. When it is so or when (which is the same thing for our purpose) it is supposed to be so, opinions will differ as to the justice or injustice of infringing it. Some maintain that no law, however bad, ought to be disobeyed by an individual citizen; that his opposition to it, if shown at all, should only be shown in endeavoring to get it altered by competent authority. This opinion (which condemns many of the most illustrious benefactors of mankind, and would often protect pernicious institutions against the only weapons which, in the state of things existing at the time, have any chance of succeeding against them) is defended by those who hold it on grounds of expediency, principally on that of the importance to the common interest of mankind, of maintaining inviolate the sentiment of submission to law. Other persons, again, hold the directly contrary opinion that any law, judged to be bad, may blamelessly be disobeyed, even though it be not judged to be unjust but only inexpedient, while others would confine the license of disobedience to the case of unjust laws; but, again, some say that all laws which are inexpedient are unjust, since every law imposes some restriction on the natural liberty of mankind, which restriction is an injustice unless legitimated by tending to their good. Among these diversities of opinion it seems to be universally admitted that there may be unjust laws, and that law, consequently, is not the ultimate criterion of justice, but may give to one person a benefit, or impose on another an evil, which justice condemns. When, however, a law is thought to be unjust, it seems always to be regarded as being so in the same way in which a breach of law is unjust, namely, by infringing somebody's right, which, as it cannot in this case be a legal right, receives a different appellation and is called a moral right. We may say, therefore, that a second case of injustice consists in taking or withholding from any person that to which he has a *moral right.*

Thirdly, it is universally considered just that each person should obtain that (whether good or evil) which he *deserves,* and unjust that he should obtain a good or be made to undergo an evil which he does not deserve. This is, perhaps, the clearest and most emphatic form in which the idea of justice is conceived by the general mind. As it involves the notion of desert, the question arises what constitutes desert? Speaking in a general way, a person is understood to deserve good if he does right, evil if he does wrong; and in a more particular sense, to deserve good from those to whom he does or has done good, and evil from those to whom he does or has done evil. The precept of returning good for evil has never been regarded as a case of the fulfillment of justice, but as one in which the claims of justice are waived, in obedience to other considerations.

Fourthly, it is confessedly unjust to *break faith* with anyone: to violate an engagement, either express or implied, or disappoint expectations raised by our own conduct, at least if we have raised those expectations knowingly and voluntarily. Like the other obligations of justice already spoken of, this one is not regarded as absolute, but as capable of being overruled by a stronger obligation of justice on the other side, or by such conduct on the part of the person concerned as is deemed to absolve us from our obligation to him and to constitute a *forfeiture* of the benefit which he has been led to expect.

Fifthly, it is, by universal admission, inconsistent with justice to be *partial*—to show favor or preference to one person over another in matters to which favor and preference do not properly apply. Impartiality, however, does not seem to be regarded as a duty in itself, but rather as instrumental to some other duty; for it is admitted that favor and preference are not always censurable, and, indeed, the cases in which they are condemned are rather the exception than the rule. A person would be more likely to be blamed than applauded for giving his family or friends no superiority in good offices over strangers when he could do so without violating any other duty; and no one thinks it unjust to seek one person in preference to another as a friend, connection, or companion. Impartiality where rights are concerned is of course obligatory, but this is involved in the more general obligation of giving to everyone his right. A tribunal, for example, must be impartial because it is bound to award, without regard to any other consideration, a disputed object to the one of two parties who has the right to it. There are other cases in which impartiality means being solely influenced by desert, as with those who, in the capacity of judges, preceptors, or parents, administer reward and punishment as such. There are cases, again, in which it means being solely influenced by consideration for the public interest, as in making a selection among candidates for a government employment. Impartiality, in short, as an obligation of justice, may be said to mean being exclusively influenced by the considerations which it is supposed ought to influence the particular case in hand, and resisting solicitation of any motives which prompt to conduct different from what those considerations would dictate.

Nearly allied to the idea of impartiality is that of *equality,* which often enters as a component part both into the conception of justice and into the practice of it, and, in the eyes of many persons, constitutes its essence. But in this, still more than in any other case, the notion of justice varies in different persons, and always conforms in its variations to their notion of utility. Each person maintains that equality is the dictate of justice, except where he thinks that expediency requires inequality. The justice of giving equal protection to the rights of all is maintained by those who support the most outrageous inequality in the rights themselves. Even in slave countries it is theoretically admitted that the rights of the slave, such as they are, ought to be as sacred as those of the master, and that a tribunal which fails to enforce them with equal strictness is wanting in justice; while, at the same time, institutions which leave to the slave scarcely any rights to enforce are not deemed unjust because they are not deemed inexpedient. Those who think that utility requires distinctions of rank do not consider it unjust that riches and social privileges should be unequally dispensed; but those who think this inequality inexpedient think it unjust also. Whoever thinks that government is necessary sees no injustice in as much inequality as is constituted by giving to the magistrate powers not granted to other people. Even among those who hold leveling doctrines, there are differences of opinion about expediency. Some communists consider it unjust that the produce of the labor of the community should be shared on any other principle than that of exact equality; others think it just that those should receive most whose wants are greatest; while others hold that those who work harder, or who produce more, or whose services are more valuable to the community, may justly claim a larger quota in the division of the produce. And the sense of natural justice may be plausibly appealed to in behalf of every one of these opinions.

Among so many diverse applications of the term "justice," which yet is not regarded as ambiguous, it is a matter of some difficulty to seize the mental link which holds them together, and on which the moral sentiment adhering to the term essentially depends. Perhaps, in this embarrassment, some help may be derived from the history of the word, as indicated by its etymology.

In most if not in all languages, the etymology of the word which corresponds to "just" points distinctly to an origin connected with the ordinances of law. *Justum* is a form of *jussum,* that which has been ordered. *Dikaion* comes directly from *dike,* a suit at law. *Recht,* from which came *right* and *righteous,* is synonymous with law. The courts of justice, the administration of justice, are the courts and the administration of law. *La justice,* in French, is the established term for judicature. I am not committing the fallacy, imputed with some show of truth to Horne Tooke of assuming that a word must still continue to mean what it originally meant. Etymology is slight evidence of what the idea now signified is, but the very best evidence of how it sprang up. There can, I think, be no doubt that the *idée mère,* the primitive element, in the formation of the notion of justice was conformity to law. It constituted the entire idea among the Hebrews, up to the birth of Christianity; as might be expected in the case of a people whose laws attempted to embrace all subjects on which precepts were required, and who believed those laws to be a direct emanation from the Supreme Being. But other nations, and in particular the Greeks and Romans, who knew that their laws had been made originally, and still continued to be made, by men, were not afraid to admit that those men might make bad laws; might do, by law, the same things, and from the same motives, which if done by individuals without the sanction of law would be called unjust. And hence the sentiment of injustice came to be attached, not to all violations of law, but only to violations of such laws as *ought* to exist, including such as ought to exist but do not, and to laws themselves if supposed to be contrary to what ought to be law. In this manner the idea of law and of its injunctions was still predominant in the notion of justice, even when the laws actually in force ceased to be accepted as the standard of it.

It is true that mankind consider the idea of justice and its obligations as applicable to many things which neither are, nor is it desired that they should be, regulated by law. Nobody desires that laws should interfere with the whole detail of private life; yet everyone allows that in all daily conduct a person may and does show himself to be either just or unjust. But even here, the idea of the breach of what ought to be law still lingers in a modified shape. It would always give us pleasure, and chime in with our feelings of fitness, that acts which we deem unjust should be punished, though we do not always think it expedient that this should be done by the tribunals. We forego that gratification on account of incidental inconveniences. We should be glad to see just conduct enforced and injustice repressed, even in the minutest details, if we were not, with reason, afraid of trusting the magistrate with so unlimited an amount of power over individuals. When we think that a person is bound in justice to do a thing, it is an ordinary form of language to say that he ought to be compelled to do it. We should be gratified to see the obligation enforced by anybody who had the power. If we see that its enforcement by law would be inexpedient, we lament the impossibility, we consider the impunity given to injustice as an evil, and strive to make amends for it by bringing a strong expression of our own and the public disapprobation to bear upon the offender. Thus the idea of legal constraint is still the generating idea of the notion of justice, though undergoing several transformations before that notion as it exists in an advanced state of society becomes complete.

The above is, I think, a true account, as far as it goes, of the origin and progressive growth of the idea of justice. But we must observe that it contains as yet nothing to distinguish that obligation from moral obligation in general. For the truth is that the idea of penal sanction, which is the essence of law, enters not only into the conception of injustice, but into that of any kind of wrong. We do not call anything wrong unless we mean to imply that a person ought to be punished in some way or other for doing it—if not by law, by the opinion of his fellow creatures; if not by opinion, by the reproaches of his own conscience. This seems the real turning point of the distinction between morality and simple expediency. It is a part of the notion of duty in every one of its forms that a person may rightfully be compelled to fulfill it. Duty is a thing which may be *exacted* from a person, as one exacts a debt. Unless we think that it may be exacted from him, we do not call it his duty. Reasons of prudence, or the interest of other people, may militate against actually exacting it, but the person himself, it is clearly understood, would not be entitled to complain. There are other things, on the contrary, which we wish that people should do, which we like or admire them for doing, perhaps dislike or despise them for not doing, but yet admit that they are not bound to do; it is not a case of moral obligation; we do not blame them; that is, we do not think that they are proper objects of punishment. How we come by these ideas of deserving and not deserving punishment will appear, perhaps, in the sequel; but I think there is no doubt that this distinction lies at the bottom of the notions of right and wrong; that we call any conduct wrong, or employ, instead, some other term of dislike or disparagement, according as we think that the person ought, or ought not, to be punished for it; and we say it would be right to do so and so, or merely that it would be desirable or laudable, according as we would wish to see the person whom it concerns compelled, or only persuaded and exhorted, to act in that manner.

This, therefore, being the characteristic difference which marks off, not justice, but morality in general from the remaining provinces of expediency and worthiness, the character is still to be sought which distinguishes justice from other branches of morality. Now it is known that ethical writers divide moral duties into two classes, denoted by the ill-chosen expressions, duties of perfect and of imperfect obligation; the latter being those in which, though the act is obligatory, the particular occasions of performing it are left to our choice, as in the case of charity or beneficence, which we are indeed bound to practice but not toward any definite person, nor at any prescribed time. In the more precise language of philosophic jurists, duties of perfect obligation are those duties in virtue of which a correlative *right* resides in some person or persons; duties of imperfect obligation are those moral obligations which do not give birth to any right. I think it will be found that this distinction exactly coincides with that which exists between justice and the other obligations of morality. In our survey of the various popular acceptations of justice, the term appeared generally to involve the idea of a personal right—a claim on the part of one or more individuals, like that which the law gives when it confers a proprietary or other legal right. Whether the injustice consists in depriving a person of a possession, or in breaking faith with him, or in treating him worse than he deserves, or worse than other people who have no greater claims—in each case the supposition implies two things: a wrong done, and some assignable person who is wronged. Injustice may also be done by treating a person better than others; but the wrong in this case is to his competitors, who are also assignable persons. It seems to me that this feature in the case—a right in some person, correlative to the moral obligation—constitutes the specific difference between justice and generosity or beneficence. Justice implies something which it is not only right to do, and wrong not to do, but which some individual person can claim from us as his moral right. No one has a moral right to our generosity or beneficence because we are not morally bound to practice those virtues toward any given individual. And it will be found with respect to this as to every correct definition that the instances which seem to conflict with it are those which most confirm it. For if a moralist attempts, as some have done, to make out that mankind generally, though not any given individual, have a right to all the good we can do them, he at once, by that thesis, includes generosity and beneficence within the category of justice. He is obliged to say that our utmost exertions are *due* to our fellow creatures, thus assimilating them to a debt; or that nothing less can be a sufficient *return* for what society does for us, thus classing the case as one of gratitude; both of which are acknowledged cases of justice, and not of the virtue of beneficence; and whoever does not place the distinction between justice and morality in general, where we have now placed it, will be found to make no distinction between them at all, but to merge all morality in justice.

Having reviewed the various meanings of justice and concluded that its "primitive element" is conformity to the law (whether that law be legal or moral), Mill now attempts to discover the origin of the feeling for justice. In particular, he is concerned with whether it is of a piece with general expediency (the utilitarian doctrine) or distinct from it. The two ingredients of justice, Mill explains, are the desire to punish one who has done wrong and an identifiable victim, both of which, he argues, are (when morally developed) based on the desire to promote the general good.

It is evident in the idea of punishment for wrongdoing against a particular individual, that the concept of rights—and rights violations—is an inherent part of justice. However, as previously noted, rights are often taken to be incompatible with utility; in many cases, protecting individual rights (for instance, the Neo-Nazi's right to free speech) seems to diminish rather than enlarge the aggregate happiness. Recognizing this problem, Mill argues that although he uses the term "right," he does not take it to mean anything more than the two ingredients of justice: the desire to punish wrongdoing and an assignable person who suffered the harm. But these are ultimately based on utility because they are explainable in terms of the promotion of the general good. Consequently, the recognition of rights that are violated by the wrongdoer are founded on utility as well.

Finally, Mill responds to the objection that justice cannot be reduced to utility because, whereas utility is always uncertain (people will forecast different consequences as well as assigning different values to outcomes), justice is incontrovertible and inflexible. But, Mill points out, this is simply not the case. Not only do different cultures have very different ideas about what is and is not just, but even within the same society (or individual), disagreement over justice is endless. In fact, the only move that keeps this disagreement from being endless is the appeal to the general good. It is not the case, then, that considerations of justice are always entertained in isolation from consequences. Thus, far from being distinct from utility, justice is in the end made possible by it.

Having thus endeavored to determine the distinctive elements which enter into the composition of the idea of justice, we are ready to enter on the inquiry whether the feeling which accompanies the idea is attached to it by a special dispensation of nature, or whether it could have grown up, by any known laws, out of the idea itself; and, in particular, whether it can have originated in considerations of general expediency.

I conceive that the sentiment itself does not arise from anything which would commonly or correctly be termed an idea of expediency, but that, though the sentiment does not, whatever is moral in it does.

We have seen that the two essential ingredients in the sentiment of justice are the desire to punish a person who has done harm and the knowledge or belief that there is some definite individual or individuals to whom harm has been done.

Now it appears to me that the desire to punish a person who has done harm to some individual is a spontaneous outgrowth from two sentiments, both in the highest degree natural and which either are or resemble instincts: the impulse of self-defense and the feeling of sympathy.

It is natural to resent and to repel or retaliate any harm done or attempted against ourselves or against those with whom we sympathize. The origin of this sentiment it is not necessary here to discuss. Whether it be an instinct or a result of intelligence, it is, we know, common to all animal nature; for every animal tries to hurt those who have hurt, or who it thinks are about to hurt, itself or its young. Human beings, on this point, only differ from other animals in two particulars. First, in being capable of sympathizing, not solely with their offspring, or, like some of the more noble animals, with some superior animal who is kind to them, but with all human, and even with all sentient, beings; secondly, in having a more developed intelligence, which gives a wider range to the whole of their sentiments, whether self-regarding or sympathetic. By virtue of his superior intelligence, even apart from his superior range of sympathy, a human being is capable of apprehending a community of interest between himself and the human society of which he forms a part, such that any conduct which threatens the security of the society generally is threatening to his own, and calls forth his instinct (if instinct it be) of self-defense. The same superiority of intelligence, joined to the power of sympathizing with human beings generally, enables him to attach himself to the collective idea of his tribe, his country, or mankind in such a manner that any act hurtful to them raises his instinct of sympathy and urges him to resistance.

The sentiment of justice, in that one of its elements which consists of the desire to punish, is thus, I conceive, the natural feeling of retaliation or vengeance, rendered by intellect and sympathy applicable to those injuries, that is, to those hurts, which wound us through, or in common with, society at large. This sentiment, in itself, has nothing moral in it; what is moral is the exclusive subordination of it to the social sympathies, so as to wait on and obey their call. For the natural feeling would make us resent indiscriminately whatever anyone does that is disagreeable to us; but, when moralized by the social feeling, it only acts in the directions conformable to the general good: just persons resenting a hurt to society, though not otherwise a hurt to themselves, and not resenting a hurt to themselves, however painful, unless it be of the kind which society has a common interest with them in the repression of.

It is no objection against this doctrine to say that, when we feel our sentiment of justice outraged, we are not thinking of society at large or of any collective interest, but only of the individual case. It is common enough, certainly, though the reverse of commendable, to feel resentment merely because we have suffered pain; but a person whose resentment is really a moral feeling, that is, who considers whether an act is blamable before he allows himself to resent it—such a person, though he may not say expressly to himself that he is standing up for the interest of society, certainly does feel that he is asserting a rule which is for the benefit of others as well as for his own. If he is not feeling this, if he is regarding the act solely as it affects him individually, he is not consciously just; he is not concerning himself about the justice of his actions. This is admitted even by anti-utilitarian moralists. When Kant (as before remarked) propounds as the fundamental principle of morals, "So act that thy rule of conduct might be adopted as a law by all rational beings," he virtually acknowledges that the interest of mankind collectively, or at least of mankind indiscriminately, must be in the mind of the agent when conscientiously deciding on the morality of the act. Otherwise he uses words without a meaning; for that a rule even of utter selfishness could not *possibly* be adopted by all rational beings—that there is any insuperable obstacle in the nature of things to its adoption—cannot be even plausibly maintained. To give any meaning to Kant's principle, the sense put upon it must be that we ought to shape our conduct by a rule which all rational beings might adopt *with benefit to their collective interest.*

To recapitulate: the idea of justice supposes two things—a rule of conduct and a sentiment which sanctions the rule. The first must be supposed common to all mankind and intended for their good. The other (the sentiment) is a desire that punishment may be suffered by those who infringe the rule. There is involved, in addition, the conception of some definite person who suffers by the infringement, whose rights (to use the expression appropriated to the case) are violated by it. And the sentiment of justice appears to me to be the animal desire to repel or retaliate a hurt or damage to oneself or to those with whom one sympathizes, widened so as to include all persons, by the human capacity of enlarged sympathy and the human conception of intelligent self-interest. From the latter elements the feeling derives its morality; from the former, its peculiar impressiveness and energy of self-assertion.

I have, throughout, treated the idea of a *right* residing in the injured person and violated by the injury, not as a separate element in the composition of the idea and sentiment, but as one of the forms in which the other two elements clothe themselves. These elements are a hurt to some assignable person or persons, on the one hand, and a demand for punishment, on the other. An examination of our own minds, I think, will show that these two things include all that we mean when we speak of violation of a right. When we call anything a person's right, we mean that he has a valid claim on society to protect him in the possession of it, either by the force of law or by that of education and opinion. If he has what we consider a sufficient claim, on whatever account, to have something guaranteed to him by society, we say that he has a right to it. If we desire to prove that anything does not belong to him by right, we think this done as soon as it is admitted that society ought not to take measures for securing it to him, but should leave him to chance or to his own exertions. Thus a person is said to have a right to what he can earn in fair professional competition, because society ought not to allow any other person to hinder him from endeavoring to earn in that manner as much as he can. But he has not a right to three hundred a year, though he may happen to be earning it; because society is not called on to provide that he shall earn that sum. On the contrary, if he owns ten thousand pounds three-per-cent stock, he *has* a right to three hundred a year because society has come under an obligation to provide him with an income of that amount.

To have a right, then, is, I conceive, to have something which society ought to defend me in the possession of. If the objector goes on to ask why it ought, I can give him no other reason than general utility. If that expression does not seem to convey a sufficient feeling of the strength of the obligation, nor to account for the peculiar energy of the feeling, it is because there goes to the composition of the sentiment, not a rational only but also an animal element—the thirst for retaliation; and this thirst derives its intensity, as well as its moral justification, from the extraordinarily important and impressive kind of utility which is concerned. The interest involved is that of security, to everyone's feelings the most vital of all interests. All other earthly benefits are needed by one person, not needed by another; and many of them can, if necessary, be cheerfully foregone or replaced by something else; but security no human being can possibly do without; on it we depend for all our immunity from evil and for the whole value of all and every good, beyond the passing moment, since nothing but the gratification of the instant could be of any worth to us if we could be deprived of everything the next instant by whoever was momentarily stronger than ourselves. Now this most indispensable of all necessaries, after physical nutriment, cannot be had unless the machinery for providing it is kept unintermittedly in active play. Our notion, therefore, of the claim we have on our fellow creatures to join in making safe for us the very groundwork of our existence gathers feelings around it so much more intense than those concerned in any of the more common cases of utility that the difference in degree (as is often the case in psychology) becomes a real difference in kind. The claim assumes that character of absoluteness, that apparent infinity and incommensurability with all other considerations which constitute the distinction between the feeling of right and wrong and that of ordinary expediency and inexpediency. The feelings concerned are so powerful, and we count so positively on finding a responsive feeling in others (all being alike interested) that *ought* and *should* grow into *must,* and recognized indispensability becomes a moral necessity, analogous to physical, and often not inferior to it in binding force.

If the preceding analysis, or something resembling it, be not the correct account of the notion of justice—if justice be totally independent of utility, and be a standard *per se,* which the mind can recognize by simple introspection of itself—it is hard to understand why that internal oracle is so ambiguous, and why so many things appear either just or unjust, according to the light in which they are regarded.

We are continually informed that utility is an uncertain standard, which every different person interprets differently, and that there is no safety but in the immutable, ineffaceable, and unmistakable dictates of justice, which carry their evidence in themselves and are independent of the fluctuations of opinion. One would suppose from this that on questions of justice there could be no controversy; that, if we take that for our rule, its application to any given case could leave us in as little doubt as a mathematical demonstration. So far is this from being the fact that there is as much difference of opinion, and as much discussion, about what is just as about what is useful to society. Not only have different nations and individuals different notions of justice, but in the mind of one and the same individual, justice is not some one rule, principle, or maxim, but many which do not always coincide in their dictates, and, in choosing between which, he is guided either by some extraneous standard or by his own personal predilections.

For instance, there are some who say that it is unjust to punish anyone for the sake of example to others, that punishment is just only when intended for the good of the sufferer himself. Others maintain the extreme reverse, contending that to punish persons who have attained years of discretion, for their own benefit, is despotism and injustice, since, if the matter at issue is solely their own good, no one has a right to control their own judgment of it; but that they may justly be punished to prevent evil to others, this being the exercise of the legitimate right of self-defense. Mr. Owen, again, affirms that it is unjust to punish at all, for the criminal did not make his own character; his education and the circumstances which surrounded him have made him a criminal, and for these he is not responsible. All these opinions are extremely plausible; and so long as the question is argued as one of justice simply, without going down to the principles which lie under justice and are the source of its authority, I am unable to see how any of these reasoners can be refuted. For in truth every one of the three builds upon rules of justice confessedly true. The first appeals to the acknowledged injustice of singling out an individual and making him a sacrifice, without his consent, for other people's benefit. The second relies on the acknowledged justice of self-defense and the admitted injustice of forcing one person to conform to another's notions of what constitutes his good. The Owenite invokes the admitted principle that it is unjust to punish anyone for what he cannot help. Each is triumphant so long as he is not compelled to take into consideration any other maxims of justice than the one he has selected; but as soon as their several maxims are brought face to face, each disputant seems to have exactly as much to say for himself as the others. No one of them can carry out his own notion of justice without trampling upon another equally binding. These are difficulties; they have always been felt to be such; and many devices have been invented to turn rather than to overcome them. As a refuge from the last of the three, men imagined what they called the freedom of the will—fancying that they could not justify punishing a man whose will is in a thoroughly hateful state unless it be supposed to have come into that state through no influence of anterior circumstances. To escape from the other difficulties, a favorite contrivance has been the fiction of a contract whereby at some unknown period all the members of society engaged to obey the laws and consented to be punished for any disobedience to them, thereby giving to their legislators the right, which it is assumed they would not otherwise have had, of punishing them, either for their own good or for that of society. This happy thought was considered to get rid of the whole difficulty and to legitimate the infliction of punishment, in virtue of another received maxim of justice, *volenti non fit injuria*—that is not unjust which is done with the consent of the person who is supposed to be hurt by it. I need hardly remark that, even if the consent were not a mere fiction, this maxim is not superior in authority to the others which it is brought in to supersede. It is, on the contrary, an instructive specimen of the loose and irregular manner in which supposed principles of justice grow up. This particular one evidently came into use as a help to the coarse exigencies of courts of law, which are sometimes obliged to be content with very uncertain presumptions, on account of the greater evils which would often arise from any attempt on their part to cut finer. But even courts of law are not able to adhere consistently to the maxim, for they allow voluntary engagements to be set aside on the ground of fraud, and sometimes on that of mere mistake or misinformation.

Again, when the legitimacy of inflicting punishment is admitted, how many conflicting conceptions of justice come to light in discussing the proper apportionment of punishments to offenses. No rule on the subject recommends itself so strongly to the primitive and spontaneous sentiment of justice as the *lex talionis,* an eye for an eye and a tooth for a tooth. Though this principle of the Jewish and of the Mohammedan law has been generally abandoned in Europe as a practical maxim, there is, I suspect, in most minds, a secret hankering after it; and when retribution accidentally falls on an offender in that precise shape, the general feeling of satisfaction evinced bears witness how natural is the sentiment to which this repayment in kind is acceptable. With many, the test of justice in penal infliction is that the punishment should be proportioned to the offense, meaning that it should be exactly measured by the moral guilt of the culprit (whatever be their standard for measuring moral guilt), the consideration what amount of punishment is necessary to deter from the offense having nothing to do with the question of justice, in their estimation; while there are others to whom that consideration is all in all, who maintain that it is not just, at least for man, to inflict on a fellow creature, whatever may be his offenses, any amount of suffering beyond the least that will suffice to prevent him from repeating, and others from imitating, his misconduct.

To take another example from a subject already once referred to. In co-operative industrial association, is it just or not that talent or skill should give a title to superior remuneration? On the negative side of the question it is argued that whoever does the best he can deserves equally well, and ought not in justice to be put in a position of inferiority for no fault of his own; that superior abilities have already advantages more than enough, in the admiration they excite, the personal influence they command, and the internal sources of satisfaction attending them, without adding to these a superior share of the world's goods; and that society is bound in justice rather to make compensation to the less favored for this unmerited inequality of advantages than to aggravate it. On the contrary side it is contended that society receives more from the more efficient laborer; that, his services being more useful, society owes him a larger return for them; that a greater share of the joint result is actually his work, and not to allow his claim to it is a kind of robbery; that, if he is only to receive as much as others, he can only be justly required to produce as much, and to give a smaller amount of time and exertion, proportioned to his superior efficiency. Who shall decide between these appeals to conflicting principles of justice? Justice has in this case two sides to it, which it is impossible to bring into harmony, and the two disputants have chosen opposite sides; the one looks to what it is just that the individual should receive, the other to what it is just that the community should give. Each, from his own point of view, is unanswerable; and any choice between them, on grounds of justice, must be perfectly arbitrary. Social utility alone can decide the preference.

How many, again, and how irreconcilable are the standards of justice to which reference is made in discussing the repartition of taxation. One opinion is that payment to the state should be in numerical proportion to pecuniary means. Others think that justice dictates what they term graduated taxation—taking a higher percentage from those who have more to spare. In point of natural justice a strong case might be made for disregarding means altogether, and taking the same absolute sum (whenever it could be got) from everyone; as the subscribers to a mess or to a club all pay the same sum for the same privileges, whether they can all equally afford it or not. Since the protection (it might be said) of law and government is afforded to and is equally required by all, there is no injustice in making all buy it at the same price. It is reckoned justice, not injustice, that a dealer should charge to all customers the same price for the same article, not a price varying according to their means of payment. This doctrine, as applied to taxation, finds no advocates because it conflicts so strongly with man's feelings of humanity and of social expediency; but the principle of justice which it invokes is as true and as binding as those which can be appealed to against it. Accordingly it exerts a tacit influence on the line of defense employed for other modes of assessing taxation. People feel obliged to argue that the state does more for the rich man than for the poor, as a justification for its taking more from them, though this is in reality not true, for the rich would be far better able to protect themselves, in the absence of law or government, than the poor, and indeed would probably be successful in converting the poor into their slaves. Others, again, so far defer to the same conception of justice as to maintain that all should pay an equal capitation tax for the protection of their persons (these being of equal value to all), and an unequal tax for the protection of their property, which is unequal. To this others reply that the all of one man is as valuable to him as the all of another. From these confusions there is no other mode of extrication than the utilitarian.

Is, then, the difference between the just and the expedient a merely imaginary distinction? Have mankind been under a delusion in thinking that justice is a more sacred thing than policy, and that the latter ought only to be listened to after the former has been satisfied? By no means. The exposition we have given of the nature and origin of the sentiment recognizes a real distinction; and no one of those who profess the most sublime contempt for the consequences of actions as an element in their morality attaches more importance to the distinction than I do. While I dispute the pretensions of any theory which sets up an imaginary standard of justice not grounded on utility, I account the justice which is grounded on utility to be the chief part, and incomparably the most sacred and binding part, of all morality. Justice is a name for certain classes of moral rules which concern the essentials of human well-being more nearly, and are therefore of more absolute obligation, than any other rules for the guidance of life; and the notion which we have found to be of the essence of the idea of justice—that of a right residing in an individual—implies and testifies to this more binding obligation.

The moral rules which forbid mankind to hurt one another (in which we must never forget to include wrongful interference with each other's freedom) are more vital to human well-being than any maxims, however important, which only point out the best mode of managing some department of human affairs. They have also the peculiarity that they are the main element in determining the whole of the social feelings of mankind. It is their observance which alone preserves peace among human beings; if obedience to them were not the rule, and disobedience the exception, everyone would see in everyone else an enemy against whom he must be perpetually guarding himself. What is hardly less important, these are the precepts which mankind have the strongest and the most direct inducements for impressing upon one another. By merely giving to each other prudential instruction or exhortation, they may gain, or think they gain, nothing; in inculcating on each other the duty of positive beneficence, they have an unmistakable interest, but far less in degree; a person may possibly not need the benefits of others, but he always needs that they should not do him hurt. Thus the moralities which protect every individual from being harmed by others, either directly or by being hindered in his freedom of pursuing his own good, are at once those which he himself has most at heart and those which he has the strongest interest in publishing and enforcing by word and deed. It is by a person's observance of these that his fitness to exist as one of the fellowship of human beings is tested and decided; for on that depends his being a nuisance or not to those with whom he is in contact. Now it is these moralities primarily which compose the obligations of justice. The most marked cases of injustice, and those which give the tone to the feeling of repugnance which characterizes the sentiment, are acts of wrongful aggression or wrongful exercise of power over someone; the next are those which consist in wrongfully withholding from him something which is his due—in both cases inflicting on him a positive hurt, either in the form of direct suffering or of the privation of some good which he had reasonable ground, either of a physical or of a social kind, for counting upon.

The same powerful motives which command the observance of these primary moralities enjoin the punishment of those who violate them; and as the impulses of self-defense, of defense of others, and of vengeance are all called forth against such persons, retribution, or evil for evil, becomes closely connected with the sentiment of justice, and is universally included in the idea. Good for good is also one of the dictates of justice; and this, though its social utility is evident, and though it carries with it a natural human feeling, has not at first sight that obvious connection with hurt or injury which, existing in the most elementary cases of just and unjust, is the source of the characteristic intensity of the sentiment. But the connection, though less obvious, is not less real. He who accepts benefits and denies a return of them when needed inflicts a real hurt by disappointing one of the most natural and reasonable of expectations, and one which he must at least tacitly have encouraged, otherwise the benefits would seldom have been conferred. The important rank, among human evils and wrongs, of the disappointment of expectation is shown in the fact that it constitutes the principal criminality of two such highly immoral acts as a breach of friendship and a breach of promise. Few hurts which human beings can sustain are greater, and none wound more, than when that on which they habitually and with full assurance relied fails them in the hour of need; and few wrongs are greater than this mere withholding of good; none excite more resentment, either in the person suffering or in a sympathizing spectator. The principle, therefore, of giving to each what they deserve, that is, good for good as well as evil for evil, is not only included within the idea of justice as we have defined it, but is a proper object of that intensity of sentiment which places the just in human estimation above the simply expedient.

Most of the maxims of justice current in the world, and commonly appealed to in its transactions, are simply instrumental to carrying into effect the principles of justice which we have now spoken of. That a person is only responsible for what he has done voluntarily, or could voluntarily have avoided, that it is unjust to condemn any person unheard; that the punishment ought to be proportioned to the offense, and the like, are maxims intended to prevent the just principle of evil for evil from being perverted to the infliction of evil without that justification. The greater part of these common maxims have come into use from the practice of courts of justice, which have been naturally led to a more complete recognition and elaboration than was likely to suggest itself to others, of the rules necessary to enable them to fulfill their double function—of inflicting punishment when due, and of awarding to each person his right.

That first of judicial virtues, impartiality, is an obligation of justice, partly for the reason last mentioned, as being a necessary condition of the fulfillment of other obligations of justice. But this is not the only source of the exalted rank, among human obligations, of those maxims of equality and impartiality, which, both in popular estimation and in that of the most enlightened, are included among the precepts of justice. In one point of view, they may be considered as corollaries from the principles already laid down. If it is a duty to do to each according to his deserts, returning good for good, as well as repressing evil by evil, it necessarily follows that we should treat all equally well (when no higher duty forbids) who have deserved equally well of *us,* and that society should treat all equally well who have deserved equally well of *it,* that is, who have deserved equally well absolutely. This is the highest abstract standard of social and distributive justice, toward which all institutions and the efforts of all virtuous citizens should be made in the utmost possible degree to converge. But this great moral duty rests upon a still deeper foundation, being a direct emanation from the first principle of morals, and not a mere logical corollary from secondary or derivative doctrines. It is involved in the very meaning of utility, or the greatest happiness principle. That principle is a mere form of words without rational signification unless one person's happiness, supposed equal in degree (with the proper allowance made for kind), is counted for exactly as much as another's. Those conditions being supplied, Bentham's dictum, "everybody to count for one, nobody for more than one," might be written under the principle of utility as an explanatory commentary. The equal claim of everybody to happiness, in the estimation of the moralist and of the legislator, involves an equal claim to all the means of happiness except in so far as the inevitable conditions of human life and the general interest in which that of every individual is included set limits to the maxim; and those limits ought to be strictly construed. As every other maxim of justice, so this is by no means applied or held applicable universally; on the contrary, as I have already remarked, it bends to every person's ideas of social expediency. But in whatever case it is deemed applicable at all, it is held to be the dictate of justice. All persons are deemed to have a *right* to equality of treatment, except when some recognized social expediency requires the reverse. And hence all social inequalities which have ceased to be considered expedient assume the character, not of simple inexpediency, but of injustice, and appear so tyrannical that people are apt to wonder how they ever could have been tolerated—forgetful that they themselves, perhaps, tolerate other inequalities under an equally mistaken notion of expediency, the correction of which would make that which they approve seem quite as monstrous as what they have at last learned to condemn. The entire history of social improvement has been a series of transitions by which one custom or institution after another, from being a supposed primary necessity of social existence, has passed into the rank of a universally stigmatized injustice and tyranny. So it has been with the distinctions of slaves and freemen, nobles and serfs, patricians and plebeians; and so it will be, and in part already is, with the aristocracies of color, race, and sex.

It appears from what has been said that justice is a name for certain moral requirements which, regarded collectively, stand higher in the scale of social utility, and are therefore of more paramount obligation, than any others, though particular cases may occur in which some other social duty is so important as to overrule any one of the general maxims of justice. Thus, to save a life, it may not only be allowable, but a duty, to steal or take by force the necessary food or medicine, or to kidnap and compel to officiate the only qualified medical practitioner. In such cases, as we do not call anything justice which is not a virtue, we usually say, not that justice must give way to some other moral principle, but that what is just in ordinary cases is, by reason of that principle, not just in the particular case. By this useful accommodation of language, the character of indefeasibility attributed to justice is kept up, and we are saved from the necessity of maintaining that there can be laudable injustice.

The considerations which have now been adduced resolve, I conceive, the only real difficulty in the utilitarian theory of morals. It has always been evident that all cases of justice are also cases of expediency; the difference is in the peculiar sentiment which attaches to the former, as contradistinguished from the latter. If this characteristic sentiment has been sufficiently accounted for; if there is no necessity to assume for it any peculiarity of origin; if it is simply the natural feeling of resentment, moralized by being made co-extensive with the demands of social good; and if this feeling not only does but ought to exist in all the classes of cases to which the idea of justice corresponds—that idea no longer presents itself as a stumbling block to the utilitarian ethics. Justice remains the appropriate name for certain social utilities which are vastly more important, and therefore more absolute and imperative, than any others are as a class (though not more so than others may be in particular cases); and which, therefore, ought to be, as well as naturally are, guarded by a sentiment, not only different in degree, but also in kind; distinguished from the milder feeling which attaches to the mere idea of promoting human pleasure or convenience at once by the more definite nature of its commands and by the sterner character of its sanctions.

DISCUSSION

Mill's argument here resembles in its strategy the arguments he presents earlier concerning virtue; he attempts to show that justice is not a "peculiar and distinct" moral quality but rather a particularly important aspect of utility. He begins by tracing the notion of justice to the concept of law (for example, among the ancient Hebrews, Greeks, and Romans) but then insists that justice is something other than law, first because there are bad laws, second because it is unthinkable that every aspect of our lives in which there is justice and injustice (for example, giving and getting grades in school) should be regulated by law. He further distinguishes justice from morality, on the grounds that justice involves rights, and then he presents us with a general argument to show that rights and justice serve social utility, thus jibing his strong belief in individual rights with his belief in utility.

Mill examines a number of ingredients in justice, among them legal rights, moral rights, "merit," what a person deserves, and impartiality, but the ingredient in justice to which he gives the most attention is that of *equality*. Mill does not mean by "equality" that everyone should receive the same out of life, nor does he even mean that everyone ought to have "equal opportunities" without regard to the overall well-being of everyone else. He means that, so far as happiness is concerned, each person's happiness (although not necessarily his or her deserving happiness) counts the same as everyone else's, or, in Bentham's words, "everybody to count for one, nobody more than one." Indeed, by the end of the chapter Mill is convinced that this principle of equality virtually follows from the principle of utility ("might be written as an explanatory commentary"). But the qualification that "all persons . . . have a *right* to equality of treatment, *except when some recognized social expediency requires the reverse,*" already includes the loophole in which the majority can persecute the minority and in which those who already have the more advantageous positions in society can convincingly claim that social expediency overrides the rights of the protesting poor.

Why should Mill—the champion of minority rights—endorse such a loophole? Because he clearly wants flexibility in his concept of justice; just as he has rejected a priori moral thinking all along, it is particularly important for him to do so here. To allow for an absolute principle of equality, for example, might under any number of circumstances lead to great unhappiness, just as to insist that all contractual rights must be upheld or all laws obeyed leaves too much room for the enforcement of deceptive agreements and bad laws.

Consider taxation, for example, a topic that is central to most discussions of distributive justice. One suggestion that at first sounds fair is that everyone should pay exactly the same. But it then becomes clear that in some circumstances—for example, when the need to tax is great and the distribution of income is extremely unequal—the misery thus caused those less well-off will be considerable. On the other hand, so-called "progressive" taxation—taxing people a higher percentage of their earnings as they earn more—strikes many people as unfair for a very different reason. One deserves what he or she earns, they say, and being taxed more leads people to work less and grumble more, thus adding to the national misery and detracting from utility considerably. In the name of equality, one might propose the more radical suggestion that everyone should be taxed so they are left with equal shares (the policy of some socialist governments), but the net resentment and inefficiency here are undeniable. And yet, one can easily imagine a small society—for example, a religious brotherhood—in which this scheme is of the greatest utility and acceptable to everyone. One might also imagine taxation by lottery, such that everyone's share is determined by chance; but the lack of both utility and justice in this suggestion—even if it might sound fair—is obvious.

How are we to choose among these alternatives, each of which has some claim to our attention? Rejecting easy and a priori answers, Mill insists that we look only to the consequences, that we actually look and see which will promote the general happiness and which will not. That is the essence of his utilitarianism, even in that "vastly more important," even "more absolute and imperative" social utility called "justice." Justice, too, whatever more noble claims have been made for it, is nothing other than a means to promote the greatest happiness of the greatest number.

Discussion Questions

1. Can justice be accounted for in terms of utility alone? What problems arise in a utilitarian account of justice?
2. Why can one not "prove" ultimate ends? Why does Mill reject the idea of proof?
3. Is it the test of something's being desirable that it is in fact desired? What qualifications must be added to make this plausible? Does the fact that something is desired thereby make it desirable?

4. What is meant by "quality" of pleasures? What new problems does this introduce into utilitarianism?
5. Is Mill's idea of "high and low" pleasure something that everyone can relate to? Does this distinction undermine his belief in equality?
6. Who is Mill's audience here? Can utilitarianism help someone become a better person? What kinds of decisions *can* it help with?

Study Questions

1. What is utilitarianism? How does Mill's conception of it differ from Bentham's conception? What is "the principle of utility"?
2. What is the justification for identifying happiness and pleasure? What role does pain play in utilitarianism? Is the avoidance of pain always the ultimate goal in utilitarianism?
3. In what sense is Mill's utilitarianism "teleological"?
4. Why does Mill say that even Kant had to appeal to the principle of utility? Is this true of Kant, would you say?
5. Does Mill ignore the question of "moral worth"? What relevance would moral worth have to the promotion of good consequences, according to the principle of utility?
6. Why does Mill think that the principle of utility entails a principle of equality? Does the one principle entail the other? What happens if one accepts the principle of utility but does not accept the principle of equality? (What happens if one accepts the principle of equality but does not accept the principle of utility?)
7. How does Mill proceed to give support (if not "proof") to the principle of utility? Outline the various steps in the argument and explain their justification. What justifies the move from "everyone wants his or her own happiness" to "everyone wants the happiness of all"?

8

Friedrich Nietzsche

Nietzsche was born in 1844, in a small town in Germany. Yet he despised Germany ("there's too much beer in the German intellect") and spent most of his adult life in Italy and Switzerland, where he became a citizen. He was trained in the classics and promised to be one of the most brilliant philologists in Basel; he was made a professor at the age of 25. Bad health (caused by an illness he caught while a medic in the Franco-Prussian War of 1870) forced him to resign his professorship, and he spent the rest of his life suffering from a number of ailments. But it was during this time too that he wrote virtually all of his astonishingly cheerful and energetic works. In 1889, in the act of throwing his arms around the neck of a horse in order to spare it a beating, Nietzsche collapsed and went hopelessly insane. He died in 1900.

If ethics is the understanding of good and evil, it is not surprising that the great moral philosophers should have spent so much of their efforts trying to clarify what is good and what is evil. But Nietzsche had something quite different in mind when he began his radical research on the nature and origins of morals, toward the end of the nineteenth century. Other philosophers—Kant most famously—took morality to be something of a given, to be clarified and justified but not questioned. Nietzsche, however, does not take morality to be a given but rather a very human—he would say "all-too-human"—invention, and, what is more, a tyrannical and destructive invention at that.

"Beyond good and evil" is one of the phrases Nietzsche frequently uses to mark his radical divorce from traditional ethics. He also calls himself an "immoralist," and he has often been called an "irrationalist." His works contain passages apparently condoning cruelty and callousness, and he writes long diatribes against such Christian virtues as pity, humility, and charity. But Nietzsche's reputation as a fanatic and as the *enfant terrible* or "bad boy" of ethics has been vastly exaggerated.

As a person, he was by all accounts gentle and considerate, soft-spoken, and witty. And although he rejects the religiously loaded concepts of "good and evil," he accepts the importance of values and is not hesitant about defending what he considers good against what he considers bad.

What is the difference between "good and evil" and "good and bad"? The first refers to that ancient conception (Nietzsche traces it to Zoroastrianism) in which good and evil are objective forces in the world, defined in the Judeo-Christian tradition by God and the devil, and culminating in the concept of *sin*—which Nietzsche despised. ("To rid the world of the concepts of Sin and Guilt: that is my goal.") "Good and bad," by contrast, refer to the strictly *psychological* question of the strength and satisfaction of our desires. What is good, Nietzsche proclaims, is what is strongest, most alive, and creative. He is not so much an immoralist or an irrationalist as he is an enthusiast. His passion radiates from his writings, and it is passion that he celebrates throughout them. On the other hand, what Nietzsche despises most is weakness and impotence, and on this ground he rejects the whole of Judeo-Christian morality and the moral emphasis on reason. In Christian morality, "only the emasculated man is the good man," he complains, in contrast to the ancient Greek warrior he idealizes. It is in this context that his comments on cruelty and suffering should be understood; it is not that Nietzsche urges cruelty, but he is concerned that the inhibitions of morality have had the effect of deadening our passions and spirit. It is not that Nietzsche likes suffering (though he had enough of it himself), but the good life, he insists, has to be created out of suffering as well as pleasure. "What does not overcome me," he writes, "makes me stronger," and—of the ancient Greeks—"how much these people must have suffered to be so beautiful."

Nietzsche's emphasis on the psychology of morals is not original (he believed that it was, even though he had already read Hume and John Stuart Mill). But, together with his vehement rejection of all objective moral standards ("there are no moral phenomena, only moralistic interpretations of phenomena"), his psychologizing clearly marks him as an ethical teleologist, who believes that the good must be defined in terms of our goals rather than in terms of any categorical principles of morals imposed from the outside (for example, the Ten Commandments). But for Nietzsche the ultimate human goal—the *summum bonum*—is not happiness. (Indeed, he calls utilitarianism "vulgar" for its emphasis on pleasure and happiness.) He sometimes says that it is "the will to power," by which he means self-assertion and expression, or what we might call "inner strength" rather than power over other people. He sometimes says that the goal is life itself (and he then defines "life" in terms of the quest for strength and "self-overcoming," that is, growth). But we would not misunderstand Nietzsche if we took his ethics to be aimed primarily at reinstating that ancient pagan ideal—the hero—in place of the bloodless bourgeois bureaucrat who in modern times represents "the good man." Nietzsche is not interested in the normal "good man" but rather in the *great* man, the more than human *Übermensch* (literally, "overman"). But if Napoleon and Caesar are mentioned as possible *Übermenschen*, it is important to note that Mozart and the great German poet Goethe are too. The vitality that Nietzsche so celebrates need not be physical but may be spiritual as well. Like Aristotle and the ancients, Nietzsche's ethics is primarily concerned with *character,* emphasizing individual virtue, and not only ignoring but rejecting universal moral rules that inhibit character and treat everyone as equal.

What is morality, that Nietzsche despises it so? He takes it to be a universal set of commandments that treats us all the same. What's wrong with that? Nietzsche's answer is that morality *appears* to benefit and protect everyone, but this in fact is not true. Instead, it benefits the weakest members of society and protects them. It is the expression of their *resentment* of the strong and successful. Therefore, it does not benefit but inhibits the strongest members of society. And if we also believe—as Nietzsche clearly does—that a society flourishes and is valuable because of the great individuals it produces, then this is a serious objection indeed. Morality is in fact the protection of the weak—a "slave" or "herd" morality.

The only good is to be found in life, in this world, in the realization of our "will to power or individual achievement and creativity," according to Nietzsche. He rejects all "other worldly" values and all authority but one's self. Is Nietzsche therefore an egoist? He would say no; in fact one of the most repeated arguments of his philosophy is his rejection of the ego, insisting that our actions are not to be understood that way (for example, "a thought comes when 'it' will, not when 'I' will"). If what we mean by "egoism" is satisfying our own interests, then Nietzsche would say that morality itself is egoistic—the expression of the resentment of the weaker members of society whose main interest it is to be protected from the strong. Furthermore, he says, it is not just a question of self-interest but rather of *whose* self-interest is in question. Nietzsche, unlike most other modern philosophers, does not believe in universal human equality. Some people are better, more alive, and more creative than others, he says, and they deserve more, too (and will take it for themselves). He is an unabashed elitist, much like the ancient philosophers Plato and Aristotle. His philosophy is "for the few," he insists—that is, for those who find themselves unhealthily inhibited by the strictures of morality and have much more to offer the world than being merely good citizens and morally proper neighbors.

THE GAY SCIENCE*

The Gay Science marks the beginning of Nietzsche's "mature" period, which saw the production of most of his greatest and most radical works. In the following story, he has a fictional madman announce "the death of God," an announcement that is to be found elsewhere in Nietzsche as well (notably in his *Thus Spake Zarathustra*) and became his most famous single phrase (challenged only by his conception of "the superman"). In this passage, however, Nietzsche does not present the "death of God" with the smug satisfaction of an atheist who has proved his point. Rather, the "madman" is filled with despair, and Nietzsche suggested that many calamities would follow in the wake of this momentous (but imaginary) event. The following section, on the other hand, presents the more exuberant side of Nietzsche's philosophy, the "joy" and "gaiety" that he insists are the most essential ingredients in any adequate ethics. He rejects the somber, even gloomy, countenance of traditional morality and suggests that the ideal should rather be an uninhibited, creative self-enjoyment. "To give style to one's character"—that is not a

*Friedrich Nietzsche, *The Gay Science*, translated by W. Kaufmann. Copyright 1974 by Random House, Inc.

prescription that modern moral philosophers have offered us. But "style" is not just superficial—a mere way of walking or a hat that a person puts on to impress new acquaintances. Style defines who a person is, and with the notion of style the entire emphasis in ethics shifts from rules (whether Kantian or utilitarian) to questions of character.

The madman.—Have you not heard of that madman who lit a lantern in the bright morning hours, ran to the market place, and cried incessantly: "I seek God! I seek God!"—As many of those who did not believe in God were standing around just then, he provoked much laughter. Has he got lost? asked one. Did he lose his way like a child? asked another. Or is he hiding? Is he afraid of us? Has he gone on a voyage? emigrated?—Thus they yelled and laughed.

The madman jumped into their midst and pierced them with his eyes. "Whither is God?" he cried; "I will tell you. *We have killed him*—you and I. All of us are his murderers. But how did we do this? How could we drink up the sea? Who gave us the sponge to wipe away the entire horizon? What were we doing when we unchained this earth from its sun? Whither is it moving now? Whither are we moving? Away from all suns? Are we not plunging continually? Backward, sideward, forward, in all directions? Is there still any up or down? Are we not straying as through an infinite nothing? Do we not feel the breath of empty space? Has it not become colder? Is not night continually closing in on us? Do we not need to light lanterns in the morning? Do we hear nothing as yet of the noise of the gravediggers who are burying God? Do we smell nothing as yet of the divine decomposition? Gods, too, decompose. God is dead. God remains dead. And we have killed him.

"How shall we comfort ourselves, the murderers of all murderers? What was holiest and mightiest of all that the world has yet owned has bled to death under our knives: who will wipe this blood off us? What water is there for us to clean ourselves? What festivals of atonement, what sacred games shall we have to invent? Is not the greatness of this deed too great for us? Must we ourselves not become gods simply to appear worthy of it? There has never been a greater deed; and whoever is born after us—for the sake of this deed he will belong to a higher history than all history hitherto."

Here the madman fell silent and looked again at his listeners; and they, too, were silent and stared at him in astonishment. At last he threw his lantern on the ground, and it broke into pieces and went out. "I have come too early," he said then; "my time is not yet. This tremendous event is still on its way, still wandering; it has not yet reached the ears of men. Lightning and thunder require time; the light of the stars requires time; deeds, though done, still require time to be seen and heard. This deed is still more distant from them than the most distant stars—*and yet they have done it themselves.*"

It has been related further that on the same day the madman forced his way into several churches and there struck up his *requiem aeternam deo.* Led out and called to account, he is said always to have replied nothing but: "What after all are these churches now if they are not the tombs and sepulchers of God?"

One thing is needful.—To "give style" to one's character—a great and rare art! It is practiced by those who survey all the strengths and weaknesses of their nature and then fit them into an artistic plan until every one of them appears as art and reason and even weaknesses delight the eye. Here a large mass of second nature has been added; there a piece of original nature has been removed—both times through long practice and daily work at it. Here the ugly that could not be removed is concealed; there it has been reinterpreted and made sublime. Much that is vague and resisted shaping has been saved and exploited for distant views; it is meant to beckon toward the far and immeasurable. In the end, when the work is finished, it becomes evident how the constraint of a single taste governed and formed everything large and small. Whether this taste was good or bad is less important than one might suppose, if only it was a single taste!

It will be the strong and domineering natures that enjoy their finest gaiety in such constraint and perfection under a law of their own; the passion of their tremendous will relents in the face of all stylized nature, of all conquered and serving nature. Even when they have to build palaces and design gardens they demur at giving nature freedom.

Conversely, it is the weak characters without power over themselves that *hate* the constraint of style. They feel that if this bitter and evil constraint were imposed upon them they would be demeaned; they become slaves as soon as they serve; they hate to serve. Such spirits—and they may be of the first rank—are always out to shape and interpret their environment as *free* nature: wild, arbitrary, fantastic, disorderly, and surprising. And they are well advised because it is only in this way that they can give pleasure to themselves. For one thing is needful: that a human being should *attain* satisfaction with himself, whether it be by means of this or that poetry and art; only then is a human being at all tolerable to behold. Whoever is dissatisfied with himself is continually ready for revenge, and we others will be his victims, if only by having to endure his ugly sight. For the sight of what is ugly makes one bad and gloomy.

THUS SPOKE ZARATHUSTRA*

Zarathustra is Nietzsche's most famous—and no doubt most difficult—book. It took the form of a long, four-part prose poem and modeled its language after the Bible. But its hero, Zarathustra, is not a familiar biblical character. (Rather, he is borrowed from the ancient Persian religion of Zoroastrianism.) And what he argues is just the opposite of the standard biblical message. There is no other life; this life is all there is. Meekness and acquiescence are not virtues: Ruthless self-examination, even self-contempt, are the ways to perfection. And happiness is not the ultimate goal; quite the contrary, it is something mediocre and pathetic. Zarathustra's "last man," portrayed here, is intended as a humiliating portrait of our desire for happiness and comfort. Thus, we can understand Zarathustra's disgust when the townspeople to whom he is preaching embrace the last man and his ideals as their own.

*Friedrich Nietzsche, "Thus Spoke Zarathustra" from *The Portable Nietzsche,* edited by Walter Kaufmann. Copyright 1954 by The Viking Press, renewed © 1982 by Viking Penguin Inc.

When Zarathustra came into the next town, which lies on the edge of the forest, he found many people gathered together in the market place; for it had been promised that there would be a tightrope walker. And Zarathustra spoke thus to the people:

"*I teach you the overman.* Man is something that shall be overcome. What have you done to overcome him?

"All beings so far have created something beyond themselves; and do you want to be the ebb of this great flood and even go back to the beasts rather than overcome man? What is the ape to man? A laughingstock or a painful embarrassment. And man shall be just that for the overman: a laughingstock or a painful embarrassment. You have made your way from worm to man, and much in you is still worm. Once you were apes, and even now, too, man is more ape than any ape.

"Whoever is the wisest among you is also a mere conflict and cross between plant and ghost. But do I bid you become ghosts or plants?

"Behold, I teach you the overman. The overman is the meaning of the earth. Let your will say: the overman *shall be* the meaning of the earth! I beseech you, my brothers, *remain faithful to the earth,* and do not believe those who speak to you of otherworldly hopes! Poison-mixers are they, whether they know it or not. Despisers of life are they, decaying and poisoned themselves, of whom the earth is weary: so let them go.

"Once the sin against God was the greatest sin; but God died, and these sinners died with him. To sin against the earth is now the most dreadful thing, and to esteem the entrails of the unknowable higher than the meaning of the earth.

"Once the soul looked contemptuously upon the body, and then this contempt was the highest: she wanted the body meager, ghastly, and starved. Thus she hoped to escape it and the earth. Oh, this soul herself was still meager, ghastly, and starved: and cruelty was the lust of this soul. But you, too, my brothers, tell me: what does your body proclaim of your soul? Is not your soul poverty and filth and wretched contentment?

"Verily, a polluted stream is man. One must be a sea to be able to receive a polluted stream without becoming unclean. Behold, I teach you the overman: he is this sea; in him your great contempt can go under.

"What is the greatest experience you can have? It is the hour of the great contempt. The hour in which your happiness, too, arouses your disgust, and even your reason and your virtue.

"The hour when you say, 'What matters my happiness? It is poverty and filth and wretched contentment. But my happiness ought to justify existence itself.'

"The hour when you say, 'What matters my reason? Does it crave knowledge as the lion his food? It is poverty and filth and wretched contentment.'

"The hour when you say, 'What matters my virtue? As yet it has not made me rage. How weary I am of my good and my evil! All that is poverty and filth and wretched contentment.'

"The hour when you say, 'What matters my justice? I do not see that I am flames and fuel. But the just are flames and fuel.'

"The hour when you say, 'What matters my pity? Is not pity the cross on which he is nailed who loves man? But my pity is no crucifixion.'

"Have you yet spoken thus? Have you yet cried thus? Oh, that I might have heard you cry thus!

"Not your sin but your thrift cries to heaven; your meanness even in your sin cries to heaven.

"Where is the lightning to lick you with its tongue? Where is the frenzy with which you should be inoculated?

"Behold, I teach you the overman: he is this lightning, he is this frenzy."

When Zarathustra had spoken thus, one of the people cried: "Now we have heard enough about the tightrope walker; now let us see him too!" And all the people laughed at Zarathustra. But the tightrope walker, believing that the word concerned him, began his performance.

Zarathustra, however, beheld the people and was amazed. Then he spoke thus:

"Man is a rope, tied between beast and overman—a rope over an abyss. A dangerous across, a dangerous on-the-way, a dangerous looking-back, a dangerous shuddering and stopping.

"What is great in man is that he is a bridge and not an end: what can be loved in man is that he is an *overture* and a *going under.*

"I love those who do not know how to live, except by going under, for they are those who cross over.

"I love the great despisers because they are the great reverers and arrows of longing for the other shore.

"I love those who do not first seek behind the stars for a reason to go under and be a sacrifice, but who sacrifice themselves for the earth, that the earth may some day become the overman's.

"I love him who lives to know, and who wants to know so that the overman may live some day. And thus he wants to go under.

"I love him who works and invents to build a house for the overman and to prepare earth, animal, and plant for him: for thus he wants to go under.

"I love him who loves his virtue, for virtue is the will to go under and an arrow of longing.

"I love him who does not hold back one drop of spirit for himself, but wants to be entirely the spirit of his virtue: thus he strides over the bridge as spirit.

"I love him who makes his virtue his addiction and his catastrophe: for his virtue's sake he wants to live on and to live no longer.

"I love him who does not want to have too many virtues. One virtue is more virtue than two, because it is more of a noose on which his catastrophe may hang.

"I love him whose soul squanders itself, who wants no thanks and returns none: for he always gives away and does not want to preserve himself.

"I love him who is abashed when the dice fall to make his fortune, and asks, 'Am I then a crooked gambler?' For he wants to perish.

"I love him who casts golden words before his deeds and always does even more than he promises: for he wants to go under.

"I love him who justifies future and redeems past generations: for he wants to perish of the present.

"I love him who chastens his god because he loves his god: for he must perish of the wrath of his god.

"I love him whose soul is deep, even in being wounded, and who can perish of a small experience: thus he goes gladly over the bridge.

"I love him whose soul is overfull so that he forgets himself, and all things are in him: thus all things spell his going under.

"I love him who has a free spirit and a free heart: thus his head is only the entrails of his heart, but his heart drives him to go under.

"I love all those who are as heavy drops, falling one by one out of the dark cloud that hangs over men: they herald the advent of lightning, and, as heralds, they perish.

"Behold, I am a herald of the lightning and a heavy drop from the cloud; but this lightning is called *overman*."

When Zarathustra had spoken these words he beheld the people again and was silent. "There they stand," he said to his heart; "there they laugh. They do not understand me; I am not the mouth for these ears. Must one smash their ears before they learn to listen with their eyes? Must one clatter like kettledrums and preachers of repentance? Or do they believe only the stammerer?

"They have something of which they are proud. What do they call that which makes them proud? Education they call it; it distinguishes them from goatherds. That is why they do not like to hear the word 'contempt' applied to them. Let me then address their pride. Let me speak to them of what is most contemptible: but that is the *last man*."

And thus spoke Zarathustra to the people: "The time has come for man to set himself a goal. The time has come for man to plant the seed of his highest hope. His soil is still rich enough. But one day this soil will be poor and domesticated, and no tall tree will be able to grow in it. Alas, the time is coming when man will no longer shoot the arrow of his longing beyond man, and the string of his bow will have forgotten how to whir!

"I say unto you: one must still have chaos in oneself to be able to give birth to a dancing star. I say unto you: you still have chaos in yourselves.

"Alas, the time is coming when man will no longer give birth to a star. Alas, the time of the most despicable man is coming, he that is no longer able to despise himself. Behold, I show you the *last man*.

"'What is love? What is creation? What is longing? What is a star?' thus asks the last man, and he blinks.

"The earth has become small, and on it hops the last man, who makes everything small. His race is as ineradicable as the flea-beetle; the last man lives longest.

"'We have invented happiness,' say the last men, and they blink. They have left the regions where it was hard to live, for one needs warmth. One still loves one's neighbor and rubs against him, for one needs warmth.

"Becoming sick and harboring suspicion are sinful to them: one proceeds carefully. A fool, whoever still stumbles over stones or human beings! A little poison now and then: that makes for agreeable dreams. And much poison in the end, for an agreeable death.

"One still works, for work is a form of entertainment. But one is careful lest the entertainment be too harrowing. One no longer becomes poor or rich: both require too much exertion. Who still wants to rule? Who obey? Both require too much exertion.

"No shepherd and one herd! Everybody wants the same, everybody is the same: whoever feels different goes voluntarily into a madhouse.

"'Formerly, all the world was mad,' say the most refined, and they blink.

"One is clever and knows everything that has ever happened: so there is no end of derision. One still quarrels, but one is soon reconciled—else it might spoil the digestion.

"One has one's little pleasure for the day and one's little pleasure for the night: but one has a regard for health.

"'We have invented happiness,' say the last men, and they blink."

And here ended Zarathustra's first speech, which is also called "the Prologue"; for at this point he was interrupted by the clamor and delight of the crowd. "Give us this last man, O Zarathustra," they shouted. "Turn us into these last men! Then we shall make you a gift of the overman!" And all the people jubilated and clucked with their tongues.

But Zarathustra became sad and said to his heart: "They do not understand me: I am not the mouth for these ears. I seem to have lived too long in the mountains; I listened too much to brooks and trees: now I talk to them as to goatherds. My soul is unmoved and bright as the mountains in the morning. But they think I am cold and I jeer and make dreadful jests. And now they look at me and laugh: and as they laugh they even hate me. There is ice in their laughter."

BEYOND GOOD AND EVIL*

Beyond Good and Evil is perhaps Nietzsche's most comprehensive book, and as the title suggests, it constitutes a sustained attack on traditional Western morality, the morality of "good and evil." But Nietzsche also attacks the theoreticians of morality, those who have tried to squeeze all the varieties of human customs and prohibitions into a single mold and have thereby tried to *justify* their own "moral prejudices." Nietzsche pursues that unusual question that so well defines his revolution in ethics: "Why should people adopt a morality at all?" Could it be that morality is really an expression, above all, of our timidity?

THE NATURAL HISTORY OF MORALS

186. The moral sentiment in Europe at present is perhaps as subtle, belated, diverse, sensitive, and refined, as the "Science of Morals" belonging thereto is

*Friedrich Nietzsche, *Beyond Good and Evil,* translated by Helen Zimmern. Copyright 1911 by The Macmillan Co.

recent, initial, awkward, and coarse-fingered:—an interesting contrast, which sometimes becomes incarnate and obvious in the very person of a moralist. Indeed, the expression, "Science of Morals" is, in respect to what is designated thereby, far too presumptuous and counter to *good* taste,—which is always a foretaste of more modest expressions. One ought to avow with the utmost fairness *what* is still necessary here for a long time, *what* is alone proper for the present: namely, the collection of material, the comprehensive survey and classification of an immense domain of delicate sentiments of worth, and distinctions of worth, which live, grow, propagate, and perish—and perhaps attempts to give a clear idea of the recurring and more common forms of these living crystallisations—as preparation for a *theory of types* of morality. To be sure, people have not hitherto been so modest. All the philosophers, with a pedantic and ridiculous seriousness, demanded of themselves something very much higher, more pretentious, and ceremonious, when they concerned themselves with morality as a science: they wanted to *give a basis* to morality—and every philosopher hitherto has believed that he has given it a basis; morality itself, however, has been regarded as something "given." How far from their awkward pride was the seemingly insignificant problem—left in dust and decay—of a description of forms of morality, notwithstanding that the finest hands and senses could hardly be fine enough for it! It was precisely owing to moral philosophers knowing the moral facts imperfectly, in an arbitrary epitome, or an accidental abridgement—perhaps as the morality of their environment, their position, their church, their *Zeitgeist,* their climate and zone—it was precisely because they were badly instructed with regard to nations, eras, and past ages, and were by no means eager to know about these matters, that they did not even come in sight of the real problems of morals—problems which only disclose themselves by a comparison of *many* kinds of morality. In every "Science of Morals" hitherto, strange as it may sound, the problem of morality itself has been *omitted;* there has been no suspicion that there was anything problematic there! That which philosophers called "giving a basis to morality," and endeavoured to realise, has, when seen in a right light, proved merely a learned form of good *faith* in prevailing morality, a new means of its *expression,* consequently just a matter-of-fact within the sphere of a definite morality, yea, in its ultimate motive, a sort of denial that it is *lawful* for this morality to be called in question—and in any case the reverse of the testing, analysing, doubting, and vivisecting of this very faith. Hear, for instance, with what innocence— almost worthy of honour—Schopenhauer represents his own task, and draw your conclusions concerning the scientificalness of a "Science" whose latest master still talks in the strain of children and old wives: "The principle," he says (page 136 of the *Grundprobleme der Ethik*), "the axiom about the purport of which all moralists are *practically* agreed: 'Do not hurt anyone, but help everyone, as much as you can.'—is *really* the proposition which all moral teachers strive to establish, . . . the *real* basis of ethics which has been sought, like the philosopher's stone, for centuries."—The difficulty of establishing the proposition referred to may indeed be great—it is well known that Schopenhauer also was unsuccessful in his efforts; and whoever has thoroughly realised how absurdly false and sentimental this proposition is, in a world whose essence is Will to Power, may be reminded that Schopenhauer, although a pessimist, *actually*—played the flute . . . daily after dinner: one may read about the matter in his biography. A question by the way: a pessimist, a repudiator of God and of the world, who *makes a halt* at morality—who assents to morality, and plays the flute to "do not hurt anyone" morals, what? Is that really—a pessimist?

187. Apart from the value of such assertions as "there is a categorical imperative in us," one can always ask: What does such an assertion indicate about him who makes it? There are systems of morals which are meant to justify their author in the eyes of other people; other systems of morals are meant to tranquillise him, and make him self-satisfied; with other systems he wants to crucify and humble himself; with others he wishes to take revenge; with others to conceal himself; with others to glorify himself and gain superiority and distinction;—this system of morals helps its author to forget, that system makes him, or something of him, forgotten; many a moralist would like to exercise power and creative arbitrariness over mankind; many another, perhaps, Kant especially, gives us to understand by his morals that "what is estimable in me, is that I know how to obey—and with you it shall not be otherwise than with me!" In short, systems of morals are only a *sign-language of the emotions.*

188. In contrast to *laisser-aller,* every system of morals is a sort of tyranny against "nature" and also against "reason"; that is, however, no objection, unless one should again decree by some system of morals, that all kinds of tyranny and unreasonableness are unlawful. What is essential and invaluable in every system of morals, is that it is a long constraint. In order to understand Stoicism, or Port-Royal, or Puritanism, one should remember the constraint under which every language has attained to strength and freedom—the metrical constraint, the tyranny of rhyme and rhythm. How much trouble have the poets and orators of every nation given themselves!—not excepting some of the prose writers of to-day, in whose ear dwells an inexorable conscientiousness—"for the sake of a folly," as utilitarian bunglers say, and thereby deem themselves wise—"from submission to arbitrary laws," as the anarchists say, and thereby fancy themselves "free," even free-spirited. The singular fact remains, however, that everything of the nature of freedom, elegance, boldness, dance, and masterly certainty, which exists or has existed, whether it be in thought itself, or in administration, or in speaking and persuading, in art just as in conduct, has only developed by means of the tyranny of such arbitrary law; and in all seriousness, it is not at all improbable that precisely this is "nature" and "natural"—and *not laisser-aller!* Every artist knows how different from the state of letting himself go, is his "most natural" condition, the free arranging, locating, disposing, and constructing in the moments of "inspiration"—and how strictly and delicately he then obeys a thousand laws, which, by their very rigidness and precision, defy all formulation by means of ideas (even the most stable idea has, in comparison therewith, something floating, manifold, and ambiguous in it). The essential thing "in heaven and in earth" is, apparently (to repeat it once more), that there should be long *obedience* in the same direction; there thereby results, and has always resulted in the long run, something which has made life worth living; for instance, virtue, art, music, dancing, reason, spirituality—anything whatever

that is transfiguring, refined, foolish, or divine. The long bondage of the spirit, the distrustful constraint in the communicability of ideas, the discipline which the thinker imposed on himself to think in accordance with the rules of a church or a court, or conformable to Aristotelian premises, the persistent spiritual will to interpret everything that happened according to a Christian scheme, and in every occurrence to rediscover and justify the Christian God:—all this violence, arbitrariness, severity, dreadfulness, and unreasonableness, has proved itself the disciplinary means whereby the European spirit has attained its strength, its remorseless curiosity and subtle mobility; granted also that much irrecoverable strength and spirit had to be stifled, suffocated, and spoiled in the process (for here, as everywhere, "nature" shows herself as she is, in all her extravagant and *indifferent* magnificence, which is shocking, but nevertheless noble). That for centuries European thinkers only thought in order to prove something—nowadays, on the contrary, we are suspicious of every thinker who "wishes to prove something"—that it was always settled beforehand what *was to be* the result of their strictest thinking, as it was perhaps in the Asiatic astrology of former times, or as it is still at the present day in the innocent, Christian-moral explanation of immediate personal events "for the glory of God," or "for the good of the soul":—this tyranny, this arbitrariness, this severe and magnificent stupidity, has *educated* the spirit; slavery, both in the coarser and the finer sense, is apparently an indispensable means even of spiritual education and discipline. One may look at every system of morals in this light: it is "nature" therein which teaches to hate the *laisser-aller,* the too great freedom, and implants the need for limited horizons, for immediate duties—it teaches the *narrowing of perspectives,* and thus, in a certain sense, that stupidity is a condition of life and development. "Thou must obey some one, and for a long time; *otherwise* thou wilt come to grief, and lose all respect for thyself"—this seems to me to be the moral imperative of nature, which is certainly neither "categorical," as old Kant wished (consequently the "otherwise"), nor does it address itself to the individual (what does nature care for the individual!), but to nations, races, ages, and ranks, above all, however, to the animal "man" generally, to *mankind.* . . .

190. There is something in the morality of Plato which does not really belong to Plato, but which only appears in his philosophy, one might say, in spite of him: namely, Socratism, for which he himself was too noble. "No one desires to injure himself, hence all evil is done unwittingly. The evil man inflicts injury on himself; he would not do so, however, if he knew that evil is evil. The evil man, therefore, is only evil through error; if one free him from error one will necessarily make him—good."—This mode of reasoning savours of the *populace,* who perceive only the unpleasant consequences of evil-doing, and practically judge that "it is *stupid* to do wrong"; while they accept "good" as identical with "useful and pleasant," without further thought. As regards every system of utilitarianism, one may at once assume that it has the same origin, and follow the scent: one will seldom err.—Plato did all he could to interpret something refined and noble into the tenets of his teacher, and above all to interpret himself into them—he, the most daring of all interpreters, who lifted the entire Socrates out of the street, as a popular theme and song, to exhibit him in endless and

impossible modifications—namely, in all his own disguises and multiplicities. In jest, and in Homeric language as well, what is the Platonic Socrates, if not—

Plato in front, Plato in back, but in the middle a Chimaera.

191. The old theological problem of "Faith" and "Knowledge," or more plainly, of instinct and reason—the question whether, in respect to the valuation of things, instinct deserves more authority than rationality, which wants to appreciate and act according to motives, according to a "Why," that is to say, in conformity to purpose and utility—it is always the old moral problem that first appeared in the person of Socrates, and had divided men's minds long before Christianity. Socrates himself, following, of course, the taste of his talent—that of a surpassing dialectician—took first the side of reason: and, in fact, what did he do all his life but laugh at the awkward incapacity of the noble Athenians, who were men of instinct, like all noble men, and could never give satisfactory answers concerning the motives of their actions? In the end, however, though silently and secretly, he laughed also at himself: with his finer conscience and introspection, he found in himself the same difficulty and incapacity. "But why"—he said to himself—"should one on that account separate oneself from the instincts! One must set them right, and the reason *also*—one must follow the instincts, but at the same time persuade the reason to support them with good arguments." This was the real *falseness* of that great and mysterious ironist: he brought his conscience up to the point that he was satisfied with a kind of self-outwitting: in fact, he perceived the irrationality in the moral judgment.—Plato, more innocent in such matters, and without the craftiness of the plebeian, wished to prove to himself, at the expenditure of all his strength—the greatest strength a philosopher had ever expended—that reason and instinct lead spontaneously to one goal, to the good, to "God"; and since Plato, all theologians and philosophers have followed the same path—which means that in matters of morality, instinct (or as Christians call it, "Faith," or as I call it, "the herd") has hitherto triumphed. Unless one should make an exception in the case of Descartes, the father of rationalism (and consequently the grandfather of the Revolution), who recognised only the authority of reason: but reason is only a tool, and Descartes was superficial. . . .

197. The beast of prey and the man of prey (for instance, Caesar Borgia) are fundamentally misunderstood, "nature" is misunderstood, so long as one seeks a "morbidness" in the constitution of these healthiest of all tropical monsters and growths, or even an innate "hell" in them—as almost all moralists have done hitherto. Does it not seem that there is a hatred of the virgin forest and of the tropics among moralists? And that the "tropical man" must be discredited at all costs, whether as disease and deterioration of mankind, or as his own hell and self-torture? And why? In favour of the "temperate zones"? In favour of the temperate men? The "moral"? The mediocre?—This for the chapter: "Morals as Timidity."

198. All the systems of morals which address themselves with a view to their "happiness," as it is called—what else are they but suggestions for behaviour adapted to the degree of *danger* from themselves in which the individuals live; recipes for their passions, their good and bad propensities, in so far as such

have the Will to Power and would like to play the master; small and great expediencies and elaborations, permeated with the musty odour of old family medicines and old-wife wisdom: all of them grotesque and absurd in their form—because they address themselves to "all," because they generalise where generalisation is not authorised; all of them speaking unconditionally, and taking themselves unconditionally; all of them flavoured not merely with one grain of salt, but rather endurable only, and sometimes even seductive, when they are over-spiced and begin to smell dangerously, especially of "the other world"? That is all of little value when estimated intellectually, and is far from being "science," much less "wisdom"; but, repeated once more, and three times repeated, it is expediency, expediency, expediency, mixed with stupidity, stupidity, stupidity—whether it be the indifference and statuesque coldness towards the heated folly of the emotions, which the Stoics advised and fostered; or the no-more-laughing and no-more-weeping of Spinoza, the destruction of the emotions by their analysis and vivisection, which he recommended so naively; or the lowering of the emotions to an innocent mean at which they may be satisfied, the Aristotelianism of morals; or even morality as the enjoyment of the emotions in a voluntary attenuation and spiritualisation by the symbolism of art, perhaps as music, or as love of God, and of mankind for God's sake—for in religion the passions are once more enfranchised, provided that . . .; or, finally, even the complaisant and wanton surrender to the emotions, as has been taught by Hafis and Goethe, the bold letting-go of the reins, the spiritual and corporeal moral license in the exceptional cases of wise old codgers and drunkards, with whom it "no longer has much danger."—This also for the chapter: "Morals as Timidity."

199. Inasmuch as in all ages, as long as mankind has existed, there have also been human herds (family alliances, communities, tribes, peoples, states, churches), and always a great number who obey in proportion to the small number who command—in view, therefore, of the fact that obedience has been most practised and fostered among mankind hitherto, one may reasonably suppose that, generally speaking, the need thereof is now innate in every one, as a kind of *formal conscience* which gives the command: "Thou shalt unconditionally do something, unconditionally refrain from something"; in short, "Thou shalt." This need tries to satisfy itself and to fill its form with a content; according to its strength, impatience, and eagerness, it at once seizes as an omnivorous appetite with little selection, and accepts whatever is shouted into its ear by all sorts of commanders—parents, teachers, laws, class prejudices, or public opinion. The extraordinary limitation of human development, the hesitation, protractedness, frequent retrogression, and turning thereof, is attributable to the fact that the herd-instinct of obedience is transmitted best, and at the cost of the art of command. If one imagine this instinct increasing to its greatest extent, commanders and independent individuals will finally be lacking altogether; or they will suffer inwardly from a bad conscience, and will have to impose a deception on themselves in the first place in order to be able to command: just as if they also were only obeying. This condition of things actually exists in Europe at present—I call it the moral hypocrisy of the commanding class. They know no other way of protecting themselves from their bad conscience than by playing the role

of executors of older and higher orders (of predecessors, of the constitution, of justice, of the law, or of God himself), or they even justify themselves by maxims from the current opinions of the herd, as "first servants of their people," or "instruments of the public weal." On the other hand, the gregarious European man nowadays assumes an air as if he were the only kind of man that is allowable; he glorifies his qualities, such as public spirit, kindness, deference, industry, temperance, modesty, indulgence, sympathy, by virtue of which he is gentle, endurable, and useful to the herd, as the peculiarly human virtues. In cases, however, where it is believed that the leader and bellwether cannot be dispensed with, attempt after attempt is made nowadays to replace commanders by the summing together of clever gregarious men: all representative constitutions, for example, are of this origin. In spite of all, what a blessing, what a deliverance from a weight becoming unendurable, is the appearance of an absolute ruler for these gregarious Europeans—of this fact the effect of the appearance of Napoleon was the last great proof: the history of the influence of Napoleon is almost the history of the higher happiness to which the entire century has attained in its worthiest individuals and periods. . . .

201. As long as the utility which determines moral estimates is only gregarious utility, as long as the preservation of the community is only kept in view, and the immoral is sought precisely and exclusively in what seems dangerous to the maintenance of the community, there can be no "morality of love to one's neighbour." Granted even that there is already a little constant exercise of consideration, sympathy, fairness, gentleness, and mutual assistance, granted that even in this condition of society all those instincts are already active which are latterly distinguished by honourable names as "virtues," and eventually almost coincide with the conception "morality": in that period they do not as yet belong to the domain of more valuations—they are still *ultra-moral*. A sympathetic action, for instance, is neither called good nor bad, moral nor immoral, in the best period of the Romans; and should it be praised, a sort of resentful disdain is compatible with this praise, even at the best, directly the sympathetic action is compared with one which contributes to the welfare of the whole, to the *res publica*. After all, "love to our neighbour" is always a secondary matter, partly conventional and arbitrarily manifested in relation to our *fear of our neighbour*. After the fabric of society seems on the whole established and secured against external dangers, it is this fear of our neighbour which again creates new perspectives of moral valuation. Certain strong and dangerous instincts, such as the love of enterprise, foolhardiness, revengefulness, astuteness, rapacity, and love of power, which up till then had not only to be honoured from the point of view of general utility—under other names, of course, than those here given—but had to be fostered and cultivated (because they were perpetually required in the common danger against the common enemies), are now felt in their dangerousness to be doubly strong—when the outlets for them are lacking—and are gradually branded as immoral and given over to calumny. The contrary instincts and inclinations now attain to moral honour; the gregarious instinct gradually draws its conclusions. How much or how little dangerousness to the community or to equality is contained in an opinion, a condition, an emotion, a disposition, or an

endowment—that is now the moral perspective; here again fear is the mother of morals. It is by the loftiest and strongest instincts, when they break out passionately and carry the individual far above and beyond the average, and the low level of the gregarious conscience, that the self-reliance of the community is destroyed; its belief in itself, its backbone, as it were, breaks; consequently these very instincts will be most branded and defamed. The lofty independent spirituality, the will to stand alone, and even the cogent reason, are felt to be dangers; everything that elevates the individual above the herd, and is a source of fear to the neighbour, is henceforth called *evil;* the tolerant, unassuming, self-adapting, self-equalising disposition, the *mediocrity* of desires, attains to moral distinction and honour. Finally, under very peaceful circumstances, there is always less opportunity and necessity for training the feelings to severity and rigour; and now every form of severity, even in justice, begins to disturb the conscience; a lofty and rigourous nobleness and self-responsibility almost offends, and awakens distrust, "the lamb," and still more "the sheep," wins respect. There is a point of diseased mellowness and effeminacy in the history of society, at which society itself takes the part of him who injures it, the part of the *criminal,* and does so, in fact, seriously and honestly. To punish, appears to it to be somehow unfair—it is certain that the idea of "punishment" and "the obligation to punish" are then painful and alarming to people. "Is it not sufficient if the criminal be rendered *harmless?* Why should we still punish? Punishment itself is terrible!"—with these questions gregarious morality, the morality of fear, draws its ultimate conclusion. If one could at all do away with danger, the cause of fear, one would have done away with this morality at the same time, it would no longer be necessary, it *would not consider itself* any longer necessary!—Whoever examines the conscience of the present-day European, will always elicit the same imperative from its thousand moral folds and hidden recesses, the imperative of the timidity of the herd: "we wish that some time or other there may be *nothing more to fear!*" Some time or other—the will and the way *thereto* is nowadays called "progress" all over Europe.

202. Let us at once say again what we have already said a hundred times, for people's ears nowadays are unwilling to hear such truths—*our* truths. We know well enough how offensively it sounds when any one plainly, and without metaphor, counts man amongst the animals; but it will be accounted to us almost a *crime,* that it is precisely in respect to men of "modern ideas" that we have constantly applied the terms "herd," "herd-instincts," and such like expressions. What avail is it? We cannot do otherwise, for it is precisely here that our new insight is. We have found that in all the principal moral judgments Europe has become unanimous, including likewise the countries where European influence prevails: in Europe people evidently *know* what Socrates thought he did not know, and what the famous serpent of old once promised to teach—they "know" to-day what is good and evil. It must then sound hard and be distasteful to the ear, when we always insist that that which here thinks it knows, that which here glorifies itself with praise and blame, and calls itself good, is the instinct of the herding human animal: the instinct which has come and is ever coming more and more to the front, to preponderance and supremacy over other

instincts, according to the increasing physiological approximation and resemblance of which it is the symptom. *Morality in Europe at present is herding-animal morality;* and therefore, as we understand the matter, only one kind of human morality, beside which, before which, and after which many other moralities, and above all *higher* moralities, are or should be possible. Against such a "possibility," against such a "should be," however, this morality defends itself with all its strength; it says obstinately and inexorably: "I am morality itself and nothing else is morality!" Indeed, with the help of a religion which has humoured and flattered the sublimest desires of the herding-animal, things have reached such a point that we always find a more visible expression of this morality even in political and social arrangements: the *democratic* movement is the inheritance of the Christian movement. That its *tempo,* however, is much too slow and sleepy for the more impatient ones, for those who are sick and distracted by the herding-instinct, is indicated by the increasingly furious howling, and always less disguised teeth-gnashing of the anarchist dogs, who are now roving through the highways of European culture. Apparently in opposition to the peacefully industrious democrats and Revolution-ideologues, and still more so to the awkward philosophasters and fraternity-visionaries who call themselves Socialists and want a "free society," those are really at one with them all in their thorough and instinctive hostility to every form of society other than that of the *autonomous* herd (to the extent even of repudiating the notions "master" and "servant"—*ni Dieu ni maître,* says a socialist formula); at one in their tenacious opposition to every special claim, every special right and privilege (this means ultimately opposition to *every* right, for when all are equal, no one needs "rights" any longer); at one in their distrust of punitive justice (as though it were a violation of the weak, unfair to the *necessary* consequences of all former society); but equally at one in their religion of sympathy, in their compassion for all that feels, lives, and suffers (down to the very animals, up even to "God"—the extravagance of "sympathy for God" belongs to a democratic age); altogether at one in the cry and impatience of their sympathy, in their deadly hatred of suffering generally, in their almost feminine incapacity for witnessing it or *allowing* it; at one in their involuntary beglooming and heart-softening, under the spell of which Europe seems to be threatened with a new Buddhism; at one in their belief in the morality of *mutual* sympathy, as though it were morality in itself, the climax, the *attained* climax of mankind, the sole hope of the future, the consolation of the present, the great discharge from all the obligations of the past; altogether at one in their belief in the community as the *deliverer,* in the herd, and therefore in "themselves."

203. We, who hold a different belief—we, who regard the democratic movement, not only as a degenerating form of political organisation, but as equivalent to a degenerating, a waning type of man, as involving his mediocrising and depreciation: where have we to fix our hopes? In *new philosophers*—there is no other alternative: in minds strong and original enough to initiate opposite estimates of value, to transvalue and invert "eternal valuations"; in forerunners, in men of the future, who in the present shall fix the constraints and fasten the knots which will compel millenniums to take *new* paths. To teach

man the future of humanity as his *will,* as depending on human will, and to make preparation for vast hazardous enterprises and collective attempts in rearing and educating, in order thereby to put an end to the frightful rule of folly and chance which has hitherto gone by the name of "history" (the folly of the "greatest number" is only its last form)—for that purpose a new type of philosophers and commanders will some time or other be needed, at the very idea of which everything that has existed in the way of occult, terrible, and benevolent beings might look pale and dwarfed. The image of such leaders hovers before *our* eyes:—is it lawful for me to say it aloud, ye free spirits? The conditions which one would partly have to create and party utilise for their genesis; the presumptive methods and tests by virtue of which a soul should grow up to such an elevation and power as to feel a *constraint* to these tasks; a transvaluation of values, under the new pressure and hammer of which a conscience should be steeled and a heart transformed into brass, so as to bear the weight of such responsibility; and on the other hand the necessity for such leaders, the dreadful danger that they might be lacking, or miscarry and degenerate:—these are *our* real anxieties and glooms, ye know it well, ye free spirits! these are the heavy distant thoughts and storms which sweep across the heaven of *our* life. There are few pains so grievous as to have seen, divined, or experienced how an exceptional man has missed his way and deteriorated; but he who has the rare eye for the universal danger of "man" himself *deteriorating,* he who like us has recognised the extraordinary fortuitousness which has hitherto played its game in respect to the future of mankind—a game in which neither the hand, nor even a "finger of God" has participated!—he who divines the fate that is hidden under the idiotic unwariness and blind confidence of "modern ideas," and still more under the whole of Christo-European morality—suffers from an anguish with which no other is to be compared. He sees at a glance all that could still *be made out of man* through a favourable accumulation and augmentation of human powers and arrangements; he knows with all the knowledge of his conviction how unexhausted man still is for the greatest possibilities, and how often in the past the type man has stood in presence of mysterious decisions and new paths:—he knows still better from his painfulest recollections on what wretched obstacles promising developments of the highest rank have hitherto usually gone to pieces, broken down, sunk, and become contemptible. The *universal degeneracy of mankind* to the level of the "man of the future"—as idealised by the sociolistic fools and shallow-pates—this degeneracy and dwarfing of man to an absolutely gregarious animal (or as they call it, to a man of "free society"), this brutalising of man into a pigmy with equal rights and claims, is undoubtedly *possible!* He who has thought out this possibility to its ultimate conclusion knows *another* loathing unknown to the rest of mankind—and perhaps also a new *mission!*

Nietzsche sees the need for the reintroduction of a lost conception, the concept of "nobility." To be sure, there were aristocrats in Europe even as he was writing, but most of them had all of the features of contemporary culture that Nietzsche had grown to despise. Above all, they were *comfortable*. What Nietzsche has in mind by "nobility" is rather an ancient paradigm, presupposing a most inegalitarian society, in which a few people are (and are recognized to be) superior to all of the others. It is here that Nietzsche introduces his much-discussed distinction between "master morality" and "slave morality," two moral "types" that are found in different proportions in most societies (and even in the same person). Master morality is a morality of self-assertion (best understood as creativity, not physical strength), and slave morality is a morality of weakness, a defensive stance that tries to get those who are superior to "level" themselves, to bring themselves down with the others and become wholly nonthreatening. Underlying Nietzsche's analysis is a biological, almost Darwinian, analysis of the necessity of struggle and the desirability of the survival of the "best." (Darwin had published his *Origin of Species* only two decades before.) Nietzsche emphasizes the importance of struggle in every human effort, and he harshly criticizes those who have become merely "weary" of the challenges of life.

WHAT IS NOBLE?

257. Every elevation of the type "man," has hitherto been the work of an aristocratic society and so it will always be—a society believing in a long scale of gradations of rank and differences of worth among human beings, and requiring slavery in some form or other. Without the *pathos of distance,* such as grows out of the incarnated difference of classes, out of the constant outlooking and downlooking of the ruling caste on subordinates and instruments, and out of their equally constant practice of obeying and commanding, of keeping down and keeping at a distance—that other more mysterious pathos could never have arisen, the longing for an ever new widening of distance within the soul itself, the formation of ever higher, rarer, further, more extended, more comprehensive states, in short, just the elevation of the type "man," the continued "self-surmounting of man," to use a moral formula in a supermoral sense. To be sure, one must not resign oneself to any humanitarian illusions about the history of the origin of an aristocratic society (that is to say, of the preliminary condition for the elevation of the type "man"): the truth is hard. Let us acknowledge unprejudicedly how every higher civilisation hitherto has *originated!* Men with a still natural nature, barbarians in every terrible sense of the word, men of prey, still in possession of unbroken strength of will and desire for power, threw themselves upon weaker, more moral, more peaceful races (perhaps trading or cattle-rearing communities), or upon old mellow civilisations in which the final vital force was flickering out in brilliant fireworks of wit and depravity. At the commencement, the noble caste was always the barbarian caste: their superiority did not consist first of all in their physical, but in their psychical power—they were more *complete* men (which at every point also implies the same as "more complete beasts").

258. Corruption—as the indication that anarchy threatens to break out among the instincts, and that the foundation of the emotions, called "life," is

convulsed—is something radically different according to the organisation in which it manifests itself. When, for instance, an aristocracy like that of France at the beginning of the Revolution, flung away its privileges with sublime disgust and sacrificed itself to an excess of its moral sentiments, it was corruption:—it was really only the closing act of the corruption which had existed for centuries, by virtue of which that aristocracy had abdicated step by step its lordly prerogatives and lowered itself to a *function* of royalty (in the end even to its decoration and parade-dress). The essential thing, however, in a good and healthy aristocracy is that it should *not* regard itself as a function either of the kingship or the commonwealth, but as the *significance* and highest justification thereof—that it should therefore accept with a good conscience the sacrifice of a legion of individuals, who, *for its sake,* must be suppressed and reduced to imperfect men, to slaves and instruments. Its fundamental belief must be precisely that society is not allowed to exist for its own sake, but only as a foundation and scaffolding, by means of which a select class of beings may be able to elevate themselves to their higher duties, and in general to a higher *existence:* like those sun-seeking climbing plants in Java—they are called *Sipo Matador,*—which encircle an oak so long and so often with their arms, until at last, high above it, but supported by it, they can unfold their tops in the open light, and exhibit their happiness.

259. To refrain mutually from injury, from violence, from exploitation, and put one's will on a par with that of others: this may result in a certain rough sense in good conduct among individuals when the necessary conditions are given (namely, the actual similarity of the individuals in amount of force and degree of worth, and their co-relation within one organisation). As soon, however, as one wished to take this principle more generally, and if possible even as *the fundamental principle of society,* it would immediately disclose what it really is—namely, a Will to the *denial* of life, a principle of dissolution and decay. Here one must think profoundly to the very basis and resist all sentimental weakness: life itself is *essentially* appropriation, injury, conquest of the strange and weak, suppression, severity, obtrusion of peculiar forms, incorporation, and at the least, putting it mildest, exploitation;—but why should one for ever use precisely these words on which for ages a disparaging purpose has been stamped? Even the organisation within which, as was previously supposed, the individuals treat each other as equal—it takes place in every healthy aristocracy—must itself, if it be a living and not a dying organisation, do all that towards other bodies, which the individuals within it refrain from doing to each other: it will have to be the incarnated Will to Power, it will endeavour to grow, to gain ground, attract to itself and acquire ascendency—not owing to any morality or immorality, but because it *lives,* and because life *is* precisely Will to Power. On no point, however, is the ordinary consciousness of Europeans more unwilling to be corrected than on this matter; people now rave everywhere, even under the guise of science, about coming conditions of society in which "the exploiting character" is to be absent:—that sounds to my ears as if they promised to invent a mode of life which should refrain from all organic functions. "Exploitation" does not belong to a depraved, or imperfect and primitive society: it belongs to the *nature* of the living being as a primary organic function; it is a consequence of the intrinsic Will to Power, which is precisely the

Will to Life.—Granting that as a theory this is a novelty—as a reality it is the *fundamental fact* of all history: let us be so far honest towards ourselves!

260. In a tour through the many finer and coarser moralities which have hitherto prevailed or still prevail on the earth, I found certain traits recurring regularly together, and connected with one another, until finally two primary types revealed themselves to me, and a radical distinction was brought to light. There is *master-morality* and *slave-morality;*—I would at once add, however, that in all higher and mixed civilisations, there are also attempts at the reconciliation of the two moralities; but one finds still oftener the confusion and mutual misunderstanding of them, indeed, sometimes their close juxtaposition—even in the same man, within one soul. The distinctions of moral values have either originated in a ruling caste, pleasantly conscious of being different from the ruled—or among the ruled class, the slaves and dependents of all sorts. In the first case, when it is the rulers who determine the conception "good," it is the exalted, proud disposition which is regarded as the distinguishing feature, and that which determines the order of rank. The noble type of man separates from himself the beings in whom the opposite of this exalted, proud disposition displays itself: he despises them. Let it at once be noted that in this first kind of morality the antithesis "good" and "bad" means practically the same as "noble" and "despicable";—the antithesis "good" and *"evil"* is of a different origin. The cowardly, the timid, the insignificant, and those thinking merely of narrow utility are despised; moreover, also, the distrustful, with their constrained glances, the self-abasing, the dog-like kind of men who let themselves be abused, the mendicant flatterers, and above all the liars:—it is a fundamental belief of all aristocrats that the common people are untruthful. "We truthful ones"—the nobility in ancient Greece called themselves. It is obvious that everywhere the designations of moral value were at first applied to *men,* and were only derivatively and at a later period applied to *actions;* it is a gross mistake, therefore, when historians of morals start questions like, "Why have sympathetic actions been praised?" The noble type of man regards *himself* as a determiner of values; he does not require to be approved of; he passes the judgment: "What is injurious to me is injurious in itself"; he knows that it is he himself only who confers honour on things; he is a *creator of values.* He honours whatever he recognises in himself: such morality is self-glorification. In the foreground there is the feeling of plentitude, of power, which seeks to overflow, the happiness of high tension, the consciousness of a wealth which would fain give and bestow:—the noble man also helps the unfortunate, but not—or scarcely—out of pity, but rather from an impulse generated by the super-abundance of power. The noble man honours in himself the powerful one, him also who has power over himself, who knows how to speak and how to keep silence, who takes pleasure in subjecting himself to severity and hardness, and has reverence for all that is severe and hard. "Wotan placed a hard heart in my breast," says an old Scandinavian Saga: it is thus rightly expressed from the soul of a proud Viking. Such a type of man is even proud of *not* being made for sympathy; the hero of the Saga therefore adds warningly: "He who has not a hard heart when young, will never have one." The noble and brave who think thus are the furthest removed from

the morality which sees precisely in sympathy, or in acting for the good of others, or in *désintéressement,* the characteristic of the moral; faith in oneself, pride in oneself, a radical enmity and irony towards "selflessness," belong as definitely to noble morality, as do a careless scorn and precaution in presence of sympathy and the "warm heart."—It is the powerful who *know* how to honour, it is their art, their domain for invention. The profound reverence for age and for tradition—all law rests on this double reverence,—the belief and prejudice in favour of ancestors and unfavourable to newcomers, is typical in the morality of the powerful; and if, reversely, men of "modern ideas" believe almost instinctively in "progress" and the "future," and are more and more lacking in respect for old age, the ignoble origin of these "ideas" has complacently betrayed itself thereby. A morality of the ruling class, however, is more especially foreign and irritating to present-day taste in the sternness of its principle that one has duties only to one's equals; that one may act towards beings of a lower rank, towards all that is foreign, just as seems good to one, or "as the heart desires," and in any case "beyond good and evil": it is here that sympathy and similar sentiments can have a place. The ability and obligation to exercise prolonged gratitude and prolonged revenge—both only within the circle of equals,—artfulness in retaliation, *raffinement* of the idea in friendship, a certain necessity to have enemies (as outlets for the emotions of envy, quarrelsomeness, arrogance—in fact, in order to be a good *friend*): all these are typical characteristics of the noble morality, which, as has been pointed out, is not the morality of "modern ideas," and is therefore at present difficult to realise, and also to unearth and disclose.—It is otherwise with the second type of morality, *slave-morality.* Supposing that the abused, the oppressed, the suffering, the unemancipated, the weary, and those uncertain of themselves, should moralise, what will be the common element in their moral estimates? Probably a pessimistic suspicion with regard to the entire situation of man will find expression, perhaps a condemnation of man, together with his situation. The slave has an unfavourable eye for the virtues of the powerful; he has a scepticism and distrust, a *refinement* of distrust of everything "good" that is there honoured—he would fain persuade himself that the very happiness there is not genuine. On the other hand, *those* qualities which serve to alleviate the existence of sufferers are brought into prominence and flooded with light; it is here that sympathy, the kind, helping hand, the warm heart, patience, diligence, humility, and friendliness attain to honour; for here these are the most useful qualities, and almost the only means of supporting the burden of existence. Slave-morality is essentially the morality of utility. Here is the seat of the origin of the famous antithesis "good" and "evil":—power and dangerousness are assumed to reside in the evil, a certain dreadfulness, subtlety, and strength, which do not admit of being despised. According to slave-morality, therefore, the "evil" man arouses fear; according to master-morality, it is precisely the "good" man who arouses fear and seeks to arouse it, while the bad man is regarded as the despicable being. The contrast attains its maximum when, in accordance with the logical consequences of slave-morality, a shade of depreciation—it may be slight and well-intentioned—at last attaches itself to the "good" man of this morality; because, according to the servile mode of thought, the good man must in any case be the *safe* man: he is good-natured, easily deceived, perhaps a little stupid, *un bonhomme.* Everywhere that slave-morality gains the ascendancy, language shows a tendency to approximate the significations of the words "good" and "stupid."—At last fundamental difference: the desire for *freedom,* the instinct for happiness and the refinements of the feeling of liberty belong as necessarily to slave-morals and morality, as artifice and enthusiasm in reverence and devotion are the regular symptoms of an aristocratic mode of thinking and estimating.—Hence we can understand without further detail why love *as a passion*—it is our European speciality—must absolutely be of noble origin; as is well known, its invention is due to the Provençal poet-cavaliers, those brilliant, ingenious men of the *"gai saber,"* to whom Europe owes so much, and almost owes itself.

261. Vanity is one of the things which are perhaps most difficult for a noble man to understand: he will be tempted to deny it, where another kind of man thinks he sees it self-evidently. The problem for him is to represent to his mind beings who seek to arouse a good opinion of themselves which they themselves do not possess—and consequently also do not "deserve,"—and who yet *believe* in this good opinion afterwards. This seems to him on the one hand such bad taste and so self-disrespectful, and on the other hand so grotesquely unreasonable, that he would like to consider vanity an exception, and is doubtful about it in most cases when it is spoken of. He will say, for instance: "I may be mistaken about my value, and on the other hand may nevertheless demand that my value should be acknowledged by others precisely as I rate it:—that, however, is not vanity (but self-conceit, or, in most cases, that which is called 'humility,' and also 'modesty')." Or he will even say: "For many reasons I can delight in the good opinion of others, perhaps because I love and honour them, and rejoice in all their joys, perhaps also because their good opinion endorses and strengthens my belief in my own good opinion, perhaps because the good opinion of others, even in cases where I do not share it, is useful to me, or gives promise of usefulness:—all this, however, is not vanity." The man of noble character must first bring it home forcibly to his mind, especially with the aid of history, that, from time immemorial, in all social strata in any way dependent, the ordinary man *was* only that which he *passed for:*—not being at all accustomed to fix values, he did not assign even to himself any other value than that which his master assigned to him (it is the peculiar *right of masters* to create values). It may be looked upon as the result of an extraordinary atavism, that the ordinary man, even at present, is still always *waiting* for an opinion about himself, and then instinctively submitting himself to it; yet by no means only to a "good" opinion, but also to a bad and unjust one (think, for instance, of the greater part of the self-appreciations and self-depreciations which believing women learn from their confessors, and which in general the believing Christian learns from his Church). . . . The vain person rejoices over *every* good opinion which he hears about himself (quite apart from the point of view of its usefulness, and equally regardless of its truth or falsehood), just as he suffers from every bad opinion: for he subjects himself to both, he *feels* himself subjected to both, by that oldest instinct of subjection which breaks forth in him.—It is "the slave" in the vain man's blood, the remains of the slave's craftiness. . . .

262. A *species* originates, and a type becomes established and strong in the long struggle with essentially constant *unfavourable* conditions. On the other hand, it is known by the experience of breeders that species which receive superabundant nourishment, and in general a surplus of protection and care, immediately tend in the most marked way to develop variations, and are fertile in prodigies and monstrosities (also in monstrous vices). Now look at an aristocratic commonwealth, say an ancient Greek *polis,* or Venice, as a voluntary or involuntary contrivance for the purpose of *rearing* human beings; there are there men beside one another, thrown upon their own resources, who want to make their species prevail, chiefly because they *must* prevail, or else run the terrible danger of being exterminated. The favour, the superabundance, the protection are there lacking under which variations are fostered; the species needs itself as species, as something which, precisely by virtue of its hardness, its uniformity, and simplicity of structure, can in general prevail and make itself permanent in constant struggle with its neighbours, or with rebellious or rebellion-threatening vassals. The most varied experience teaches it what are the qualities to which it principally owes the fact that it still exists, in spite of all gods and men, and has hitherto been victorious: these qualities it calls virtues, and these virtues alone it develops to maturity. It does so with severity, indeed it desires severity; every aristocratic morality is intolerant in the education of youth, in the control of women, in the marriage customs, in the relations of old and young, in the penal laws (which have an eye only for the degenerating): it counts intolerance itself among the virtues, under the name of "justice." A type with few, but very marked features, a species of severe, warlike, wisely silent, reserved and reticent men (and as such, with the most delicate sensibility for the charm and *nuances* of society) is thus established, unaffected by the vicissitudes of generations; the constant struggle with uniform *unfavourable* conditions is, as already remarked, the cause of a type becoming stable and hard. Finally, however, a happy state of things results, the enormous tension is relaxed; there are perhaps no more enemies among the neighbouring peoples, and the means of life, even of the enjoyment of life, are present in superabundance. With one stroke the bond and constraint of the old discipline severs: it is no longer regarded as necessary, as a condition of existence—if it would continue, it can only do so as a form of *luxury,* as an archaïsing *taste.* Variations, whether they be deviations (into the higher, finer, and rare), or deteriorations and monstrosities, appear suddenly on the scene in the greatest exuberance and splendour; the individual dares to be individual and detach himself. At this turning-point of history there manifest themselves, side by side, and often mixed and entangled together, a magnificent, manifold, virgin-forest-like up-growth and up-striving, a kind of *tropical tempo* in the rivalry of growth, and an extraordinary decay and self-destruction, owing to the savagely opposing and seemingly exploding egoisms, which strive with one another "for sun and light," and can no longer assign any limit, restraint, or forbearance for themselves by means of the hitherto existing morality. It was this morality itself which piled up the strength so enormously, which bent the bow in so threatening a manner:—it is now "out of date," it is getting "out of date." The dangerous and disquieting point has been reached when the greater, more manifold, more comprehensive life *is lived*

beyond the old morality; the "individual" stands out, and is obliged to have recourse to his own law-giving, his own arts and artifices for self-preservation, self-elevation, and self-deliverance. Nothing but new "Whys," nothing but new "Hows," no common formulas any longer, misunderstanding and disregard in league with each other, decay, deterioration, and the loftiest desires frightfully entangled, the genius of the race overflowing from all the cornucopias of good and bad, a portentous simultaneousness of Spring and Autumn, full of new charms and mysteries peculiar to the fresh, still inexhausted, still unwearied corruption. Danger is again present, the mother of morality, great danger; this time shifted into the individual, into the neighbour and friend, into the street, into their own child, into their own heart, into all the most personal and secret recesses of their desires and volitions. What will the moral philosophers who appear at this time have to preach? They discover, these sharp onlookers and loafers, that the end is quickly approaching, that everything around them decays and produces decay, that nothing will endure until the day after tomorrow, except one species of man, the incurably *mediocre.* The mediocre alone have a prospect of continuing and propagating themselves—they will be the men of the future, the sole survivors; "be like them! become mediocre!" is now the only morality which has still a significance, which still obtains a hearing.—But it is difficult to preach this morality of mediocrity! it can never avow what it is and what it desires! it has to talk of moderation and dignity and duty and brotherly love—it will have difficulty *in concealing its irony!*

263. There is an *instinct for rank,* which more than anything else is already the sign of a *high* rank; there is a *delight* in the *nuances* of reverance which leads one to infer noble origin and habits. The refinement, goodness, and loftiness of a soul are put to a perilous test when something passes by that is of the highest rank, but is not yet protected by the awe of authority from obtrusive touches and incivilities: something that goes its way like a living touchstone, undistinguished, undiscovered, and tentative, perhaps voluntarily veiled and disguised. He whose task and practice it is to investigate souls, will avail himself of many varieties of this very art to determine the ultimate value of a soul, the unalterable, innate order of rank to which it belongs: he will test it by its *instinct for reverence.* "Difference breeds hatred:" the vulgarity of many a nature spurts up suddenly like dirty water, when any holy vessel, any jewel from closed shrines, any book bearing the marks of great destiny, is brought before it; while on the other hand, there is an involuntary silence, a hesitation of the eye, a cessation of all gestures, by which it is indicated that a soul *feels* the nearness of what is worthiest of respect. The way in which, on the whole, the reverence for the *Bible* has hitherto been maintained in Europe, is perhaps the best example of discipline and refinement of manners which Europe owes to Christianity: books of such profoundness and supreme significance require for their protection an external tyranny of authority, in order to acquire the *period* of thousands of years which is necessary to exhaust and unriddle them. Much has been achieved when the sentiment has been at last instilled into the masses (the shallow-pates and the boobies of every kind) that they are not allowed to touch everything, that there are holy experiences before which they must take off their shoes and keep away the unclean hand—it is almost their highest advance

towards humanity. On the contrary, in the so-called cultured classes, the believers in "modern ideas," nothing is perhaps so repulsive as their lack of shame, the easy insolence of eye and hand with which they touch, taste, and finger everything; and it is possible that even yet there is more *relative* nobility of taste, and more tact for reverence among the people, among the lower classes of the people, especially among peasants, than among the newspaper-reading *demimonde* of intellect, the cultured class. . . .

265. At the risk of displeasing innocent ears, I submit that egoism belongs to the essence of a noble soul, I mean the unalterable belief that to a being such as "we," other beings must naturally be in subjection, and have to sacrifice themselves. The noble soul accepts the fact of his egoism without question, and also without consciousness of harshness, constraint, or arbitrariness therein, but rather as something that may have its basis in the primary law of things:—if he sought a designation for it he would say: "It is justice itself." He acknowledges under certain circumstances, which made him hesitate at first, that there are other equally privileged ones; as soon as he has settled this question of rank, he moves among those equals and equally privileged ones; with the same assurance, as regards modesty and delicate respect, which he enjoys in intercourse with himself—in accordance with an innate heavenly mechanism which all the stars understand. It is an *additional* instance of his egoism, this artfulness and self-limitation in intercourse with his equals—every star is a similar egoist; he honours *himself* in them, and in the rights which he concedes to them, he has no doubt that the exchange of honours and rights, as the *essence* of all intercourse, belongs also to the natural condition of things. The noble soul gives as he takes, prompted by the passionate and sensitive instinct of requital, which is at the root of his nature. The notion of "favour" has, among equals, neither significance nor good repute; there may be a sublime way of letting gifts as it were light upon one from above, and of drinking them thirstily like dew-drops but for those arts and displays the noble soul has no aptitude. His egoism hinders him here: in general, he looks "aloft" unwillingly—he looks either *forward,* horizontally and deliberately, or downwards—*he knows that he is on a height.*

ON THE GENEALOGY OF MORALS*

In his next book, *On the Genealogy of Morals,* Nietzsche pursues the idea of "master" and "slave morality" in far more historical detail, tracing the origins and growth of slave morality. (We now simply think of it as "morality," and philosophers like Kant have tried to justify it as universal.) A "genealogy" is an account of one's ancestry, in this case, the ancestry of a set of ideas and institutions. Nietzsche then applies the same technique to an examination of the related question, "Where did our ideas of obligation and responsibility come from?" His answer, again, is that such ideas are not natural but carefully cultivated by society, in part as a matter of personal pride and self-aggrandizement.

*Friedrich Nietzsche, *The Birth of Tragedy and the Genealogy of Morals,* translated by Francis Golffing. Copyright © 1956 by Doubleday & Company, Inc.

1. The English psychologists to whom we owe the only attempts that have thus far been made to write a genealogy of morals are no mean posers of riddles, but the riddles they pose are themselves, and being incarnate have one advantage over their books—they are interesting. What are these English psychologists really after? One finds them always, whether intentionally or not, engaged in the same task of pushing into the foreground the nasty part of the psyche, looking for the effective motive forces of human development in the very last place we would wish to have them found, e.g., in the inertia of habit, in forgetfulness, in the blind and fortuitous association of ideas: always in something that is purely passive, automatic, reflexive, molecular, and, moreover, profoundly stupid. What drives these psychologists forever in the same direction? A secret, malicious desire to belittle humanity, which they do not acknowledge even to themselves? A pessimistic distrust, the suspiciousness of the soured idealist? Some petty resentment of Christianity (and Plato) which does not rise above the threshold of consciousness? Or could it be a prurient taste for whatever is embarrassing, painfully paradoxical, dubious and absurd in existence? Or is it, perhaps, a kind of stew—a little meanness, a little bitterness, a bit of anti-Christianity, a touch of prurience and desire for condiments? . . . But, again, people tell me that these men are simply dull old frogs who hop and creep in and around man as in their own element—as though man were a bog. However, I am reluctant to listen to this, in fact I refuse to believe it; and if I may express a wish where I cannot express a conviction, I do wish wholeheartedly that things may be otherwise with these men—that these microscopic examiners of the soul may be really courageous, magnanimous, and proud animals, who know how to contain their emotions and have trained themselves to subordinate all wishful thinking to the truth—any truth, even a homespun, severe, ugly, obnoxious, un-Christian, unmoral truth. For such truths do exist.

2. All honor to the beneficent spirits that may motivate these historians of ethics! One thing is certain, however, they have been quite deserted by the true spirit of history. They all, to a man, think unhistorically, as is the age-old custom among philosophers. The amateurishness of their procedure is made plain from the very beginning, when it is a question of explaining the provenance of the concept and judgment *good*. "Originally," they decree, "altruistic actions were praised and approved by their recipients, that is, by those to whom they were useful. Later on, the origin of that praise having been forgotten, such actions were felt to be good simply because it was the habit to commend them." We notice at once that this first derivation has all the earmarks of the English psychologists' work. Here are the key ideas of utility, forgetfulness, habit, and, finally, error, seen as lying at the root of that value system which civilized man had hitherto regarded with pride as the prerogative of all men. This pride must now be humbled, these values devalued. Have the debunkers succeeded?

Now it is obvious to me, first of all, that their theory looks for the genesis of the concept *good* in the wrong place: the judgment *good* does not originate with those to whom the good has been done. Rather it was the "good" themselves, that is to say the noble, mighty, highly placed, and high-minded who decreed themselves and their actions to be good, i.e., belonging to the highest rank, in contradistinction to all that was base, low-minded and plebeian. It was only this *pathos of distance* that authorized them to create values and name them—what was utility to them? The notion of utility seems singularly inept to account for such a quick jetting forth of supreme value judgments. Here we come face to face with the exact opposite of that lukewarmness which every scheming prudence, every utilitarian calculus presupposes—and not for a time only, for the rare, exceptional hour, but permanently. The origin of the opposites *good* and *bad* is to be found in the pathos of nobility and distance, representing the dominant temper of a higher, ruling class in relation to a lower, dependent one. (The lordly right of bestowing names is such that one would almost be justified in seeing the origin of language itself as an expression of the rulers' power. They say, "This *is* that or that"; they seal off each thing and action with a sound and thereby take symbolic possession of it.) Such an origin would suggest that there is no *a priori* necessity for associating the word *good* with altruistic deeds, as those moral psychologists are fond of claiming. In fact, it is only after aristocratic values have begun to decline that the egotism-altruism dichotomy takes possession of the human conscience; to use my own terms, it is the herd instinct that now asserts itself. Yet it takes quite a while for this instinct to assume such sway that it can reduce all moral valuations to that dichotomy—as is currently happening throughout Europe, where the prejudice equating the terms *moral, altruistic,* and *disinterested* has assumed the obsessive force of an *idée fixe*. . . .

10. The slave revolt in morals begins by rancor turning creative and giving birth to values—the rancor of beings who, deprived of the direct outlet of action, compensate by an imaginary vengeance. All truly noble morality grows out of triumphant self-affirmation. Slave ethics, on the other hand, begins by saying *no* to an "outside," an "other," a non-self, and that *no* is its creative act. This reversal of direction of the evaluating look, this invariable looking outward instead of inward, is a fundamental feature of rancor. Slave ethics requires for its inception a sphere different from and hostile to its own. Physiologically speaking, it requires an outside stimulus in order to act at all; all its action is reaction. The opposite is true of aristocratic valuations; such values grow and act spontaneously, seeking out their contraries only in order to affirm themselves even more gratefully and delightedly. Here the negative concepts, *humble, base, bad,* are late, pallid counterparts of the positive, intense and passionate credo, "We noble, good, beautiful, happy ones." Aristocratic valuations may go amiss and do violence to reality, but this happens only with regard to spheres which they do not know well, or from the knowledge of which they austerely guard themselves: the aristocrat will, on occasion, misjudge a sphere which he holds in contempt, the sphere of the common man, the people. On the other hand we should remember that the emotion of contempt, of looking down, provided that it falsifies at all, is as nothing compared with the falsification which suppressed hatred, impotent vindictiveness, effects upon its opponent, though only in effigy. There is in all contempt too much casualness and nonchalance, too much blinking of facts and impatience, and too much inborn gaiety for it ever to make of its object a downright caricature and monster.

. . . All this stands in utter contrast to what is called happiness among the impotent and oppressed, who are full of bottled-up aggressions. Their happiness is purely passive and takes the form of drugged tranquillity, stretching and yawning, peace, "sabbath," emotional slackness. Whereas the noble lives before his own conscience with confidence and frankness (*gennaios* "nobly bred" emphasizes the nuance "truthful" and perhaps also "ingenuous"), the rancorous person is neither truthful nor ingenuous nor honest and forthright with himself. His soul squints; his mind loves hide-outs, secret paths, and back doors; everything that is hidden seems to him his own world, his security, his comfort; he is expert in silence, in long memory, in waiting, in provisional self-depreciation, and in self-humiliation. A race of such men will, in the end, inevitably be cleverer than a race of aristocrats, and it will honor sharpwittedness to a much greater degree, i.e., as an absolutely vital condition for its existence. Among the noble, mental acuteness always tends slightly to suggest luxury and overrefinement. The fact is that with them it is much less important than is the perfect functioning of the ruling, unconscious instincts or even a certain temerity to follow sudden impulses, court danger, or indulge spurts of violent rage, love, worship, gratitude, or vengeance. When a noble man feels resentment, it is absorbed in his instantaneous reaction and therefore does not poison him. Moreover, in countless cases where we might expect it, it never arises, while with weak and impotent people it occurs without fail. It is a sign of strong, rich temperaments that they cannot for long take seriously their enemies, their misfortunes, their *misdeeds;* for such characters have in them an excess of plastic curative power, and also a power of oblivion. (A good modern example of the latter is Mirabeau, who lacked all memory for insults and meannesses done him, and who was unable to forgive because he had forgotten.) Such a man simply shakes off vermin which would get beneath another's skin—and only here, if anywhere on earth, is it possible to speak of "loving one's enemy." The noble person will respect his enemy, and respect is already a bridge to love. . . . Indeed he requires his enemy for himself, as his mark of distinction, nor could he tolerate any other enemy than one in whom he finds nothing to despise and much to esteem. Imagine, on the other hand, the "enemy" as conceived by the rancorous man! For this is his true creative achievement: he has conceived the "evil enemy," the Evil One, as a fundamental idea, and then as a pendant he has conceived a Good One—himself.

11. The exact opposite is true of the noble-minded, who spontaneously creates the notion *good,* and later derives from it the conception of the *bad.* How ill-matched these two concepts look, placed side by side: the bad of noble origin, and the *evil* that has risen out of the cauldron of unquenched hatred! The first is a by-product, a complementary color, almost an afterthought; the second is the beginning, the original creative act of slave ethics. But neither is the conception of good the same in both cases, as we soon find out when we ask ourselves who it is that is really evil according to the code of rancor. The answer is: precisely the good one of the opposite code, that is the noble, the powerful— only colored, reinterpreted, reenvisaged by the poisonous eye of resentment. And we are the first to admit that anyone who knew these "good" ones only as enemies would find them evil enemies indeed. For these same men who,

amongst themselves, are so strictly constrained by custom, worship, ritual, gratitude, and by mutual surveillance and jealousy, who are so resourceful in consideration, tenderness, loyalty, pride and friendship, when once they step outside their circle become little better than uncaged beasts of prey. Once abroad in the wilderness, they revel in the freedom from social constraint and compensate for their long confinement in the quietude of their own community. They revert to the innocence of wild animals: we can imagine them returning from an orgy of murder, arson, rape, and torture, jubilant and at peace with themselves as though they had committed a fraternity prank—convinced, moreover, that the poets for a long time to come will have something to sing about and to praise. Deep within all these noble races there lurks the beast of prey, bent on spoil and conquest. This hidden urge has to be satisfied from time to time, the beast let loose in the wilderness. This goes as well for the Roman, Arabian, German, Japanese nobility as for the Homeric heroes and the Scandinavian vikings. The noble races have everywhere left in their wake the catchword "barbarian." And even their highest culture shows an awareness of this trait and a certain pride in it (as we see, for example, in Pericles' famous funeral oration, when he tells the Athenians: "Our boldness has gained us access to every land and sea, and erected monuments to itself *for both good and evil.*") This "boldness" of noble races, so headstrong, absurd, incalculable, sudden, improbable (Pericles commends the Athenians especially for their *rathumia*), their utter indifference to safety and comfort, their terrible pleasure in destruction, their taste for cruelty—all these traits are embodied by their victims in the image of the "barbarian," the "evil enemy," the Goth or the Vandal. The profound and icy suspicion which the German arouses as soon as he assumes power (we see it happening again today) harks back to the persistent horror with which Europe for many centuries witnessed the raging of the blond Teutonic beast. If it were true, as passes current nowadays, that the real meaning of culture resides in its power to domesticate man's savage instincts, then we might be justified in viewing all those rancorous machinations by which the noble tribes, and their ideals, have been laid low as the true instruments of culture. But this would still not amount to saying that the *organizers* themselves represent culture. Rather, the exact opposite would be true, as is vividly shown by the current state of affairs. These carriers of the leveling and retributive instincts, these descendants of every European and extra-European slavedom, and especially of the pre-Aryan populations, represent human retrogression most flagrantly. Such "instruments of culture" are a disgrace to man and might make one suspicious of culture altogether. One might be justified in fearing the wild beast lurking within all noble races and in being on one's guard against it, but who would not a thousand times prefer fear when it is accompanied with admiration to security accompanied by the loathsome sight of perversion, dwarfishness, degeneracy? And is not the latter our predicament today? What accounts for our repugnance to man—for there is no question that he makes us suffer? Certainly not our fear of him, rather the fact that there is no longer anything to be feared from him; that the vermin "man" occupies the entire stage; that, tame, hopelessly mediocre, and savorless, he considers himself the apex of historical evolution; and not entirely without justice, since he is still somewhat removed from the mass of sickly and effete creatures whom Europe is beginning to stink of today. . . .

16. Let us conclude. The two sets of valuations, good/bad and good/evil, have waged a terrible battle on this earth, lasting many millennia; and just as surely as the second set has for a long time now been in the ascendant, so surely are there still places where the battle goes on and the issue remains in suspension. It might even be claimed that by being raised to a higher plane the battle has become much more profound. Perhaps there is today not a single intellectual worth his salt who is not divided on that issue, a battleground for those opposites.

"GUILT," "BAD CONSCIENCE," AND RELATED MATTERS

1. To breed an animal with the right to make promises—is not this the paradoxical problem nature has set itself with regard to man? and is it not man's true problem? That the problem has in fact been solved to a remarkable degree will seem all the more surprising if we do full justice to the strong opposing force, the faculty of oblivion. Oblivion is not merely a *vis inertiae,* as is often claimed, but an active screening device, responsible for the fact that what we experience and digest psychologically does not, in the stage of digestion, emerge into consciousness any more than what we ingest physically does. The role of this active oblivion is that of a concierge: to shut temporarily the doors and windows of consciousness; to protect us from the noise and agitation with which our lower organs work for or against one another; to introduce a little quiet into our consciousness so as to make room for the nobler functions and functionaries of our organism which do the governing and planning. This concierge maintains order and etiquette in the household of the psyche; which immediately suggests that there can be no happiness, no serenity, no hope, no pride, no *present,* without oblivion. A man in whom this screen is damaged and inoperative is like a dyspeptic (and not merely *like* one): he can't be done with anything. . . . Now this naturally forgetful animal, for whom oblivion represents a power, a form of strong health, has created for itself an opposite power, that of remembering, by whose aid, in certain cases, oblivion may be suspended—specifically in cases where it is a question of promises. By this I do not mean a purely passive succumbing to past impressions, the indigestion of being unable to be done with a pledge once made, but rather an active not wishing to be done with it, a continuing to will what has once been willed, a veritable "memory of the will"; so that, between the original determination and the actual performance of the thing willed, a whole world of new things, conditions, even volitional acts, can be interposed without snapping the long chain of the will. But how much all this presupposes! A man who wishes to dispose of his future in this manner must first have learned to separate necessary from accidental acts; to think causally; to see distant things as though they were near at hand; to distinguish means from ends.

In short, he must have become not only calculating but himself calculable, regular even to his own perception, if he is to stand pledge for his own future as a guarantor does.

2. This brings us to the long story of the origin or genesis of responsibility. The task of breeding an animal entitled to make promises involves, as we have already seen, the preparatory task of rendering man up to a certain point regular, uniform, equal among equals, calculable. The tremendous achievement which I have referred to in *Daybreak* as "the custom character of morals," that labor man accomplished upon himself over a vast period of time, receives its meaning and justification here—even despite the brutality, tyranny, and stupidity associated with the process. With the help of custom and the social straitjacket, man was, in fact, made calculable. However, if we place ourselves at the terminal point of this great process, where society and custom finally reveal their true aim, we shall find the ripest fruit of that tree to be the sovereign individual, equal only to himself, all moral custom left far behind. This autonomous, more than moral individual (the terms *autonomous* and *moral* are mutually exclusive) has developed his own, independent, long-range will, which dares to make promises; he has a proud and vigorous consciousness of what he has achieved, a sense of power and freedom, of absolute accomplishment. This fully emancipated man, master of his will, who dares to make promises—how should he not be aware of his superiority over those who are unable to stand security for themselves? Think how much trust, fear, reverence he inspires (all three fully *deserved*), and how, having that sovereign rule over himself, he has mastery too over all weaker-willed and less reliable creatures! Being truly free and possessor of a long-range, pertinacious will, he also possesses a scale of values. Viewing others from the center of his own being, he either honors or disdains them. It is natural to him to honor his strong and reliable peers, all those who promise like sovereigns: rarely and reluctantly; who are chary of their trust; whose trust is a mark of distinction; whose promises are binding because they know that they will make them good in spite of all accidents, in spite of destiny itself. Yet he will inevitably reserve a kick for those paltry windbags who promise irresponsibly and a rod for those liars who break their word even in uttering it. His proud awareness of the extraordinary privilege responsibility confers has penetrated deeply and become a dominant instinct. What shall he call that dominant instinct, provided he ever feels impelled to give it a name? Surely he will call it his *conscience.*

The final three selections are taken from some of Nietzsche's last, most belligerent works. In the first, *Twilight of the Idols,* he reconsiders the traditional ethical emphasis on the importance of rationality and "nature" in morality and the war against the passions that is so frequently part of it. In the second, *The Antichrist,* he summarizes his harshest indictment against Christian morality—that in the name of the "highest values" it imposes upon us "corrupt," "decadent," and *nihilistic* values. In the third selection, from his unpublished notes compiled under his own (unused) title, *The Will to Power,* he again explores the notion of "moral evolution" and condemns its tendency to promote mediocrity and herd mentality.

TWILIGHT OF THE IDOLS*

MORALITY AS ANTI–NATURE

All passions have a phase when they are merely disastrous, when they drag down their victim with the weight of stupidity—and a later, very much later phase when they wed the spirit, when they "spiritualize" themselves. Formerly, in view of the element of stupidity in passion, war was declared on passion itself, its destruction was plotted; all the old moral monsters are agreed on this: *il faut tuer les passions.*[1] The most famous formula for this is to be found in the New Testament, in that Sermon on the Mount, where, incidentally, things are by no means looked at from a height. There it is said, for example, with particular reference to sexuality: "If thy eye offend thee, pluck it out." Fortunately, no Christian acts in accordance with this precept. *Destroying* the passions and cravings, merely as a preventive measure against their stupidity and the unpleasant consequences of this stupidity—today this itself strikes us as merely another acute form of stupidity. We no longer admire dentists who "pluck out" teeth so that they will not hurt any more.

To be fair, it should be admitted, however, that on the ground out of which Christianity grew, the concept of the "spiritualization of passion" could never have been formed. After all the first church, as is well known, fought *against* the "intelligent" in favor of the "poor in spirit." How could one expect from it an intelligent war against passion? The church fights passion with excision in every sense: its practice, its "cure," is *castratism.* It never asks: "How can one spiritualize, beautify, deify a craving?" It has at all times laid the stress of discipline on extirpation (of sensuality, of pride, of the lust to rule, of avarice, of vengefulness). But an attack on the roots of passion means an attack on the roots of life: the practice of the church is *hostile to life.*

The same means in the fight against a craving—castration, extirpation—is instinctively chosen by those who are too weak-willed, too degenerate, to be able to impose moderation on themselves; by those who are so constituted that they require *La Trappe,* to use a figure of speech, or (without any figure of speech) some kind of definitive declaration of hostility, a *cleft* between themselves and the passion. Radical means are indispensable only for the degenerate; the weakness of the will—or, to speak more definitely, the inability *not* to respond to a stimulus—is itself merely another form of degeneration. The radical hostility, the deadly hostility against sensuality, is always a symptom to reflect on: it entitles us to suppositions concerning the total state of one who is excessive in this manner. . . .

---

[1]"One must kill the passions."

I reduce a principle to a formula. Every naturalism in morality—that is, every healthy morality—is dominated by an instinct of life; some commandment of life is fulfilled by a determinate canon of "shalt" and "shalt not"; some inhibition and hostile element on the path of life is thus removed. *Anti-natural* morality—that is, almost every morality which has so far been taught, revered, and preached—turns, conversely, *against* the instincts of life: it is *condemnation* of these instincts, now secret, now outspoken and impudent. When it says, "God looks at the heart," it says No to both the lowest and the highest desires of life, and posits God as the *enemy of life.* The saint in whom God delights is the ideal eunuch. Life has come to an end where the "kingdom of God" begins.

Once one has comprehended the outrage of such a revolt against life as has become almost sacrosanct in Christian morality, one has, fortunately, also comprehended something else: the futility, apparentness, absurdity, and *mendaciousness* of such a revolt. A condemnation of life by the living remains in the end a mere symptom of a certain kind of life: the question whether it is justified or unjustified is not even raised thereby. One would require a position *outside* of life, and yet have to know it as well as one, as many, as all who have lived it, in order to be permitted even to touch the problem of the *value* of life: reasons enough to comprehend that this problem is for us an unapproachable problem. When we speak of values, we speak with the inspiration, with the way of looking at things, which is part of life: life itself forces us to posit values; life itself values through us when we posit values. From this it follows that even that anti-natural morality which conceives of God as the counterconcept and condemnation of life is only a value judgment of life—but of what life? of what kind of life? I have already given the answer: of declining, weakened, weary, condemned life. Morality, as it has so far been understood—as it has in the end been formulated once more by Schopenhauer, as "negation of the will to life"— is the very *instinct of decadence,* which makes an imperative of itself. It says: "Perish!" It is a condemnation pronounced by the condemned.

Let us finally consider how naive it is altogether to say: "Man *ought* to be such and such!" Reality shows us an enchanting wealth of types, the abundance of a lavish play and change of forms—and some wretched loafer of a moralist comments: "No! Man ought to be different." He even knows what man should be like, this wretched bigot and prig: he paints himself on the wall and comments, *"Ecce homo!"* But even when the moralist addresses himself only to the single human being and says to him, "You ought to be such and such!" he does not cease to make himself ridiculous. The single human being is a piece of *fatum* from the front and from the rear, one law more, one necessity more for all that is yet to come and to be. To say to him, "Change yourself!" is to demand that everything be changed, even retroactively. And indeed there have been consistent moralists who wanted man to be different, that is, virtuous—they wanted him remade in their own image, as a prig: to that end, they *negated* the world! No small madness! No modest kind of immodesty!

Morality, insofar as it *condemns* for its own sake, and *not* out of regard for the concerns, considerations, and contrivances of life, is a specific error with which one ought to have no pity—an *idiosyncrasy of degenerates* which has caused immeasurable harm.

We others, we immoralists, have, conversely, made room in our hearts for every kind of understanding, comprehending, and *approving*. We do not easily negate; we make it a point of honor to be *affirmers*. More and more, our eyes have opened to that economy which needs and knows how to utilize all that the holy witlessness of the priest, of the *diseased* reason in the priest, rejects—that economy in the law of life which finds an advantage even in the disgusting species of the prigs, the priests, the virtuous. *What* advantage? But we ourselves, we immoralists, are the answer.

What alone can be *our* doctrine? That no one *gives* man his qualities—neither God, nor society, nor his parents and ancestors, nor he himself. (The nonsense of the last idea was taught as "intelligible freedom" by Kant—perhaps by Plato already.) No one is responsible for man's being there at all, for his being such-and-such, or for his being in these circumstances or in this environment. The fatality of his essence is not to be disentangled from the fatality of all that has been and will be. Man is not the effect of some special purpose, of a will, and end; nor is he the object of an attempt to attain an "ideal of humanity" or an "ideal of happiness" or an "ideal of morality." It is absurd to wish to devolve one's essence on some end or other. We have invented the concept of "end": in reality there is no end.

One is necessary, one is a piece of fatefulness, one belongs to the whole, one is in the whole; there is nothing which could judge, measure, compare, or sentence our being, for that would mean judging, measuring, comparing, or sentencing the whole. But there is nothing besides the whole. That nobody is held responsible any longer, that the mode of being may not be traced back to a *causa prima,* that the world does not form a unity either as a sensorium or as "spirit"—that alone is the great liberation; with this alone is the innocence of becoming restored. The concept of "God" was until now the greatest objection to existence. We deny God, we deny the responsibility in God: only thereby do we redeem the world.

My demand upon the philosopher is known, that he take his stand *beyond* good and evil and leave the illusion of moral judgment *beneath* himself. This demand follows from an insight which I was the first to formulate: that *there are altogether no moral facts.* Moral judgments agree with religious ones in believing in realities which are no realities. Morality is merely an interpretation of certain phenomena—more precisely, a misinterpretation. Moral judgments, like religious ones, belong to a stage of ignorance at which the very concept of the real and the distinction between what is real and imaginary, are still lacking; thus "truth," at this stage, designates all sorts of things which we today call "imaginings." Moral judgments are therefore never to be taken literally: so understood, they always contain mere absurdity. Semeiotically, however, they remain invaluable: they reveal, at least for those who know, the most valuable realities of cultures and inwardnesses which did not know enough to "understand" themselves. Morality is mere sign language, mere symptomatology; one must know what it is all about to be able to profit from it.

THE ANTICHRIST*

REVALUATION OF ALL VALUES

What is good? Everything that heightens the feeling of power in man, the will to power, power itself.

What is bad? Everything that is born of weakness.

What is happiness? The feeling that power is *growing,* that resistance is overcome.

Not contentedness but more power; not peace but war; not virtue but fitness (Renaissance virtue, *virtù,* virtue that is moraline-free).

The weak and the failures shall perish: first principle of *our* love of man. And they shall even be given every possible assistance.

What is more harmful than any vice? Active pity for all the failures and all the weak: Christianity. . . .

It is a painful, horrible spectacle that has dawned on me: I have drawn back the curtain from the *corruption* of man. In my mouth, this word is at least free from one suspicion: that it might involve a moral accusation of man. It is meant—let me emphasize this once more—*moraline-free.* So much so that I experience this corruption most strongly precisely where men have so far aspired most deliberately to "virtue" and "godliness." I understand corruption, as you will guess, in the sense of decadence: it is my contention that all the values in which mankind now sums up its supreme desiderata are *decadence-values.*

I call an animal, a species, or an individual corrupt when it loses its instincts, when it chooses, when it prefers, what is disadvantageous for it. A history of "lofty sentiments," of the "ideals of mankind"—and it is possible that I shall have to write it—would almost explain too *why* man is so corrupt. Life itself is to my mind the instinct for growth, for durability, for an accumulation of forces, for *power:* where the will to power is lacking there is decline. It is my contention that all the supreme values of mankind *lack* this will—that the values which are symptomatic of decline, *nihilistic* values, are lording it under the holiest names.

THE WILL TO POWER**

Whose Will to Power Is Morality? The *common factor* of all European history since the time of Socrates is the attempt to make the *moral values* dominate

---

*Friedrich Nietzsche, "The Antichrist" from *The Portable Nietzsche,* edited by Walter Kaufmann. Copyright 1954 by The Viking Press, renewed © 1982 by Viking Penguin Inc.

**Friedrich Nietzsche, *The Will to Power,* translated by Walter Kaufmann. Copyright 1967 by Random House.

all other values, in order that they should not be only the leader and judge of life, but also of: (1) knowledge, (2) Art, (3) political and social aspirations. . . .

What is the meaning of this *will to power on the part of moral values,* which has played such a part in the world's prodigious evolutions?

Answer: Three powers lie concealed behind it: (1) the instinct of the *herd* opposed to the strong and independent; (2) the instinct of all *sufferers* and all *abortions* opposed to the happy and well-constituted; (3) the instinct of the mediocre opposed to the exceptions. . . .

The Tendency of Moral Evolution Every one's desire is that there should be no other teaching and valuation of things than those by means of which he himself succeeds. Thus the *fundamental tendency* of the *weak* and *mediocre* of all times, has been to *enfeeble the strong and to reduce them to the level of the weak: their chief weapon in this process was the moral principle.* The attitude of the strong towards the weak is branded as evil: the higher states of the strong become bad bywords. . . .

The instinct of the herd values the *juste milieu* and the *average* as the highest and most precious of all things: the spot where the majority is to be found, and the air that it breathes there. In this way it is the opponent of all order of rank; it regards a climb from the level to the heights in the same light as a descent from the majority to the minority. The herd regards the *exception,* whether it be above or beneath its general level, as something which is antagonistic and dangerous to itself.

The more dangerous a quality seems to the herd, the more completely it is condemned. . . .

My teaching is this, that the herd seeks to maintain and preserve one type of man, and that it defends itself on two sides—that is to say, against those which are decadents from its ranks (criminals, etc.), and against those who rise superior to its dead level. The instincts of the herd tend to a stationary state of society; they merely preserve. They have no creative power. . . .

DISCUSSION

Unlike most other philosophers, Nietzsche does not try to *justify* morality; instead, he tries to analyze and *explain* it through psychology. What we call "morality," he argues, is in fact a "herd" or "slave morality," which was invented for the protection of the weak and coerces and inhibits those who could do more than merely "be moral." Thus, he insists that there are "no moral facts" and no objective moral order but rather a "tyranny against nature" invented by those whose natures are weak and insecure. A virtue such as humility, for example, inhibits our natural tendency to be proud and outspoken about our own accomplishments—which of course does not bother those who have nothing to be proud about (earlier, Hume had made the same point). There is nothing "right" about humility, or, for that matter, about pride. But pride is "natural"; humility is not. Pride is a manifestation of strength and accomplishment; humility is a mark of meekness and self-denial.

Accordingly, Nietzsche distinguishes his two kinds of moral perspectives—master and slave moralities. Master morality is the nobility of great desires, expressing what we feel, without the inhibitions of universal rules. This is not to say that masters must be cruel or inconsiderate; Nietzsche even says at one point that the strong have a *duty* to help the weak, but this as a mark of character rather than a moral obligation. Slave morality is prompted not by desire and passion, however, but by fear and a sense of inadequacy. For the slave, "good" comes to mean just the opposite of what it means to the master—self-denial instead of self-fulfillment. In turn, the master's "good" becomes slave morality's "evil" and the Christian concept of sin. Denying one's passions becomes morally imperative for everyone; expressing or pursuing one's passion is universally prohibited—which is no inconvenience, of course, to those of little passion.

Nietzsche claims that he is giving us a "genealogy" when he traces the origins of "slave morality" to the literal slaves of ancient Egypt and early Rome. Similarly, he claims that he is simply explaining two types of morality when he distinguishes master and slave moral concepts. But it is clear that the terms "master" and "slave" are anything but neutral, and that although Nietzsche is sympathetic to the plight of the slaves, he prefers and defends the former and despises the latter. Furthermore, Nietzsche spends so much of his philosophical energy attacking (slave) morality and its metaphysical supports in Christianity that his ethics too often appears to be simply negative—or what he calls "nihilism"—a brutal attack that leaves nothing in its place. But Nietzsche would have been offended by this view of his work, which he repeatedly called a "Yes-saying" to life and an expression of the ultimate freedom and "cheerfulness." He saw nihilism rather as a product of morality itself and he saw his rejection of (slave) morality and religion ("God is dead") as a liberating force in our lives, an opening up of infinite possibilities: "Every hazard is permitted. . . . The sea, *our* sea, lies open there. Perhaps there has never been so open a sea."

Discussion Questions

1. In what sense does Nietzsche claim to be a "psychologist in the matter of morals"? What is he looking for when he asks, "What does such an assertion [for example, 'there is a categorical imperative'] indicate about the person who makes it?"
2. What is the *Übermensch?* Why and in what way is he (or she) "more than human"? What kind of ideal is Nietzsche holding up to us here?
3. What's wrong with weakness?
4. What is so bad about socialism and democracy (which Nietzsche links together as a single phenomenon)?
5. What's wrong with "humility"? (Would Aristotle agree?)
6. What is wrong with taking the main terms of morality as essentially impersonal or "disinterested"? Isn't this the very essence of morals?
7. "There are altogether no moral facts." What does this mean?
8. What is wrong with trying to "improve mankind"?

Study Questions

1. If Nietzsche were in an argument with John Stuart Mill about utilitarianism, what would Nietzsche say about Mill's basic premise, that everyone desires his or her own happiness (pleasure)?

2. What is "slave morality," and why is our own morality a version of it? What is the origin of slave morality? What is its motivation?

3. Why is every morality "tyranny against nature"? Why does Nietzsche attack the dominance of reason in morals? In what way does he thus resemble Hume? In what way does he differ from Hume? What would Nietzsche say about the role of the "moral sentiments" in ethics?

4. Why does Nietzsche so despise Christianity and Judeo-Christian morality? Could one defend Christianity and morality without invoking the considerations Nietzsche rejects? Is Christian morality based fundamentally on resentment and weakness? Does Nietzsche insist that *all* Christians are so motivated?

5. What does Nietzsche have against Socrates? Why does he link Socrates with Christianity?

6. Nietzsche credits the ancient Hebrew for "the miracle of the inversion of valuations" that defines slave morality. What is this "inversion," and how does it work? How does slave morality translate the values of "master morality" into its own terms?

7. What is "noble"? In what ways does Nietzsche's morality agree with that of Plato and Aristotle? In what ways is it clearly different?

8. Is Nietzsche a teleologist in ethics? Why does he insist that "man is not the effect of some special purpose, of a will, an end; nor is he the object of an attempt to attain an 'ideal of humanity' or an 'ideal of happiness' or an 'ideal of morality'?" What does he mean when he writes, "We have invented the concept of 'end'; in reality there is no end"?

9

Jean-Paul Sartre

Sartre was born in Paris in 1905, and he continued to live there for virtually the whole of his life. He studied philosophy and for a short time taught in the provinces, which he hated. He joined the army at the outbreak of World War II, was captured, and spent some time in a German prison camp, reading the German philosophers (Hegel and Heidegger) and resolving to dedicate his life writing in the cause of freedom. *Being and Nothingness* was published in 1943 and quickly became the classic text of the new fashion, "existentialism." Sartre's politics moved further and further to the left, but, although a Marxist, he never joined the Communist party, which he considered dogmatic and immoral. He spent his life with Simone de Beauvoir, herself an accomplished philosopher, novelist, and journalist. He died in 1980, at the age of 75.

Jean-Paul Sartre is generally recognized as *the* "existentialist." The word is his, and the dozens of other philosophers associated with existentialism—including many who have disclaimed their association—are judged to be more or less "existential" philosophers by their proximity to Sartre's ideas. One can summarize those ideas in two words—"freedom" and "responsibility." Freedom, Sartre tells us, is the primary condition of human existence, the brute fact that we can and must make choices and, consequently, "make ourselves" into what we will be. Responsibility follows freedom; to have choices and to be able to make a difference is to be responsible for what one chooses and the difference one makes. This includes, of course, *not* choosing, because—Sartre keeps reminding us—not to choose is to *choose* not to choose, whether through willful ignorance, or indecision, or any number of other devices for denying responsibility—which he calls "bad faith" *(mauvaise foi)*.

Like Nietzsche and Camus, Sartre rejects the whole history of ethical justifications. The world is not rational, and we have no reason to expect it to conform to our demands. There is no God, Sartre insists, and therefore no one and nothing to give purpose to the universe or meaning to life. Furthermore, he argues in his popular 1947 lecture, *Existentialism Is a Humanism* (reprinted in part here), there is no one or nothing to give an "essence"—a distinctive purpose or reason—to our existence. There is no human nature, in other words, just our freedom, and it is our responsibility to use as we will. *We* give purpose and meaning to our lives, and there is no one and nothing to assure us that it is the "right" purpose or meaning. This is the human condition, and it is the point of Sartre's philosophy, not to give us an ethical code or rules to live by, but to keep reminding us of this frightening but inescapable freedom and the responsibility that goes along with it.

Sartre started in philosophy as a student of *phenomenology*—a method formulated by the German-Czech philosopher Edmund Husserl at the beginning of this century. The key to phenomenology is the careful investigation of human experience itself, and it is there that Sartre grounds his ethical views. Our basic freedom is first of all a phenomenological finding; that is, a careful examination of our every practical experience shows that the possibility of choice is always there. (A similar point had been argued by Kant—who was decidedly not an existentialist—when he argued that freedom was the necessary "postulate" of practical reason.)

Sartre divides the world into two kinds of "being," which he calls "being-in-itself" *(être-en-soi)* and "being-for-itself" *(être-pour-soi).* The first is the being of things. Things simply are what they are; they don't worry about what they ought to be. The second is the being of human consciousness; it is incomplete, aware of the future and the various possibilities for the future. Accordingly, we have a "double property," the facts about ourselves and our interpretation and use of those facts—which Sartre calls facticity and transcendence, respectively. Human beings are always worried about what they will be and what they ought to be. But, because there is no God and because we are endowed (or cursed) with continuous choices, we have no basis for choosing one course of action, one way of life, rather than another. Our basic emotion, accordingly, is anxiety—about what we are, what we will do, what we will be. (In an early novel, Sartre says that our most basic philosophical feeling is rather *nausea*, but his outlook improves at least slightly later on.)

Our lives, according to Sartre, are always incompletely formed, "indeterminate." Not only can we change our plans for the future, but we also change our past. Suppose you are a pre-med student, working hard to get into medical school and remembering with pride how long you have wanted to be a doctor and the various jobs and responsibilities you have had with that end in mind. But when you flunk your organic chemistry course, your view drastically changes. Not only do you give up your plan to go to medical school, but you stop thinking about your past in pre-med terms. Now you have decided to be an architect, and so you weave a tale of continued creativity and interest in buildings. The facts of the past may stay the same, but the stories we create around them—and what facts are deemed relevant or not—change significantly.

What we would like, according to Sartre, is to be both free and determined, that is, to be able to choose but at the same time "know who we are." But there is no "knowing who we are" because we are not yet anything or anyone in particular, and we cannot be free and at the same time determined. This ideal of being both free and determined is, as a matter of fact, the conception of God that many medieval philosophers (notably Augustine) defended, which leads Sartre to say, somewhat blasphemously, that what we all really want is to be God. But Sartre is not really interested in theology here; what concerns him is the fact that our lives embody an impossible, ultimate wish. There is no *summum bonum;* there is only frustration and the illusion of temporary happiness. "Man is a useless passion," he writes in one of the bleaker passages of *Being and Nothingness,* his most important existentialist treatise, excerpted in this chapter.

It would be a mistake, however, to see Sartre as a pessimist, with a tragic and gloomy picture of human life. Shortly before he died in 1980, Sartre insisted in an interview that he had "never had an unhappy day in his life." His plays and novels exude a mischievous sense of humor, and he claims throughout his works that (his) existentialism is in fact the most optimistic philosophy, because it gives each of us the freedom and responsibility to take charge of our own lives and frees us from the constraints falsely imposed on us by authoritative appeals to "human nature," what is natural "or God's Will."

EXISTENTIALISM IS A HUMANISM*

. . . For in truth this is of all teachings the least scandalous and the most austere: it is intended strictly for technicians and philosophers. All the same, it can easily be defined.

The question is only complicated because there are two kinds of existentialists. There are, on the one hand, the Christians, amongst whom I shall name Jaspers and Gabriel Mercel, both professed Catholics; and on the other the existential atheists, amongst whom we must place Heidegger as well as the French existentialists and myself. What they have in common is simply the fact that they believe that *existence* comes before *essence*—or, if you will, that we must begin from the subjective. What exactly do we mean by that?

If one considers an article of manufacture—as for example, a book or a paper-knife—one sees that it has been made by an artisan who had a conception of it; and he has paid attention, equally, to the conception of a paper-knife and to the pre-existent technique of production which is a part of that conception and is, at bottom, a formula. Thus the paper-knife is at the same time an article producible in a certain manner and one which, on the other hand, serves a definite purpose, for one cannot suppose that a man would produce a paper-knife without knowing what it was for. Let us say, then, of the paper-knife that its essence—that is to say the sum of the formulae and the qualities which made its production and its definition possible—precedes its existence. The presence of such-and-such a paper-knife or book is thus determined before my eyes. Here, then, we are viewing the world from a technical standpoint, and we can say that production precedes existence.

When we think of God as the creator, we are thinking of him, most of the time, as a supernatural artisan. Whatever doctrine we may be considering,

*Jean-Paul Sartre, *Existentialism Is a Humanism,* translated by P. Mairet. Copyright © 1949 by The Philosophical Library, Inc.

whether it be a doctrine like that of Descartes, or of Leibnitz himself, we always imply that the will follows, more or less, from the understanding or at least accompanies it, so that when God creates he knows precisely what he is creating. Thus, the conception of man in the mind of God is comparable to that of the paper-knife in the mind of the artisan: God makes man according to a procedure and a conception, exactly as the artisan manufactures a paper-knife, following a definition and a formula. Thus each individual man is the realisation of a certain conception which dwells in the divine understanding. In the philosophic atheism of the eighteenth century, the notion of God is suppressed, but not, for all that, the idea that essence is prior to existence; something of that idea we still find everywhere, in Diderot, in Voltaire and even in Kant. Man possesses a human nature; that "human nature," which is the conception of human being, is found in every man; which means that each man is a particular example of an universal conception, the conception of Man. In Kant, this universality goes so far that the wild man of the woods, man in the state of nature and the bourgeois are all contained in the same definition and have the same fundamental qualities. Here again, the essence of man precedes that historic existence which we confront in experience.

Atheistic existentialism, of which I am a representative, declares with greater consistency that if God does not exist there is at least one being whose existence comes before its essence, a being which exists before it can be defined by any conception of it. That being is man or, as Heidegger has it, the human reality. What do we mean by saying that existence precedes essence? We mean that man first of all exists, encounters himself, surges up in the world—and defines himself afterwards. If man as the existentialist sees him is not definable, it is because to begin with he is nothing. He will not be anything until later, and then he will be what he makes of himself. Thus, there is no human nature, because there is no God to have a conception of it. Man simply is. Not that he is simply what he conceives himself to be, but he is what he wills, and as he conceives himself after already existing—as he wills to be after that leap towards existence. Man is nothing else but that which he makes of himself. That is the first principle of existentialism. . . .

Before that projection of the self nothing exists; not even in the heaven of intelligence: man will only attain existence when he is what he purposes to be. Not, however, what he may wish to be. For what we usually understand by wishing or willing is a conscious decision taken—much more often than not—after we have made ourselves what we are. I may wish to join a party, to write a book or to marry—but in such a case what is usually called my will is probably a manifestation of a prior and more spontaneous decision. If, however, it is true that existence is prior to essence, man is responsible for what he is. Thus, the first effect of existentialism is that it puts every man in possession of himself as he is, and places the entire responsibility for his existence squarely upon his own shoulders. And, when we say that man is responsible for himself, we do not mean that he is responsible only for his own individuality, but that he is responsible for all men. The word "subjectivism" is to be understood in two senses, and our adversaries play upon only one of them. Subjectivism means, on the one hand, the freedom of the individual subject and, on the other, that man cannot pass beyond human subjectivity. It is the latter which is the deeper meaning of existentialism. When we say that man chooses himself, we do mean that every one of us must choose himself; but by that we also mean that in choosing for himself he chooses for all men. For in effect, of all the actions a man may take in order to create himself as he wills to be, there is not one which is not creative, at the same time, of an image of man such as he believes he ought to be. To choose between this or that is at the same time to affirm the value of that which is chosen; for we are unable ever to choose the worse. What we choose is always the better; and nothing can be better for us unless it is better for all. If, moreover, existence precedes essence and we will to exist at the same time as we fashion our image, that image is valid for all and for the entire epoch in which we find ourselves. Our responsibility is thus much greater than we had supposed, for it concerns mankind as a whole. If I am a worker, for instance, I may choose to join a Christian rather than a Communist trade union. And if, by that membership, I choose to signify that resignation is, after all, the attitude that best becomes a man, that man's kingdom is not upon this earth, I do not commit myself alone to that view. Resignation is my will for everyone, and my action is, in consequence, a commitment on behalf of all mankind. Or if, to take a more personal case, I decide to marry and to have children, even though this decision proceeds simply from my situation, from my passion or my desire, I am thereby committing not only myself, but humanity as a whole, to the practice of monogamy. I am thus responsible for myself and for all men, and I am creating a certain image of man as I would have him to be. In fashioning myself I fashion man.

This may enable us to understand what is meant by such terms—perhaps a little grandiloquent—as anguish, abandonment and despair. As you will soon see, it is very simple. First, what do we mean by anguish? The existentialist frankly states that man is in anguish. His meaning is as follows—When a man commits himself to anything, fully realising that he is not only choosing what he will be, but is thereby at the same time a legislator deciding for the whole of mankind—in such a moment a man cannot escape from the sense of complete and profound responsibility. There are many, indeed, who show no such anxiety. But we affirm that they are merely disguising their anguish or are in flight from it. Certainly, many people think that in what they are doing they commit no one but themselves to anything: and if you ask them, "What would happen if everyone did so?" they shrug their shoulders and reply, "Everyone does not do so." But in truth, one ought always to ask oneself what would happen if everyone did as one is doing; nor can one escape from that disturbing thought except by a kind of self-deception. The man who lies in self-excuse, by saying "Everyone will not do it," must be ill at ease in his conscience, for the act of lying implies the universal value which it denies. By its very disguise his anguish reveals itself. This is the anguish that Kierkegaard called "the anguish of Abraham." You know the story: An angel commanded Abraham to sacrifice his son: and obedience was obligatory, if it really was an angel who had appeared and said, "Thou, Abraham, shalt sacrifice thy son." But anyone in such a case would wonder, first, whether it was indeed an angel and secondly, whether I am really Abraham. Where are the proofs? A certain mad woman who suffered from hallucinations said that people were telephoning to her, and giving her orders. The doctor asked, "But who is it that speaks to you?" She replied: "He says it is God." And what, indeed, could prove to her that it was God? If an angel appears to me, what is the proof that it is an angel; or, if I hear voices, who can prove that they proceed from heaven and not from hell, or from my own subconsciousness or some pathological condition? Who can prove that they are really addressed to me?

Who, then, can prove that I am the proper person to impose, by my own choice, my conception of man upon mankind? I shall never find any proof whatever; there will be no sign to convince me of it. If a voice speaks to me, it is still I myself who must decide whether the voice is or is not that of an angel. If I regard a certain course of action as good, it is only I who choose to say that it is good and not bad. There is nothing to show that I am Abraham: nevertheless I also am obliged at every instant to perform actions which are examples. Everything happens to every man as though the whole human race had its eyes fixed upon what he is doing and regulated its conduct accordingly. So every man ought to say, "Am I really a man who has the right to act in such a manner that humanity regulates itself by what I do?" If a man does not say that, he is dissembling his anguish. Clearly, the anguish with which we are concerned here is not one that could lead to quietism or inaction. It is anguish pure and simple, of the kind well known to all those who have borne responsibilities. When, for instance, a military leader takes upon himself the responsibility for an attack and sends a number of men to their death, he chooses to do it and at bottom he alone chooses. No doubt he acts under a higher command, but its orders, which are more general, require interpretation by him and upon that interpretation depends the life of ten, fourteen or twenty men. In making the decision, he cannot but feel a certain anguish. All leaders know that anguish. It does not prevent their acting, on the contrary it is the very condition of their action, for the action presupposes that there is a plurality of possibilities, and in choosing one of these, they realise that it has value only because it is chosen. Now it is anguish of that kind which existentialism describes, and moreover, as we shall see, makes explicit through direct responsibility towards other men who are concerned. Far from being a screen which could separate us from action, it is a condition of action itself.

And when we speak of "abandonment"—a favourite word of Heidegger— we only mean to say that God does not exist, and that it is necessary to draw the consequences of his absence right to the end. The existentialist is strongly opposed to a certain type of secular moralism which seeks to suppress God at the least possible expense. Towards 1880, when the French professors endeavoured to formulate a secular morality, they said something like this:—God is a useless and costly hypothesis, so we will do without it. However, if we are to have morality, a society and a law-abiding world, it is essential that certain values should be taken seriously; they must have an *a priori* existence ascribed to them. It must be considered obligatory *a priori* to be honest, not to lie, not to beat one's wife, to bring up children and so forth; so we are going to do a little work on this subject, which will enable us to show that these values exist all the same, inscribed in an intelligible heaven although, of course, there is no God. In other words—and this is, I believe, the purport of all that we in France call radicalism—nothing will be changed if God does not exist; we shall re-discover the same norms of honesty, progress and humanity, and we shall have disposed of God as an out-of-date hypothesis which will die away quietly of itself. The existentialist, on the contrary, finds it extremely embarrassing that God does not exist, for there disappears with Him all possibility of finding values in an intelligible heaven. There can no longer be any good *a priori,* since there is no infinite and perfect consciousness to think it. It is nowhere written that "the good" exists, that one must be honest or must not lie, since we are now upon the plane where there are only men. Dostoyevsky once wrote "If God did not exist, everything would be permitted"; and that, for existentialism, is the starting point. Everything is indeed permitted if God does not exist, and man is in consequence forlorn, for he cannot find anything to depend upon either within or outside himself. He discovers forthwith, that he is without excuse. For if indeed existence precedes essence, one will never be able to explain one's action by reference to a given and specific human nature; in other words, there is no determinism—man is free, man *is* freedom. Nor, on the other hand, if God does not exist, are we provided with any values or commands that could legitimise our behaviour. Thus we have neither behind us, nor before us in a luminous realm of values, any means of justification or excuse. We are left alone, without excuse. That is what I mean when I say that man is condemned to be free. Condemned, because he did not create himself, yet is nevertheless at liberty, and from the moment that he is thrown into this world he is responsible for everything he does. The existentialist does not believe in the power of passion. He will never regard a grand passion as a destructive torrent upon which a man is swept into certain actions as by fate, and which, therefore, is an excuse for them. He thinks that man is responsible for his passion. Neither will an existentialist think that a man can find help through some sign being vouchsafed upon earth for his orientation: for he thinks that the man himself interprets the sign as he chooses. He thinks that every man, without any support or help whatever, is condemned at every instant to invent man. . . .

As an example by which you may the better understand this state of abandonment, I will refer to the case of a pupil of mine, who sought me out in the following circumstances. His father was quarreling with his mother and was also inclined to be a "collaborator"; his elder brother had been killed in the German offensive of 1940 and this young man, with a sentiment somewhat primitive but generous, burned to avenge him. His mother was living alone with him, deeply afflicted by the semi-treason of his father and by the death of her eldest son, and her one consolation was in this young man. But he, at this moment, had the choice between going to England to join the Free French Forces or of staying near his mother and helping her to live. He fully realised that this woman lived only for him and that his disappearance—or perhaps his death—would plunge her into despair. He also realised that, concretely and in fact, every action he performed on his mother's behalf would be sure of effect in the sense of aiding her to live, whereas anything he did in order to go and fight would be an ambiguous action which might vanish like water into sand and serve no purpose. For instance, to set out for England he would have to wait indefinitely in a Spanish camp on the way through Spain; or, on arriving in England or in Algiers he might be put into an office to fill up forms. Consequently, he found himself confronted by two very different modes of action: the one concrete, immediate but directed towards only one individual; and the other an action addressed to an end infinitely greater, a national collectivity, but for that very reason ambiguous—and it might be frustrated on the way. At the same time, he was hesitating between two kinds of morality; on the one side the morality of sympathy, of personal devotion and, on the other side, a morality of wider scope but of more debatable validity. He had to choose between those two. What could help him to choose? Could the Christian doctrine? No. Christian doctrine says: Act with charity, love your neighbour, deny yourself for others, choose the way which is hardest, and so forth. But which is the harder road? To whom does one owe the more brotherly love, the patriot or the mother? Which is the more useful aim, the general one of fighting in and for the whole community, or the precise aim of helping one particular person to live? Who can give an answer to that *a priori?* No one. Nor is it given in any ethical scripture. The Kantian ethic says, Never regard another as a means, but always as an end. Very well; if I remain with my mother, I shall be regarding her as the end and not as a means: but by the same token I am in danger of treating as means those who are fighting on my behalf; and the converse is also true, that if I go to the aid of the combatants I shall be treating them as the end at the risk of treating my mother as a means.

If values are uncertain, if they are still too abstract to determine the particular, concrete case under consideration, nothing remains but to trust in our instincts. That is what this young man tried to do; and when I saw him he said, "In the end it is feeling that counts; the direction in which it is really pushing me is the one I ought to choose. If I feel that I love my mother enough to sacrifice everything else for her—my will to be avenged, all my longings for action and adventure—then I stay with her. If, on the contrary, I feel that my love for her is not enough, I go." But how does one estimate the strength of a feeling? The value of his feeling for his mother was determined precisely by the fact that he was standing by her. I may say that I love a certain friend enough to sacrifice such or such a sum of money for him, but I cannot prove that unless I have done it. I may say, "I love my mother enough to remain with her," if actually I have remained with her. I can only estimate the strength of this affection if I have performed an action by which it is defined and ratified. But if I then appeal to this affection to justify my action, I find myself drawn into a vicious circle. . . .

What is at the very heart and centre of existentialism is the absolute character of the free commitment, by which every man realises himself in realising a type of humanity—a commitment always understandable, to no matter whom in no matter what epoch—and its bearing upon the relativity of the cultural pattern which may result from such absolute commitment. One must observe equally the relativity of Cartesianism and the absolute character of the Cartesian commitment. In this sense you may say, if you like, that every one of us makes the absolute by breathing, by eating, by sleeping or by behaving in any fashion whatsoever. There is no difference between free being—being as self-committal, as existence choosing its essence—and absolute being. And there is no difference whatever between being as an absolute, temporarily localised—that is, localised in history—and universally intelligible being. . . .

. . . Existentialism is nothing else but an attempt to draw the full conclusions from a consistently atheistic position. . . . Not that we believe God does exist, but we think that the real problem is not that of His existence; what man needs is to find himself again and to understand that nothing can save him from himself, not even a valid proof of the existence of God. In this sense existentialism is optimistic, it is a doctrine of action, and it is only by self-deception, by confusing their own despair with ours that Christians can describe us as without hope.

BEING AND NOTHINGNESS*

BAD FAITH

. . . What are we to say is the being of man who has the possibility of denying himself? . . . It is best to choose and to examine one determined attitude which is essential to human reality and which is such that consciousness instead of directing its negation outward turns it toward itself. This attitude, it seems to me, is *bad faith (mauvaise foi)*. . . .

Take the example of a woman who has consented to go out with a particular man for the first time. She knows very well the intentions which the man who is speaking to her cherishes regarding her. She knows also that it will be necessary sooner or later for her to make a decision. But she does not want to realize the urgency; she concerns herself only with what is respectful and discreet in the attitude of her companion. She does not apprehend this conduct as an attempt to achieve what we call "the first approach"; that is, she does not want to see possibilities of temporal development which his conduct presents. She restricts this behavior to what is in the present; she does not wish to read in the phrases which he addresses to her anything other than their explicit meaning. If he says to her, "I find you so attractive!" she disarms this phrase of its sexual background; she attaches to the conversation and to the behavior of the speaker, the immediate meanings, which she imagines as objective qualities. The man who is speaking to her appears to be sincere and respectful as the table is round or square, as the wall coloring is blue or gray. The qualities thus

*Jean-Paul Sartre, *Being and Nothingness,* translated by Hazel Barnes. Copyright © 1956 by The Philosophical Library, Inc.

attached to the person she is listening to are in this way fixed in a permanence like that of things, which is no other than the projection of the strict present of the qualities into the temporal flux. This is because she does not quite know what she wants. She is profoundly aware of the desire which she inspires, but the desire cruel and naked would humiliate and horrify her. Yet she would find no charm in a respect which would be only respect. In order to satisfy her, there must be a feeling which is addressed wholly to her *personality—i.e.,* to her full freedom—and which would be a recognition of her freedom. But at the same time this feeling must be wholly desire; that is, it must address itself to her body as object. This time then she refuses to apprehend the desire for what it is; she does not even give it a name; she recognizes it only to the extent that it tran-scends itself toward admiration, esteem, respect and that it is wholly absorbed in the more refined forms which it produces, to the extent of no longer figuring anymore as a sort of warmth and density. But then suppose he takes her hand. This act of her companion risks changing the situation by calling for an immedi-ate decision. To leave the hand there is to consent in herself to flirt, to engage her-self. To withdrew it is to break the troubled and unstable harmony which gives the hour its charm. The aim is to postpone the moment of decision as long as pos-sible. We know what happens next; the young woman leaves her hand there, but she *does not notice* that she is leaving it. She does not notice because it happens by chance that she is at this moment all intellect. She draws her companion up to the most lofty regions of sentimental speculation; she speaks of Life, of her life, she shows herself in her essential aspect—a personality, a consciousness. And during this time the divorce of the body from the soul is accomplished; the hand rests inert between the warm hands of her companion—neither consenting nor resisting—a thing.

We shall say that this woman is in bad faith. But we see immediately that she uses various procedures in order to maintain herself in this bad faith. She has disarmed the actions of her companion by reducing them to being only what they are; that is, to existing in the mode of the in-itself. But she permits herself to enjoy his desire, to the extent that she will apprehend it as not being what it is, will recognize its transcendence. Finally while sensing profoundly the pres-ence of her own body—to the degree of being disturbed perhaps—she realizes herself as *not being* her own body, and she contemplates it as though from above as a passive object to which events can *happen* but which can neither provoke them nor avoid them because all its possibilities are outside of it. What unity do we find in these various aspects of bad faith? It is a certain art of form-ing contradictory concepts which unite in themselves both an idea and the nega-tion of that idea. The basic concept which is thus engendered utilizes the double property of the human being, who is at once a *facticity* and a *transcendence*. These two aspects of human reality are and ought to be capable of a valid coor-dination. But bad faith does not wish either to coordinate them or to surmount them in a synthesis. Bad faith seeks to affirm their identity while preserving their differences. It must affirm facticity as *being* transcendence and transcen-dence as *being* facticity, in such a way that at the instant when a person appre-hends the one, he can find himself abruptly faced with the other. . . .

If man is what he is, bad faith is forever impossible and candor ceases to be his ideal and becomes instead his being. But is man what he is? And more generally, how can he *be* what he is when he exists as consciousness of being? If candor or sincerity is a universal value, it is evident that the maxim "one must be what one is" does not serve solely as a regulating principle for judgments and concepts by which I express what I am. It posits not merely an ideal of knowing but an ideal of *being;* it proposes for us an absolute equivalence of being with itself as a prototype of being. In this sense it is necessary that we *make ourselves* what we are. But what *are we* then if we have the constant obligation to make ourselves what we are, if our mode of being is having the obligation to be what we are?

Let us consider this waiter in the café. His movement is quick and forward, a little too precise, a little too rapid. He comes toward the patrons with a step a little too quick. He bends forward a little too eagerly; his voice, his eyes express an interest a little too solicitous for the order of the customer. Finally there he returns, trying to imitate in his walk the inflexible stiffness of some kind of automaton while carrying his tray with the recklessness of a tight-rope-walker by putting it in a perpetually unstable, perpetually broken equilibrium which he perpetually re-establishes by a light movement of the arm and hand. All his behavior seems to us a game. He applies himself to chaining his movements as if they were mechanisms, the one regulating the other; his gestures and even his voice seem to be mechanisms; he gives himself the quickness and pitiless rapidity of things. He is playing, he is amusing himself. But what is he playing? We need not watch long before we can explain it: he is playing at *being* a waiter in a café. There is nothing there to surprise us. The game is a kind of marking out and investigation. The child plays with his body in order to explore it, to take inventory of it; the waiter in the café plays with his condition in order to *realize* it. This obligation is not different from that which is imposed on all tradesmen. Their condition is wholly one of ceremony. The public demands of them that they realize it as a ceremony; there is the dance of the grocer, of the tailor, of the auctioneer, by which they endeavor to persuade their clientele that they are nothing but a grocer, an auctioneer, a tailor. A grocer who dreams is offensive to the buyer, because such a grocer is not wholly a grocer. Society demands that he limit himself to his function as a grocer, just as the soldier at attention makes himself into a soldier-thing with a direct regard which does not see at all, which is no longer meant to see, since it is the rule and not the interest of the moment which determines the point he must fix his eyes on (the sight "fixed at ten paces"). There are indeed many precautions to imprison a man in what he is, as if we lived in perpetual fear that he might escape from it, that he might break away and suddenly elude his condition.

In a parallel situation, from within, the waiter in the café can not be immediately a café waiter in the sense that this inkwell *is* an inkwell, or the glass is a glass. It is by no means that he can not form reflective judgments or concepts concerning his condition. He knows well what it "means"; the obligation of getting up at five o'clock, of sweeping the floor of the shop before the restaurant opens, of starting the coffee pot going, *etc.* He knows the rights which it allows:

the right to tips, the right to belong to a union, *etc.* But all these concepts, all these judgments refer to the transcendent. It is a matter of abstract possibilities, of rights and duties conferred on a "person possessing rights." And it is precisely this person *who I have to be* (if I am the waiter in question) and who I am not. It is not that I do not wish to be this person or that I want this person to be different. But rather there is no common measure between his being and mine. It is a "representation" for others and for myself, which means that I can be he only in *representation.* But if I represent myself as him, I am not he; I am separated from him as the object from the subject, separated *by nothing,* but this nothing isolates me from him. I cannot be he, I can only play *at being* him; that is, imagine to myself that I am he. And thereby I affect him with nothingness. In vain do I fulfill the functions of a café waiter. I can be he only in the neutralized mode, as the actor is Hamlet, by mechanically making the *typical gestures* of my state and by aiming at myself as an imaginary café waiter through those gestures taken as an "analogue." What I attempt to realize is a being-in-itself of the café waiter, as if it were not just in my power to confer their value and their urgency upon my duties and the rights of my position, as if it were not my free choice to get up each morning at five o'clock or to remain in bed, even though it meant getting fired. As if from the very fact that I sustain this role in existence I did not transcend it on every side, as if I did not constitute myself as one *beyond* my condition. Yet there is no doubt that I *am* in a sense a café waiter—otherwise could I not just as well call myself a diplomat or a reporter? But if I am one, this cannot be in the mode of being-in-itself. I am a waiter in the mode of *being what I am not.*

Furthermore we are dealing with more than mere social positions; I am never any one of my attitudes, any one of my actions. The good speaker is the one who *plays at* speaking, because he cannot *be speaking.* The attentive pupil who wishes to *be* attentive, his eyes riveted on the teacher, his ears open wide, so exhausts himself in playing the attentive role that he ends up by no longer hearing anything. . . .

Under these conditions what can be the significance of the ideal of sincerity except as a task impossible to achieve, of which the very meaning is in contradiction with the structure of my consciousness. To be sincere, we said, is to be what one is. That supposes that I am not originally what I am. But here naturally Kant's "You ought, therefore you can" is implicitly understood. I can *become* sincere; this is what my duty and my effort to achieve sincerity imply. But we definitely establish that the original structure of "not being what one is" renders impossible in advance all movement toward being in itself or "being what one is." And this impossibility is not hidden from consciousness; on the contrary, it is the very stuff of consciousness; it is the embarrassing constraint which we constantly experience; it is our very incapacity to recognize ourselves, to constitute ourselves as being what we are. It is this necessity which means that, as soon as we posit ourselves as a certain being, by a legitimate judgment, based on inner experience or correctly deduced from *a priori* or empirical premises, then by that very positing we surpass this being—and that not toward another being but toward emptiness, toward *nothing.*

How then can we blame another for not being sincere or rejoice in our own sincerity since this sincerity appears to us at the same time to be impossible? How can we in conversation, in confession, in introspection, even attempt sincerity since at the very time when we announce it we have a prejudicative comprehension of its futility? Let us take an example: A homosexual frequently has an intolerable feeling of guilt, and his whole existence is determined in relation to this feeling. One will readily foresee that he is in bad faith. In fact it frequently happens that this man, while recognizing his homosexual inclination, while avowing each and every particular misdeed which he has committed, refuses with all his strength to consider himself *"a paederast."* His case is always "different," peculiar; there enters into it something of a game, of chance, of bad luck; the mistakes are all in the past; they are explained by a certain conception of the beautiful which women cannot satisfy; we should see in them the results of a restless search, rather than the manifestations of a deeply rooted tendency, *etc., etc.* Here is assuredly a man in bad faith who borders on the comic since, acknowledging all the facts which are imputed to him, he refuses to draw from them the conclusion which they impose. His friend, who is his most severe critic, becomes irritated with this duplicity. The critic asks only one thing—and perhaps then he will show himself indulgent: that the guilty one recognize himself as guilty, that the homosexual declare frankly—whether humbly or boastfully matters little—"I am a paederast." We ask here: Who is in bad faith? The homosexual or the champion of sincerity?

The homosexual recognizes his faults, but he struggles with all his strength against the crushing view that his mistakes constitute for him a *destiny.* He does not wish to let himself be considered as a thing. He has an obscure but strong feeling that a homosexual is not a homosexual as this table is a table or as this red-haired man is red-haired. It seems to him that he has escaped from each mistake as soon as he has posited it and recognized it; he even feels that the psychic duration by itself cleanses him from each misdeed, constitutes for him an undetermined future, causes him to be born anew. Is he wrong? Does he not recognize in himself the peculiar, irreducible character of human reality? His attitude includes then an undeniable comprehension of truth. But at the same time he needs this perpetual rebirth, this constant escape in order to live; he must constantly put himself beyond reach in order to avoid the terrible judgment of collectivity. Thus he plays on the word *being.* He would be right actually if he understood the phrase "I am a paederast" in the sense of "I am not what I am." That is, if he declared to himself, "To the extent that a pattern of conduct is defined as the conduct of a paederast and to the extent that I have adopted this conduct, I am a paederast. But to the extent that human reality cannot be finally defined by patterns of conduct, I am not one." But instead he slides surreptitiously toward a different connotation of the word "being." He understands "not being a paederast" in the sense in which this table is not an inkwell. He is in bad faith.

But the champion of sincerity is not ignorant of the transcendence of human reality, and he knows how at need to appeal to it for his own advantage. He makes use of it even and brings it up in the present argument. Does he not wish, first in the name of sincerity, then of freedom, that the homosexual reflect on himself and acknowledge himself as a homosexual? Does he not let the other understand that such a confession will win indulgence for him? What does this mean if not that the man who will acknowledge himself as a homosexual will no longer be *the same* as the homosexual whom he acknowledges being and that he will escape into the region of freedom and of good will? The critic asks the man then to be what he is in order no longer to be what he is. It is the profound meaning of the saying, "A sin confessed is half pardoned." The critic demands of the guilty one that he constitute himself as a thing, precisely in order no longer to treat him as a thing. And this contradiction is constitutive of the demand of sincerity. Who cannot see how offensive to the Other and how reassuring for me is a statement such as, "He's just a paederast," which removes a disturbing freedom from a trait and which aims at henceforth constituting all the acts of the Other as consequences following strictly from his essence. That is actually what the critic is demanding of his victim—that he constitute himself as a thing, that he should entrust his freedom to his friend as a fief, in order that the friend should return it to him subsequently—like a suzerain to his vassal. The champion of sincerity is in bad faith to the degree that in order to reassure himself, he pretends to judge, to the extent that he demands that freedom as freedom constitute itself as a thing. We have here only one episode in that battle to the death of consciousnesses which Hegel calls "the relation of the master and the slave." A person appeals to another and demands that in the name of his nature as consciousness he should radically destroy himself as consciousness, but while making this appeal he leads the other to hope for a rebirth beyond this destruction. . . .

Bad faith is possible only because sincerity is conscious of missing its goal inevitably, due to its very nature. I can try to apprehend myself as *"not being cowardly,"* when I *am* so, only on condition that the "being cowardly" is itself "in question" at the very moment when it exists, on condition that it is itself *one* question, that at the very moment when I wish to apprehend it, it escapes me on all sides and annihilates itself. The condition under which I can attempt an effort in bad faith is that in one sense, I *am not* this coward which I do not wish to be. But if I *were not* cowardly in the simple mode of not-being-what-one-is-not, I would be "in good faith" by declaring that I am not cowardly. Thus this inapprehensible coward is evanescent; in order for me not to be cowardly, I must in some way also be cowardly. That does not mean that I must be "a little" cowardly, in the sense that "a little" signifies "to a certain degree cowardly—and not cowardly to a certain degree." No. I must at once both be and not be totally and in all respects a coward. Thus in this case bad faith requires that I should not be what I am; that is, that there be an imponderable difference separating being from non-being in the mode of being of human reality.

But bad faith is not restricted to denying the qualities which I possess, to not seeing the being which I am. It attempts also to constitute myself as being what I am not. It apprehends me positively as courageous when I am not so. And that is possible, once again, only if I am what I am not. . . .

Although the considerations which are about to follow are of interest primarily to the ethicist, it may nevertheless be worthwhile after these descriptions and arguments to return to the freedom of the for-itself and try to understand what the fact of this freedom represents for human destiny.

The essential consequence of our earlier remarks is that man being condemned to be free carries the weight of the whole world on his shoulders; he is responsible for the world and for himself as a way of being. We are taking the word "responsibility" in its ordinary sense as "consciousness (of) being the incontestable author of an event or of an object." In this sense the responsibility of the for-itself is overwhelming since he is the one by whom it happens that *there is* a world; since he is also the one who makes himself be, then whatever may be the situation in which he finds himself, the for-itself must wholly assume this situation with its peculiar coefficient of adversity, even though it be insupportable. He must assume the situation with the proud consciousness of being the author of it, for the very worst disadvantages or the worst threats which can endanger my person have meaning only in and through my project; and it is on the ground of the engagement which I am that they appear. It is therefore senseless to think of complaining since nothing foreign has decided what we feel, what we live, or what we are.

Furthermore this absolute responsibility is not resignation; it is simply the logical requirement of the consequences of our freedom. What happens to me happens through me, and I can neither affect myself with it nor revolt against it nor resign myself to it. Moreover everything which happens to me is *mine.* By this we must understand first of all that I am always equal to what happens to me *qua* man, for what happens to a man through other men and through himself can be only human. The most terrible situations of war, the worst tortures do not create a non-human state of things; there is no non-human situation. It is only through fear, flight, and recourse to magical types of conduct that I shall decide on the non-human, but this decision is human, and I shall carry the entire responsibility for it. But in addition the situation is *mine* because it is the image of my free choice of myself, and everything which it presents to me is *mine* in that this represents me and symbolizes me. Is it not I who decide the coefficient of adversity in things and even their unpredictability by deciding myself?

Thus there are no *accidents* in life; a community event which suddenly bursts forth and involves me in it does not come from the outside. If I am mobilized in a war, this war is *my* war; it is in my image and I deserve it. I deserve it first because I could always get out of it by suicide or by desertion; these ultimate possibles are those which must always be present for us when there is a question of envisaging a situation. For lack of getting out of it, I have *chosen* it. This can be due to inertia, to cowardice in the face of public opinion, or because I prefer certain other values to the value of the refusal to join in the war (the good opinion of my relatives, the honor of my family, *etc.*). Any way you look at it, it is a matter of a choice. This choice will be repeated later on again and again without a break until the end of the war. Therefore we must agree with the statement by J. Romains, "In war there are no innocent victims." If therefore I have preferred war to death or to dishonor, everything takes place as if I bore the entire responsibility for this war. Of course others have declared it, and one might be tempted perhaps to consider me as a simple accomplice. But this notion of complicity has only a juridical sense, and it does not hold here. For it depended on me that for me and by me this war should not exist, and I have decided that it does exist. There was no compulsion here, for the compulsion could have got no hold on a freedom. I did not have any excuse; . . . the peculiar character of human-reality is that it is without excuse. Therefore it remains for me only to lay claim to this war.

But in addition the war is *mine* because by the sole fact that arises in a situation which I cause to be and that I can discover it there only be engaging myself for or against it, I can no longer distinguish at present the choice which I make of myself from the choice which I make of the war. To live this war is to choose myself through it and to choose it through my choice of myself. There can be no question of considering it as "four years of vacation" or as a "reprieve," as a "recess," the essential part of my responsibilities being elsewhere in my married, family, or professional life. In this war which I have chosen I choose myself from day to day, and I make it mine by making myself. If it is going to be four empty years, then it is I who bear the responsibility for this.

Finally, . . . each person is an absolute choice of self from the standpoint of a world of knowledges and of techniques which this choice both assumes and illumines; each person is an absolute upsurge at an absolute date and is perfectly unthinkable at another date. It is therefore a waste of time to ask what I should have been if this war had not broken out, for I have chosen myself as one of the possible meanings of the epoch which imperceptibly led to war. I am not distinct from this same epoch; I could not be transported to another epoch without contradiction. Thus I *am* this war which restricts and limits and makes comprehensible the period which preceded it. In this sense we may define more precisely the responsibility of the for-itself if to the earlier quoted statement, "There are no innocent victims," we add the words, "We have the war we deserve." Thus, totally free, undistinguishable from the period for which I have chosen to be the meaning, as profoundly responsible for the war as if I had myself declared it, unable to live without integrating it in *my* situation, engaging myself in it wholly and stamping it with my seal, I must be without remorse or regrets as I am without excuse; for from the instant of my upsurge into being, I carry the weight of the world by myself alone without anything or any person being able to lighten it.

Yet this responsibility is of a very particular type. Someone will say, "I did not ask to be born." This is a naïve way of throwing greater emphasis on our facticity. I am responsible for everything, in fact, except for my very responsibility, for I am not the foundation of my being. Therefore everything takes place as if I were compelled to be responsible. I am *abandoned* in the world, not in the sense that I might remain abandoned and passive in a hostile universe like a board floating on the water, but rather in the sense that I find myself suddenly alone and without help, engaged in a world for which I bear the whole responsibility without being able, whatever I do, to tear myself away from this responsibility for an instant. For I am responsible for my very desire of fleeing responsibilities. To make myself passive in the world, to refuse to act upon things and upon Others is still to choose myself, and suicide is one mode among others of being-in-the-world. Yet I find an absolute responsibility for the fact that my facticity (here the fact of my birth) is directly inapprehensible and even inconceivable, for this fact of my birth never appears as a brute fact but always across a projective reconstruction of my for-itself. I am ashamed of being born or I am astonished at it or I rejoice over it, or in attempting to get rid of my life I affirm that I live and I assume this life as bad. Thus in a certain sense I *choose* being born. This choice itself is integrally affected with facticity since I am not able not to choose, but this facticity in turn will appear only in so far as I surpass it toward my ends. Thus facticity is everywhere but inapprehensible; I never encounter anything except my responsibility. That is why I can not ask, "*Why* was I born?" or curse the day of my birth or declare that I did not ask to be born, for these various attitudes toward my birth—*i.e.,* toward the *fact* that I realize a presence in the world—are absolutely nothing else but ways of assuming this birth in full responsibility and of making it *mine.* Here again I encounter only myself and my projects so that finally my abandonment—*i.e.,* my facticity—consists simply in the fact that I am condemned to be wholly responsible for myself. I am the being which is in such a way that in its being its being is in question. And this "is" of my being *is* as present and inapprehensible.

Under these conditions since every event in the world can be revealed to me only as an *opportunity* (an opportunity made use of, lacked, neglected, *etc.*), or better yet since everything which happens to us can be considered as a *chance* (*i.e.,* can appear to us only as a way of realizing this being which is in question in our being) and since others as transcendences-transcended are themselves only *opportunities* and *chances,* the responsibility of the for-itself extends to the entire world as a peopled-world. It is precisely thus that the for-itself apprehends itself in anguish; that is, as a being which is neither the foundation of its own being nor of the Other's being nor of the in-itselfs which form the world, but a being which is compelled to decide the meaning of being—within it and everywhere outside of it. The one who realizes in anguish his condition as *being* thrown into a responsibility which extends to his very abandonment has no longer either remorse or regret or excuse; he is no longer anything but a freedom which perfectly reveals itself and whose being resides in this very revelation. But as we pointed out . . . , most of the time we flee anguish in bad faith.

DISCUSSION

The central claim of Sartre's existentialist philosophy is that we are free to choose what we are and what we will be. But it is essential that we do not take him to be saying what is clearly nonsense, that a person can do anything he or she chooses to do. A person raised in Detroit cannot choose to have been raised in Marseilles, and a person born to be five-foot-eight cannot choose to be six-foot-ten. We have all wished—after a moment of tragedy—that we could relive the last few hours and act differently; but that is impossible. What we can do, however, is to choose what we are to make out of the circumstances in which we find ourselves. A Jew in France during the Nazi occupation could not change the fact that he or she was a Jew, but could and had to choose whether to hide that fact, or flee the country, or join the underground resistance forces, or sacrifice him- or herself as a possible example of Nazi atrocities. We cannot choose to succeed in what we try to do, but we can always choose to try. That is Sartre's basic point, and it is the one point that he relentlessly refuses to let us forget.

To forget, to pretend that we have no choice in the matter or cannot do anything about it, is bad faith. Bad faith is, first of all, pretending that there is nothing to be done or nothing we can do; at the extreme limits (which were the daily condition during the war) you could always choose to risk or sacrifice your life to make a point. In more modest circumstances, you can always quit a job rather than do what you disapprove of (for example, resigning as contractor because the assignment is to destroy a neighborhood) or drop a class if you disapprove of the way it is taught. Of course there is always a cost; the contractor may have trouble getting another job, and the student may have trouble getting another course (or getting out of this one). But cost does not eliminate choice. The choice remains; it is just a question of what we choose.

Bad faith can also be appealing our decisions to something outside of ourselves. Insisting that we did something because "God willed it" is a way of not taking responsibility for our own actions; so is appealing an action to the law, as in, "it's the law" or "I'm just doing my job." We can always break the law, protesting as we do so that it is a bad law. Appeals to morality may also be instances of bad faith; sometimes we decide to lie (for example, when it is a "white" lie); other times we do not. It is bad faith, therefore, to insist that, when we do not lie, it is because of a moral principle. We support the principle by refusing to lie, but we do not refuse to lie because of the principle. (What would Immanuel Kant and John Stuart Mill say about this?)

It is in this context that we are to understand Sartre's celebrated example about the young man who must choose to join the army or stay with his grieving mother. Appeal to principles will not help him; he must choose. But this dramatic case, in which the two sides are evenly balanced, is no different from our every choice, according to Sartre. We are always in a position in which, in addition to choosing our particular course of action, we are also choosing to exemplify a kind of character and to support a principle of some sort, whether implicit in our actions or explicit in our explanations of our actions. It is with this in mind that Sartre evokes the very Kantian image of our always acting not just for ourselves but for all of humanity. We, in our every action, try to demonstrate what we think humanity ought to be.

There is a problem with bad faith, however, no matter how morally moving that concept. Sartre seemingly portrays bad faith as if anything we do, other than acknowledge our responsibility for choosing—and the facts of the case—is going to be bad faith. But according to Sartre's own arguments, the facts of the case are in part determined by our choices, and our choices—needless to say—are circumscribed by the facts. This makes it look as if there is no escaping bad faith, that we are guilty of manipulating the facts or rationalizing our choices no matter what we do. The example of the homosexual displays this difficulty. Our decisions (our *transcendence*) shape the facts; thus, it is not clear exactly what the facts that we must accept should be. How do we avoid bad faith—as Sartre is clearly urging us? And what is "bad" about bad faith?

This problem raises another, more fundamental to the entire outlook of Sartre's philosophy. In his emphasis on freedom of choice, Sartre neglects one of the main ingredients—if not the main ingredient—in any ethics: what we have called an ethos, a community of shared values and interests. The entire thrust of Sartre's philosophy is precisely to separate ourselves from any such uncritical participation in a community and to stress the picture of each individual in isolation, facing the world and having to make his or her choices—alone. It is a vision of life that is quite common in the late twentieth century, but the question is whether an ethics is possible in light of it. Indeed, Sartre himself had doubts about this, and his later work—especially his massive *Critique of Dialectical Reason* in 1960—is very much an attempt to redefine the nature of community and say how it is possible.

Discussion Questions

1. Why are we a "useless passion"? How can Sartre insist that he is an "optimist"?
2. Why is there no "human nature"? Is Sartre denying that we have instincts and other "natural" inclinations and motives? Give an example in which a clearly "natural" desire is nevertheless a matter of self-conscious choice. Give an example in which a supposed feature of "human nature" is a matter of self-conscious choice.
3. What should Sartre's student have done? Why?
4. "The genius of Proust is the sum of Proust's works." What does this mean?
5. Can we rationally choose to be dishonest, for Sartre? How would he disagree with Kant on this issue?
6. In what way does Sartre's concept of man as a legislator differ from Kant's?

Study Questions

1. What is "existentialism"? Sartre defines his position by insisting that there is no God. How, then, would religious or theistic existentialism be possible? Could "existence (still) precede essence"?
2. Is Sartre a teleologist? A deontologist? Explain.
3. In what sense are we *always* free, according to Sartre? Is this plausible? To what extent is it an (*a priori*) conclusion based on Sartre's division of the world into consciousness (being-for-itself) and the being of things (being-in-itself)? To what extent is it a reasonable observation about people's actual behavior and motivation?
4. What is "bad faith"? Why is it bad?
5. Why should we always act as if we were acting for all of humanity? Is Sartre here repeating the categorical imperative? What are the differences? What are the similarities?
6. What is "abandonment"? What is "despair"?
7. Sartre says that everyone is responsible for the war (written during World War II). He also said that "we were never more free than during the German occupation (of Paris)." How would you make sense of these two extreme and conscientiously perverse statements?
8. What follows from the claim that God does not exist?

10

Bertrand Russell

Bertrand Russell was born in 1872 to an aristocratic and intellectually prominent family (John Stuart Mill was his godfather). He was educated at Cambridge University and taught there for many years, eventually losing his position because of his opposition to World War I (Russell was a bold and outspoken social critic all his life, and he later lost a second academic position at City College, New York. He was also twice imprisoned because of his antiwar and antinuclear protests). While at Cambridge he worked and was close friends with the most prominent philosophers of his time, including G. E. Moore, Alfred North Whitehead, and Ludwig Wittgenstein. Although his most famous contributions to philosophy were in logic and epistemology, his writing ranged over the entire intellectual landscape of his time, including ethics, education, politics, history, religion, and science; in 1950, he was awarded the Nobel Prize for Literature. Widely regarded as one of the greatest minds of the twentieth century, Russell died in 1970, at the age of 97.

Bertrand Russell is sometimes seen as a dry logician whose principal contributions to philosophy were specialized, theoretical works such as *Principles of Mathematics* (1903), *Principia Mathematica* (with Alfred North Whitehead, 1910, 1912, 1913) and such essays as "On Denoting" (1905) and "The Philosophy of Logical Atomism" (1918, 1919). It is certainly true that his contributions to logic, the philosophy of mathematics, and the branch of philosophy often referred to as "analytic philosophy" are among the most important in the twentieth century. But in life Russell was anything but dry and technical; he was first and foremost a social and political radical, and much of his mature intellectual effort was expended on the pressing questions of what constituted the good life for humans in the twentieth century. His many (and often controversial) works on ethical and political questions included his "Ethics (1) and (2)" (1910), *Philosophical Essays* (1910), *Prospects of Industrial Civilization* (1923), *Principles of Social Reconstruction* (1926), *On*

Education (1926), *Why I Am Not a Christian* (1927), *Marriage and Morals* (1929), and *The Conquest of Happiness* (1930).

Although Russell struggled with ethical theory throughout his philosophical career, he never completed—nor even attempted—a complete ethical system like those we see in, for example, the work of Kant and Mill. What is most interesting about Russell as a moral philosopher is the struggle itself: in the selections that follow, we see one of the most capable minds of the 20th century trying first one ethical theory, then another, testing this idea of moral good, discarding that one. The process is marvelous to watch, and is reminiscent of Plato's depiction of one of Socrates's conversations about ethics or virtue. Russell is in effect having a long moral conversation with himself and with his time (and, if we read him, with us as well). It seems fitting that this conversation does not conclude with a definitive answer; indeed, as Russell wrote in his *Problems of Philosophy,* even if philosophy does not necessarily provide us with answers, at least it teaches us to ask better and better questions.

In his early work on ethics, Russell continued the project begun by his friend G. E. Moore. In Moore's *Principia Ethica* (1903) he attempts to show that the object of ethical inquiry, the good, cannot be defined or analyzed, but must be *intuited* when it is present in an act or object. Thus, Moore's theory of ethics is often referred to as *intuitionism.* Russell sees the appeal of Moore's position: if we can intuit those acts and objects that are good, an ethical theory need not, and indeed cannot, further explain why such acts or objects are good. Ethical goodness will not be revealed analytically; rather, it will reveal itself intuitively to the thinker who conscientiously investigates the good in its many and various instances. Ethics, therefore, becomes a matter of observation and induction, rather than a set of universal rational principles.

In our first two selections, Russell advances a similar view, augmenting it, however, with a version of utilitarianism. Russell argues that we can in fact intuit morally good values that are subjectively right for us. He writes, "We are to consider then the suggestion that an act is moral when an agent approves it, and immoral when he disapproves it; using *moral* to mean *subjectively right* and *immoral* to mean *subjectively wrong."* Moral goodness is a matter of the intuitive operation of the mind of some particular human subject, and each individual's conscience will tell that individual—after proper reflection—what is morally right and morally wrong. However, choosing what is morally right is not in itself sufficient, because a person can intuit the good and in good conscience commit an act which is nonetheless misguided. We are all capable of making moral mistakes, despite the fact that we acted in good conscience. Accordingly, we must also determine what is objectively *right,* and here Russell appeals to a utilitarian standard, arguing that what is an objectively right act is "the most fortunate act," the act "that will have the best consequences." The ideal moral situation, then, is when our acts are both good (approved by our intuiting conscience) and right (producing the best consequences). This will be achieved only by "an appropriate amount of candid reflection" (he quite reasonably adds that the more difficult the decision is, the more you should think about it before acting). When after due reflection, we recognize that an act is both good and right, we can say that it has objective (he sometimes says "intrinsic") value. But finding such "objectively valuable acts" or "judgments of intrinsic value" is notoriously difficult, and, anticipating his own later objections to his argument, he concludes: "The making of such judgments [of objective value] we did not undertake; for if the reader agrees, he could make them himself, and if he disagrees without falling into any of the possible confusions, there is no way of altering his opinion."

ETHICS AND OBJECTIVITY*

In judging of conduct we find at the outset two widely divergent methods, of which one is advocated by some moralists, the other by others, while both are practiced by those who have no ethical theory. One of these methods, which is that advocated by Utilitarians, judges the rightness of an act by relation to the goodness or badness of its consequences. The other method, advocated by intuitionists, judges by the approval or disapproval of the moral sense or conscience. I believe that it is necessary to combine both theories in order to get a complete account of right and wrong. There is, I think, one sense in which a man does right when he does what will probably have the best consequences, and another in which he does right when he follows the dictates of his conscience, whatever the probably consequences may be. (There are many other senses which we may give to the word *right,* but these two seem to be the most important.) Let us begin by considering the second of these senses.

The question we have to ask ourselves is: What do we mean by the dictates of the moral sense? If these are to afford a definition of right conduct, we cannot say that they consist in judging that such and such acts are *right,* for that would make our definition circular.

We shall have to say that the moral sense consists in a certain specific emotion of *approval* towards an act, and that an act is to be called right when the agent, at the moment of action, feels this emotion of approval towards the action which he decides to perform. There is certainly a sense in which a man ought to perform any act which he approves, and to abstain from any act which he disapproves; and it seems also undeniable that there are emotions which may be called approval and disapproval. Thus this theory, whether adequate or not, must be allowed to contain a part of the truth.

It is, however, fairly evident that there are other meanings of right conduct, and that, though there is an emotion of approval, there is also a judgment of approval, which may or may not be true. For we certainly hold that a man who has done an action which his conscience approved may have been mistaken, and that in some sense his conscience ought not to have approved his action. But this would be impossible if nothing were involved except an emotion. To be mistaken implies a judgment; and thus we must admit that there is such a thing as a *judgment* of approval. If this were not the case we could not reason with a man as to what is right; what he approves would be necessarily right for him to do, and there could be no argument against his approval. We do in fact hold that when one man approves of a certain act, while another disapproves, one of them

*Bertrand Russell, *Philosophical Essays,* London: Longmans Green, 1910.

is mistaken, which would not be the case with a mere emotion. If one man likes oysters and another dislikes them, we do not say that either of them is mistaken.

Thus there is a judgment of approval, and this must consist of a judgment that an act is, in a new sense, right. The judgment of approval is not merely the judgment that we feel the emotion of approval, for then another who disapproved would not necessarily hold our judgment of approval to be mistaken. Thus in order to give a meaning to the judgment of approval, it is necessary to admit a sense of *right* other than *approved.* In this sense, when we approve an act we judge that it is right, and we may be mistaken in so judging. This new sense is *objective,* in the sense that it does not depend upon the opinions and feelings of the agent. Thus a man who obeys the dictates of his conscience is not always acting rightly in the objective sense. When a man does what his conscience approves, he does what he *believes* to be objectively right, but not necessarily what *is* objectively right. We need, therefore, some other criterion than the moral sense for judging what is objectively right.

It is in defining objective rightness that the consequences of an action become relevant. More moralists, it is true, deny the dependence upon consequences; but that is to be attributed, I think, to confusion with the subjective sense. When people argue as to whether such and such an action is right, they always adduce the consequences which it has or may be expected to have. A statesman who had to decide what is the right policy, or a teacher who has to decide what is the right education, will be expected to consider what policy or what education is likely to have the best results. Whenever a question is at all complicated, and cannot be settled by following some simple rule, such as "thou shalt not steal," or "thou shalt not bear false witness," it is at once evident that the decision cannot be made except by consideration of consequences.

But even when the decision can be made by a simple precept, such as not to lie or not to steal, the justification of the precept is found only by consideration of consequences. A code such as the Decalogue, it must be admitted, can hardly be true *without exception* if the goodness or badness of consequences is what determines the rightness or wrongness of actions; for in so complex a world it is unlikely that obedience to the Decalogue will always produce better consequences than disobedience. Yet it is a suspicious circumstance that breaches of those of the Ten Commandments which people still hold it a duty to obey do, as a matter of fact, have bad consequences in the vast majority of instances, and would not be considered wrong in a case in which it was fairly certain that their consequences would be good. This latter fact is concealed by a question-begging addition of moral overtones to words. Thus, e.g., "thou shalt do no murder," would be an important precept if it were interpreted, as Tolstoy interprets it, to mean "thou shalt not take human life." But it is not so interpreted; on the contrary, some taking of human life is called "justifiable homicide." Thus murder comes to mean "unjustifiable homicide"; and it is a mere tautology to say, "Thou shalt do no unjustifiable homicide." That this should be announced from Sinai would be as fruitless as Hamlet's report of the ghost's message: "There's not a villain, in all Denmark, but he's an arrant knave." As a matter of fact, people do make a certain classification of homicides, and decide that certain kinds are justifiable and certain others unjustifiable. But there are many doubtful cases: tyrannicide, capital punishment, killing in war, killing in self-defense, killing in defense of others, are some of these. And if a decision is sought, it is sought usually by considering whether the consequences of actions belonging to these classes are on the whole good or bad. Thus the importance of precepts such as the Ten Commandments lies in the fact that they give simple rules, obedience to which will in almost all cases have better consequences than disobedience; and the justification of the rules is not wholly independent of consequences.

In common language the received code of moral rules is usually presupposed, and an action is only called *immoral* when it infringes one of these rules. Whatever does not infringe them is regarded as permissible, so that on most of the occasions of life no one course of action is marked out as along *right*. If a man adopts a course of action which, though not contrary to the received code, will probably have bad consequences, he is called unwise rather than immoral. Now, according to the distinction we have made between objective and subjective rightness, a man may well act in a way which is objectively wrong without doing what is subjectively wrong, i.e., what his conscience disapproves. An act (roughly speaking, I shall return to this point presently) is *immoral* when a man's conscience disapproves it, but is judged only unwise or injudicious when his conscience approves it, although we judge that it will probably have bad consequences. Now the usual moral code is supposed, in common language, to be admitted by every man's conscience, so that when he infringes it, his action is not merely injudicious, but immoral; on the other hand, where the code is silent, we regard an unfortunate action as objectively but not subjectively wrong, i.e., as injudicious, but not immoral.

The acceptance of a moral code has the great advantage that, in so far as its rules are objectively right, it tends to harmonize objective and subjective rightness. Thus it tends to cover all frequent cases, leaving only the rarer ones to the individual judgment of the agent. Hence when new sorts of cases become common, the moral code soon comes to deal with them; thus each profession has its own code concerning cases common in the profession, though not outside it. But the moral code is never itself ultimate; it is based upon an estimate of probable consciences, and is essentially a method of leading men's judgment to approve what is objectively right and disapprove what is objectively wrong. And when once a fairly correct code is accepted, the exceptions to it become very much fewer than they would otherwise be, because one of the consequences of admitting exceptions is to weaken the code, and this consequence is usually bad enough to outweigh the good resulting from admitting such and such an exception. This argument, however, works in the opposite direction with a grossly incorrect code; and it is to be observed that most conventional codes embody some degree of unwarrantable selfishness, individual, professional, or national, and are thus in certain respects worthy of detestation.

What is objectively right, then, is in some way dependent on consequences. The most natural supposition to start from would be that the objectively right act, under any circumstances, is the one which will have the best consequences. We will define this as the *most fortunate* act. The most fortunate act, then, is the one which will produce the greatest excess of good over evil, or the least excess of evil over good (for there may be situations in which every possible act will have consequences that are on the whole bad). But we cannot maintain that the most fortunate act is always the one which is objectively right, in the sense that it is what a wise man will hold that he ought to do. For it may happen that the act which will in fact prove the most fortunate is likely, according to all the evidence at our disposal, to be less fortunate than some other. In such a case, it will be, at least in one sense, objectively wrong to go against the evidence, in spite of the actual good result of our doing so. There have certainly been some men who have done so much harm that it would have been fortunate for the world if their nurses had killed them in infancy. But if their nurses had done so the action would not have been objectively right, because the probability was that it would not have the best effects. Hence it would seem we must take account of probability in judging of objective rightness; let us then consider whether we can say that the objectively right act is the one which will *probably* be most fortunate. I shall define this as the *wisest* act. The *wisest* act, then, is that one which, when account is taken of all available data, gives us the greatest expectation of good on the balance, [or the least expectation of evil on the balance]. There is, of course, a difficulty as to what are to be considered available data; but broadly we can distinguish, in any given state of knowledge, things capable of being foreseen from things which are unpredictable.

We must now return to the consideration of subjective rightness, with a view to distinguishing conduct which is merely mistaken from conduct which is immoral or blameworthy. We here require a new sense of *ought,* which it is by no means easy to define. In the objective sense, a man ought to do what is objectively right. But in the subjective sense, which we have now to examine, he sometimes ought to do what is objectively wrong. For example, we saw that it is often objectively right to give less consideration to an unimportant question of conduct than would be required for forming a trustworthy judgment as to what is objectively right. Now it seems plain that if we have given to such a question the amount and kind of consideration which is objectively right, and we then do what *appears* to us objectively right, our action is, in some sense, subjectively right, although it may be objectively wrong. Our action could certainly not be called a sin, and might even be highly virtuous, in spite of its objective wrongness. It is these notions of what is sinful and what is virtuous that we have now to consider.

The first suggestion that naturally occurs is that an act is subjectively right when it is judged by the agent to be objectively right, and subjectively wrong when it is judged to be objectively wrong. I do not mean that it is subjectively right when the agent judges that it is the act which, of all that are possible, will probably have the best results; for the agent may not accept the above account of objective rightness. I mean merely that it is the one towards which he has the judgment of approval. A man may judge an act to be right without judging that its conscience will be probably the best possible; I only contend that, when he *truly* judges it to be right, then its consequences will probably be the best possible. But his judgment as to what is objectively right may err, not only by a wrong estimate of probable consequences, or by failing to think of an act which he might have thought of, but also by a wrong theory as to what constitutes objective rightness. In other words, the definition I gave of objective rightness is not meant as an analysis of the meaning of the word, but as a mark which in fact attaches to all objectively right actions and to no others.

We are to consider then the suggestion that an act is moral when the agent approves it, and immoral when he disapproves it; using *moral* to mean *subjectively right* and *immoral* to mean *subjectively wrong*. This suggestion, it is plain, will not stand without much modification. In the first place, we often hold it immoral to approve some things and disapprove others, unless there are special circumstances to excuse such approval or disapproval. In the second place, unreflecting acts, in which there is no judgment either of approval or disapproval, are often moral or immoral. For both these reasons the suggested definition must be regarded as inadequate.

The doctrine that an act is never immoral when the agent thinks it right has the drawback (or the advantage) that it excuses almost all the acts which would be commonly condemned. Very few people deliberately do what, at the moment, they believe to be wrong; usually they first argue themselves into a belief that what they wish to do is right. They decide that it is their duty to teach so-and-so a lesson, that their rights have been so grossly infringed that if they take no revenge there will be an encouragement to injustice, that without a moderate indulgence in pleasure a character cannot develop in the best way, and so on and so on. Yet we do not cease to blame them on that account. . . .

We may therefore say that an act is moral when it is one which the agent would judge to be right after an appropriate amount of candid thought, or, in the case of acts which are best when they are unreflecting, after the amount and kind of thought requisite to form a first opinion. An act is immoral when the agent would judge it to be wrong after an appropriate amount of reflection. It is neither moral nor immoral when it is unimportant and a small amount of reflection would not suffice to show whether it was right or wrong.

We may now sum up our discussion of right and wrong. When a man asks himself: "what ought I to do?" he is asking what conduct is *right* in an objective sense. He cannot mean: "What ought a person to do who holds my views as to what a person ought to do?" for his views as to what a person ought to do are what will constitute his answer to the question: "What ought I to do?" But the onlooker, who thinks that the man has answered this question wrongly, may nevertheless hold that, in acting upon his answer, the man was acting rightly in a second, subjective, sense. This second sort of right action we call *moral* action. We hold that an action is *moral* when the agent would judge it to be *right* after an appropriate amount of candid thought, or after a small amount in the case of acts which are best when they are unreflecting; the appropriate amount of thought being dependent upon the difficulty and the importance of the decision. And we hold that an action is *right* when, of all that are possible, it is the one which will probably have the best results. There are many other meanings of *right,* but these seem to be the meanings required for answering the questions: "What ought I to do?" and "What acts are immoral?"

We may now sum up our whole discussion of ethics. The most fundamental notions in ethics, we agreed, are the notions of intrinsic good and evil. These are wholly independent of other notions, and the goodness or badness of a thing cannot be inferred from any of its other qualities, such as its existence or nonexistence. Hence what actually occurs has no bearing on what ought to occur, and what ought to occur has no bearing on what does occur. The next pair of notions with which we were concerned were those of objective right and wrong. The objectively right act is the act which a man will hold that he ought to perform when he is not mistaken. This, we decided, is that one, of all the acts that are possible, which will probably produce the best results. Thus in judging what actions are *right* we need to know what results are *good*. When a man is mistaken as to what is objectively right, he may nevertheless act in a way which is subjectively right; thus we need a new pair of notions, which we called *moral* and *immoral*. A moral act is virtuous and deserves praise; an immoral act is sinful and deserves blame. A moral act, we decided, is one which the agent would have judged right after an appropriate amount of candid reflection, where the appropriate amount of reflection depends upon the difficulty and importance of his decision. The making of such judgments we did not undertake; for if the reader agrees, he could make them himself, and if he disagrees without falling into any of the possible confusions, there is no way of altering his opinion.

SUBJECTIVISM*

In our next reading, Russell rejects his (and Moore's) idea that values have any objective existence. He now advocates an ethical theory he calls sometimes *subjectivism,* other times *the subjectivity of values,* which insists that differences in values are merely differences in taste, and nothing more. There are no objective virtues or vices, no acts that are intrinsically good or intrinsically evil. He argues that "good" and "bad" are merely expressions of individual desire: that which I desire, I call "good," that which I do not desire (or actively avoid) I call "bad." You, my neighbor, may very well have different desires, and therefore different "goods" and "bads;" systems of ethics, Russell thinks, are simply my (or some philosopher's) attempt to impose my "goods" and "bads" on you. Sounding very much like Nietzsche (a philosopher Russell read, but did not admire) he writes: "All systems of ethics embody the desires of those who advocate them, but this is concealed in a mist of words." He admits that some will find this theory "immoral," but responds that, in general, people are less selfish and more inclined toward kind and generous acts than many moralists suppose. In a powerful (and distinctly Aristotelian) formulation, he concludes that "It is, in fact, not by ethical theory, but by the cultivation of large and generous desires, through intelligence, happiness, and freedom from fear, that men can be brought to act . . . in a manner that is consistent with the general happiness of mankind."

*Bertrand Russell, *Religion and Science.* New York: Henry Holt, 1935.

It is obvious, to begin with, that the whole idea of good and bad has some connection with *desire. Prima facie,* anything that we all desire is "good," and anything that we all dread is "bad." If we all agreed in our desires, the matter could be left there, but unfortunately our desires conflict. If I say, "What I want is good," my neighbor will say, "No, what *I* want." Ethics is an attempt—though not, I think, a successful one—to escape from this subjectivity. I shall naturally try to show, in my dispute with my neighbor, that my desires have some quality which makes them more worthy of respect than his. If I want to preserve a right of way, I shall appeal to the landless inhabitants of the district; but he, on his side, will appeal to the landowners. I shall say: "What use is the beauty of the countryside if no one sees it?" He will retort: "What beauty will be left if trippers are allowed to spread devastation?" Each tries to enlist allies by showing that his own desires harmonize with those of other people. When this is obviously impossible, as in the case of a burglar, the man is condemned by public opinion, and his ethical status is that of a sinner.

The theory which I have been advocating is a form of the doctrine which is called the "subjectivity" of values. This doctrine consists in maintaining that, if two men differ about values, there is not a disagreement as to any kind of truth, but a difference of taste. If one man says, "Oysters are good," and another says, "*I* think they are bad," we recognize that there is nothing to argue about. The theory in question holds that all differences as to values are of this sort, although we do not naturally think them so when we are dealing with matters that seem to us more exalted than oysters. The chief ground for adopting this view is the complete impossibility of finding any arguments to prove that this or that has intrinsic value. If we all agreed, we might hold that we know values by intuition. We cannot *prove,* to a color-blind man, that grass is green and not red. But there are various ways of proving to him that he lacks a power of discrimination which most men possess, whereas in the case of values there are no such ways, and disagreements are much more frequent than in the case of colors. Since no way can be even imagined for deciding a difference as to values, the conclusion is forced upon us that the difference is one of tastes, not one as to any objective truth.

The consequences of this doctrine are considerable. In the first place, there can be no such thing as "sin" in any absolute sense; what one man calls "sin" another may call "virtue," and though they may dislike each other on account of this difference, neither can convict the other of intellectual error. Punishment cannot be justified on the ground that the criminal is "wicked," but only on the ground that he has behaved in a way which others wish to discourage. Hell, as a place of punishment for sinners, becomes quite irrational.

In the second place, it is impossible to uphold the way of speaking about values which is common among those who believe in Cosmic Purpose. Their argument is that certain things which have been evolved are "good," and therefore the world must have had a purpose which was ethically admirable. In the language of subjective values, this argument becomes: "Some things in the world are to our liking, and therefore they must have been created by a Being with our tastes, Whom, therefore, we also like, and Who, consequently, is good." Now it seems fairly evident that, if creatures having likes and dislikes were to exist at all, they were pretty sure to like *some* things in their environment, since otherwise they would find life intolerable. Our values have been evolved along with the rest of our constitution, and nothing as to any original purpose can be inferred from the fact that they are what they are.

Those who believe in "objective" values often contend that the view which I have been advocating has immoral consequences. This seems to me to be due to faulty reasoning. There are, as has already been said, certain ethical consequences of the doctrine of subjective values, of which the most important is the rejection of vindictive punishment and the notion of "sin." But the more general consequences which are feared, such as the decay of all sense of moral obligation, are not to be logically deduced. Moral obligation, if it is to influence conduct, must consist not merely of a belief, but of a desire. The desire, I may be told, is the desire to be "good" in a sense which I no longer allow. But when we analyze the desire to be "good" it generally resolves itself into a desire to be approved, or, alternatively, to act so as to bring about certain general consequences which we desire. We have wishes which are not purely personal, and, if we had not, no amount of ethical teaching would influence our conduct except through fear of disapproval. The sort of life that most of us admire is one which is guided by large impersonal desires; now such desires can, no doubt, be encouraged by example, education, and knowledge, but they can hardly be created by the mere abstract belief that they are good, nor discouraged by an analysis of what is meant by the word "good."

When we contemplate the human race, we may desire that it should be happy, or healthy, or intelligent, or warlike, and so on. Any one of these desires, if it is strong, will produce its own morality; but if we have no such general desires, our conduct, whatever our ethic may be, will serve social purposes only in so far as self-interest and the interests of society are in harmony. It is the business of wise institutions to create such harmony as far as possible, and for the rest, whatever may be our theoretical definition of value, we must depend upon the existence of impersonal desires. When you meet a man with whom you have a fundamental ethical disagreement—for example, if you think that all men count equally, while he selects a class as alone important—you will find yourself no better able to cope with him if you believe in objective values than if you do not. In either case, you can influence his conduct only through influencing his desires: if you succeed in that, his ethic will change, and if not, not.

Some people feel that if a general desire, say, for the happiness of mankind, has not the sanction of absolute good, it is in some way irrational. This is due to a lingering belief in objective values. A desire cannot, in itself, be either rational or irrational. It may conflict with other desires, and therefore lead to unhappiness; it may rouse opposition in others, and therefore be incapable of gratification. But it cannot be considered "irrational" merely because no reason can be given for feeling it. We may desire A because it is a means to B, but in the end, when we have done with mere means, we must come to something which we desire for no reason, but not on that account "irrationally." All systems of ethics embody the desires of those who advocate them, but this fact is concealed in a mist of words. Our desires are, in fact, more general and less purely selfish than many moralists imagine; if it were not so, no theory of ethics would make moral improvement possible. It is, in fact, not by ethical theory, but by the cultivation of large and generous desires through intelligence, happiness, and freedom from fear, that men can be brought to act more than they do at present in a manner that is consistent with the general happiness of mankind. Whatever our definition of the "Good," and whether we believe it to be subjective or objective, those who do not desire the happiness of mankind will not endeavor to further it, while those who do desire it will do what they can to bring it about.

A CRITIQUE OF SUBJECTIVISM*

In the preceding passage from *Religion and Science* (1935), Russell strongly rejected his previous objectivism in ethics in favor of subjectivism, making ethics a matter of personal taste. By 1954, however, with the horrors of World War II and the dangers of nuclear warfare permanently imprinted in his mind (a year later, in 1955, he and Albert Einstein would release their famous "Russell-Einstein Manifesto" against the use of nuclear weapons), Russell recants his earlier subjectivism. The following selection gives us Russell's final—and, as he later decides, failed—attempt to find an objective foundation for ethical belief.

If we say, "Cruelty is wrong," or "You ought to love your neighbor as yourself," are we saying something which has impersonal truth or falsehood, or are we merely expressing our own preferences? If we say, "Pleasure is good and pain is bad," are we making a statement, or are we merely expressing an emotion which would be more correctly expressed in a different grammatical form, say, "Hurrah for pleasure, and away dull care"? When men dispute or go to war about a political issue, is there any sense in which one side is more in the right than the other, or is there merely a trial of strength? What is meant, if anything, by saying that a world in which human beings are happy is better than one in which they are unhappy? I, for one, find it intolerable to suppose that when I say, "Cruelty is bad" I am merely saying, "I dislike cruelty," or something equally subjective. What I want to discuss is whether there is anything in ethics that is not, in the last analysis, subjective.

To put the same problem in more technical language: When we examine what purport to be ethical statements, we find that they differ from statements asserting matters of fact by the presence of one or both of two terms, "ought" and "good," or their synonyms. Are these terms, or equivalents of them, part of any minimum vocabulary of ethics? Or are they definable in terms of desires and

*Bertrand Russell, *Human Society in Ethics and Politics,* pp. 92–100. Copyright 1954 by George Allen and Unwin. Reprinted by permission of the publisher.

emotions and feelings? And, if so, do they have essential reference to the desires and emotions and feelings of the person using the words, or have they a reference to the general desires and emotions and feelings of mankind? There are words such as "I," "here," "now," which have a different meaning for each different person who uses them, or even on each different occasion when they are used. Such words I call "egocentric." Our question is: Are ethical terms egocentric?

In discussing the above questions I shall repeat in abbreviated form arguments which have occurred elsewhere, but this time we must arrive at decisions, and not, as before, leave many questions open.

One possible theory is that "ought" is indefinable, and that we know by ethical intuition one or more propositions about the kinds of acts that we ought, or ought not, to perform. There is no *logical* objection to this theory, and I am not prepared to reject it decisively. It has, however, a grave drawback, namely, that there is no general agreement as to what sorts of acts ought to be performed, and that the theory affords no means of deciding who is in the right where there is disagreement. It thus becomes, in practice though not in theory, an egocentric doctrine. If A says, "You ought to do this" and B says, "No, you ought to do that," you only know that these are their opinions, and you have no means of knowing which, if either, is right. You can only escape from this conclusion by saying dogmatically: "Whenever there is a dispute as to what ought to be done, I am in the right, and those who disagree with me are mistaken." But as those who disagree will make a similar claim, ethical controversy will become merely a clash of rival dogmas. These considerations lead us to abandon "ought" as the fundamental ethical term. Let us see whether we can do any better with the concept "good."

We shall call something "good" if it has value on its own account, independently of its effects. Perhaps, since the term "good" is ambiguous, we shall do well to substitute the term "intrinsic value." Thus the theory that we are now to examine is the theory that there is an indefinable which we are calling "intrinsic value," and that we know, by a different kind of ethical intuition from that considered in connection with "ought," that certain kinds of things possess intrinsic value. The term has a negative, to which we will give the name "disvalue." A possible ethical intuition of the sort appropriate to our present theory would be: "Pleasure has intrinsic value and pain has intrinsic disvalue." We shall now define "ought" in terms of intrinsic value: An act "ought" to be performed if, of those that are possible, it is the one having the most intrinsic value. To this definition we must add the principle: "The act having most intrinsic value is the one likely to produce the greatest balance of intrinsic value over intrinsic disvalue, or the smallest balance of intrinsic disvalue over intrinsic value." An intrinsic value and an intrinsic disvalue are defined as equal when the two together have zero intrinsic value.

This theory, like its predecessor, is not logically refutable. It has the advantage, over the theory which makes "ought" fundamental, that there are many fewer disagreements as to what has intrinsic value than as to what ought to be done. And when we examine disagreements as to what ought to be done, we find, usually, though perhaps not always, that they are derived from disagreements as to the effects of actions. A savage may believe that infringing a taboo causes death; some sabbatarians believe that working on Sunday leads to defeat in war. Such considerations suggest that moral rules are really based on an estimate of consequences even when they seem to be absolute. And if we judge the morality of an act by its consequences, we seem driven to adopt some such definition of "ought" as that suggested at the end of the last paragraph. Our present theory is, therefore, a definite improvement upon the theory which makes "ought" indefinable.

There are, however, still objections, some analogous to the former ones, and some of a new kind. Although there is more agreement as to intrinsic value than as to rules of conduct, there are still some disagreements that are serious. One of these is as to vindictive punishment. Is there intrinsic value in inflicting pain upon those whose acts have intrinsic disvalue? Believers in hell must answer in the affirmative, and so must all those who believe that the purpose of the criminal law should not be merely deterrent and reformatory. Some stern moralists have maintained that pleasure has no intrinsic value, but I do not think they were quite sincere in this, as they maintained at the same time that the virtuous will be happy in heaven. The question of vindictive punishment is more serious, because, as in the case of disagreement about moral rules, there is no way in which the matter can be argued: if you think it good and I think it bad, neither of us can advance any reasons whatever in support of our belief.

There is a consideration of quite another kind, which, while not conclusive, tends to throw doubt on the view that intrinsic value is indefinable. When we examine the things to which we are inclined to attach intrinsic value, we find that they are all things that are desired or enjoyed. It is difficult to believe that anything would have value in a universe devoid of sentience. This suggests that "intrinsic value" may be definable in terms of desire or pleasure or both.

If we say, "Pleasure is good and pain is bad," do we mean anything more than "We like pleasure and dislike pain"? It seems as if we must mean something more than this, but this is certainly a part of what we mean. We cannot attribute intrinsic value to everything that is desired, because desires conflict, for instance in a war, where each side desires its own victory. We could perhaps evade this difficulty by saying that only states of mind have intrinsic value. In that case, if A and B compete for something which only one of them can have, we shall say that there is intrinsic value in the pleasure of the victor, whichever he may be. There is now nothing which one of the two judges to have intrinsic value, while the other judges that the same thing has intrinsic disvalue. A may admit that the pleasure which B would derive from victory would have intrinsic value, but may argue that B's victory is nevertheless to be prevented if possible, on account of its effects. Thus we shall now consider the definition: "Intrinsic value" means "the property of being a state of mind desired by the person who experiences it." This differs very little from the view that the good is pleasure. We come even nearer to the good as pleasure if we substitute "enjoyed" for "desired" in the above definition.

I do not think the statement "The good is pleasure" is quite correct, but I think that most of the difficulties of ethics are the same when this statement is adopted as when we adopt one which seems to me more exact. I shall, therefore, for the sake of simplicity, adopt hypothetically, for the moment, the hedonistic definition of the good. It remains to examine how this definition can be connected with our ethical feelings and convictions. . . .

What, on this theory, shall we say about praise and blame? Blame, when it is deliberate, is both an emotion and a judgment: I feel a dislike of the act that I blame, and I judge that I do right in feeling this dislike. The emotion is just a fact, and raises no theoretical issue, but the judgment is a more difficult matter. I certainly do not *mean,* when I judge an act to be right, that it is the act best calculated to maximize pleasure, for, if I did, it would be logically impossible to dispute hedonism, which it is not. Perhaps the judgment is not really a judgment, but another emotion, namely, an emotion of approval toward my likes or dislikes. According to this view, when I deliberately, and not impulsively, blame an act, I dislike the act, and feel toward my dislike an emotion of approval.

Another person, who disagrees with me about ethics, may disapprove of my approval; he will express his feeling in which *seems* to be a judgment, saying, "You ought not to have blamed that act," or something equivalent. But on our present theory he is still expressing an emotion; neither he nor I is making any assertion, and therefore our conflict is only practical, not theoretical.

If we define "right," the matter is different. We can then have a *judgment,* "This is right." If our definition is not to have paradoxical results, our definition of "right" must be such that usually, when an act is right according to our definition, it is one toward which we feel the emotion of approval, and when it is wrong, it is one toward which we feel disapproval. We are thus led to seek for some common property of as many as possible of the acts commonly approved (or disapproved). If *all* had such a common property, we should have no hesitation in defining this as "right." But we do not find anything quite so convenient as this. What we do find is that most of the acts toward which people feel the emotion of approval have a certain common property, and that the exceptional acts, which have not this property, tend to be no longer approved of when people have become clearly aware of their exceptional character. We may then say, in a sense, that approval of such acts is mistaken.

We can now set up a series of fundamental propositions and definitions in Ethics.

(1) Surveying the acts which arouse emotions of approval or disapproval, we find that, as a general rule, the acts which are approved of are those believed likely to have, on the balance, effects of certain kinds, while opposite effects are expected from acts that are disapproved of.

(2) Effects that lead to approval are defined as "good," and those leading to disapproval as "bad."

(3) An act of which, on the available evidence, the effects are likely to be better than those of any other act that is possible in the circumstances, is defined as "right"; any other act is "wrong." What we "ought" to do is, by definition, the act which is right.

(4) It is right to feel approval of a right act and disapproval of a wrong act.

These definitions and propositions, if accepted, provide a coherent body of ethical propositions, which are true (or false) in the same sense as if they were propositions of science. . . .

Although, on the above theory, ethics contains statements which are true or false, and not merely optative or imperative, its basis is still one of emotion and feeling, the emotion of approval and the feeling of enjoyment or satisfaction, the former being involved in the definition of "right" and "wrong," the latter in that of "intrinsic value." And the appeal upon which we depend for the acceptance of our ethical theory is not the appeal to the facts of perception, but to the emotions and feelings which have given rise to the concepts of "right" and "wrong," "good" and "bad."

FREEDOM AND HAPPINESS*

In the least formal of the selections presented here, Russell offers us a meditation on society, humans within their societies, freedom, and (now, distinctly spiritual) happiness.

When you are talking of the external conditions of happiness—I am going to talk mostly of the conditions in your own mind, about the internal conditions— a person must have, of course, enough to eat and the necessaries of life and what is needed for the care of children. When you have those things you have as much as really contributes to happiness. Beyond that you only multiply cares and anxiety. So that I don't think enormous wealth is the solution. I should say, for the external conditions of happiness, that in this country, as far as the material problem of the production of goods is concerned, you have quite solved it. If the goods that are produced were distributed with any justice, that certainly would be a real contribution towards happiness. Your problem here is two-fold. It is first a political problem: to secure the advantages of your unrivalled production for a wider circle. On the other hand, it is the psychological problem of learning how to get the good out of these material conditions that have been created by our industrial age. That, I think, is where we modern people have failed most—on the psychological side, on the side of being able to enjoy the opportunities which we have created. I think that this is due to a number of causes.

I should attribute it partly to the effect of Puritanism in decay. Puritanism in its heyday was a conception of life which filled people's minds and made them in their way happy. Anything which fills people's minds makes them happy. But people nowadays don't believe in the Puritan way; they retain certain principles which are connected with Puritanism, though not perhaps quite obviously. They

*Bertrand Russell, *Human Society in Ethics and Politics*. Copyright 1954 by George Allen and Unwin. Reprinted by permission of the publisher.

have, in the first place, a certain kind of moral outlook, that is, a tendency to be looking out for opportunities to find fault with others, a tendency to think that it is very important to keep up certain rules of conduct. There are a number of old, inherited taboos and rules which people don't think about but simply go on with because they always have been there. These do not touch the core of the matter. The thing that has survived most out of Puritanism is a contempt for happiness—not a contempt for pleasure, *a contempt for happiness!* You find among rebels a very great desire for pleasure but a very small realization of happiness as against pleasure, and that has gone through our whole conception of pleasure and of happiness.

Another thing that we owe to it is the belief in work. In America I have spent most of my time in preaching idleness. I made up my mind when I was young that I would not be restrained from preaching a doctrine merely because I have not practiced it. I have not been able to practice the doctrine of idleness, because the preaching of it takes up so much time. I don't mean idleness in the literal sense, for most people, the great majority of us white people, don't enjoy sitting in the sun and doing nothing; we like to be busy. What I mean by idleness is simply work or activity which is not part of your regular professional job. Under the influence of this dogma, Puritanism has forced us to retain in our operative beliefs the notion that the important part of our life is work. That, at any rate, applies to the major portion of mankind: that the important part of what we do is getting on in our business, and getting a fortune which we can leave to our descendants, and they, in turn, get a larger fortune to leave to theirs. This whole business has taken the place of living for Heaven, for in the old Puritan days we tried to forgo pleasures in life in order to get to Heaven.

Heaven has disappeared, but the idea of living in order to leave a large fortune has not disappeared, and the kind of a life which is required for the one purpose is much the same that is required for the other—the foregoing of enjoyment for the sake of future benefits. That we have retained from the old Puritan outlook, and that, I think, is not in its modern form a very fine or noble thing. In the old days there was something splendid about it, but in this modern form it is not anything that we should particularly admire, and for the sake of it we do forego everything that would make life civilized, free and happy. . . .

I think that if we are going to have a true morality, if we are going to have an outlook upon life which is going to make life richer and freer and happier, it must not be a repressive outlook, it must not be an outlook based upon any kind of restrictions or prohibitions; it must be an outlook based upon the things that we love rather than those that we hate. There are a number of emotions which guide our lives, and roughly you can divide them into those that are repressive and those that are expansive. Repressive emotions are cruelty, fear, jealousy; expansive emotions are such as hope, love of art, impulse of constructiveness, love, affection, intellectual curiosity, and kindliness; and they make more of life instead of less. I think that the essence of true morality consists in living by the expansive impulses and not by the repressive ones.

What I am saying has, I am afraid, very revolutionary consequences to which I cannot hope to win the assent of everyone. There will be many who think that my deductions are not deductions to be accepted. For example, love and jealousy are—the one expansive and the other repressive. Now, in our traditional morality, when you subject it to psychological analysis and see whence it has sprung, you will all have to admit that jealousy has been the main-spring; it has been jealousy that has given rise to it. I don't myself feel that it is very probable that a code rising in that way and from that source can be the best possible. It seems to me far more likely that one arising out of the positive emotions would be better than one arising out of the negative, and that such restrictions as would have to be placed on freedom should arise out of affection or kindliness for other persons, and not out of the sheer repressive emotion of jealousy. If you apply *that* principle it leads to a better development of character and more wholesome type of person, a person freed from many of the cruelties which limit the conventional moralist.

There is a very strong element of cruelty in traditional morals—part of the satisfaction which every moralist derives from his morality is that it gives him the justification for inflicting pain. We all know that the infliction of punishment is to a great many people delightful. There was once a prime minister who traveled from Constantinople to Antioch, and spent there eight hours watching his enemy being tortured. I think that the impulse toward pleasure in the suffering of others is one which arises through people thwarting their natural emotions, through the fact that they have not been able to find a free outlet for their creative impulses.

I do not positively *know* whether that is really the basis of a great deal of cruelty, but I cannot help thinking that an enormous mass of the cruelty that we see in the world is from unconscious envy. That is a very deep-seated feeling in human nature, and when you have a nice, convenient code to embody it, of course it is very popular.

I don't know whether I can quite convey to you the kind of way in which it seems to me that one can live most happily. I find things in the Gospels which illustrate the sort of thing I mean—not texts which are very often quoted, but, for example, "Take no thought what ye shall eat, or what ye shall drink, or wherewithal ye shall be clothed." If you really lived upon that principle— which, by the way, forbids all discussion of the Volstead Act—you would find life very delightful. There is a certain kind of liberation, a certain kind of care-free attitude, which, if you can once acquire it, makes you able to go through the world untroubled, not distressed by all the minor annoyances that arise. The gist of the matter is to be rid of fear. Fear lies very deep in the heart of man, fear has been the source of most religions; fear has been the source of most moral codes; fear is our instincts; fear is encouraged in our youth, and fear is at the bottom of all that is bad in the world. When once you are rid of fear you have the freedom of the universe. Of course, you all know about the sort of dark superstitions of more barbarous ages, when men, women and children were sacrificed to the gods out of fear. This superstition we see to be dark and absurd, but our own superstitions do not strike us in the same light. Now, I am not prepared to say that no great disaster can ever overtake us, but I say this, that the fear of those things that might overtake us is a greater evil than the things themselves, and it would be far better to go through life not fearing, and come to some disaster, than go through life creeping, wise, and cautious, and burdened—never having enjoyed life at any moment and yet dying peacefully in your bed.

I think we want our lives to be expansive and creative, we want to live to a very great extent upon impulse; and when I say impulse I don't mean every transitory impulse of every passing moment—I mean those major impulses that really govern our lives. There are in some people great artistic impulses, in others scientific, and in others this or that form of affection or creativeness. And if you deny those impulses, provided that they do not infringe upon the liberty of another, you stunt your growth, I know, for instance, any number of men who are Socialists, and who spend their lives as journalists writing for the most conservative papers. These men may get pleasure out of life, but I don't believe that it is possible for them to get happiness. Happiness is at an end for any man who denies himself one of those fundamental impulses about which life ought to grow.

I should say precisely the same thing about the private affections. Where a really strong or powerful affection exists, the man or woman who goes against it suffers the same kind of damage—it is the same kind of inner destruction of something precious and valuable; all the poets have said so. We have accepted it when it was said in verse, because nobody takes verse seriously, but if it is said in prose and in public we think it is very dreadful.

I don't know why everybody is allowed to say a host of things in private that he is not allowed to say in public. I think it is about time we said the same things in public that we say in private. Walt Whitman, in praise of the animals, says: "They don't grunt and sweat over their condition—not one of them is respectable or unhappy throughout the whole world." I must say I have a very great affection for Walt Whitman. He illustrates what I mean—how the man who lives expansively lives in a kindly way; how he is free from cruelty, from the desire to stop other people from doing what they want.

I think it is very important to get that idea into one's head—that every artificial morality means the growth of cruelty. Of course, we cannot live like Walt Whitman's animals, because man has foresight and memory, and, having foresight, he has to organize his life into a unit. That is where we develop our superstitions. And you know quite well that it would not do if you followed each whim without a certain amount of discipline, and I don't want you to think that there is not a need of discipline. There is, but it should be that discipline that comes from within, from the realization of one's own needs, from the feeling of something which one wishes to achieve. Nothing of importance is ever achieved without discipline. I feel myself sometimes not wholly in sympathy with some modern educational theorists, because I think that they underestimate the part that discipline plays. But the discipline you have in your life should be one determined by your own desires and your own needs, not put upon you by society or authority. . . .

In our private relations we all get so busy that we have not time to develop affections for others as they deserve to be developed; we have not time for sympathy, the understanding for all those things that make the beauty of human relations, because we all are so busy, and when we are not busy we are tired. You have in this country, on the average, if the goods produced in this country were divided equally, much more than anybody needs for happiness, and it would be possible to live on a very much smaller amount of work and yet have enough; you could then develop and cultivate those things that make for happiness. You would have freedom. A man does not have freedom if he has to indulge all day in an activity which is not one he likes: that is as bad as a treadmill. We cannot always be doing delightful things, but we can for the greater part of the day; and I think that in the advanced industrial nations a better ideal of private happiness is probably the thing that is most wanted. More important even than political and economic reconstructions is the realization of the things that really make for human happiness.

We should not be so ready to go to war if our lives were happier. It is to my mind quite an amazing thing to see the extraordinary feebleness in the modern world of what you might call the will to live. There is a will to work, but not a will to live; you don't find that the prospect of wholesale destruction is considered intolerable. You don't find that people are willing to sacrifice money and power in order that they may be rid of the menace of war; they don't really want to be rid of it. A happy nation would not be willing to sacrifice life, health and happiness for the idle business of fighting, and possibly winning. This comes because our lives are too collective and too little individual. We, living as we do, forced by the mechanical mold of our civilization more and more to resemble each other, we, I say, more and more live by mass emotions and less and less by the individual, personal ones. In that way the individual gets sacrificed. A life where the individual is sacrificed is not one where the individual is going to have a strong love for life. . . .

I have been talking rather lightly to you, but the thing that I mean is something immensely living and a real kind of liberation—being free in this world, free of the universe, so that the things that happen to you no longer worry you, the things that occur no longer seem to matter. There is a kind of fire that can live in the soul of every man and woman, and when you have that you don't care any longer about the little things of which our lives are so full. You can live in that way—you can live freely and expansively. You will find that when you let those fears drop off you are closer to others, you can enjoy friendship in a different degree. The whole world is more interesting, more living—there is something there that is infinitely more valuable. Whoever has once tasted it knows that it is infinitely better than those things gotten by other methods. It is an old secret—it has been taught by all teachers and been forgotten by their priests; it is that secret of being in close contact with the world, of not having the walls of self so rigid that you cannot see what is beyond. The moralist is concerned to think "How virtuous I am," and he also is an egoist like the rest. It is not in that world of hard immorals that you will find the life that is happy and free. It is in the kind of life where you have lost fear because a little hurt is worth enduring—it comes from the knowledge of the fact that there is something better than the avoidance of hurt—there is the securing of a kind of intense union with the world, a kind of intense love, something glowing, warm, like a personal affection and yet universal. If you can achieve that you will know the secret of a happy life.

1. Can we "intuit" the good? Does it make sense, as Jiminy Cricket put it, to "always let your conscience be your guide"?
2. What if anything is the difference between aesthetic judgments and moral judgments? Is it in fact the case that the difference between our society and the society of Nazi Germany is as much a matter of taste as the difference between, say, pepperoni pizza with anchovies or without? If not, why not?
3. What ethical principles might Russell appeal to in support of his pacifism and his opposition to nuclear warfare?
4. Imagine a conversation between Kant, Nietzsche, and Russell of his "Freedom and Happiness" period. How do you think the conversation would run? Would anyone change his mind?
5. What does Russell mean when he says that "an enormous mass of the cruelty we see in the world is from unconscious envy"? Do you agree?
6. Which position would you rather be in: that of Kant, who believes he knows what moral good is, or that of Russell, who is never quite sure? Are there good reasons to applaud a little moral uncertainty? Would Socrates have something to say?

Study Questions

1. Why does Russell distinguish between "morally good" and "objectively right"? Explain how Russell supplements intuitionism with utilitarianism, and why.
2. What are the four ethical "fundamental propositions and definitions" Russell proposes in his response to (his own) subjectivism? Explain them in nontechnical language.
3. What is subjectivism in ethics? How might it be defended? Attacked?
4. Why does Russell think that freedom is so important to happiness?
5. How might the Russell of his last period have critiqued Utilitarianism?
6. Why does Russell reject his early intuitionist view?

11

John Rawls

John Rawls was born in 1921 and was a professor emeritus at Harvard University, where he taught for many years. He is the author of numerous articles and books, including his most recent book, *Political Liberalism,* in which he answers many of the critics of the work excerpted here, *A Theory of Justice.* His work has inspired an almost unprecedented amount of discussion and commentary by many of the best thinkers in the field of political philosophy. The publication of *A Theory of Justice* was followed shortly by Robert Nozick's (1939–2002) *Anarchy, State, and Utopia,* which did for libertarianism what Rawls's work accomplished for liberalism. Together these two Harvard philosophers began a debate that continues more than 25 years later.

John Rawls's *A Theory of Justice* was published in 1971 and is often credited with revitalizing the field of political philosophy. Although it is usually considered in light of its contribution to political theory (in particular its defense of liberalism), it contains a substantial account of ethics as well. In fact, Rawls suggests that moral development, and hence moral theory, can be studied only in light of some "particular theory of justice." That is, to talk about our moral obligations and rights is to necessarily invoke some account of what the ideal, or ideally just, society looks like. Ethics and politics, then, are intimately connected, a point made by Aristotle some 2,000 years earlier.

The first two-thirds of *A Theory of Justice* is concerned with laying out Rawls's account of the just society. In so doing, Rawls makes use of an impressive array of historical contributions to political and ethical thought. Aristotle, Kant, other social contract theorists (such as Locke and Rousseau), Mill, and a host of other thinkers influence the complex account of the just society that Rawls painstakingly builds for us. His basic idea is that of "justice as fairness." The primary role for this understanding of justice in political theory concerns the allocation of rights and duties such that the benefits made possible by the cooperative efforts of individuals in society are fairly distributed.

Rawls's starting point is the question of which basic principles would lead to the best (most fair or just) distribution. To answer this, he looks for "the principles that free and rational persons concerned to further their own interests would accept in an initial position of equality as defining the fundamental terms of their association." This single sentence contains much of Rawls's entire theory and merits careful unpacking.

First, there are the features that characterize the social contract approach (as illustrated by Hobbes in this volume). The basic idea is to arrive at the ideal form of social union, or civil society, by asking what rules we would agree to commit ourselves to, independent of any artificial constraints (such as preexisting laws, relationships, duties, etc.). Posing the question in this way emphasizes three features of human beings that Rawls will make much of: equality, rationality, and freedom. According to both traditional and Rawlsian social contract theory, people come to the bargaining table (to decide which rules to adopt) as inherently free and equal beings who are capable of deliberating on how to best further their own self-interests.

A second aspect of Rawls's quoted statement is that it also spells out (not accidentally) the main strands of contemporary liberal theory. As Jeremy Waldron writes in a recent collection of essays on liberalism: "Liberals are committed to a conception of freedom and of respect for the capacities and the agency of individual men and women, and . . . these commitments generate a requirement that all aspects of the social world should either be made acceptable or be capable of being made acceptable to every last individual." Although there are many camps within liberal ideology, all liberals hold at minimum that persons are inherently equal, capable of formulating and acting upon their own life plans, and deserving of the opportunity to do so. As we shall see, Rawls takes great care to ensure that these capacities are realizable in the just society.

Third, there is a strong Kantian element to Rawls's approach. This is evidenced in the first place by the way in which Rawls pictures the original agreement, or contract, taking place. Instead of making the unlikely claim that the social contract was a specific, historical event, Rawls describes it as a *hypothetical* contract (thus, he asks what principles people *would* choose if they were in such a position). What we are to imagine, then, is that we are in the ahistorical position of beginning entirely anew, of building society from scratch. To ensure fairness Rawls adds a proviso to this "original position," and that is what he calls "the veil of ignorance." He describes it as follows:

> Among the essential features of this situation is that no one knows his place in society, his class position or social status, nor does any one know his fortune in the distribution of natural assets and abilities, his intelligence, strength, and the like. I shall even assume that the parties do not know their conceptions of the good or their special psychological propensities. The principles of justice are chosen behind a veil of ignorance.

Thus, like Kant, Rawls is claiming that in order to choose rightly we must ignore that part of us that is known empirically and that is, in many cases, purely accidental. For instance, if you were born into a secure, wealthy family with a broad range of opportunities available, you will probably have a very different outlook on the world and the proper function of government than if you were born to a homeless, single woman. Just as Kant asserted that our particular circumstances and inclinations (good or bad) have no place in moral reasoning, so Rawls is claiming that our luck in the lottery of natural skills and social position is irrelevant morally and politically. This is not to say that Rawls denies the impact of social differences; his theory addresses them directly. Rather, the point of the veil of ignorance is to ensure that such social differences are not operative at the time of choosing the basic principles.

A THEORY OF JUSTICE*

JUSTICE AS FAIRNESS

Rawls introduces his project by asserting that justice is the most essential quality for any society to have. No matter how efficient, affluent, or otherwise successful a society may be, if it lacks justice, it is no good. A corollary to this claim is the demand that all persons be treated with equal respect based on their intrinsic worth (again we see Kant's influence). It is the choice of principles in the original position, with its veil of ignorance, that guarantees that both these conditions are met.

1. The Role of Justice

Justice is the first virtue of social institutions, as truth is of systems of thought. A theory however elegant and economical must be rejected or revised if it is untrue; likewise laws and institutions no matter how efficient and well-arranged must be reformed or abolished if they are unjust. Each person possesses an inviolability founded on justice that even the welfare of society as a whole cannot override. For this reason justice denies that the loss of freedom for some is made right by a greater good shared by others. It does not allow that the sacrifices imposed on a few are outweighed by the larger sum of advantages enjoyed by many. Therefore in a just society the liberties of equal citizenship are taken as settled; the rights secured by justice are not subject to political bargaining or to the calculus of social interests. The only thing that permits us to acquiesce in an erroneous theory is the lack of a better one; analogously, an injustice is tolerable only when it is necessary to avoid an even greater injustice. Being first virtues of human activities, truth and justice are uncompromising. . . .

Now let us say that a society is well-ordered when it is not only designed to advance the good of its members but when it is also effectively regulated by a public conception of justice. That is, it is a society in which (1) everyone accepts and knows that the others accept the same principles of justice, and (2) the basic social institutions generally satisfy and are generally known to satisfy these principles. In this case while men may put forth excessive demands on one another, they nevertheless acknowledge a common point of view from which their claims may be adjudicated. If men's inclination to self-interest makes their vigilance against one another necessary, their public sense of justice makes their secure association together possible. Among individuals with disparate aims and purposes a shared conception of justice establishes the bonds of civic friendship; the general desire for justice limits the pursuit of other ends. One may think of a public conception of justice as constituting the fundamental charter of a well-ordered human association. . . .

2. The Subject of Justice

Many different kinds of things are said to be just and unjust: not only laws, institutions, and social systems, but also particular actions of many kinds, including decisions, judgments, and imputations. We also call the attitudes and dispositions of persons, and persons themselves, just and unjust. Our topic, however, is that of social justice. For us the primary subject of justice is the basic structure of society, or more exactly, the way in which the major social institutions distribute fundamental rights and duties and determine the division of advantages from social cooperation. By major institutions I understand the political constitution and the principal economic and social arrangements. Thus the legal protection of freedom of thought and liberty of conscience, competitive markets, private property in the means of production, and the monogamous family are examples of major social institutions. Taken together as one scheme, the major institutions define men's rights and duties and influence their life-prospects, what they can expect to be and how well they can hope to do. The basic structure is the primary subject of justice because its effects are so profound and present from the start. The intuitive notion here is that this structure contains various social positions and that men born into different positions have different expectations of life determined, in part, by the political system as well as by economic and social circumstances. In this way the institutions of society favor certain starting places over others. These are especially deep inequalities. Not only are they pervasive, but they affect men's initial chances in life; yet they cannot possibly be justified by an appeal to the notions of merit or desert. It is these inequalities, presumably inevitable in the basic structure of any society, to which the principles of social justice must in the first instance apply. These principles, then, regulate the choice of a political constitution and the main elements of the economic and social system. The justice of a social scheme depends essentially on how fundamental rights and duties are assigned and on the economic opportunities and social conditions in the various sectors of society. . . .

A conception of social justice, then, is to be regarded as providing in the first instance a standard whereby the distributive aspects of the basic structure of society are to be assessed. This standard, however, is not to be confused with the principles defining the other virtues, for the basic structure, and social arrangements generally, may be efficient or inefficient, liberal or illiberal, and many other things, as well as just or unjust. A complete conception defining principles for all the virtues of the basic structure, together with their respective weights when they conflict, is more than a conception of justice; it is a social ideal. The principles of justice are but a part, although perhaps the most important part, of such a conception. A social ideal in turn is connected with a conception of society, a vision of the way in which the aims and purposes of social cooperation are to be understood. . . .

In these preliminary remarks I have distinguished the concept of justice as meaning a proper balance between competing claims from a conception of justice as a set of related principles for identifying the relevant considerations which determine this balance. I have also characterized justice as but one part of a social ideal, although the theory I shall propose no doubt extends its everyday sense. This theory is not offered as a description of ordinary meanings but as an account of certain distributive principles for the basic structure of society. I assume that any reasonably complete ethical theory must include principles for this fundamental problem and that these principles, whatever they are, constitute its doctrine of justice. The concept of justice I take to be defined, then, by the role of its principles in assigning rights and duties and in defining the appropriate division of social advantages. A conception of justice is an interpretation of this role.

Now this approach may not seem to tally with tradition. I believe, though, that it does. The more specific sense that Aristotle gives to justice, and from which the most familiar formulations derive, is that of refraining from *pleonexia*, that is, from gaining some advantage for oneself by seizing what belongs to another, his property, his reward, his office, and the like, or by denying a person that which is due to him, the fulfillment of a promise, the repayment of a debt, the showing of proper respect, and so on. It is evident that this definition is framed to apply to actions, and persons are thought to be just insofar as they have, as one of the permanent elements of their character, a steady and effective desire to act justly. Aristotle's definition clearly presupposes, however, an account of what properly belongs to a person and of what is due to him. Now such entitlements are, I believe, very often derived from social institutions and the legitimate expectations to which they give rise. There is no reason to think that Aristotle would disagree with this, and certainly he has a conception of social justice to account for these claims. The definition I adopt is designed to apply directly to the most important case, the justice of the basic structure. There is no conflict with the traditional notion.

3. The Main Idea of the Theory of Justice

My aim is to present a conception of justice which generalizes and carries to a higher level of abstraction the familiar theory of the social contract as found, say, in Locke, Rousseau, and Kant. In order to do this we are not to think of the original contract as one to enter a particular society or to set up a particular form of government. Rather, the guiding idea is that the principles of justice for the basic structure of society are the object of the original agreement. They are the principles that free and rational persons concerned to further their own interests would accept in an initial position of equality as defining the fundamental terms of their association. These principles are to regulate all further agreements; they specify the kinds of social cooperation that can be entered into and the forms of government that can be established. This way of regarding the principles of justice I shall call justice as fairness.

Thus we are to imagine that those who engage in social cooperation choose together, in one joint act, the principles which are to assign basic rights and duties and to determine the division of social benefits. Men are to decide in advance how they are to regulate their claims against one another and what is to be the foundation charter of their society. Just as each person must decide by rational reflection what constitutes his good, that is, the system of ends which it is rational for him to pursue, so a group of persons must decide once and for all what is to count among them as just and unjust. The choice which rational men would make in this hypothetical situation of equal liberty, assuming for the present that this choice problem has a solution, determines the principles of justice.

In justice as fairness the original position of equality corresponds to the state of nature in the traditional theory of the social contract. This original position is not, of course, thought of as an actual historical state of affairs, much less as a primitive condition of culture. It is understood as a purely hypothetical situation characterized so as to lead to a certain conception of justice. Among the essential features of this situation is that no one knows his place in society, his class position or social status, nor does any one know his fortune in the distribution of natural assets and abilities, his intelligence, strength, and the like. I shall even assume that the parties do not know their conceptions of the good or their special psychological propensities. The principles of justice are chosen behind a veil of ignorance. This ensures that no one is advantaged or disadvantaged in the choice of principles by the outcome of natural chance or the contingency of social circumstances. Since all are similarly situated and no one is able to design principles to favor his particular condition, the principles of justice are the result of a fair agreement or bargain. For given the circumstances of the original position, the symmetry of everyone's relations to each other, this initial situation is fair between individuals as moral persons, that is, as rational beings with their own ends and capable, I shall assume, of a sense of justice. The original position is, one might say, the appropriate initial status quo, and thus the fundamental agreements reached in it are fair. This explains the propriety of the name "justice as fairness": it conveys the idea that the principles of justice are agreed to in an initial situation that is fair. The name does not mean that the concepts of justice and fairness are the same, any more than the phrase "poetry as metaphor" means that the concepts of poetry and metaphor are the same.

Justice as fairness begins, as I have said, with one of the most general of all choices which persons might make together, namely, with the choice of the first principles of a conception of justice which is to regulate all subsequent criticism and reform of institutions. Then, having chosen a conception of justice, we can suppose that they are to choose a constitution and a legislature to enact laws, and so on, all in accordance with the principles of justice initially agreed upon. Our social situation is just if it is such that by this sequence of hypothetical agreements we would have contracted into the general system of rules which defines it. Moreover, assuming that the original position does determine a set of principles (that is, that a particular conception of justice would be chosen), it will then be true that whenever social institutions satisfy these principles those engaged in them can say to one another that they are cooperating on terms to which they would agree if they were free and equal persons whose relations with respect to one another were fair. They could all view their arrangements as meeting the stipulations which they would acknowledge in an initial situation that embodies widely accepted and reasonable constraints on the choice of principles. The general recognition of this fact would provide the basis for a public acceptance of the corresponding principles of justice. No society can, of course, be a scheme of cooperation which men enter voluntarily in a literal sense; each person finds himself placed at birth in some particular position in some particular society, and the nature of this position materially affects his life prospects. Yet a society satisfying the principles of justice as fairness comes as close as a society can to being a voluntary scheme, for it meets the principles which free and equal persons would assent to under circumstances that are fair. In this sense its members are autonomous and the obligations they recognize self-imposed.

One feature of justice as fairness is to think of the parties in the initial situation as rational and mutually disinterested. This does not mean that the parties are egoists, that is, individuals with only certain kinds of interests, say in wealth, prestige, and domination. But they are conceived as not taking an interest in one another's interests. They are to presume that even their spiritual aims may be opposed, in the way that the aims of those of different religions may be opposed. Moreover, the concept of rationality must be interpreted as far as possible in the narrow sense, standard in economic theory, of taking the most effective means to given ends. I shall modify this concept to some extent, as explained later, but one must try to avoid introducing into it any controversial ethical elements. The initial situation must be characterized by stipulations that are widely accepted.

In working out the conception of justice as fairness one main task clearly is to determine which principles of justice would be chosen in the original position. . . . It may be observed . . . that once the principles of justice are thought of as arising from an original agreement in a situation of equality, it is an open question whether the principle of utility would be acknowledged. Offhand it hardly seems likely that persons who view themselves as equals, entitled to press their claims upon one another, would agree to a principle which may require lesser life prospects for some simply for the sake of a greater sum of advantages enjoyed by others. Since each desires to protect his interests, his capacity to advance his conception of the good, no one has a reason to acquiesce in an enduring loss for himself in order to bring about a greater net balance of satisfaction. In the absence of strong and lasting benevolent impulses, a rational man would not accept a basic structure merely because it maximized the algebraic sum of advantages irrespective of its permanent effects on his own basic rights and interests. Thus it seems that the principle of utility is incompatible with the conception of social cooperation among equals for mutual advantage. It appears to be inconsistent with the idea of reciprocity implicit in the notion of a well-ordered society. Or, at any rate, so I shall argue.

I shall maintain instead that the persons in the initial situation would choose two rather different principles: the first requires equality in the assignment of basic rights and duties, while the second holds that social and economic inequalities, for example inequalities of wealth and authority, are just only if they result in compensating benefits for everyone, and in particular for the least advantaged members of society. These principles rule out justifying institutions on the grounds that the hardships of some are offset by a greater good in the aggregate. It may be expedient but it is not just that some should have less in order that others may prosper. But there is no injustice in the greater benefits earned by a few provided that the situation of persons not so fortunate is thereby improved. The intuitive idea is that since everyone's well-being depends upon a scheme of cooperation without which no one could have a satisfactory life, the division of advantages should be such as to draw forth the willing cooperation of everyone taking part in it, including those less well situated. Yet this can be expected only if reasonable terms are proposed. The two principles mentioned seem to be a fair agreement on the basis of which those better endowed, or more fortunate in their social position, neither of which we can be said to deserve, could expect the willing cooperation of others when some workable scheme is a necessary condition of the welfare of all. Once we decide to look for a conception of justice that nullifies the accidents of natural endowment and the contingencies of social circumstance as counters in quest for political and economic advantage, we are led to these principles. They express the result of leaving aside those aspects of the social world that seem arbitrary from a moral point of view. . . .

DISCUSSION

After an extended discussion of the original position, the choice situation, and the actors involved, Rawls offers the two principles he claims would be chosen by the parties in the hypothetical social contract. They are as follows:

First Principle
> Each person is to have an equal right to the most extensive total system of equal basic liberties compatible with a similar system of liberty for all.

Second Principle
> Social and economic inequalities are to be arranged so that they are both
>> (a) to the greatest benefit of the least advantaged, consistent with the just savings principle, and
>> (b) attached to offices and positions open to all under conditions of fair equality of opportunity.

The sorts of liberties protected by the first principle include the following:

. . . political liberty (the right to vote and to be eligible for public office) together with freedom of speech and assembly; liberty of conscience and freedom of thought; freedom of the person along with the right to hold (personal) property; and freedom from arbitrary arrest and seizure as defined by the concept of the rule of law.

The second principle (in particular [a], which Rawls calls the difference principle), however, allows for differences between citizens. Such differences concern primarily differences in income, wealth, and positions of authority. According to "the difference principle," such inequalities are allowable only insofar as a person's gains not only do not come at the expense of those less fortunate, but positively benefit the "least advantaged" members of society. Although this principle is not the focus of Rawls's moral theory, and as such, will not be our primary concern, a brief explanation is warranted.

Recall that Rawls has argued that our starting point in life (including social position, wealth, natural assets, family, and so on) is entirely a matter of luck and therefore undeserved. For this reason, Rawls imposes the veil of ignorance in his quest for justice as fairness; fairness has to do with getting what we are entitled to or deserve. Given the enormous impact that differences in wealth, income, and social position obviously have, the fact that they are in themselves morally undeserved is problematic to say the least. On the other hand, Rawls points to the benefits of allowing such differences: "The greater expectations allowed to entrepreneurs encourages them to do things which raise the long-term prospects of laboring class [sic]. Their better prospects act as incentives so that the economic process is more efficient, innovation proceeds at a faster pace, and so on." Accordingly, social and economic inequalities are both desirable and potentially unjust (assuming justice as fairness). Rawls adds the difference principle as a response to these opposing effects: We can allow inequalities and the benefits that accrue as a result, but only if the injustice of the undeserved starting points is counterbalanced by benefiting those who were not so lucky.

Finally, Rawls adds an important restriction on how these are to be applied, namely, that the first principle has priority over the second. That is, the guarantee of individual liberty cannot be compromised; in any social scheme, the demand for basic, individual liberties must be met before any other goal is pursued. The two principles are addressed respectively to those aspects in which everyone is alike and equally worthy (the first principle) and those in which inequalities will be acceptable (the second principle). And as required by both the Kantian and the liberal doctrines, the former can never be sacrificed for the latter. In other words, a person's liberties cannot be used as a bargaining chip; people may not be used as a mere means to an end, regardless of the desirability of that end. Accordingly, Rawls claims that the principle of utility—which focuses on the aggregate happiness rather than individual well-being and rights—would not be acceptable to those in the original position.

GOODNESS AS RATIONALITY

In Part Three, Rawls addresses himself to the ethical dimensions of the well-ordered society. He assumes that the principles discussed in Part One have been chosen and implemented and are, for the most part, respected and complied with by all. What is striking at this point is how much remains to be said. In particular, what is required is to give content to the idea of the good life within a just society. All we have so far is a formal scheme in which people's liberties are guaranteed to the greatest extent possible, along with some rules of distributive justice, as characterized by the second principle. (Compare this approach with the doctrines of Augustine, Plato, or Aristotle, all of whom start out with very definite, substantive goals and arrange the formal rules around them.)

This system of formal rules is, in fact, a typical feature of liberalism and can be summed up by the slogan "The right is prior to the good." The basic idea is that humans are (and should be) self-determining beings—beings who are capable of finding out and pursuing what is good *for them.* There is no single right answer to the question, "What is the good life?" Rather, it is something that each person, as a rational, free being, must determine for him- or herself. However, to make that determination and then be able to pursue it, a certain amount of control over our own destinies is required, and that is where "the right" comes in. In particular, we will be unable to pursue our goals if we are constantly in danger of being attacked or murdered, if our belongings are stolen, if we are not allowed to think or talk to others or study, and so on.

The right, then, is the public system of rules and principles (primarily in the form of rights) that regulates our basic interactions but that leaves us free to autonomously pick out our own good. These principles are equally applicable to all citizens, regardless of their preferred conception of the good life; the principles of right are neutral with regard to competing claims concerning the best way to live. For Rawls, the right is determined by his two principles of justice (recall that the veil of ignorance prevented the participants from knowing anything about their conception of the good), which, even if applied perfectly, nevertheless leave almost entirely open what sorts of lives will be pursued in the society in which they are respected. The good, on the other hand, involves substantive value judgments, which vary from citizen to citizen and often conflict. Rawls's liberal emphasis on freedom, autonomy, and equality inevitably leads him to claim that it is not the state's business to determine its citizens' life plans, or to choose among them, but only to ensure that a multiplicity of rational life plans are possible.

In this section, Rawls develops two accounts of the good: what he calls the thin and the full theories. The former applies to the stage at which the principles are chosen and, as such, is meant to be applicable no matter what the circumstances; the full theory applies only after the principles are in place and actually presupposes a just and stable society. Both are defined in terms of rationality but apply to different sorts of assessments. The thin theory, with which we begin, concerns only what Rawls calls artifacts and social roles and is based on the desirability of certain properties given that something's function. Thus, a good knife is one with a sharp edge because it is a knife's function to cut. It is, then, rational to want such a property in a knife; thus, goodness is equated with rational desirability.

Generally speaking, the thin theory of the good is based on the rationality of desiring certain properties (in whatever is being assessed) for the advancement of our ends—no matter what those ends are. Thus, regardless of what sort of life we are pursuing, Rawls argues that it is rational to want more rather than less of what he calls the primary goods (wealth, opportunities, liberty, and self-respect). This account of the good is, according to Rawls, purely descriptive insofar as it merely describes what would be useful in the promotion of a chosen end, without evaluating the end itself.

60. The Need for a Theory of the Good

So far I have said very little about the concept of goodness. It was briefly mentioned earlier when I suggested that a person's good is determined by what is for him the most rational plan of life given reasonably favorable circumstances. All along I have assumed that in a well-ordered society citizens' conceptions of their good conform to the principles of right publicly recognized and include an appropriate place for the various primary goods. But the concept of goodness has been used only in a rather thin sense. And in fact I shall distinguish between two theories of the good. The reason for doing this is that in justice as fairness the concept of right is prior to that of the good. In contrast with teleological theories, something is good only if it fits into ways of life consistent with the principles of right already on hand. But to establish these principles it is necessary to rely on some notion of goodness, for we need assumptions about the parties' motives in the original position. Since these assumptions must not jeopardize the prior place of the concept of right, the theory of the good used in arguing for the principles of justice is restricted to the bare essentials. This account of the good I call the thin theory: its purpose is to secure the premises about primary goods required to arrive at the principles of justice. Once this theory is worked out and the primary goods accounted for, we are free to use the principles of justice in the further development of what I shall call the full theory of the good.

In order to clarify these matters, let us recall where a theory of the good has already played a role. First of all, it is used to define the least favored members of society. The difference principle assumes that this can be done. It is true that the theory need not define a cardinal measure of welfare. We do not have to know how disadvantaged the least fortunate are, since once this group is singled out, we can take their ordinal preferences (from the appropriate point of view) as determining the proper arrangement of the basic structure. Nevertheless, we must be able to identify this group. Further, the index of well-being and the expectations of representative men are specified in terms of primary goods. Rational individuals, whatever else they want, desire certain things as prerequisites for carrying out their plans of life. Other things equal, they prefer a wider to a narrower liberty and opportunity, and a greater rather than a smaller share of wealth and income. That these things are good seems clear enough. But I have also said that self-respect and a sure confidence in the sense of one's own worth is perhaps the most important primary good. And this suggestion has been used in the argument for the two principles of justice. Thus the initial definition of expectations solely by reference to such things as liberty and wealth is provisional; it is necessary to include other kinds of primary goods and these raise deeper questions. Obviously an account of the good is required for this; and it must be the thin theory. . . .

Summing up these points, we need what I have called the thin theory of the good to explain the rational preference for primary goods and to explicate the notion of rationality underlying the choice of principles in the original position. This theory is necessary to support the requisite premises from which the principles of justice are derived. But looking ahead to other questions yet to be discussed, a more comprehensive account of the good is essential. Thus the definition of beneficent and supererogatory acts depends upon such a theory. So likewise does the definition of the moral worth of persons. . . . Eventually we shall have to consider whether being a good person is a good thing for that person, if not in general, then under what conditions. In some circumstances at least, for example those of a society well-ordered or in a state of near justice, it turns out, I believe, that being a good person is indeed a good. This fact is intimately connected with the good of justice and the problem of the congruence of a moral theory. We need an account of the good to spell all this out. The characteristic feature of this full theory, as I have said, is that it takes the principles of justice as already secured, and then uses these principles in defining the other moral concepts in which the notion of goodness is involved. Once the principles of right are on hand, we may appeal to them in explaining the concept of moral worth and the good of the moral virtues. Indeed, even rational plans of life which determine what things are good for human beings, the values of human life so to speak, are themselves constrained by the principles of justice. But clearly, to avoid moving in a circle, we must distinguish between the thin and the full theory, and always keep in mind which one we are relying upon.

Finally, when we come to the explanation of the social values and the stability of a conception of justice, a wider interpretation of the good is required. For example, one basic psychological principle is that we have a tendency to love those who manifestly love us, those who with evident intention advance our good. In this instance our good comprises final ends and not only primary goods. Moreover, in order to account for the social values, we need a theory that explains the good of activities, and in particular the good of everyone's willingly acting from the public conception of justice in affirming their social institutions. When we consider these questions we can work within the full theory. Sometimes we are examining the processes by which the sense of justice and moral sentiments are acquired; or else we are noting that the collective activities of a just society are also good. There is no reason for not using the full theory, since the conception of justice is available.

However, when we ask whether the sense of justice is a good, the important question clearly is that defined by the thin theory. We want to know whether having and maintaining a sense of justice is a good (in the thin sense) for persons who are members of a well-ordered society. Surely if the sentiment of justice is ever a good, it is a good in this special case. And if within the thin theory it turns out that having a sense of justice is indeed a good, then a well-ordered society is as stable as one can hope for. Not only does it generate its own supportive moral attitudes, but these attitudes are desirable from the standpoint of rational persons who have them when they assess their situation independently from the constraints of justice. This match between justice and goodness I refer to as congruence; and I shall examine this relation when we take up the good of justice. . . .

Rawls now extends his account of goodness as rationality to plans of life: "The rational plan for a person determines his good." Just as there are better and worse choices of tools for a particular job, there are better and worse plans of life for any individual person. The rational person chooses the best, or most effective, means in either case. But how are we to assess something as amorphous as a life plan? Whereas the choice of which saw to use to cut down a tree is both indicated by common sense and something that we can determine through experimentation, the same does not seem to be immediately true of the "task" of life. It is for this reason that Rawls introduces the Aristotelian principle: "Other things equal, human beings enjoy the exercise of their realized capacities (their innate or trained abilities), and this enjoyment increases the more the capacity is realized, or the greater its complexity." Thus, a good (rational) plan of life is one that enables a person to develop and utilize his or her skills and assets to the greatest degree possible (subject to various qualifications). Note that this is still a part of the thin theory of the good insofar as it leaves entirely open which ends will be pursued; goodness is still a purely formal and instrumental notion to this point.

63. The Definition of Good for Plans of Life

I should say a few things about the rather complex notion of a rational plan. It is fundamental for the definition of good, since a rational plan of life establishes the basic point of view from which all judgments of value relating to a particular person are to be made and finally rendered consistent. Indeed, with certain qualifications we can think of a person as being happy when he is in the way of a successful execution (more or less) of a rational plan of life drawn up under (more or less) favorable conditions, and he is reasonably confident that his plan can be carried through. Someone is happy when his plans are going well, his more important aspirations being fulfilled, and he feels sure that his good fortune will endure. Since plans which it is rational to adopt vary from person to person depending upon their endowments and circumstances and the like, different individuals find their happiness is doing different things. The gloss concerning favorable circumstances is necessary because even a rational arrangement of one's activities can be a matter of accepting the lesser evil if natural conditions are harsh and the demands of other men oppressive. The achievement of happiness in the larger sense of a happy life, or of a happy period of one's life, always presumes a degree of good fortune. . . .

The aim of deliberation is to find that plan which best organizes our activities and influences the formation of our subsequent wants so that our aims and interests can be fruitfully combined into one scheme of conduct. Desires that tend to interfere with other ends, or which undermine the capacity for other activities, are weeded out; whereas those that are enjoyable in themselves and support other aims as well are encouraged. . . . If this conception of plans is sound, we should expect that the good things in life are, roughly speaking, those activities and relationships which have a major place in rational plans. And primary goods should turn out to be those things which are generally necessary for carrying out such plans successfully whatever the particular nature of the plan and of its final ends. . . .

65. The Aristotelian Principle

. . . the Aristotelian Principle runs as follows: other things equal, human beings enjoy the exercise of their realized capacities (their innate or trained abilities), and this enjoyment increases the more the capacity is realized, or the greater its complexity. The intuitive idea here is that human beings take more pleasure in doing something as they become more proficient at it, and of two activities they do equally well, they prefer the one calling on a larger repertoire of more intricate and subtle discriminations. For example, chess is a more complicated and subtle game than checkers, and algebra is more intricate than elementary arithmetic. Thus the principle says that someone who can do both generally prefers playing chess to playing checkers, and that he would rather study algebra than arithmetic. We need not explain here why the Aristotelian Principle is true. Presumably complex activities are more enjoyable because they satisfy the desire for variety and novelty of experience, and leave room for feats of ingenuity and invention. They also evoke the pleasures of anticipation and surprise, and often the overall form of the activity, its structural development, is fascinating and beautiful. Moreover, simpler activities exclude the possibility of individual style and personal expression which complex activities permit or even require, for how could everyone do them in the same way? That we should follow our natural bent and the lessons of our past experience seems inevitable if we are to find our way at all. Each of these features is well illustrated by chess, even to the point where grand masters have their characteristic style of play. Whether these considerations are explanations of the Aristotelian Principle or elaboration of its meaning, I shall leave aside. I believe that nothing essential for the theory of the good depends upon the question. . . .

The Aristotelian Principle is a principle of motivation. It accounts for many of our major desires, and explains why we prefer to do some things and not others by constantly exerting an influence over the flow of our activity. Moreover, it expresses a psychological law governing changes in the pattern of our desires. Thus the principle implies that as a person's capacities increase over time (brought about by physiological and biological maturation, for example, the development of the nervous system in a young child), and as he trains these capacities and learns how to exercise them, he will in due course come to prefer the more complex activities that he can now engage in which call upon his newly realized abilities. The simpler things he enjoyed before are no longer sufficiently interesting or attractive. If we ask why we are willing to undergo the stresses of practice and learning, the reason may be (if we leave out of account external rewards and penalties) that having had some success at learning things in the past, and experiencing the present enjoyments of the activity, we are led to expect even greater satisfaction once we acquire a greater repertoire of skills. There is also a companion effect to the Aristotelian Principle. As we witness the exercise of well-trained abilities by others, these displays are enjoyed by us and arouse a desire that we should be able to do the same things ourselves. We want to be like those persons who can exercise the abilities that we find latent in nature. . . .

Now accepting the Aristotelian Principle as a natural fact, it will generally be rational, in view of the other assumptions, to realize and train mature capacities. Maximal or satisfactory plans are almost certainly plans that provide for doing this in significant measure. Not only is there a tendency in this direction postulated by the Aristotelian Principle, but the plain facts of social interdependency and the nature of our interests more narrowly construed incline us in the same way. A rational plan—constrained as always by the principles of right—allows a person to flourish, so far as circumstances permit, and to exercise his realized abilities as much as he can. Moreover, his fellow associates are likely to support these activities as promoting the common interest and also to take pleasure in them as displays of human excellence. To the degree, then, that the esteem and admiration of others is desired, the activities favored by the Aristotelian Principle are good for other persons as well. . . .

Now it may be objected that there is no reason to suppose that the Aristotelian Principle is true. Like the idealist notion of self-realization, to which it bears a certain resemblance, it may have the ring of a philosopher's principle with little to support it. But it seems to be borne out by many facts of everyday life, and by the behavior of children and some of the higher animals. Moreover, it appears to be susceptible to an evolutionary explanation. Natural selection must have favored creatures of whom this principle is true. Aristotle says that men desire to know. Presumably we have acquired this desire by a natural development, and indeed, if the principle is sound, a desire to engage in more complex and demanding activities of any kind as long as they are within our reach. Human beings enjoy the greater variety of experience, they take pleasure in the novelty and surprises and the occasions for ingenuity and invention that such activities provide. The multiplicity of spontaneous activities is an expression of the delight that we take in imagination and creative fantasy. Thus the Aristotelian Principle characterizes human beings as importantly moved not only by the pressure of bodily needs, but also by the desire to do things enjoyed simply for their own sakes, at least when the urgent and pressing wants are satisfied. The marks of such enjoyed activities are many, varying from the manner and way in which they are done to the persistence with which they are returned to at a later time. Indeed, we do them without the incentive of evident reward, and allowing us to engage in them can itself act often as a reward for doing other things. Since the Aristotelian Principle is a feature of human desires as they now exist, rational plans must take it into account. The evolutionary explanation, even if it is correct, is not of course a justification for this aspect of our nature. In fact, the question of justification does not arise. The question is rather: granted that this principle characterizes human nature as we know it, to what extent is it to be encouraged and supported, and how is it to be reckoned with in framing rational plans of life?

The role of the Aristotelian Principle in the theory of the good is that it states a deep psychological fact which, in conjunction with other general facts and the conception of a rational plan, accounts for our considered judgments of value. The things that are commonly thought of as human goods should turn out to be the ends and activities that have a major place in rational plans. The principle is part of the background that regulates these judgments. Provided that it is true, and leads to conclusions matching our convictions about what is good and bad (in reflective equilibrium), it has a proper place in moral theory. Even if this conception should not be true of some persons, the idea of a rational long-term plan still applies. We can work out what is good for them in much the same way as before. Thus imagine someone whose only pleasure is to count blades of grass in various geometrically shaped areas such as park squares and well-trimmed lawns. He is otherwise intelligent and actually possesses unusual skills, since he manages to survive by solving difficult mathematical problems for a fee. The definition of the good forces us to admit that the good for this man is indeed counting blades of grass, or more accurately, his good is determined by a plan that gives an especially prominent place to this activity. Naturally we would be surprised that such a person should exist. Faced with his case, we would try out other hypotheses. Perhaps he is peculiarly neurotic and in early life acquired an aversion to human fellowship, and so he counts blades of grass to avoid having to deal with other people. But if we allow that his nature is to enjoy this activity and not to enjoy any other, and that there is no feasible way to alter his condition, then surely a rational plan for him will center around this activity. It will be for him the end that regulates the schedule of his actions, and this establishes that it is good for him. I mention this fanciful case only to show that the correctness of the definition of a person's good in terms of the rational plan for him does not require the truth of the Aristotelian Principle. The definition is satisfactory, I believe, even if this principle should prove inaccurate, or fail altogether. But by assuming the principle we seem able to account for what things are recognized as good for human beings taking them as they are. Moreover, since this principle ties in with the primary good of self-respect, it turns out to have a central position in the moral psychology underlying justice as fairness.

Although it was necessary to invoke only the minimalist, thin theory of the good for the choice of principles, once those principles are in place (and the right ensured), we can and must say a good deal more about the good person and the good life. Rawls now proposes the full theory of the good in which we come to make substantive moral judgments, in particular judgments about the good person and the question of moral worth. Goodness is still, however, based on rationality, or what Rawls calls "an instrumental or economic theory of value." That is, the good person will be defined by means of those properties (the "broad-based properties") that are useful for members of an association to have, both for the individual who has the properties and those who are affected by that person.

Morality, then, is not something with which we begin and then build society around (it is not, Rawls says, *a priori*) but rather a product of community life. We begin from the original position with the knowledge that we shall all have a better life if we cooperate than we would if we were each to go it alone (even assuming that were possible). We then attempt, through the principles of justice, to secure the minimal conditions necessary to pursue our own conceptions of the good life. Only when those are in place, do we turn to questions of morality—morality presupposes society. Alternatively, society is prior to morality; moral worth then will be defined in terms of what is useful for (or rational to want in) communal life.

66. The Definition of Good Applied to Persons

Having defined a person's good as the successful execution of a rational plan of life, and his lesser goods as parts thereof, we are in a position to introduce further definitions. In this way the concept of goodness is applied to other subjects that have an important place in moral philosophy. But before doing this we should note the assumption that the primary goods can be accounted for by the thin theory of the good. That is, I suppose that it is rational to want these goods whatever else is wanted, since they are in general necessary for the framing and the execution of a rational plan of life. The persons in the original position are assumed to accept this conception of the good, and therefore they take for granted that they desire greater liberty and opportunity, and more extensive means for achieving their ends. With these objectives in mind, as well as that of securing the primary good of self-respect, they evaluate the conceptions of justice available to them in the original position.

That liberty and opportunity, income and wealth, and above all self-respect are primary goods must indeed be explained by the thin theory. The constraints of the principles of justice cannot be used to draw up the list of primary goods that serves as part of the description of the initial situation. The reason is, of course, that this list is one of the premises from which the choice of the principles of right is derived. To cite these principles in explaining the list would be a circular argument. We must assume, then, that the list of primary goods can be accounted for by the conception of goodness as rationality in conjunction with the general facts about human wants and abilities, their characteristic phases and requirements of nurture, the Aristotelian Principle, and the necessities of social interdependence. At no point can we appeal to the constraints of justice. But once we are satisfied that the list of primary goods can be arrived at in this way, then in all further applications of the definition of good the constraints of right may be freely invoked. I shall not argue the case for the list of primary goods here, since their claims seem evident enough. I shall, however, come back to this point from time to time, especially in connection with the primary good of self-respect. In what follows I take the list as established and apply the full theory of the good. The test of this theory is that it should fit our considered judgments of value in reflective equilibrium. . . .

Now many philosophers have been willing to accept some variant of goodness as rationality for artifacts and roles, and for such nonmoral values as friendship and affection, the pursuit of knowledge and the enjoyment of beauty, and the like. Indeed, I have emphasized that the main elements of goodness as rationality are extremely common, being shared by philosophers of markedly different persuasions. Nevertheless, it is often thought that this conception of the good expresses an instrumental or economic theory of value that does not hold for the case of moral worth. When we speak of the just or the benevolent person as morally good, a different concept of goodness is said to be involved. I wish to argue, however, that once the principles of right and justice are on hand, the full theory of goodness as rationality can in fact cover these judgments. The reason why the so-called instrumental or economic theory fails is that what is in effect the thin theory is applied directly to the problem of moral worth. What we must do instead is to use this theory only as a part of the description of the original position from which the principles of right and justice are derived. We can then apply the full theory of the good without restrictions and are free to use it for the two basic cases of a good person and a good society. Developing the thin into the full theory via the original position is the essential step.

Several ways suggest themselves for extending the definition to the problem of moral worth, and I believe that at least one of these will serve well enough. First of all, we might identify some basic role or position, say that of citizen, and then say that a good person is one who has to a higher degree than the average the properties which it is rational for citizens to want in one another. Here the relevant point of view is that of a citizen judging other citizens in the same role. Second, the notion of a good person could be interpreted as requiring some general or average assessment so that a good person is one who performs well in his various roles, especially those that are considered more important. Finally, there may exist properties which it is rational to want in persons when they are viewed with respect to almost any of their social roles. Let us say that such properties, if they exist, are broadly based. To illustrate this idea in the case of tools, the broadly based properties are efficiency, durability, ease of maintenance, and so on. These features are desirable in tools of most any kind. Much less broadly based properties are properties such as keeps its cutting edge, does not rust, and so on. The question whether some tools have these would not even arise. By analogy, a good person, in contrast to a good doctor or a good farmer, and the like, is one who has to a higher degree than the average person the broadly based properties (yet to be specified) that it is rational for persons to want in one another.

Offhand it seems that the last suggestion is the most plausible one. It can be made to include the first as a special case and to capture the intuitive idea of the second. There are, however, certain complications in working it out. The first thing is to identify the point of view from which the broadly based properties are rationally preferred and the assumptions upon which this preference is founded. I note straightway that the fundamental moral virtues, that is, the strong and normally effective desires to act on the basic principles of right, are undoubtedly among the broadly based properties. At any rate, this seems bound to be true so long as we suppose that we are considering a well-ordered society, or one in a state of near justice, as I shall indeed take to be the case. Now since the basic structure of such a society is just, and these arrangements are stable with respect to the society's public conception of justice, its members will in general have the appropriate sense of justice and a desire to see their institutions affirmed. But it is also true that it is rational for each person to act on the principles of justice only on the assumption that for the most part these principles are recognized and similarly acted upon by others. Therefore the representative member of a well-ordered society will find that he wants others to have the basic virtues, and in particular a sense of justice. His rational plan of life is consistent with the constraints of right, and he will surely want others to acknowledge the same restrictions. In order to make this conclusion absolutely firm, we should also like to be sure that it is rational for those belonging to a well-ordered society who have already acquired a sense of justice to maintain and even to strengthen this moral sentiment. I shall discuss this question later; for the present I suppose that it is the case. Thus with all these presumptions on hand, it seems clear that the fundamental virtues are among the broadly based properties that it is rational for members of a well-ordered society to want in one another.

A further complication must be considered. There are other properties that are presumably as broadly based as the virtues, for example, intelligence and imagination, strength and endurance. Indeed, a certain minimum of these attributes is necessary for right conduct, since without judgment and imagination say, benevolent intentions may easily lead to harm. On the other hand, unless intellect and vigor are regulated by a sense of justice and obligation, they may only enhance one's capacity to override the legitimate claims of others. Certainly it would not be rational to want some to be so superior in these respects that just institutions would be jeopardized. Yet the possession of these natural assets in the appropriate degree is clearly desirable from a social point of view; and therefore within limits these attributes are also broadly based. Thus while the moral virtues are included in the broadly based properties, they are not the only ones in this class.

It is necessary, then, to distinguish the moral virtues from the natural assets. The latter we may think of as natural powers developed by education and training, and often exercised in accordance with certain characteristic intellectual or other standards by reference to which they can be roughly measured. The virtues on the other hand are sentiments and habitual attitudes leading us to act on certain principles of right. We can distinguish the virtues from each other by means of their corresponding principles. I assume, then, that the virtues can be singled out by using the conception of justice already established; once this conception is understood, we can rely on it to define the moral sentiments and to mark them off from the natural assets.

A good person, then, or a person of moral worth, is someone who has to a higher degree than the average the broadly based features of moral character that it is rational for the persons in the original position to want in one another. Since the principles of justice have been chosen, and we are assuming strict compliance, each knows that in society he will want the others to have the moral sentiments that support adherence to these standards. Thus we could say alternatively that a good person has the features of moral character that it is rational for members of a well-ordered society to want in their associates. Neither of these interpretations introduce any new ethical notions, and so the definition of goodness as rationality has been extended to persons. In conjunction with the theory of justice which has the thin account of the good as a subpart, the full theory seems to give a satisfactory rendering of moral worth. . . .

Some philosophers have thought that since a person qua person has no definite role or function, and is not to be treated as an instrument or object, a definition along the lines of goodness as rationality must fail. But as we have seen, it is possible to develop a definition of this sort without supposing that persons hold some particular role, much less that they are things to be used for some ulterior purpose. It is true, of course, that the extension of the definition to the case of moral worth makes many assumptions. In particular, I assume that being a member of some community and engaging in many forms of cooperation is a condition of human life. But this presumption is sufficiently general so as not to compromise a theory of justice and moral worth. Indeed, it is entirely proper, as I have noted previously, that an account of our considered moral judgments should draw upon the natural circumstances of society. In this sense there is nothing a priori about moral philosophy. It suffices to recall by way of summation that what permits this definition of the good to cover the notion of moral worth is the use of the principles of justice already derived. Moreover, the specific content and mode of derivation of these principles is also relevant. The main idea of justice as fairness, that the principles of justice are those that would be agreed to by rational persons in an original position of equality, prepares the way for extending the definition of good to the larger questions of moral goodness. . . .

DISCUSSION

Goodness as rationality has two parts: the thin and the full theories of the good. The former is that which is used when choosing the principles of justice, prior to any definite knowledge about our particular place in society or the ends that we might pursue. The full theory comes in only after the basic issue of the right has been settled and allows us to give meaning to moral concepts, in particular that of moral worth. Both accounts, however, are based on rationality, and we might clarify the differences between them by stating the precise sense of rationality being used.

The concept of goodness as rationality is incomplete until we answer the question of rational for what purpose. The sort of *instrumental* rationality that Rawls relies upon clearly presupposes a purpose, and it is rational to value particular properties because they enable us to achieve that purpose. Now in the thin theory of the good, we are concerned with any purpose the participants in the original position might have. Thus, the primary goods of wealth, opportunities, liberties, and self-respect are valued because they will be helpful in attaining *any* end we might choose. In the full theory of the good, the question of rational for what is answered in terms of persons, their relationships in society, and the ways in which they might flourish. Given the greater specificity of these purposes, Rawls offers a much more detailed account of what is good, including the Aristotelian principle and the traditional moral virtues.

One final note on goodness as rationality: In this view, morality is characterized as very much in the service of human beings. That is, moral constraints are not the result of coming to accept some eternal truths, values, or duties that exist independently of those whom they constrain. Rather, we begin with the individuals who will be subject to the moral rules and ask what will work for them. Thus, again Rawls denies that there is anything a priori about moral philosophy. This way of viewing the basis of morality may have less grandeur than Plato's Forms, Kant's universal reason, or Augustine's City of God, but it offers the clear advantage of being justifiable from a much greater range of perspectives.

THE SENSE OF JUSTICE

In this final excerpt, Rawls poses a fundamental question in ethics, namely, Why be moral? Having established both the principles of right (the principles of justice) and a definition of the good, Rawls now turns to why we should accept that any of it will work. For both his theory of justice and his full theory of the good rely, in the end, on our having certain fairly specific desires and motivations: comprehension of the principles of justice and the desire to uphold them (at least most of the time), concern over how other members of society view us, the ability to incorporate the flourishing of others into our own lives, and respect for the life plans of others even when they don't affect us. But what if people are, in general, indifferent to such values? He rightly states: "However attractive a conception of justice might be on other grounds, it is seriously defective if the principles of moral psychology are such that it fails to engender in human beings the requisite desire to act upon it." It remains to be shown, then, that people are psychologically disposed to choose and maintain the principles of justice and the theory of the good that is built on them.

Rawls frames his answer in terms of stability, contending that if people are motivated in the relevant ways, they will (again, for the most part) uphold the principles of justice, thereby engendering justice as fairness over the long run. Moreover, if we can show that individuals are naturally disposed to run their lives according to such principles, it turns out that the good for society as a whole (justice) and the good for the individual coincide. This is what Rawls refers to as the congruence of the just and the good. To establish this congruence, Rawls traces the development of the moral sentiments, or what he calls "the sense of justice."

69. The Concept of a Well-Ordered Society

At the beginning I characterized a well-ordered society as one designed to advance the good of its members and effectively regulated by a public conception of justice. Thus it is a society in which everyone accepts and knows that the others accept the same principles of justice, and the basic social institutions satisfy and are known to satisfy these principles. Now justice as fairness is framed to accord with this idea of society. The persons in the original position are to assume that the principles chosen are public, and so they must assess conceptions of justice in view of their probable effects as the generally recognized standards. Conceptions that might work out well enough if understood and followed by a few or even by all, so long as this fact were not widely known, are excluded by the publicity condition. We should also note that since principles are consented to in the light of true general beliefs about men and their place in society, the conception of justice adopted is acceptable on the basis of these facts. There is no necessity to invoke theological or metaphysical doctrines to support its principles, nor to imagine another world that compensates for and corrects the inequalities which the two principles permit in this one. Conceptions of justice must be justified by the conditions of our life as we know it or not at all.

Now a well-ordered society is also regulated by its public conception of justice. This fact implies that its members have a strong and normally effective desire to act as the principles of justice require. Since a well-ordered society endures over time, its conception of justice is presumably stable: that is, when institutions are just (as defined by this conception), those taking part in these arrangements acquire the corresponding sense of justice and desire to do their part in maintaining them. One conception of justice is more stable than another if the sense of justice that it tends to generate is stronger and more likely to override disruptive inclinations and if the institutions it allows foster weaker impulses and temptations to act unjustly. The stability of a conception depends upon a balance of motives: the sense of justice that it cultivates and the aims that it encourages must normally win out against propensities toward injustice. To estimate the stability of a conception of justice (and the well-ordered society that it defines), one must examine the relative strength of these opposing tendencies.

It is evident that stability is a desirable feature of moral conceptions. Other things equal, the persons in the original position will adopt the more stable scheme of principles. However attractive a conception of justice might be on other grounds, it is seriously defective if the principles of moral psychology are such that it fails to engender in human beings the requisite desire to act upon it. Thus in arguing further for the principles of justice as fairness, I should like to show that this conception is more stable than other alternatives. This argument from stability is for the most part in addition to the reasons so far adduced. I wish to consider this notion in more detail both for its own sake and to prepare the way for the discussion of other matters such as the basis of equality and the priority of liberty. . . .

The task of this chapter is to explain how justice as fairness generates its own support and to show that it is likely to have greater stability than the traditional alternatives, since it is more in line with the principles of moral psychology. To this end, I shall describe briefly how human beings in a well-ordered society might acquire a sense of justice and the other moral sentiments. . . .

According to Rawls, our moral development takes place in three stages: the morality of authority, the morality of association, and the morality of principles. Throughout this account, Rawls assumes that the society in which such development is taking place is "well-ordered." That is, the basic institutions governing social interactions are just, and they are recognized as such by members of the community. In other words, the basic principles chosen from the original position have been implemented. It is only within this sort of social arrangement that the requisite moral sentiments can develop.

In the first stage of moral development, the morality of authority, the child in the well-ordered society (which includes families) develops a sense of trust through interaction with his or her parents. This begins, however, only with the child's realization that the love of those parents can be counted on. In response, the child returns that love, seeks approval, and learns to regulate his or her behavior in order to gain it. Thus the child begins with self-interest; he or she is willing to give love only if guaranteed a return on it. However, once such reciprocity is evident, the child begins to develop genuine feelings for others. Although not in command of the abstract moral principles that tell us *why* an action is wrong, the child at this stage is nonetheless able to discern and follow rules imposed by those in authority. When those rules are broken, a sense of guilt is developed along with the already existing love and trust.

Once the child engages with the larger community, he or she begins to develop the morality of association. This stage includes not only the basic rules learned from those in authority, but the more complex standards of conduct that make cooperative endeavors possible. Rather than the simple categories of allowed and prohibited acts as encountered in the first stage, the child now learns to discern far more subtle moral injunctions. These new standards are based on social roles, cooperation, and the purposes and aims of the various associations which sprout up in the just society. Rawls describes this stage as follows:

> In due course a person works out a conception of the whole system of
> cooperation that defines the association and the ends which it serves. He knows
> that others have different things to do depending upon their place in the
> cooperative scheme. Thus he eventually learns to take up their point of view and
> to see things from their perspective.

In this way, the child eventually emerges with a sense of right and wrong that is referenced to the interests, actions, and points of view of others. But because it is only through such cooperation that a person can flourish, these ties of fellow feeling and concern for others remain in the individual's own interests. They are at the same time, however, the basis for the maintenance of "just (or fair) rules, bonds of friendship and mutual trust . . . thereby holding them ever more securely to the scheme."

In the final stage, the morality of principles, it is respect for justice itself, rather than simply a means-end sort of reasoning, that is operative. Although the morality of association will take us a long way, Rawls rightly points out that it will be limited by particular ties, specific circumstances, and actual associations. If the concrete goals and players are unknown, the morality of association tells us little or nothing. Yet justice ought not to depend upon such circumstantial factors; if an act is right, it is so regardless of whether we know those whom it will affect. Rawls states that "our moral sentiments display an independence from the accidental circumstances of our world, the meaning of this independence being given by the description of the original position and its Kantian interpretation." It is only when we come to be attached to the principles themselves that we have developed the full sense of justice.

Rawls concludes:

> For one who understands and accepts the contract doctrine, the sentiment of justice is not a different desire from that to act on principles that rational individuals would consent to in an initial situation which gives everyone equal representation as a moral person. Nor is it different from wanting to act in accordance with principles that express men's nature as free and equal rational beings. The principles of justice answer to these descriptions and this fact allows us to give an acceptable interpretation to the sense of justice. In the light of the theory of justice we understand how the moral sentiments can be regulative in our life and have the role attributed to them by the formal conditions on moral principles. Being governed by these principles means that we want to live with others on terms that everyone would recognize as fair from a perspective that all would accept as reasonable. The ideal of persons cooperating on this basis exercises a natural attraction upon our affections.

In this account, Rawls suggests that our moral development is both natural and socially conditioned. The psychological tendencies he refers to are largely based on natural feelings of trust and reciprocity: the child's response to (fair) parental control and attention, the citizen's development of "fellow feeling" as a result of joint endeavors, and finally the individual's acceptance of the principles of justice for their own sake—all develop naturally *given the right social conditions.* The most important prerequisite condition, according to Rawls, is the existence of just institutions and rules governing those subject to them. In other words, it is what Rawls claims free and rational individuals would choose from the original position. He states early on in *The Theory of Justice* that "On a contract doctrine the moral facts are determined by the principles which would be chosen in the original position." But equally important, as pointed out in the introduction to this section, those principles of justice that are chosen must reflect a fairly accurate picture of the way people actually (naturally) are. The sense of justice, then, develops naturally in human beings if the community within which they live nurtures it.

One final point is one for which Rawls has been both praised and condemned, namely, that the principles of both justice and morality seem to be self-serving on Rawls's account. This aspect is conspicuously clear in the social contractarian approach to the original position: Rawls claims that the participants come to the bargaining table in order to further their own good. They are basically indifferent (but not necessarily hostile) to the interests of other participants. (As we will see, however, the distinction between self-interested and altruistic behavior may not be as sharp as we might think: Pursuing our own interests may well involve consideration of the interests of others.)

Those who applaud such an approach to moral and political obligations point out that there is an almost elegant simplicity to it. It begins with what is an undeniable aspect of human nature—that we all seek our own good—without relying on other potentially dubious claims such as the existence of an all-powerful God

(Augustine), the possibility of pure practical reason (Kant), or the positing of a higher level of reality (Plato's Forms). In a broad sense, Rawls ends up in roughly the same place as other ethical theorists; he offers (among other things) a set of rules and regulations that are meant to limit the ways in which we might act based on a theory of good and evil, right and wrong. But the route by which he arrives is cleaner, so to speak. If he is correct, we needn't advance unprovable assumptions such as those just mentioned; we have all we need in humans as they undeniably present themselves, at least at times. Morality and political obligation can be derived from our own self-interest. (Unlike the debate over whether there is such a thing as natural altruism, the existence of natural self-interest is taken for granted.) Without social limitations (political and moral), genuinely human life—that is, a life that incorporates our intellectual, spiritual, and emotional needs as well as our physical ones—would be impossible for all.

We have in one sense come full circle and returned to the philosopher with which we began, Plato. He, too, claimed that to be just, or righteous, was ultimately in our own interest. Although Plato's reasons for asserting this justification for moral behavior differ in important ways from Rawls's (in particular, the former's theory relies heavily on the immortality of the soul, whereas Rawls is very much centered in the this life), the end result is the same in an important sense. Why be moral? Because without morality you are lost. The advantages to such a foundation with regard to the motivation to be moral should be obvious. No longer are we confronted with the stark dichotomy between what we want to do and what we ought to do. Although we may not always see it, the two come to the same thing. The just and the good, Rawls says, are congruent. There is enormous comfort in finding that what is good for others and what is good for us coincides; we can, then, in a sense, have our cake and eat it too.

We mentioned, however, that Rawls has been condemned on this same point. Although this is not the place for an extended discussion of political philosophy, it is worth mentioning that Rawls's theory as presented here has been found to be seriously flawed by proponents of a school of thought known as communitarianism. Although communitarians offer a number of criticisms of liberal theory, the one with which we shall be concerned is the charge of "asocial individualism." There are a number of forms this complaint takes; however, the basic gist of it is that liberals such as Rawls offer a seriously bankrupt account of human beings. Not only is it simply false to assert that people could be so utterly indifferent to their surroundings, relationships, and own personal traits as required by the original position, but it's difficult to see why this might be desirable, according to the communitarians. If humans are inherently social beings, why claim that they construct their society as though they were not? Alternatively (and perhaps more dramatically), why should we assume as the basis of our *moral* theory that the essence of human nature is to seek our own good without any regard for the good of others? Again, this is not the place for an extended discussion of the debate between liberals and communitarians; suffice it to say that Rawls and his fellow liberal theorists do have responses to the communitarian objections, and the debate is still very much alive.

Perhaps the philosopher to whom Rawls most obviously owes a debt is Kant. As discussed, the original position with its social contract approach and the veil of ignorance is clearly Kantian in nature. But perhaps even more fundamentally, the central importance of the guarantee of individual liberties (formalized in the requirement that the first principle be satisfied before any other goal is pursued) shows Rawls to hold a very Kantian conception of persons. To say that a person's basic liberties cannot be violated regardless of the beneficial outcome to others is to echo the imperative against using persons as mere means. Third, in his rejection of utilitarianism Rawls explicitly sides with Kant and advocates a deontological theory over a teleological one. The basis for this claim is found both in the priority of individual liberties as just discussed and in the broader concept of the right as being prior to the good. He says of justice as fairness that it "is a deontological theory, one that either does not specify the good independently from the right, or does not interpret the right as maximizing the good."

Even though these strands are fundamentally Kantian, Rawls's theory also shares some aspects of utilitarianism, despite his repeated rejection of that theory. For instance, as in the utilitarian doctrine, Rawls very much believes that morality is for the sake of the human beings to which it applies. Unlike theories that posit some other worldly goal (such as Augustine and Plato) or characterize morality as some sort of eternal law that applies regardless of circumstances (Kant), Rawls and the utilitarians conceive of morality as being in the service of persons, and not vice versa. Morality exists in this view to enable us to live happier, more fruitful lives. Moreover, both utilitarians and Rawls (who, again, would never consider himself a utilitarian) begin with natural emotions rather than a sense of duty or ultimate purpose. For the utilitarians it is the desire for happiness that gets the ball rolling, while for Rawls it is the sort of natural feelings of trust, desire for approval and respect, and ultimately, belief in reciprocity that form the basis of the sense of justice, or moral sentiments. (It should be noted that while desire for happiness is the cornerstone of Mill's *Utilitarianism,* he too makes use of the sorts of fellow-feeling—what he referred to as a "contagion of sympathy"—that Rawls builds on.)

Finally, it is clear that Aristotle has a special place in Rawls's theory, as explicitly evidenced by the Aristotelian Principle. Although he disagrees with Aristotle about the existence of a single, species-determined *telos,* Rawls obviously does adopt a teleological approach once the principles of justice are in place. (Recall that throughout this discussion of moral development he assumes just institutions and participants who uphold them.)

So what are we to make of Rawls's moral theory? Are these varied and potentially conflicting influences a sign of strength or of confusion? Is it more like a well-ordered army with appropriate hierarchies or a crazy quilt with disparate patterns thrown together? We can answer favorably only if the various influences are put together in such a way that each performs a function without nullifying or contradicting that which another strand is meant to do. And this is arguably the case. The main thing to keep in mind is that Rawls proceeds in two very separate stages. In the first we choose the principles of justice or right and rely only on the thin theory of the good, while in the second we fill in more substantive values and provide the full theory of the good, *assuming a just society.* Given these very different tasks (and the very different presuppositions that go with them), radically distinct tools (theories) may well be needed.

In the first stage, we cannot assume anything by way of fellow-feeling or cooperation because what we are to choose from the original position is the basis for that cooperation and the sentiments that will arise from it. It is Kant, then, who does the heavy lifting at this stage. His theory ensures—above all—fairness and universal respect for the equal dignity of each and every person. Likewise, the views of the other social contract theorists, and their approach generally, are appropriate at this stage because prior to the relationships and cooperative ventures made possible by the principles of justice, we assume only that each person seeks to advance his or her own interests.

However, once the principles of justice are in place, the picture changes entirely. We no longer need to establish the basic protection of individuals (the principles of right or justice) because we are assuming that they are agreed upon and respected. This frees us up to ask much deeper questions about what is good for persons (rather than simply what is right procedurally). It is at this point that the Aristotelian Principle comes to play such an important part. It is only after we have achieved a certain degree of order in social life (through the first stage) that we can even think about the pursuit of long-term goals, conceptions of rational plans of life, the development of our natural capacities, and so on. Once we are able to focus on such ends, though, we naturally move toward what we have characterized as utilitarian tendencies: the idea that moral rules should be for the benefit of those to whom they apply and, equally, that such rules should be built around the human goals that will lead to happiness and fulfillment as given by the Aristotelian Principle.

Discussion Questions

1. How convincing do you find Rawls's account of moral development? What happens to his just society if this turns out to be mistaken?
2. What are the Kantian aspects of Rawls's theory? In what ways do his views differ from Kant?
3. What are the virtues according to Rawls? Does this definition account for all the traditional virtues? Can you think of a virtue that would not be included?
4. What is a well-ordered society? Do we live in one?

Study Questions

1. What is the original position, and what role is the veil of ignorance supposed to play? How likely is it that we could shed so much knowledge of ourselves even for a short time?
2. Why does Rawls characterize his theory of justice as fairness? Can you think of other social arrangements that might be more fair?
3. Why are there two theories of the good? How do they differ? What do they have in common?
4. What does Rawls mean by "goodness as rationality"? How does his account of rationality compare with Kant's notion of reason? With Aristotle's theory of practical reason?
5. What is the social contract approach, and how does Rawls make use of it? What are the benefits of such a theory?
6. Why must the first principle be satisfied before the second? What would a utilitarian say about this requirement?
7. In what way is the just congruent with the good? Why should this matter?
8. What is the Aristotelian Principle, and what use does Rawls make of it in his theory of the good?
9. What is the "morality of principles"? Why is this the last stage in the development of a sense of justice?

Glossary

absolute   ultimate, without exception, applicable to everybody, everywhere. If a principle is an absolute principle, then it holds without exception and without regard for any particular circumstances or persons. For a value to be absolute is for it *not* to be relative or subjective. Many people believe that God is the absolute being. (See also **objective, universal law.**)

action   what a person (or any agent) does. In ethics, it is important to be able to explain what happens as the result of a person's action (will or intentions) and attribute responsibility for that action.

aesthetics   the study of art and beauty. Philosophers of aesthetics are concerned with how we make judgments about taste, about what is good or bad in art; with what beauty is, and how we perceive art. Aesthetic judgments are often contrasted with moral judgment.

agape   one of the three kinds of love distinguished by the ancient Greeks, contrasted with erotic (sexual) love. (See **love.**)

agency   ethicists talk in terms of agency when they want to talk about attributing responsibility for actions, and when they talk about what kinds of beings can be considered morally responsible.

agent   any person or being who performs an action.

altruism   the moral intention to do good for other people. (Some theorists would add, "and *not* for yourself.") Someone who's altruistic is *neither* selfish nor egoistic. Some philosophers equate being moral with being altruistic, but many do not.

amoralism   the belief that actions are neither moral nor immoral, that moral terms are irrelevant and that there are no binding rules for social behavior, except for prudential (self-interested) and pragmatic (practical) rules of thumb.

amoralist   one who believes that people's actions are neither moral nor immoral.

anatman   the Buddhist concept of "no-self." Most Buddhists believe that the false belief in a self tends to mislead humans into forming those attachments to the world that create suffering.

anthropologist a person who describes the ethical (and other) behavior of people in various societies.

anthropology the study of human beings, what they do, and what they believe. Anthropology does not offer a prescriptive ethical theory or justifications for such beliefs but only describes them.

apodeictic knowledge about what *must* be (in contrast to either what *could* be or what *might* be). An apodeictic claim is stated in terms of necessity, not in terms of either possibility or contingency. There are good examples of apodeictic claims in geometry; for instance, we know apodeictically that the sum of the squares of the sides of a right triangle equals the square of the hypotenuse, because it couldn't be any other way. Our knowledge of something is apodeictic if it *doesn't even make sense* to talk about alternatives. Kant claimed that the categorical imperative is apodeictic.

a posteriori knowledge based on sense experience. Literally, "a posteriori" means "after," i.e., "after having experienced." A posteriori knowledge is based on the senses—seeing, smelling, hearing, feeling, tasting, and touching. ("After" is used in a logical sense, not as "after" in time.) Some philosophers (called "empiricists") think that all knowledge (except merely logical truth) comes from sense experience. (See empiricism.)

a priori knowledge based on pure rationality. Literally, "a priori" means "before," i.e., "before experience." A priori knowledge is whatever we know without having to see, smell, hear, feel, taste or touch. ("Before" is used in the logical sense, not in time; that is, it is in the sense of having *prior*-ity.) Some philosophers think that our most important knowledge—the principles that lie at the basis of all knowledge—comes from pure reason, or logic. One such philosopher was Kant (by whom the term was most famously used). He claimed that not only mathematical or logical truths but also moral truths are a priori and purely rational. Thus, according to Kant, we can figure out what's ultimately right to do by rational deliberation and not solely on the basis of our own (limited) experience.

arete the ancient Greek word for "virtue." Literally, it means, "specific excellence." Most generally, it's the quality that makes any particular thing a *good example* of its *kind*. For instance, a virtue, or arete, of a knife is its sharpness (Aristotle's example). The virtues of a human being are those qualities that specifically make a person excellent as a human being, for instance, courage, a sense of honor, and cultivated intelligence.

assertoric knowledge or statements that are about what is the case, the kind of statement that expresses a fact. (An assertion is an assertoric statement.) Kant distinguished assertoric imperatives from both hypothetical imperatives and the categorical imperative.

atman the self. The self is central to Hindu thought, but is usually rejected in Buddhist thought.

autonomy independence or self-determination. Sometimes "autonomy" is used as a synonym for "free will." Ethicists often talk about autonomy, because if people are *not* autonomous, it would be impossible to talk about their being responsible for their actions. Kant defined "autonomy" as, "subjection of the will to its own law," in other words, the ability to make yourself do what you tell yourself to do. Autonomy is sometimes contrasted with "heteronomy," doing what other people tell you without deliberation or affirmation on your own part.

bad faith in Sartre, the tendency to treat our choices as already determined by circumstances, to deny responsibility and make excuses. (To confuse our "transcendence" for our "facticity.")

benevolence concern for and the advancement of the good of others.

categorical imperative   the absolute moral law that binds every rational creature. "Categorical" means applicable absolutely, without conditions. An "imperative" is a command or order. Anyone who is rational, no matter what era or culture or world they live in, is bound by their rationality to obey certain general rules or principles—for example, "treat others as you (or anyone) ought to be treated" and "treat others as ends and not merely as means." Philosophers use this term when referring to Kant, who coined it. Kant defined the categorical imperative as "the supreme, absolute moral law of rational autonomous beings." According to Kant, the categorical imperative is the foundation of morality; it tells us what our duty is.

choice   a decision between two or more alternatives. Usually, philosophers talk about a "choice" as appropriate only for an autonomous agent. Some philosophers insist that a person can choose only among *actions* and that a person can choose only the *means* to an ultimate end or goal. Some philosophers, on the other hand, think that a person can also choose among ultimate *ends* or goals.

conscience   usually appealed to in the ethical theory known as intuitionism, the part of the mind where moral knowledge may be revealed to an agent who reflects carefully on moral problems or situations.

consequentialism   an ethical theory that claims that actions are judged according to their consequences. A consequentialist is a person who believes that the only consideration that makes an action right or wrong, good or bad, is its result. So, for example, a consequentialist might say that, if premarital sex is wrong, it is wrong *only* because some people (e.g., naive teenagers) would be hurt or upset by it, not because it's forbidden by God or Society or otherwise *immoral*. Utilitarianism is a consequentialist theory.

contingent   what *could* (or might not) be, as opposed to either what *must* be or what *cannot* be. A fact, or state of affairs, is contingent if it happens to be the case, but might just as easily have turned out not to be the case. For example, a person's existence is contingent; although you are in fact alive, your parents might not have conceived you. (They might never have even met.) You can imagine a world in which you didn't exist. Philosophers often talk about contingent existence in contrast to necessary existence, for example, the necessary existence of God according to such authors as Augustine.

deontology   any type of ethical theory in which right action is considered to be right in and of itself. A deonotologist claims that one *knows* what his or her duty is (*deon* comes from the ancient Greek word for *duty*). Deontological ethical theories (for example, Kant's theory) are typically contrasted to teleological ethical theories. That is, in deontological ethics, what is *right* to do is not defined in terms of the good.

descriptive statements   claims about how things are (or seem to be). In ethics, descriptive statements are typically sociological and psychological claims about how people *do in fact* behave, or about what people *do in fact* value. Philosophers talk about "descriptive" in contrast to "prescriptive" statements; a descriptive claim says something about what is rather than about what ought to be. For instance, an anthropologist might make descriptive statements about the morality of a certain culture.

dialectic   logical argumentation. There are three basic senses in which philosophers use the word "dialectic." The first comes originally from Plato and describes the way Socrates debates with other people. In this first sense, then, dialectic means the back-and-forth, question-and-answer style in which people talk together as they try to get a handle on the truth. The second sense comes from the German philosopher G. W. F. Hegel and describes the way that knowledge and value systems change over history. This sense of "dialectic" is a grand extension of the Platonic sense, applied over very long time periods; the theories and dogmas of any particular historical period are always in a sense responses to the theories and dogmas that came before them and then provoke new theories and dogmas in response to themselves. The third sense of "dialectic" comes from Marx, who was (as Hegel predicted) responding to Hegel and again changed the meaning of "dialectic." According to Marx, the changes in history came about, not through refinement of ideas, but through changes in the way people lived their lives, through wars and revolutions and technological advances, and through changes in the economic structure of society. This third sense of "dialectic" has given rise to the Marxist philosophy of "dialectical materialism" because it's about the back-and-forth movement of concrete, physical things. In all three senses, "dialectic" is the mechanism by which things change, by way of conflict and confrontation but also in continuation with its predecessors.

disinterestedness   observation or relation without emotional investment. Some philosophers claim that a person can make objective judgments only about matters in which he or she is disinterested. Kant, in particular, argued that disinterestedness was essential in both ethical and aesthetic judgments.

distributive justice   takes each person's "due" to be his or her "fair share" of the goods and necessities of his or her society. Thus, distributive justice is concerned with allocations, with the distribution to people of what they need and want. Some philosophers take the term "fair share" here to mean an "equal" share. Other philosophers insist that one's fair share must be proportional to the effort and contribution one has made; while still others, Karl Marx, for instance, take the term "fair share" to mean "enough to meet one's needs." (See **justice.**)

divine   about or belonging to God, or the gods. Moral laws, natural laws, and rights have often been claimed to be divine or have divine origins. The Ten Commandments, for example, came to us with the authority of God and are therefore considered divinely ordained.

dukha   suffering. The problem of human suffering—Why do we suffer? Can we free ourselves from it?—is central to all religious thought, but is particularly important to Hinduism, Buddhism, and Jainism. Arthur Schopenhauer, a German philosopher who was heavily influenced by Asian philosophy and religion, also made the problem of suffering the keystone of his philosophy.

duty (duties)   what a person ought to do, a moral obligation. There are (at least) two different kinds of duties, however: duties that are defined by a particular social role or position (e.g., as chairman of the committee, as the night watchman) and duties that are binding on everyone, regardless of social role or position. Philosophers usually focus on the second sense, in which the word "duty" has a special *moral* status. Not all ethicists base their theories on a concept of duty because not all ethicists think that right action is to be defined in terms of obligation. But some ethical theories—deontological theories—insist that obligation (to God, or to the law, or to other people) is the basis of all morality.

egoism   giving priority to your own interest. (This is not the same as egotism—thinking too highly of yourself.) Philosophers talk about two kinds of egoism, **ethical egoism** and **psychological egoism.**

Ethical egoism is any theory that states that people *ought* to pursue their own interests. Thus, ethical egoism is a prescriptive theory about how people should behave in order to do what's *morally* right. Some defenders of modern capitalism, for example, argue that each person ought to pursue his or her own welfare, and the nation as a whole will benefit. An ethical egoist need not also be a psychological egoist; indeed, he or she may think that acting in one's own self-interest takes a special effort or exceptional talent (some of Nietzsche's writings can be interpreted this way).

Psychological egoism is any theory that states that people *do in fact* always pursue their own interests. In other words, psychological egoism is a descriptive theory about how people actually behave. An ethicist who is a psychological egoist had better believe that it's *moral* to act in one's own interest, because such a theory claims that we can't act in any other way.

In general, egoism includes any ethical or psychological theory of self-interest. (See **enlightened egoism, self-interest.**)

elitism   a bias toward the upper class or preference for some "better" class of people. The word "aristocracy," literally translated, means "rule by the best." Aristotle's ethics has been called elitist because he believed that only wealthy, well-educated men were capable of doing the things that lead to happiness. In our egalitarian ("all men [and women] are created equal") society, to be called an elitist is something of a moral criticism.

emotivism   any ethical theory that claims that ethical statements are neither true nor false and cannot be proven but are really only statements about how someone feels. An emotivist is therefore a kind of a skeptic (see **skepticism**), who denies ethical knowledge and the possibility of any single correct, absolute morality. David Hume was an early skeptic who was also an emotivist, but emotivism has particularly blossomed in the twentieth century. A. J. Ayer, for example, argued that moral judgments were essentially the same as exclamations, like "Hooray!" or "Yuck!" Emotivism is one species of "noncognitivism" (the claim that ethical claims cannot be known). (See **noncognitivism.**)

empiricism   any theory of knowledge that claims that all knowledge is based on sense experience. There are some things that we obviously learn through experience—that summer comes after spring, for instance. But what about that $2 + 2 = 4$? A thoroughgoing empiricist would claim that a person learns even mathematical truths through sense perception (for instance, by putting two fingers next to two other fingers and *counting* up to four so that, eventually, you *know* $2 + 2 = 4$. (Alternatively, an empiricist might insist that $2 + 2 = 4$ just tells us, trivially, what "2" means.) Philosophical empiricism takes as its model the methods of empirical science, in which knowledge is gained by observation. In ethics, empiricism typically favors a descriptive, experience-based approach to morality. (David Hume is an empiricist in ethics as well as in other philosophical matters.) The name for the most directly opposing theory of knowledge is "rationalism."

end   the purpose or goal of an action. In ethics, this technical meaning of the word "end" is extremely important. (In this sense, it does not mean "finish" or "termination"—although achieving the end of some activities may signal the end or finish of the activity as well.) Philosophers contrast "ends" and "means"—the goal of an activity and its instruments and strategies. Thus, one of the most important ethical questions is, "Do the ends justify the means?" An activity may involve more than one end, and there can be different levels and priorities to ends; for instance, the end of reading this philosophy book may be to do well in philosophy class, but the end of doing well in philosophy class may be to be a better educated, more interesting person, the end of which, in turn, might be argued to be happiness. (See **teleology.**)

enlightened egoism   the view that unselfish or moral behavior is actually in one's own interest. An ethical theory based on enlightened egoism claims that everybody's self-interest is best satisfied when we all obey the moral rules. Also called "enlightened self-interest." (See **egoism, prudence, self-interest.**)

enlightened self-interest   prudent, long-term, usually cooperative self-interest. (See **enlightened egoism.**)

entitlement   a legitimate claim to something. Rights are a kind of entitlement. (See **rights.**) A person might be entitled to something for different reasons: because he or she inherited it, because he or she worked hard to earn it, because he or she paid for it, because it was promised by the government or a friend. Some philosophers claim that the only real entitlements are legal and based on law or specific contracts, whereas others claim that there are entitlements that people have regardless of any particular system of law or explicit agreements. Entitlements typically entail duties; if you are entitled to something, someone (or other) has a duty to provide it for you. (See **duty, rights.**)

epistemology   the study of knowledge or any theory of knowledge. ("Logos" in ancient Greek means, roughly, "reason." "Episteme" means "knowledge.") An epistemologist is a philosopher who inquires into what sorts of things can be known by people, how it is that people know what they know, and how people learn what they know. (The study of psychology is largely based on eighteenth-century epistemology.) Although there are many epistemological theories, philosophers often group them into two basic "camps," rationalism and empiricism.

eros   erotic or sexual love. (See **love.**)

ethical egoism   See **egoism.**

ethical hedonism   See **hedonism.**

ethics   theories of value, virtue, or of right (valuable) action. "Ethics" comes from an ancient Greek word, *ethé,* which means "character." The word "ethics" accordingly has two basic meanings: first, the values that one accepts and practices; second, the views that one has *about* those values. Sometimes philosophers use the words, "ethics" and "morals" synonymously, but they often make a distinction between "morals"—a set of rules of conduct—and "ethics"—a broader study of the values of society and, possibly, the justification of moral rules. There are many kinds of ethical theories, and many versions of each basic kind of theory. (See **deontology, emotivism, hedonism, teleology.**) An **ethicist** is a person who inquires into what's right and wrong, good and bad, desirable or undesirable, virtuous or vicious.

ethnocentricity   basing a general moral theory on the (rather specific) beliefs of a particular ethnic group. Calling a theory "ethnocentric" is an objection to the theory suggesting that it is only applicable to, or only for the good of, for example, people of European or Anglo-American ancestry. For instance, some moral theories make claims about the rightness of "civilized" behavior, where "civilization" is peculiar to the mores of European society; or a theory will discuss "morality" where "morality" means "Christian belief." Any absolutist ethics makes claims that apply to everybody, but if other cultures' beliefs do not comply with the theory, it is important to question whether it is the culture or rather the theory that is wrong. (Any relativist, by way of contrast, will take the differing moral standards of different cultures as a datum and claim that virtually all ethical theories, by their very nature, are ethnocentric.)

ethos   the character of a culture. "Ethos" is an ancient Greek word for "character" and was mostly used in talking about the Greek city-state. We now use the term to refer to the character of a particular nation, culture, or ethnic group. The Greek word ethé, from which we get our word "ethics," is derived from "ethos." Thus, the Greeks, at least, thought the two concepts were closely related; what one believes is right and wrong has a lot to do with the values and beliefs of his or her society. Our ethos helps define for us what the good life is in our culture and what roles are appropriate for certain people in our culture, etc. For instance, the value of working hard is often said to be part of the American ethos. (See **ethics, mores.**)

eudaimonia   roughly translated (from the Greek), happiness. Eudaimonia is the ancient Greek word for "good living." Aristotle claimed that eudaimonia is the goal of human life and the basis of all ethical behavior. While it is most often translated as "happiness," eudaimonia means more than just a pleasant feeling. It's what we might call "true happiness"; a full, satisfying, interesting life.

excellence   in Aristotle, determined according to a thing or a being's function: the fulfillment of that function in the best possible way.

existentialism   according to Jean-Paul Sartre, who coined the term, a theory that claims that "existence precedes essence," that we aren't born with a specific character (given us by God or nature) but rather we *make* ourselves into what we are. A person therefore defines for him- or herself what it means to be human, what it means to be good, and what kind of person he or she will be, through the choices he or she makes in life. Existentialists generally believe in radical freedom of the will, that our choices are not directed or determined by God or nature or society. (See **will.**) Of course, that implies that a person bears the sole *responsibility* for all his or her actions, too. There are no excuses.

external sanction   a reward or punishment imposed by someone other than the agent. The term comes from John Stuart Mill, who claimed that all morality had two natural sanctions. There is an external sanction (external to us)—our reputation in the eyes of others. We are motivated to act morally so that our friends and mentors will show approval for our actions. There are also internal sanctions. (See **internal sanction** and **sanction.**)

facticity   in Sartre, those aspects of our situation which precede choice, "the facts."

fellow-feeling   in Mill, the connection between the pursuit of one's own happiness and concern for the happiness of others.

In Rawls, the result of feelings of trust and reciprocity which naturally develop in communal living, and the basis for our sense of morality.

freedom   in Kant, the ability to make choices (in particular the choice to will in accordance with the moral law) and thus the basis for morality.

In Sartre, the essential feature of human nature, the need to make choices and be responsible.

grace   in the Judeo-Christian tradition, the belief that God may of his own free choice bestow salvation on a person or even an entire race.

happiness   in Aristotle, the state in which one is living well or thriving.

In Augustine, salvation in the next world.

In Mill, pleasure and the absence of pain.

hedonism   the claim that pleasure is the only thing that's good. A person who believes in hedonism or acts primarily for the sake of pleasure is a **hedonist.** An acting hedonist acts in order to obtain pleasure. A theoretical hedonist claims that everything one does is done in order to increase pleasure or reduce pain. There are two kinds of hedonisms: **ethical hedonism** and **psychological hedonism.**

Ethical hedonism is the claim that people *ought* to seek pleasure, that pleasure is the moral good. Thus, an ethical hedonist is making a prescriptive claim about how people should behave. A hedonist *might* want to reject all traditional moral rules, including prudence, as distractions from or antagonists to pleasure, but he or she *could* be a hedonist and still believe in a traditional set of moral rules. To do this, he or she would have to interpret morality, or prudence, as rules that are meant to increase people's pleasure and security (which is a precondition for many pleasures) in the long run. John Stuart Mill's Utilitarianism is an example of this type of hedonism. (See **egoism, prudence, self-interest, utilitarianism.**)

Psychological hedonism is the claim that *in fact* what people seek is pleasure. A psychological hedonist is only making a descriptive claim about how people actually behave. A psychological hedonist might well also argue that people *ought* to seek pleasure, since they can't do otherwise. He or she might still want to distinguish, however, between different kinds and qualities of pleasure.

holism   the claim that you can't understand the part(s) unless you understand the whole. In ethics, this means that particular actions don't make any sense except in reference to their historical, social, and personal context. For example, we can't say whether (the equivalent of) $3.85 is a fair hourly wage for a thirteenth-century Chinese worker without knowing much more about the circumstances and conditions of Chinese workers; similarly, we can't say in the abstract whether wrestling a tiger is brave or not (it might just be stupid). Holism insists that we have to understand the general context comprehending the particular action of a particular person.

humanism   the belief that human welfare is the ultimate moral good. A humanist judges goodness and badness in terms of benefit or liability to human life. In ethics, humanism is typically contrasted to uncompromising religious views; where a divine morality claims that God's commands are the ultimate authority for our actions, a humanist would claim that human standards by themselves are the only authority people need. Jean-Paul Sartre's existentialism is one sort of philosophical humanism, but humanism need not be opposed to religion as such.

hypothetical imperative   a conditional command. "Hypothetical" means "not necessarily," or "just supposing"; an "imperative" is a command or order. A hypothetical imperative is a command that you need to obey only *if* certain conditions hold. For example, "*If* you want a good grade in philosophy class, *then* learn what a hypothetical imperative is!" is a hypothetical imperative. Philosophers usually use this term in reference to Kant, who contrasted hypothetical imperatives with moral commands, which he called "categorical." Kant insisted that moral commands are not conditional. (See **categorical imperative.**)

inclination   a person's tendency, preference, or wish. In ethics, the word "inclination" usually refers to one's emotions, moods, and desires, especially the appetites such as hunger and thirst, but also natural sentiments such as compassion. Thus, our inclinations contrast with other, more rational or deliberate intentions. Kant used the term "inclination" as a specific contrast to duty. Other philosophers, such as Mill or Aristotle, claim that our moral duty ultimately serves our inclinations. In other words, that what we *ought* to do is, fortunately, usually what we really *want* to do as well.

incontinence   the inability to control oneself. In ethics, "incontinence" refers to the specific moral problem of not being able to *do* what one knows to be morally right. Moral incontinence may be a lack of control over one's passions or emotions, which may distract us from doing what's right. Incontinence is particularly a problem for Plato and Aristotle, because they both claimed that virtue was a type of knowledge. (Knowing what's right, how could one then do wrong?)

instrumental   of use toward some further purpose. "Instrumental" includes the word "instrument"; therefore, it is clear that something instrumental is used as a tool to further some end. In epistemology, instrumental reason is sometimes compared with pure reason, where instrumental reasoning is calculating the means to some end or working out the steps to a conclusion that's presupposed by some goal or other. In ethics, an instrumental good is compared with an intrinsic good, where instrumental goods are good only because they help us achieve some other, more important good, whereas an intrinsic good is good in itself and not aimed at any further end. For instance, Aristotle claims that money is an instrumental good because it's only good *for buying things;* it's the things it can buy that are the real goods. Of course, a good could be instrumental and intrinsic at the same time: watching a good movie may be interesting in itself and also restful, informative, or a good excuse for socializing. (See **end, intrinsic, reason.**)

intention   the will to do something, the basis of a decision. In ethics, the word "intention" refers to the psychological cause of action but also to how people describe and justify their actions to themselves.

internal sanction   self-punishment or rewards that are part of an act or accomplishment—for example, the pain of guilt or shame following an inconsiderate or foolish action, or the feeling of pride and self-satisfaction that comes along with virtues that are "their own reward." The term comes from John Stuart Mill (in his defense of Utilitarianism) who wanted to show that the principle of utility was the principle underlying all our moral decisions. He claimed that in addition to external sanctions (such as our reputation in the eyes of others), we are motivated to act morally by an internal sanction (internal to us) which is our *conscience,* feeling proud or guilty about what we do. (See also **external sanction and sanction.**)

intrinsic   in and of itself. In ethics, "intrinsic" is used in reference to goodness or value, to distinguish instrumentally good things (things that are good only because they're needed in order to obtain other good things) from things that are good in themselves. Pleasure, health, and knowledge are often said to be intrinsic goods because they seem (typically) to be ends in themselves and not tools for obtaining some higher goods. (See **end, instrumental.**)

intuitionism   in ethics, the thesis that the truth of values or moral judgments may be directly perceived (or "intuited") by subjects who reflect thoroughly about moral situations. Usually these moral intuitions are said to be revealed in the subject's conscience.

justice   what is right, what ought to be done in any social arrangement. Justice, of course, is one of the central concepts and concerns of ethics. Most generally, justice is the correct or proper way to treat others, and thus it is centrally concerned with how societies ought to function and how a person ought to function within society. Philosophers over the years have offered many definitions, analogies, and arguments concerning what justice is. One definition that seems to cover all bases is from Plato's *Republic:* "giving to each his or her due." Of course, what's *due* a person can mean many things and employ many standards. Philosophers tend to divide justice into two more or less distinct concerns: **distributive justice** and **retributive justice.**

justification   demonstrating the correctness of your beliefs or actions. The word "justification" comes from the word "justice," and because "justice" means "giving or getting what's due (what's right or proper)," "justification" means "proving that something is due (right or proper)." In philosophy, the word "justification" refers both to giving a sound reason or argument for what you take to be right or true and to establishing an authority or reason that *makes* your belief right or true. A justification of morality might show how moral rules are rational or sound or might establish God's existence and moral authority.

logical positivism   in a theory that emphasizes scientific method over and above any alternative philosophical approach. The logical positivists of the "Vienna Circle" at the turn of the twentieth century came from different disciplines but all insisted that science would solve what were formerly religious or philosophical questions—if, that is, they were meaningful questions at all. The discipline of philosophy, according to the positivists, should confine itself to the analysis of language and furthering scientific research, in order to make our outlook toward the world more scientific.

love   in philosophers talk about different *kinds* of love and disagree about its place in ethics. Both the early Greeks and Christian philosophy put love at the very core of ethics, but most modern theories (deontology and utilitarianism, for example), relegate it to the margins or ignore it altogether. The ancient Greeks distinguished **agape, eros,** and **philia:**

Agape   is what we would now call "brotherly love." It is the kind of love that we can and possibly do feel for everybody, or for the whole world—for "thy neighbor," in general. If "God is Love," as the typical Biblical claim goes, then He is agape love.

Eros   is the root of our word, "erotic." It means "sexual desire" or "attraction." Plato, and much, much later, Sigmund Freud, claimed that eros is the motivation behind many more of our choices and actions than we usually recognize. Eros is the most closely related of these three types of love to what we usually mean by "romantic" or "erotic" love.

Philia   forms part of the root of our words, "philosophy" and "philanthropy." It refers to love within groups of intimate associates and generally means "friendship." Aristotle insisted that "no man would choose to live without friends," and he meant by "friend" a person with whom a person had a long-lasting, fulfilling relationship full of high regard. The "philosopher" is "the friend of wisdom," a person who cares for wisdom and wants to live his or her life sharing in it.

master morality   in Nietzsche, a value system that esteems personal excellence.

maxim   in the principle of a person's action. Philosophers usually use this word in reference to Kant, for whom maxims were essential to the test of duty. Kant defined a "maxim" as "a subjective principle of volition," that is, the way we would describe the reasoning behind our own action. For instance, if you're going to the supermarket, your maxim might be, "I will go to the supermarket because I'm out of bread"; or if you were going to cheat on an exam your maxim might be, "I will glance at the test of the person sitting next to me because I'm unsure of the answers and I want to pass." If you were keeping a promise, your maxim might be, "I will keep my promise because it's the right thing to do." A maxim, the reasons for our action, may or may not be morally right reasons, but there is always some reason why we behave as we do.

metaphysics   in the study of "first principles," of ultimate reality. "Meta" is the Latin term for "after" or "beyond," and "physics" includes all the natural sciences. Thus, "metaphysics" includes inquiries about the foundations of Nature, which constitute the object of study of the natural sciences. Metaphysics is the philosophical inquiry into reality—the creation, existence, and order of whatever there really *is*. Some philosophers (some of the ancient Greeks and the European medievals) took metaphysics to be basically the inquiry into the nature and existence of God or the gods. Others (most modern and contemporary philosophers), take metaphysics to be the inquiry into the nature and existence of the objective world.

moksha   in Hinduism and Jainism, release or liberation from the suffering of life, usually accompanied by a profound (and largely incommunicable) understanding of truth.

monotheism   the belief that there is only one God, usually accompanied by the belief that this one God created the universe and assumes responsibility for it.

morality   in the rules of right conduct. Often, philosophers use the term "morality" synonymously with "ethics." But the two words have different connotations. Ethics has to do with the general, practical questions about how to live our lives. Morality, on the other hand, has to do with objective rules about especially important human activities. The Ten Commandments, for instance, are (for the most part) a statement of morality. Kant's and Mill's ethical theories are also clearly moral ones—they both claim that there are discernable objective rules and/or goals for human conduct (although Kant and Mill disagree about what those objective rules are).

morals   in the quality of the habits and character of a person or a society. The word comes from "mores," a society's sense of right conduct and customs. (See **mores.**) Morals are often taken to be instances of morality, i.e., practices and actions in accordance with, or in obedience to, the laws or principles of morality. (See **morality.**) But some philosophers (for instance, David Hume) use the term to refer primarily to the qualities of character as such, without special reference to any overarching set of rules or principles.

moral skepticism   in the refusal to accept that there are irrefutable moral truths.

mores   in a particular society's sense of good conduct; particular customs and traditions. Our word "morality" is derived from "mores." Both mores and morality dictate how people ought to behave, but mores differ from morality in three possible ways: (1) Mores are culturally relative. They are based in a particular culture and they most likely change from one society to the next; morality, on the other hand, is supposed to be objective, universal, and not at all relative. (See **relativism, universal law.**) (2) Mores may include rules but may not be explicitly rule governed, as morality is often said to be. A society's mores may include its ideals and common beliefs (some of which may be encoded in rules, such as what vows ought to be taken at a wedding ceremony) but they need not be so encoded. Our rather loosely defined belief in "rugged individualism" is a part of our American mores. (3) Mores cover a broader spectrum of behavior than does morality and includes "less important" things than morals, such as what counts as "courteous" and "polite" in a society.

natural law   in universal and necessary law, a "higher" law. Both scientists and ethicists use the term "natural law" to mean laws that apply to everything in nature. In science, a natural law is descriptive of all physical objects (like the law of gravity); in ethics, natural law is prescriptive to all moral agents by virtue of their rationality. Philosophers contrast "natural law" with "conventional law," where the latter means human law or government. Thus, natural law is the law "higher" than the "laws of the land"; it's the law over which a government has no special jurisdiction. For example, the "inalienable rights" protected by the American Constitution are such because they are based in natural law. (See **rights.**)

necessity   in what must be; what could not possibly be otherwise. For philosophers, necessity means logical necessity—something is necessary only if it would be a logical contradiction to suggest that it could be any other way. To say that something is necessary is a much stronger claim than to say that it's either possible (in other words, that it *might* be) or contingent (in other words, it *might* not be). For instance, many philosophers have claimed that God's existence is necessary; that it doesn't make any sense at all to talk about the world unless there is a God who makes it intelligible and ordered. (See **apodeictic.**)

nihilism   in belief in nothing. A nihilist can claim, descriptively, that in fact nothing really exists (for instance, that there's no God, or no Justice, or that everything is just illusions and there's nothing real behind them). On the other hand, a nihilist could claim, prescriptively, that there ought not to be anything, that nothing is good, and so we ought to undo everything. Obviously, nihilism, especially in this second sense, is a very frightening doctrine. Some philosophers, especially Nietzsche and the existentialists, have been accused of nihilism (in the first sense), because they seemed to believe that people *make* the world everything it is (in other words, that there's nothing in the world besides human thought and opinion). Nietzsche and many existentialists claim, on the contrary, that their philosophy is life-affirming and that the Judeo-Christian tradition is nihilist by virtue of its appeal to the "other-worldly" and its denial of some human values and pleasures. In general, it is no compliment to be called a nihilist.

nirvana   in Buddhism, release or liberation from the suffering of life, usually accompanied by a profound (and largely incommunicable) understanding of truth.

noncognitivism   in an ethical theory that claims that there is no moral knowledge as such, only attitudes and opinions. Emotivists are noncognitivists because they claim that morality is nothing but a matter of emotion, not knowledge. (See **emotivism.**)

objective   in true as such, whether or not people accept it, and not affected by personal opinions or prejudices. An objective truth is therefore something that everybody, no matter what his or her culture or personal biases, ought to be able to recognize as true.

Philosophers talk about "objective truth" in contrast to both "relative truth" (something that is true in one culture and false in another) and "subjective truth" (something that is true for one person, and false for another). (See **relativism.**) In a much weaker formulation, "objective truth" is used synonymously with "intersubjectivity"; something is objectively true if we can all agree it's true. Usually, though, philosophers mean something much stronger by the term—namely, that what is objectively true is what we all *ought* to agree is true, because it is true. (See **absolute, universal law.**)

objectivism in ethics, the thesis that values or moral judgments may have objective existence.

ontology in what exists, or the study of what exists. "Onto" is from the ancient Greek word, meaning "to be"; thus, ontology is the philosophical study of existence (where existence means *everything* that exists). Philosophers have attempted to understand what exists by naming, categorizing, and grouping things, by ordering or prioritizing everything, and so on. The system that results from a particular philosopher's inquiry into existence is also called his or her ontology, i.e., what he or she claims really exists and is the order of things. Not surprisingly, ontology is the most abstract of philosophical inquiries. For philosophers of religion, it is also an inquiry into God or God's nature. For Jean-Paul Sartre, on the other hand, ontology is first of all the study of what it is to be a human being. (See **metaphysics.**)

particular in an individual thing or relationship. Because ethics is so often the search for universal principles and values, some philosophers have objected that no such generalities can be found. According to this objection, we do not have universally valid duties, nor is there a single good that is good for everybody. Rather, we have special obligations toward each individual with whom we relate or in each new situation that we encounter. In a political sense, a particularist would claim that each individual or group in the state has its own interests, which cannot be generalized to apply to all the citizens or groups. Usually, then, this emphasis on the particular insists that the basis of morality is not some abstract good but rather consists in loyalties to concrete communities or individuals.

pathos in a feeling of sympathy or pity. "Pathos" comes from the ancient Greek *pathas* meaning "emotion" or "sensation." Philosophers of aesthetics and ethics talk about pathos as the basis of beauty in tragic art or of morality, respectively. For instance, Aristotle claimed that a good tragedy was specifically aimed at bringing out the audience members' feelings of pity and fear, and theories of morals that emphasize sentiments (such as Hume's) and the Christian claim that suffering is the path to salvation both claim that morality is rooted in our human pathos. Nietzsche drew a relation between these two concepts of pathos when he claimed that Christian morality was the replaying of a tragedy.

phenomenology in the philosophical study of conscious experience. A "phenomenon" is an "experienced event." It is an occurrence *as experienced by a conscious mind.* Phenomenologists claim that since everything we know is known through and in a mind, or consciousness, the task of philosophy (especially epistemology) is to describe and analyze conscious experience. A phenomenologist is concerned with questions such as, "What is the experience of knowing something like?" and "What is the experience of moral reasoning like?" Although many philosophers have concerned themselves with these questions, the term "phenomenology" is usually used in reference to twentieth-century French and German thinkers, especially Jean-Paul Sartre, and is closely related to existentialism.

philia in friendship. (See **love.**)

philosophy in the study of "first principles," the "love of wisdom." "Philia" is the ancient Greek term for "love," as in "friendship," and "sophia" is the ancient Greek for "wisdom." But one of the things that philosophers dispute about most is the definition of their discipline: some think of what philosophers do—or ought to do, if they are to be called "philosophers"—in a very narrow sense, like helping and grounding the sciences and such defining key terms as "knowledge" and "goodness." Some philosophers have a very broad definition of what they do, searching for the truth or understanding the meaning of life. The role of ethics in philosophy depends very much on the scope of such definitions.

platonic   in with reference to Plato, the Greek philosopher of the fourth century B.C. Plato is one of the greatest philosophers of all times; as one philosopher put it, "All of the history of philosophy has been a footnote to Plato." "Platonic love" is a concept that played an enormous role in late medieval ethics. In common parlance, "platonic" love is usually used to refer to "nonsexual" love but, on the basis of Plato's writings (especially *The Symposium*), Platonic love came to mean the love for "higher" things, ultimately God.

pluralism   in a philosophy that insists that there is more than one truth, one right, one set of values. Also, a political theory that advocates diversity in the state. A political pluralist claims that a nation that has citizens from many cultural and ethnic backgrounds is the best society. But then there is a problem: How can very different and opposing sets of values be reconciled? Pluralism poses a particular problem to contemporary philosophers. As a result, pluralists tend to look for new kinds of ethical or political theories that are not ethnocentric and that emphasize tolerance and mutual understanding rather than uncompromising insistence on a single correct set of values. (See **ethnocentricity.**)

polemics   in aggressive and often exaggerated argument for one's opinion.

practical syllogism   in ethical reasoning, according to Aristotle. A "syllogism" is a classic form of proof: It states a number of premises (typically two in a classic syllogism) and then draws a conclusion from them. For instance, the most popular philosophical example is: "(a) All men are mortal. (b) Socrates is a man. (c) Therefore, Socrates is mortal." A syllogism is "practical" when it has to do with our actions or practices. Aristotle claimed that people make ethical decisions by using a syllogism; for example, (a) "The good for a human being is happiness." (b) "This virtuous act will contribute to my happiness." (c) "Therefore, I ought to do this act."

prescriptive statements   in claims about how things ought to be. In ethics, prescriptive statements are usually claims about how people *ought* to behave, about what they *should do*. Philosophers talk about prescriptive statements as a way of contrasting them to descriptive ones; in other words, a prescriptive claim says something about what ought to be the case rather than about what is the case. For example, normative ethics is a set of prescriptions for behavior. (See **descriptive statements.**)

prescriptivism   in a theory that claims that moral statements are recommendations of certain behavior. Prescriptivists (like emotivists) distinguish statements about values from statements of fact; the latter are descriptive and the former, prescriptive. Prescriptivism is a form of noncognitivism (See **noncognitivism.**)

prudence   in acting in our long-term self-interest. It's easy to see, even if we believe that morality is really only self-interest, that satisfying our immediate self-interest isn't always advisable. Although you may like ice cream very much, you like your health and your handsome figure more; so, in your *own self-interest* over the long term, you regulate your ice-cream intake. In doing this, you are acting prudently. Prudence is giving your interests a certain priority. Some philosophers (such as the ancient Greek hedonist Epicurus, and even Aristotle) claim that all ethics is really the counsel of prudence. Others (such as Kant) claim that, although morality may sometimes correspond with prudence, it is essential that morality be much more than mere prudence. (See **enlightened egoism, morality.**)

psychological egoism See **egoism.**

psychological hedonism See **hedonism.**

rational in accordance with reason. Whatever a philosopher's image of "reason" is, (and through history, there have been many candidates) most philosophers agree that their conversations and theories ought to be rational; in other words, they ought to make sense and be intelligible to other human beings. Some philosophers claim that the natural world is itself rational and therefore intelligible. Very recently, in the late nineteenth century, a great many philosophers (particularly the existentialists) began to question the rationality of both the world and our attitudes toward the world. (See **rationalism, reason.**)

rationalism in a theory that takes reason as the ultimate authority in all matters of knowledge, belief, or behavior. Kant, a most famous rationalist, insisted that we know the ultimate laws of nature through reason, not through experience alone, and we ascertain the ultimate principles of morality through pure practical reason, not through experience at all. Rationalism is typically contrasted with "empiricism"—the view that all of our knowledge and wisdom comes from experience, not reason. (See **a priori, empiricism.**)

reason in that which makes the world intelligible. Most philosophers use the term "reason" to name a human faculty; it is because people have reason that we can understand the universe as comprehensible. Reason has often been elevated to the status of a quasi-divine mode of access to the true world (e.g., in Plato), and it has been denigrated to the role of a mere calculating instrument (e.g., by Hume). Some philosophers, however (e.g., Hegel), use the term "reason" to talk about some power or faculty of the world (of Nature or of God or of History), claiming, for instance, that because there is reason in Nature, Nature is in principle intelligible. Not only rationalists rely on reason, of course; empiricists and even most relativists rely on the faculty of reason as well. (See **rationality.**)

reasons in explanations and/or justifications. Reasons account for an action, e.g., by attributing a psychological cause (a motive or intention, the aim of the action). Reasons justify an action by showing why that action was the proper one to perform, for example, by showing that its consequences were beneficial or by demonstrating that, from the limited point of view of the agent, it seemed to be the best course of action available. In philosophy—a self-consciously rational discipline—all claims need to be justified with reasons.

relativism in a theory that claims that what's right or true differs from culture to culture. Relativism as a philosophical stance has grown more popular in the modern age, since the discoveries of explorers, colonizers, and anthropologists showed us that there are radically different belief structures in different societies. A person who believes in such differences is a **relativist.** A relativist would claim that what's right or true is always relative to the particular circumstances and beliefs of a people (or a person); in other words, it's true or right *for someone.* If truth or morality is relative, then, it is *not* absolute or universal, and if the relativist is correct, it would seem as if there is no cross-cultural (or interpersonal) objective standard to appeal to when trying to decide what is right. At the extremes, it has been argued that a relativist could not even find a ground on which to condemn the atrocities of the Nazis. But then, of course, it must be questioned *to whom* such horrendous values are supposed to be relative—not the Jews, Catholics, and Gypsies they slaughtered by the millions, not those millions of Germans who silently despised the actions of their government, perhaps not even to those Nazis themselves who later repented and regretted their actions. The Nazi question is illustrative, however, because it underscores the point that relativism (except extreme relativism) does not eliminate duty and responsibility so much as it affirms them, at least within the group to which a person's values are relative. A relativist believes that a person is bound to the morality of his or her culture, indeed, absolutely bound to his or her culture. We could also argue that the fact of relativism obliges us to respect others all the more. Even relativism, therefore, can have its absolutes. (See **absolute, subjective.**)

responsibility   in Sartre, accountability, by reason of one's choices in life.

retributive justice   in takes each person's "due" to mean "what he or she deserves," with particular reference to retribution for wrongdoing. When philosophers talk about retributive justice, they talk about rewards and, especially, punishments. To be just, rewards must be merited and appropriate to the task for which they're given; punishments must be warranted and appropriate to the crime for which they're administered. It would be unjust to be executed for missing a dentist's appointment, but it is probably just to have your license taken away for drunk driving. One of the classic statements of retributive justice is from the Bible's Old Testament: "An eye for an eye, a tooth for a tooth." (See **justice.**)

right (rights)   in a justified claim, whether by virtue of law, contract, or morality. For example, every American has the right to free speech, by virtue of that body of law called the "Constitution" and its amendments. If you sign a contract promising to pay a painter for his work, he then has a right to that payment. On the other hand, every sensitive creature has the right not to be tortured, not by virtue of any law or understanding but simply by virtue of the basic moral imperative that says, "Don't be cruel."

sanction   in authorization, or (as a verb) to authorize. "Sanction" is usually used to refer to a punishment or a reward, but it can refer to any incentive offered by an authority, to do or not to do something—a license, a tax break, etc. In other words, a sanction is the "official" recognition of a person's action. The "authority" here could be any authority— God, natural law, reason, etc. For instance, you could say that the natural sanction for being clumsy is falling down; that the customary sanction for doing good work is a raise in pay; for speeding, a hefty fine. (See **external sanction** and **internal sanction.**)

secular   in worldly and social, as opposed to relating to religion and the Church. With the separation of Church and state in some countries in the Modern Age, it became important to devise a secular education and establish secular authorities to replace the once absolute authority of the Church. In philosophy and science, it has become increasingly important to devise secular explanations of morality and nature, to find scientific and philosophical ways of explaining the world without reference to God. In the nineteenth and twentieth centuries, the movement to secularize education has become associated with humanism, and many philosophers and others have dubbed the contemporary Western worldview to be "secular-humanist." (See **humanism.**)

self-interest   in a person's own advantage. When a person acts in his or her own self-interest, his or her goal in acting is his or her own good—perhaps a financial return, perhaps elevation in the eyes of his or her peers, perhaps a feeling of victory. Clearly, people often do act in their own self-interest; what moral philosophers wonder about is whether they *always* do so and whether they *ought* to do so. It is also open to question what our *own good* really is. Usually, acting in our own self-interest is not considered morally wrong; rather, it is morally neutral, of no moral worth. However, a few philosophers have thought otherwise. Philosophers who claim that we ought to act in our own self-interest are a variety of ethical egoist—ethical hedonists (who claim that "our own good" is "pleasure"), enlightened egoists (who claim that "our own good" is "long-term fulfillment"). (See **egoism, enlightened egoism, enlightened self-interest, hedonism, prudence.**)

self-love   in concern for and the advancement of one's own good (not equivalent to selfishness).

skepticism   in doubt; distrust of the seemingly obvious, especially distrust of the senses. A philosophical skeptic is a person who doubts not just some particular claim to knowledge or right behavior but knowledge and right behavior as such. A skeptic doubts whether human beings can ever really know anything at all, including the correct principles of morality. For instance, a skeptic might say that our senses cannot be considered a reliable source of knowledge because they often mislead us. (A far-away sound sounds higher in pitch than it would if it were nearby.) So, too, a skeptic might use the existence of differing moralities in different societies to argue that there is no morality as such, only differing practices in different cultures. Put differently, there is no way to *justify* morality, except by showing that it "fits" into a particular society at a particular time. There have been skeptics throughout the history of philosophy; the best-known modern skeptic is David Hume. (See **emotivism, empiricism, epistemology, justification, rationalism, relativism.**)

slave morality   in the true nature of any rule-governed, objective theory of morals, according to Nietzsche. Nietzsche claimed that morality emerged historically as a complex and ingenious defense invented by slavish peoples to combat their masters. Morality, he thought, was a Judeo-Christian "trick" that seemed to put God and the authority or Reason "on their side"—against the "evil" ruling or masterly class (Egypt, Babylon, Rome). Nietzsche pointed out that slave morality is essentially prohibitive— it consists mainly of "Thou shalt *nots*" (in contrast, for instance, to Aristotle's emphasis on positive virtues). The goal of these prohibitions was *equality,* an effort to bring masterful people down to the slave's level. Morality, thus understood, is "slavish"; it is a sign of weakness and resentment.

social contract   in an implicit pact among all the members of society, which is the basis of all moral obligations to each other. Some moral philosophers, called "contractarians," claim that a good government, or a good social structure, is one that everybody either does, would, or could (in principle) agree to. Contractarians claim that a good legal code or social code is one which every person does or would obligate him or her *self* to (rather than one that is, say, commanded by a king or some other external authority). The social contract is a hypothetical scenario that displays how such a "contract" might be arrived at. For instance, Thomas Hobbes claimed that the social contract ensured the protection of everyone from everyone else in return for their obedience to a monarch. For some philosophers, the social contract is meant to serve as a basis for a better society in the future; for others, the social contract is a myth that represents the implicit basis of our existing society. (See **distributive justice, enlightened egoism, self-interest.**)

Socratic method   in eliciting and sharpening the opinions of others by asking them questions. In one Platonic dialogue, Socrates compares his profession with that of a midwife. A midwife helps people give birth to healthy babies; a philosopher, according to Socrates, helps people give birth to healthy ideas. Socrates almost never stated or argued his opinions; rather, he asked others to state their opinions and then challenged them and argued with them. Socrates claimed that only the truth (a "healthy" idea) could stand up to such questioning, and therefore, that this questioning was the only way to get at the truth. Still, some of the people he picked on didn't like it very much.

sophist   in a teacher of public speaking, for lawyers and politicians. "Sophist" is the ancient Greek root for our word "sophisticated," describing someone who appears to be (but may or may not actually be) very knowledgeable. The original sophists in ancient Greece did not use the Socratic method, or questioning, to teach. Rather, they claimed that they knew all about morality, law, and politics and that they could explain these weighty matters directly to anyone willing and able to pay their fee. Socrates gave them a rather bad name, claiming, in effect, that their self-interested motives indicated that they did not know as much about law and morality as they claimed to. Yet he found them to be sharp thinkers with beliefs that he felt strongly compelled to challenge; hence, in most of the dialogues, Plato pits Socrates against one or another sophist: Protagoras, Gorgias, Euthyphro, and in the *Republic,* Glaucon.

subjective   in believed or felt by an individual. If truth is subjective, then it can differ from person to person. The belief that knowledge, truth, or morality is subjective is a kind of relativism. A subjectivist claims that what is right or true is always right or true *for someone.* If truth and morality are subjective, then they are *not* objective. In fact, if the subjectivist is right, then there are no objective standards at all to which we can appeal when trying to decide what's true or right. Existentialists sometimes claim that truth and morals are subjective. (See **objective, relativism.**)

subjectivism   in ethics, the thesis that values or moral judgments are purely subjective, and thus true only insofar as they are true for particular subjects.

summum bonum   in the "highest good," in Latin. "Summum bonum" are the Latin words used to describe Aristotle's ultimate end and medieval philosophers' notions of God. God is, for these thinkers, the supreme good from which all other good things are derived. It implies a hierarchy of good things, or ends, and the "summum" is at the top of the hierarchy, the good *for the sake of which* all other goods are good or useful. Aristotle argued that happiness was the summum bonum *for man;* the good for the sake of which we do everything else. (See **end, instrumental, intrinsic, teleology.**)

syllogism   in Aristotle, a form of argument, usually involving a major premise (a universal statement), a minor premise (a particular statement), followed by a conclusion.

teleology   in any theory that explains an object or an action by reference to the end or result that it achieves. "Telos" is the ancient Greek word for "end" (in the sense of "goal," or "result"). Thus, "teleology" means "the study of ends," or how ends are ordered in relation to each other, and how each thing is ordered to its end. In philosophy, there are both teleological metaphysics (which claims that everything *exists* for a purpose), and teleological ethics (which claims that all actions *are good* only insofar as they achieve some good end). Aristotle had both: He claimed that everything that existed did so for a purpose and had a natural end—knives must exist *for* cutting, trees *for* growing, etc.— and that in fact, nature as a whole existed for the sake of its end. John Stuart Mill was a teleological ethicist: he claimed that all actions were justified only insofar as they produced a good—which he claimed was pleasure or happiness. (See **end, intrinsic, *summum bonum.***)

transcendence   in Sartre, the realm of our choices, plans, possibilities.

universal law   in any law that applies to everything, everywhere. The laws of nature, (such as the law of gravity) are generally thought to be universal laws—everything is subject to them; there are no exceptions. Universal law is used in contrast to "ordinary" law, the law of a particular nation, "conventional" law. Human beings, when they make laws for countries, make laws that are only locally binding. Nature and God, on the other hand, make laws that are universally binding. Some philosophers have claimed as well that there are laws other than natural laws that apply universally. For example, Kant claimed that the categorical imperative, the moral law, obligated everybody, everywhere, as strongly as a law of nature and was therefore universal. Some political theorists have claimed that natural rights are given us by a universal law. (See **absolute, categorical imperative, natural law, objective.**)

utilitarianism   in any moral theory that claims that actions are good only insofar as they increase the amount of happiness (and decrease the amount of suffering) in the world. Utilitarians believe that actions ought to be performed according to the "principle of utility," which is, "do that action which provides the greatest happiness for the greatest number." Thus, what makes a good action good, according to a utilitarian, are its consequences. Utilitarianism is one kind of teleological ethics. (See **teleology.**) Both the number of people happily affected and the amount of happiness each one gets is important in determining the right course of action in any given situation. The principle of utility always accompanies a principle of equality—in other words, one person's unit of happiness (a "utile") is always considered equal to anyone else's unit of happiness. The simplest and earliest form of utilitarianism, therefore, is a form of **act utilitarianism.** To decide what to do in any given situation, then, one should assess the consequences of each course of action and do whichever "adds up" to the most happiness. A detailed and sophisticated version of this was defended by Jeremy Bentham in the early nineteenth century. Later utilitarians—notably John Stuart Mill—revised utilitarianism considerably, but they all maintain some form or other of the principle of utility. One such revision is called **rule utilitarianism.** Rule utilitarians claim that the principle of utility applies to rules, not individual acts; in other words, people should "obey that rule which provides the greatest happiness for the greatest number." For instance, a rule utilitarian might say that over the course of history, more people have been made happier by obeying the Ten Commandments than would have been if they hadn't obeyed them. (See **consequentialism, enlightened egoism, teleology.**)

vice in a bad or immoral character trait. Vice is the opposite of virtue and is included in our word "vicious." Vices are bad traits. They tend to be antisocial and conducive to distrust and social conflict. Philosophers talk about vices particularly in the context of an ethical theory concerned with the virtues. Aristotle had such a virtue-based ethical theory, as did some medieval theologians, notably St. Thomas Aquinas. Aristotle's list of vices included such unenviable traits as conceit, mock modesty, vulgarity, and miserliness—traits that were, to his mind, irrational and extreme. It is worth noting that the list of Christian vices includes some traits that Aristotle considered virtues, e.g., pride and anger. (See **virtue.**)

virtue in a good or moral character trait. Virtue is the opposite of vice and is the base of the word "virtuous." Virtues are good traits. They tend to be socially beneficial and promote social harmony. Some philosophers have had virtue-based ethical theories, notably Aristotle and, more recently, David Hume. The virtues are states of character that make it virtually "automatic" for a person to do the right thing. For Aristotle, the virtues included honesty, pride, generosity, and friendliness. (See **vice.**)

will in the power to choose and implement a person's own actions.

wisdom in Aristotle, knowledge of the invariable principles regarding the most noble objects and the ability to apply them.

wu-wei literally, "non-action," the greatest virtue according to the Taoist philosopher Lao-Tze. Sometimes described as "acting naturally."

Index